CONTENTS

MODERN

Real Estate Practice IN

NEW YORK FOR SALESPERSONS AND BROKERS

EIGHTH EDITION

Edith Lank

Dearborn™
Real Estate Education

President: Roy Lipner
Publisher: Evan Butterfield
Development Editor: Christopher Oler
Production Coordinator: Daniel Frey
Typesetter: Janet Schroeder
Creative Art Director: Lucy Jenkins
Cover Design: Gail Chandler

Published by Dearborn™ Real Estate Education,
a division of Dearborn Financial Publishing, Inc.®
30 South Wacker Drive
Chicago, IL 60606-1719
www.dearbornRE.com

03   04   05   10   9   8   7   6   5   4   3   2   1

Library of Congress Cataloging-in-Publication Data

Lank, Edith.
    Modern real estate practice in New York / Edith Lank.-- 8th ed.
        p. cm.
Includes index.
    ISBN 0-7931-4264-4
    1. Vendors and purchasers--New York (State) 2. Real estate
business--Law and legislation--New York (State) 3. Real property--New
York (State) I. Title.
    KFN5166.L359 2003
    346.74704'37—dc22

                                                                        2993018081

CHAPTER 22
General Business Law   372

CHAPTER 23
Construction and Development   391

CHAPTER 24
Conveyance of Real Property   412

CHAPTER 25
Property Management   420

CHAPTER 26
Taxes and Assessments   441

PREFACE

This eighth, 21st-century edition of *Modern Real Estate Practice in New York* has been completely updated to reflect changes in the real estate industry as well as requirements for prelicensing courses set forth in the Department of State's syllabus. Each topic follows closely the state outlines for the salespersons' and brokers' courses.

Like previous editions, this one is dedicated to hundreds of thousands of real estate students and instructors whose enthusiastic acceptance has made this the best-selling real estate textbook in the Empire State. Once again, many valuable suggestions for the new edition have come from those who use the book.

Those suggestions have always played a great part in the evolution of the text. For this eighth edition, we paid particular attention to your classroom needs and the state's syllabus. We also made every effort to make this textbook learning-friendly, using classroom-tested features such as highlighted key terms and concepts and margin notes. Web addresses are included.

This edition owes a great debt to alert reader Gerry Hoffman, and to Judith J. Deickler, GRI, and Rhonda Brown, Esq. Anthony Agelire, RETC of Greater New York, Beverly L. Deickler, Esq., William R. Deickler, William R. Deickler Contracting, Inc., Robert Stack and Anna Y. Tam, American Real Estate School, and Jane A. Willson, Expo Services, Ltd., made excellent contributions. Their combined criticisms and comments have made this the best edition yet of *Modern Real Estate Practice in New York*.

Professor Karen Morris, Esq., and William Lippman, Esq., provided valuable help with the chapter on General Business Law and the chapters that deal with agency. Eileen Taus, Westchester Board of REALTORS®, again served as a valuable resource. Thanks are due also to John Piper, Karen Van DeViver, and Sandra Kleps of the Greater Rochester Association of REALTORS®.

The author is grateful for contributions to the book over the years from Babette Yuhas of the Greater Syracuse Board of REALTORS®; Arthur Elfenbein, New York University Real Estate Institute, and Professor Patrick Falci, St. John's University. For contributions to this and earlier editions, thanks also go to Frank Langone, RETC of Greater New York; and Mary Manfred, Real Estate Learning Center, Inc.

The author would also like to thank the following instructors for their assistance with earlier editions: Peter A. Karl III, SUNY Institute of Technology; Anthony J. DiChiara, GRI, ME, MS, Niagara University; Wendy A. Tilton, New York University; Uri Shamir, Queens College; James V. Pugliese, CRB, GRI, Coldwell Banker Prime Properties; Richard J. Sobelsohn, The Sobelsohn School; Samuel Irlander, New York University Real Estate Institute; D. J. Sperano, Fingerlakes Community College/Corning Community College; Anna Y. Tam, American Real Estate School; Michael K. Brady, IFA, RAM, State University of New York; James R. Trevitt, Broome County Board of REALTORS®;

Michael D. Jesmer, Syracuse Real Estate, Inc.; and Richard Levin, Don Milton and David M. Alexander, all of the Greater Rochester Association of REALTORS®.

Special contributions to earlier editions came from George M. Vaughn, GRI, CRB, CRS, LTG; Anthony Agelire; Paul Desseault; Thomas E. DeCelle; Rolando Santiago; Charles E. Davis; Peter Karl III; Leon Katzen, Esq.; William Lang, Jr.; George Lasch; John Mataraza; James Myers, Esq.; Thomas Thomassian; Dorothy Tymon, and Chris E. Wittstruck, Esq.

Assistance and encouragement has also been gratefully received from Amy Penzabene, Gail Bates, Mary Anne Moore, William Stavola, Willard Roff, and Joseph Amello of the New York Department of State; Charles M. Staro, Georgianne Bailey, and Mark Morano of the New York State Association of REALTORS®; Bonnie May and Thomas R. Viola of the State Division of Housing and Community Renewal; Liz Duncan and Jeff Lubar with the National Association of REALTORS®; P. Gilbert Mercurio of the Westchester County Board of REALTORS®; Hung Pham, Barbara Portman, John Viteretti, and Antonio F. Brown; and bankers Rose Bernstein, Gaye Greene, and Bill Mattle.

Robert Kyle and Anita Constant first sponsored this book. Carol Luitjens, Daniel Frey, Evan Butterfield, Louise Benzer, and Christopher Oler helped the eighth edition through the editorial process.

Valuable help has also come from attorneys Michael Wallender, counsel to the New York State Association of REALTORS®, Demetrios Cortisides, Paul Anderson, Abraham Berkowitz, Demetrios Coritsidis, Donald Friedman, Harold Geringer, David Henehan, Benjamin Henszey, Ezra Katzen, James Loeb, Robert Mendohlson, Joseph M. O'Donnell, Louis Ryen, Karen Schafer, Sally Smith, Christine Van Benschoten, and Garrett Lacara.

Among REALTORS® who offered suggestions and assistance are Ronald Baroody, Thomas Carozza, John Cyr, Barry Deickler, Ruth De Roo, Thomas Galvin, Harold Kahn, Norman Lank, William Lester, Robert Michaels, Norman Schwartz, John Sobeck, Michael Stucchio, John Tyo, Thomas Wills III, Rex Vail, Jeff Wolk, and Rita Scharg.

Thanks are due also to instructors Newt Alderman, Joseph DiIanni, John Alberts, Professor Kenneth Beckerink, Cindy Faire, Jim Foley, John Keaton, Eli Kimels, Nicholas Morabito, Joseph O'Donnell, Edween Reagh, Alvin Schwartz, Professor U. Shamir, Marcia Spada, Larry Rockefeller, Jonathan Easterling, Marie Esposito, Richard Fuchs, Irving Levine, Stephen Mendolla, Selwyn Price, Dominic Telesco, Christine di Grande Jones, and Harry Goldberg.

Instructors are encouraged to write to the publisher on school letterheads for the complementary instructor's manual that accompanies this textbook. The author would also like to recommend to them the Real Estate Educators Association, which may be contacted at www.reea.org. The association offers workshops, publications, and conferences, and has a chapter in New York State.

Part of the fascination of the real estate field is the way it changes and adapts to new economic and social conditions. The author always enjoys discussing new information, suggestions, and criticism with students and instructors who contact:

Edith Lank
240 Hemingway Drive
Rochester, NY 14620
585-473-4973
edithlank@aol.com

■ ABOUT THE AUTHOR

Edith Lank has been a licensed broker in New York for more than 30 years and has taught real estate at St. John Fisher College. Her award-winning weekly column on real estate, distributed by Creators Syndicate, has appeared in newspapers in Buffalo, Rochester, Syracuse, Schenectady, Amsterdam, Elmira, Brooklyn, Binghamton, Kingston, Ithaca, Middletown, Westchester and Rockland counties, and Long Island, as well as in 100 other newspapers around the country and various Web pages.

She has hosted her own television and radio shows, and is a frequent speaker at Associations of REALTORS® functions. Edith has published eight books on real estate, including *The 201 Questions Every Homebuyer and Homeseller Must Ask, The Homebuyer's Kit,* and *The Homeseller's Kit,* all available from Dearborn Financial Publishing, Inc.® Her work has been honored by the Monroe County Bar Association, Women in Communications, local and national associations of REALTORS®, the National Association of Real Estate Editors, the Real Estate Educators Association, and Governor Mario Cuomo. A graduate of Penn Yan Academy and Syracuse University, she is a member of Phi Beta Kappa and is listed in *Who's Who.*

■ USEFUL WEB LINKS

WWWeb.Link

Current rates: *www.bankrate.com*

Data on comparable sales by neighborhood: *www.domania.com*

New York Department of State, real estate page. Licensing, exam information, rules and regulations: *www.dos.state.ny.us*

Shop for mortgages: *www.eloan.com*

Environmental Protection Agency: *www.epa.gov*

Credit reporting: *www.equifax.com*

Credit reporting: *www.experian.com*

Fannie Mae home page: *www.fanniemae.com*

Federal Emergency Management Agency, flood zones: *www.fema.gov*

Microsoft's large real estate site: *www.homeadvisor.com*

VA loan information: *homeloans.va.gov*

Fannie Mae information for buyers and sellers: *www.homepath.com*

Rent stabilization and rent regulation: *www.houseingnyc.com*

Mortgage calculators, current rates: *www.hsh.com*

U.S. Department of Housing and Urban Development, FHA:
www.hud.gov/mtgprog.html

Daily real estate news headlines and stories: *www.inman.com*

International Real Estate Digest: *www.ired.com*

Shop for mortgages: *www.lendingtree.com*

Current rates, loan process: *www.loanlibrary.com*

New York city: *www.nyc.gov*

State of New York Mortgage Agency, SONYMA loans: *www.nyhomes.org*

National Association of REALTORS®, nationwide MLS: *www.realtor.com*

Reverse mortgages for seniors: *www.reversemortgage.org*

U.S. Department of Agriculture, rural development home loans:
www.rurdev.usda.gov/rhs/index.html

Credit reporting: *www.transunion.com*

Financing for veterans: *www.valoans.com*

1

LICENSE LAW

Joan wants to earn money at home. Neighbor Shanice suggests Joan do telemarketing, phoning homeowners to see if anyone is interested in selling. Shanice, who has a real estate license, will give Joan $25 for every lead that results in a listing. Joan has no real estate license, but Shanice says this is not illegal because Joan won't do any actual listing or selling. Is there a problem here?

Like every other state, New York has enacted real estate license laws to protect the public from incompetent or dishonest brokers and salespersons and to maintain high standards in the real estate industry. The licensee who is not familiar with the law's requirements could face fines and loss of license.

■ KEY TERMS

administrative discipline

apartment information
   vendor

apartment-sharing agent

appraiser

Article 12-A

Article 78 procedure

associate broker

blind ad

commingling

continuing education

denial, suspension, or
   revocation of license

Department of State (DOS)

escrow

irrevocable consent

kickback

misdemeanor

mortgage banker

mortgage broker

net listing

pocket card

real estate broker

real estate salesperson

reciprocity

record of association

revocation

sponsoring broker

suspension

termination of association
   notice

violation

■ PURPOSE OF REAL ESTATE LICENSE LAWS

The New York **Department of State,** Division of Licensing Services, has the power to issue licenses and enforce the real estate license law. The law is enforced through fines; reprimands; and the **denial, suspension, or revocation of licenses.** The Department currently licenses more than 57,000 salespersons and 48,000 brokers.

State Board of Real Estate.   The Division of Licensing Services shares regulatory duties with New York's State Board of Real Estate, which has 15 members. At least 5 are real estate brokers; the remainder are members of the public, and the Secretary of State serves as chairperson. The board has the power to promulgate rules and regulations in some legal areas and also examines applicants, approves real estate schools, and helps enforce the real estate laws.

Violation of the license law is a misdemeanor punishable by up to a year in jail and a fine of up to $1,000.

The New York Real Property Law, **Article 12-A,** which went into effect in 1922, is the main source of law for real estate licenses in New York. Copies of the law and regulations may be obtained by writing to

New York Department of State
Division of Licensing Services
84 Holland Avenue
Albany, NY 12208

WWWeb.Link

The Licensing Division maintains a consumer assistance phone line in Albany at 518-474-4664, and a Web page at *www.dos.state.ny.us/lcns/realest.html.* The e-mail address is info@dos.state.ny.us. New York State's TTY phone number is 1-800-662-1220.

Who Must Be Licensed?

Any person who for another and for a fee performs any of the activities described in the license law must hold a real estate license unless specifically exempted.

Broker.   A **real estate broker** is any person, firm, partnership, or corporation that for another and for a fee (or the expectation of a fee) performs any of the following services:

1. Negotiates any form of real estate transaction
2. Lists or attempts to list real property for sale
3. Negotiates a loan secured by a mortgage
4. Negotiates a lease
5. Collects rents for more than one client
6. Sells a lot or parcel of land by auction
7. Negotiates the sale of a parcel of subdivided land
8. Exchanges real property
9. Relocates commercial or residential tenants

10. Engages in the sale of condominiums and cooperatives
11. Sells a business that has more than half its value in real estate.

Soliciting, processing, placing, and negotiating mortgage loans on one to four-family dwellings for a fee also requires registration with the state banking department as a mortgage broker.

Salesperson.   A **real estate salesperson** is one who assists in any of the services performed by a broker. A broker is authorized to operate his or her own real estate business; a salesperson may work only in the name of and under the supervision of a sponsoring broker. The salesperson may never accept a commission from anyone except his or her supervising or principal broker.

Associate broker.   A license as **associate broker** is available for the broker who chooses to work in the role of a salesperson under the sponsorship and supervision of another broker. The associate broker must meet all the qualifications for a broker's license and pass the broker's examination, but he or she transacts business in the name of the **sponsoring broker,** exactly as a salesperson would. An associate broker may also hold broker's license to work independently as well.

Exceptions.   The provisions of the license law requiring licensure do not apply to the following:

- Public officers while they are performing their official duties
- Persons acting under order of a court (executors, guardians, referees, receivers, administrators)
- Attorneys licensed in New York, not required to take the licensing examination. (An attorney who employs real estate salespersons, however, must obtain a real estate broker's license.)
- A resident manager employed by one owner to manage rental property when the leasing of units or the collection of rents is part of the manager's regular duties
- Certain authorized tenant organizations and not-for-profit corporations enforcing the housing code of the City of New York

REALTOR®.   The word REALTOR® has nothing to do with state licensing. It refers to a member of a private trade organization, the National Association of REALTORS®. (See Chapter 19.)

■ QUALIFICATIONS FOR LICENSURE

A licensed salesperson must

- be 18 or older;
- never have been convicted of a felony (some exceptions are made for an executive pardon, a certificate of good conduct from a parole board, or a certificate of relief from disabilities);
- be either a citizen or a legal permanent resident of the United States;

TABLE 1.1	Salesperson	Broker
Requirements for Licensing in New York	At least 18	At least 19
	No felony*	No felony*
	Permanent resident of U.S.	Permanent resident of U.S.
	Sponsoring broker	Full year's experience*
	45-hour course	90 hours' study
	Pass state exam ($15)	Pass state exam ($15)
	$50 (two years) license fee	$150 (two years)

* Some exceptions possible

■ successfully complete a 45-hour prelicensing course approved by the Department of State;
■ pass the state's licensing examination; and
■ have a sponsoring broker before obtaining the license.

Table 1.1 shows the requirements for salespersons' and brokers' licenses.

A licensed broker must meet the same requirements, except that the minimum age is 19, the required courses of study total 90 hours, and a sponsoring broker no longer will be needed. Instead, the prospective broker must submit proof of one full year's experience as a licensed salesperson or two years' equivalent experience, subject to approval by the Department of State, in some other aspect of real estate, or proof of a license from a state with which New York has a **reciprocity** agreement. (See Table 1.1.) The experience requirement is based on a point system, which will be discussed in Chapter 19.

An associate broker must meet all the same requirements as any other broker, but also must submit the name of a sponsoring broker.

Education Requirements

The Department of State certifies certain educational institutions to offer two qualifying education courses. One qualifying course covers the necessary 45 hours' instruction for a salesperson's license; the second 45-hour qualifying course completes the 90-hour prelicensing requirement for a broker. The courses must be taken in order. Topics to be covered and the time devoted to each are set by law. Successful completion of each course requires at least 36 hours' attendance and the passing of a final examination.

■ LICENSE EXAMINATIONS

Walk-in examinations are open to any interested person, either before or after completion of the 45-hour qualifying course. Applicants should arrive well before the scheduled times. Space is available on a first-come, first-served basis.

Same day license status. Walk-in examinations at the Albany, Rochester, and New York City test centers offer a chance for immediate licensure that same day. The candidate who passes must bring the license fee as well as the examination fee and a fully completed application that shows successful completion of the prelicensing course and the signature of the sponsoring broker. This allows individuals to begin their real estate salesperson careers immediately. The certificate is valid until a permanent license is issued.

Other locations for salespersons and brokers licensing examinations are as follows. For examination dates and times, call the Division of Licensing Services at 518-474-4429, or visit the Web site listed on page 2.

Albany
84 Holland Avenue
Basement

Binghamton
State Office Building
44 Hawley Street
15th Floor

Buffalo
State Office Bldg.
65 Court Street
Main Floor Hearing Room, Part 5

Franklin Square
V.F.W. Hall
68 Lincoln Road
Basement

Hauppauge
State Office Bldg.
250 Veterans Memorial Highway
Basement Conference Room 1

Newburgh
Orange Ulster BOCES Adult
Ed Center
471 Broadway, 2nd Floor

New York City
123 William Street
19th Floor

Plattsburgh
Clinton County Community College
Lake Shore Drive
Route 9 South

Rochester
Finger Lakes DDSO (Monroe
Development Center)
620 Westfall Road

Syracuse—Brokers
333 East Washington St.
Main Floor, Hearing Room A

Syracuse—Salesperson
American Postal Workers Union
407 East Taft Road
North Syracuse

Utica
State Office Bldg.
207 Genesee Street
1st Floor, Room 110C

Watertown
State Office Bldg.
317 Washington Street
11th Floor

The examinations cover material from the prelicensing courses and test a fair knowledge of the English language. One hour is allowed for the salesperson's test, two and one-half hours for the broker's.

Examinees should bring to the examination a government-issued signature photo ID, two number-two pencils, and a check or money order for $15 payable to the Department of State (no cash is accepted). An identifying thumbprint will be taken. Scrap paper is furnished and must be turned in before the applicant leaves the room. Calculators are allowed but must be noiseless and hand-held with no tape printout. Passing grade is 70. For those who fail, unlimited retakes are allowed, with a $15 fee for each.

Except with same day licensure, notice of success or failure is mailed to the applicant's home address promptly. If the slip is marked "Passed," it is good for no more than two years toward a license application. If two years elapse without a license application, the state examination must be repeated.

■ LICENSING PROCEDURE

The salesperson's license application (Figure 1.1) is provided by the school where the 45-hour course was successfully completed and is signed by the broker who will supervise the new licensee and be responsible for his or her actions. It is accompanied by a $50 license fee and proof that the applicant has passed the state licensing exam.

The broker's application includes details of all past transactions during the apprenticeship period as a salesperson, with information about transactions during the required year's full-time activity as a licensed salesperson or during two years' equivalent experience in general real estate.

The applicant for an associate broker's license not only lists past transactions but also includes the signature of the principal broker with whose firm the new associate broker will be working.

Both applications include a child support statement, certifying whether applicants have any obligation to pay child support and, if so, whether they are four months or more in arrears.

Fees

The Department of State charges the following application fees:

- Broker, original license and renewal: $150
- Associate broker, original license and renewal: $150
- Salesperson, original license and renewal: $50
- Branch office, original and renewal: $150
- License examination: $15

Issuing the License

Each license is good for two years. Each licensee is issued a license and pocket card from the Department of State (DOS).

A salesperson's principal broker keeps the salesperson's license; the pocket card must be carried by the salesperson. Broker's licenses must be prominently displayed in the place of business; the salesperson's may be, if the broker wishes.

Licensing corporations, partnerships, and other legal entities.   A license issued to a corporation entitles a designated officer to act as a broker, but that person also must secure a license personally. One officer may act as the real estate broker under the corporate or business license. Every other officer or partner who wishes to act as a broker must secure another license, which will expire on the same day as the corporate or business license. An officer or partner of a licensed corporation or other legal entity may not be licensed as a real estate salesperson or associate broker.

FIGURE   1.1

Real Estate Salesperson Application

OFFICE USE ONLY	CLASS	KEY	UNIQUE ID NUMBER	CASH NUMBER	FEE
	4				$ 50

E W S _____ / _____   B _____ / _____

Real Estate Salesperson Application

Read the Instruction Sheet for details before completing this application form. You must answer each question and TYPE or PRINT responses in ink.

APPLICANT'S LAST NAME   FIRST NAME   M.I.   SUFFIX

HOME ADDRESS -NUMBER AND STREET (P.O. BOX MAY BE ADDED TO ENSURE DELIVERY)   APT/UNIT

CITY   STATE   ZIP+4   COUNTY

SPONSORING BROKER OR FIRM NAME (EXACTLY AS IT APPEARS ON THE BROKER'S LICENSE)

OFFICE ADDRESS WHERE APPLICANT WILL BE PERMANENTLY STATIONED - NUMBER AND STREET

CITY   STATE   ZIP+4   COUNTY

DAYTIME TELEPHONE NUMBER   SOCIAL SECURITY NUMBER OR FEDERAL ID NUMBER (*SEE PRIVACY NOTIFICATION*)
(   )

E-MAIL ADDRESS (IF ANY)

1   BACKGROUND DATA

1. What is your date of birth? _____

                                                                                    YES   NO

2. Have you ever been convicted in this state or elsewhere of any criminal offense that is a misdemeanor or a felony? . . . .   ____   ____
   ➡**IF "YES,"** submit a written explanation giving the place, court jurisdiction, nature of the offense, sentence and/or other disposition. You must provide a copy of the accusatory instrument (e.g., indictment, criminal information or complaint) and a Certificate of Disposition. If you possess or have received a Certificate of Relief from Disabilities, Certificate of Good Conduct or Executive Pardon, you must provide a copy of same.

3. Are there any criminal charges (misdemeanors or felonies) pending against you in any court in this state or elsewhere? . . . .   ____   ____
   ➡**IF "YES,"** you must provide a copy of the accusatory instrument (e.g., indictment, criminal information or complaint).

4. Has any license or permit issued to you or a company in which you are or were a principal in New York State or elsewhere ever been revoked, suspended or denied? . . . .   ____   ____
   ➡**IF "YES,"** you must provide all relevant documents, including the agency determination, if any.

5. Have you ever applied for or been issued a real estate broker's or salesperson's license in this state?   ____   ____

   ➡**IF "YES,"** in what year? _____ Under what name? _____

   UID # (if applicable)   _____

Real Estate Salesperson Application (continued)

Real Estate Salesperson Application

2   Certification of Satisfactory Completion

_____
(Name of School)

Real Estate Salesperson Course (Code) #S- _____

This certifies that _____ has satisfactorily completed a 45-hour salesperson
(Name of Student)

qualifying course in real estate approved by the Secretary of State in accordance with the provisions of Chapter 868
of the Laws of 1977; that attendance of the student was in compliance with the law and that a passing grade was
achieved on the final examination. The course was completed on _____ .

Authorized Signature

X_____   *Date* _____

(School Seal)

3   Child Support Statement — *You must complete this section. If you do not complete it, your application will be returned.*

"X" A or B, below

I, the undersigned, do hereby certify that (You *must* "X" A or B below):

A. [   ] **I am not under obligation to pay child support**.   (SKIP "B" and go directly to **Applicant Affirmation**).

B. [   ] I am under obligation to pay child support   (You must "X" any of the four statements below that are true and apply to you):

    [   ]   I do *not* owe four or more months of child support payments.

    [   ]   I am making child support payments by income execution or court approved payment plan or by a plan agreed to by the parties.

    [   ]   My child support obligation is the subject of a pending court proceeding.

    [   ]   I receive public assistance or supplemental social security income.

4   Applicant Affirmation — I affirm, under the penalties of perjury, that the statements made in this application are true and correct. I further affirm that I have read and understand the provisions of Article 12-A of the Real Property Law and the rules and regulations promulgated thereunder.

Applicant's Signature

X _____   *Date* _____

F I G U R E   1.1

Real Estate Salesperson Application (continued)

Real Estate Salesperson Application

5   Association Statement — I am sponsoring this application in accordance with the Real Property Law, §441.1(d).

Broker Name _____   Date _____

Broker Signature _____

Broker Print Name _____

Please remember to include with this application any required explanations and statements along with your application fee (payable to NYS Department of State).

It is important that you notify this division of any changes
to your business address so you can continue to receive renewal
notices and any other notifications pertinent to your license.

DOS-0022 (Rev. 11/02)   PAGE 3 OF 3

◾ MAINTAINING A LICENSE

Various license laws and regulations affect a licensee's business practices.

Change of business address, status, or name.   All licensees must notify the department in writing of any change in their business address. A filing fee of $10 must accompany all such notifications. Failure to notify the department of a change is grounds for suspension of a license. When a broker moves his or her office to a different address, the broker must cross out the former address on the license and pocket card of each licensee and replace it with the new address. The broker also must complete a change-of-address form and send it to the DOS with the appropriate fee. Each individual licensee affiliated with that broker also must complete a change-of-address form and send it to the DOS.

Those desiring a license status change (such as from associate broker to broker); change of employment; or name change must submit the appropriate form and a $10 fee to the DOS.

Commissions.   No individual may legally accept a commission or other compensation for performing any of the activities regulated by the license law unless he or she holds a valid New York real estate license at the time the activity is performed. A salesperson may not accept a commission from anyone other than his or her supervising broker. Brokers may not receive compensation from more than one party to a transaction without the knowledge and consent of all parties involved (dual compensation). Brokers may share commissions only with their own salespersons and associate brokers or with other licensed brokers.

The law against sharing a commission with any unlicensed person effectively prohibits **kickbacks** to either buyers or sellers.

Disclosure of interest.   Licensees may neither buy nor acquire an interest in property listed with them for their own account without first making their true position known to the owners involved. Similarly, licensees may not act as brokers or salespersons in the sale of property in which they have an interest without revealing the interest to all parties to the transaction.

Offers to purchase.   All offers to purchase property must be presented promptly to the owner of the property.

■ TERMINATION OR CHANGES IN ASSOCIATION

When a salesperson or associate broker terminates an association with a broker, the supervising broker must file a **termination of association notice** with the Department of State, submit a $10 fee, and return the license to the licensee. The license may then be moved to a new sponsoring broker by establishing a new **record of association** with the DOS. The fee for filing a record of association is $10.

Revocation or suspension of a broker's license automatically causes the licenses of those affiliated with the broker to be suspended, pending a change of association.

A real estate salesperson who terminates his or her association with a broker must turn over to the broker any and all listing information obtained during the association. This is required whether the information was originally given to the salesperson by the broker or acquired by the salesperson during the association.

■ RENEWAL AND CONTINUING EDUCATION

Real estate licenses must be renewed every two years. A licensee who does not renew within two years of expiration must retake the licensing examination. Online renewal is available at the DOS Web site.

Continuing education. To renew a license, a licensee must complete 22.5 hours of **continuing education** every two years. Active licensed brokers who have been continuously licensed and active as full-time salespersons and/or brokers for the preceding 15 years and attorneys licensed to practice in New York State are exempt from the continuing education requirement.

A list of approved continuing education courses can be obtained by calling 518-486-3803, or e-mailing licensing@dos.state.ny.us.

The hours may be accumulated in modules as short as three-hour courses. Distance learning is available through the Internet or on CD-ROM.

■ BROKERAGE MANAGEMENT IN ACCORDANCE WITH LICENSE LAWS

Brokers must follow a variety of laws and regulations as they operate their brokerage businesses.

Place of business. Every New York real estate broker must maintain a principal place of business within the state (with the rare exception of some nonresident brokers).

Business name and sign. Any business name used by a New York real estate broker must be approved by the Department of State. A sign readable from the sidewalk must be posted conspicuously on the outside of the building. If the office is located in an apartment building, office building, or hotel, the broker's name and the words "Licensed Real Estate Broker" must be posted in the space that lists the names of the building's occupants.

Branch offices. A broker may maintain a branch office or offices; a separate license must be maintained for each. The principal broker must pay expenses for the branch office and supervise it closely.

Maintaining documents. Every real estate broker must maintain a file of all agency disclosure forms, listings, offers, closing statements, and certain other documents for a period of three years. (Most brokers keep all records indefinitely as a matter of good business practice.)

Delivery of documents. A real estate broker must immediately deliver to all parties signing the document duplicate originals of any document relating to a real estate transaction prepared by the broker or one of his or her salespeople.

Care and handling of funds. A real estate broker must not **commingle** money or other properties belonging to others with his or her own funds. The broker who holds other people's money must maintain a separate, federally insured New York bank account (**escrow** or trust account) to be used exclusively for the deposit of these monies and must deposit them immediately. Within a reasonable time period the broker must render an account of the funds to the client and remit any funds collected to the proper party. Interest earned, if any, does not belong to the broker.

Obligations to Other Parties and Other Brokers

The license law expressly prohibits a broker from interfering with or trying to frustrate other parties' existing contracts.

No broker may accept the services of any other broker's associates without that broker's knowledge, and brokers may not pay other broker's associates directly without that broker's knowledge.

Brokers are prohibited from negotiating the sale, lease, or exchange of any property directly with an owner who has an existing written contract that grants exclusive authority to another broker. This means that brokers may not interfere with another broker's exclusive listing agreement.

■ OTHER LICENSES OR REGISTRATIONS INVOLVING REAL ESTATE

An **apartment information vendor's** license is available to anyone older than 18 who is trustworthy and able to maintain a $5,000 interest-bearing escrow account. The license is renewable annually for a $400 fee. Apartment information vendors engage in the business of furnishing information concerning the location and availability of residential rental property, including apartments. They must provide prospective tenants a contract or receipt with specific information regarding the services they offer. They also must display a sign in all offices bearing the same information, post their license in all offices, and notify the Department of State of any changes in name or address.

An **apartment-sharing agent** finds roommates and arranges for sharing of homes. The one-year license costs $400, and the agent must maintain a trust account of $2,500.

Certification or licensing of **appraisers** is not required for all appraisal work but is necessary for most appraisals related to mortgage loans. New York State licenses and certifies appraisers at different levels, depending on the applicants' experience, education, and examinations. Requirements are detailed in Chapter 14.

Mortgage banking companies. **Mortgage bankers** are not thrift institutions and offer neither checking nor savings accounts. Because they do not use depositors' money, they are subject to considerably less regulation than thrift institutions. They make real estate loans that may later be sold to investors (with the mortgage company receiving a fee if it continues servicing the loans). Mortgage bankers originate a large percentage of all home loans. Mortgage bankers must file a $50,000 surety bond with the Superintendent of Banks, or establish a trust fund in the same amount that can be used to reimburse customers, if it is determined that the mortgage banker has charged improper fees. They are not mortgage *brokers*.

TABLE 1.2

States Offering Reciprocity with New York Licenses

Arkansas	Broker and Sales two years' licensure and current. (Business and residence must be in Arkansas.)
Connecticut	Broker and Sales—current licensure only. (Business and residence must be in Connecticut.)
Georgia	Broker and Sales—two years' licensure and current. (Business and residence must be in Georgia.)
Massachusetts	Broker only—two years' licensure and current. (Business and residence must be in Massachusetts.)
Nebraska	Broker and Sales—two years' licensure and current. (Business and residence must be in Nebraska.)
Oklahoma	Broker only—two years' licensure and current. (Business and residence must be in Oklahoma.)
West Virginia	Broker and Sales—current licensure only. (Business and residence must be in West Virginia.)

All need *current* certification (dated within six [6] months, from the real estate commission where license was obtained); completed application; irrevocable consent form; and the appropriate fee.

Applicants seeking a reciprocal real estate salesperson's license must be sponsored by a broker holding a current New York State broker's license.

Mortgage brokers.   **Mortgage brokers** are registered with the State Banking Department to bring borrowers and lenders together. They charge a fee, often of the borrower, for their services. The Superintendent of Banks may require a mortgage broker to obtain a surety bond or establish a trust fund in the amount of $25,000.

Licensing Nonresidents

Nonresidents of New York may be licensed as New York real estate brokers or salespersons by conforming to all the provisions of the license law except maintaining a place of business within the state. Some New Jersey brokers, for example, hold licenses in both states.

The department will recognize the license issued to a real estate broker or salesperson by another state if the laws of his or her home state permit licenses to be issued to New York licensees without requiring that he or she take that state's licensing examination. (See Table 1.2.) If a particular state's laws do not include these provisions, the nonresident applicant must pass the licensing examination.

Every nonresident applicant must file an **irrevocable consent** form, which makes it easier for the nonresident to be sued in New York State.

■ ADVERTISEMENTS

Advertising must not be misleading in any way. All real estate advertisements must contain the name of the broker's firm and must clearly indicate that the party who placed the ad is a real estate broker. **Blind ads** that contain only a telephone number are prohibited.

On Web sites as well as in print ads, a salesperson's name may not be displayed more prominently than the broker's or firm's name. Any Internet ad must contain a link to the firm's Web site.

All advertisements that state that a property is in the vicinity of a geographic area or territorial subdivision must include as part of the advertisement the name of the geographic area or territorial subdivision in which the property actually is located.

For Sale signs.   A broker must obtain an owner's consent to place a For Sale sign on the owner's property.

■ SUSPENSION AND REVOCATION OF LICENSES

The Division of Licensing Services may hear complaints and/or initiate investigations into any alleged **violations** of the license law or its rules and regulations. Anyone found guilty of untrustworthiness or incompetence may have his or her license suspended **(suspension)** or revoked **(revocation)** or may be fined or reprimanded **(administrative discipline).** Untrustworthiness or incompetence may include any of the following acts:

- Making any substantial misrepresentation (defined as a false statement or the concealment of a material fact, done in order to induce someone to take a certain action, whether done maliciously, ignorantly, or carelessly)
- Making any false promise likely to influence, persuade, or induce
- Making a false statement or misrepresentation through agents, salespersons, advertising, or otherwise
- Accepting, if a salesperson, a commission or valuable consideration for any real estate service from any person except the licensed broker with whom the salesperson is associated
- Acting for or receiving compensation from more than one party in a transaction without the knowledge of all parties involved
- Failing within a reasonable amount of time to account for or remit any monies belonging to others that come into his or her possession
- Being untrustworthy or incompetent to act as a real estate licensee
- Paying a commission or valuable consideration to any person for services performed in violation of the law
- Obtaining a license falsely or fraudulently or making a material misstatement in the license application
- Negotiating with an owner or a landlord with knowledge that the owner or landlord has an exclusive written contract with another broker
- Offering a property for sale or lease without the authorization of the owner
- Accepting the services of any salesperson who is employed by another broker
- Giving legal opinions or performing title examinations
- Entering into a **net listing** contract (when a seller authorizes a broker to procure a specified amount of money for the property and allows the broker to keep any money above the specified amount obtained from the sale)

- Discriminating because of race, creed, color, national origin, age, sex, disability, sexual orientation, or marital status in the sale, rental, or advertisement of housing or commercial space
- Failing to provide definitions of exclusive-right-to-sell and exclusive-agency listings
- Engaging in improper, fraudulent, or dishonest dealing
- Committing any violation of license law

Investigation of complaint and hearing. If the Department feels that a complaint warrants further investigation, it will send an investigator to interview the alleged violator about the charge. In some cases the investigation is preceded by a formal letter of complaint from the Department. If the investigation results in sufficient evidence, the Department will conduct a hearing. Individuals accused of violation of the law may defend themselves or be represented by an attorney. The Department investigates roughly 2,500 complaints annually, with about 1,000 resulting in disciplinary action.

Penalties. An offender who has received any sum of money as commission, compensation, or profit in connection with a license law violation may be held liable for up to four times that amount in damages in addition to having his or her license suspended or revoked. If a license is revoked, one year must pass before a new license application is made.

The Department of State also may impose a fine not to exceed $1,000. Violation of the license law also constitutes a **misdemeanor,** and a licensee may be tried in criminal court in addition to the DOS hearing. Criminal actions can be prosecuted by the attorney general of the State of New York. A misdemeanor is punishable by a fine of not more than $1,000 and/or imprisonment for not more than one year.

Appeal. The action of the Department of State is subject to review. Any determination in granting or renewing a license, revoking or suspending a license, or imposing a fine or reprimand may be appealed to the Secretary of State. Judicial appeal is made through an **Article 78 procedure,** an appeal to the New York State Supreme Court.

Revocation of broker's license. Revocation of a broker's license automatically suspends the licenses of all salespeople affiliated with that broker until they find another supervising broker and their licenses are reissued.

When a salesperson is accused of violating the license law, the supervising broker is also held accountable if the broker knew or should have known of the violation or, having found out about the problem, retained any fees or commissions arising from the transaction.

■ UNLICENSED REAL ESTATE ASSISTANTS

In today's real estate market, many real estate agents find that using unlicensed assistants is very useful. These assistants can do a fair amount of paperwork and legwork, leaving the agents free to use their time finding clients and negotiating transactions. However, it is imperative that unlicensed assistants refrain from performing any real estate activities for which a license is required. According to the Department of State, an unlicensed assistant may safely engage in the following activities:

- Answer the phone, forward calls, and take messages
- Arrange appointments, by telephone, for the licensee
- Follow up on loan commitments after a contract has been negotiated and generally secure status reports on the loan progress
- Assemble documents for closing
- Write ads for the approval of the broker and place approved classified advertising
- Type contract forms for the approval of the broker
- Compute commission checks
- Place signs on or remove them from properties
- Order items of repair as directed by the broker
- Prepare flyers and promotional information for approval by the broker
- Schedule appointments for licensees to show listed property
- Gather information for a comparative market analysis
- Gather information for an appraisal
- Monitor licenses and personnel files
- Perform secretarial and clerical duties such as typing letters and filing

DOS Determinations.   In recent years, the DOS has acted in cases like the following:

- Associate broker failed to provide the required written disclosure of agency (as explained in Chapter 3); DOS fined him $500. The principal broker also was fined and penalized.
- Salesperson lied on her license renewal application and said she had completed continuing education requirements. An audit turned up the false statement. DOS revoked her license.
- Salesperson did not lie on license renewal, but frankly stated he had failed to complete the continuing education courses required. DOS suspended his license until he provided proof he completed the courses.
- Broker's license was suspended because he failed to pay child support, not to be reinstated until Family Court confirmed he was up to date with his payments.
- Broker had misappropriated rental income he was collecting on behalf of a landlord, and when ordered to make restitution, paid with bad checks. DOS revoked his license, and indicated it could not be reinstated until the full sum was repaid to the landlord together with interest.

■ CASE STUDY

The Facts

Peter and Kathleen contacted a licensed broker, Roger, about a house they had seen advertised. Roger told them he would be representing them as a buyers' agent, but did not give them any written disclosure form.

About six months later, another broker contacted Peter and Kathleen and told them about a house just listed by his firm by trustees acting for their mother. The list price was $259,000. After viewing the property, Peter and Kathleen contacted Roger and asked if he would appraise the house for them. He assured them he could be trusted and agreed to perform the appraisal for between $350 and $400. The appraisal was not actually performed.

Roger, having learned about the house, promptly showed it to Mr. and Mrs. S. This second couple made several offers, and learning that Peter and Kathleen were offering full price, made a final offer for $260,000 with a 30-day closing. All offers were presented at the same time, and none was accepted. Ten days later, Peter went directly to the listing agent's office and signed an offer for $265,000, with closing and other terms to the sellers' satisfaction.

Peter and Kathleen's offer was accepted, the property closed, and the commission was paid to the listing office.

Roger sued the trustees, seeking a commission of $15,600 on the grounds that he had earned a commission by producing buyers ready, willing, and able to pay $260,000, which was more than the asking price. He testified that one of the two trustees had agreed to those terms.

Courts have held in the past that a broker has performed the service for which he was hired by producing a buyer ready, willing, and able to meet the seller's terms. They have also held that commission is earned at the meeting of the minds.

If you were the judge, how would you have ruled?

Roger lost the suit, and appealed. The Appellate judge ruled against him, concluding there had been no meeting of the minds between the trustees and the second couple, particularly as regards the closing date.

DOS Opinion

The Department of State revoked Roger's license and that of his company, on the grounds that Roger

- failed to provide Peter and Kathleen with a written disclosure of whether he was acting as a buyer's or seller's agent;
- never made clear for which party he was acting. He assured Peter and Kathleen he was representing them, but later stated he was representing the trustees and that they owed him a commission (untrustworthiness and incompetency);
- accepted Peter and Kathleen as principals when he agreed to perform the appraisal for them. (He breached his duty by failing to perform the

appraisal and by showing another couple the house Peter and Kathleen had called to his attention);

■ involved Peter and Kathleen in the lawsuit, a "gross demonstration of untrustworthiness";

■ sued for a commission to which he was not entitled, a "demonstration of untrustworthiness";

■ engaged in "fraudulent practices" by promising Peter and Kathleen they could trust him, failing to make the appraisal he had promised, and misusing the information they gave him about the house in order to show it to another couple; and

■ acted as an undisclosed dual agent for both Peter and Kathleen and the trustees;

Roger's loss of license makes it clear that the Department of State will insist that

■ brokers make it clear whom they are representing;

■ written disclosure forms be signed at first substantive contact with buyers and sellers; and

■ dual agency requires the informed consent of all parties to the transaction.

■ SUMMARY

In New York, licensees must be permanent residents of the United States, must never have been convicted of a felony, and must pass state examinations before licensure. A salesperson must have completed a prescribed 45-hour qualifying course, be at least 18 years old, and be sponsored by a licensed broker. A broker must be at least 19 years old, with an additional 45 hours of approved study and one full year's experience as a licensed salesperson. Some exceptions to these requirements are possible.

The real estate license, which covers a two-year period, costs $50 for a salesperson and $150 for a broker. An associate broker license designates a fully qualified broker who chooses to remain in a salesperson's capacity under a supervising broker. Those exempt from licensing requirements include New York State attorneys, public officials while performing their public duties, and persons acting under court order. A license is not required of a resident manager employed by only one owner to collect rents. Certain tenant organizations in New York City may also perform real estate services without being licensed.

Every residential broker must have a principal place of business within the state, post a sign readable from the sidewalk or in the lobby of an office building, obtain a separate license for each branch office, and display the principal broker's license prominently. Brokers who handle other people's money must maintain a separate escrow account for those funds. The broker must immediately deliver duplicate originals of all documents to the persons signing them and must keep a file of all documents relating to real estate transactions for at least three years.

Commissions may be collected only by the supervising broker and may be shared only with other brokers and the broker's own associated salespersons and associate brokers. Advertisements must contain the name of the broker's firm.

Laws, rules, and regulations governing licensees are administered by the New York Department of State, which may, after hearings, suspend or revoke licenses. Violations of these laws, rules, and regulations is also a misdemeanor.

QUESTIONS

1. Joan, who has no real estate license, canvasses homeowners by phone to see if they are interested in selling their homes. Shanice, who is licensed, gives Joan $25 for every lead she turns up. Does this violate license law?

   a. No, because the gift is not more than $25.
   b. No, because Joan does not actually list or sell property.
   c. Yes, because Shanice is paying compensation for services that require licensure.
   d. Yes, because Joan is using a home telephone with no broker's sign outside her house.

2. Real estate license laws were instituted to

   a. raise revenue through license fees.
   b. limit the number of brokers and salespersons.
   c. match the federal government's requirements.
   d. protect the public and maintain high standards.

3. In New York, real estate licenses are under the supervision of the

   a. Real Estate Commission.
   b. Board of REALTORS®.
   c. Department of State.
   d. Department of Education.

4. Tom Swift, a New York resident, needs a real estate license to

   a. give his cousin advice about pricing her home for the market.
   b. write a lease for a tenant in a building he owns.
   c. accept a TV set from a grateful neighbor for whom he arranged a home equity loan.
   d. sell the house of his dead aunt while he is settling her estate.

5. The sponsoring broker's name must be at last as conspicuous as a salesperson's name on

   a. business cards.
   b. Internet advertising.
   c. classified ads.
   d. All of the above

6. A duly licensed salesperson may accept a bonus from

   a. a grateful seller.
   b. a grateful buyer.
   c. another salesperson.
   d. None of the above

7. A fully qualified broker who chooses to act as a salesperson under another broker's sponsorship is licensed as a(n)

   a. adjunct salesperson.
   b. sales associate.
   c. associate broker.
   d. principal broker.

8. To obtain a broker's license, one must reach the age of

   a. 18.   c. 20.
   b. 19.   d. 21.

9. A broker must have completed how many hours of prescribed study?

   a. 15   c. 45
   b. 30   d. 90

10. Which of the following meets a requirement for a broker's license in New York State?

    a. Completion of 50 hours in real estate courses
    b. Age of at least 18
    c. One year's experience as a licensed salesperson
    d. Membership in the New York State Association of REALTORS®

11. Generally, real estate licenses are good for a period of

    a. one year.   c. three years.
    b. two years.   d. four years.

12. A nonresident broker seeking a New York license must

    a. post a bond of $5,000.
    b. be a citizen of the United States.
    c. find a New York attorney to act as a sponsor.
    d. file an affidavit allowing himself or herself to be sued in New York State.

13. In the office a broker must display

    a. all brokers' licenses.
    b. all salespersons' licenses.
    c. no licenses.
    d. only salespersons' licenses.

14. Salesperson Jackson told the telephone company to print the following ad under Real Estate in the Yellow Pages: Alissia Jackson, Licensed Salesperson, Residential Property a Specialty, 473-4973. She should have included her

    a. area code.
    b. broker's name.
    c. office address.
    d. home phone number.

15. A violation of the license law is legally classified as a(n)

    a. revocation.   c. misdemeanor.
    b. offense.   d. felony.

16. The Department of State has revoked Ted Toller's license for fraud. Which of the following is true?

    a. Toller may appeal the revocation.
    b. His salespersons may continue in business for 90 days, because they were not found guilty.
    c. Toller may continue his business for 90 days if he posts a bond with the DOS.
    d. Toller may have his license reinstated if he signs an irrevocable consent form.

17. If a principal broker loses her license, her associated salespersons must immediately

    a. appoint one of their number to serve as supervisor.
    b. stop listing and selling.
    c. obtain brokers' licenses.
    d. move the office to another location.

18. A salesperson need *not* be

    a. licensed by the state.
    b. at least 18 years old.
    c. already experienced in real estate.
    d. supervised by a broker.

19. Don Houseknecht lists his house with Bob Broker. Don offers a bonus commission of $500 to the agent who brings a good buyer before Thanksgiving. Sally Salesperson, who is associated with the cooperating firm of Orville Otherbroker, effects the sale on November 1. Sally may collect that bonus from

    a. Don.   c. Bob.
    b. Orville.   d. no one.

20. A broker must post a sign at the place of business

    a. inside the broker's office.
    b. on the office mailbox.
    c. above each salesperson's desk.
    d. visible from the sidewalk or in a lobby.

21. A real estate broker must keep all documents for the DOS pertaining to a real estate transaction on file for how long?

    a. Two years   c. Seven years
    b. Three years   d. Indefinitely

22. The term *commingling* pertains to

    a. mixing the broker's funds with escrow deposits.
    b. soliciting the services of another broker's salespersons.
    c. failing to deliver duplicate originals of contracts.
    d. promoting business at social gatherings.

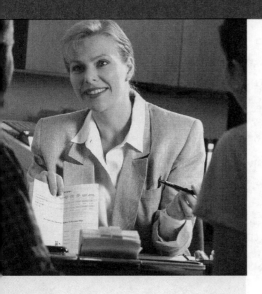

2

THE LAW OF AGENCY

Bob Broker listed the Bensons' attractive house for sale, decided he'd like to live there himself, and offered to pay the full asking price. When the sale closed, Bob collected the commission originally agreed on. Was there a conflict of interest?

The real estate practitioner needs a thorough knowledge of the law of agency to avoid violations of fiduciary duty.

■ KEY TERMS

accountability

agency

agency coupled with an interest

agent

brokerage

buyer's broker

client

commission

confidentiality

customer

disclosure

dual agency

express agency

fiduciary

fiduciary duties

fiduciary relationship

fraud

general agent

implied agency

informed consent

kickbacks

latent defects

law of agency

listing agreement

loyalty

meeting of the minds

misrepresentation

obedience

power of attorney

principal

procuring cause of sale

puffing

ratification

ready, willing, and able buyer

reasonable care

self-dealing

special agent

subagent

undisclosed dual agency

undivided loyalty

universal agent

■ OVERVIEW OF AGENCY DISCUSSION

In this chapter, the basic **law of agency** is covered, with emphasis on the duties of agents to their clients and standards for dealing with their customers. Chapter 3 (Agency and Real Estate Brokerage) discusses the various types of possible agency relationships and the need for brokers to develop policies for disclosure of representation.

■ WHAT IS AN AGENT?

Real estate brokers and salespersons are commonly referred to as agents. Legally, however, the term refers to strictly defined legal relationships. In the case of real estate, it is a relationship between licensees and buyers, sellers, landlords, or tenants. In the law of agency (the body of law that governs these relationships), the following terms have specific definitions:

■ **Agent**—the individual who is authorized and consents to represent the interests of another person. In the real estate business the broker firm is the agent of the seller, buyer, landlord, or tenant.
■ **Principal**—the individual who hires and delegates to the agent the responsibility of representing his or her interests.
■ **Agency**—the fiduciary relationship between the principal and the agent.
■ **Fiduciary**—the relationship of trust and confidence to the principal between the agent and the principal.
■ **Client**—the principal.
■ **Customer**—the third party with whom the agent deals on behalf of the principal.

There is a distinction between the duties owed by the agent to a client and the treatment owed to a customer. The *client* is the principal to whom the agent gives *advice* and *counsel* and whose interest must be put above the interest of all others. The agent is entrusted with certain *confidential information* and has *fiduciary responsibilities* (discussed in greater detail later) to the principal. In contrast, the *customer* is entitled only to factual information and fair and honest dealings as a consumer but does not receive advice and counsel or confidential information about the principal. The agent works for the principal and with the customer.

Types of Agents

An agent may be classified as a universal agent, general agent, or special agent. A **universal agent** has authority to represent the principal in *all matters that can be delegated.* The universal agent can enter into any contract on behalf of the principal without prior permission. He or she can act for the principal in a broad range of areas. This type of agency is often created by a written document known as a **power of attorney.**

A **general agent** is empowered to represent the principal in a *specific range of matters.* The general agent may bind the principal to any contract within the scope of the agent's authority. This type of authority also can be created by a power of attorney. A property manager is usually a general agent.

A **special agent** is authorized to represent the principal in *one specific transaction or business activity under detailed instructions*. A real estate broker is usually a special agent. If hired by a seller, the broker's duty is limited to finding a ready, willing, and able buyer for the property. If hired by the buyer, the broker's duty is limited to finding a suitable property for the buyer. As a special agent, the broker is not authorized to bind the principal to any contract.

An **agency coupled with an interest** is a relationship in which the agent has some interest in the property being sold. Such an agency *cannot be revoked by the principal, nor can it be terminated on the principal's death*. For example, a broker might supply the financing for a condominium development, provided the developer agrees to give the broker the exclusive right to sell the completed condo units. Because this agent has a special interest in the transaction, the developer may not revoke the listing agreement after the broker provides the financing.

■ CREATION OF AGENCY

An agency relationship can be created by either an oral or a written agency agreement between the principal and the agent. It can also be implied from words or conduct. Of course, to ensure that all parties have a clear understanding of the agency relationship, it is in everyone's best interest to create an agency relationship with a written agreement.

The most common way of creating an agency relationship is through an *express agreement* (an agreement that is expressed in words, either spoken or written). A written agreement that creates an **express agency** relationship between a seller and a real estate broker is called a **listing agreement.** A listing agreement authorizes the broker to find a buyer or tenant for the owner's property. An agency relationship also can be created between a buyer or tenant and a broker by the use of a document called a *buyer agency agreement*. A buyer agency agreement describes the activities and responsibilities the principal expects from the broker in finding the appropriate property for purchase or lease.

An agency also could be created with an *implied agreement*. This occurs when both the principal and the agent act as if an agency exists, even though they have not expressly entered into an agreement. Providing services that are accepted by the principal can create an **implied agency** relationship. For instance, a broker advises a seller on a fair listing price, gives helpful hints on how the seller can make the house more marketable, shows the property to several buyers, and continually refers to himself or herself as the *seller's agent*. The seller sets the listing price according to the broker's advice, makes the recommended repairs to the house, and agrees to numerous showings. In this case, there may be an implied agency relationship.

When someone claims to be an agent but there is no agreement, the principal may establish an agency by ratification—in other words, by accepting the benefits of the previously unauthorized act.

The requirement for written agency disclosure (discussed in Chapter 3) reduces the chances for misunderstanding in a residential transaction. However, it is often difficult for customers to understand the complexities of the law of agency. Buyers easily can assume that when they contact a broker to show them property, the broker becomes "their agent." *In the end it is a person's actions that control the creation of an agency relationship, not just his or her words.*

Compensation.   It is commonly assumed that a person is the agent of the one who pays the compensation. However, this is not true. The source of compensation does not determine agency; the agent does not necessarily represent the person who pays the commission. In fact, agency can exist even if there is no fee involved (a *gratuitous agency*). Buyers, sellers, and brokers can make any agreement they choose about compensating the broker, regardless of which one is the agent's principal. For example, the seller could agree to pay a commission to a broker who is the buyer's agent. Written agency agreements should always state how the agent is to be compensated.

■ AGENCY AND BROKERAGE

The business of bringing buyers and sellers or landlords and tenants together in the marketplace is known as **brokerage.**

The principal who employs the broker may be a seller, a prospective buyer, an owner who wishes to lease property, or someone seeking property to rent. The broker acts as the *agent* of the principal, who usually compensates the broker with a **commission** or fee for having successfully performed the service for which the broker was employed. The principal is also known as the *client*.

Seller as Principal

If a seller contracts with a broker to market the seller's real estate, the broker becomes an *agent of the seller*; the seller is the *principal*, the broker's *client*. A buyer who contacts the broker to review properties listed with the broker's firm is the broker's customer. Though obligated to deal honestly with all parties to a transaction and to comply with all aspects of the license law, the broker is strictly *accountable only to the principal—in this case the seller*.

The listing contract for residential properties usually authorizes the broker to use licensees employed by the broker as well as the services of other cooperating brokers in marketing the seller's real estate. The salesperson is considered an agent of his or her managing broker, and also a **subagent** of any seller who is using the firm's services. The cooperating agent, the broker from another company who finds the buyer, may be acting as

- a *subagent* of the seller;
- an agent for the listing broker (broker's agent); or
- an agent for the buyer.

Buyer as Principal

The practice of buyers hiring brokers to find the desired real estate is becoming more common. In this situation the broker and the buyer usually draw up an agreement that details the nature of the property desired, the amount of the broker's compensation, and how it is to be paid. (See the sample buyer agency agreement in Chapter 3.) The buyer becomes the *principal*, the broker's *client*. In this case the broker, as agent, is the **buyer's broker** and is strictly account-able to the buyer. The seller becomes the *customer*.

The same relationships apply when a prospective tenant hires a broker to locate property for rent.

Broker as Principal

A broker is licensed to act as the principal's agent and thus can collect a commission for performing his or her assigned duties. A salesperson or associate broker, on the other hand, has no authority to make contracts or receive compensation directly from a principal. All of a salesperson's activities must be performed in the name of his or her supervising broker. The broker is fully responsible for the real estate actions of all salespeople licensed under him or her.

The salesperson functions as an *agent* of the broker and a *subagent* of the principal (the buyer or the seller). Thus, both the broker and the broker's salespersons and associate brokers have a fiduciary relationship with the prin-cipal.

Importance of Agency Law to Licensees

Agency law has become an increasingly vital topic for all real estate agents. While most of the legal principles of agency law have remained unchanged for decades, the practical application of those laws to real estate agents has dramatically changed the face of the real estate business in recent years.

Whom does the agent represent?   In the early 1980s the Federal Trade Commission found that the public was totally confused about whom a real estate agent was working for. When buyers who bought property listed by a different firm were asked whom they thought the selling agent was working for, more than 70 percent said they believed the selling agent was working for them. The reality was that in the vast majority of these transactions, the agent was legally bound to represent and work for the best interests of the seller.

Many states began drafting legislation that would require agents to disclose whom they represented to all the parties involved. In 1991, New York enacted a disclosure law that, in the opinion of many, was a model for the nation. (Agency disclosure is discussed in Chapter 3.)

Basic Agency Relationships

Before we discuss the fiduciary responsibilities owed to principals by their agents, it is important to take a quick look at the types of agency relationships that may exist in a given transaction. The first agency relationship is between the seller and the listing broker. The broker agrees to perform diligently to find a ready, willing, and able buyer. The seller is the principal; the broker is the agent.

The broker typically has licensed salespeople to help list and market property. The salespeople are the agents of the broker and the subagents of the seller.

FIGURE   2.1

Agent's
Responsibilities

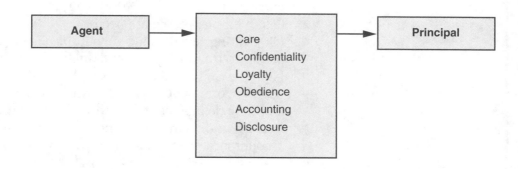

Both the listing broker and the affiliated salespeople owe their fiduciary duties to the seller (unless otherwise agreed).

The listing broker and cooperating brokers (other members of a multiple-listing service, or MLS) will begin to market the listed property. As they do so, they work with various prospective buyers. Cooperating brokers and salespeople who choose to represent the seller owe their fiduciary duties to the seller, not the buyer. However, some cooperating brokers may be working under a buyer-agency agreement and represent the buyer. They owe their fiduciary duties to the buyer, not the seller. Others may work not as subagents but simply as cooperating borkers.

■ FIDUCIARY RESPONSIBILITIES

A broker has the right to reject agency contracts that in his or her judgment violate the law, ethics, or high standards of the office. After a brokerage relationship has been established, however, the broker owes the principal the duty to exercise care, skill, and integrity in carrying out instructions.

An agent's **fiduciary relationship** with his or her principal is a relationship of trust and confidence. (Other types of fiduciaries include trustees, executors, and guardians.) If the principal could not count on the agent to act in the principal's best interest, the agency relationship would be meaningless.

Fiduciary Duties to the Principal

The relationship created by agency carries with it certain **fiduciary duties** that the broker must fulfill: the duties of care, confidentiality, loyalty, obedience, accounting, and disclosure, which can be memorized as CC-LOAD. (See Figure 2.1.)

Care.   The broker must exercise **reasonable care** while transacting business entrusted to him or her by the principal. Real estate brokers are expected to have special skills and expertise in the real estate field. They must be knowledgeable about real property laws, land-use issues, financing, transfer of title, and the like.

Brokers should be skilled in the following areas:

- Valuing property (to determine a reasonable listing price and a reasonable purchase price)
- Clarifying the principal's needs
- Discovering pertinent facts about the neighborhood, the property, and the parties to the transaction and disclosing this information to the principal
- Filling in and explaining in simple terms the purpose and effect of the contract forms involved (the listing agreement or buyer agency agreement and the purchase contract) while never engaging in the practice of law
- Recommending that the principal seek expert advisers (such as attorneys, accountants, or inspectors) when appropriate
- Making best efforts to sell or find the property
- Explaining different financing options available from local lenders
- Negotiating offers and counteroffers
- Meeting contract deadlines

If a broker represents the seller, care and skill include helping the seller arrive at an appropriate and realistic listing price, discovering facts that affect the seller and disclosing them, and properly presenting the contracts that the seller signs. It also means making reasonable efforts to market the property, such as advertising, holding open houses, and helping the seller evaluate the terms and conditions of offers to purchase.

For example, suppose a broker sells a home a few days after the listing agreement is signed. While the seller is initially pleased with the quick sale, she later realizes that the broker set the listing price too low. The seller also discovers that plans for a nearby shopping center were approved a few months ago. When the shopping center is completed in eight months, her property will be worth even more. The broker, who claimed to be an expert on her neighborhood, had no idea about the new shopping center. There were also several clauses in the sales contract that the seller didn't understand. When she asked the broker about them, he shrugged off her concern. Now she realizes that the clauses were important and were not to her advantage. If she had understood their effect, she would have consulted an attorney. The broker breached his duty to exercise reasonable care and skill when fulfilling the terms of the agency contract. He should have had a basic knowledge about property values, new developments in the neighborhood, and the importance of contract terms. And he certainly should have recommended that the seller consult an attorney before signing the contract or make the contract subject to the approval of her attorney.

A broker who represents the buyer will be expected to help the buyer locate suitable property and evaluate property values, neighborhood, and property conditions; discover financing alternatives; and handle offers and counteroffers with the buyer's interest in mind. For example, the buyers' broker might discover that the seller is facing foreclosure if the property is not sold promptly. The broker doesn't relay that information to the buyers. If they had known, they might have bought the property for less than they offered. The broker violated fiduciary duty to the buyer.

The broker is liable to the principal for any loss resulting from the broker's negligence or carelessness.

Confidentiality.   An agent may not disclose any confidential information learned from or about the principal. For example, if the agent is representing the seller, information about the principal's financial condition may not be disclosed to potential buyers, including the fact that the principal will accept a price lower than the listing price. The same rule applies to any confidential facts that might harm the principal's bargaining position, such as the fact that the seller must quickly move out of the area. Similarly, a buyer's broker would not reveal the buyer's readiness to pay more if necessary.

Confidential information never may be revealed, even if it would mean a larger commission or a quicker closing date for the agent. Even after the agency relationship has terminated—for instance, after the sale has closed—confidential information should be kept confidential.

A broker may not maintain **confidentiality**, however, if the information is something he or she is obligated to disclose because of the duty to deal honestly with a customer. For example, if the broker knows about a hazardous condition on the property, it must be disclosed to the buyer.

Loyalty.   The duty of **loyalty** dictates that an agent must always place the principal's interests above those of other persons, including the agent's own interests. The seller's agent, for example, must try to obtain the highest possible price, the buyer's agent to obtain the lowest. The agent must never take advantage of a chance to profit at the principal's expense.

For example, an offer with a lower purchase price may be in the seller's best interest because of the financing terms, closing date, or other concessions. The agent must try his or her best to negotiate such an offer, even though it may mean a smaller commission for the agent.

Obedience.   The fiduciary relationship obligates the broker to obey the principal's instructions in accordance with the contract. This duty of **obedience** is not absolute, however. The broker may not obey any instructions that are unlawful or unethical. For example, the broker may not follow instructions to make the property unavailable to members of a minority group or to conceal a defect in the property.

If a broker knows or has reason to suspect that the client will ask him or her to do something unlawful or unethical, the broker should either refuse to accept the listing or should terminate the listing if it already exists.

Accounting.   Brokers must be able to report the status of all funds entrusted to them. Real estate license laws require that brokers give duplicate originals of all documents to all parties affected by such documents and keep copies of them on file for three years. In addition, brokers must immediately deposit all funds entrusted to them in special trust, or escrow, accounts. It is illegal for brokers to commingle (mix) such monies with personal funds or to retain any interest such monies earn. This duty to account to the principal is sometimes referred to as **accountability.**

Disclosure.   It is the broker's duty to pass on to the principal all facts or information the broker obtains that could affect the principal's decisions. The duty of **disclosure** is sometimes known as the *duty of notice.* It includes not only useful information the broker knew but also relevant information or *material facts* that the agent should have known. (A material fact is any fact that is important to a person making a decision.)

In the course of a transaction, principals must make critical decisions. Agents must supply their clients with all the material facts, so that the principals may make informed choices.

The broker must volunteer pertinent information whether or not the client knows enough to ask for it. For example, a broker has presented an offer to her principal, the seller. The offer involves seller financing (the buyer will make a small down payment, and the seller will finance the difference between the down payment and the purchase price). The broker knows that the buyer has a history of defaulting on his obligations. Even though the seller does not ask the broker about the buyer's credit history, the broker must express a concern and perhaps recommend the seller require that the buyer obtain a preapproved mortgage. In many cases, a broker may be held liable for damages for failure to disclose material facts.

Some of the types of information it is imperative to disclose include the following:

- The relationship between an agent and other parties to the transaction. For instance, if the agent is representing the seller and the buyer is a relative of the agent, the agent must disclose that fact to the seller. Other relationships that must be disclosed include close friends and close business associates.
- Whether the agent is acting for himself or herself. New York forbids brokers and salespersons to buy or sell property in which they have a personal interest without informing the seller or purchaser of that interest. It is prudent to make such a disclosure in writing as part of the purchase contract before it is signed. If a buyer's broker has a similar type of relationship with the property seller, that relationship must be fully disclosed to the buyer.
- The existence of other offers. All offers should be immediately submitted to the principal until the sale is closed. The seller's agent must remember that it is up to the principal to reject or accept an offer; it is not the agent's job to evaluate the offers and submit only the most favorable. Failing to submit all offers immediately is a violation of license law.
- The status or form of the earnest money deposit. The seller's agent always must inform the principal if the earnest money is in the form of a promissory note or a postdated check. If the broker fails to do so and the

seller cannot collect on the note or check, the broker may be liable to the seller for the amount of the deposit.

- The buyer's financial condition. If the seller's broker knows of any negative information about the buyer, he or she must inform the seller at once. The buyer's broker, however, must keep the buyer's financial condition confidential, unless to do so would breach the agent's duty to treat the seller fairly.

- The value of the property. One of the reasons sellers use real estate brokers to market their properties and buyers use brokers to help them purchase properties is that brokers have expertise in the area of property values. Brokers must always give their true opinions of a property's value, and should never inflate that value to obtain a listing or complete a sale. The broker would be wise to disclose the sale prices of comparable properties, including those the broker should know about if he or she had studied the marketplace.

- Any commission split. The listing broker should disclose to the seller any fee-sharing arrangement with a cooperating broker. This means that the listing broker must describe to the seller the general company policy regarding cooperating with subagents, cooperating agents, and buyer agents.

- Contract provisions. The broker must explain to his or her client the important provisions of any contract the client is going to sign. If the client requires anything more than a simple explanation, the broker must advise the client to seek competent legal advice.

- Property deficiencies. If a broker represents a buyer, he or she must disclose the deficiencies of a property as well as contract or financing issues that are not to the buyer's benefit. The buyer's broker should also suggest the lowest price the buyer should pay based on comparable values and how long a property has been listed or why the seller is selling.

Breach of Fiduciary Duties

If agents breach their fiduciary duties, they may be subject to a variety of penalties. Some of these penalties can be imposed regardless of whether the agent's breach of duties caused the principal any actual harm. Penalties for breaching fiduciary duties may include

- loss of the commission;
- loss of the agent's license or other disciplinary action by the state;
- adverse judgment in a civil suit; and
- rescission (voiding) of the transaction by court order.

Scope of Authority

While agents must fulfill their fiduciary responsibilities, they must also act within the scope of their authority. Real estate agents, who are almost always special agents, have only the authority granted to them by their listing or buyer broker agreements. For example, the listing broker is authorized to find a ready, willing, and able buyer, but generally has no authority to sign contracts for the seller, initial changes to an offer, receive the purchase price on behalf of the seller, or permit early occupancy.

The authority granted to a listing broker should be stated expressly in the listing agreement. In a typical listing contract, the seller specifically authorizes the broker to place a sign on the property, advertise, show property, cooperate with other brokers, use the services of the local MLS, and accept earnest money deposits. Usually, the broker is not given the right to sign contracts, although in exceptional cases, the broker may be appointed as attorney-in-fact under a separately granted power of attorney.

A buyer's broker is generally given the authority to seek out appropriate property. The broker is not usually given the right to sign a purchase contract on behalf of the buyer.

Agent's Responsibilities to Other Parties in the Transaction

Even though an agent's primary responsibility is to the principal, the agent also has obligations to third parties. The duties to the third party or customer include

- honest and fair dealing; and
- disclosure of material facts that the licensee knows or should know that affect the desirability or value of the property (or the buyer's ability to complete the transaction) and that are not discoverable by the customer.

Opinion versus fact. Whatever the specific topic, brokers, salespeople, and other staff members must be careful about the statements they make to third parties. They must be sure that the customer understands whether the statement is an *opinion* or a *fact*. Statements of opinion are only permissible as long as they are offered as opinions and without any *intention to deceive*.

For instance, a broker is showing a house to a buyer and says, "This house has the best view in the neighborhood." This statement is obviously a statement of opinion, and because the buyer can look out the window and judge the view for himself, the statement is not made with an intent to deceive.

Statements that are an exaggeration of a property's benefits are called **puffing.** If the broker said, in the previous example, "This house has the best view in the whole county—no, the whole state!" her statement would be considered puffing. It is an obvious exaggeration. Puffing is considered a sales tactic and is legal. However, real estate agents must be careful to make sure that their "puffing" is not accepted by buyers as fact. For instance, telling a prospective buyer that a home "will appreciate at least 50 percent in the next five years" may be an exaggeration, but it is also a misleading statement that a buyer could easily accept as a fact. Licensees must be sure that none of their statements can be interpreted as *fraudulent*. **Fraud** is the *intentional misrepresentation of a material fact in such a way as to harm or take advantage of another person*. Misrepresentation is discussed in more detail below.

Environmental concerns. Disclosure of environmental health hazards, which can render properties unsalable, also may be required. Frequently the buyer or the buyer's mortgage lender will request inspections or tests to determine the presence or level of risk. Licensees are urged to obtain advice from state and local authorities responsible for environmental regulation whenever toxic waste dumping; contaminated soil or water; nearby chemical or nuclear facilities; or health hazards such as radon, mold, asbestos, or lead paint may be present.

Latent defects.   Brokers and salespersons should be aware that some courts have ruled that a seller is responsible for revealing to a buyer any material (important) latent defects relating to the property. A **latent** (or hidden) **defect** is one that is not discoverable by ordinary, reasonable inspection. Regardless of whether the agent represents the buyer or the seller, the broker likewise is responsible for disclosing known hidden defects to the buyer. Buyers have been able either to rescind the sales contract or to receive damages when latent defects are not revealed. Examples of such hidden defects include a leaking underground oil storage tank, a buried drain tile that causes water to accumulate, and a driveway built partly on adjoining property.

New York courts are continuing to rule on the duties of real estate agents toward their customers. While the traditional principle of caveat emptor (let the buyer beware) is still the law, it has been modified in certain circumstances to require that both the seller and the broker disclose known material facts. To protect himself or herself from liability in this area, a broker should ask the seller for all the pertinent facts about the physical condition of the property. The broker does not have to complete a detailed physical inspection; asking the seller for all pertinent facts should be sufficient. Although a seller may be understandably reluctant to discuss such facts, the broker can assure the seller that such disclosure will protect the seller from potential liability, protect the broker from potential liability, and enable the broker to market the property in the most effective way possible.

According to the Department of State Division of Licensing Services, it is not the broker's duty to verify all of the seller's representations, unless the broker uses such representations in marketing the property. However, if the broker knows *or has reason to know* that the seller has indeed made a misrepresentation or failed to disclose material facts, the broker is required to make a full disclosure.

New York State requires sellers to furnish perspective buyers with a 48-item Property Condition Disclosure Statement, discussed in Chapter 3.

In a New York Supreme Court Appellate Division case, *Stambovsky v. Akley* (the haunted house case), a seller was held responsible for failing to disclose a house was haunted. The court did rule that the broker was not at fault.

To clear up the problem of "stigmatized" properties, a 1995 amendment to the New York State Real Property Law (Section 443-a) provides that an owner, occupant, or agent need not disclose the fact that the property is or is suspected to be the site of a homicide, suicide, other death, or any other felony. The fact that the property was ever owned or occupied by someone who had or was suspected to have HIV infection or AIDS or any disease highly unlikely to be transmitted through occupancy of a dwelling may not be disclosed either.

Megan's Law.   New York courts have held that brokers have no obligation to search the state records on which convicted pedophiles must register their addresses. A buyer's broker should, however, advise clients that the registry is available for public inspection.

To gain information about the possibility that crimes have been committed on the property, a prospective purchaser may submit a written inquiry; and the seller or the seller's agent may choose whether or not to respond to the inquiry.

Misrepresentations. One of the most common complaints against real estate agents is that of **misrepresentation.** Misrepresentations violate the broker's obligation of honesty and fair dealing.

To successfully sue a real estate agent for misrepresentation, the plaintiff (the one bringing the suit) must be able to prove that

- the broker made a misstatement (oral or written) to the buyer or failed to disclose a material fact to the buyer that should have been disclosed;
- the broker either knew or should have known that the statement was not accurate or that the information should have been disclosed;
- the buyer reasonably relied on such statement; and
- the buyer was damaged as a result of that reliance.

Misrepresentation can be an affirmative statement, such as "A new roof was put on this house three years ago" when the broker knows the roof is 12 years old. It can also be a failure to disclose a latent defect (discussed earlier). For instance, if the broker knows the basement regularly floods but does not disclose that fact to the buyer, the broker is guilty of misrepresentation.

The misstatement does not have to be intentional to be misrepresentation. A real estate agent can be liable for misrepresentation if he or she knew or *should have known* about the falsity of the statement.

Brokers around the country have been held liable for misrepresentations in the following types of cases:

- Termite infestation. The broker, acting for the seller, plastered over termite damage.
- Free of liens and encumbrances. The broker mistakenly told the buyer that the seller owned the property free and clear of all encumbrances.
- Filled land. The broker made an unauthorized statement to the buyer that the property was not a "filled lot." (The house later sank when the fill settled.)
- Easements. When a buyer asked a broker about easements on a property, the broker said not to worry. Three months later, the city used the easement to lay water pipes.
- Zoning. The broker misrepresented the property's zoning.

If a contract to purchase real estate is obtained as a result of misstatements made by a broker or salesperson, the contract may be disaffirmed or renounced by the purchaser. In such a case the broker will lose a commission. If either party suffers loss because of misrepresentations, the broker can be held liable for damages.

For the buyer's broker, a hidden defect requiring disclosure to the seller would be the buyer's financial inability or unwillingness to complete the purchase.

Dual agency.   Sometimes a broker may have the opportunity to receive compensation from both the buyer and the seller in a transaction. An agent cannot, however, give **undivided loyalty** to two or more principals in the same transaction. Thus, real estate license laws prohibit a broker from representing and/or collecting compensation from both parties to a transaction without their prior knowledge and consent. More difficult to handle is the situation in which a seller's broker, for example, emotionally adopts a buyer and unconsciously begins to work for the buyer's best interest, so that an unintended and illegal **dual agency** results. One could be acting as a dual agent even if not being paid by both parties.

A common complaint against agents is that of **undisclosed dual agency,** which occurs when an agent acts in the best interests of one party to a transaction while legally representing the other. An example might be when a buyer's agent sells a close relative's property to a client without the **informed consent** of that client.

Self-dealing.   Problems can also occur when brokers list property, then decide to buy it themselves and collect the agreed-on commission. This is referred to as **self-dealing**. At that point those brokers represent themselves but continue to act as the sellers' agents as well. It is advisable for agents in this position to give up the listing, collect no commission, and just represent themselves as buyers.

■ THE BROKER'S COMPENSATION

The broker's compensation is specified in the listing agreement, management agreement, or other contract with the principal and is subject to negotiation between the parties. Compensation usually is computed as a percentage of the total amount of money involved, but it could be a flat fee or other consideration. It usually is considered to be earned when the broker has accomplished the work for which he or she was hired after a seller accepts an offer from a ready, willing, and able buyer. A **ready, willing, and able buyer** is one who is *prepared to buy on the seller's terms, is financially capable, and is ready to take positive steps to complete the transaction.*

Many listing agreements contain a preclusive agreement (an "as, if, and when" clause), providing that the broker will not collect the commission unless and until the sale has actually closed. The broker, however, is usually entitled to a commission if the transaction is not completed for any of the following reasons:

- The owner changes his or her mind and refuses to sell.
- The owner commits fraud with respect to the transaction.

- The owner is unable to deliver possession within a reasonable time.
- The owner insists on terms not in the listing (for example, the right to restrict the use of the property).
- The owner and the buyer agree to cancel the transaction.

In other words, *a broker generally is due a commission if a sale is not consummated because of the seller's default.* In rare situations the commission may still be due even when it is the buyer who defaults.

The broker is entitled to a fee if he or she is the procuring cause of sale; produces a ready, willing, and able buyer; or brings about a meeting of the minds. If several brokers disagree as to which one brought about a sale, the one with the best claim to be the procuring cause is that broker who brought the parties into agreement, as evidenced by the sales contract. A **meeting of the minds** is said to have taken place when the parties are in agreement on price, down payment, financing method, and other essential terms.

New York's Real Property Law makes it illegal for a broker to share a commission with unlicensed people. This regulation forbids any form of gift or compensation, such as giving a TV set to a friend for providing a valuable lead or paying finder's fees and portions of the commission. **Kickbacks,** the return of part of the commission as gifts or money to buyers or sellers, are also prohibited.

Compensation by both parties is permissible if there is full knowledge and consent of both parties.

Salesperson's Compensation

The compensation of a salesperson is set by agreement between broker and salesperson. A broker may pay a salary to a salesperson or, more commonly, a share of the commissions from transactions originated by a salesperson (the commission "split"). *The salesperson may never accept compensation from any buyer or seller, and may not accept compensation from any broker except the one broker with whom he or she is associated, except with the full knowledge of his or her broker* (Article 175.B).

A salesperson may, however, accept compensation from a former broker for fees earned while still associated with that broker.

■ TERMINATION OF AGENCY

Because the agency relationship involves so many responsibilities, it is important to know how agencies are created and how they are terminated. An agency relationship may be terminated at any time (except when coupled with an interest) for any of the following reasons:

- Death or incompetence of either party
- Destruction or condemnation of the property
- Expiration of the terms of the agency
- Mutual agreement to terminate the agency

<table>
<tr><td>

AN AGENCY MAY BE TERMINATED BY

- death or incompetence of either party;
- destruction or condemnation of the property;
- expiration of the terms;
- mutual agreement;
- renunciation by agent;
- revocation by principal;
- bankruptcy; or
- completion of the purpose.

</td><td>

- Renunciation by the agent or revocation by the principal (In New York the principal acting in good faith always has the power to cancel a listing at any time. The principal may, however, be required to reimburse the broker for expenses if the principal cancels before the agency's expiration. Damages could be awarded to the agent if the principal acted in bad faith.)
- Bankruptcy of either party
- Completion or fulfillment of the purpose for which the agency was created

</td></tr>
</table>

The question of when an agency relationship ends can be important. For example, suppose agent John listed and sold Margaret's property. Three weeks after closing, Margaret shows up at one of John's open houses. Is Margaret still John's client? Probably not, but John must clarify this with Margaret. Because it is often difficult to treat a former client as a customer, some firms will obtain a written dual agency consent agreement from both parties or enter into a buyer agency relationship with the former client.

The broker may not disclose to a new client information obtained in confidence from a former client during the agency relationship. Even though the agency relationship may have terminated, the duty of confidentiality has not.

■ SUMMARY

Real estate brokerage is the bringing together, for a fee or commission, of people who wish to buy, sell, exchange, or lease real estate.

Real estate brokerage is governed by the law of agency.

An agency may be created by an express agreement, either written or oral, or by an implied agreement.

A real estate broker is the agent, hired by either a buyer or a seller of real estate, to sell or find a particular parcel of real estate. The person who hires the broker is the principal or client. Who pays the commission does not determine who the principal is. The principal and the agent have a fiduciary relationship under which the agent owes the principal the duties of care, confidentiality, loyalty, obedience, accounting, and disclosure. Agents are not, however, required to reveal the existence of "stigmas" on a property.

Third parties in a transaction are the broker's customers, who are owed only fair and honest treatment. New York requires disclosure of agency as the licensee begins to work with a client or customer.

The salesperson is the broker's agent and the seller's subagent (or, if specifically retained as such, the buyer's agent).

Agency can be ended by death or incompetence of either party, destruction of the property, expiration of the terms of the agency, mutual agreement, cancellation by either party, bankruptcy of either party, or completion of the purpose for which the agency was created.

QUESTIONS

1. The relationship between broker and seller is generally a(n)
   a. special agency.
   b. general agency.
   c. ostensible agency.
   d. universal agency.

2. A broker hired by an owner to sell a parcel of real estate must comply with
   a. any instructions of the owner.
   b. the law of agency.
   c. the principle of estoppel.
   d. all instructions of the buyer.

3. A buyer's broker is told by the buyer that he had filed for bankruptcy the year before. The buyer's broker
   a. should discuss with the buyer her duty to reveal the bankruptcy to the MLS.
   b. has a duty of fair dealing toward the seller and must discuss the buyer's finances with the seller honestly.
   c. may politely refuse to provide any information to the seller that would violate her duty of confidentiality to the buyer.
   d. has no responsibility to the seller, because she is the buyer's agent.

4. A listing may be terminated when either broker or principal
   a. gets married.
   b. goes bankrupt.
   c. overfinances other property.
   d. becomes terminally ill.

5. When retained by the buyer, the broker owes a prospective seller
   a. obedience to lawful instructions.
   b. confidentiality about the seller's financial situation.
   c. honest, straightforward treatment.
   d. undivided loyalty.

6. The salesperson who sincerely tries to represent both buyer and seller is practicing
   a. fraud.   c. dual agency.
   b. puffing.   d. general agency.

7. A seller who wishes to cancel a listing agreement in New York
   a. must cite a legally acceptable reason.
   b. may not cancel without the agent's consent.
   c. may be held liable for money and time expended by the broker.
   d. may not sell the property for six months afterward.

8. A broker is entitled to collect a commission from both the seller and the buyer when
   a. the broker holds a state license.
   b. the buyer and the seller are related.
   c. both parties know about and agree to such a transaction.
   d. both parties have attorneys.

9. A house was purchased in 1950 for $4,500. The seller knows properties have appreciated and asks the broker to try to sell it for $100,000. The broker knows the value could be more than $200,000. The broker should
   a. take the listing as offered and sell it quickly.
   b. purchase the house himself for the full $100,000, including in the contract that he is a licensed broker.
   c. buy the house through his aunt, who has a different last name.
   d. tell the seller that the house is worth much more.

10. An example of a latent defect would be a
    a. large crack in the dining room ceiling.
    b. roof with warped shingles.
    c. used-car lot next door.
    d. malfunctioning septic tank.

11. Commissions usually are earned when
    a. the buyer makes a purchase offer.
    b. the seller accepts the buyer's offer without conditions.
    c. a new mortgage has been promised by the lender.
    d. the title to the property is searched.

12. Even if a proposed transaction does not go through, the broker sometimes may collect a commission if the
    a. buyer turns out to be financially unable.
    b. seller refuses to do repairs required by the lender.
    c. seller simply backs out.
    d. lender does not appraise the house for the sales price.

13. A meeting of the minds occurs when the
    a. seller signs a listing agreement.
    b. buyer is introduced to the seller.
    c. buyer and seller agree on the price and terms of the sale.
    d. final closing (settlement) of the transaction takes place.

14. George signed a 120-day listing with Bay Realty. After 60 days George decided not to sell. He told Bay Realty he no longer wanted them to market his house. When is the agency of Bay Realty terminated?
    a. On the 121st day
    b. After a reasonable time
    c. On the 61st day
    d. When the listing expires

15. A seller's broker must disclose to a prospective buyer that the
    a. septic tank doesn't work well.
    b. last owner was murdered there.
    c. seller has AIDS.
    d. house is haunted.

16. Bob Broker buys a property listed with his firm and collects the agreed-on commission. In this transaction, Bob
    a. may have a conflict of interest.
    b. represents both the buyer and seller.
    c. may be considered to be self-dealing.
    d. All of the above

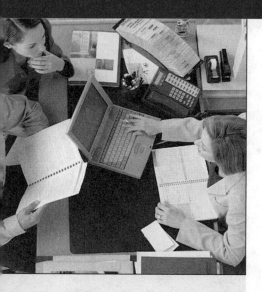

3

AGENCY AND REAL ESTATE BROKERAGE

The Murphys have approached broker Susan to help them in their search for a new house, explaining that they need help in finding the right property and negotiating the best deal with the seller. After some discussion, Susan realizes that one of her listed properties would be perfect for their needs. Can Susan adequately represent the Murphys without violating her duties as an agent of the seller?

Traditionally, real estate agents represented the sellers in real estate transactions, but it has become increasingly common for agents to represent buyers instead. Real estate agents must be prepared to act in the best interest of their clients, while still dealing honestly with other parties.

■ **KEY TERMS**

blanket unilateral offer of subagency
broker's agent
buyer agency
dual agency
exclusive-agency listing
exclusive right to represent

exclusive-right-to-sell listing
first substantive contact
implied creation of a subagency
informed consent
listing broker

open listing
seller agency
selling broker
single agency
subagency
undisclosed dual agency
vicarious liability

■ NEW YORK AGENCY DISCLOSURE REQUIREMENTS

New York's Real Property Law section 443 (RPL 443) requires that brokers and salespersons give prospective sellers and buyers (or landlords and tenants) a disclosure statement that describes the roles of sellers' agents, buyers' agents, listing brokers' agents, and dual agents. (See Figure 3.1.) The buyer or seller must sign an acknowledgment certifying that he or she has read the disclosure form and understands the role of the particular agent in the transaction. The written disclosure is intended, among other things, to warn members of the public not to reveal to the other party's agent any information they'd prefer to keep confidential.

RPL 443 applies to residential transactions involving the sale or lease of one to four-unit residential property. A listing agent must obtain the seller's signed acknowledgment before entering a listing agreement. A buyer agent must obtain the buyer's signed acknowledgment before entering an agreement to represent the buyer.

Signed acknowledgments.   A seller's agent must provide the disclosure and obtain the acknowledgment from all prospective buyers or their buyer agents at the time of the **first substantive contact.** A first substantive contact with a buyer occurs when the buyer walks into the agent's office and begins discussing his or her real estate needs or financial situation. Similarly, buyer agents must provide the disclosure to the seller or the seller's agent at the time of first substantive contact. That might occur when the seller begins explaining his or her reasons for selling or simply greets an agent who is showing someone through the property. A copy of the required disclosure is shown in Figure 3.1.

Finally, if a purchase agreement is entered into between a buyer and seller, both must sign a second acknowledgment regarding the role of any agent in the transaction, unless both parties are represented by attorneys who arrange for and prepare the contract (as is customary in the area of New York City).

Copies of the signed agency disclosure forms obtained in the course of a broker's business must be maintained for three years. If any buyer or seller refuses to sign the forms, the agent may make a written affirmation that the disclosure form was provided to that party. (See Figure 3.2.) This statement can be kept in the broker's file in place of the signed acknowledgment.

RPL 443 also provides for broker's agents. A **broker's agent** is a cooperating broker who is an agent of the listing broker but not strictly a subagent of the seller. A broker's agent has fiduciary duties to the seller, but the seller is not liable for acts of the broker's agent unless the seller specifically authorizes those acts. (Although this concept came directly from the Department of State, it remains to be seen whether this limited liability will be upheld by the courts.)

A second disclosure requirement is found in DOS (Department of State) Regulation 175.7, which states, "A real estate broker shall make it clear for which party he is acting and he shall not receive compensation from more

FIGURE 3.1

Agency Disclosure Form

DISCLOSURE REGARDING REAL ESTATE AGENCY RELATIONSHIPS

Before you enter into a discussion with a real estate agent regarding a real estate transaction, you should understand what type of agency relationship you wish to have with that agent.

New York State law requires real estate licensees who are acting as agents of buyers or sellers of property to advise the potential buyers or sellers with whom they work of the nature of their relationship and the rights and obligations it creates.

SELLER'S OR LANDLORD'S AGENT

If you are interested in selling or leasing real property you can engage a real estate agent as a seller's agent. A seller's agent, including a listing agent under a listing agreement with the seller, acts solely on behalf of the seller. You can authorize a seller's or landlord's agent to do other things including hire subagents, broker's agents or work with other agents such as buyer's agents on a cooperative basis. A subagent is one who has agreed to work with the seller's agent, often through a multiple listing service. A subagent may work in a different real estate office.

A seller's agent has, without limitation, the following fiduciary duties to the seller: reasonable care, undivided loyalty, confidentiality, full disclosure, obedience and a duty to account.

The obligations of a seller's agent are also subject to any specific provisions set forth in an agreement between the agent and the seller.

In dealings with the buyer, a seller's agent should (a) exercise reasonable skill and care in performance of the agent's duties; (b) deal honestly, fairly and in good faith; and (c) disclose all facts known to the agent materially affecting the value or desirability of property, except as otherwise provided by law.

BUYER'S OR TENANT'S AGENT

If you are interested in buying or leasing real property, you can engage a real estate agent as a buyer's or tenant's agent. A buyer's agent acts solely on behalf of the buyer. You can authorize a buyer's agent to do other things including hire subagents, broker's agents or work with other agents such as seller's agents on a cooperative basis.

A buyer's agent has, without limitation, the following fiduciary duties to the buyer: reasonable care, undivided loyalty, confidentiality, full disclosure, obedience and a duty to account.

The obligations of a buyer's agent are also subject to any specific provisions set forth in an agreement between the agent and the buyer.

In dealings with the seller, a buyer's agent should (a) exercise reasonable skill and care in performance of the agent's duties; (b) deal honestly, fairly and in good faith and (c) disclose all facts known to the agent materially affecting the buyer's ability and/or willingness to perform a contract to acquire seller's property that are not inconsistent with the agent's fiduciary duties to the buyer.

BROKER'S AGENTS

As part of your negotiations with a real estate agent you may authorize your agent to engage other agents whether you are a buyer/tenant or seller/landlord. As a general rule, those agents owe fiduciary duties to your agent and to you. You are not vicariously liable for their conduct.

AGENT REPRESENTING BOTH SELLER AND BUYER

A real estate agent acting directly or through an associated licensee can be the agent of both the seller/landlord and the buyer/tenant in a transaction but only with the knowledge and informed consent, in writing, of both the seller/landlord and the buyer/tenant.

In such a dual agency situation, the agent will not be able to provide the full range of fiduciary duties to the buyer/tenant and seller/landlord.

The obligations of an agent are also subject to any specific provisions set forth in an agreement between the agent and the buyer/tenant and seller/landlord.

An agent acting as a dual agent must explain carefully to both the buyer/tenant and seller/landlord that the agent is acting for the other party as well. The agent should also explain the possible effects of dual representation, including that by consenting to the dual agency relationship the buyer/tenant and seller/landlord are giving up their right to undivided loyalty.

A BUYER/TENANT OR SELLER/LANDLORD SHOULD CAREFULLY CONSIDER THE POSSIBLE CONSEQUENCES OF A DUAL AGENCY RELATIONSHIP BEFORE AGREEING TO SUCH REPRESENTATION.

GENERAL CONSIDERATIONS

You should carefully read all agreements to ensure that they adequately express your understanding of the transaction. A real estate agent is a person qualified to advise about real estate. If legal, tax or other advice is desired, consult a competent professional in that field.

Throughout the transaction you may receive more than one disclosure form. The law requires each agent assisting in the transaction to present you with this disclosure form. You should read its contents each time it is presented to you considering the relationship between you and the real estate agent in your specific transaction.

ACKNOWLEDGMENT OF PROSPECTIVE BUYER/TENANT

(1) I have received and read this disclosure notice.
(2) I understand that a seller's/landlord's agent, including a listing agent, is the agent of the seller/landlord exclusively, unless the seller/landlord and buyer/tenant otherwise agree.
(3) I understand that subagents, including subagents participating in a multiple listing service, are agents of the seller/landlord exclusively.
(4) I understand that I may engage my own agent to be my buyer's/tenant's broker.

(5) I understand that the agent presenting this form to me, _____ of _____
　　　　　　　　　　　　　　　　　　　　　　　(name of licensee)　　　　　　　　　　　　　　　　(name of firm)

is (check applicable relationship) ☐ an agent of the seller/landlord ☐ my agent as a buyer's/tenant's agent.

Dated _____ Buyer/Tenant _____　　Dated _____ Buyer/Tenant _____

ACKNOWLEDGMENT OF PROSPECTIVE SELLER/LANDLORD

(1) I have received and read this disclosure notice.
(2) I understand that a seller's/landlord's agent, including a listing agent, is the agent of the seller/landlord exclusively, unless the seller/landlord and buyer/tenant otherwise agree.
(3) I understand that subagents, including subagents participating in a multiple listing service, are agents of the seller/landlord exclusively.
(4) I understand that a buyer's/tenant's agent is the agent of the buyer/tenant exclusively.

(5) I understand that the agent presenting this form to me, _____ of _____
　　　　　　　　　　　　　　　　　　　　　　　(name of licensee)　　　　　　　　　　　　　　　　(name of firm)

is (check applicable relationship) ☐ my agent as a seller's/landlord's agent ☐ an agent of the buyer/tenant.

Dated _____ Seller/Landlord _____　　Dated _____ Seller/Landlord _____

ACKNOWLEDGMENT OF PROSPECTIVE BUYER/TENANT AND SELLER/LANDLORD TO DUAL AGENCY

(1) I have received and read this disclosure notice.
(2) I understand that a dual agent will be working for both the seller/landlord and buyer/tenant.
(3) I understand that I may engage my own agent as a seller's/landlord's agent or a buyer's/tenant's agent.
(4) I understand that I am giving up my right to the agent's undivided loyalty.
(5) I have carefully considered the possible consequences of a dual agency relationship.

(6) I understand that the agent presenting this form to me, _____ of _____
　　　　　　　　　　　　　　　　　　　　　　　(name of licensee)　　　　　　　　　　　　　　　　(name of firm)

is ☐ a dual agent working for both the buyer/tenant and seller/landlord, acting as such with the consent of both the buyer/tenant and seller/landlord and following full disclosure to the buyer/tenant and seller/landlord.

Dated _____ Buyer/Tenant _____　　Dated _____ Seller/Landlord _____

Dated _____ Buyer/Tenant _____　　Dated _____ Seller/Landlord _____

ACKNOWLEDGMENT OF THE PARTIES TO THE CONTRACT

(1) I have received, read and understand this disclosure notice.
(2) I understand that _____ of _____
　　　　　　　　　　　(name of real estate licensee)　　　　　　　　　(name of firm)

is (check applicable relationship) ☐ an agent of the seller/landlord ☐ an agent of the buyer/tenant ☐ a dual agent working for both the buyer/tenant and seller/landlord, acting as such with the consent of both buyer/tenant and seller/landlord and following full disclosure to the buyer/tenant and seller/landlord.

I also understand that _____ of _____
　　　　　　　　　　　　　(name of real estate licensee)　　　　　　　　　(name of firm)

is (check applicable relationship) ☐ an agent of the seller/landlord ☐ an agent of the buyer/tenant ☐ a dual agent working for both the buyer/tenant and seller/landlord, acting as such with the consent of both buyer/tenant and seller/landlord and following full disclosure to the buyer/tenant and seller/landlord.

Dated _____ Buyer/Tenant _____　　Dated _____ Seller/Landlord _____

Dated _____ Buyer/Tenant _____　　Dated _____ Seller/Landlord _____

GRAR 7/95

F I G U R E   3.2

Disclosure Affirmation

DECLARATION PURSUANT TO SECTION 443 (3) (F) OF THE REAL PROPERTY LAW

State of New York)
) ss.:

_____ (name), being duly sworn, deposes and says:

1. I am the principal broker/associate broker/licensed salesperson affiliated with _____ (name of agency).
2. I make this Affidavit in compliance with Section 443 (3) (F) of the New York State Real Property Law.
3. On the _____ day of _____ , 199____ , I presented to _____ (name of buyer or seller) the disclosure forms required pursuant to Section 443 of the Real Property Law. The form of the Disclosure Form as presented is attached to this statement.
4. The above named buyer/seller refused to execute an acknowledgment of the receipt of this disclosure form despite my request that it be executed.
5. A copy of this statement and additional copies of the Disclosure Form are being mailed to the person(s) named in paragraph 3, contemporaneously with the execution of this Affidavit.

_____
                               (Name)

than one party except with the full knowledge and consent of all parties." This requirement applies to all types of transactions, not just residential.

The requirement regarding compensation from more than one party is not strictly limited to compensation related to the sale itself; *it applies to any compensation that is in any way related to the transaction.* Thus a selling agent who accepts compensation for arranging the buyer's loan (mortgage broker's commission), must disclose this to the parties, in addition to sharing in the commission split for the sale

Signing an agency disclosure form does not in and of itself create an agency relationship. It is not a contract between agent and client. Merely having a prospective buyer sign the acknowledgment that a disclosure form stated the broker was acting as a buyer's agent is not legally sufficient to create buyer agency. The relationship should be established through a separate written buyer-agency agreement, similar to the listing agreement used by sellers' agents.

■ AGENCY ALTERNATIVES

An agent is someone who represents a principal in a transaction. The agent owes the principal the duties of *reasonable care, confidentiality, loyalty, obedience, accounting,* and *disclosure of any facts* that might affect the principal's decisions. Agency relationships between a broker and a seller are usually created through *listing agreements,* in which a broker agrees to act as the agent of a seller. Agency relationships between a broker and a buyer are usually created through *buyer-agency agreements.*

Real estate brokers frequently enlist the help of other brokers to market their listed properties. A common example is *a multiple-listing service* (MLS) for residential properties, in which participating brokers agree to share commissions between the **listing broker** and the **selling broker** (the one who finds the buyer). This arrangement may create a **subagency**—in which the selling broker is acting as a subagent of the seller—or the selling broker may be acting as the *broker's agent.*

Because a real estate transaction involves two parties—the buyer and the seller—it is possible for an agent to represent either one or both. In a **single agency,** the agent represents only one party. A single agency can be a traditional **seller agency,** in which the agent represents the seller, or a **buyer agency,** in which the agent represents the buyer. In a **dual agency,** the agent represents both parties in the same transaction. The New York Department of State regards the exercise of dual agency with great suspicion. (Dual agency without full written disclosure to and approval of all parties is, of course, illegal.)

■ SUBAGENCY

When a broker accepts a listing from a seller, the agency relationship is clear: the broker becomes the seller's agent. By extension, any salespersons who work for the broker become subagents of the seller, because they are agents of the broker. The situation is less clear, however, in the case of another broker who procures a buyer for the property. Is the other broker acting as a subagent of the seller, an agent of the buyer, or an agent of the listing broker?

Blanket offer of subagency. Traditionally, one of the most common ways that a subagency was created was through participation in an MLS. By agreeing to submit a listing to the MLS, the seller agreed to a **blanket unilateral offer of subagency** to all participating brokers. However, the seller is now allowed to choose whether to offer subagency or simply to have the listing broker cooperate with other brokers regardless of whom they represent.

Brokerage without subagency. As a principal, the seller is liable for actions not only of the listing agent but also of subagents. This potentially enormous liability—for human rights violations among other problems—is the reason some sellers do not want to offer subagency.

If a seller does not wish to offer subagency to MLS members but still wants to gain exposure through an MLS, he or she can direct that the listing agent may split the commission with another broker who produces the buyer, without the other broker acting as the seller's subagent. The seller agrees to pay the selling broker part of the commission but does not risk being held liable for any statements or actions on the part of the selling broker. With more and more buyers being represented by their own brokers these days, this simple offer of cooperation and commission sharing solves problems that used to arise about how the buyer's broker is to be paid.

Selective offer of subagency. Not all properties are submitted to an MLS. For instance, nonresidential properties often are listed exclusively with only one broker. Sometimes a listing broker wants to work cooperatively with only a few select brokers to find a buyer. Although these arrangements are usually informal—they typically are little more than an oral agreement to a commission split—they may result in the **implied creation of a subagency.** As a result, the cooperating broker would have fiduciary responsibilities toward the seller, and the seller would be liable for the acts of the cooperating broker.

To avoid potential conflicts, these cooperation agreements should be put in writing, with the responsibilities of all parties clearly defined. In addition, the listing broker must disclose such relationships to the seller and obtain the seller's informed consent for the creation of subagencies.

Disclosure of subagency.   The relationship between a subagent (selling broker) and a principal (seller) in a real estate transaction is not clearly understood by many buyers. Buyers who use a selling broker's services to find a property often believe the broker is working on their behalf when, in fact, the broker has a fiduciary duty to act in the best interest of the seller.

For example, Jameson is looking for a house. She contacts Mendez, a broker, who shows her many houses over the course of several weeks. Jameson tells Mendez the kind of house she is looking for and gives him information about her ability to buy and her time frame for buying. By the time Jameson finds a house she is interested in, she feels very comfortable with Mendez and begins to think of Mendez as her real estate agent. In fact, Mendez is a subagent of the seller. Jameson makes an offer on the house, telling Mendez that she is willing to pay up to $8,000 more than her initial offer. Mendez has a duty to relay this information to the seller, who immediately counteroffers with a higher selling price. Because she wrongly believed Mendez to be acting on her behalf, Jameson will end up paying more for the house than she otherwise might have.

The written Agency Disclosure Statement shown in Figure 3.1, which Jameson should have received at the outset, should have warned her that Mendez, however helpful, was working for the seller and could not keep her information confidential.

■ DUAL AGENCY

In a *dual agency*, the broker represents both buyer and seller in the same transaction. Because the buyer and seller have competing goals, dual agency represents an inherent conflict of interest for the broker. It is often impossible for a dual agent to fully satisfy the fiduciary requirements of confidentiality and full disclosure with respect to both parties in a transaction. Consequently, dual agency by its nature may involve something less than full representation of each client and must be undertaken with care.

Informed Consent

Dual agency is legal; however, only with the informed consent of both parties. To ensure informed consent, it is good practice to have a *written document* signed by both principals. This document should indicate that the principals consent to the dual agency and understand that

- the agent may not provide undivided loyalty to either principal;
- the principals' confidential information regarding pricing strategy will be protected, as well as any other information agreed to by the principals;
- the agent may be paid fees as specified, either by one or by both principals;
- dual agency does involve potential conflicts of interest because one principal may feel compromised unfairly or that one might be favored over the other;
- if either principal is uncomfortable with the dual agency process, he or she should not proceed; and
- the principals should have obtained their attorneys' advice before proceeding in a dual agency situation.

RPL 443 provides a special form of acknowledgment for consensual dual agency transactions. This acknowledgment is required by law, but the broker also may have the parties sign a more specific consent to dual agency that spells out the precise nature of the relationship of the parties in the particular transaction. (See Figure 3.3.)

When dual agency exists but is not fully disclosed or consented to by the parties, the broker faces serious consequences. These include loss of license or other disciplinary action, loss of commission on the sale, and liability for damages if the sale is rescinded. Because of these risks, brokers must be constantly aware of the potential for undisclosed dual agency situations.

Undisclosed Dual Agency

A broker does not have to embark intentionally on a dual agency situation to suffer the consequences of undisclosed dual agency. In fact, **undisclosed dual agency** *is often unintentional.* Although the buyer and seller may specifically request that a broker act as a dual agent, a dual agency situation may arise without the broker's realizing it. Examples of such situations include in-house sales and sales by cooperating brokers who are acting as buyers' agents.

In-house sales.   Whenever a broker takes a listing, the broker and all salespeople who work for the broker become agents or subagents of the seller. This is true for all salespeople in all offices of the brokerage. Any time that a salesperson or broker acts as a buyer agent (either explicitly or implicitly) with respect to any of the firm's own listings, dual agency exists, and appropriate steps must be taken to avoid liability.

Company policy.   The possibility of dual agency should be discussed with clients at the time the agency agreement (listing or buyer agency) is entered. Clients should be informed of the possibility of in-house sales and of the policy of the broker's office regarding such sales.

F I G U R E   3.3

Dual Agency Consent Form

6/30/95

INFORMED CONSENT TO DUAL AGENCY

Property Address: _____

Seller(s): _____

Name of Brokerage Firm: _____ **("Broker")**

Listing Salesperson: _____

Buyer(s): _____

Selling Salesperson: _____

1. **Consent to Dual Agency:**
   The Seller and Buyer acknowledge and agree that Broker and the listing and selling salespersons are undertaking a Consensual Dual Agency representation in the sale of the above property. Seller and Buyer have previously been informed of the possibility of a dual agency arising if a buyer client becomes interested in a seller client's property. Seller and Buyer have consented to this dual representation and hereby confirm their consent by signing below after reading the following description of the type of representation to be provided.

2. **Description of Broker's Role: Confidentiality and Disclosure of Information:**
   Because Broker is acting as agent for both Seller and Buyer in this transaction, Broker shall make every reasonable effort to remain impartial to Seller and Buyer. Seller and Buyer acknowledge that, prior to the time this Addendum was entered into, Broker acted as (exclusive) agent of the Seller and acted as (exclusive) agent of the Buyer. In those separate roles, Broker may have obtained information which, if disclosed, could harm the bargaining position of the party providing such information to Broker. Seller and Buyer agree that Broker shall not be obligated or liable to either party for refusing or failing to disclose information which in the sole discretion of Broker would harm one party's bargaining position but would benefit the other party.

   Nothing contained herein shall prevent Broker from disclosing to Buyer any known material defects that affect the property value. Broker agrees not to disclose confidential information to the other party, such as (a) to Buyer information about what price or terms Seller will accept other than the Listing Price and terms or (b) to Seller information about what price or terms Buyer will agree to other than any written offering price. In the event that Seller and Buyer do not enter into an agreement for the purchase and sale of Seller's property to Buyer, or in the event that the purchase and sale provided for in a contract of sale between Seller and Buyer does not close in accordance with its terms, this dual agency and this Consent may be terminated by any party, by mailing written notice to the others.

3. **Description of Seller's and Buyer's Role:**
   Seller and Buyer acknowledge that they are aware of the implications and consequences of Broker's dual agency role to facilitate a transaction, rather than act as an advocate for one party over the other, and that they have determined that the benefits of entering into this transaction, with the Broker acting as a dual agent outweigh those implications and consequences.

   Seller and Buyer acknowledge that they have been advised to seek independent legal counsel in order to assist them with any matter relating to a purchase and sale contract and any other aspect of the transaction. Seller and Buyer agree to indemnify and hold Broker harmless against all claims, damages, losses, expenses or liabilities arising from Broker's role as a dual agent except those arising from Broker's intentional wrongful acts or violation of the Real Property Law of the State of New York. Seller and Buyer shall have a duty to protect their own interests and should read this Consent carefully to ensure that it accurately sets forth the terms which they want included in the transaction.

   Both BUYER and SELLER understand and agree that BROKER shall have the right to collect a commission or fee from the transaction, pursuant to existing agreements, and acknowledge that it has been disclosed that BROKER will collect a fee of $_____ or _____% of the sales price which shall be paid as a cost of this transaction from the proceeds to be paid by BUYER to SELLER. Any prior agreements to the contrary are hereby superseded.

4. **Consequences of Dual Agency:**
   Seller and Buyer are giving up their right to have Broker's undivided loyalty to act at all times solely in their individual best interests to the exclusion of all other interests. Dual Agency may thus deprive Buyer and Seller of benefits they may have otherwise received in a Single Agency relationship. For example, as a seller represented by an Agent, Seller has the right to expect that Seller's agent will attempt to obtain the full asking price for the property. As a buyer, represented by an Agent, Buyer has the right to expect the Agent to work toward bringing about a transaction at the lowest possible price. A Dual Agent will not work on behalf of either party regarding price.

Dual Agency Consent Form (continued)

5.   **Fiduciary Duties:**
In theory, a Dual Agent owes both the buyer and seller the same fiduciary duties as if the Agent represented each alone. These duties include loyalty, obedience, disclosure, confidentiality, reasonable care, diligence and the duty to account. By consenting to dual agency, the conflicting duties to Buyer and Seller are reconciled by mutual agreement to forego them. The duty of undivided loyalty is forfeited in a Dual Agency relationship and instead the Dual Agent is required to act with fairness to each party. In addition, most of the other fiduciary obligations are affected because of the contrasting motivations of Buyer and Seller, who have agreed that the consensual dual agent will not favor the interests of one over those of the other.

6.   **Disputes:**
In the event a dispute arises between Buyer and Seller, Broker may elect to withdraw from the transaction.

7.   **Description of Limited Agency Services:**
WHAT BROKER AND ITS SALESPERSONS CAN DO FOR SELLERS AND BUYERS WHEN ACTING AS A DUAL AGENT:
>   We will treat the Seller and Buyer honestly and fairly.
>   We will provide helpful information about the property and neighborhood to the Buyer.
>   We will respond accurately to questions about the property.
>   We will disclose all material facts about the property that are known to us.
>   We will disclose financial qualifications of the Buyer to the Seller.
>   We can explain real estate terms and procedures.
>   We can help the Buyer to arrange for property inspections.
>   We can help the Buyer compare financing alternatives.
>   We will provide information about comparable properties so the Seller and Buyer may make an educated decision on what price to accept and/or offer.
>   We will work diligently to facilitate the sale and will advise when experts should be retained (lawyer, tax accountant, architect, etc.)
>   We will act as a mediator and make recommendations for compromise between Seller and Buyer.

WHAT BROKER AND ITS SALESPERSONS CANNOT DISCLOSE TO SELLERS AND BUYERS.
>   We cannot disclose confidential information that we may know about the Seller and/or Buyer (e.g., motivation, to sell/buy; price/terms; negotiating strategy), without written permission of the Seller and/or Buyer.
>   We cannot disclose the price the Seller will take other than the listing price without written permission of the Seller.
>   We cannot disclose the price the Buyer is willing to pay without written permission of the Buyer.
>   We cannot recommend or suggest a price the Buyer should offer or pay for the property.
>   We cannot recommend or suggest a price the Seller should accept or counter.

8.   **Role of Salesperson:**
The salesperson who has executed this Informed Consent To Dual Agency as the "Listing Salesperson" agrees that she(he) will continue to represent the interests of the Seller in all negotiations, discussions and procedures relating to this transaction. The person whose signature is set forth below and is designated as "Selling Salesperson" agrees that she(he) will continue to represent the interests of the Buyer in all negotiations, discussions and procedures relating to this transaction. Broker will act as an intermediary with respect to Seller and Buyer and except for the fiduciary duty to account for any monies which come into Broker's possession and the duty to exercise reasonable care, Broker will not have fiduciary duties to either Seller or Buyer to provide "undivided loyalty or obedience." If the salesperson who acted as the Listing Salesperson is also the Selling Salesperson, then such Salesperson will act as an intermediary with respect to Seller and Buyer.

By signing below, you approve and agree that Broker and its salespersons may act as dual agents in this transaction.

_____
Buyer   Date

_____
Buyer   Date

Broker

By:_____

_____
Seller   Date

_____
Seller   Date

_____
Selling Salesperson

_____
Listing Salesperson

The Selling Salesperson whose signature appears above acknowledges that Buyer has signed this Consent before signing any written offer to purchase the property. The Listing Salesperson whose signature appears above acknowledges that the Seller has signed this Consent before signing the acceptance of an offer or a counter offer.

F:\WPDOCS\WCBR3213\ICDA.EIS

■ SINGLE AGENCY

In a single agency, the broker represents only one of the parties in a transaction, either the buyer or the seller. The party represented by the broker is the *broker's client*, and other parties or their agents are treated as customers by the broker. If the broker's client is the seller, the broker deals with buyers or their agents as customers only. If the buyer is the broker's client, sellers are treated as customers.

A single agency broker may choose to represent only sellers (seller agency) or only buyers (buyer agency), but also may choose to represent either, one at a time. This can lead to potential conflicts. A buyer client (principal) might be interested in a property listed by a seller client (also a principal). When such situations arise, the single agency broker could formally terminate the agency relationship with the buyer. If this occurs, the broker also should inform the seller of the previous agency relationship with the buyer, although he or she may not disclose confidential information that was obtained during the time the buyer was a client. The broker may not, for example, disclose to the seller that the buyers are willing to pay x number of dollars for a property they really like because this is information the broker learned while representing those buyers. This situation would require careful handling.

Handling In-House Sales

A substantial part of many brokerage businesses consists of *sales of in-house listings* (listings generated by that same broker or the broker's licensees). As agents of the broker and subagents of the seller, all salespersons in the brokerage have an obligation to use their best efforts to find a buyer for properties that are listed with the brokerage. In-house sales also avoid the need to split the commission with another brokerage.

In-house sales are perfectly legal, as long as the buyer is informed that the salesperson is acting as an agent of the seller and the salesperson does not do anything to imply that he or she is representing the buyer. Complications can and do arise, however, especially in the case where a buyer (customer) has a current or previous agency (client) relationship with the broker. In these cases, an undisclosed dual agency may be the result.

For example, Jane lists her home for sale with ABC Realty, and she also asks ABC to help her find a new home. She decides to make an offer on Fred's property, which is also listed with ABC. Because ABC is the agent of both Jane and Fred (as sellers), this situation gives rise to a dual agency. ABC cannot act as the selling broker in Jane's purchase from Fred without the informed consent of both parties.

Designated Agency

The Department of State has approved a technique by which the in-house dual agency problem can be handled when a firm's buyer-client expresses interest in property that same company has listed. The Secretary of State has stated that "you (the managing broker) can designate one of your agents to represent the buyer and another to represent the seller. If designated agents are appointed, the firm continues as a dual agent representing both the buyer and seller in the same transaction. The designated agents, however, will, by virtue of the new agreement with the buyer and seller, function as single agents giving undivided loyalty to their respective clients." Informed consent (by both parties) to dual agency and then informed consent to the designated agent arrangement must be obtained.

A designated agency agreement suggested by the New York State Association of REALTORS® can be found in Chapter 19.

Handling Cooperative Sales

Cooperation among brokers, either selectively or through an MLS, is common practice in the real estate industry. When a property is sold through a broker who is not the listing broker, it is important to clarify the agency relationships among all of the people involved. The cooperating or selling broker (or his or her salesperson) must inform the listing agent whether he or she is acting as a subagent of the seller, as an agent of the buyer, or simply as a broker's agent with no agency relationship with either buyer or seller. The relationship would affect the amount of information a listing agent would share about the seller's motivation or financial situation.

■ AGENCY FORMS

The majority of agency relationships of any type are created by written agreement between the agent and the principal. In the case of real estate agency, the relationship between the seller and the listing agent is defined by the *listing agreement*. The relationship between the buyer and the agent is defined by the *buyer-agency agreement*.

In large commercial leasing transactions it is not unusual for a broker to represent a tenant as a client. All the same requirements for disclosure, loyalty, and confidentiality apply to a tenant agency.

Listing Agreements

The three common types of listings are the *exclusive-right-to-sell listing*, the *exclusive-agency listing*, and the *open listing*. The primary difference between these types of listings relates to the conditions under which the broker will have earned a commission. Their similarities and differences are examined in Table 3.1.

THREE COMMON TYPES OF LISTING AGREEMENTS

1. Exclusive right to sell
2. Exclusive agency
3. Open listing

Exclusive-right-to-sell listing.   The **exclusive-right-to-sell listing** provides the greatest protection for the broker. The broker under this arrangement has earned a commission if the property is sold during the listing term, regardless of who procures the buyer.

Exclusive-agency listing.   An **exclusive-agency listing** entitles the broker to a commission if the property is sold during the listing term, unless the seller acting alone is the one who procures the buyer. If the seller procures the buyer without involving any broker, no commission is due.

Open listing.   The **open listing** is the least restrictive of the three types. In an open listing the seller may employ any number of brokers and need pay a commission only to that broker who successfully produces a ready, willing, and able buyer. A seller who personally sells the property without the aid of any of the

TABLE 3.1

Listing Agreements

Type of Listing	Seller	Agent	Other Broker
Exclusive-Right-to-Sell Listing	x	x	x
Exclusive-Agency Listing		x	x
Open Listing		x	

brokers is not obligated to pay any of them a commission. A listing contract generally creates an open listing unless the wording specifically provides otherwise.

While the open listing may seem the most favorable to the seller, it usually means that no one agent is motivated to spend a great deal of time or advertising money on the property, because no compensation will be due if someone else sells it first.

When a broker represents a landlord in procuring tenants for a property, the most common agreement is the *exclusive right to rent*, which is similar to the exclusive right to sell. The broker earns a commission if the property is leased during the term of the agreement, regardless of who procures the tenant.

Net listing.   With a net listing the broker is free to offer the property for sale at any price. If the property is sold, the broker pays the seller only a certain net amount previously agreed on and keeps anything above that. This type of listing is *illegal* in New York. It lends itself to fraud and is seldom in the seller's best interest.

Multiple listing.   Not a type of listing, an MLS is organized within a geographic area by a group of brokers who agree to distribute and share listing information.

The multiple-listing agreement, while not actually a separate form of listing, is in effect an exclusive-right-to-sell or exclusive-agency agreement with an additional authority to distribute the listing to other brokers who belong to the MLS. The obligations among member brokers of a multiple-listing organization vary widely. Most provide that on sale of the property the commission will be divided between the listing broker and the selling broker. Terms for division of the commission vary by individual arrangement among brokers.

Under most multiple-listing contracts the broker who secures the listing is not only authorized but obligated to turn the listing over to the MLS within a definite period of time so that it can be distributed to other member brokers.

The Internet and multiple listing.   Many individual brokers showcase their listings on their own Web pages (virtual office Web sites, VOWs). Larger groups of listings are found on local, regional, and statewide multiple-listing Internet sites. Meanwhile, *Realtor.com* and *Microsoft's HomeAdvisor.com* compete for the largest number of nationwide listings. In addition, several sites offer exposure to For-Sale-By-Owner (FSBO) properties.

As a result, most homebuyers today use the Internet to browse the market, particularly at the start of their searches. In the end, however, most sales are eventually made through the services of a face-to-face real estate broker.

Termination of listings.   A listing, like any agency relationship, may be ended for any of the following reasons:

- Performance of the object (sale of the property)
- Expiration of the time period stated in the agreement
- Abandonment by a broker who spends no time on the listing
- Revocation by the owner (although the owner may be liable for the broker's expenses)
- Cancellation by the broker or by mutual consent
- Bankruptcy, death, or insanity of either party
- Destruction of the property
- A change in property use by outside forces (such as a change in zoning)

All listings should specify a definite period of time during which the broker is to be employed. The use of automatic extensions of time in exclusive listings is illegal in New York.

Information needed for listing agreements.   When taking a listing, the broker must obtain as much information as possible on the parcel of real estate. This ensures that all possible contingencies can be anticipated, particularly when the listing will be shared in a multiple-listing arrangement. Some of the information accompanies the actual listing contract; some is furnished to prospective buyers on separate information sheets. It includes the following (where appropriate):

- Names and addresses of owners
- Adequate description of the property
- Size of lot (frontage and depth; if irregular, square footage)
- Number and size of rooms and total square footage
- Construction and age of the building
- Information relative to the neighborhood (schools, transportation)
- Current taxes
- Amount of existing financing
- Utilities and average payments
- Appliances to be included in the transaction
- Date of occupancy or possession
- Possibility of seller financing
- Zoning classification (especially important for vacant land)
- Detailed list of exactly what personal property and fixtures will or will not be included in the sales price

The agent should search the public records for information on zoning, lot size, and yearly taxes. The true tax figure should be used, disregarding any present veteran's, aged, disabled, senior apartment, "Gold Star" parent, STaR, or religious exemption, or any addition for unpaid water bills.

Property Condition Disclosure Statement

Property Condition Disclosure Statement

Name of seller or sellers: _____

Property address: _____

The Property Condition Disclosure Act requires the seller of residential real property to cause this disclosure statement or a copy thereof to be delivered to a buyer or buyer's agent prior to the signing by the buyer of a binding contract of sale.

Purpose of Statement:

This is a statement of certain conditions and information concerning the property known to the seller. This disclosure statement is not a warranty of any kind by the seller or by any agent representing the seller in this transaction. It is not a substitute for any inspections or tests and the buyer is encouraged to obtain his or her own independent professional inspections and environmental tests and also is encouraged to check public records pertaining to the property.

A KNOWINGLY FALSE OR INCOMPLETE STATEMENT BY THE SELLER ON THIS FORM MAY SUBJECT THE SELLER TO CLAIMS BY THE BUYER PRIOR TO OR AFTER THE TRANSFER OF TITLE. IN THE EVENT A SELLER FAILS TO PERFORM THE DUTY PRESCRIBED IN THIS ARTICLE TO DELIVER A DISCLOSURE STATEMENT PRIOR TO THE SIGNING BY THE BUYER OF A BINDING CONTRACT OF SALE, THE BUYER SHALL RECEIVE UPON THE TRANSFER OF TITLE A CREDIT OF FIVE HUNDRED DOLLARS AGAINST THE AGREED UPON PURCHASE PRICE OF THE RESIDENTIAL REAL PROPERTY.

"Residential real property" means real property improved by a one to four family dwelling used or occupied, or intended to be used or occupied, wholly or partly, as the home or residence of one or more persons, but shall not refer to (a) unimproved real property upon which such dwellings are to be constructed or (b) condominium units or cooperative apartments or (c) property on a homeowners' association that is not owned in fee simple by the seller.

Instructions to the seller:

(a) Answer all questions based upon your actual knowledge.
(b) Attach additional pages with your signature if additional space is required.
(c) Complete this form yourself.
(d) If some items do not apply to your property, check "NA" (non-applicable). If you do not know the answer check "UNKN" (unknown).

Seller's Statement:

The seller makes the following representations to the buyer based upon the seller's actual knowledge at the time of signing this document. The seller authorizes his or her agent, if any, to provide a copy of this statement to a prospective buyer of the residential real property. The following are representations made by the seller and are not the representations of the seller's agent.

General Information

1. How long have you owned the property? _____

2. How long have you occupied the property? _____

3. What is the age of the structure or structures? _____
    Note to buyer- If the structure was built before 1978 you are encouraged to investigate for the presence of lead based paint.

4. Does anybody other than yourself have a lease, easement or any other right to use or occupy any part of your property other than those stated in documents available in the public record, such as rights to use a road or path or cut trees or crops? Yes No UNKN NA

5. Does anybody else claim to own any part of your property? Yes No UNKN NA (if yes, explain below)

1

Property Condition Disclosure Statement (continued)

6. Has anyone denied you access to the property or made a formal legal claim challenging your title to the property? Yes No UNKN NA (if yes, explain below)

7. Are there any features of the property shared in common with adjoining land owners or a homeowners association, such as walls, fences or driveways? Yes No UNKN NA (if yes describe below)

8. Are there any electric or gas utility surcharges for line extensions, special assessments or homeowner or other association fees that apply to the property? Yes No UNKN NA (if yes, explain below)

9. Are there certificates of occupancy related to the property? Yes No UNKN NA (if no, explain below)

Environmental

Note to Seller - In this section, you will be asked questions regarding petroleum products and hazardous or toxic substances that you know to have been spilled, leaked or otherwise been released on the property or from the property onto any other property. Petroleum products may include, but are not limited to, gasoline, diesel fuel, home heating fuel, and lubricants. Hazardous or toxic substances are products that could pose short- or long-term danger to personal health or the environment if they are not properly disposed of, applied or stored. These include, but are not limited to, fertilizers, pesticides and insecticides, paint including paint thinner, varnish remover and wood preservatives, treated wood, construction materials such as asphalt and roofing materials, antifreeze and other automotive products, batteries, cleaning solvents including septic tank cleaners, household cleaners and pool chemicals and products containing mercury and lead.

Note to Buyer - If contamination of this property from petroleum products and/or hazardous or toxic substances is a concern to you, you are urged to consider soil and groundwater testing of this property.

10. Is any or all of the property located in a designated floodplain? Yes No UNKN NA (if yes, explain below)

11. Is any or all of the property located in a designated wetland? Yes No UNKN NA (if yes, explain below)

12. Is the property located in an agricultural district? Yes No UNKN NA (if yes, explain below)

13. Was the property ever the site of a landfill? Yes No UNKN NA (if yes, explain below)

14. Are there or have there ever been fuel storage tanks above or below the ground on the property? Yes No UNKN NA
    If yes, are they currently in use? Yes No UNKN NA Location(s) _____
    Are they leaking or have they ever leaked? Yes No UNKN NA (if yes, explain below)

15. Is there asbestos in the structure? Yes No UNKN NA (if yes, state location or locations below)

16. Is lead plumbing present? Yes No UNKN NA (if yes, state location or locations below)

17. Has a radon test been done? Yes No UNKN NA (if yes, attach a copy of the report)

18. Has motor fuel, motor oil, home heating fuel, lubricating oil or any other petroleum product, methane gas, or any hazardous or toxic substance spilled, leaked or otherwise been released on the property or from the property onto any other property? Yes No UNKN NA (if yes, describe below)

19. Has the property been tested for the presence of motor fuel, motor oil, home heating fuel, lubricating oil, or any other petroleum product, methane gas, or any hazardous or toxic substance? Yes No UNKN NA (if yes, attach report(s))

Structural
20. Is there any rot or water damage to the structure or structures? Yes No UNKN NA (if yes, explain below)

21. Is there any fire or smoke damage to the structure or structures? Yes No UNKN NA (if yes, explain below)
22. Is there any termite, insect, rodent or pest infestation or damage? Yes No UNKN NA (if yes, explain below)

2

F I G U R E   3.4

Property Condition Disclosure Statement (continued)

23.   Has the property been tested for termite, insect, rodent or pest infestation or damage?
Yes No UNKN NA (if yes, please attach report(s))

24.   What is the type of roof/roof covering (slate, asphalt, other.)? _____
Any known material defects? _____
How old is the roof? _____
Is there a transferable warrantee on the roof in effect now? Yes No UNKN NA (if yes, explain below)

25.   Are there any known material defects in any of the following structural systems: footings, beams, girders, lintels, columns or partitions. Yes No UNKN NA (if yes, explain below)

Mechanical Systems & Services

26.   What is the water source (circle all that apply - well, private, municipal, other)? If municipal, is it metered?
Yes No UNKN NA

27.   Has the water quality and/or flow rate been tested? Yes No UNKN NA (if yes, describe below)

28.   What is the type of sewage system (circle all that apply – public sewer, private sewer, septic or cesspool)?
If septic or cesspool, age? _____
Date last pumped? _____
Frequency of pumping? _____
Any known material defects? Yes No UNKN NA (if yes, explain below)

29.   Who is your electric service provider? _____
What is the amperage? _____
Does it have circuit breakers or fuses? _____
Private or public poles? _____
Any known material defects? Yes No UNKN NA (if yes, explain below)

30.   Are there any flooding, drainage or grading problems that resulted in standing water on any portion of the property? Yes No UNKN NA (if yes, state locations and explain below)

31.   Does the basement have seepage that results in standing water? Yes No UNKN NA (if yes, explain below)

Are there any known material defects in any of the following (if yes, explain below. Use additional sheets if necessary):

32. Plumbing system?   Yes No UNKN NA
33. Security system?   Yes No UNKN NA
34. Carbon monoxide detector?   Yes No UNKN NA
35. Smoke detector?   Yes No UNKN NA
36. Fire sprinkler system?   Yes No UNKN NA
37. Sump pump?   Yes No UNKN NA
38. Foundation/slab?   Yes No UNKN NA
39. Interior walls/ceilings?   Yes No UNKN NA
40. Exterior walls or siding?   Yes No UNKN NA
41. Floors?   Yes No UNKN NA
42. Chimney/fireplace or stove?   Yes No UNKN NA
43. Patio/deck?   Yes No UNKN NA
44. Driveway?   Yes No UNKN NA
45. Air conditioner?   Yes No UNKN NA
46. Heating system?   Yes No UNKN NA
47. Hot water heater?   Yes No UNKN NA
48. The property is located in the following school district _____ UNKN

3

Property Condition Disclosure Statement (continued)

Note: Buyer is encouraged to check public records concerning the property (e.g. tax records and wetland and flood plain maps)

The seller should use this area to further explain any item above. If necessary, attach additional pages and indicate here the number of additional pages attached.

_____

_____

_____

_____

_____

_____

_____

Seller's Certification:
SELLER CERTIFIES THAT THE INFORMATION IN THIS PROPERTY CONDITION DISCLOSURE STATEMENT IS TRUE AND COMPLETE TO THE SELLER'S ACTUAL KNOWLEDGE AS OF THE DATE SIGNED BY THE SELLER. IF A SELLER OF RESIDENTIAL REAL PROPERTY ACQUIRES KNOWLEDGE WHICH RENDERS MATERIALLY INACCURATE A PROPERTY CONDITION DISCLOSURE STATEMENT PROVIDED PREVIOUSLY, THE SELLER SHALL DELIVER A REVISED PROPERTY CONDITION DISCLOSURE STATEMENT TO THE BUYER AS SOON AS PRACTICABLE. IN NO EVENT, HOWEVER, SHALL A SELLER BE REQUIRED TO PROVIDE A REVISED PROPERTY CONDITION DISCLOSURE STATEMENT AFTER THE TRANSFER OF TITLE FROM THE SELLER TO THE BUYER OR OCCUPANCY BY THE BUYER, WHICHEVER IS EARLIER.

Seller_____ date_____

Seller_____ date_____

Buyer's Acknowledgment:
Buyer acknowledges receipt of a copy of this statement and buyer understands that this information is a statement of certain conditions and information concerning the property known to the seller. It is not a warranty of any kind by the seller or seller's agent and is not a substitute for any home, pest, radon or other inspections or testing of the property or inspection of the public records.

Buyer_____ date_____

Buyer_____ date_____

For a copy of the Property Condition Disclosure Statement, go to *www.dos.state.ny.us*

Seller disclosures.   For one to four-family dwellings, each buyer, before any binding contract of sale is signed, is entitled to receive a Property Condition Disclosure Statement from the seller. (See Figure 3.4.) The Statement starts with "1. How long have you owned the property?" and proceeds through questions about property's environment, structure, and mechanical conditions, to "48. The property is located in the following school district_____." Any buyer who does not receive the Statement is entitled to a $500 credit toward purchase. The Disclosure Statement is shown in Figure 3.5.

New York state requires that a functioning carbon monoxide detector and smoke alarm be installed in every one or two-family house, co-op, or condo offered for sale. All sellers of housing built before 1978 must disclose the presence of known lead-based paint or lead-related hazards to prospective buyers, both at the time of listing and later before the closing. (See Figure 3.5.) The disclosure would be included with the sample listing contract shown in Figure 3.6. Sellers or landlords must also provide a HUD/EPA booklet on the subject.

Environmental hazards.   When property is listed, questions should be raised about the possible presence of environmental hazards. The real estate broker must not assume expertise in these matters. It is enough to be alert for situations that might raise a red flag and to recommend, where it seems indicated, that the seller consult a licensed engineer. In some situations an environmental audit may be indicated. As always, troublesome questions can be taken to an attorney. Environmental hazards are of increasing importance, not only because buyers may suffer damage to their health but also because in some cases purchasers have been held responsible for cleanup of existing problems.

Rental property.   In the sale of multifamily dwellings and other income-producing properties, the seller should be ready to present a statement of income and expenses, preferably prepared by an accountant. A rent roll should show the name of each tenant, amount of rent, expiration date of each lease, and amount of security deposits. The listing agent should verify zoning and the legality of existing use. The seller should be informed of the necessity for a certificate of occupancy at transfer. Arranging with tenants to show the property at reasonable times also is important.

Truth-in-Heating Law.   New York's Truth-in-Heating Law requires the seller to furnish, on written request, two past years' heating and cooling bills to any prospective buyer of a one or two-family home. Sellers also must furnish a statement of the extent and type of insulation they have installed together with any information they may have about insulation installed by previous owners.

Other government requirements.   If HUD has determined that the property is in a flood-prone area, a buyer may need to obtain flood insurance before placing certain kinds of mortgages. The listing agent can anticipate this by consulting a flood area map at the time of listing. Maps may be ordered from the Federal Emergency Management Agency, Flood Map Distribution Center, 6930 (A-F) San Tomas Road, Baltimore, MD 21227-6227, or by calling toll-free 1-800-333-1363. The Web site is *www.fema.gov*.

WWWeb.Link

F I G U R E   3.5

Disclosure of Lead-Based Paint and Lead-Based Hazards

LEAD-BASED PAINT OR LEAD-BASED PAINT HAZARD ADDENDUM

It is a condition of this contract that, until midnight of _____ , Buyer shall have the right to obtain a risk assessment or inspection of the Property for the presence of lead-based paint and/or lead-based paint hazards* at Buyer's expense. This contingency will terminate at that time unless Buyer or Buyer's agent delivers to the Seller or Seller's agent a written inspection and/or risk assessment report listing the specific existing deficiencies and corrections needed, if any. If any corrections are necessary, Seller shall have the option of (i) completing them, (ii) providing for their completion, or (iii) refusing to complete them. If Seller elects not to complete or provide for completion of the corrections, then Buyer shall have the option of (iv) accepting the Property in its present condition, or (v) terminating this contract, in which case all earnest monies shall be refunded to Buyer. Buyer may waive the right to obtain a risk assessment or inspection of the Property for the presence of lead-based paint and/or lead based paint hazards at any time without cause.

*Intact lead-based paint that is in good condition is not necessarily a hazard. See EPA pamphlet "Protect Your Family From Lead in Your Home" for more information.

Disclosure of Information on Lead-Based Paint and Lead-Based Paint Hazards

Lead Warning Statement

Every Buyer of any interest in residential real property on which a residential dwelling was built prior to 1978 is notified that such property may present exposure to lead from lead-based paint that may place young children at risk of developing lead poisoning. Lead poisoning in young children may produce permanent neurological damage, including learning disabilities, reduced intelligence quotient, behavioral problems, and impaired memory. Lead poisoning also poses a particular risk to pregnant women. The Seller of any interest in residential real property is required to provide the Buyer with any information on lead-based paint hazards from risk assessments or inspections in the Seller's possession and notify the Buyer of any known lead-based paint hazards. A risk assessment or inspection for possible lead-based paint hazards is recommended prior to purchase.

Seller's Disclosure (initial)

_____ (a) Presence of lead-based paint and/or lead-based paint hazards (check one below):
   Known lead-based paint and/or lead-based paint hazards are present in the housing (explain).
   _____
   _____
   Seller has no knowledge of lead-based paint and/or lead-based paint hazards in the housing.
_____ (b) Records and reports available to the Seller (check one below):
   Seller has provided the Buyer with all available records and reports pertaining to lead-based paint and/or lead-based paint hazards in the housing (list documents below).
   _____
   _____
   Seller has no reports or records pertaining to lead-based paint and/or lead-based paint hazards in the housing.

Buyer's Acknowledgment (initial)

_____ (c) Buyer has received copies of all information listed above.
_____ (d) Buyer has received the pamphlet *Protect Your Family from Lead in Your Home.*
_____ (e) Buyer has (check one below):
   Received a 10-day opportunity (or mutually agreed upon period) to conduct a risk assessment or inspection for the presence of lead-based paint and/or lead-based paint hazards; or
   Waived the opportunity to conduct a risk assessment or inspection for the presence of lead-based paint and/or lead-based paint hazards.

Agent's Acknowledgment (initial)

_____ (f) Agent has informed the Seller of the Seller's obligations under 42 U.S.C. 4582(d) and is aware of his/her responsibility to ensure compliance.

Certification of Accuracy

The following parties have reviewed the information above and certify, to the best of their knowledge, that the information provided by the signatory is true and accurate.

Buyer: _____ (SEAL) Date _____
Buyer: _____ (SEAL) Date _____
Agent: _____ Date _____
Seller: _____ (SEAL) Date _____
Seller: _____ (SEAL) Date _____
Agent: _____ Date _____

Some municipalities may have restrictive ordinances regarding aquifer protection zones, wetlands protection, or steep slopes. Listing agents should keep current with all potential restrictions on use of land.

New York State requirements.   The New York Real Property Law requires that the broker have attached to or printed on the reverse side of an exclusive agreement for a one to three-family dwelling a separately signed statement to the following effect:

> *An exclusive-right-to-sell listing means that if you, the property owner, find a buyer for your house or if another broker finds a buyer, you must pay the agreed-on commission to the present broker.*
>
> *An exclusive-agency listing means that if you, the property owner, find a buyer, you will not have to pay a commission to the broker. However, if another broker finds a buyer, you will owe a commission to both the selling broker and your present broker.*

If an exclusive listing of residential property is obtained by a broker who is a member of an MLS, the listing agreement must allow the seller to choose whether all negotiated offers to purchase will be submitted through the listing broker or through the selling broker.

Sample listing agreement.   The individual specifics of a listing may vary from area to area. Following is a section-by-section analysis of a sample agreement; the numbered items in the list refer to the specific provisions of the contract. (See Figure 3.6, used by the Westchester Putnam Multiple Listing Service.)

1. Exclusive right to sell. The title specifies that this document is an "exclusive right to sell" the property.
2. Date. The date of the listing contract is the date it is executed (signed); this may not always be the date the contract becomes effective.
3. Names. The names of all persons having an interest in the property should be specified.
4. Broker or firm. The name of the broker or firm entering into the listing must be clearly stated in the agreement, along with the property address.
5. Contract. This section establishes the document as a bilateral contract and states the promises by both parties that create and bind the agreement.
6. Termination of agreement. Both the exact time and the date should be stated to avoid misunderstandings.
7. Listing price. Many brokers prefer not to refer to this as the *asking price*.
8. Commission rate. This important paragraph establishes the broker's rate of commission. Each brokerage firm is free to set its own fee schedule and to negotiate commission rates if it wishes to. The paragraph also makes an offer of subagency to other members of the MLS and states whether the seller will allow the listing agent to offer part of the commission to a buyer's broker.
9. Extension clause. This section, permitted in New York, protects the broker if, after the listing expires, the owner sells the property to someone with whom the original broker had dealt during the listing period. This

extension clause does not apply if the owner has relisted the property with another agent.

10. Negotiation. The owner agrees to refer all inquiries to the agent and chooses to have any offers submitted by either the listing agent or the selling agent, who may belong to a different firm.

11. Multiple-listing service. The agent will circulate information on the listing to all members of the MLS immediately. In some other areas the listing office may have one, two, or three days of "office exclusive" before the listing is submitted to the MLS.

12. Fair housing. Both parties agree to comply with local, state, and federal fair housing laws.

13. For Sale sign. The agent may not place a sign on the property without authorization.

14. Requirements. The owner(s) must sign this agreement before it is acceptable for publication.

15. Rental. If the owner wishes to rent the property during the life of the agreement, the agent has sole and exclusive right to act as the rental agent. The owner will pay the agent a commission for this service.

16. Termination. The agent is entitled to payment for advertising expenses, damages, and commission if the owner terminates the agreement before it expires.

17. Additional points. Anything not illegal may be agreed on by seller and agent. For example, an understanding that "no commission will be due if seller's brother purchases within 30 days" would go here.

18. In-house sales. A broker must notify the seller and the buyer that a dual agency situation exists and that both the seller and buyer can dissolve their agency agreement with the broker or with informed consent continue with the broker serving as a consensual dual agent.

19. Signatures. The contract should be signed by all owners. The sales associate signs on behalf of the broker or firm; the contract is not made with the individual salesperson.

20. Definitions. The seller must receive an explanation of types of listings.

21. Civil rights legislation. This clause serves to alert the owner that both federal and state legislation protect against discrimination.

22. Owner's acknowledgment. The seller acknowledges notification of listing definitions.

■ BUYER AGENCY

In a buyer-agency relationship, the broker represents the buyer as a client, rather than treating the buyer as merely a customer. Buyer agency allows the broker to provide services to buyers that might otherwise be inappropriate, such as assistance in negotiating the terms of the contract to the buyer's best advantage. The buyers who specifically retain their own agents would be subject to **vicarious liability** for the acts of their agents, just as sellers are for theirs.

Compensating Buyer Agents

An agency relationship does not depend on the source of the agent's compensation. Buyer agents may be compensated by either the buyer or the seller.

F I G U R E   3.6

Listing Agreement

(1) **EXCLUSIVE RIGHT TO SELL AGREEMENT**

THIS AGREEMENT is effective (2) _____ ,19___, and confirms that (3) _____ has (have) appointed
(4) _____ to act as Agent for the sale of property known as _____ , New
York.

(5) In return for the Agent's agreement to use Agent's best efforts to sell the above property, the Owner(s) agree(s) to grant the Agent the exclusive right to sell this property under the following terms and conditions:

PERIOD OF AGREEMENT

1.   This agreement shall be effective from the above date and shall expire at midnight on (6) _____ , 19___.

PRICE AT WHICH PROPERTY WILL BE OFFERED AND AUTHORITY

2.   The property will be offered for sale at a list price of (7) _____ and shall be sold, subject to negotiation, at such price and upon such terms to which Owner(s) may agree. The word Owner refers to each and ALL parties who have ownership interest in the property and the undersigned represent(s) they are the sole and exclusive owners and are fully authorized to enter into this agreement.

(8) **COMMISSION TO BE PAID TO AGENT**

3.   The Agent shall be entitled to and Owner shall pay to Agent one commission of _____ of the selling price. Both the Owner(s) and the Agent acknowledge that the above commission rate was not suggested nor influenced by anyone other than the parties to this Agreement. Owner(s) hereby authorizes Agent to make an offer of cooperation to any other licensed real estate broker with whom Agent wishes to cooperate. Any commission due for a sale brought about by a Sub-Agent (another broker who is authorized by Agent to assist in the sale of Owner(s) property) or to an authorized Buyer(s) Agent shall be paid by the Agent from the commission received by the Agent pursuant to this Paragraph.

        The commission offered by Agent to Sub-Agents shall be _____ of the gross selling price. The commission offered by Agent to Buyer(s) Agents shall be _____ of the gross selling price.

        In the event that Owner(s) authorizes Agent to compensate a Buyer('s) Agent, Owner(s) acknowledges Owner's(s') understanding that such Buyer's Agent is not representing Owner(s) as Sub-Agent and that the Buyer's Agent will be representing only the interests of the prospective purchaser.

(9) **OWNER(S) OBLIGATIONS AFTER THE EXPIRATION OF THIS AGREEMENT**

4.   Owner(s) understands and agrees to pay the commission referred to in paragraph 3, if this property is sold or transferred or is the subject of a contract of sale within _____ months after the expiration date of this agreement involving a person with whom the Agent or a Cooperating Broker or the Owner(s) negotiated or to whom the property is offered, quoted or shown during the period of this listing agreement. Owner(s) will not, however, be obligated to pay such commission if Owner(s) enters into a valid Exclusive Listing Agreement with another New York State licensed real estate broker after the expiration of this agreement.

(10) **WHO MAY NEGOTIATE FOR OWNER(S)**

5.   Owner(s) agree(s) to direct all inquiries to the Agent. Owner(s) elect(s) to have all offers submitted through Agent ___ or Cooperating Agent ___.

(11) **SUBMISSION OF LISTING TO MULTIPLE LISTING SERVICE**

6.   Both Owner(s) and Agent agree that the Agent immediately is to submit this listing agreement to the Westchester Multiple Listing Service, Inc. ("WMLS"), for dissemination to its Participants. No provision of this agreement is intended to nor shall be understood to establish or imply any contractual relationship between the Owner(s) and WMLS nor has WMLS in any way participated in any of the terms of this agreement, including the commission to be paid. Owner(s) acknowledge(s) that the Agent's ability to submit this listing to WMLS or to maintain such listing amongst those included in any compilation of listing information made available by WMLS, is subject to Agent's continued status as a member in good standing of the Westchester County Board of REALTORS, Inc., and Agent's status as a Participant in good standing of WMLS.

(12) **FAIR HOUSING**

7.   Agent and Owner agree to comply fully with local, state and federal fair housing laws against discrimination on the basis of race, color, religion, sex, national origin, handicap, age, marital status and/or familial status, children or other prohibited factors.

Listing Agreement (continued)

(13) AUTHORIZATION FOR "FOR SALE" SIGN AND OTHER SERVICES

8.   Agent __ is (__ is not) authorized to place a "For Sale" sign on the property. Owner acknowledges that Agent has fully explained to Owner(s) the services and marketing activities which Agent has agreed to provide.

(14) REQUIREMENTS FOR PUBLICATION IN WMLS COMPILATION

9.   This listing agreement is not acceptable for publication by WMLS unless and until the Owner(s) has duly signed this agreement and an acknowledgement reflecting receipt of the definitions of "Exclusive Right to Sell" and "Exclusive Agency" required by the New York State Department of State - Division of Licensing Services.

(15) RENTAL OF PROPERTY

10.   Should the Owner(s) desire to rent the property during the period of this agreement, Agent is hereby granted the sole and exclusive right to rent the property, exclusive "FOR RENT" sign privilege and the Owner(s) agrees to pay Agent a rental commission of _____. The applicable commission for the lease term is due and will be paid __ upon the execution of the lease __ upon the date of occupancy. The commission for each and any subsequent renewal thereof, is due and will be paid upon the commencement of each renewal term.

(16) TERMINATION

11.   Owner(s) understands that if Owner(s) terminates the Agent's authority prior to the expiration of its term, Agent shall retain its contract rights (including but not limited to recovery of its commission, advertising expenses and/or any other damages) incurred by reason of an early termination of this agreement.

(17) ADDITIONAL POINTS

12.   Additional Points of Agreement, if any:_____

(18) IN-HOUSE SALES

13.   If the Broker has an agency relationship with the buyer ["buyer's broker"], and that buyer expresses interest in property owned by a seller who also has an agency relationship with the Broker ["seller's broker"], a conflict has arisen.

The Broker shall immediately advise both the buyer client and the seller client of the pertinent facts including the fact that a dual agency situation has arisen, and that the **following options are available:**

[a] **The Broker and buyer could dissolve their Agency relationship.** The buyer may then seek to retain another broker, and/or an attorney, or may represent (her)himself. This would release the buyer from any Broker employment contract which was entered into with the Broker.   Broker may continue to act as agent for the seller.

[b] **The Broker and the seller could dissolve their Agency relationship.** The seller may then seek to retain another broker, and/or an attorney, or may represent (her)himself. This would release the seller from any listing agreement which was entered into with Broker. The Broker may continue to act as Agent for the buyer.

[c] **With fully informed consent, the buyer and seller may elect to continue with the brokerage firm serving as a consensual dual agent, which is the exception to the general rule that agents serve one principal.** As a dual agent, the firm and its licensee agents have a duty of fairness to both principals. By mutual agreement the buyer and seller may identify who will negotiate for each principal. For example: [a] the licensee who signed the buyer as a principal of the brokerage firm may negotiate on behalf of the buyer principal and [b] the licensee who signed the seller as a principal of the firm may negotiate on behalf of the seller principal.

In either case, the brokerage commission will be paid by the seller in accordance with the listing agreement with the seller, unless different arrangements have been negotiated.

As a dual agent, the firm and its agents cannot furnish undivided loyalty to either party.

As a dual agent, the firm and its licensee agents have a duty not to disclose confidential information given by one principal to the other principal, such as the price one is willing to pay or accept. Such information may already be known to the firm and its agents. If the information is of such a nature that the agent cannot fairly give advice without disclosing it, the agent cannot properly continue to act as an agent.

The buyer, seller and broker shall memorialize the option of their mutual choice by executing a statutory disclosure notice. If there is no mutual agreement, the proposed transaction between buyer and seller shall not be pursued.

F I G U R E   3.6

Listing Agreement (continued)

(19) ALL MODIFICATIONS TO BE MADE IN WRITING

14.   Owner(s) and Agent agree that no change, amendment, modification or termination of this agreement shall be binding on any party unless the same shall be in writing and signed by the parties.

(OWNER) _____ (DATE) _____   (AGENT) _____

(OWNER) _____ (DATE) _____   By: _____
                                                             (Authorized Representative)   (DATE)

Owner's Mailing Address: _____   Agent's Address: _____

_____   _____

Owner's Telephone: _____   Agent's Telephone: _____

(20) DEFINITIONS

In accordance with the requirements of the New York State Department of State the undersigned Owner(s) does (do) hereby acknowledge receipt of the following:

1.   Explanation of "Exclusive Right to Sell" listing;
2.   Explanation of "Exclusive Agency" listing;
3.   A list of Participants of Westchester Multiple Listing Service, Inc.

EXPLANATION OF EXCLUSIVE RIGHT TO SELL: (As worded verbatim by the Department of State)

An "exclusive right to sell" listing means that if you, the owner of the property find a buyer for your house, or if another broker finds a buyer, you must pay the agreed commission to the present broker.

EXPLANATION OF EXCLUSIVE AGENCY: (As worded verbatim by the Department of State)

An "exclusive agency" listing means that if you, the owner of the property find a buyer, you will not have to pay a commission to the broker. However, if another broker finds a buyer, you will owe a commission to both the selling broker and your present broker.

(21) "THE FAIR HOUSING ACT"

The Civil Rights Act of 1968 known as the Federal Fair Housing Law makes illegal any discrimination based on race, color, religion, sex or national origin in connection with the sale or rental of housing. The 1988 amendment to this Act (The Fair Housing Amendments Act of 1988) expands the coverage of this law to handicapped persons and families with children. Agent and Owner agree to comply fully with State and local statutes and Federal Fair Housing laws.

Article X of the REALTOR Code of Ethics states:

"REALTORS shall not deny equal professional services to any person for reasons of race, color, religion, sex, handicap, familial status or national origin. REALTORS shall not be parties to any plan or agreement to discriminate against a person or persons on the basis of race, color, religion, sex, handicap, familial status or national origin."

(22) _____

Owner

_____

Owner

Naturally, the way in which fees are to be paid should be stated in writing and clearly understood well in advance to avoid potential conflict between the buyer and the broker.

Seller-paid fee. The seller might agree to pay the buyer's broker fee, particularly during negotiations with a buyer who may be short of cash. In fact, this is probably the most common method of compensation today. The payment of fees does not determine whom an agent represents. As long as the agency relationship is clear and explicit, it does not matter legally whether the buyer or the seller pays the fee.

The seller may pay the buyer's broker's fee through a commission split or by crediting the buyer a specific amount out of the sales proceeds at closing. The most common method is *the commission split,* where the listing broker has written authorization to split the commission with the buyer's broker.

For the most part, the fact that buyers have their own agents has no significant impact on the overall compensation paid to the agents in a transaction. Whether the cooperating agent is a subagent or a buyer's agent, the fees are substantially the same in most instances.

Buyer-paid fee. Buyer-agent compensation also can be paid directly by the buyer. This arrangement has the advantage of avoiding any appearance that the buyer's agent is acting as a subagent of the seller and also gives the buyer's agent greater control over getting paid. The compensation may take the form of an hourly rate, a flat fee, or a percentage commission.

■ Hourly rate. Under an hourly rate arrangement, the broker actually is acting as a consultant. The hourly fee is payable whether or not the buyer actually purchases a property.

■ Percentage fee. A percentage fee is based on the sales price of the home the buyer purchases. The primary benefit of this arrangement is that real estate agents and their clients are accustomed to a percentage arrangement. The obvious disadvantage is that the broker may have a conflict of interest, because the higher the price, the higher the fee.

■ Flat fee. Under this arrangement, the buyer's broker is paid a flat fee if the buyer purchases a house located through the broker. The amount of the fee is based on the broker's estimate of the work and skills involved.

Some buyer's agent agreements provide that the buyer is obligated to pay the fee but is entitled to a credit for any amount the seller agrees to pay. Thus, the buyer would not pay the buyer's broker fee in a typical MLS sale, where the buyer's broker will get a split of the listing broker's commission. However, the buyer would be obligated to pay the fee if the seller had not listed the property or offered any commission to a selling broker.

As always, if the agent is paid by both parties, both must understand the arrangement and give their consent.

Working Relationships with Buyers

Buyers as customers. Not every buyer wants to be represented by an agent. Some buyers like working with several different brokers. Some buyers, especially experienced buyers, are happy with the services provided by a seller's agent: help in finding a suitable property, information about property values, help in preparing and presenting their offer, and aid in securing financing. All of these services can be provided to a customer by an agent representing a seller.

Buyers as clients. Other buyers, however, want more than customer services. They need and want advice, something the seller's broker cannot provide them with. These are the buyers who will benefit most from buyer agency.

Buyer-Agency Agreements

Agreements between buyers and buyer agents are sometimes referred to as *buyer listings, buyer representation agreements,* or *buyer-agency agreements.* Like a listing agreement, a buyer-agency agreement is also an employment contract. In this case, however, the broker is employed as the buyer's agent. The purpose of the agreement is to find a suitable property. An agency agreement gives the buyer a degree of representation that is possible only in a fiduciary relationship.

Types of buyer-agency agreements. There are three basic types of buyer-agency agreements:

1. Exclusive buyer-agency agreement. The buyer is legally bound to compensate the agent whenever he or she purchases a property of the type described in the contract. The broker is entitled to payment regardless of who located the property. Even if the buyer finds the property independently, the agent is entitled to payment. The broker has an **exclusive right to represent** the buyer.
2. Exclusive-agency buyer-agency agreement. The broker is entitled to payment only if he or she locates the property that the buyer ultimately purchases. The buyer is free to find a suitable property without being obligated to pay the agent.
3. Open buyer-agency agreement. This agreement permits the buyer to enter into similar agreements with an unlimited number of brokers. The buyer is obligated to compensate only the broker who locates the property ultimately purchased by the buyer.

A broker also may wish to represent a buyer with respect to a single property only. In this arrangement, the buyer agrees to pay the broker a fee if the buyer purchases a specific property. The broker does not reveal the exact location of the property until the agreement is signed.

In any buyer-agency agreement, the buyer's broker should clarify the types of services to be offered to the buyer client (in addition to the traditional services rendered by real estate licensees to buyers as customers). These could include such tasks as the structuring of the transaction, investment analysis, assistance in development, assistance in financing, and negotiating the sale. Naturally, a buyer's broker must advise the buyer to seek professional legal, tax, or other experts should the need arise.

As with a listing agreement, the time and date of termination should be specified to prevent later conflicts. If the broker wants to be reimbursed for a sale that takes place on a certain property after the buyer agency agreement terminates, the broker should insert an extension clause like that found in most listing agreements. Of course, buyer-agency agreements can be terminated by mutual consent.

Sometimes a buyer may want to purchase a property listed by the buyer's broker. In this case, the buyer's broker would be put in the position of acting as a dual agent. Another type of conflict would arise if the broker were showing more than one buyer client the same property. The buyer-agency agreement should anticipate these types of conflicts. For instance, some agreements provide that the broker will represent the buyer in all cases except in-house listings. Many agreements include an acknowledgment by the buyer that the broker may represent more than one buyer and that if more than one buyer is interested in the same property, it will not be considered a conflict of interest.

An example of a buyer-agency agreement appears in Figure 3.7.

■ SUMMARY

Real estate agents may act in a variety of capacities. Agency relationships exist between a broker and client, between a broker and his or her salespersons, and between cooperating brokers. It is vital that agents understand their relationships to the parties in a transaction and act accordingly.

New York requires brokers and salespersons to provide a written disclosure of agency at first substantive contact with prospective buyers or sellers. The disclosure is repeated when the principal enters into a listing agreement or a buyer agency agreement.

Single agents represent only one party in a transaction, the buyer or the seller. Buyer agents represent buyers, although their compensation may be provided by the seller. Seller agents represent the seller. Unless a cooperating agent (selling agent) specifically rejects an agency relationship with a seller, he or she may be deemed a subagent of the seller in the transaction. Listing agents should always obtain the informed consent of the seller before entering cooperative agreements that create subagencies. Sellers are free to avoid vicarious liability by refusing offers of subagency.

A dual agent represents both the buyer and the seller in the same transaction. Unless both parties have given their informed consent to this form of representation, dual agency is strictly forbidden and can result in severe penalties. Dual agency can arise or be implied in many situations, often without conscious action by the agent. In-house sales, cooperating brokers who are buyer agents, and broker or salesperson self-dealing are all situations of potential dual agency. The state allows designated agents within one firm to represent

F I G U R E   3.7

Exclusive Buyer Agency Agreement

EXCLUSIVE BUYER AGENCY AGREEMENT

COMMISSIONS OR FEES FOR REAL ESTATE SERVICES TO BE PROVIDED ARE NEGOTIABLE BETWEEN REALTOR AND CLIENT. THIS IS A LEGALLY BINDING AGREEMENT. YOU MAY WISH TO CONSULT AN ATTORNEY BEFORE SIGNING IT. FOR THE PURPOSES OF THIS AGREEMENT THE TERM "BUYER" SHALL BE USED TO DESCRIBE PROSPECTIVE PURCHASER(S) OR TENANT(S).

1. APPOINTMENT OF BROKER
By this agreement,_____("Buyer") appoints

_____ ("REALTOR")
as Buyer's exclusive agent, subject to the terms and conditions stated in this Agreement.

By appointing REALTOR as Buyer's exclusive agent, Buyer agrees to conduct all negotiations for the types of property described in Section 2 below through REALTOR and to refer to REALTOR all contact made with Buyer about such properties from other brokers, salespersons, sellers and others during the term of this Agreement.

2. PURPOSE OF AGENCY
Buyer desires to purchase / lease real property (which may include items of personal property) described as follows:
Type: ( ) Residential ( ) Commercial ( ) Residential Income ( ) Industrial ( ) Vacant Land ( ) Other
General Description:

_____

_____

Approximate Price Range: $ _____ to $ _____

General Location:_____

_____

Preferred Terms:_____

_____

Other:_____

3. TERM OF AGENCY: REALTOR's authority to act as Buyer's exclusive agent under this Agreement shall begin _____and shall end at midnight _____.

4. REALTOR'S REPRESENTATIONS AND SERVICES: REALTOR represents that REALTOR is duly licensed under the laws of the State of New York as a real estate broker. REALTOR will assist Buyer in locating property of the type described in Section 2 of this Agreement and to negotiate for Buyer any offer by Buyer to purchase or lease such property. During the term of this Agreement, REALTOR will give Buyer information describing and identifying properties which appear to REALTOR to substantially meet the terms set forth in Section 2.

5. COMPENSATION OF REALTOR: In consideration of the services performed by REALTOR under the terms of this Agreement, Buyer agrees to pay REALTOR the following fee(s): (Initial all applicable sections).

_____a. Non-Refundable Retainer: Buyer shall pay REALTOR a Non-Refundable Retainer of $ _____ to be paid to REALTOR herewith whether or not Buyer purchases or leases any property.
        _____ This Retainer shall be credited against the Hourly Fee described in subsection (b) below or the Transaction Fee described in subsection (c) below.
_____b. Hourly Fee: Buyer will pay REALTOR at the rate of $ _____per hour for all services performed by REALTOR under the terms of this Agreement, to be billed _____and to be paid within five (5) days after Buyer receives a bill for such services from REALTOR.

F I G U R E   3.7

Exclusive Buyer Agency Agreement (continued)

_____ This Hourly Fee shall be credited against the Transaction Fee described in subsection (c) below and shall be kept by REALTOR whether or not a Transaction Fee is earned.

_____c. Transaction Fee: Buyer shall pay REALTOR a Transaction Fee which is the lesser of $ _____ or_____% of the purchase or total lease price (and renewals and/or expansions, if applicable) of any property purchased or leased by Buyer. This Transaction Fee shall be due and payable upon closing of the Purchase and Sale Contract or Lease providing, however, if such Contract or Lease fails to close due to default by the Buyer this Transaction Fee shall become immediately due and payable to REALTOR.   REALTOR is authorized to attempt to obtain payment of the Transaction Fee from the Seller or Lessor of the property , but Buyer shall have the obligation to pay REALTOR the Transaction Fee set forth in this Agreement if REALTOR cannot obtain payment of such fee from the Seller or Lessor of the property. If within_____ days after the expiration of this Agreement, Buyer purchases or leases any property which REALTOR has submitted to Buyer during the term of this Agreement, Buyer will pay REALTOR the Transaction Fee stated above.

_____d. Other: _____

6. OTHER POTENTIAL BUYERS: Buyer understands that other potential buyers have entered or may enter into similar agency contracts with REALTOR which may involve the purchase or lease, through REALTOR, of the same or similar property or properties as Buyer is attempting to purchase or lease. Buyer consents to REALTOR'S representation of such other buyers.

7. CONFLICTING INTERESTS: If REALTOR has an ownership interest in or is an agent for any owner in the sale or lease of any property in which Buyer expresses an interest (e.g. a "company listing"), REALTOR shall immediately notify Buyer of such facts. In such event, if Buyer decides to purchase or lease such property, Buyer will acknowledge the ownership interest of REALTOR or REALTOR'S contractual relationship with that owner and will allow REALTOR to act as dual agent for Buyer and owner. While acting in a dual agency capacity, REALTOR may not, without the express permission of the respective party, disclose to the other party that owner will accept a price less than the listing price or that Buyer will pay a price greater than the price offered. Furthermore, REALTOR'S position as dual agent shall be neutral with respect to both parties, and REALTOR shall act effectively as a mediator between the parties. Buyer is encouraged to refer to New York State DISCLOSURE REGARDING REAL ESTATE AGENCY RELATIONSHIPS, a copy of which is delivered herewith.

8. NONDISCRIMINATION: REALTOR and Buyer agree that all actions carried out under this Agreement shall be in full compliance with local, state and federal fair housing laws against discrimination on the basis of race, creed, color, religion, national origin, sex, familial status, marital status, age or disabilities.

9. PROFESSIONAL COUNSEL: REALTOR hereby recommends that Buyer seek legal, tax, property financing, property inspection, appraisal, environmental engineering and other professional advice (if appropriate) relating to any proposed transaction. Buyer agrees that Buyer will not rely on REALTOR for such professional advice nor rely on REALTOR for payment for such services.

10. OTHER _____

_____

11. ENTIRE AGREEMENT AND ASSIGNABILITY: This Agreement constitutes the complete agreement between REALTOR and Buyer relating to the exclusive agency of REALTOR for Buyer. No modification of any terms of this Agreement shall be valid or binding unless such modification is in writing and signed by Buyer and REALTOR. This agreement is not assignable without written approval of Buyer and REALTOR.

Date:_____   _____BUYER

_____BUYER

REALTOR: _____   BY: _____

buyer and seller separately, when in-house sales are made. The supervising broker in the firm, however, remains a dual agent.

Seller's agents are hired through the use of listing contracts; buyer's agents through buyer-agency agreements.

New York State sets certain minimum requirements to be included in listing agreements.

QUESTIONS

1. The law of agency applies to
   a. real estate brokers only.
   b. real estate salespersons only.
   c. persons holding power of attorney only.
   d. any fiduciary authorized to represent another.

2. Broker John Brown owes customer Susie Smith
   a. loyalty.
   b. fairness and honesty.
   c. confidentiality.
   d. accounting.

3. The Agency Disclosure form must be presented, explained, and signed
   a. when the customer makes an offer.
   b. when the seller accepts an offer.
   c. at the first substantive contact.
   d. when the seller and buyer first meet.

4. The acknowledgment to the sales contract need not be signed when
   a. attorneys represent both parties and prepare the contract.
   b. the closing is delayed.
   c. there is no earnest money deposit.
   d. the closing is in escrow.

5. In a single agency agreement in which a broker represents a seller
   a. the buyer is the client.
   b. the seller is the client.
   c. the seller is the customer.
   d. the buyer is a subagent.

6. The broker receives the most incentive to market property when he or she has a(n)
   a. open listing.
   b. exclusive-agency listing.
   c. net listing.
   d. exclusive-right-to-sell listing.

7. Cooperating brokers must inform the listing agent if they are acting as
   a. subagents of the seller.
   b. buyers' agents.
   c. brokers' agents.
   d. All of the above

8. A buyer's agent owes the seller
   a. loyalty.
   b. confidentiality.
   c. honest and fair business dealing.
   d. accounting.

9. An agency relationship is determined by
   a. the source of compensation.
   b. how well the parties know each other.
   c. agreement between the principal and the agent.
   d. first substantive contact.

10. Undisclosed dual agency may result in broker Joan Jones
    a. losing her license.
    b. losing the commission.
    c. being liable for damages.
    d. All of the above

11. When broker Tony Thomas purchases for himself an MLS-listed property, there is a possibility of
    a. collecting both sides of the commission.
    b. designated agency.
    c. a unilateral offer of cooperation.
    d. undisclosed dual agency.

12. Real Property Law section 443 disclosure requirements apply only to
    a. sale or lease of one to four-unit residential properties.
    b. all types of real estate transactions.
    c. mortgage financing arrangements.
    d. commercial properties.

13. When listing a property, ABC Realty best protects its chances of earning a commission if the listing is a(n)

a. exclusive-right-to-sell listing.
b. for sale by owner.
c. exclusive-agency listing.
d. open listing.

14. Broker Susan represents Murphy as a buyer's agent. She wants to show Murphy property a seller has listed with her. If broker Susan shows Murphy the property, she

a. will have done nothing wrong.
b. must disclose to the seller that she is also representing the buyer.
c. must first get the informed, written consent of both the buyer and the seller to her acting as a dual agent in the transaction.
d. must first notify the Secretary of State that she intends to represent both the buyer and the seller.

4

ESTATES AND INTERESTS

After the Foxes moved into a rented house, they installed an ornate wrought-iron handrail for steps leading from their lawn to the sidewalk. The landlord refused to reimburse them for money spent on the handrail, which angered Tom Fox so much that he decided to remove it. Does he have the right to?

The real estate professional needs to understand the nature of real estate and how it differs from personal property.

■ KEY TERMS

act of waste	freehold estates	remainder interest
agricultural real estate	general partnership	remainderman
air rights	grant	residential real estate
beneficiary	homestead	reversionary interest
bundle of legal rights	improvement	right of survivorship
chattels	industrial real estate	riparian rights
commercial real estate	interest	severalty
common elements	joint tenancy	sole proprietorship
condominium	joint venture	special-purpose real estate
convey	land	subsurface rights
conveyance	leasehold estates	surface rights
cooperative	life estate	syndicate
co-ownership	limited liability company	tenancy by the entirety
corporation	limited partnership	tenant in common
curtesy	littoral rights	title
devise	parcel	trade fixture
dower	partition	trust
emblements	partnership	trustee
escheat	personal property	trustor
estate in land	real estate	undivided interest
fee simple	real property	unities of interest, posses-
fixture		sion, time, and title

F I G U R E   4.1

The Bundle of Legal Rights

- Possession
- Control
- Enjoyment
- Exclusion
- Disposition

■ REAL ESTATE TRANSACTIONS

The purchase or rental of real estate is quite different from dealings in personal property such as automobiles, groceries, or television sets. Even the simplest of real estate transactions brings into play a body of complex laws.

RIGHTS OF OWNERSHIP INCLUDE
■ possession;
■ control of property;
■ enjoyment;
■ exclusion; and
■ disposition.

Real property has often been described as a **bundle of legal rights.** A person who purchases real estate is actually buying the rights previously held by the seller. These *rights of ownership* include the right to *possession*; the right to *control the property* within the framework of the law; the right of *enjoyment* (to use the property in any legal manner); the right of *exclusion* (to keep others from entering or occupying the property); and the right of *disposition* (to be able to sell or otherwise transfer the property). (See Figure 4.1.) Within these ownership rights are included further rights: to **devise** (leave by will), mortgage, encumber, cultivate, explore, lease, license, dedicate, give away, abandon, share, trade, or exchange the property.

■ LAND, REAL ESTATE, AND REAL PROPERTY

The words *land, real estate,* and *real property* often are used to describe the same thing. There are, however, important differences.

Land

The term **land** refers to more than just the surface of the earth; it includes things permanently attached to the land by nature only, such as trees and water. Land ownership also includes minerals and substances below the earth's surface together with the air above up to infinity.

Thus *land* is defined as the *earth's surface extending downward to the center of the earth and upward to infinity, including things permanently attached by nature only.* (See Figure 4.2.)

A specific tract of land is commonly referred to as a **parcel,** which has specific boundaries.

Land and Real Estate

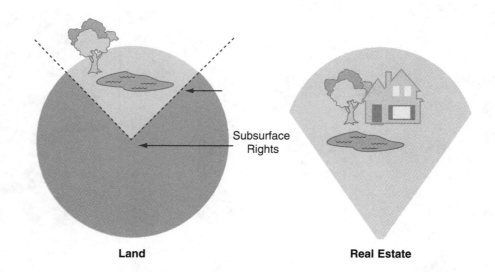

Subsurface
Rights

Land   **Real Estate**

Real Estate

The term *real estate* is broader than the term land and includes all permanent improvements—buildings on the land as well as streets, utilities, sewers, and other *man-made additions* to the property.

Real estate is defined as the *earth's surface extending downward to the center of the earth and upward into space, including all things permanently attached to it by nature and by people.* (See Figure 4.2.)

Real Property

The term *real property* is broader still and includes the *bundle of legal rights of ownership.*

Thus *real property* is defined as the *earth's surface extending downward to the center of the earth and upward into space, including all things permanently attached to it by nature and by people, as well as the interests, benefits, and rights included in ownership.* (See Figure 4.3.)

In everyday usage, the term *real estate* or *realty* is commonly used for *real property.*

Subsurface rights, the rights to the natural resources lying below the earth's surface, may be owned separately.

A landowner, for example, may sell to an oil company the rights to any oil and gas found in the land. The landowner then could sell the land to a purchaser and in the sale reserve the rights to all coal that may be found in the land. After these sales, three parties have ownership interests in this real estate: (1) the oil company owns all oil and gas; (2) the seller owns all coal; and (3) the new landowner owns the rights to the remaining real estate.

Real Property

The Bundle
of Rights

Real Property

Mineral rights also may be leased. Much of the farmland in southwestern New York State is subject to oil and gas leases.

The rights to use the airspace above the land may be sold or leased independently of the land itself. Such **air rights** are an increasingly important part of real estate, particularly in large cities, where air rights over railroads have been purchased to construct huge office buildings like the Met-Life Building in New York City. For the construction of such a building, the developer must purchase not only the air rights above the land but also numerous small portions of the actual land to construct the building's foundation supports.

Until the development of airplanes, air rights were considered to be unlimited. Today, however, the courts permit reasonable interference with these rights by aircraft, as long as the owner's right to use and occupy the land is not interfered with. Governments and airport authorities often purchase air rights next to an airport to provide glide patterns for aircraft.

With the continuing development of solar power, courts may consider tall buildings that block sunlight from smaller buildings to be interfering with the smaller buildings' rights to solar energy.

The rights in one parcel of real property could therefore be owned by many people: (1) an owner of the **surface rights;** (2) an owner of subsurface mineral rights; (3) an owner of subsurface gas and oil rights; and (4) an owner of the air rights.

Riparian rights are the owner's rights in land bordering a river or stream. In New York, persons owning land bordering nonnavigable streams own the property to the midpoint of the stream. Those whose land borders navigable

Riparian Rights

streams own the property to the high-water mark (the limit of the rise of medium tides); the riverbed belongs to the state. (See Figure 4.4.)

Closely related to riparian rights are the **littoral rights** of owners whose land borders large lakes, bays, and oceans. They may enjoy unrestricted use of the water but own the land only up to the high-water mark. (See Figure 4.5.) All land below this point is owned by the government.

Riparian and littoral rights may not be sold separately or kept when the land is sold. Where land adjoins streams, an owner is entitled to all *accretions*, increases resulting from the deposit of soil by the action of the water or wind. An owner also may lose land through gradual *erosion* or through *avulsion*, due to a change in the channel of a stream.

■ REAL PROPERTY VERSUS PERSONAL PROPERTY

Nearly everything that can be owned may be classified as either real or personal property.

Personal property is *all property that does not fit the definition of real estate*. Personal property is *movable*, or mobile. Items of personal property, also

Littoral Rights

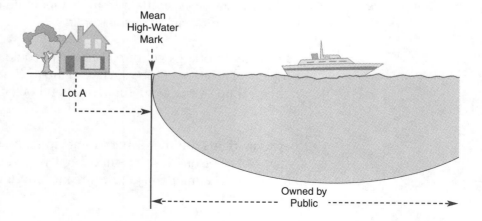

FIGURE   4.6

**Real versus
Personal Property**

Real Estate	Personal Property
Land and anything permanently attached to it	Movable items not attached to real estate; items severed from real estate

Fixture	Trade Fixture
Item of personal property converted to real estate by attaching it to the real estate with the intention that it become permanently a part thereof	Item of personal property attached to real estate that is owned by a tenant and is used in a business; legally removable by tenant

referred to as **chattels,** include possessions such as refrigerators, drapes, clothing, money, bonds, and bank accounts. (See Figure 4.6.)

It is possible to change an item of real estate to personal property. A growing tree is real estate, but if the owner cuts down the tree and thereby severs it from the earth, it becomes personal property. The process is known as *severance*.

The reverse situation is also possible. Personal property can be changed to real estate. If an owner buys cement, stones, and sand and constructs a concrete walk, materials that were originally personal property are changed into real estate because they have become a permanent improvement on the land.

Trees and crops are generally considered in two classes: (1) Trees, perennial bushes, and grasses that do not require yearly cultivation are considered real estate; and (2) Annual crops of wheat, corn, vegetables, and fruit, known as **emblements,** are generally considered personal property. A mobile home is usually considered personal property unless it is permanently attached to the land by a foundation.

Fixtures

An article of personal property that has been permanently attached to land or a building is known as a **fixture** and becomes part of the real estate. Examples of fixtures are furnaces, elevator equipment, kitchen cabinets, light fixtures, and sinks. Almost any item that has been added as a *permanent part* of a building is considered a fixture.

FOUR LEGAL TESTS OF A FIXTURE:

1. The adaptation of the article to the real estate
2. The method of annexation of the item
3. The intention and relationship of the parties
4. The existence of an agreement

Legal tests of a fixture.   Courts apply four basic tests to determine whether an article is a fixture (and therefore a part of the real estate) or removable personal property. These tests are based on (1) the adaptation of the article to the real estate; (2) the method of annexation (attachment) of the item; (3) the intention and relationship of the parties; and (4) the existence of an agreement.

Although these tests seem simple, court decisions do not always agree on whether something is a fixture. Annexation alone is not a final test. The front door key, for example, is not attached, but it is clearly a fixture that belongs with the house.

The distinction between personal and real property is of great importance in the sale of real estate. When a contract for the sale of property is being negotiated, buyers and sellers must be guided by clear written agreements about what "goes with" the real estate being sold.

Trade fixtures.   An article owned by a tenant and attached to a rented space for use in conducting a business is a **trade fixture.** Examples of trade fixtures are bowling alley equipment, store shelves, and restaurant equipment. Agricultural fixtures such as chicken coops and toolsheds also are included in this definition. (See Figure 4.6.)

Trade fixtures remain the personal property of the tenant and may be removed on or before the last day the property is rented. The tenant must, however, restore the property to its original condition, repairing holes left by bolts, for example. Trade fixtures not removed become the property of the landlord.

Uses of Real Estate

Real estate brokers deal with many different types of real property. (See Figure 4.7.) Real estate generally can be classified in these categories:

> **FIVE BASIC CATEGORIES OF REAL PROPERTY:**
> 1. Residental
> 2. Commercial
> 3. Industrial
> 4. Agricultural
> 5. Special-purpose

- **Residential**—all property used for housing, from acreage to small city lots, both single-family and multifamily, in urban, suburban, and rural areas
- **Commercial**—business property including offices, shopping malls, theaters, hotels, and parking facilities
- **Industrial**—warehouses, factories, land in industrial districts, and research facilities (Industrial property is sometimes referred to as *manufacturing property* in New York City.)
- **Agricultural**—farms, timberland, pastureland, and orchards
- **Special-purpose**—religious institutions, schools, cemeteries, hospitals, and government-held lands

■ ESTATES (OWNERSHIP) IN LAND

A buyer's choice of ownership type will affect his or her legal right to sell in the future without the consent of others and also the right to leave the property to chosen heirs. The real estate practitioner needs to understand various forms of ownership so that buyers, sellers, tenants, and landlords can be alerted to the need for legal input to avoid future problems. This chapter discusses various interests in real estate and the basic forms of real estate ownership.

The amount and kind of **interest** (ownership) that a person has in real property is an **estate in land.** Estates in land are either freehold estates or leasehold estates (those involving rentals).

FIGURE 4.7

Uses of Real Property

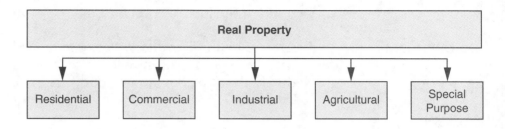

Freehold estates exist indefinitely for a lifetime or forever. The freehold estates recognized in New York are: (1) fee simple, (2) qualified (determinable) fee, (3) fee on condition; and (4) life estates.

The first three of these estates continue for an indefinite period and can be inherited after the owner's death. A life estate ends at the death of the person on whose life it is based.

Leasehold estates are estates for a specific period of time. They are classified as personal property.

■ *Estate for years:* Commonly established by a lease, written, or (if for a period of less than one year) oral. An estate for years gives the tenant possession of the property for a fixed time.

■ *Periodic estate, estate at will, estate at sufferance:* These leasehold estates are covered at length in Chapter 7. Each lasts for an indefinite length of time.

Fee Simple Estate

An estate in **fee simple** is the *most complete type of ownership in real estate.* A fee simple estate is one in which the owner is entitled to all rights in the property. There is no time limit—it is said to run forever. On the death of its owner the estate passes to the owner's heirs. The terms *fee, fee simple,* and *fee simple absolute* are basically the same. New York law provides that a **grant** (sale or gift) of real property automatically **conveys** (transfers) fee simple ownership unless the terms of the grant show a clear intention to convey a lesser estate.

Qualified Fee Estate

Sometimes a gift or sale provides that the real property must be used for a specific purpose. The deed that transfers the property might state Smith gives the land "to the Jones Foundation so long as it is used for a wildlife preserve." If the Jones Foundation later builds a corporate headquarters on the land, ownership will *automatically* revert to Smith (or Smith's heirs); the Jones Foundation owned only a *qualified fee.*

Fee on Condition

A *fee on condition* is slightly different. The deed transferring ownership to the Jones Foundation might have been worded so that if the land were ever used for any purpose except a wildlife preserve, the land would *not automatically revert* back to Smith. Smith or Smith's heirs would, however, have the right to file suit in court to recover the property.

Real estate brokers and salespersons need to know just enough about qualified fee and fee on condition to alert sellers and buyers to the need for legal counsel if such a situation is encountered.

Life Estates

A **life estate** is *limited to the life of some specific person.* The owner does not have the right to pass ownership to heirs, because the life estate ends with the death of the owner or a third party. Life estates may be *ordinary* or *pur autre vie.*

An *ordinary life estate* lasts as long as the owner, the life tenant, is alive. A may leave a life estate to B, who will have full ownership for the rest of his or her life. B does not, however, have the right to leave the property to anyone at death. A has already established who will become the next owner.

A life estate *pur autre vie* (for another life) lasts as long as a particular third party, named by the original owner, is alive. Mrs. A might, for example, leave her home to son B, to be owned by B "as long as my brother, Felix, is alive and living in the home." B (or B's heirs) would be complete owner of the property, but only until Felix's death.

Remainder and reversion.   The person who sets up the life estate provides for the future ownership of the property. After the death of the life tenant the property may revert to the original owner or pass to someone else. (See Figure 4.8.)

- **Remainder interest:** Mr. A may leave the family homestead to the second Mrs. A for her lifetime with the provision that it pass, at her death, to the son of his first marriage, A, Jr. During Mrs. A's lifetime, A, Jr., owns a *remainder interest* and is known as a **remainderman.**
- **Reversionary interest:** Mr. A may give his home to poor relative B for B's lifetime with the provision that at B's death ownership reverts (returns) to A (or, if A has died, to A's heirs). During B's lifetime Mr. A owns a *reversionary interest.*

A life tenant's interest in real property is true ownership. The life tenant may not, however, permanently injure the land or property, acts known in legal terms as an **act of waste.** A life tenant is entitled to all income and profits arising from the property. A life interest could theoretically be sold, leased, mortgaged, or given away, but it always will terminate (end) on the death of the person against whose life the estate is measured.

Not Used in New York State

A husband's interest in the real estate of his deceased wife is called **curtesy.** **Dower** is the interest that a wife has in the real estate of her deceased husband. New York law no longer recognizes dower and curtesy.

In a community property state (California is a conspicuous example), property acquired during the marriage is presumed to belong equally to husband and wife, with the exception of gifts and inheritances. New York is not a community property state and recognizes no special community property rights in real estate.

F I G U R E   4.8

Life Estate

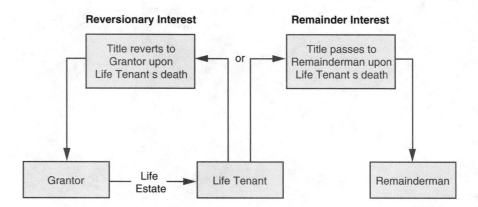

In some states the estate known as **homestead** gives the owner special rights in property used as a family home. New York does not have any special right of homestead.

■ FORMS OF OWNERSHIP

A fee simple estate in land may be held (1) in **severalty,** where **title** (ownership) is held by one owner; (2) in **co-ownership,** where title is held by two or more persons; or (3) in **trust,** where title is held by a third person for the benefit of another.

The form by which property is owned is important to the real estate broker for two reasons: (1) *the form of ownership existing when a property is sold determines who must sign the various documents involved* (listing contract, acceptance of offer to purchase, sales contract, and deed); and (2) *the purchaser must determine in what form he or she wishes to take title*. When questions about these forms are raised, the real estate broker should recommend that the parties seek legal advice.

The word **tenant,** when used with various forms of ownership, does not refer to someone who is renting the property. Instead it means the owner.

Severalty

Severalty is the ownership of property by one person only. Ownership is severed or separated from any form of co-ownership and is also referred to as *sole ownership*. When the owner dies, the property passes to the owner's heirs or as otherwise provided by the owner's will.

Co-Ownership

When title to one parcel of real estate is owned by two or more persons or organizations, those parties are said to be *co-owners*. New York recognizes the following forms of ownership: (1) tenancy in common; (2) joint tenancy; and (3) tenancy by the entirety.

FIGURE   4.9

Tenancy in Common

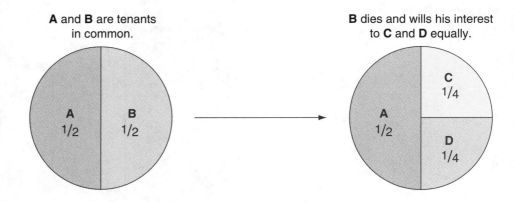

A and B are tenants
in common.

B dies and wills his interest
to C and D equally.

Tenancy in common.   A **tenant in common** owns an **undivided interest** in the property. Although an owner may have, say, a one-half or one-third interest in a property, it is impossible to distinguish physically which specific half or third of the property is owned. The deed creating a tenancy in common may or may not state the fractional interest held by each co-owner. If no fractions are stated, each owns an equal share. For example, if five people hold title, each would own an undivided one-fifth interest. On the death of a co-owner, his or her interest would pass to heirs or devisees named in the owner's will (and the tenancy in common would continue). (See Figure 4.9.)

A second important characteristic of a tenancy in common is that *each owner* may sell, convey, mortgage, or transfer that interest *without the consent* of the other co-owners.

In New York a **conveyance** (sale or gift) to persons not married to each other automatically creates a tenancy in common unless otherwise stated in the deed. Property inherited by two or more persons is owned by them as tenants in common unless the will states otherwise.

When an unmarried couple buys a home together, they have a decision to make. If one dies, should that person's share go to heirs named in a will or, if there is no will, to what the state calls *natural heirs:* spouse, parents, siblings, children? If so, they will take title as tenants in common. If, however, they would like the surviving partner to become complete owner automatically, their deed should make it clear they are taking title as joint tenants.

Joint tenancy.   With **joint tenancy,** the property is owned by a group made up of two or more persons. The death of one of the joint tenants simply means there is one fewer person in the group. The remaining joint tenants automatically receive the share owned by the deceased tenant, by **right of survivorship,** no matter what that person's will might have ordered. Only the last survivor, who becomes sole owner, may dispose of the property by will. (See Figure 4.10.)

FIGURE   4.10

**Joint Tenancy with
Right of Survivorship**

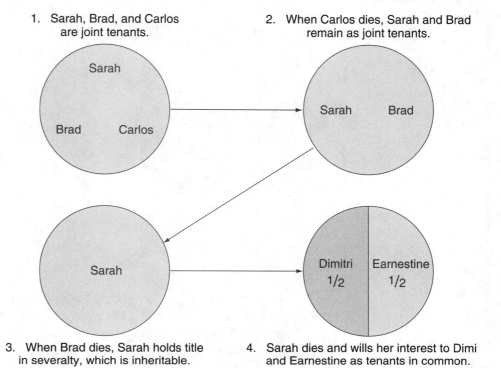

1. Sarah, Brad, and Carlos
   are joint tenants.

2. When Carlos dies, Sarah and Brad
   remain as joint tenants.

3. When Brad dies, Sarah holds title
   in severalty, which is inheritable.

4. Sarah dies and wills her interest to Dimi
   and Earnestine as tenants in common.

Creating joint tenancies.   To create a joint tenancy in New York, language in the deed must specifically state that title is taken in that form of ownership.

Four unities are required to create a joint tenancy:

1. **Unity of *time*—**All joint tenants acquire their interest at the same time.
2. **Unity of *title*—**All joint tenants acquire their interest by the same deed.
3. **Unity of *interest*—**All joint tenants hold equal ownership interests.
4. **Unity of *possession*—**All joint tenants hold an undivided interest in the property move.

Terminating joint tenancies.   While a joint tenant is free to convey (sell or give away) his or her interest in the jointly held property, doing so will destroy the joint tenancy. For example, if A, B, and C hold title as joint tenants and A sells her interest to D, then D will own a one-third interest as a tenant in common with B and C, who will continue to own their two-thirds interest as joint tenants. (See Figure 4.11.) If D dies, one-third interest will go to D's heir. If B dies, C will own two-thirds.

Joint tenancies also may be terminated by bankruptcy or foreclosure sale proceedings.

Lee, Sims, and Tobey
are joint tenants.

Lee

Sims   Tobey

Lee sells her interest to Wilbur.

Wilbur

Sims   Tobey

Wilbur becomes a tenant in common
with Sims and Tobey as joint tenants.

Termination of co-ownership by partition suit. Tenants in common or joint tenants may file in court a suit to **partition** the land. The right of partition is a legal way to end co-ownership when the parties do not agree. If the court determines that the land cannot be physically divided (acreage, for example), it will order the real estate sold and the proceeds divided among the co-owners. Such a forced sale, however, may not yield full market value.

Tenancy by the entirety. A **tenancy by the entirety** is a *special joint tenancy between husband and wife. (It is used in New York, but not in all states.)* The owners must be husband and wife when they receive the property. They have rights of survivorship, but there is no right to partition.

In New York a conveyance to a married couple automatically creates in them a tenancy by the entirety unless the deed specifies otherwise. Divorce breaks a tenancy by the entirety, and the ex-spouses immediately become tenants in common.

■ TRUSTS

Property owners may provide for their own financial care and/or that of others by establishing trusts. Such trusts may be created by agreement during a property owner's lifetime (inter vivos or living trust) or established by will after the owner's death (testamentary trust).

There are three parties to a trust: the trustor, the trustee, and the beneficiary or beneficiaries. The individual creating a trust, the **trustor,** makes an agreement conveying assets to the **trustee** with the understanding that the trustee will assume certain duties. These duties include the care and investment of the trust assets to produce income. After payment of operating expenses and trustee's fees, this income is paid to or used for the benefit of one or more

beneficiaries. These trusts may continue for the beneficiaries' lifetimes or until the beneficiaries reach certain ages.

■ OWNERSHIP OF REAL ESTATE BY BUSINESS ORGANIZATIONS

Ownership by a business organization makes it possible for many people to hold an interest in the same parcel of real estate. Investors may be organized in various ways to finance a real estate project. Sometimes real estate is owned by the organization itself, sometimes directly by the investors. Business organizations may be categorized as partnerships, corporations, syndicates, or limited liability companies. The purchase or sale of real estate by any business organization involves complex legal questions, and legal counsel is required.

All of the following types of business organizations contrast with **sole proprietorship,** a business owned by one individual.

Partnerships

An association of two or more people to carry on a business as co-owners and share in the business's profits and losses is a **partnership.** Partnerships are classified as general and limited. In a **general partnership** all partners participate to some extent in the operation and management of the business and may be held personally liable for business losses and obligations. A **limited partnership** includes general partners as well as limited (popularly known as "silent") partners. The business is run by the general partner or partners. The limited partners do not participate, and each can be held liable for the business's losses *only to the extent of his or her investment.* The limited partnership is a popular method of organizing investors in a real estate project. If a general partner dies, the partnership is dissolved, unless the partnership agreement provides otherwise.

Corporations

A **corporation** is an artificial person or legal entity created under the laws of the state from which it receives its charter. Because the corporation is a legal person, real estate ownership by a corporation is an *ownership in severalty.* A corporation is managed and operated by its *board of directors,* which is elected by the shareholders.

As a legal entity, a corporation exists indefinitely (in perpetuity). The death of one of the shareholders, officers, or directors does not affect title to property owned by the corporation.

Individuals participate, or invest, in a corporation by purchasing stock. Because stock is *personal property,* stockholders do not have a direct ownership interest in real estate owned by a corporation. Each stockholder's liability for the corporation's losses usually is limited to the amount of his or her investment.

Limited Liability Company

The **limited liability company** is a hybrid entity that combines the freedom to manage the company offered by partnerships with the limited liability for all the owners and income tax advantages offered by corporations. The owners pay taxes on earnings and profits received from the limited liability company.

Syndicates

A **syndicate** is *a joining together of two or more people or firms to carry out one or more business projects.* It may be organized into a number of ownership forms, including co-ownership (tenancy in common, joint tenancy), partnership, trust, limited liability company, or corporation.

A **joint venture** is an organization of two or more people or firms to carry out a *single project*. A joint venture lasts for a limited time and is not intended to establish a permanent relationship.

The real estate practitioner who organizes or sells a real estate venture involving investors who expect to benefit without active participation should be alert for special registration or licensing required by the state department of law for syndication activity.

■ COOPERATIVE AND CONDOMINIUM OWNERSHIP

In this century apartment dwellers have turned to arrangements under which they own their living space. Cooperative ownership was the first to develop; condominium ownership appeared later.

Cooperative Ownership

Under the usual **cooperative** arrangement, title to land and building is held by a *corporation*. Tenants buy stock in the corporation and receive proprietary leases to their apartments. As stockholders they exercise control over the administration of the building through an elected board of directors. Barring any violation of antidiscrimination laws, directors usually may approve or disapprove of prospective purchasers of the apartment leases. Tenants contribute monthly fees to cover maintenance costs, the corporation's property taxes, and the overall mortgage on the building.

The corporation, however, is financially vulnerable. If other tenants cannot pay their monthly charges, the owner/occupant may lose out in the event of a forced sale of the property. Cooperative ownership is found in and around New York City more than in other parts of the state.

Although the stock in a cooperative is considered personal property, a real estate license is needed for the sale of cooperatives. In addition, the Internal Revenue Service allows the owners of cooperative apartments to treat the units as if they were real estate for income tax purposes.

Condominium Ownership

The owner of each **condominium** apartment holds a *fee simple title* to his or her dwelling unit and also to a percentage of the other parts of the building and land, known as the **common elements.**

The condominium form of ownership is often used for apartment buildings. These may range from freestanding highrise buildings to town house arrangements. Common elements include such items as the land, walls, hallways, elevators, stairways, and roof. Lawns and recreational facilities such as swimming pools, clubhouses, and golf courses also may be considered common elements.

In addition, condominium ownership is sometimes used for commercial property or office buildings. The word *condominium* could apply even to a group of single detached houses whose ownership was organized in this fashion.

The owner of a condominium unit receives a separate tax bill and may mortgage the individual living unit. Default in the payment of taxes or a mortgage loan by one unit owner may result in a foreclosure sale of that owner's unit but will not affect the ownership of the other unit owners.

Operation and administration.   In New York State, the condominium property is customarily administered by an association of unit owners or a board of managers elected by the unit owners. It may manage the property on its own or engage a professional property manager. Owners pay monthly charges for maintenance expenses.

Town house ownership is a hybrid form. Town house occupants own the land directly beneath their unit and the living unit, including roof and basement, in fee simple. Sometimes a small lawn or patio is individually owned as well. Single houses on extra-small lots, in what is known as *cluster housing*, sometimes use this form of ownership. A town house owner becomes a member of a homeowners' association, which owns the common elements.

Time-sharing is a variation of condominium ownership in which the buyer receives the right to use a living unit, usually in a resort area, for a specific portion of a year. The buyer might own an undivided one-twelfth interest together with a right to use the facility for one month of the year.

■ OTHER WAYS TITLE IS TRANSFERRED

When a person dies leaving no will and no relatives who qualify as natural heirs, his or her real estate becomes the property of the State of New York, through the process known as **escheat.** Land is, rarely, acquired through long use without the owner's consent in a complex legal process known as *adverse possession*. Both of these processes are discussed in Chapter 24.

■ SUMMARY

Even the simplest real estate transactions involve a complex body of laws. The person who buys real estate receives not only the land itself but also the legal rights to use the land in certain ways.

Land includes not only the earth's surface but also the mineral deposits under the earth and the air above it. The term *real estate* further includes man-made improvements attached to the land. Real property includes real estate plus the bundle of legal rights associated with its ownership.

The same parcel of real estate may be owned and controlled by different parties, one owning surface rights, another owning air rights, and yet another owning the subsurface rights.

Ownership of land also includes the right to use the water on or adjacent to it. Riparian rights give the owner of land next to water that cannot be navigated by boat ownership to the middle of the stream. A river that can be navigated belongs to the landowner only up to the high-water mark; the riverbed belongs to the state. Littoral rights are held by owners of land bordering large lakes and oceans and include use of the water and ownership of the land up to the high-water mark.

All property that does not fit the definition of real estate is classified as personal property, also known as *chattels*. When articles of personal property are permanently attached to land, they may become fixtures and part of the real estate. Personal property installed by a tenant for a business purpose, however, is classified as a trade fixture, remains personal property, and may be removed.

Real property can be classified according to its general use as residential, commercial, industrial, agricultural, or special-purpose.

An estate is the amount and kind of interest a person holds in land. Freehold estates are estates of indefinite length. Leasehold estates involve the right to use the property for a specified length of time without owning it. They concern landlords and tenants.

Estates that can be inherited include fee simple, fee on condition, and qualified fee estates. Life estates can be granted for the life of the new owner or for the life of some third party (pur autre vie). At the end of the life estate, ownership can go back to the original owner (reverter) or pass to a designated third party (remainder). Homestead in New York is not an estate, and community property is not part of New York law.

Sole ownership or ownership in severalty indicates that title is held by one person or entity.

Title to real estate can be held at the same time by more than one person. It is important for purchasers to recognize the issues involved in the manner of taking title, which include their ability to will the property or transfer it without the consent of the other joint owner. Title questions should be discussed with an attorney prior to purchasing jointly owned property.

Under tenancy in common an individual owner may own an unequal share, may sell his or her interest, and has the right to leave the share to any designated beneficiaries. When two or more persons not married to each other hold title to real estate, they own it as tenants in common unless their deed specifically states some other intention.

Joint tenancy involves two or more owners with the right of survivorship. Upon the death of one owner that person's share passes to the remaining co-owner(s). The intention to establish joint tenancy with right of survivorship must be stated clearly in their deed, and four unities must exist. Both tenants in common and joint tenants have the right to force a sale by partition.

Tenancy by the entirety is a special joint tenancy for property acquired by husband and wife. Unless their deed specifically states they wish to own the property in another way, they will own it by the entirety. Neither can force a sale by partition. Divorce changes their ownership to tenancy in common.

Real estate ownership also may be held in trust. Title to the property is conveyed by the trustor to a trustee, who administers it for the benefit of a beneficiary.

Various types of business organizations may own real estate. A corporation is a legal entity and holds title to real estate in severalty. A partnership or limited liability company may own real estate in its own name. A syndicate is an association of two or more persons or firms who join together for the purpose of making investments. Many syndicates are joint ventures organized for only a single project.

With cooperative ownership, title to the property, often an apartment building, is held by a corporation that pays taxes, principal, and interest on the building's mortgage, and operating expenses. The purchaser of an apartment receives shares in the corporation and a long-term lease to the living unit and pays monthly charges to cover a share of expenses.

Under condominium ownership each occupant/owner holds fee simple title to a living unit plus a share of the common elements. Each owner receives an individual tax bill and may mortgage the unit. Expenses for operating the building are collected by a condominium owners' association through monthly assessments. In town house ownership each occupant usually owns the land directly below the unit, and a homeowners' association may own the common elements.

QUESTIONS

1. A specific tract of land is known as a
   a. devise.   c. chattel.
   b. parcel.   d. littoral.

2. The definition of land includes
   a. sewers, roads, and streets.
   b. buildings permanently attached.
   c. the right of enjoyment.
   d. the airspace above the surface.

3. Real property is often referred to as a *bundle of legal rights*. Among these is the right of
   a. navigation.   c. avulsion.
   b. exclusion.   d. emblement.

4. Ben Jones, owner of a farm in Steuben County, may find that an oil company wants to lease his
   a. littoral rights.
   b. subsurface rights.
   c. air rights.
   d. riparian rights.

5. Man-made, permanent additions to land are called
   a. fixtures.   c. improvements.
   b. parcels.   d. trade fixtures.

6. When a building is to be constructed above land owned by another, the builder purchases the landowner's
   a. riparian rights.
   b. subsurface rights.
   c. air rights.
   d. littoral rights.

7. Dana Fox owns land along the Mohawk River and as the owner has certain
   a. riparian rights.
   b. subsurface rights.
   c. air rights.
   d. littoral rights.

8. When Miriam Enton sells her farm, which of the following will not be a part of the real estate?
   a. Fences
   b. Permanent buildings
   c. Farm equipment
   d. Growing trees

9. Two months into the one-year rental period the tenant installs awnings over the front windows. Which of the following is true?
   a. Tenant must remove the awnings before the lease is up.
   b. Awnings are considered personal property due to their permanent nature.
   c. Tenant may not remove the awnings.
   d. Awnings are considered trade fixtures.

10. When Sally opened her hair salon, she installed three shampoo basins, four large plate-glass mirrors, and custom work-station counters. Just before the expiration of the lease, she has the right to remove
    a. everything but the shampoo basins because they are attached to the plumbing.
    b. only the mirrors, and then only if holes in the walls are repaired.
    c. all of the items mentioned above.
    d. nothing, because all of the items became fixtures when they were attached.

11. Fred and Celia Tomkins are building a deck off their kitchen. A dealer has just unloaded a truckload of lumber onto their driveway. At this point the lumber is considered
    a. a chattel.   c. a fixture.
    b. real estate.   d. a trade fixture.

12. When the Tomkinses' deck is completed, the lumber will be considered
    a. a chattel.   c. a parcel.
    b. real estate.   d. a trade fixture.

13. The owner who signs a contract promising to sell all the real estate without listing any exceptions has no right to take his
    a. tomato plants.
    b. drapes.
    c. portable dishwasher.
    d. dining room chandelier.

14. Special-purpose real estate includes
    a. apartment houses.
    b. churches.
    c. factories.
    d. shopping malls.

15. Property that is part of the commercial market includes
    a. office buildings for lease.
    b. apartments for rent.
    c. churches.
    d. factories.

16. The most complete ownership recognized by law is a(n)
    a. life estate.
    b. fee simple estate.
    c. leasehold estate.
    d. estate at will.

17. Julia inherited her cousin's house, but it is hers only as long as the dog, Buster, is alive and well and living in the house. When Buster dies, the house is to go to her cousin's son. The cousin's son is a
    a. beneficiary.   c. life tenant.
    b. remainderman.   d. limited partner.

18. John and Mary Alessi owned a small apartment house by the entirety. Mary had a will leaving half her estate to John and half to her daughter Susan. After Mary was killed in an automobile accident, Susan owned how much of the apartment house?
    a. None   c. One-third
    b. One-quarter   d. One-half

19. Ownership of real property by one person is called ownership in
    a. trust.   c. entirety.
    b. severalty.   d. condominium.

20. A house was purchased by Howard Evers and Tinker Chance. Evers paid one-third of the cost, and Chance paid the balance. The seller's deed conveyed the property "to Howard Evers and Tinker Chance" without further explanation. Evers and Chance are
    a. joint tenants.
    b. tenants in common, each owning a one-half undivided interest.
    c. tenants in common, with Evers owning an undivided one-third interest.
    d. general partners in a joint venture.

21. If property is held by two or more owners as tenants in common, on the death of one owner the ownership of his or her share will pass to the
    a. remaining owner or owners.
    b. heirs or whoever is designated under the deceased owner's will.
    c. surviving owner and/or his or her heirs.
    d. deceased owner's surviving spouse.

22. In New York a deed conveying property to a married couple, such as to "Frank Peters and Marcia Peters, husband and wife," creates a
    a. joint tenancy.
    b. tenancy by the entirety.
    c. tenancy in common.
    d. periodic tenancy.

23. Which of the following statements applies equally to joint tenants and tenants by the entireties?
    a. There is no right to file a partition suit.
    b. The survivor becomes complete owner.
    c. There may be more than two owners.
    d. The deed must state the type of tenancy desired.

24. An artificial person created by legal means is known as a

    a. trust.

    b. corporation.

    c. limited partnership.

    d. joint tenancy.

25. A syndicate formed to carry out a single business project for a limited time is commonly known as a

    a. joint venture.

    b. corporation.

    c. limited partnership.

    d. joint tenancy.

CHAPTER FIVE

LIENS AND EASEMENTS

Eric buys a vacation cottage, and the seller tells him she has always used an easement to go across the next-door neighbor's land to the lake. Eric worries about whether he will have that same right, or whether the neighbor might deny him lake access now that ownership has changed.

Real estate brokers often come up against claims by nonowners as they follow through on real estate transactions: a shared driveway, an old judgment placed against a seller's property, a neighbor's garage built six inches over the property line. Agents need a working knowledge of the concepts and vocabulary involved so they can assist attorneys in clearing up encumbrances.

■ KEY TERMS

adverse possession
affidavit of entitlement to
   commission
appurtenant
cloud on the title
corporation franchise
   tax
deed restrictions
dominant estate
easement
easement appurtenant
easement by condemnation
easement by grant

easement by necessity
easement by prescription
easement in gross
encroachment
encumbrance
estate taxes
general lien
involuntary lien
judgment
license
lien
lis pendens
mechanic's lien

mortgage lien
notice of pending legal
   action
party wall
priority
right-of-way
servient estate
specific lien
subordination agreement
tacking
tax lien
voluntary lien

F I G U R E   5.1
General Liens

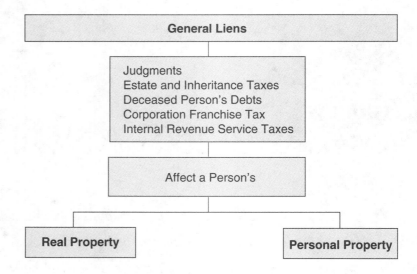

ENCUMBRANCES

An **encumbrance** is a right or interest in a property held by a party who is not the owner of the property. Encumbrances fall into two categories:

1. *Liens:* financial claims against the property
2. *Usage encumbrances:* restrictions, easements, and encroachments

LIENS

A *financial claim against real estate that provides security for a debt or obligation of the property owner* is a **lien**. If the claim is not paid, the lienholder, or creditor, may ask a court to order the real estate sold for full or partial satisfaction of the debt, a process known as *foreclosure of the lien*.

A lien may be voluntary or involuntary. A **voluntary lien** is created by the owner's action, such as placing a mortgage loan. An **involuntary lien** is created by law. A real estate tax lien, for example, is an involuntary lien; it is placed on the property without any action by the property owner.

Liens may also be classified as either general or specific. As illustrated in Figure 5.1, **general liens** usually affect all the property of a debtor, both real and personal. They include judgments, estate and inheritance taxes, debts of a deceased person, corporation franchise taxes, and federal and state income taxes.

Specific liens, on the other hand, are secured by a specific parcel of real estate and affect only that particular property. As illustrated in Figure 5.2, these include mechanics' liens, mortgages, real estate taxes, special assessments, liens for certain public utilities, vendors' liens, vendees' liens, and surety bail bond liens.

ENCUMBRANCES MAY DIVIDE INTO TWO GENERAL CLASSIFICATIONS:

1. Liens—financial claims against the property
2. Usage encumbrances—restrictions, easements, and encroachments

FIGURE   5.2

Specific Liens

- *Real estate taxes* (discussed further in Chapters 12 and 26) have first claim against the property.
- *Judgments* are court orders to pay a debt, such as an unpaid bill. They become liens against all real property owned by an individual in that county when they are docketed (filed) in the county clerk's office. They also may be filed in other counties in New York State and against personal property.
- *Mechanics' liens* are placed against a specific property by workers or suppliers who have not been paid for labor or materials used in construction, improvement, or repairs of that property.

■ EFFECTS OF LIENS ON TITLE

If the buyer agreed, an owner could sell a parcel of real estate even though it was encumbered by a lien. The lien, however, remains with the property because liens and other encumbrances *run with the land*; that is, they will bind successive owners. If steps are not taken to clear them up, they become appurtenant.

Liens attach to property, not to the property owner. Although a purchaser who buys real estate subject to a lien may not be personally responsible for payment of the debt, the property is still encumbered, and the creditor could take court action to foreclose the lien.

Priority of Liens

Tax liens.   Real estate taxes and special assessments (tax liens) generally take **priority** over all other liens. If the property goes through a court-ordered sale to satisfy unpaid debts or obligations, outstanding real estate taxes and special assessments will be paid from the proceeds *first*. The remainder will be used to pay other outstanding liens in the order of their priority. For example, if the courts ordered a parcel of land sold to satisfy a judgment lien entered in the public record on February 7, 1999, subject to a first mortgage lien recorded January 22, 1994, and to this year's as-yet-unpaid real estate taxes, the proceeds of the sale would be distributed in the following order:

1. To the taxing bodies for this year's real estate taxes
2. To the mortgage lender for the entire amount of the mortgage loan outstanding as of the date of the sale (if proceeds remain after payments of taxes)

```
┌─────────────────────────────────────────┐
│   Real estate taxes/special assessments  │
└─────────────────────────────────────────┘

┌─────────────────────────────────────────┐
│                                          │
│   Property            1024 First St.     │
│                       Anytown USA        │
│                                          │
│                                          │
│     10-14-93 First Mortgage lien...      │
│     USA---Federal Savings & Loan         │
│     2-17-94--Mechanic's lien filed       │
│     J.W. Adams Construction              │
│     3-1-95--Second Mortgage lien--       │
│     American Finance Company             │
│                                          │
└─────────────────────────────────────────┘
```

3. To the creditor named in the judgment lien (if any proceeds remain after paying the first two items)
4. To the foreclosed-on landowner (if any proceeds remain after paying the first three items plus costs of foreclosure)

Liens other than general taxes and special assessments take priority from the date of recording in the public records of the county where the property is located. (See Figure 5.3.)

Subordination agreements. Subordination agreements are written agreements between lienholders to change the priority of mortgage, judgment, and other liens under certain circumstances.

■ LIENS OTHER THAN REAL ESTATE TAXES

Aside from real estate tax and special assessment liens, the following types of liens may be charged against real property either by the owner (voluntarily) or by an outside party (involuntarily).

Mortgage Liens

A **mortgage lien** is a voluntary lien on real estate given to a lender by a borrower as security for a loan. It becomes a lien on real property when the mortgage funds are disbursed and the mortgage document is signed by the borrower (mortgagor) and delivered to the mortgagee (lender). The lender files or records the mortgage in the office of the county clerk or register of the county where the property is located. Mortgage lenders generally require a *first mortgage lien;* this means that (aside from taxes) no other liens against the property will take priority over the mortgage lien. Second mortgages and home equity loans do not, of course, have first priority. When the debt is fully paid, the lien is removed from the property by filing a satisfaction certificate signed by the lender.

Mechanics' Liens

A mechanic's lien covers a situation in which an owner has not paid for work done on the property or the general contractor has been paid but has not paid subcontractors or suppliers of materials. A claim for a mechanic's lien must be placed within four months of the completion of the work on a single dwelling and eight months on other buildings. A mechanic's lien is valid for one year and may be renewed.

New York's lien law allows some brokers' claims for leasing commissions to be filed as mechanics' liens. On the theory that the negotiation of a long-term lease constitutes an improvement of commercial property, a broker may enter a mechanic's lien in the public records for unpaid commissions. Such a lien may be filed only if the property is to be used for other than residential purposes, if the lease is for three years or longer, and if the broker was working under a written commission agreement. The lien must be filed within eight months of the date when the commission became due.

Similarly, real property law allows a broker to file an **affidavit of entitlement to commission** for negotiation of a contract for the purchase or lease of any real property. Such an affidavit, although entered in the public records, *does not become a lien* against the property. A broker who sells or leases a commercial or industrial property, however, may file a lien for commissions due.

Judgments.   A **judgment** is a decree issued by a court. When the decree provides for money to be awarded to the creditor, it is referred to as a *money judgment*. A judgment differs from a mortgage in that a specific parcel of real estate was never given as security for the debt.

A judgment becomes a *general involuntary lien on all real property* in the county owned by the debtor when it is docketed (filed, recorded) with the county clerk. Transcripts of the lien also may be docketed in any other county in New York if the creditor wishes.

A judgment is a lien against real property for ten years and can be renewed for ten more.

A judgment takes priority from the date the judgment is docketed in the county clerk's office. Judgments are enforced through the sale of the debtor's real or personal property by a sheriff. If the sale yields enough to satisfy the debt after any liens with priority have first been satisfied, the sheriff's report of sale will show that the sale yielded sufficient money to satisfy the debt and the record will be cleared of the judgment.

A judgment also can be satisfied, of course, by the debtor's payment of the debt in full. Debtors who pay such a debt and fail to record a satisfaction piece—a document that states that the debt has been paid in full—are often surprised to find the judgment still on their credit records years later.

Lis pendens.   Considerable time may elapse between the filing of a lawsuit and the rendering of a judgment or other decree. When any suit is filed that affects title to a parcel of real estate (such as an action for specific performance), a **lis pendens** (or **notice of pending legal action**) is immediately recorded to give notice to interested parties, such as prospective purchasers and lenders, that there is a **cloud on the title.**

Other Liens

Federal **estate taxes** and state *inheritance taxes* (as well as the debts of deceased persons) are *general involuntary liens* that encumber a deceased person's real and personal property. These are normally paid or cleared in probate court proceedings.

A *vendor's lien* is a *seller's claim* in cases where the seller did not receive the full agreed-on purchase price.

A *vendee's lien* is a *buyer's claim* against a seller's property in cases where the seller failed to deliver title. This may occur when property is purchased under an installment contract (contract for deed, land contract) and the seller fails to deliver title after all other terms of the contract have been satisfied.

Municipalities that furnish water or services such as refuse collection are given the right to a lien on the property of an owner who refuses to pay bills.

A real estate owner who must stand trial for a crime may choose to put up real estate instead of cash as surety for bail (or other family members may pledge their real estate). The execution and recording of such a *surety bail bond* creates a lien enforceable by the state if the accused person does not appear in court.

New York State levies a **corporation franchise tax** on corporations as a condition of allowing them to do business in the state. Such a tax is a lien on all property, real and personal, owned by the corporation. New York City also imposes a tax on corporations doing business in the city, which becomes a lien on the corporation's property.

An *environmental lien* may be levied by the federal government for costs and damages incurred in removal or remedial action under the Comprehensive Environmental Response, Compensation, and Liability Act (CERCLA), the environmental cleanup act. The lien attaches only to the property subject to the cleanup.

An *Internal Revenue Service (IRS) tax lien* results from failure to pay any portion of federal income or withholding taxes. It is a lien on all the taxpayers's real and personal property.

Other liens include those for unpaid condominium common charges in favor of the board of managers or condominium association; liens for unpaid maintenance or other charges in favor of a cooperative corporation; and liens for New York State income and transfer taxes and some Uniform Commercial Code (UCC) filings.

F I G U R E   5.4

FIGURE   5.4

Easements

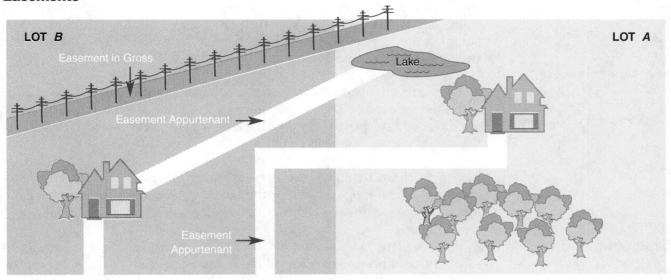

■ DEED RESTRICTIONS

Private agreements that affect the use of land are **deed restrictions** *and covenants.*
They usually are placed by the owner when the property is sold, and they may
be included in the deed. *Deed restrictions* typically are imposed by a developer
to maintain specific standards in a subdivision or to require that a property
be used for a specific purpose. For example, property owners in a subdivision
may not be allowed to park recreational vehicles in the street.

■ EASEMENTS

A right acquired by one party to use the land of another party for a special
purpose is an **easement**. Easements commonly are created by written agreement between the parties. An easement may be either **appurtenant** or in gross.

Easement Appurtenant

The permanent right to use another's land for the benefit of a neighboring
parcel is an **easement appurtenant**. For example, A and B own properties in
a lake resort community, but only A's property borders the lake. A may grant
B an easement across A's property to give B access to the beach. (See
Figure 5.4.) An easement appurtenant *runs with the land* (is permanent), so
that if B sells the property to C, C acquires the same right-of-way over A's
land. If A sells to D, B still owns the easement. Easements appurtenant involve
two adjoining parcels of land. The public often refers to such an easement as
a **right-of-way.**

An easement appurtenant is ended if the two adjoining parcels are merged into one, owned by a single owner. It also may be terminated if the owner of the dominant estate (tenement) releases or abandons the easement. In some cases, an easement was only meant to last for a specific length of time, and automatically expires. An easement by necessity would be terminated if the need for it no longer existed.

FOUR TYPES OF EASEMENTS:

1. Appurtenant
2. In gross
3. By necessity
4. By prescription

The property that benefits is called the **dominant estate;** the one that is used is the **servient estate.** In the case of the right-of-way, B's property, which can use the neighbor's land, is the dominant estate; A's property, which must allow the use, is the servient estate.

Less often encountered are the terms **easement by grant** (one created deliberately, usually through a deed, by the landowner) and **easement by condemnation** (the government's right to use land, for example, as a sidewalk).

Easement in Gross

A mere right to use the land of another is an easement in gross. Such an easement does not involve any adjoining estate. Common examples are the right to run high-tension, telephone, or cable TV lines. In Figure 5.4, utility lines run by right of an easement along the boundary line between the lots.

Easement by Necessity

In certain cases, if the only access to a parcel is through another's property, the owner may acquire an **easement by necessity** to reach his or her land. In Figure 5.4, A owns an easement by necessity, from the road across B's land.

Easement by Prescription

Under specific circumstances one may acquire the permanent right to *use* another's property by doing so for a period (in New York State) of ten years, creating an easement by prescription. **Tacking** allows consecutive owners to accumulate the ten years' usage. (A similar process, *adverse possession*, sometimes allows the user to acquire actual *ownership*; see Chapter 24.) Through *tacking*, a party who did not use the property for the entire required period may still claim an easement by prescription. The parties must have been *successors in interest*, such as an ancestor and heir, a landlord and tenant, or a seller and buyer.

Party Walls

A **party wall** is shared by two buildings and constructed on the boundary line between two owners' lots. Each owns his or her side of the **party wall** and an easement right in the other half. A party wall may not be demolished without the consent of both owners. Each owner is responsible for maintaining his or her half.

Encroachments

When a building, fence, or driveway extends illegally beyond the land of its owner and covers some land of an adjoining owner or a street, an **encroachment** arises. Encroachments usually are disclosed by either a physical inspection of the property or a survey. A survey shows the location of all improvements on a property and whether any improvements extend over the lot lines. If a building encroaches on neighboring land, the neighbor may be able to recover damages or secure removal of the portion of the building that encroaches. Encroachments of ten years may give rise to ownership by adverse possession.

■ LICENSES

Not classified as an encumbrance because it is not a permanent right, a privilege to enter the land of another for a specific purpose is known as a **license**. Examples of license include permission to park in a neighbor's driveway or to erect a billboard. The permission given by a license may be withdrawn.

■ SUMMARY

Encumbrances against real estate may be in the form of liens, deed restrictions, easements, and encroachments.

Liens are financial claims against the real and personal property of a debtor. Liens are either general, covering all real and personal property of a debtor/owner, or specific, covering only the one parcel of real estate described in the mortgage, tax bill, building or repair contract or other document. Liens can be enforced by court-ordered foreclosure, that is, sale of the property to satisfy unpaid debt(s).

With the exception of real estate tax liens, which come first, the priority of liens is generally determined by the order in which they are placed in the public records.

Mortgage liens are given to lenders to provide security for mortgage loans. Mechanics' liens protect general contractors, subcontractors, and material suppliers whose work adds value to real estate.

A judgment is a court decree obtained by a creditor, usually for a monetary award from a debtor. When docketed (filed), it becomes a lien on all the debtor's real property in the county where it was docketed, and it may be similarly docketed in any other county in New York State. Lis pendens, or notice of pending legal action, is a recorded notice that a lawsuit is awaiting trial in court and may result in a judgment.

Federal estate taxes and state inheritance taxes are general liens against a deceased owner's property. A vendor's lien is a seller's claim against a purchaser who has not paid the entire purchase price, and a vendee's lien is a purchaser's claim against a seller under an installment contract who has not conveyed title.

Deed restrictions are placed on land by sellers who wish to control future uses of the property.

An easement is a permanent right one has to use land owned by another. Easements appurtenant involve two neighboring tracts. The tract benefited is known as the *dominant estate;* the tract subject to the easement is called the *servient estate.* An easement in gross is a right such as that granted to utility companies to maintain poles, wires, and pipelines.

An encroachment is the physical intrusion of some improvement on another's land. A license is temporary permission to enter another's property for a specific purpose.

QUESTIONS

1. Which of the following is considered a lien on real estate?
   a. An easement running with the land
   b. An unpaid mortgage loan
   c. A public footpath
   d. A license to erect a billboard

2. Contractor Hammond was hired to build a room addition to the Elkins's home. Hammond completed the work several weeks ago but still has not been paid. In this situation Hammond is entitled to a mechanic's lien, which will be a
   a. general lien.   c. lis pendens.
   b. specific lien.   d. voluntary lien.

3. Which of the following liens usually would be given highest priority?
   a. A mortgage dated last year
   b. The current real estate tax
   c. A mechanic's lien for work started before the mortgage was made
   d. A judgment rendered yesterday

4. Jim Chard was not paid for roofing the Hills' ranch home. How long does he have to file a mechanic's lien?
   a. Four months   c. One year
   b. Eight months   d. Ten years

5. Jim's mechanic's lien will remain against the property for at least
   a. four months.   c. one year.
   b. eight months.   d. ten years.

6. A homeowner's neighbor plans to file a suit against the homeowner because of a boundary dispute. When the neighbor learns that the property is for sale, which of the following will she and her attorney use to protect her interest?
   a. Lis pendens
   b. Prescription
   c. Affidavit of entitlement
   d. Satisfaction piece

7. When the Cratchetts failed to pay for Tim's orthopedic surgery, Dr. Welby obtained a money judgment, which, upon docketing, becomes a lien against the Cratchetts'
   a. vacant land.   c. apartment house.
   b. home.   d. All of the above

8. Donna Majors sold David Berel a parcel of real estate; title has passed, but to date Berel has not paid the purchase price in full as originally agreed. If Majors does not receive payment, which of the following could she use to enforce the payment?
   a. Mortgage lien   c. Lis pendens
   b. Vendee's lien   d. Vendor's lien

9. When the Cratchetts pay off their doctor's judgment, they should
   a. record a satisfaction certificate.
   b. put a lis pendens on the apartment house.
   c. notify their mortgagee.
   d. grant an easement appurtenant.

10. Rhonda buys a summer cottage that has a mechanic's lien against it, placed by the workman who was not paid by the former owner, Jim, for constructing a dock. The lien now
    a. is void.
    b. remains as a claim against the property.
    c. is Jim's responsibility only.
    d. is considered satisfied.

11. A telephone company runs its poles and wires with the rights granted by an easement
    a. by necssity.   c. by prescription.
    b appurtenant.   d. in gross.

12. The farmer who allowed promoters to run the Woodstock rock festival on his land granted them a(n)
    a. easement by necessity.
    b. dominant estate.
    c. voluntary lien.
    d. license.

13. To establish an easement by prescription in New York, a person must use another's property for an uninterrupted period of

a. 5 years.   c. 15 years.
b. 10 years.   d. 20 years.

14. Rayburn's neighbor Jones regularly uses Rayburn's driveway to reach Jones's garage on Jones's property. Jones has an easement over Rayburn's driveway. Rayburn's property is properly called

a. the dominant estate.
b. an estate.
c. a leasehold.
d. the servient estate.

15. A shared driveway agreement will probably take the form of a(n)

a. voluntary lien.
b. easement appurtenant.
c. affidavit of entitlement.
d. certificate of satisfaction.

16. A party wall

a. straddles a boundary line.
b. faces a main road.
c. is located only on a servient estate.
d. is owned by one party.

17. Eric buys a vacation cottage whose previous owner had an easement appurtenant for access to the lake across a neighbor's land. If Eric wants to reach the lake, he must

a. renegotiate with the neighbor.
b. apply to a court for an easement by necessity.
c. pay a token rental to the neighbor.
d. simply go ahead and use the crossing.

18. The lien with first claim against real estate is

a. the property tax.
b. a mechanic's lien.
c. a first mortgage.
d. whatever lien was first recorded.

19. Linda Allen owns a condominium apartment in Manhattan; a cabin on three acres in the Catskills, where she keeps a boat; and a house in Florida. If one of her creditors sues her in Manhattan and obtains a judgment, that judgment may be placed as a lien against the

a. Manhattan apartment only.
b. apartment and cabin.
c. apartment, cabin, and boat.
d. apartment, cabin, boat, and Florida house.

20. Deed restrictions are created by a

a. seller.
b. buyer.
c. neighborhood association.
d. government agency.

21. The right to run a power line across the back of someone's property is an example of an easement

a. in gross.   c. by necessity.
b. by prescription. d. in common.

REAL ESTATE INSTRUMENTS: DEEDS

Norm and Michelle bought a farm from Michelle's parents. Recently Norm heard that a quitclaim deed offers the least protection to the property owner. That's all he received when they bought the farm, and he's worried. If Michelle died, could her parents take the farm back? Are there steps he should take?

A deed is a written instrument by which a property owner as "grantor" conveys and transfers to a "grantee" an ownership interest in real estate. Deeds must be understood (though never drawn up) by the real estate practitioner.

The transfer of title to real property is known as alienation—the removal of ownership. In most cases it is voluntary, done deliberately by the grantor. In some cases, described more fully in Chapter 24, the transfer is done without the owner's intentions, as when property is taken by the government in a condemnation proceeding. Such transfers are known as involuntary alienation.

■ KEY TERMS

accession
alluvion
attorney-in-fact
avulsion
bargain and sale deed
bargain and sale deed
  with covenant
benchmark
consideration
conveyance
covenants
datum
dedication/dedication
  by deed
deed

delivery and
  acceptance
description
devise
escheat
executor, executrix
executor's deed
full covenant and
  warranty deed
grantee/grantor
intestate
involuntary/voluntary
  alienation
legal description
metes and bounds
monuments

plat of subdivision
point (place) of
  beginning
probate
quitclaim deed
rectangular survey
  system
referee's deed
seisin
special warranty
  deed
survey
testate/testator
title
warranty deed

■ LEGAL DESCRIPTIONS

One of the essential elements of a valid deed is an adequate **description** of the *land* being conveyed. (The deed does not usually describe buildings on the land.) A **legal description** is *an exact way of describing real estate that will be accepted in a court of law.*

Legal descriptions never should be changed or combined without information from a competent authority such as a surveyor or title attorney. Street address and property tax account number, although helpful for quick reference to what is being described, are not usually acceptable as legal descriptions.

Land can be described by three methods:

1. Metes and bounds
2. Government survey
3. Reference to a plat (map) filed in the county clerk's office in the county where the land is located, a tax map, or a prior recorded instrument

In New York a legal description may combine different descriptive methods. Also used is reference to a previously recorded deed or mortgage.

Metes and Bounds

A **metes-and-bounds** description uses the boundaries and measurements of the land in question. A metes-and-bounds description is defined as description by "distance and direction."

It starts at a definite point called the **point (place) of beginning** (POB) and proceeds clockwise around the boundaries of the tract by reference to measurements and directions. A metes-and-bounds description always ends at the point where it began (the POB).

In a metes-and-bounds description **monuments** are fixed objects used to establish boundaries. In the past, natural objects such as stones and large trees were commonly used as monuments. Today man-made markers are more common because natural objects may change or be removed. An example of a metes-and-bounds description of a parcel of land (shown in Figure 6.1) appears below.

> *A tract of land located in the City of Elmira, County of Chemung, State of New York, described as follows: Beginning at the intersection of the east line of Jones Road and the south line of Skull Drive; thence east along the south line of Skull Drive 200 feet; thence south 15 degrees east 216.5 feet, more or less, to the center thread of Red Skull Creek; thence northwesterly along the center line of said creek to its intersection with the east line of Jones Road; thence north 105 feet, more or less, along the east line of Jones Road to the place of beginning.*

Metes-and-bounds descriptions are used everywhere, from rural undeveloped areas to Manhattan, with street intersections used as monuments.

FIGURE 6.1

Metes-and-Bounds Tract

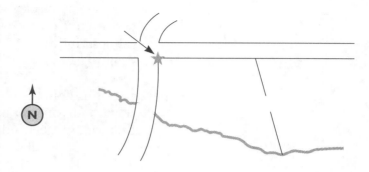

Rectangular (Government) Survey System

The **rectangular survey system,** sometimes called the *government survey method*, was established by Congress in 1785 as a standard method for describing western lands acquired by the government. It is seldom used in New York or any of the other 13 original states.

The rectangular survey system is based on sets of intersecting lines: principal meridians and base lines. *Principal meridians* are north and south lines; *base lines* run east and west. They are located by reference to degrees of longitude and latitude.

Townships.   Using these meridians and base lines, land is surveyed into six-mile-square *townships*, each with identifying reference numbers. Each township contains 36 square miles.

Sections.   A township is further divided into 36 numbered *sections*. Sections are numbered 1 through 36, as shown in Figure 6.2. Section 1 is always in the northeast, or upper right-hand, corner.

FIGURE 6.2

Sections in a Township

Each section contains one square mile, or *640 acres*. As illustrated in Figure 6.3, each section may be divided into smaller parcels for reference purposes. The southeast quarter is a 160-acre tract; this would be abbreviated as SE¼. Quartersections can be divided into quarters or halves and further divided by quarters. The SE¼ of SE¼ of SE¼ of Section 1 would be a ten-acre square in the lower right-hand corner of Section 1.

Recorded Plat of Subdivision

The third method of land description is by *lot and map number* referring to a **plat of subdivision** filed with the clerk of the county where the land is located. The recorded plat of subdivision method is also known as the *block and lot method*.

The first step in subdividing land is the preparation of a *plat (map)* by a licensed surveyor or engineer, as illustrated in Figure 6.4. On this plat the land is divided into blocks and lots, and streets or access roads for public use are indicated. Lots are assigned numbers or letters. Lot sizes and street details are indicated. When properly signed and approved, the subdivision plat may be recorded in the county in which the land is located.

In describing a lot from a recorded subdivision plat, the lot number, name or number of the subdivision plat, and name of the county and state are used. For example:

THAT TRACT OR PARCEL OF LAND, situated in the Town of Brighton, County of Monroe, and State of New York, known and designated as Lot No. 8 of the Fertile Acres Tract. Said Lot is situated on Dearing Lane and is of the dimensions shown on a map of Fertile Acres filed in the Monroe County Clerk's Office in Liber 125 of Maps at page 95.

FIGURE 6.4

Subdivision Plat Map

The word *liber* is Latin for *book*. Sometimes a *reel* number is used, referring to a specific reel of microfilm records.

Preparation and Use of a Survey

A licensed surveyor is trained and authorized to locate a given parcel of land. A *survey* sets forth the legal description. A survey map shows the location and dimensions of the parcel and the location, size and shape of buildings on the lot. Surveys may be required for conveying a portion of a given tract of land, placing a mortgage loan, showing the location of new construction, locating roads and highways, and determining legal descriptions.

■ MEASURING ELEVATIONS

Air Lots

The owner of a parcel of land may subdivide the air above the land into *air lots*. This type of description is found in titles to tall buildings located on air rights or to condominium units.

F I G U R E   6.5

Benchmark

Datum

A point, line, or surface from which elevations are measured or indicated is a **datum,** defined by the United States Geodetic Survey as mean sea level at New York harbor. Many large cities have established a local official datum. In preparing a subdivision plat for condominium use, a surveyor describes each condominium unit by reference to the elevation of the floors and ceilings above the city datum.

Benchmarks.   To aid surveyors, permanent reference points called **benchmarks** have been established throughout the United States. (See Figure 6.5.)

Condominium

A sufficient description of condominium property must include (1) a description of the land on which the building and improvements are located; (2) a designation of the unit conveyed as listed in the declaration, filed in accordance with the *New York Condominium Act*; and (3) a description of the common interest or the percentage of the common interest that is conveyed with the unit.

◼ DEEDS

A **deed** is a *written instrument by which an owner of real estate intentionally conveys his or her right, title, or interest in a parcel of real estate.* Sometimes a deed transfers only a part of the owner's interest.

All deeds must be in writing, in accordance with the requirements of the statute of frauds. The owner, who grants (sells or gives the land) is referred to as the **grantor,** and the new owner (who receives the title) is called the **grantee.** A deed is always *executed* (signed) by the grantor (or other authorized person).

Occasionally, in mortgage assumptions and condominium transfers, it also is signed by the grantee.

Requirements for a Valid Conveyance

The requirements for a valid **conveyance** by deed are

◼ a *grantor* having the legal capacity to execute (sign) the deed;

REQUIREMENTS FOR A VALID DEED

- Legally capable grantor
- Identifiable grantee
- Recital of consideration
- Granting clause
- Habendum clause
- Description of any limitations on conveyances
- Legal description
- Exceptions and reservations
- Grantor's signature and acknowledgment
- Delivery and acceptance

- a *grantee* named with reasonable certainty so that he or she can be easily identified;
- a *recital of consideration;*
- a *granting clause* (words of conveyance) ;
- a *habendum clause* (to define ownership);
- designation of any limitations on the conveyance of a full fee simple estate;
- an *adequate description* (a legal description) of the property conveyed;
- *exceptions and reservations* affecting the title;
- the *signature of the grantor, and (if the deed is to be recorded) acknowledgment*; and
- *delivery* of the deed and *acceptance* by the grantee to pass title.

Grantor.   In New York a person must be of sound mind and have reached the age of 18 to effect a valid conveyance. A contract executed by an incompetent or a minor is *voidable* by the courts; that is, it may be set aside in a lawsuit conducted on behalf of the incompetent or minor. A minor may also void (or rescind) a contract upon reaching the age of 18. A minor who is married, however, may convey property used as a home as if he or she had reached the age of 18.

Grantee.   To be valid, a deed must name a grantee in such a way that he or she is readily identifiable. In New York both grantee and grantor must be identified by address if the deed is to be recorded.

Consideration.   To be valid all deeds must contain a clause acknowledging the grantor's receipt of consideration. **Consideration** is something of value given in an exchange for the transfer of the real property. Where a purchase price is not involved, "love and affection" may be sufficient consideration, though often it is customary to recite a *nominal* consideration such as "$10.00 and other good and valuable consideration." In New York State the full dollar amount of consideration is seldom stated in the deed, except when the instrument is signed by a fiduciary such as an executor or trustee, by an attorney-in-fact pursuant to a power of attorney, or by a referee when the property is bought at a foreclosure auction.

Granting clause (words of conveyance).   A deed must contain words in the *granting clause* that state the grantor's intention to transfer (convey) ownership of the property.

If more than one grantee is involved, the granting clause should cover the creation of their specific rights in the property. The clause might state, for example, that the grantees will take title as joint tenants or tenants in common. This is especially important because specific wording is necessary to create a joint tenancy.

Deeds that convey the entire fee simple interest of the grantor usually contain wording such as "to Jacqueline Smith and to her heirs and assigns forever." A deed creating a life estate would convey property "to Jacqueline Smith for the duration of her natural life."

Habendum clause.   To define or explain the ownership to be enjoyed by the grantee, a *habendum clause* follows the granting clause. The habendum clause begins with the words "to have and to hold." Its provisions must agree with those set down in the granting clause.

Exceptions and reservations.   A grantor may reserve some right in the land for his or her own use (an easement, for instance). A grantor also may place certain restrictions on a grantee's use of the property. A developer, for example, can restrict the number of houses that may be built on a one-acre lot in a subdivision. Such restrictions may be stated in the deed or contained in a previously recorded document (such as the subdivider's master deed) that is expressly mentioned in the deed.

Description of real estate.   For a deed to be valid it must contain an adequate description of the real estate conveyed. Land is considered adequately described if a competent surveyor can locate the property from the description used.

Signature of grantor.   A deed must be signed by *all grantors*. New York permits a grantor's signature to be executed by an **attorney-in-fact,** a person who has been given power of attorney to sign for the grantor. Usually the power of attorney must be recorded in the county where the property is located. Because the power of attorney ends on the death of the person granting the authority, evidence must be submitted that the grantor is alive at the time the attorney-in-fact signs the deed. This is typically done with a phone call placed during the closing.

An *acknowledgment* is a declaration made by a person who is signing a document before an authorized public officer. The term *acknowledgment* also refers to a document or section in a document that states that the person signing the deed or other document is known to the officer or has produced sufficient identification. It provides evidence that the signature is genuine. A deed could be valid without an acknowledgment, but it could not be placed in the public records.

Although an acknowledgment is usually made before a *notary public*, it can also be taken by a judge, justice of the peace, or other qualified person.

An acknowledgment is not required to make a deed valid, but in New York all deeds, mortgages, and similar documents must be acknowledged before they can be recorded (entered in the public records). In some cases they can be signed before a witness, who would then swear to the validity of the signature before an authorized public official.

From a purely practical point of view a deed that is not acknowledged is not satisfactory and could cause problems. To help ensure good title, a grantee should always require acknowledgment of the grantor's signature on a deed so that it may be recorded. Further requirements before a deed may be recorded are detailed in Chapter 24.

Delivery and acceptance. Before a transfer of title by deed can take effect, there must be an actual **delivery** of the deed by the grantor and **acceptance** by the grantee. *Title is said to pass when a deed is delivered.* (**Title** *is the right to the entire bundle of rights inherent in real property ownership.*)

In England during the Middle Ages, when few people were literate, transfer of title occurred in the following manner: The seller took the buyer into the field in question, and they walked the boundaries together ("beating the bounds"). Then the seller reached down, took up a clod of earth to represent the whole field, and handed it to the buyer. At the moment when the buyer seized the clod he became owner of the land. Today a document is used instead of a clod of earth, but title still transfers at the moment of delivery and acceptance, and the owner is still said to be *seized* of the property. The Middle English word **seisin** still denotes ownership and control.

Execution of Corporate Deeds

A corporation can convey real estate only after a resolution passed by its *board of directors.* If all or a substantial portion of a corporation's real estate is being conveyed, the holders of at least two-thirds of the stock also must approve.

Rules pertaining to religious corporations and not-for-profit corporations vary widely and may require a court order authorizing the conveyance. Because the legal requirements must be followed explicitly, an attorney should be consulted for all corporate conveyances.

Types of Deeds

The forms of deeds used in New York are

- full covenant and warranty deed,
- bargain and sale deed with covenant against grantor's acts,
- bargain and sale deed without covenant against grantor's acts,
- quitclaim deed,
- executor's deed, and
- referee's deed.

> **COMMON FORMS OF DEEDS**
> - Full covenant and warranty deed
> - Bargain and sale deed with covenant against grantor's acts
> - Bargain and sale deed without covenant against grantor's acts
> - Quitclaim deed
> - Executor's deed
> - Referee's deed

Warranty Deeds. For a purchaser of real estate, a **full covenant and warranty deed** provides the *greatest protection* of any deed (shown in Figure 6.6). In it the grantor makes certain **covenants,** or warranties, which are legal promises that the grantee will have unchallenged ownership. The basic warranties are

- *covenant of seisin (ownership):* The grantor warrants that he or she is the owner of the property and has the right to convey it.
- *covenant against encumbrances:* The grantor warrants that the property is free from any liens or encumbrances except those specifically stated in the deed.
- *covenant of quiet enjoyment:* The grantor guarantees that the grantee's title is good against anyone who challenges the grantee's ownership.
- *covenant of further assurance:* The grantor promises to obtain and deliver any instrument needed to make the title good.
- *covenant of warranty forever:* The grantor promises that if at any time in the future the title fails, he or she will be liable.

F I G U R E   6.6

Full Covenant and Warranty Deed

Standard N.Y. B.T.U. Form 8003 — 8-13 — Warranty Deed With Full Covenants — Individual or Corporation. (single sheet)   35-3100-021
Form 31-21

THIS INDENTURE, made the   day of   , nineteen hundred and
BETWEEN

party of the first part, and

party of the second part,

WITNESSETH, that the party of the first part, in consideration of Ten Dollars and other valuable consideration paid by the party of the second part, does hereby grant and release unto the party of the second part, the heirs or successors and assigns of the party of the second part forever,

ALL that certain plot, piece or parcel of land, with the buildings and improvements thereon erected, situate, lying and being in the

TOGETHER with all right, title and interest, if any, of the party of the first part of, in and to any streets and roads abutting the above-described premises to the center lines thereof; TOGETHER with the appurtenances and all the estate and rights of the party of the first part in and to said premises; TO HAVE AND TO HOLD the premises herein granted unto the party of the second part, the heirs or successors and assigns of the party of the second part forever.

AND the party of the first part, in compliance with Section 13 of the Lien Law, covenants that the party of the first part will receive the consideration for this conveyance and will hold the right to receive such consideration as a trust fund to be applied first for the purpose of paying the costs of the improvement and will apply the same first to the payment of the cost of the improvement before using any part of the total of the same for any other purpose.

AND the party of the first part covenants as follows: that said party of the first part is seized of the said premises in fee simple, and has good right to convey the same; that the party of the second part shall quietly enjoy the said premises; that the said premises are free from incumbrances, except as aforesaid; that the party of the first part will execute or procure any further necessary assurance of the title to said premises; and that said party of the first part will forever warrant the title to said premises.

The word "party" shall be construed as if it read "parties" whenever the sense of this indenture so requires.

IN WITNESS WHEREOF, the party of the first part has duly executed this deed the day and year first above written.

IN PRESENCE OF:

These covenants in a **warranty deed** are not limited to matters that occurred during the time the grantor owned the property; they extend back to all previous owners. The grantee is entitled to money damages if any of the warranties are ever breached.

A deed in New York must contain a *lien covenant,* stating that the seller holds the proceeds of the sale in trust against unpaid improvements to the property.

In New York State the seller need not deliver a full covenant and warranty deed unless the purchase agreement requires it. In many upstate areas the warranty deed is the one used most commonly. In other areas a bargain and sale deed with covenant is more usual.

Bargain and sale deed with covenant against grantor's acts (special warranty deed). With these deeds the grantors imply that they have title to the property and add only one covenant, stating that they have done nothing to encumber the property while it was in their possession. This deed is used in most sale transactions and by fiduciaries (executors and trustees). The grantors are willing to warrant about the time they owned the property but not about previous owners.

This **bargain and sale deed with covenant** (against grantor's acts) is normally used in real estate transactions in the New York City area; the buyer may look to title insurance for protection in the event of future title problems. In most other states this deed is known as a **special warranty deed.**

Bargain and sale deed without covenant. A bargain and sale deed without covenant contains no warranties. It does, however, *imply* that the grantor holds title to the property. The grantee has little legal recourse if defects later appear in the title. The bargain and sale deed without covenant is also commonly used in New York City, as well as in foreclosure and tax sales and as a *referee's deed.*

Quitclaim deeds. A quitclaim deed provides the grantee with the least protection. It carries no covenant or warranties and conveys only whatever interest the grantor may have. If the grantor has no interest in the property, the grantee will acquire nothing and will have no claim against the grantor. A quitclaim deed can convey title as effectively as a warranty deed if the grantor has good title, but it provides no guarantees.

A quitclaim deed commonly is used for simple transfers within a family and for property transferred during divorce settlements. A quitclaim deed also can be used to clear a cloud on a title when persons who may or may not have some claim to property are asked to "sign off."

Executor's and referee's deeds. An **executor's deed** is a bargain and sale deed with covenant; a *referee's deed* contains no covenants or warranties although it does *imply* seisin (ownership). The *full consideration* (sales price) usually is stated in these cases so that it is a matter of public record.

■ DEDICATION BY DEED

The developer who turns the road in a new subdivision over to the local government does so by the process known as **dedication.** A quitclaim deed is often used for the process.

■ NATURAL PROCESSES

Land owners are entitled to any additional soil (**alluvion**) added to their property by lakes, rivers or streams. The right of ownership to such new land is called **accession.** Land lost by erosion or the sudden tearing away of land by earthquake or tidal waves is lost to the land owner by the process of **avulsion**.

■ CONVEYANCE AFTER DEATH

A will differs from a deed in that it does not transfer property until the death of the person signing the will (the *testator*).

Probate or administration is the process by which the property of a deceased person is distributed, under the supervision of the surrogate court in the county where the decedent (the person who died) lived.

If the decedent left a will (died **testate**), he or she (the **testator** or *testatrix*) may have named an **executor** or **executrix** to carry out the provisions of the will. If not, during the process of probate the court appoints an administrator. Heirs who receive real estate through a will are known as *devisees*. Transferring real property through a will is called **devising** *it*.

When a person dies **intestate** (without leaving a will), property goes by intestate succession to what the law calls *natural heirs*—surviving spouse, children and relatives. The Statute of Descent and Distribution lists those persons who are in a close enough degree of kinship to be considered natural heirs. Where neither a will nor natural heirs can be found, the property passes to the State of New York through the process known as **escheat.**

Details of the making and execution of wills and of intestate administration can be found in Chapter 24.

■ SUMMARY

Documents affecting interests in real estate must contain a legal description that accurately identifies the property involved. Land is described by (1) metes and bounds, (2) rectangular (government) survey, and (3) recorded plat of subdivision.

In a metes-and-bounds description the actual location of monuments is an important consideration. The description always must enclose a tract of land; the boundary line must end at the point at which it started.

The rectangular survey system is not used in New York. It involves surveys based on principal meridians. Land is surveyed into squares 36 miles in area, called *townships*. Townships are divided into 36 sections of one square mile each. Each square mile contains 640 acres.

Land can be subdivided into lots by means of a recorded plat of subdivision. An approved map giving the size, location, and designation of lots and specifying the location and size of streets is filed in the county clerk's or recorder's office of the county where the land is located.

A survey is the usual method of certifying the legal description of a parcel of land. Surveys often are required when a mortgage or new construction is involved.

Air lots, condominium descriptions, and other measurements of vertical elevations may be computed from the U.S. Geodetic Survey datum, which is mean sea level in New York harbor. Most large cities have established local datums. The elevations from these datums are further supplemented by reference points, called benchmarks.

The voluntary transfer of an owner's title is made by a deed, executed (signed) by the owner as grantor to the purchaser or donee as grantee.

Among the most common requirements for a valid deed are a grantor with legal capacity to contract, a readily identifiable grantee, a granting clause, a legal description of the property, a recital of consideration, exceptions and reservations on the title, and the signature of the grantor. In addition, the deed should be acknowledged before a notary public or other officer to provide evidence that the signature is genuine and to allow recording. Title to the property passes when the grantor delivers a deed to the grantee who accepts it.

A general warranty deed provides the greatest protection of any deed by binding the grantor to certain covenants or warranties. A bargain and sale deed with covenant warrants only that the real estate has not been encumbered by the grantor. A bargain and sale deed without covenant carries with it no warranties but implies that the grantor holds title to the property. A quitclaim deed carries no warranties whatsoever and conveys only whatever interest, if any, the grantor may or may not possess in the property.

QUESTIONS

1. When Norm and his wife bought a farm from her parents, they received only a quitclaim deed. This was most likely because
   a. that's the type often used for in-family transactions.
   b. he will own the farm only during his wife's lifetime.
   c. he and his wife own as tenants by the entirety.
   d. a mortgage was involved.

2. If Tom Flock buys a new home in the Buffalo subdivision known as Vista Ridge, his land probably bears a legal description based on
   a. the rectangular survey.
   b. metes and bounds.
   c. the recorded plat.
   d. the street address.

3. When someone dies leaving no will and no natural heirs, his or her property goes to
   a. local charities.
   b. the federal government.
   c. the State of New York.
   d. an escrow fund.

4. Someone who dies without leaving a will is said to have died
   a. devised.
   b. conveyed.
   c. probated.
   d. intestate.

5. The least acceptable legal method for identifying property is
   a. the rectangular survey.
   b. lot and block.
   c. the street address.
   d. metes and bounds.

6. It is essential that every deed be signed by the
   a. grantor.
   b. grantee.
   c. grantor and grantee.
   d. devisee.

7. Title to property transfers at the moment a deed is
   a. signed.
   b. acknowledged.
   c. delivered and accepted.
   d. recorded.

8. Consideration in a deed refers to
   a. gentle handling of the document.
   b. something of value given by each party.
   c. the habendum clause.
   d. the payment of transfer tax stamps.

9. A declaration before a notary or other official providing evidence that a signature is genuine is an
   a. affidavit.
   b. acknowledgment.
   c. affirmation.
   d. estoppel.

10. A notary's acknowledgment of the signature on a deed is necessary
    a. for the deed to be valid.
    b. for the deed to be recorded.
    c. before transfer tax can be paid.
    d. to give constructive notice of the transfer.

11. Arthur signs a deed to Michelle as grantee, has it acknowledged, and receives payment from her. Arthur arranges to meet Michelle the next morning at the courthouse to give the deed to her. Michelle will own the property
    a. immediately because she has paid for it.
    b. the next morning when she receives the deed.
    c. when she records the deed.
    d. as soon as she signs the deed the next morning.

12. The grantee receives greatest protection with what type of deed?
    a. Quitclaim
    b. Warranty
    c. Bargain and sale with covenant
    d. Executor's

13. A bargain and sale deed with covenant against grantor's acts is commonly used
    a. by executors.
    b. upstate.
    c. in divorce settlements.
    d. to clear cloud from a title.

14. According to the accompanying plat map (Figure 6.7), which of the following lots has the most frontage on Manassas Lane?
    a. Lot 10, Block B   c. Lot 8, Block A
    b. Lot 11, Block B   d. Lot 7, Block A

15. On the plat, how many lots have easements?
    a. One   c. Three
    b. Two   d. Four

FIGURE 6.7

Plat Map of Braddock Estates

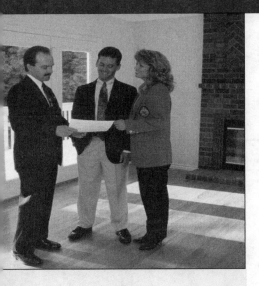

7

REAL ESTATE INSTRUMENTS: LEASES

Connie Smith has lived comfortably in her apartment for the first two years of a three-year lease. Now she has been asked to show the premises to potential buyers of the building. She is considering refusing to let anyone in, because she doesn't want to be turned out with a month's notice by a new landlord.

Leases spell out the rights of landlords and tenants, and real estate brokers need to know the provisions that may be included in leases as well as those prohibited by law.

■ **KEY TERMS**

actual eviction

assignment

constructive eviction

estate for years

graduated lease

gross lease

ground lease

holdover tenant

implied warranty of
    habitability

index lease

lease

leasehold estate

lessee/lessor

month-to-month tenancy

net lease

New York General
    Obligations Law

percentage lease

periodic estate

proprietary lease

quiet enjoyment

security deposit

statute of frauds

sublease

suit for possession

tenancy at sufferance

tenancy at will

T A B L E 7.1	Type of Estate	Distinguishing Characteristics
Leasehold Estates	Estate for Years	For Definite Period of Time
	Periodic Estate	Automatically Renews
	Tenancy at Will	For Indefinite Period of Time
	Tenancy at Sufferance	Without Landlord's Consent

■ LEASING REAL ESTATE

A **lease** is a contract between an owner of real estate (known as the **lessor**) and a tenant (the **lessee**) that transfers the right to possession and use of the owner's property, usually for a specified period of time. The agreement sets forth the length of time the contract is to run, the amount to be paid by the lessee for the right to use the property, and the rights and obligations of the parties.

The landlord grants the tenant the right to occupy the premises and use them for purposes stated in the lease. In return the landlord retains the right to receive payment for the use of the premises as well as a *reversionary right* to retake possession after the lease term has expired.

The **statute of frauds** requires that a lease for a term of more than one year be in writing to be enforceable. It also should be signed by both lessor and lessee. A lease for one year or less can be binding (legally enforceable) even if it is not written.

■ LEASEHOLD ESTATES

A tenant's right to occupy land is called a **leasehold estate.** Just as there are several types of freehold (ownership) estates, there are various leasehold estates. The four most important are the (1) estate for years; (2) periodic estate, or estate from period to period; (3) tenancy at will; and (4) tenancy at sufferance. (See Table 7.1.) All are recognized in New York State.

Estate for Years

A leasehold estate that continues for a definite period of time, whether for years, months, weeks, or even days, is called an **estate for years.** It always has a specific starting and ending time. When that time expires, the lessee is required to leave. No notice is required to end the lease when the time is up. A lease for years may be terminated ahead of time by mutual consent, but otherwise neither party may terminate without showing that the other has breached the lease agreement.

An estate for years need not last for years or even for one year. The main point is that it begins and ends at a specific time.

Periodic Estate

Periodic estates, sometimes called *estates from period to period,* continue for an indefinite length of time without a specific expiration date. They may run for a certain amount of time: month to month, week to week, or year to year. The agreement is automatically renewed for similar succeeding periods until one of the parties gives notice to terminate.

A month-to-month tenancy is created when a tenant takes possession with no definite termination date and pays rent on a monthly basis.

A New York tenant who remains in possession of leased premises after expiration of the lease is known as a **holdover tenant.** If the landlord accepts rent, a tenancy from month to month is created. Or, if the lease term is longer than one month, the landlord may commence proceedings to remove a tenant who has held over.

To *terminate* a periodic estate, either the landlord or the tenant must give *proper notice.* To end a month-to-month tenancy, New York State requires one month's written notice; New York City requires 30 days' notice. Notice must be given at least one day before a date on which rent is due. If rent is due on September 1, the landlord who wants the tenant to vacate by October 1 must give notice no later than August 31.

> **FOUR TYPES OF LEASEHOLD ESTATES:**
> 1. Estate for years
> 2. Periodic estate
> 3. Tenancy at will
> 4. Tenancy at sufferance

Tenancy at Will

An estate that gives the tenant the right to possess with the consent of the landlord and no definite period of time is a **tenancy at will.** It might occur when property has been put on the market and the landlord gives the present tenant (who has no lease) permission to remain until the indefinite time when the sale is closed. The term is indefinite, but the tenancy may be terminated by giving proper notice. Unlike other tenancies, an estate at will is automatically terminated by the death of either landlord or tenant.

Tenancy at Sufferance

A **tenancy at sufferance** arises when a tenant continues, after his or her rights have expired, to occupy the premises *without the consent of the landlord.* Examples of estates at sufferance might be when a tenant for years *fails to leave* at the expiration of the lease and when a mortgagor refuses to leave after a foreclosure sale. In New York a tenant may be charged up to double rent for the period while he or she is in possession as a tenant at sufferance or holdover tenant.

■ TYPICAL LEASE PROVISIONS

The lease may be written, oral, or implied, depending on the circumstances. New York State requires a *plain-English* format for residential leases. The requirements for a valid lease are essentially the same as those for any other real estate contract. In New York the eight essentials of a valid lease include the following:

1. *Capacity to contract:* The parties must be sane adults.
2. *A demising clause:* The lessor agrees to let and the lessee to take the premises.

3. *Description of the premises:* A description of the leased premises should be clearly stated. If the lease covers land, the legal description of the real estate should be used. If the lease is for part of a building, such as office space or an apartment, the space itself should be clearly described.
4. A *clear statement of the term* (duration) of the lease must be provided.
5. *Specification of the rent and how it is to be paid:* In New York, unless the lease states otherwise, rent is considered due in arrears rather than in advance.
6. *The lease must be in writing* if it is to be for more than one year.
7. *Signatures:* A lease should be signed by both parties.
8. *Delivery:* The lease must be delivered by landlord to tenant, with duplicate originals for each.

Use of Premises

A lessor may restrict a lessee's use of premises through provisions included in the lease. This is most important in leases for stores or commercial space. A lease may provide, for example, that the leased premises are to be used *only* as a real estate office. In the absence of such limitations, a lessee may use the premises for any lawful purpose.

Disabled tenants are entitled to make any reasonable alterations that are necessary to accommodate their disabilities. These tenants must pay for the alterations themselves, and landlords may require that a tenant restore the premises to their former state at the end of the lease term.

Term of Lease

The term of a lease is the period for which it will run, and it should be set out precisely. The date of the beginning of the term and the date of its ending should be stated, together with a statement of the total period of the lease: for example, "for a term of five years beginning June 1, 1999, and ending May 31, 2004."

Security Deposits

Many leases require that a tenant provide a **security deposit** to guarantee payment of rent or safeguard against a tenant's destruction of the premises. Where trade fixtures are to be installed, the landlord may want an extra deposit to ensure that the property will be restored to its original state when they are removed.

Under the **New York General Obligations Law** a landlord must hold all security deposits in trust and *must not commingle* them with his or her own funds because *such deposits continue to belong to the tenants who have advanced them.* If the building contains six or more units, the landlord must notify tenants in writing where security funds are being held in a New York interest-bearing bank account and must turn over to the tenants all but 1 percent of any interest earned. A tenant may choose to receive interest annually or at the end of the lease. Any provisions in a lease requiring a tenant to waive any provisions of this law are void. The rules also apply to mobile home parks.

A landlord who conveys rental property must turn over any security deposits to the new owner within five days of the deed's delivery. The landlord also must notify tenants by registered or certified mail that their deposits have been turned over and must include the new owner's name and address. The new owner is responsible for eventual return of the security deposits to the extent received from the grantor. However, if the building contains six or more dwelling units, the new owner is responsible for all security deposits, even if he or she never received them.

Under New York's *Emergency Tenant Protection Act* (ETPA) certain apartments are rent-stabilized in New York City and some other locations throughout the state. For a rent-stabilized apartment no more than one month's rent may be charged for security deposit.

■ LEGAL PRINCIPLES OF LEASES

New York provides that a lease can be recorded. Memoranda of leases that exceed three years in duration also may be recorded. The recording places the world on notice of the long-term rights of the tenant. Commercial leases are sometimes recorded.

When there is a written nonresidential lease of more than three years, a lien for a commission may be placed on the premises if the brokerage services were performed pursuant to a written contract.

Lead Paint Notification

For any residence constructed before 1978, the tenant must be given a booklet about lead paint hazards before signing a lease. The requirement does not apply to rentals for fewer than 100 days, studio apartments, zero-bedroom lofts, housing exclusively intended for the elderly, and premises already determined to be lead-free by a certified inspector.

Details about the booklet and enforcement of the requirement may be found in Chapter 16.

Improvements

The tenant may make improvements with the landlord's permission, but any such alterations generally become the property of the landlord; they become fixtures. A tenant may, however, be given the right to install trade fixtures. It is customary to provide that such trade fixtures may be removed by the tenant before the lease expires, provided the tenant restores the premises to their original condition.

Maintenance of Premises

Every residential New York lease, oral or written, is considered to contain an implied warranty (*or covenant*) of habitability. The landlord guarantees that the leased property is fit for human habitation and that the tenant will not be subjected to any conditions that could endanger life, health, or safety. The tenant is entitled to what is known as **quiet enjoyment,** undisturbed occupancy. The landlord is required to maintain dwelling units in a habitable condition and to make any necessary repairs to common elements such as hallways, stairs, or elevators. The tenant does not have to make any repairs (unless otherwise provided in the lease) but must return the premises in the same condition they were received with allowances for ordinary wear and tear.

FIGURE 7.1

Assignment versus Subletting

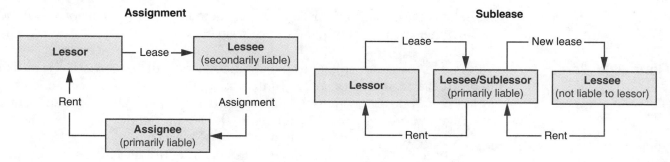

Assignment and Subleasing

The tenant may assign or sublease if the lease terms do not prohibit it. A tenant who transfers the entire remaining term of a lease assigns the lease. One who transfers less than all of the term but retains some of the rights and obligations subleases. (See Figure 7.1.) The original tenant's interest in the real estate is known as a *sandwich lease*. In most cases the **sublease** or **assignment** of a lease does not relieve the original tenant of the obligation to make rental payments unless the landlord agrees to waive such liability.

If the building contains four or more residential units and the landlord unreasonably withholds consent to assignment, the lease may not be assigned, but the tenant is released from the lease with 30 days' notice. If the landlord unreasonably withholds consent to a request to sublet, the tenant may nevertheless sublet the unit.

New York's *Real Property Law* sets guidelines for a detailed written request from the tenant; the landlord's right to ask for additional information within 10 days; and the landlord's written response, including the reasons for any denial, within 30 days. The landlord's failure to respond is considered consent for the sublet.

Special regulations apply to the subletting of rent-stabilized apartments: For a furnished sublet, the original tenant may charge the subtenant as much as 10 percent more than the original rent figure; the landlord may in turn collect an additional 5 percent from the original tenant. The original tenant must establish that the apartment is his or her primary residence and will be reoccupied. A rent-stabilized apartment may not be sublet for more than half of any four-year period. The original tenant, not the subtenant, is entitled to the right of a renewal lease and any right resulting from a co-op conversion.

Apartment Sharing

In New York State a lease may not restrict occupancy of an apartment to the named tenant and that tenant's immediate family. (Landlords may, however, limit the total number of occupants to comply with health laws on overcrowding.) The apartment may be shared with one additional occupant and that occupant's dependent children. If the lease names more than one tenant and one of them moves out, that tenant may be replaced with another occupant and that person's dependent children. At least one of the original tenants named in the lease or that person's spouse must continue to occupy the shared apartment as a primary residence.

Tenants must inform their landlords of the name of any occupant within 30 days after the occupant moves into an apartment.

Renewals

Sometimes a lease contains a clause stating that it will be *automatically renewed unless* the tenant gives *notice* of intent not to renew. No such clause is valid in New York unless the landlord reminds the tenant about the automatic renewal provision 15 to 30 days before the tenant's notice would be due.

The occupant of a rent-stabilized apartment is entitled to a one-year or two-year renewal.

Many leases contain an *option* that grants the lessee (the tenant) the privilege of *renewing* the lease but requires that the lessee give *notice* on or before a specific date of intention to exercise the option. Some leases grant to the lessee the option to purchase the leased premises; the provisions for the option to purchase vary widely. Any option should contain all the essential elements of an offer to purchase.

Termination of Lease

A written lease for a definite period of time expires at the end of that time period; no separate notice is required to terminate. Oral and written leases that do not specify a definite expiration date (such as a month-to-month or year-to-year tenancy or a tenancy at will) may be terminated by giving proper written notice.

The tenant who signs a lease for senior housing has the right to cancel within three days of signing.

When the conditions of a lease are breached, a landlord may terminate the lease and evict the tenant. This action must be handled through a court proceeding. The landlord who wishes to be rid of a tenant is not allowed to use threats of violence, change locks, discontinue essential services like water or heat, or seize the tenant's possessions.

It is possible for the parties to agree to cancel the lease. The tenant may offer to surrender the lease, and acceptance by the landlord will result in termination. A tenant who abandons leased property, however, remains liable for the rent. The terms of the specific lease will usually dictate whether the landlord is obligated to try to rerent the space.

When the property is sold, *the lease does not terminate*. If a landlord conveys leased real estate, the new owner takes the property subject to the rights of the tenant. The lease *survives* the sale and continues as it was.

If a tenant dies, the lease remains in effect; the deceased lessee's estate is bound by the terms of the lease. New York State provides, however, that the estate may assign the lease or sublet, subject to the landlord's consent. If consent is unreasonably withheld, the lease is terminated.

A lease may be terminated by any tenant aged 62 or older who has been accepted in an adult care facility, residential health facility, or housing unit receiving subsidies for housing senior citizens or who is moving to a relative's home for health care. The landlord is entitled to 30 days' notice and a copy of a document of admission to the new facility. The lease may also be cancelled by a tenant who is called up for military service.

Breach of Lease

When a tenant breaches any lease provision, the landlord may sue for a judgment to cover past-due rent, damages to the premises, or other defaults. Likewise, when a landlord breaches any lease provision, the tenant is entitled to remedies. The landlord's nonperformance of some obligation under a non-residential lease, short of eviction, does not, however, affect the tenant's obligation to pay rent.

In New York, grounds for which the landlord can institute proceedings include nonpayment of rent, illegal use of the premises, remaining in possession after expiration of the lease without permission, and bankruptcy or insolvency of the tenant.

Suit for possession—actual eviction.   When a tenant breaches a lease or improperly retains possession, the landlord may regain possession through a **suit for possession** or summary proceeding to recover possession of real estate. This process is known as **actual eviction.** The landlord must serve *notice* on the tenant before commencing the suit. In New York, only a three-day notice must be given before filing a suit for possession based on a default in payment of rent. When a court issues a judgment for possession, the tenant must leave peaceably, or the landlord can have the judgment enforced by a sheriff, constable, or marshal, who will *forcibly remove* the tenant and his or her possessions.

Tenants' remedies—constructive eviction.   If a landlord breaches any clause of a lease agreement, the tenant has the right to sue, claiming a judgment for damages against the landlord. If an action or omission on the landlord's part results in the leased premises becoming uninhabitable for the purpose intended in the lease, the tenant may have the right to abandon the premises. This action, called **constructive eviction,** terminates the lease if the tenant can prove that the premises have become unusable because of the landlord's neglect. To claim constructive eviction, the tenant must actually move from the premises while the uninhabitable condition exists.

For example, a lease requires that the landlord furnish steam heat; because of the landlord's failure to repair a defective heating plant, the heat is not provided. If this results in the leased premises becoming uninhabitable, the tenant may abandon them. Some leases provide that if the failure to furnish heat is accidental and not the landlord's fault, it is not grounds for constructive eviction.

T A B L E   7.2

Types of Leases

Type of Lease	Legal Effect	Landlord Pays
Gross Lease Residential (also small commercial)	Basic Rent	Property Charges (taxes, repairs, insurance, etc.)
Net Lease Commercial/Industrial	Basic Rent Plus Most or All Property Charges	Few or No Property Charges, Mortgage (if any)
Percentage Lease Commercial/Industrial	Basic Rent Plus Percent of Gross Sales (may pay some or all property costs)	Any Agreed Property Charges

■ PRO-TENANT LEGISLATION

In New York State a landlord may not legally retaliate because a tenant joins a tenants' organization. If the landlord fails to furnish heat as stipulated in the lease, tenants in New York may pay a utility company directly and deduct the sum from rent due. In New York City at least one-third of the tenants of a multiple-unit dwelling, acting together, may start a special court proceeding to use their rent money to remedy conditions dangerous to life, health, or safety. Retaliatory evictions are illegal.

■ TYPES OF LEASES

Three primary types of leases are outlined in Table 7.2.

Gross Lease

In a **gross lease** the tenant pays a *fixed rental* and the landlord pays all taxes, insurance, mortgage payments, repairs, and the like (usually called *property charges*). This type of lease most often is used for residential rentals.

Net Lease

The **net lease** provides that in addition to the rent the *tenant pays some or all of the property charges*. The monthly rental paid is net income for the landlord. Leases for commercial or industrial buildings, ground leases, and long-term leases are often net leases. With a *triple-net lease*, the tenant pays taxes, insurance, and all other expenses except debt service (mortgage payments).

Percentage Lease

Either a gross lease or a net lease may be a **percentage lease,** normally used for retail business locations.

> **THREE TYPES OF LEASES:**
>
> 1. Gross lease
> 2. Net lease
> 3. Percentage lease

The percentage lease provides for a minimum fixed rental fee plus a percentage of the tenant's business income that exceeds a stated minimum. For example, a lease might provide for a minimum monthly rental of $1,200 with the further agreement that the tenant pay an additional amount each month equivalent to 5 percent of all gross sales in excess of $30,000. The percentage charged in such leases varies widely with the nature of the business.

Other Lease Types

Several types of leases allow for increases in the rent during the lease period. Two of the more common ones are the **graduated lease,** which provides for increases in rent at set future dates, and the **index lease,** which allows rent to be increased or decreased periodically based on changes in the government cost-of-living index.

Proprietary leases.   The owner of a cooperative apartment, who buys shares in the corporation that owns the building, does not specifically own his or her apartment. Instead, the owner receives a **proprietary lease** to the living unit.

Ground leases.   When a landowner leases land to a tenant who agrees to *erect a building on it,* the lease is referred to as a **ground lease.** It is usually for a long enough term to make it worth the tenant's while to invest in the building. These leases are generally *net leases* that require the lessee to pay rent as well as real estate taxes, insurance, upkeep, and repairs. Net ground leases often run for terms of 50 years or longer, and a lease for 99 years is not impossible. Although these leases are considered personal property, leaseholders may have some of the rights and obligations of real property owners.

Oil and gas leases.   When oil companies lease land to explore for oil and gas, a special agreement must be negotiated. Usually the landowner receives a cash payment for executing the lease. If no well is drilled within the period stated, the lease expires.

If oil and/or gas is found, the landowner usually receives a fraction of its value as a royalty. In this case the lease will continue for as long as oil or gas is obtained in significant quantities. Oil and gas leases are common across the southern tier and in the western part of New York State. An oil or gas lease constitutes a cloud on title, and a buyer may refuse to purchase unless he or she has specifically agreed to take title subject to such a lease.

■ SUMMARY

A lease grants someone the right to use the property of another for a certain period in return for consideration.

A leasehold estate that runs for a specific length of time creates an estate for years, whereas one that runs for an indefinite period creates a periodic tenancy (year to year, month to month) or a tenancy at will. A leasehold estate is generally classified as personal property.

The requirements of a valid lease include the capacity to contract, a demising clause, description of premises, statement of terms, rent, and signatures. The state statute of frauds requires that any lease for more than a year be in writing. Most leases also include clauses relating to rights and obligations of the landlord and tenant: the use of the premises, subletting, judgments, maintenance of the premises, and termination of the lease period.

In New York an oral lease is valid if it is for a period of one year or less. A lease for three years or more, if properly acknowledged, may be entered in the public records. State law requires that the owner of six or more residential units hold security deposits in an interest-bearing New York bank account with all interest less a 1 percent fee due the tenant. State law gives the tenant in any building with four or more residential units the right to sublet, subject to the landlord's consent, which may not be unreasonably withheld.

Leases may be terminated by the expiration of the lease period, mutual agreement of the parties, or a breach of the lease by either landlord or tenant. Neither the death of the tenant nor the landlord's sale of the rental property terminates a lease.

On a tenant's default on any of the lease provisions, a landlord may sue for a money judgment or for actual eviction where a tenant has improperly retained possession of the premises. If the premises have become uninhabitable (whether or not due to the landlord's negligence), the tenant may refuse to pay rent until the problem is remedied.

Basic types of leases include net leases, gross leases, and percentage leases, classified according to the method used in determining the rental rate of the property.

QUESTIONS

1. A lease is considered to be
   a. a freehold estate.
   b. personal property.
   c. a reversionary interest.
   d. real property.

2. Tracy Peters agrees to rent her upstairs apartment to Beverly Ashton for the next six months. Beverly has a(n)
   a. estate for years.
   b. periodic estate.
   c. tenancy at will.
   d. tenancy at sufferance.

3. Willie James agrees to rent his upstairs apartment to Dana Gibson from month to month. To end the arrangement, Willie must
   a. file a court suit to recover possession.
   b. give at least 60 days' notice from the day the rent is due.
   c. give at least one month's notice from a day before the rent is due.
   d. simply refuse to accept the next month's rent on the day it is due.

4. A tenant's lease has expired, the tenant has neither left nor negotiated a renewal lease, and the landlord has said she does not want the tenant to remain. The tenancy is called a(n)
   a. estate for years.
   b. periodic estate.
   c. tenancy at will.
   d. tenancy at sufferance.

5. Mary Withers sells her six-unit apartment building in Queens to George Brown. Now
   a. George may give all the tenants 30 days' notice.
   b. tenants should collect their security deposits from Mary.
   c. George must renegotiate all leases with the tenants.
   d. Mary must turn over security deposits to George.

6. Connie Smith fears that if the building is sold, a new landlord may not honor the year remaining on her apartment lease. Actually, the new owner
   a. would have to give her 90 days' notice to move.
   b. must honor the lease but may charge double rent.
   c. must abide by the terms of her original lease.
   d. can terminate her rental only if he intends to occupy the apartment himself.

7. An automatic renewal clause in a lease
   a. is not allowed on rent-stabilized apartments.
   b. is granted every tenant in a building with four or more units.
   c. is illegal in New York State.
   d. requires notice from the landlord calling the tenants' attention to the clause.

8. Jane Miller's apartment lease agreement states that it will expire on April 30, 2004. When must her landlord give notice that her tenancy is to terminate?
   a. January 31, 2004
   b. February 28, 2004
   c. April 1, 2004
   d. No notice is required.

9. If a tenant falls three months behind in rent payments, a landlord may
   a. turn down the heat.
   b. move out the tenant's possessions, storing them carefully.
   c. start a court suit for possession.
   d. All of the above

10. In Question 9 the landlord who turns down the heat has terminated the lease through
    a. the demising clause.
    b. constructive eviction.
    c. payment in arrears.
    d. assigning the lease.

11. With a triple-net lease, the tenant pays

    a. rent only.
    b. rent plus a share of business profits.
    c. rent plus any increase in property taxes.
    d. everything but the mortgage.

12. A ground lease is usually

    a. terminable with 30 days' notice.
    b. based on percentages.
    c. long term.
    d. a gross lease.

13. The landlord must furnish a lead-paint information booklet

    a. within 100 days after the lease is signed.
    b. if the building is intended exclusively for those older than 55.
    c. only if the building contains six or more units.
    d. for buildings constructed before 1978.

14. Ms. Doran manufactures knitwear in a small rented building. In addition to monthly rent she pays heat, light, and property taxes on the building. She probably has a

    a. net lease.   c. percentage lease.
    b. periodic lease.   d. security lease.

15. In New York a tenant usually may sublet an apartment if the

    a. new tenant is paying a premium over the rent.
    b. building contains four or more living units.
    c. lease is for three years or more.
    d. original tenant has a written lease.

16. Terrence says to Jim, "I'll let you rent my attic apartment for $500 a month until the first of the year." Jim agrees. The agreement

    a. constitutes a binding lease.
    b. is invalid because it is not in writing.
    c. binds the landlord only.
    d. will be enforceable only if it is recorded.

17. A gross lease is most likely to be used for rental of

    a. an apartment.
    b. a factory building.
    c. land under a post office.
    d. a farm.

18. Before entering into an oral or written lease, prospective tenants must be given a lead paint warning if the property

    a. is an office building.
    b. was built before 1978.
    c. contains six or more units.
    d. has asbestos siding.

REAL ESTATE INSTRUMENTS: CONTRACTS

Laura Secord always meant to take her grandmother's antique chandelier from the dining room after she sold the house. She told the buyers so the day they first saw the place. But when they moved in and found the chandelier missing, they took Laura to small claims court. Laura doesn't know how she can prove she told them about it.

The real estate business makes use of many different types of contracts, including listing agreements, leases, and sales contracts. Brokers and salespeople can help prevent misunderstandings among buyers, sellers, landlords, and tenants if they understand how contracts work.

■ KEY TERMS

agreement in writing and signed	executory contract	release
"as is"	express contract	rescission
assignment	forbearance	rider
bilateral contract	implied contract	right of first refusal
breach of contract	laches	specific performance
competent parties	land contract	statute of frauds
consideration	legality of object	statute of limitations
contingency	liquidated damages	"time is of the essence"
contract	memorandum of sale	unenforceable contract
counteroffer	novation	Uniform Commercial Code
earnest money deposit	offer and acceptance	unilateral contract
equitable title	option	valid contract
escape clause	parol evidence rule	voidable contract
executed contract	real estate sales contract	void contract

■ CONTRACT LAW

> **A CONTRACT MAY BE**
> ■ expressed or implied;
> ■ unilateral or bilateral;
> ■ executory or executed; and
> ■ valid, unenforceable, voidable, or void.

A **contract** is a *voluntary agreement between legally competent parties to perform or refrain from performing some legal act, supported by legal consideration.*

Depending on the situation and the nature or language of the agreement, a contract may be

■ expressed or implied;
■ unilateral or bilateral;
■ executory or executed; and
■ valid, unenforceable, voidable, or void.

Express and Implied Contracts

In an **express contract** the parties state the terms and show their intentions in words. An express contract may be either oral or written. A listing agreement is an *express* contract between seller and broker that names the broker as fiduciary representative (agent) of a seller.

In an **implied contract** the agreement of the parties is demonstrated by their acts and conduct. The patron who orders a meal in a restaurant has implied a promise to pay for the food.

Bilateral and Unilateral Contracts

Contracts also may be classified as either bilateral or unilateral. In a **bilateral contract** both parties promise to do something; one promise is given in exchange for another. A real estate sales contract is a bilateral contract because the seller promises to sell a parcel of real estate to the buyer, who promises to pay a certain sum of money. "I will do this, *and* you will do that." "OK."

A **unilateral contract,** on the other hand, is a one-sided agreement whereby one party makes a promise to be kept only if a second party does something. The second party is not legally obligated to act; however, if the second party does comply, the first party must keep the promise. An option is a real estate example of a unilateral contract. "I will sell you the property for $150,000 within two years if you wish." ("I will do this if you do that.") Only the owner is bound by an option; the other party is free either to buy or not to buy. An open listing is another example of a unilateral contract.

Executed and Executory Contracts

A contract may be classified as either executed or executory. An **executed contract** is one in which both parties have fulfilled their promises and performed the contract. An **executory contract** exists when something remains to be done. A *real estate sales contract* is executory before final settlement; after the closing it is executed.

Validity of Contracts

A contract can be described as valid, void, voidable, or unenforceable (see Table 8.1), depending on the circumstances.

A **valid contract** complies with all the essential elements (which will be discussed later in this chapter) and is binding and enforceable on both parties.

A **void contract** is one that has no legal effect because it does not meet the essential elements of a contract. One of those essential elements is that a con-

TABLE 8.1

Legal Effects of Contract

Type of Contract	Legal Effect	Example
Valid	Binding and Enforceable on Both Parties	Agreement Complying with Essentials of a Valid Contract
Void	No Legal Effect	Contract for an Illegal Purpose
Voidable	Valid, but May Be Disaffirmed by One Party	Contract with a Minor
Unenforceable	Valid Between the Parties, but Neither May Force Performance	Certain Oral Agreements

tract be for a legal purpose; thus a contract to commit a crime, or to pay interest higher than allowed by usury law, would be void.

A **voidable contract** is one that seems on the surface to be valid but may be voided, or disaffirmed, by one of the parties. For example, a contract entered into with a minor usually is voidable; a minor generally is permitted to disaffirm a real estate contract within a reasonable time after reaching legal age. A voidable contract is considered by the courts to be valid if the party that could disaffirm the agreement does not do so within a reasonable period of time.

An **unenforceable contract** also seems on the surface to be valid; however, neither party can successfully sue the other to force performance. For example, if one party tries to enforce an otherwise valid contract after the statute of limitations has expired, the contract is unenforceable. Unenforceable contracts are said to be "valid as between the parties" because if both desire to go through with it, they can do so.

Elements Essential to a Valid Contract

The five essentials of a valid contract are

1. **competent parties:** To enter into a binding contract in New York, a person must be at least 18 years old and of sound mind. A married person younger than 18 is considered an adult for the purposes of buying a principal residence.
2. **offer and acceptance:** This requirement, also called *mutual assent*, means there must be a meeting of the minds. The contract must express all the agreed-on terms and must be clearly understood by the parties.
3. **consideration:** The agreement must be based on good and valuable consideration. Consideration is what the parties promise in the agreement to give to or receive from each other. Consideration may consist of legal tender, exchange of value, or mutual promises. The promises might consist of a pledge to perform some act or of **forbearance**, a promise to refrain from doing something. The price or amount must be stated definitely and payable in exchange for the deed or right received.
4. **legality of object:** To be valid and enforceable, a contract must not involve a purpose that is illegal or against public policy.
5. **agreement in writing and signed:** New York's **statute of frauds** requires that certain types of contracts be in writing. These include all contracts for the sale of real estate and for leasing real property for more than one year.

The **parol evidence rule** states that the written contract takes precedence over oral agreements or promises. A promise that is not in the written contract may not be legally binding.

Undue influence and duress.   Contracts signed by a person under duress or undue influence are voidable (may be canceled) by such person or by a court. Extreme care should be taken when one or more of the parties to a contract is elderly, sick, in great distress, or under the influence of drugs or alcohol. To be valid, every contract must be signed as the free and voluntary act of each party.

Performance of Contract

A contract may call for a specific time by which the agreed-on acts must be completely performed. In addition, some contracts provide that **"time is of the essence."** This means that the contract must be performed within the time limit specified. Any party who has not performed on time is guilty of a breach of contract. This powerful phrase is a two-edged sword, and brokers should leave its use to attorneys.

When a contract does not specify a date for performance, the acts it requires should be performed within a reasonable time, depending on the situation. A real estate contract usually names a date and place for closing. If that date comes and goes without settlement, the contract is still valid, and either party has the right to a reasonable adjournment. Either party may later make time of the essence; again, that action should be taken only with a lawyer's advice.

Assignment and Novation

Often after a contract has been signed, one party wants to withdraw without actually ending the agreement. This may be accomplished through either assignment or novation.

Assignment refers to a transfer of rights and/or duties under a contract. Generally, rights may be assigned to a third party unless the agreement forbids such an assignment. Most contracts include a clause that either permits or forbids assignment.

A contract also may be performed by **novation,** or the substitution of a *new* contract for an existing agreement. The new agreement may retain the same parties or substitute a new party for either (*novation of the parties*). A real estate example might be the assumption of a present mortgage by the new owner of a property, with the lender releasing the original borrower and substituting the new one.

Discharge of Contract

A contract may be completely performed, with all terms carried out, or it may be breached (broken) if one of the parties defaults. There are also various other methods by which a contract may be discharged (ended):

■ *Partial performance* of the terms along with a written acceptance by the person for whom acts have not been done or to whom money has not been paid

■ *Substantial performance*, in which one party has performed most of the contract but does not complete all details exactly as the contract requires, which may be sufficient to force payment with certain adjustments for any damages suffered by the other party

■ *Impossibility of performance*, in which an act required by the contract cannot be legally accomplished

■ *Mutual agreement* of the parties to cancel

■ *Operation of law,* as in the voiding of a contract by a minor, as a result of fraud, owing to the expiration of the statute of limitations, or because of alteration of a contract without written consent of all parties involved

Default—Breach of Contract

A **breach of contract** is a violation of any of the terms or conditions of a contract without legal excuse.

If a seller defaults, the buyer has three alternatives:

1. The buyer may *rescind, or cancel, the contract* and recover the earnest money deposit.
2. The buyer may file a court suit, known as an action for specific performance, to force the seller to perform the contract *(that is, sell the property).*
3. The buyer may *sue the seller for compensatory damages.*

If the *buyer defaults,* the seller may pursue one of the following courses:

■ The seller may *declare the contract forfeited.* The right to forfeit usually is provided in the terms of the contract, and the seller usually is entitled to retain the earnest money and all payments received from the buyer.
■ The seller may *rescind the contract;* that is, he or she may cancel, or terminate, the contract as if it had never been made.
■ The seller may *sue for specific performance.* This may require that the seller offer a valid deed to the buyer to show that the seller is ready to meet the contract terms.
■ The seller may *sue for compensatory damages.*

Statute of limitations.   New York allows a specific time limit of *six years* during which parties to a contract may bring legal suit to enforce their rights. Any party who does not take steps to enforce his or her rights within this statute of limitations may lose those rights. The six-year period applies to contracts, foreclosures, mortgages, and cases of fraud. Lawsuits to recover real property have a ten-year statute of limitations in New York.

The principle of **laches** is similar to that of the statute of limitations. Laches is an undue delay or failure to assert a claim or right that can result in the loss of that claim or right.

■ CONTRACTS USED IN THE REAL ESTATE BUSINESS

The written agreements most commonly used by brokers and salespeople are independent contractor agreements, listing agreements, buyers' broker agreements, real estate sales contracts, option agreements, contracts for deed, and leases.

Broker's Authority to Prepare Documents

The New York Department of State specifically states that the real estate broker's license does not confer the right to draft legal documents or give legal advice. However, a decision by the New York Appellate Court has stated that a broker has a right to complete a simple contract. No court decisions have yet been made as to what constitutes a "simple" contract.

The preparation of legal documents by a broker may result in the loss of commissions, loss of license, or other penalties or damages. In upstate areas many brokers fill in the blanks on forms or simple sales contracts; in the New York City area the seller's attorney usually prepares the sales contract.

The *Duncan and Hill* decision recommended that New York State brokers and salespersons who prepare purchase and sales contracts protect themselves against charges of unauthorized practice of law by making the contracts subject to (effective only after) approval by attorneys for both the buyer and seller. An attorney then may ask for changes to protect the client's interest; any such changes constitute a counteroffer and need not be accepted by the other party.

On the subject of real estate licensees writing purchase contracts, the Attorney General of the State of New York has concluded that a broker may use a contract form that has been approved by a recognized bar association in conjunction with a recognized REALTORS® association, provided that

- the form requires only that the broker fill in nonlegal provisions such as the names of the parties, date and location of the closing, description of the property, and sale price; and
- the document clearly and prominently indicates on its face that it is a legally binding document and recommends that the parties seek advice from their lawyers before signing.

The attorney general's opinion also states that brokers may not add provisions to standard "fill in the blanks" contracts unless they make the entire contract subject to the review and approval of each party's attorney.

Contract forms.   *Printed forms* are used for many contracts because many transactions are similar in nature. The use of printed forms raises three problems: (1) what information should be used to *fill in the blanks*; (2) what printed matter is not applicable to a particular sale and can be *ruled out* by drawing lines through the unwanted words; and (3) what clauses or agreements (called *riders*) are to be *added*. All changes and additions usually are initialed by both parties. Additional agreements should be drawn up by attorneys, not brokers.

Listing Agreements

Listing agreements are contracts that establish the rights of the broker as agent and of the buyer or seller as principal. Explanations of the types of listing agreements are presented in Chapter 3.

Sales Contracts

A **real estate sales contract** sets forth all details of the agreement between a buyer and a seller for the purchase and sale of a parcel of real estate. Depending on the locality, this agreement may be known as an *offer to purchase*, a *contract of purchase and sale*, an *earnest money agreement*, a *binder and deposit receipt*, or other variations of these titles. New York does not mandate any specific form of listing or sales contract. An example of a real estate contract form used by some brokers appears as Figure 8.1.

For simple transactions, real estate brokers are allowed to fill in the blanks on this contract, which was published by a REALTORS® organization after consultation with the local bar association. Among other provisions, it provides for input by buyer's and seller's attorneys if desired.

In a few localities, notably in and around New York City, brokers prepare a non-binding **memorandum of sale,** data sheet, or terms sheet. This sheet of information states the essential terms of the agreement. The parties agree to have a formal and complete contract of sale drawn up by an attorney. Throughout the state, a preliminary memorandum might be used in any situation where the details of the transaction are too complex for a standard sales contract form.

The contract of sale is the most basic document in the sale of real estate because it sets out in detail the agreement between the buyer and the seller and establishes their legal rights and obligations. *The contract, in effect, dictates the contents of the deed* and is a blueprint for closing the sale.

Offer and acceptance.   One of the essential elements of a valid contract of sale is a *meeting of the minds*, whereby the buyer and seller agree on the terms of the sale. This usually is accomplished through the process of offer and acceptance.

A broker lists an owner's real estate for sale at the price and conditions set by the owner. A party who wants to purchase the property at those terms or some other terms is found. Upstate, an offer to purchase is drawn up, signed by the prospective buyer, and presented by the broker to the seller. This is an *offer*. If the seller agrees to the offer *exactly as it was made* and signs the contract, the offer has been *accepted*, and the contract is *valid*. The broker then must advise the buyer of the seller's acceptance, obtain lawyers' approval if the contract calls for it, and deliver a duplicate original of the contract to each party.

In some downstate areas the broker prepares a precontract agreement, known as a *binder*, which may or may not be legally enforceable but usually contains many of the essential terms that will later be included in a contract. It also may acknowledge receipt of an earnest money deposit. In the New York City area purchase offers often are handled by attorneys.

Any attempt by the seller to change the terms proposed by the buyer ("Okay, except that . . .") creates a **counteroffer.** The buyer is no longer bound by the original offer because the seller has, in effect, rejected it. The buyer nay accept the seller's counteroffer or reject it or, if desired, make another counteroffer. Any change in the last offer made results in a counteroffer until one party finally agrees completely with the other party's last offer and both parties sign the final contract.

A contract is not considered valid until the person making the offer has been *notified of the other party's acceptance*.

Equitable title.   A buyer who signs a contract to purchase real estate does not receive title to the land; only delivery of a deed can actually convey title. However, after the contract is signed, the buyer has a contract right known as **equitable title.** In New York a buyer under a land contract also acquires equitable title. If the parties decide not to go through with the purchase and sale, they usually enter into a written release, freeing each other from any obligation under the contract.

Destruction of premises.   New York State has adopted *the Uniform Vendor and Purchaser Risk Act*, which provides that the seller (vendor) bears any loss, most commonly from a fire, that occurs before the title passes or the buyer (vendee) takes possession.

Earnest money deposits.   It is customary, but not essential, for a purchaser to provide a cash deposit when making an offer to purchase real estate. This cash deposit, commonly referred to upstate as earnest money and downstate as a *down payment* or *contract deposit, gives evidence of the buyer's intention to carry out the terms of the contract.* It is often held by one of the brokers involved in the sale (upstate) or the seller's attorney (New York City area). The state requires that each sales contract name the person holding the deposit and the bank where it is to be held. If the offer is not accepted, the **earnest money deposit** is returned immediately to the would-be buyer.

The deposit generally should be sufficient to discourage the buyer from defaulting, compensate the seller for taking the property off the market, and cover any expenses the seller might incur if the buyer defaults. A purchase offer with no earnest money is, however, valid. Most contracts provide that the deposit and interest earned on it, if any, becomes the seller's property if the buyer defaults. The seller might also claim further damages.

Earnest money must be held by a broker or lawyer in a special *trust,* or *escrow, bank account.* This money may not be *commingled,* or mixed, with a broker's personal funds. A broker may not use such funds for personal use; this illegal act is known as *conversion.*

A broker need not open a special escrow account for each earnest money deposit received. One account into which all such funds are deposited is sufficient. A broker should maintain full, complete, and accurate records of all earnest money deposits.

Parts of a sales contract.   In New York the six essentials of a valid contract for the sale of real property are

1. contract in writing;
2. competent parties;
3. agreement to buy and sell;
4. adequate description of the property;
5. consideration (price and terms of payment); and
6. signatures of the parties. (The signature of a witness is not essential for a valid contract.)

Important, although not essential, for a valid contract are provisions covering

- the grantor's agreement to convey (should specify type of deed); and
- the place and time of closing.

Further included in most sales contracts are the following:

- Encumbrances to which the deed will be made subject
- Earnest money deposit
- Mortgage financing the buyer plans to obtain and other contingencies
- Possession by the buyer
- Title evidence
- Prorations and adjustments

SIX ELEMENTS REQUIRED FOR A VALID REAL ESTATE CONTRACT:

1. Contract in writing
2. Competent parties
3. Agreement to buy and sell
4. Adequate description of the property
5. Consideration
6. Signatures of the parties

- Destruction of the premises before closing
- Default by either party
- Miscellaneous provisions

Miscellaneous provisions.   In recent years, increasing awareness of consumers' rights has increased the number of disclosures that must be made to a buyer before that person is bound by a purchase contract. Among these in New York State are disclosure of agency relationships and disclosures relating to possible problems with lead paint, agricultural districts, and electric service.

When the purchaser intends to secure an FHA or a VA loan, an accompanying **rider** provides that the contract may be voided if the property is appraised by the lending institution for less than the sale price. The FHA requires that before signing a purchase contract, its borrowers acknowledge receipt of a notice that the FHA's appraiser is concerned mainly with overall value and not with detailed condition. The notice states that FHA recommends (but does not require) that the buyer retain a home inspector. Sometimes provisions are added stipulating that seller or buyer will furnish satisfactory reports on such items as termite or insect infestation, or quality of a private water supply.

In some transfers a certificate of occupancy must be obtained from a municipality; the contract should make it clear whose responsibility this will be.

With regard to personal property or appliances being transferred with the real estate, the buyer usually agrees to accept them in their present condition, **"as is."**

The purchaser may want the right to inspect the property shortly before settlement.

Contingencies are happenings without which the contract will not be performed. Among the more common are the buyer's need to secure a specific loan, the purchaser's right to a satisfactory engineer's and environmental report on the property within a specified time period, approval of the contract by a family member or the purchaser's attorney within a short period of time, and the buyer's need to sell a present home before buying the next one.

Where the buyer has another home that must be sold first, the seller may insist on an **escape clause,** or *kickout*. Such a provision allows the seller to look for another offer, with the original purchaser retaining the right, if challenged, either to firm up the first sales contract (dropping the contingency) or to void the contract. If the first buyer chose to drop out, the seller would then be free to accept the other offer.

Liquidated damages are an amount of money, agreed to in advance by buyer and seller, that will serve as total compensation if one party does not live up to the contract. If a sales contract specifies that the earnest money deposit will serve as liquidated damages, the seller will be entitled to only the deposit if the buyer refuses to perform for no good reason. The seller who does agree to accept the deposit as liquidated damages may not sue later for any further damages.

Plain-language requirement (Sullivan Law).   New York law requires that certain written agreements for the sale or lease of residential property be written in a clear and coherent **manner** with words that are common in everyday usage. The copy also must be appropriately divided and captioned in its various sections. The plain-language requirement does not apply to agreements involving amounts over $50,000. Figure 8.1 is an example of a plain-English contract.

Lead-Based Paint Hazard Disclosure.   A buyer who purchases almost any residential property built before 1978 must be furnished with a booklet discussing lead-based paint hazards. Any purchase contract involving the sale of pre-1978 residential property must allow the buyer ten days in which to investigate potential lead-based paint hazards, before the contract becomes binding. Buyers and sellers may, however, agree to shorten or waive this time period (this agreement must be included in the purchase contract itself).

Cooperative Apartment Contracts

Because a cooperative apartment is owned by a corporation, the buyer of a co-op apartment does not receive a deed to real estate. Instead, he or she buys shares in the corporation and receives a proprietary lease to a unit in the building. These shares are personal property rather than real property. They can usually be financed, but through a loan under the **Uniform Commercial Code** (UCC) rather than a mortgage. The IRS, however, treats the owner's interest on the loan as it does mortgages.

The board of directors that manages a cooperative building is involved in any sale because it usually has the right to approve or disapprove of prospective tenants (owners), as long as its decisions are not based on discrimination against any classes protected by fair housing laws. The board may charge the seller a "flip" tax at the time of sale.

Condominium Sales

The buyer of a condominium receives fee simple title to his or her unit "from the plaster in" and also a percentage of ownership of the common elements. Special contracts are used for condominium sales. In some cases, the condominium association must release its **right of first refusal** before the condo may be sold to an outsider.

Chapter 23 contains details on initial sale and resale of condominiums and cooperatives, which are much more complex, involving submission of offering plans (the black book), financial plans, marketing statements, and other documents subject to approval by the state's attorney general.

Option Agreements

An **option** is a *contract by which an optionor (owner) gives an optionee (prospective purchaser or lessee) the right to buy or lease the owner's property at a fixed price within a stated period of time.* The optionee pays a fee (the agreed-on consideration) for this right and has no other obligation. The optionee is free to decide within the specified time to either buy or lease the property or allow the option to expire. The owner is bound to sell if requested; the optionee is not bound to buy. An option is often used by a tenant, who may then choose either to buy or to remain as a tenant. Options must contain all the terms required for a valid contract of sale.

FIGURE   8.1

Purchase and Sale Contract for Residential Property

PURCHASE AND SALE CONTRACT
FOR RESIDENTIAL PROPERTY

Plain English Form published by and only for use of the Greater Rochester Association of REALTORS®, Inc.
and the Monroe County Bar Association.
**COMMISSIONS OR FEES FOR THE REAL ESTATE SERVICES TO BE PROVIDED ARE NEGOTIABLE BETWEEN REALTOR®
AND CLIENT.**
When Signed, This Document Becomes A Binding Contract. Buyer or Seller May Wish to Consult Their Own Attorney.

TO: _____ (Seller) FROM: _____ (Buyer)

OFFER TO PURCHASE

Buyer offers to purchase the property described below from Seller on the following terms:

1. Property Description. Property known as _____ in the
❏ Town ❏ City ❏ Village of _____, State of New York, Zip _____ also known as
Tax No. _____ including all buildings and any other
improvements and all rights which the Seller has in or with the property. Approximate Lot Size: _____.
Description of buildings on property: _____.

2. Other Items Included in Purchase. The following items, if any, now in or on the property are included in this purchase and sale, which Seller represents are owned by Seller: All heating, plumbing, septic and private water systems, lighting fixtures, flowers, shrubs, trees, window shades and blinds, curtain and traverse rods, storm windows, storm doors, screens, awnings, TV antennae, satellite dish and all related equipment and accessories, water softeners, sump pumps, window boxes, mail box, shed, fences, underground pet containment fencing with control devices, wall-to-wall carpeting and runners, exhaust fans, hoods, garbage disposal, electric garage door opener and remote control devices, intercom equipment, humidifier, security systems and security codes, smoke detectors, all fireplace screens and enclosures, swimming pool and all related equipment and accessories, central vacuum and all related equipment and accessories, and the following, if built-in: cabinets, mirrors, microwave ovens, stoves, ovens, dishwashers, trash compactors, shelving, basketball apparatus, outdoor playsets, and air conditioning (except window units). Buyer agrees to accept these items in their present conditions. Other items to be included in the purchase and sale are: _____
_____.
Items not included are: _____.
Seller represents that Seller has good title to all of the above items to be transferred to Buyer, and will deliver a Bill of Sale for the above items at closing.
❏ Seller shall cause any heating, plumbing, air conditioning, electrical systems and included appliances to be in working order at the time of closing, except for _____. The prior sentence shall not be construed as a warranty or guarantee after closing.

3. Price & Payment: The purchase price is _____ Dollars
$_____. Buyer shall receive credit at closing for any deposit made hereunder. The balance of the purchase price shall be paid as follows: (Check and complete applicable provisions.)
❏ (a) Seller agrees to pay a loan fee of: ❏ ____% of the mortgage amount, ❏ ____% of the purchase price, or ❏ $_____
      toward any of the following applicable expenses as authorized by the Buyer's mortgage lender (not to exceed actual expenses paid): closing costs, prepaid items/escrows, points, buy down fees, FHA up front MIP, or VA funding fee.
❏ (b) Official bank draft or certified check at closing.
❏ (c) Mortgage Assumption pursuant to the terms and conditions of the Mortgage Assumption Addendum.
❏ (d) Seller Financing pursuant to the terms and conditions of the Seller Financing Addendum.

4. Contingencies. Buyer makes this offer subject to the following contingencies. If any of these contingencies is not satisfied by the dates specified, then either Buyer or Seller may cancel this contract by written notice to the other. (Check and complete applicable provisions.)
❏ (a) **Mortgage Contingency.** This offer is subject to Buyer obtaining and accepting a _____
      mortgage loan commitment in an amount not to exceed $_____at an interest rate not to exceed
      _____%, for a term of _____ years. Buyer shall immediately apply for this loan and shall have until
      _____, 20____ to obtain and accept a written mortgage commitment. The conditions of any such mortgage commitment shall not be deemed contingencies of this contract but shall be the sole responsibility of Buyer.
      If the loan commitment requires repairs, replacements, or improvements to be made, or painting to be done, before closing, then Seller shall do the work and install the materials and improvements needed or have the same done, at Seller's expense. However, if the cost of doing so exceeds $_____, Seller shall not be obligated to have such work done, and Buyer will be allowed either to receive credit at closing for the above amount and incur any necessary expenses to comply with the loan commitment requirements, or to cancel this contract by written notice to Seller, and any deposit shall be returned to Buyer. Acceptance of a written mortgage commitment by Buyer shall be deemed a waiver and satisfaction of this contingency.

_____
Seller's Initials

_____
Buyer's Initials

F I G U R E   8.1

Purchase and Sale Contract for Residential Property (continued)

❏ (b) **Sale and Transfer of Title Contingency.** This offer is contingent upon the sale and transfer of title of Buyer's existing property pursuant to the terms and conditions of the Sale and Transfer of Title Contingency Addendum.

❏ (c) **Attorney Approval.** This contract is subject to the written approval of attorneys for Buyer and Seller within _____ calendar days, *excluding Sundays and public holidays*, from date of acceptance (the Approval Period). If either attorney (i) does not provide written approval within the Approval Period or (ii) makes written objection to or conditionally approves (collectively, the Objections) the contract within the Approval Period and the Objection is not cured by written approval by both attorneys and all of the parties within the Approval Period, then (A) either Buyer or Seller may cancel this contract by written notice to the other and any deposit shall be returned to the Buyer or (B) the approving attorney may notify the other party (with a copy to any attorney listed below) in writing that no approval has been received and that the noticed party has five (5) calendar days, *inclusive of Sundays and public holidays*, from receipt of the notice (Grace Period) to provide written attorney approval or disapproval of the contract. The approving attorney shall provide to the noticed party (with a copy to any attorney listed below) a copy of the approving attorney's approval letter, whether conditional or not, along with the written notice of the Grace Period. If written attorney approval or disapproval is not provided to the approving attorney within the Grace Period, then this Attorney Approval contingency shall be deemed waived by the noticed party and any conditions in the approving attorney's approval letter shall be deemed accepted by the noticed party.

❏ (d) **Waiver of Attorney Approval.** This offer is not subject to the Buyer's attorney approval.

❏ (e) **Property Inspection Contingency.** This offer is contingent upon inspection(s) of the property pursuant to the terms and conditions of the Property Inspection Addendum.

❏ (f) **Other Contingencies.** _____

_____

5. Closing Date and Place. Transfer of title shall take place at the _____ County Clerk's Office or at the offices of Buyer's lender on or before _____, 20 _____.

6. Possession of Property.

❏ (a) Buyer shall have possession of the property on the day of closing, in broom-clean condition, with all keys to the property delivered to Buyer at closing.

❏ (b) Seller shall have the right to retain possession for _____ calendar days after closing at the cost of $ _____ per day inclusive of real property taxes, plus utilities. At closing, a key to the property shall be delivered to Buyer. At delivery of possession to Buyer, the property shall be in broom-clean condition and the remaining keys to the property shall be delivered to Buyer.

❏ (c) Buyer shall have right of early possession for _____ calendar days prior to closing at the cost of $ _____ per day inclusive of real property taxes, plus utilities. At possession, the property shall be in broom-clean condition and a key to the property shall be delivered to Buyer; the remaining keys shall be delivered to Buyer at closing.

In the event of retained possession or early possession, the parties shall enter into a written possession agreement, the form of which shall be the Monroe County Bar Association's recommended form, which agreement shall require a security deposit of $ _____.

7. Title and Related Documents. Seller shall provide the following documents in connection with the sale:

A. Deed. Seller will deliver to Buyer at closing a properly signed and notarized Warranty Deed with lien covenant (or Executor's Deed, Administrator's Deed or Trustee's Deed, if Seller holds title as such).

B. Abstract, Bankruptcy and Tax Searches, and Instrument Survey Map. Seller will furnish and pay for and deliver to Buyer or Buyer's attorney at least 15 calendar days prior to the date of closing, fully guaranteed tax, title and United States Court Searches dated or re-dated after the date of this contract with a local tax certificate for Village, or City taxes, if any, and an instrument survey map dated or re-dated after the date of this contract. Seller will pay for the map or re-dated map and for continuing such searches to and including the day of closing. Any survey map shall be prepared or re-dated and certified to meet the standards and requirements of Buyer's mortgage lender and the Monroe County Bar Association.

C. Other Documents. Seller agrees to furnish a smoke alarm affidavit at closing and to cooperate in executing any documents required by federal or state laws for transfer of title to residential property.

8. Marketability of Title. The deed and other documents delivered by Seller shall be sufficient to convey good marketable title to the property in fee simple, free and clear of all liens and encumbrances. However, Buyer agrees to accept title to the property subject to restrictive covenants of record common to the tract or subdivision of which the property is a part, provided these restrictions have not been violated, or if they have been violated, that the time for anyone to complain of the violations has expired. Buyer also agrees to accept title to the property subject to public utility easements along lot lines as long as those easements do not interfere with any buildings now on the property or with any improvements Buyer may construct in compliance with all present restrictive covenants of record and zoning and building codes applicable to the property. Except for waterfront property, Buyer also agrees to accept title to the property subject to fence encroachments of less than one foot onto the property, as long as the fence placement does not: (i) impair access to the property from a public or private right of way and/or (ii) render the property in violation of: (a) any applicable building, zoning and/or subdivision requirements and/or (b) any easements, agreements, or restrictive covenants of record.

9. Objections to Title. If Buyer raises a valid written objection to Seller's title which indicates that the title to the property is unmarketable, Seller may cancel this contract by giving prompt written notice of cancellation to Buyer and Buyer's deposit shall be returned. However, if Seller is able to cure the title objection on or before the closing date, or if the title objection is insurable and Buyer is willing to accept insurable title, then this contract shall continue in force until the closing date, subject to the Seller curing the title objection and/or providing insurable title at Seller's expense. If Seller fails to cure the title objection on or before the closing date, or, if Buyer is unwilling to accept insurable title, Buyer may cancel this contract by giving prompt written notice of cancellation to Seller and Buyer's deposit shall be returned.

Seller's Initials

Buyer's Initials

F I G U R E   8.1

Purchase and Sale Contract for Residential Property (continued)

10. Recording Costs, Mortgage Tax, Transfer Tax and Closing Adjustments. Seller will pay the real property transfer tax and special additional mortgage recording tax, if applicable. Buyer will pay mortgage assumption charges, if any, and will pay for recording the deed and the mortgage, and for the mortgage tax. The following, as applicable, will be prorated and adjusted between Seller and Buyer as of the date of closing, excluding any delinquent items, interest and penalties: current taxes computed on a fiscal year basis, rent payments, fuel oil on the property, water charges, pure water charges, sewer charges, mortgage interest, current common charges or assessments, prepaid FHA Mortgage Insurance Premium (MIP) of approximately $_____, with the exact amount to be calculated at closing in accordance with FHA formulae. Any FHA insurance premium which is not prepaid, but rather paid monthly, shall be adjusted at closing. If there is a water meter at the property, Seller shall furnish an actual reading to a date not more than 5 days before the closing date set forth in this contract. At closing the water charges and any sewer rent shall be apportioned on the basis of such actual reading.

11. Zoning. Seller represents that the property is in full compliance with all zoning and building ordinances for use as a _____. If applicable laws require it, the Seller will furnish at or before closing, a Certificate of Occupancy for the property, dated within 90 days of the closing, with Seller completing the work and installing the materials and improvements needed to obtain a Certificate of Occupancy. However, if the cost of obtaining a Certificate of Occupancy exceeds $_____, Seller shall not be obligated to have such work done, and Buyer will be allowed either to receive credit at closing for the amount recited above, and incur the necessary expenses to obtain the Certificate of Occupancy, or to cancel this contract by written notice to Seller, and any deposit shall be returned to Buyer.

12. Risk of Loss. Risk of loss or damage to the property by fire or other casualty until transfer of title shall be assumed by the Seller. If damage to the property by fire or such other casualty occurs prior to transfer, Buyer may cancel this contract without any further liability to Seller and Buyer's deposit is to be returned. If Buyer does not cancel but elects to close, then Seller shall transfer to Buyer any insurance proceeds, or Seller's claim to insurance proceeds payable for such damage.

13. Condition of Property. Buyer agrees to purchase the property and any items included in the purchase **AS IS** except as provided in paragraph 2, subject to reasonable use, wear, tear, and natural deterioration between now and the time of closing. However, this paragraph shall not relieve Seller from furnishing a Certificate of Occupancy as called for in paragraph 11, if applicable. Buyer shall have the right to inspect the property within 48 hours before the time of closing, and Seller agrees that all utilities shall be on at that time.

14. Services. Seller represents the property is serviced by: ❏ Public Sewers, ❏ Septic System, ❏ Public Water, ❏ Private Well, ❏ Other _____.

15. Deposit to Listing Broker. Buyer ❏ has deposited ❏ will deposit within two calendar days of acceptance $_____ in the form of a _____ with _____ (Escrow Agent) at _____ (Bank), which deposit is to become part of the purchase price or returned if not accepted or if this contract thereafter fails to close for any reason not the fault of the Buyer. If Buyer fails to complete Buyer's part of this contract, Seller is allowed to retain the deposit to be applied to Seller's damages, and may also pursue other legal rights Seller has against the Buyer, including but not limited to a lawsuit for any real estate brokerage commission paid by the Seller.

16. Real Estate Broker.
❏ (a) The parties agree that _____ brought about this purchase and sale.
❏ (b) It is understood and agreed by Buyer and Seller that no broker brought about this purchase and sale.

17. Life of Offer. This offer shall expire on _____, 20_____, at _____ .m.

18. Responsibility of Persons Under This Contract; Assignability. If more than one person signs this contract as Buyer, each person and any party who takes over that person's legal position will be responsible for keeping the promises made by Buyer in this contract. If more than one person signs this contract as Seller, each person or any party who takes over that person's legal position, will be fully responsible for keeping the promises made by Seller. However, this contract is personal to the parties and may not be assigned by either without the other's consent.

19. Entire Contract. This contract when signed by both Buyer and Seller will be the record of the complete agreement between the Buyer and Seller concerning the purchase and sale of the property. No oral agreements or promises will be binding. Seller's representations in this contract shall not survive after closing.

20. Notices. All notices under this contract shall be in writing and deemed delivered upon receipt. Any notices relating to this contract may be given by the attorneys for the parties.

21. Seller's Property Condition Disclosure Statement (check one).
❏ (a) Seller has provided Buyer with Seller's Property Condition Disclosure Statement which is attached to and made a part of this contract.
❏ (b) Seller has not provided Buyer with Seller's Property Condition Disclosure Statement, and Seller shall credit Buyer $500.00 at closing in lieu of such Statement.

_____
Seller's Initials

_____
Buyer's Initials

F I G U R E   8.1

Purchase and Sale Contract for Residential Property (continued)

22. Addenda. The following Addenda are incorporated into and attached to and made a part of this contract:

❑ Agricultural/Farming Disclosure	❑ Mediation	❑ Sale & Transfer of Title Contingency
❑ All Parties Agreement (FHA/VA)	❑ Mortgage Assumption	❑ Seller Financing
❑ Electric Availability	❑ Property Condition Disclosure Statement	❑ Services (Septic & Water)
❑ Lead Compliance	❑ Property Inspection	❑ Utility Surcharge

❑ Other: _____.

Dated: _____   BUYER _____

Witness: _____   BUYER _____

❑ ACCEPTANCE OF OFFER BY SELLER   ❑ COUNTER OFFER BY SELLER

Seller certifies that Seller owns the property and has the power to sell the property. Seller accepts the offer and agrees to sell on the terms and conditions above set forth.

❑ Waiver of Seller's attorney approval. This offer is not subject to Seller's attorney approval.

Dated: _____   SELLER _____

Witness: _____   SELLER _____

_____   **ADMINISTRATIVE INFORMATION** _____

Property Address: _____   MLS# _____

Seller: _____   **Buyer:** _____

Address: _____   Address: _____

_____ Zip: _____   _____ Zip: _____

Phones: (H) _____ (W) _____   Phones: (H) _____ (W) _____

Attorney: _____   **Attorney:** _____

Address: _____   Address: _____

_____ Zip: _____   _____ Zip: _____

Phone: _____ Fax: _____   Phone: _____ Fax: _____

Listing Broker: _____   **Selling Broker:** _____

Address: _____   Address: _____

_____ Zip: _____   _____ Zip: _____

Phone: _____ Fax: _____   Phone: _____ Fax: _____

Listing Agent: _____   **Selling Agent:** _____

Other: _____ ID # _____   Other: _____ ID# _____

_____
Seller's Initials

_____
Buyer's Initials

Land Contracts

A real estate sale can be made under a **land contract,** sometimes called a *contract for deed* or *an installment contract*. Under a typical land contract the seller, also known as the *vendor*, retains ownership, while the buyer, known as the *vendee*, moves in and has an equitable interest in the property. Each land contract is different, but in a common form the buyer agrees to give the seller a down payment and pay regular installments of principal and interest over a number of years. The buyer also agrees to pay real estate taxes, insurance premiums, repairs, and upkeep on the property. Although the buyer obtains possession when the contract is signed by both parties, *the seller is not obligated to execute (sign) and deliver a deed to the buyer until the terms of the contract have been satisfied*. Depending on the agreement, this might occur when the buyer can obtain a regular mortgage loan and pay off the balance due on the contract.

Real estate is occasionally sold with the new buyer's assuming an existing land contract from the original buyer/vendee. Generally, the seller/vendor must approve the new purchaser.

Land contracts require extensive legal input from lawyers experienced in real estate matters. The broker who negotiates a land contract should consult attorneys for both parties at every step of the way and refrain from specifying any detailed terms in the agreement.

Local Forms

To gain familiarity with the forms used in a local area, the student should go to brokers or real estate companies and ask for copies of the sales contract, listing agreement, and other forms they use. More general forms also can be obtained at a title or abstract company and some banks and savings and loan associations, or they may be purchased at local office supply and stationery stores.

Rescission

With contracts for the purchase of some types of personal property, the buyer has three days in which to reconsider and rescind (cancel) the contract. No such right of **rescission** applies to contracts for the purchase of real estate (with certain exceptions, e.g., when lead-based paint laws apply).

Borrowers who change their minds about a mortgage loan have three days in which to cancel the transaction if the mortgage was for *refinance* of presently owned property. No right of rescission, however, applies to mortgage loans used for the *purchase* of real estate.

■ SUMMARY

A contract is defined as an agreement made by competent parties with adequate consideration, to take or to refrain from some lawful action.

Contracts may be classified according to whether the parties' intentions are expressed or are implied by their actions. They also may be classified as bilateral, when both parties have obligated themselves to act, or unilateral, when one party is obligated to perform only if the other party does. In addition, contracts may be classified according to their legal enforceability as valid, void, voidable, or unenforceable.

An executed contract is one that has been fully performed. An executory contract is one in which some act remains to be performed.

The essentials of a valid contract are (1) competent parties, (2) offer and acceptance, (3) consideration, (4) legality of object, and (5) agreement in writing and signatures of the parties.

In many types of contracts either party may transfer his or her rights and obligations by assignment of the contract or novation (substitution of a new contract).

A party who has suffered a loss because of the other party's default may sue for damages to cover the loss. A party who insists on completing the transaction may ask for specific performance of the terms of the contract; a court may order the other party to comply with the agreement.

A real estate sales contract binds a buyer and a seller to a definite transaction as described in the contract. The buyer is bound to purchase the property for the amount stated in the agreement. The seller is bound to deliver title, free from liens and encumbrances (except for those allowed by the contract).

The *Duncan and Hill* court decision cautioned real estate brokers to make any sales contracts they draw up subject to approval by the parties' attorneys. The Department of State expects licensees to limit their assistance in drawing up sales contracts to filling in the blanks on forms approved by local bar associations. Any unusual or complicated provisions must be drawn up by attorneys.

Under an option agreement, the optionee purchases from the optioner, for a limited time period, the exclusive right to purchase or lease the optioner's property. A land contract, or installment contract, is an agreement under which a buyer purchases a seller's real estate on time. The buyer takes possession of and responsibility for the property but does not receive the deed immediately.

QUESTIONS

1. Laura Secord told her buyers, when they first looked at her house, that she intended to remove her grandmother's antique chandelier. It was not mentioned in the contract. Now they are suing her. A judge is likely to say that

   a. Laura's oral announcement was enough; she could take the chandelier.
   b. the chandelier should remain because of the rule of parol evidence.
   c. because the chandelier wasn't mentioned in the written contract, it remained personal property.
   d. there was no legal way Laura could have retained the chandelier.

2. Markus Barnes drives into a filling station and tops off his gas tank. He is obligated to pay for the fuel through what kind of contract?

   a. Express   c. Oral
   b. Implied   d. Voidable

3. A contract is said to be *bilateral* if

   a. one of the parties is a minor.
   b. the contract has yet to be fully performed.
   c. only one party to the agreement is bound to act.
   d. all parties to the contract are bound to act.

4. A contract for the sale of real estate that does not state the consideration to be paid for the property would be

   a. implied.   c. void.
   b. executory.   d. enforceable.

5. During the period of time after a real estate sales contract is signed but before title actually passes, the status of the contract is

   a. voidable.   c. executed.
   b. executory.   d. implied.

6. Derrick Smith, who is 17 years old, signs a contract to buy a home for himself. The contract is

   a. voidable.   c. executed.
   b. optional.   d. unilateral.

7. A buyer signed an offer to purchase a property for $10,000 less than the asking price and deposited $5,000 with the broker. The owner cannot be reached to tell him of the signed document. At this point the document is a(n)

   a. voidable contract.
   b. offer.
   c. executory agreement.
   d. implied contract.

8. Consideration offered in exchange for a deed might take the form of

   a. love and affection.
   b. a purchase-money mortgage.
   c. cash.
   d. Any of the above

9. Under the statute of frauds, any contract for the sale of real estate must be

   a. drawn up by a lawyer.
   b. on a preprinted form.
   c. in writing.
   d. accompanied by an earnest money deposit.

10. The buyer of a home built before 1978 must be given a lead paint disclosure statement

    a. when the property is first inspected.
    b. by the mortgage lender.
    c. before signing a purchase offer.
    d. at closing.

11. In New York State, who may fill in the blanks on purchase contracts?

    a. Seller's attorney
    b. Buyer's attorney
    c. Real estate broker
    d. Any of the above, according to local custom

12. If a real estate sales contract does not state that time is of the essence and the stipulated date of transfer comes and goes without a closing, the contract is then

    a. binding for only 30 more days.
    b. novated.
    c. still valid.
    d. automatically void.

13. Tom has a contract to buy Blackacre but would rather let his friend Mary buy it instead. If the contract allows, Mary can acquire Tom's right to buy by the process known as

a. assignment.
b. substantial performance.
c. subordination.
d. mutual consent.

14. A suit for specific performance of a real estate contract asks for

a. money damages.
b. a new contract.
c. a deficiency judgment.
d. a forced sale or purchase.

15. When a small change is made in a contract by crossing out one word or figure and inserting another, to eliminate future arguments, the usual procedure is to

a. write a letter to each party listing the changes.
b. have each party write a letter approving the changes.
c. redraw the entire contract.
d. have both parties initial or sign in the margin near each change.

16. A broker listed a vacant building for sale at 6 percent commission. Marketing the property proved lengthy and difficult, and advertising costs mounted. Finally the seller accepted an offer brought in by the broker. Before the closing the broker insisted the commission be raised to 10 percent. The seller refused to pay more than 6 percent. At that point the

a. sale cannot close.
b. seller need pay only 6 percent.
c. seller has violated the fiduciary relationship.
d. broker and seller should compromise on 8 percent.

17. The Foxes offer in writing to purchase a house for $140,000, drapes included, with the offer to expire Saturday at noon. The Wolfs reply in writing on Thursday, accepting $140,000 but excluding the drapes. On Friday while the Foxes are considering this counteroffer, the Wolfs decide to accept the original offer, drapes included, and state that in writing. At this point the Foxes

a. must buy and have a right to insist on the drapes.
b. are not bound to buy and can forget the whole thing.
c. must buy but are not entitled to the drapes.
d. must buy and can deduct the value of the drapes from the $140,000.

18. In New York State a valid contract for the sale of real estate must include

a. an earnest money deposit.
b. an adequate description of the property.
c. the signatures of witnesses.
d. All of the above

19. The sales contract says Timothy Jones will purchase only if his wife flies up to New York and approves the sale by the following Saturday. Mrs. Jones's approval is a

a. contingency.   c. warranty.
b. reservation.   d. consideration.

20. When the buyer promises to purchase only if he can sell his own present home, the seller gains some protection from an

a. escrow.   c. equitable title.
b. option.   d. escape clause.

21. Real estate licensees who fill in the blanks on purchase contracts can protect themselves by making the contracts subject to

a. operation of law.
b. novation.
c. approval by the party's attorneys.
d. specific performance.

22. An option to purchase binds
    a. the buyer only.
    b. the seller only.
    c. neither buyer nor seller.
    d. both buyer and seller.

23. Failure to fulfill one's obligations under a contract is called a
    a. novation.   c. delinquency.
    b. default.   d. defect.

24. The purchaser of real estate under an installment contract
    a. generally pays no interest charge.
    b. receives title immediately.
    c. is not required to pay property taxes for the duration of the contract.
    d. is called a *vendee*.

25. The consumer has the right to change his or her mind and rescind the transaction within three days after a
    a. land contract.
    b. firm purchase contract.
    c. refinance mortgage.
    d. lease option.

TITLE AND CLOSING COSTS

When they buy their house next Monday, the O'Briens have been told to bring a cashier's check for the money they will need. But what about the fuel oil the seller put in the tank? The year's taxes the seller already paid? Interest due on the mortgage they are assuming? How will they know how much to bring?

Final closing of a real estate sale (also called *settlement* or *transfer of title*) involves many financial details to be settled between the buyer and seller. Even more important, however, is the buyer's need to receive unchallenged ownership, or clear title.

■ **KEY TERMS**

abstract of title
accrued item
actual notice
adjustments
affidavit
attorney's opinion of title
caveat emptor
chain of title
closing statement
coinsurance clause
constructive notice

credit
debit
escrow
evidence of title
homeowner's insurance
    policy
liability insurance
marketable title
mortgage reduction
    certificate
prepaid item
proration

public records
Real Estate Settlement
    Procedures Act (RESPA)
reconciliation
replacement cost
suit to quiet title
survey
title insurance policy
Torrens system
Uniform Settlement
    Statement

■ PUBLIC RECORDS AND RECORDING

Before purchasing a parcel of real estate, the prospective buyer wants to be sure that the seller can convey good title to the property. The present owner of the real estate undoubtedly purchased from a previous owner, so the same question has been asked many times in the past.

Recording Acts

Parties interested in real estate may record, or file, documents affecting real estate in the *public records*, to give notice to the world of their interest.

Public records are maintained by the recorder of deeds, registrar, county clerk, county treasurer, city clerk and collector, and clerks of various courts of record. Records involving taxes, special assessments, ordinances, and zoning and building also are open for anyone's inspection.

Necessity for Recording

A deed or mortgage may not be effective as far as later purchasers are concerned unless it has been recorded. The public records should reveal the condition of the title, and a purchaser should be able to rely on a search of the records.

In New York, to give subsequent purchasers constructive notice of a person's interest, all deeds, mortgages, or other written instruments affecting an interest in real estate must be recorded in the county clerk's office of the county where the real estate is located (or, in four of the New York City counties, the Register's Office). All documents must be properly acknowledged and show proof of payment of the real estate transfer tax on deeds or the mortgage tax on mortgages before the documents will be accepted for recording.

A deed will not be accepted for recording in counties outside the city of New York unless it is accompanied by a *real property transfer report*, which will be used by the New York State Board of Equalization and Assessment. A real estate transfer tax (form TP584) **affidavit** (sworn statement) also must be filed. In New York City a deed may not be recorded unless it is accompanied by a *multiple dwelling registration statement* or an affidavit that no statement is due, an affidavit stating that the property contains a smoke alarm, and a New York City Real Property Transfer Tax Form.

The county clerk's office maintains general indexes of instruments recorded in that office. Documents are also recorded in the Office of the New York City Register in borough offices in Manhattan (New York County), Brooklyn (Kings County), the Bronx (Bronx County), and Jamaica (Queens County).

Notice

Through the legal maxim of **caveat emptor** ("let the buyer beware"), the courts hold prospective real estate buyers or mortgagees (lenders) responsible for inspecting the property and searching the public records to find out the interests of other parties. **Constructive notice** assumes that the information is available, so the buyer or lender could have learned it.

Constructive notice, or what a person can find out, is distinguished from **actual notice,** or what the person *actually knows*. An individual who has searched the public records and inspected the property has actual notice of the information learned.

Unrecorded liens.   A special search may be needed for unrecorded liens. Estate taxes and franchise taxes are placed against all real estate owned either by a decedent at the time of death or by a corporation at the time the franchise tax became a lien; these liens also are not recorded.

Recording sales contracts.   Occasionally it is desirable to record a real property sales contract. Any document to be recorded must be acknowledged. If neither the buyer nor seller can be reached for an acknowledgment, it will be sufficient if a witness to their signatures appears before a notary.

Chain of Title

The **chain of title** shows the record of ownership of the property over a period of time. An **abstract of title** is a condensed history of all the instruments affecting a particular parcel of land.

In New York, chains of title frequently date back to a grant from the king of England or a grant to a Dutch patroon.

Through the chain of title, the sequence of owners can be traced from its origin to its present owner. When this cannot be done, there is a *gap* in the chain. In such cases ownership usually must be established by a court action called a **suit to quiet title,** or an Article 15 proceeding.

■ EVIDENCE OF TITLE

When dealing with an owner of real estate, a purchaser or lender requires satisfactory proof that the seller or borrower is the owner and has good title to the property. This documentary proof is called **evidence of title.**

Generally four forms of title evidence are used: (1) abstract of title and lawyer's opinion, (2) title insurance policy, (3) Torrens certificate, and (4) certificate of title. *A deed is not proof of title*. It proves the grantee received the property but does not prove the grantor had good title in the first place. The only effective proof is one of the evidences of title, based on an adequate search of the public records.

Abstract of Title and Lawyer's Opinion

An abstract of title is a brief history of the instruments appearing in the county record that affect title to the parcel in question. The abstractor lists and summarizes each instrument in order, along with information about taxes, judgments, special assessments, and the like. *An abstractor does not, however, pass judgment on or guarantee the condition of the title*.

The abstract illustrated in Figure 9.1 shows that on June 3, 1947, Ida Hughey mortgaged her property at 47 Rowley Street to Rochester Savings Bank for $5,000. The rubber stamp on the record shows that the mortgage was paid off in 1958. The mortgage document evidently carried two legal descriptions: one by plat of subdivision, the other by metes and bounds.

In 1952 Hughey granted a five-year lease on the property to Michael and Mildred Franco, who recorded the document. The next year the Francos bought the property. This particular abstract later goes on to report a driveway easement the Francos negotiated with their neighbors to the north and then

F I G U R E   9.1

Portion of an Abstract

A B S T R A C T   O F   T I T L E

- T O -

#47   W e s t   s i d e   R o w l e y   S t r e e t ,   b e i n g

P a r t   o f   L o t s   #27   a n d   28   o f   t h e

B r o o k s   T r a c t   (N .   P a r t)   i n   t h e

C i t y   o f   R o c h e s t e r

Maps: Liber 2 of Maps, page 120 and 138
Liber 3 of Maps, page 45
1935 Hopkins Atlas, Vol. 1, Plate 4

1   Ida May Hughey   Mortgage to secure $5000.00
-TO-   Dated   June 3, 1947
Rochester Savings Bank   same day
47 Main Street West   same day at 12:30 P. M.
Rochester, New York   Liber 1800 of Mortgages, page 344

(t) Conveys land in the City of Rochester, being on the

west side of Rowley Street in said City and being part of lots

Nos. 27 and 28 in the Brooks Tract as shown on a map of said

Tract made by M. D. Rowley, surveyor, May 15, 1869 and filed

in Monroe County Clerk's Office and counded and described as

follows:

Beginning at a point in the west line of Row<u>e</u>ly

Street 15 feet northerly from the southeast corner of said

lot #27; thence northerly on the west line of Rowley Street,

<u>forth</u> (40) feet; thence westerly on a line parallel with the

south line of said lot #27, 121 feet; thence southerly on a

line parallel with the west line of Rowley Street, 40 feet;

thence easterly 121 feet to the place of beginning.

F I G U R E   9.1

Portion of an Abstract (continued)

Being the same premises conveyed to the mortgagor by Liber 2258 of Deeds, page 178.

Subject to any restrictions and public utility easements of record.

- -

2   Ida May Hughey, Landlord   Lease

        -To-   Dated May 23, 1952
                      Ack.   same day
Michael Franco   Rec.   August 4, 1952
Mildred Franco,his wife,
Tenants, 17 Glendale Park, Liber 2769 of Deeds, page 290
Rochester, N.Y.,(Second
parties not certified)

First party leases to second parties premises described as #47 Rowley Street, Rochester, New York, being a 12 room house for a term of 5 years commencing July 16, 1952 and ending July 15, 1957 on certain terms and conditions set forth herein.

Second parties shall have the right of renewal on the same terms and conditions as herein for an additional period of 5 years provided that written notice of intention to renew is served upon Landlord or her assigns at least 30 days prior to end of initial term hereof.

- -

3   Ida May Hughey,   Warranty Deed

      -To-   Dated Oct. 30, 1953
                      Ack. Same day
Michele Franco, Mildred   Rec. Same day at 10:50 A.M.
Franco, his wife, as
tenants by the entirety,   Liber 2861 of Deeds, page 411
#47 Rowley St., Rochester,
N.Y. (Second parties not
certified).

Conveys same as #1.

Subject to all covenants, easements and restrictions

traces the property through several later owners with mortgages placed and paid off along the way.

Where the abstract will be used for proof of title, the seller's attorney usually orders the abstract continued to cover the current date. It is then submitted to the buyer's attorney, who *examines the entire document*. The attorney must evaluate all the material and prepare a written report for the purchaser. This report is called an **attorney's opinion of title.** (Abstracts with attorneys' opinions of title are not customary in New York City.)

Mortgage lenders prefer that the seller's title be proved by the use of title insurance, which is required in all commercial transactions and is required by the secondary market for residential loans that are to be resold.

Title Insurance

A **title insurance policy** protects the policyholder against loss if a defect in the owner's title is challenged by anyone at any time. The policy is paid for only once and is in force for the whole period of ownership.

When a seller, buyer, or lender applies for a policy, the title company examines the title records. If it is satisfied, it agrees to insure against certain undiscovered defects, usually those that may be found in the public records and such items as forged documents, documents of incompetent grantors, incorrect marital statements, and improperly delivered deeds. Exactly which defects the company will insure against depends on the type of policy; the New York State Insurance Department sets standards. The policy amount is the purchase price in the case of an owner's policy and the loan amount in the case of the lender's policy.

On completing the examination, the title company usually issues a report of title or a commitment to issue a title policy. An owner's policy usually coverage against unrecorded documents, unrecorded defects of which the policyholder has knowledge, rights of parties in possession, and facts discoverable by survey. The insurance company agrees to defend the title at its own expense and to reimburse the policyholder up to the amount of the policy for damages sustained by reason of any defect not excepted. Title companies in New York must offer a homeowner the right to purchase insurance covering future market value.

Title companies issue various forms of policies, the most common of which are the *owner's* title insurance policy (a *fee policy*) and the *mortgagee* or *lender* title insurance policy. The owner's policy protects the owner and his heirs or devisees. The mortgagee policy protects the lender's interests.

The Torrens System

The **Torrens system** is a legal registration system used to verify ownership and encumbrances. Registration in the Torrens system provides evidence of title without the need for an additional search of the public records. At any time the Torrens certificate in the registrar's office reveals the owner of the land and all mortgages, judgments, and similar liens. It does not reveal federal or state taxes and some other items. The Torrens system is no longer used in New York.

**Certificate
of Title**

With an older system, which still may be used for transfers where no lending institution is involved, a *certificate of title prepared by an attorney* is used, and no abstract is prepared. The attorney examines the public records and issues a certificate of title that expresses his or her opinion of the title's status. It is not, however, a title insurance policy and does not carry the full protection of such a policy. The person who sustains damages by relying on it may look to the lawyer for satisfaction.

**Marketable
Title**

Under the terms of the usual real estate sales contract, the seller is required to deliver marketable or insurable title to the buyer at the closing. Generally a **marketable title** is one that is free from significant defects (other than those specified in the sales contract), will not expose the purchaser to lawsuits that threaten his or her quiet enjoyment of the property, and would be accepted by a reasonably well-informed and prudent person. Proper evidence of title is proof that the title is in fact marketable.

A buyer cannot be forced to accept a conveyance that is materially different from the one bargained for in the sales contract; he or she cannot be forced to buy a problem. Questions of marketable title must be raised by a purchaser (or the purchaser's attorney) before acceptance of the deed. If a buyer accepts a deed with unmarketable title, the only available legal recourse is to sue the seller under the covenants or warranty (if any) contained in the deed.

■ CLOSING THE TRANSACTION

Although salespeople usually are not burdened with the technicalities of closing, they must clearly understand what takes place. A real estate specialist should be able to assist in preclosing arrangements and advise the parties in estimating expenses and the approximate amounts the buyer will need and the seller will receive at the closing.

Generally the closing of a real estate transaction involves a gathering of interested parties at which the promises made in the *real estate sales contract are kept,* or *executed;* that is, a deed is delivered in exchange for the purchase price. In many sales transactions two closings actually take place at this time: (1) the closing of the buyer's loan and the disbursement of mortgage funds in exchange for the note and mortgage, and (2) the closing of the sale.

As discussed in Chapter 8, a sales contract is the blueprint for the completion of a real estate transaction. The buyer must be sure that the seller is delivering good title and that the property is in the promised condition. This involves inspecting the title evidence; the deed the seller will give; any documents representing the removal of undesired liens and encumbrances; and any survey, physical and/or environmental inspection, termite report, or leases (if there are tenants on the premises). The seller must be sure that the buyer has obtained financing and has the funds to complete the purchase. Both parties should inspect the closing statement to ensure that all monies involved in the transaction have been properly accounted for. In New York State, the parties usually are represented by attorneys.

When everything is in order, the exchange is made and all pertinent documents then are recorded.

Where Closings Are Held and Who Attends

Closings may be held at a number of locations, including the offices of the title company, the lending institution, the office of one of the parties' attorneys, the broker's office, the office of the county clerk (or other local recording official), or an escrow company. Those attending a closing may include any of the following interested parties: buyer, seller, real estate agent(s), attorney(s) for the seller and/or buyer, representatives for the lending institutions involved, and representatives of the title insurance company.

Broker's Role at Closing

Depending on the locality, the broker's role at a closing can vary from conducting the proceedings to not even being present. A broker's job is essentially over when there has been a meeting of the minds. At that point, according to New York State customs, attorneys take over. Even so, a broker's service generally continues after the contract is signed as he or she advises the parties in practical matters, aids the buyer with a mortgage application, and makes sure all details are taken care of so that the closing can proceed smoothly. In this capacity the broker might make arrangements for such items as appraisals, termite inspections, and repairs or might suggest sources of these services to the parties. An agent can arrange for and accompany the last-minute walk-through of the property most buyers now request just before the closing.

Lender's Interest in Closing

When a buyer is obtaining a new loan, the lender wants to protect its security interest in the property to make sure that the buyer is getting good, marketable title and that tax and insurance payments are maintained so that there will be no liens with greater priority than the mortgage lien and the insurance will be paid up if the property is damaged or destroyed.

For this reason the lender frequently requires the following items: (1) a title insurance policy; (2) a fire and hazard insurance policy with receipt for the premium; (3) additional information such as a survey, a termite or other inspection report, or a certificate of occupancy (for newly constructed buildings, multiple dwellings, and in areas in and around New York City, all buildings); (4) representation by its own attorney at the closing; and (5) establishment of a reserve, or escrow, account for tax and insurance payments. (In New York State, lenders are required to pay interest on escrow accounts for owner-occupied properties.)

Homeowners' Insurance

Where mortgaging is involved, the buyer must bring to the closing proof of insurance on the property and, occasionally, proof of flood insurance. The insurance policy or binder usually names the lender as lienholder and copayee in case of loss under the policy.

Although it is possible for a homeowner to obtain individual policies for each type of risk, most residential property owners take out insurance in the form of a packaged **homeowner's insurance policy.** These standardized policies insure holders against the destruction of their property by fire or windstorm, injury to others that occurs on the property, and theft of any personal property on the premises that is owned by the insured or members of his or her family.

The homeowner's policy also includes **liability insurance** for personal injuries to others resulting from the insured's acts or negligence, voluntary medical payments and funeral expenses for accidents sustained by guests or resident employees on the property of the owner, and physical damage to the property of others caused by the insured.

Characteristics of homeowners' packages.   There are four major forms of homeowners' policies. The *basic* form, known as *HO-1*, provides property coverage against fire or lightning; glass breakage; windstorm or hail; explosion; riot or civil commotion; damage by aircraft; damage from vehicles; damage from smoke; vandalism and malicious mischief; theft; and loss of property removed from the premises when endangered by fire or other perils.

Increased coverage is provided under a *broad* form, known as *HO-2*, that also covers falling objects; weight of ice, snow, or sleet; collapse of the building or any part of it; bursting, cracking, burning, or bulging of a steam or hot water heating system or of appliances used to heat water; accidental discharge, leakage, or overflow of water or steam from within a plumbing, heating, or air-conditioning system; freezing of plumbing, heating and air-conditioning systems, and domestic appliances; and injury to electrical appliances, devices, fixtures, and wiring from short circuits or other accidentally generated currents.

Further coverage is provided by *comprehensive* forms *HO-3*, the most popular form, and *HO-5*. These policies cover all possible perils except flood, earthquake, war, and nuclear attack. Other policies include *HO-4*, a form designed specifically for apartment renters, and *HO-6*, a broad-form policy for condominium owners. Apartment and condominium policies generally provide fire and windstorm, theft, and public liability coverage for injuries or losses sustained within the unit but usually do not extend to cover losses or damages to the structure. The structure is insured by either the landlord or the condominium owners' association.

Claims.   Most homeowners' insurance policies contain a **coinsurance clause.** This provision typically requires that the insured maintain fire insurance on the property equal to at least 80 percent of the **replacement cost** of the dwelling (not including the price of the land). With such a policy the owner may make a claim for the cost of the repair or replacement of the damaged property without deduction.

In any event, *the total settlement may not exceed the face value of the policy.* Because of coinsurance clauses, it is important that homeowners review their policies regularly to be certain that the coverage is equal to at least 80 percent of the current replacement cost of their homes. Some policies carry automatic increases in coverage to adjust for inflation.

Federal Flood Insurance Program

Property owners in certain areas must obtain flood damage insurance before they can obtain federally related mortgages. Federally related loans include those made by banks, savings and loan associations, or other lenders whose deposits are insured by federal agencies (FDIC or FSLIC); those insured by the FHA or guaranteed by the VA; mortgages administered by the U.S. Department of Housing and Urban Development; and loans intended to be sold by

WWWeb.Link

the lender to Fannie Mae, Ginnie Mae, or Freddie Mac. An owner may be able to avoid purchasing flood insurance if he or she can furnish a survey showing that the lowest part of the building is above the 100-year flood mark. Information on national flood insurance is available from 1-800-358-9616, online at *www.fema.gov*, or by writing to the Federal Emergency Mangement Agency at Box 1038, Jessup, MD 20794.

RESPA Requirements

The federal **Real Estate Settlement Procedures Act (RESPA)** ensures that the buyer in a *residential* real estate transaction has knowledge of all settlement costs. *RESPA requirements apply when the purchase is financed by a federally related mortgage loan.*

RESPA regulations apply to transactions involving new first mortgage loans, refinance loans, second mortgages, home equity loans, and lines of credit. When a transaction is covered by RESPA, the following requirements must be met:

- *Special information booklet:* Lenders must give a copy of the HUD booklet *Settlement Costs and You* to every person from whom they receive or for whom they prepare a loan application.
- *Good-faith estimate of settlement costs:* At the time of the loan application or within three business days, the lender must provide the borrower with a good-faith estimate of the settlement costs the borrower is likely to incur. A lender who requires use of a particular attorney or title company to conduct the closing must state whether it has any business relationship with that firm and must estimate the charges for this service.
- *Uniform Settlement Statement (HUD Form 1):* Loan closing information must be prepared on a special HUD form, the **Uniform Settlement Statement,** designed to detail all financial particulars of a transaction. (See Figure 9.2.) The completed statement must itemize all charges imposed by the lender. Items paid for before the closing must be clearly marked as such on the statement and are omitted from the totals. On the borrower's request the closing agent must permit the borrower to inspect the settlement statement, to the extent that the figures are available, one business day before the closing. Lenders must retain these statements for two years after the date of closing unless the loan (and its servicing) is sold or otherwise disposed of.
- *Prohibition against kickbacks:* RESPA explicitly prohibits the payment of kickbacks, or unearned fees; for example, when an insurance agency pays a kickback to a lender for referring one of the lender's recent customers to the agency. This prohibition does *not* include fee splitting between cooperating brokers or members of multiple-listing services, brokerage referral arrangements, or the division of a commission between a broker and his or her salespeople. (RESPA is administered by HUD.)

■ THE TITLE PROCEDURE

On the date when the sale is actually completed, that is, the date of delivery of the deed, the buyer has a title commitment or an abstract that was issued several days or weeks before the closing. For this reason the title or abstract company is usually required to make a second search of the public records. A last-minute search is often made at the moment of closing.

F I G U R E 9.2

RESPA Uniform Settlement Statement

A. **Settlement Statement**	U.S. Department of Housing and Urban Development	OMB Approval No. 2502-0265

B. Type of Loan

1. ☐ FHA 2. ☐ FmHA 3. ☒ Conv. Unins.	6. File Number:	7. Loan Number:	8. Mortgage Insurance Case Number:
4. ☐ VA 5. ☐ Conv. Ins.			

C. Note: This form is furnished to give you a statement of actual settlement costs. Amounts paid to and by the settlement agent are shown. Items marked "(p.o.c.)" were paid outside the closing; they are shown here for informational purposes and are not included in the totals.

D. Name & Address of Borrower:	E. Name & Address of Seller:	F. Name & Address of Lender:
Brook Redemann 22 King Court Riverdale, ED 00000	John Iuro and Joanne Iuro 3045 North Racine Avenue Riverdale, ED 00000	Thrift Federal Savings 1100 Fountain Plaza Riverdale, ED 00000

G. Property Location: 3045 North Racine Avenue Riverdale, ED 00000	H. Settlement Agent: Open Door Real Estate Co.	
	Place of Settlement: 720 Main Street Riverdale, ED 00000	I. Settlement Date: June 15, 200-

J. Summary of Borrower's Transaction		K. Summary of Seller's Transaction	
100. Gross Amount Due From Borrower		**400. Gross Amount Due To Seller**	
101. Contract sales price	$115,000.00	401. Contract sales price	$115,000.00
102. Personal property		402. Personal property	
103. Settlement charges to borrower (line 1400)	4,892.09	403.	
104.		404.	
105.		405.	
Adjustments for items paid by seller in advance		**Adjustments for items paid by seller in advance**	
106. City/town taxes to		406. City/town taxes to	
107. County taxes to		407. County taxes to	
108. Assessments to		408. Assessments to	
109.		409.	
110.		410.	
111.		411.	
112.		412.	
120. Gross Amount Due From Borrower	119,892.09	**420. Gross Amount Due To Seller**	$115,000.00
200. Amounts Paid By Or In Behalf Of Borrower		**500. Reductions In Amount Due To Seller**	
201. Deposit or earnest money	23,000.00	501. Excess deposit (see instructions)	
202. Principal amount of new loan(s)	92,000.00	502. Settlement charges to seller (line 1400)	8,285.00
203. Existing loan(s) taken subject to		503. Existing loan(s) taken subject to	
204.		504. Payoff of first mortgage loan	57,964.47
205.		505. Payoff of second mortgage loan	
206.		506.	
207.		507.	
208.		508.	
209.		509.	
Adjustments for items unpaid by seller		**Adjustments for items unpaid by seller**	
210. City/town taxes to		510. City/town taxes to	
211. County taxes 1/1 to 6/15	790.63	511. County taxes 1/1 to 6/15	790.63
212. Assessments to		512. Assessments to	
213.		513.	
214.		514.	
215.		515.	
216.		516.	
217.		517.	
218.		518.	
219.		519.	
220. Total Paid By/For Borrower	115,790.63	**520. Total Reduction Amount Due Seller**	67,040.10
300. Cash At Settlement From/To Borrower		**600. Cash At Settlement To/From Seller**	
301. Gross Amount due from borrower (line 120)	119,892.09	601. Gross amount due to seller (line 420)	115,000.00
302. Less amounts paid by/for borrower (line 220)	(115,790.63)	602. Less reductions in amt. due seller (line 520)	(67,040.10)
303. Cash ☒ From ☐ To Borrower	$ 4,101.46	**603. Cash** ☒ To ☐ From Seller	$ 47,959.90

Section 5 of the Real Estate Settlement Procedures Act (RESPA) requires the following: • HUD must develop a Special Information Booklet to help persons borrowing money to finance the purchase of residential real estate to better understand the nature and costs of real estate settlement services; • Each lender must provide the booklet to all applicants from whom it receives or for whom it prepares a written application to borrow money to finance the purchase of residential real estate; • Lenders must prepare and distribute with the Booklet a Good Faith Estimate of the settlement costs that the borrower is likely to incur in connection with the settlement. These disclosures are manadatory.

Section 4(a) of RESPA mandates that HUD develop and prescribe this standard form to be used at the time of loan settlement to provide full disclosure of all charges imposed upon the borrower and seller. These are third party disclosures that are designed to provide the borrower with pertinent information during the settlement process in order to be a better shopper.

The Public Reporting Burden for this collection of information is estimated to average one hour per response, including the time for reviewing instructions, searching existing data sources, gathering and maintaining the data needed, and completing and reviewing the collection of information.

This agency may not collect this information, and you are not required to complete this form, unless it displays a currently valid OMB control number.

The information requested does not lend itself to confidentiality.

F I G U R E   9.2

RESPA Uniform Settlement Statement (continued)

L. Settlement Charges

		Paid From Borrowers Funds at Settlement	Paid From Seller's Funds at Settlement
700. Total Sales/Broker's Commission based on price $ 115,000.00 @ 6 % = 6,900.00			
Division of Commission (line 700) as follows:			
701. $	to		
702. $	to		
703. Commission paid at Settlement			$ 6,900.00
704.			
800. Items Payable In Connection With Loan			
801. Loan Origination Fee %		$ 920.00	
802. Loan Discount %		1,840.00	
803. Appraisal Fee 250.00 to Swift Appraisal		POC	
804. Credit Report 60.00 to Amce Credit Bureau		POC	
805. Lender's Inspection Fee			
806. Mortgage Insurance Application Fee to			
807. Assumption Fee			
808.			
809.			
810.			
811.			
900. Items Required By Lender To Be Paid In Advance			
901. Interest from 6/16 to 6/30 @$25.556 /day		383.34	
902. Mortgage Insurance Premium for months to			
903. Hazard Insurance Premium for 1 years to Hite Insurance Co.		345.00	
904. years to			
905.			
1000. Reserves Deposited With Lender			
1001. Hazard insurance 2 months@$ 28.75 per month		57.50	
1002. Mortgage insurance months@$ per month			
1003. City property taxes months@$ per month			
1004. County property taxes 7 months@$ 143.75 per month		1,006.25	
1005. Annual assessments months@$ per month			
1006. months@$ per month			
1007. months@$ per month			
1008. months@$ per month			
1100. Title Charges			
1101. Settlement or closing fee to			
1102. Abstract or title search to			
1103. Title examination to			
1104. Title insurance binder to			10.00
1105. Document preparation to			
1106. Notary fees to			
1107. Attorney's fees to		300.00	400.00
(includes above items numbers:			
1108. Title insurance to			540.00
(includes above items numbers:			
1109. Lender's coverage $ 395.00			
1110. Owner's coverage $ 145.00			
1111.			
1112.			
1113.			
1200. Government Recording and Transfer Charges			
1201. Recording fees: Deed $ 20.00 ; Mortgage $ 20.00 ; Releases $ 20.00		40.00	20.00
1202. City/county tax/stamps: Deed $; Mortgage $			
1203. State tax/stamps: Deed $; Mortgage $			115.00
1204. Record 2 documents to clear title			40.00
1205.			
1300. Additional Settlement Charges			
1301. Survey to			175.00
1302. Pest inspection to			85.00
1303.			
1304.			
1305.			
1400. Total Settlement Charges (enter on lines 103, Section J and 502, Section K)		$ 4,892.09	$ 8,285.00

The title company will ask the seller to sign an *affidavit of title*. This is a sworn statement in which the seller assures the title company that since the date of the title examination there have been no judgments, bankruptcies, or divorces involving the seller; no repairs or improvements that have not been paid for; and that he or she is in possession of the premises. Through this affidavit the title company obtains the right to sue the seller if his or her statements in the affidavit prove incorrect.

Checking the Premises

The buyer should inspect the property to determine the interests of any parties in possession. A *survey* is frequently required so that the purchaser will know the location, size, and legal description of the property. The buyer also should make a last-minute inspection before closing to check that the house remains in the condition originally presented and that the seller is leaving any personal property stipulated in the sales contract. This inspection right is often set forth in a clause in the purchase and sale agreement. At closing the seller will sign an affidavit stating that there is at least one functioning smoke alarm and a carbon monoxide detector on the premises.

Homeseller's Tax Exclusion

The IRS (and New York State) allow a homeseller's exclusion from capital gains tax of up to $250,000 ($500,00 for a married couple filing jointly) if the home has been owned and occupied as a principal residence for at least "an aggregate" of 24 months during the five years before the sale. At closing, the homeseller signs a statement that the transaction qualifies for the exclusion, and no report of the sale is due to the IRS. Under certain circumstances, including job transfer, health problems, and death in the family, a prorated portion of the exclusion can be used for a sale after less than two years of occupancy and ownership.

Releasing Existing Liens

When the purchaser pays cash or obtains a new mortgage to purchase the property, the seller's existing mortgage usually is paid in full and released in the public record. To know the exact amount required to pay the existing mortgage, the seller secures a current *payoff statement* from the mortgagee. The same procedure is followed for any other liens that must be released before the buyer takes title.

When the buyer is assuming the seller's existing mortgage loan, the buyer needs to know the exact balance of the loan as of the closing date. The buyer receives a **mortgage reduction certificate** (sometimes referred to as an *estoppel certificate*) from the lender, stating the exact balance due and the last interest payment made.

■ CLOSING IN ESCROW

In the western United States most transactions are closed in escrow, but the system is seldom used in New York.

In an **escrow** closing, a third party coordinates the closing activities. The escrow agent may be an attorney, a title company, a trust company, an escrow company, or the escrow department of a lending institution. Buyer and seller deposit all pertinent documents, money, and other items with the escrow agent. When all conditions of the escrow agreement have been met, the agent pays the purchase price to the seller and records the deed and mortgage (if a new mortgage has been executed by the purchaser). Buyer and seller may never meet.

■ PREPARATION OF CLOSING STATEMENTS

A typical real estate sales transaction involves numerous expenses for both parties in addition to the purchase price. There are a number of property expenses that the seller will have paid in advance or that the buyer will pay in the future. The financial responsibility for these items must be *prorated* (adjusted or divided) between the buyer and seller. In closing a transaction it is customary to account for all these items by preparing a written statement to determine how much money the buyer needs and how much the seller will net after the broker's commission and expenses. There are many different formats of closing, or settlement, statements, but all are designed to achieve the same results.

Closing statements in New York are prepared by the buyer's and seller's attorneys or bank representatives. The broker should, however, be able to give the seller an estimate of sale costs. In addition the buyer must be prepared with the proper amount of money to complete the purchase (in the form of a certified check), and again the broker should be able to assist by making a reasonably accurate estimate.

How the Closing Statement Works

The completion of a **closing statement** involves an accounting of the parties' debits and credits. A **debit** is a charge, an amount that the party being debited owes and must pay at the closing. A **credit** is an amount entered in a person's favor: an amount that the party already has paid, an amount that he or she must be reimbursed for, or an amount the buyer promises to pay in the form of a loan.

To determine the amount the buyer needs at the closing, the buyer's debits are totaled. Any expenses and prorated amounts for items prepaid by the seller are added to the purchase price. Then the buyer's credits are totaled. These would include the earnest money (already paid), the balance of the loan the buyer is obtaining or assuming, and the seller's share of any prorated items that the buyer will pay in the future. Finally, the total of the buyer's credits is subtracted from the total amount the buyer owes (debits) to arrive at the actual amount of cash the buyer must bring to the closing. Usually the buyer brings a bank cashier's check or a certified personal check.

A similar procedure is followed to determine how much money the seller actually will receive. The seller's debits and credits are totaled separately. The credits include the purchase price plus the buyer's share of any prorated items that the seller has prepaid. The seller's debits include expenses, the seller's share of prorated items to be paid later by the buyer, and the balance of any mortgage loan or other lien that the seller is paying off. Finally the total of the seller's charges is subtracted from the total credits to arrive at the amount the seller will receive. The closing statement represents a **reconciliation** of each party's financial obligations.

Expenses

In addition to the sales price, taxes, interest, and the like, a number of other expenses and charges, including the following items, may be involved in a real estate transaction.

Broker's commission.   The broker's commission is paid by the seller when the broker is the seller's agent. When the buyer has employed the broker, either party may pay the commission, according to agreement.

Attorney's fees.   If either party's attorney will be paid from the closing proceeds, that party will be charged with the expense in the closing statement.

Recording expenses.   Charges for recording documents vary from one county to another. A county might charge $5.50 for recording a document plus $3.00 per page. Thus a single-page deed would cost $8.50 to record, while the charge for a four-page mortgage would be $17.50.

The seller usually pays recording charges (filing fees) needed to clear all defects and furnish the purchaser with clear title. Items usually charged to the seller include the recording of satisfaction of mortgages, quitclaim deeds, affidavits, and satisfaction of mechanic's lien claims. Items usually charged to the purchaser include recording the deed and any new mortgage.

Transfer tax.   Any *New York State* conveyance is taxed at a rate of $2 per $500 or fraction thereof of the consideration paid minus the amount of any mortgage being assumed. (Those who inspect old deeds to estimate sales prices should know that before 1983 the rate was $.55 per $500.) The transfer tax must be paid, usually by the seller, when the deed is recorded. Local taxes also may be due. Shares in a cooperative are taxed at the same rate.

New York City levies a transfer tax of 1 percent on sales of less than $500,000 on one to three-family dwellings. Other transfers require payment of a higher city tax. The tax is paid by the grantor when the deed is recorded.

Personal property transferred with the real estate (drapes, for example) is covered by a bill of sale and is subject not to transfer tax but to state sales tax unless it is included in the sale of the real estate without additional consideration.

State mortgage tax.   New York State imposes a tax of $.75 for each $100 or fraction thereof for every mortgage recorded within the state, and in many counties there is an additional $.25 for each $100 or fraction thereof. The first $10,000 of a mortgage for any one or two-family residence is taxed lower, at a rate of $.50 for each $100. If the mortgage covers property improved by a structure with six or fewer cooking units, the mortgagee must pay a portion of the mortgage tax— $.25 for each $100 or fraction thereof. Private lenders do not pay the $.25 portion; lending institutions do. When a land contract is recorded, mortgage tax is due on the amount borrowed. Local mortgage taxes also may be imposed. In counties that levy additional tax, none is due on the first $10,000 of the loan for a one or two-family residence.

Title expenses.   The responsibility for title expenses varies according to the contract, which usually follows local custom. If the buyer's attorney inspects the evidence or if the buyer purchases title insurance policies, the buyer is charged for these expenses. In some situations the title or abstract company makes two searches of the public records: the first shows the status of the seller's title on the date of the sales contract or at some time before closing, and the second continues through the date on which the purchaser's deed is recorded. In some areas the seller pays for the initial search and the purchaser pays for the redate charge. (There often is no redate charge if the closing occurs within six months of the initial search.) In other areas it is customary that the buyer pay for the full search.

Loan fees.   When the purchaser is securing a mortgage to finance the purchase, the lender (mortgage company) usually charges a service charge or an origination fee. The fee is a flat charge and is usually paid by the purchaser at the time the transaction is closed. The buyer also may be charged an assumption fee for assuming the seller's financing and in some cases may pay discount points. As discussed in Chapter 10, the seller also may be charged discount points.

Tax reserves and insurance reserves (escrows).   A *reserve* is a sum of money set aside to be used later for a particular purpose. The mortgage lender usually requires that the borrower establish and maintain a reserve so that there will be sufficient funds to pay property taxes and renew hazard insurance when these items become due. To set up the reserve, the borrower makes a lump-sum payment to the lender when the mortgage money is paid out (usually at the time of closing). After that the borrower pays into the escrow account an amount equal to one month's portion of the *estimated* general tax and insurance premium as part of the monthly PITI payment to the mortgage company.

Additional fees.   An FHA borrower owes a lump sum for prepayment of the mortgage insurance premium if it is not being financed as part of the loan. A VA mortgagor pays a fee directly to the VA at closing. If a conventional loan carries private mortgage insurance, the buyer prepays one year's insurance premium at closing.

Appraisal fees.   When the buyer obtains a mortgage, the lender usually requires an appraisal, which the buyer pays for.

Survey fees.   A purchaser who obtains new mortgage financing customarily pays the survey fees. In some cases the sales contract may require that the seller furnish a survey.

Prorations

Most closings involve the dividing of financial responsibility between the buyer and seller for items such as loan interest on an assumed mortgage, taxes, rents, fuel oil, and utility bills. These allowances are called **prorations** or **adjustments.** Prorations are necessary to ensure that expenses are divided fairly between the seller and the buyer. For example, when the coming year's property taxes have been paid in advance, the seller is entitled to partial reimbursement at the closing. If the buyer assumes the seller's existing mortgage, the seller usually owes the buyer a credit for accrued interest through the date of closing.

Accrued items are owed by the seller but eventually will be paid by the buyer. The seller therefore gives the buyer credit for these items at closing. Because interest usually is paid in *arrears* (the opposite of in *advance*), each payment covers interest for the preceding month. At a midmonth closing the seller who has not made the current month's payment would owe six weeks' back interest on a mortgage.

Prepaid items are items to be prorated (such as taxes or fuel oil left in the tank) that have been paid for by the seller but not fully earned (not fully used up). They are therefore credits to the seller.

General rules for prorating.   The rules or customs governing the computation of prorations for the closing of a real estate sale vary:

- In New York it is generally provided that the buyer owns the property on the closing date. In practice, however, either buyer or seller may be charged with that day's expenses.
- Mortgage interest, real estate taxes, water bills, and similar expenses are computed in some areas by using *360 days in a year and 30 days in a month.* In other areas prorations are computed using the actual number of days in the calendar month of closing.
- *Special assessments* for municipal improvements such as sewers, water mains, or streets are usually paid in annual installments over several years. Sellers are sometimes required to pay off special assessments entirely. In other cases buyers may agree to assume future installments.
- *Rents* are usually adjusted on the basis of the actual number of days in the month of closing. The buyer often will agree in the contract or by a separate letter to collect any uncollected rents for the current month and remit a share to the seller.
- *Security deposits* generally are transferred by the seller to the buyer; the tenant must be notified of the transfer of deposit.

Accounting for Credits and Charges

Items accounted for in the closing statement fall into two general categories: (1) prorations or other amounts due to either the buyer or seller (credit to) and paid for by the other party (debit to) and (2) expenses or items paid by the seller or buyer (debit only).

Items Credited to Buyer (debited to seller)	Items Credited to Seller (debited to buyer)
1. Buyer's earnest money*	1. Sale price*
2. Unpaid principal balance of outstanding mortgage being assumed by buyer*	2. Fuel oil on hand, usually figured at current market price
3. Interest on existing assumed mortgage not yet paid (accrued)	3. Insurance and tax reserve (if any) when mortgage is being assumed by buyer
4. Portion of current rent collected in advance	4. Refund to seller of prepaid water charge or similar expenses
5. Purchase-money mortgage	5. Portion of general real estate tax paid in advance
6. Unpaid water bills	

Items with an asterisk (*) are not prorated; they are entered in full as listed. The *buyer's earnest money*, while credited to the buyer, *is not usually debited to the seller.* The buyer receives a credit because he or she has already paid that amount toward the purchase price. Under the usual sales contract the money is held by the broker or attorney in escrow until the settlement, when it will be included as part of the total amount due the seller. If the seller is paying off an existing loan and the buyer is obtaining a new one, these two items are accounted for with a debit only to the seller for the amount of the payoff and a credit only to the buyer for the amount of the new loan.

Accounting for expenses.   Expenses paid out of the closing proceeds are usually debited only to the party making the payment.

■ THE ARITHMETIC OF PRORATION

There are three basic methods of calculating prorations:

1. The yearly charge is divided by a 360-day year or 12 months of 30 days each.
2. The monthly charge *is divided by the actual number of days in the month of closing* to determine the amount.
3. The yearly charge *is divided by 365* to determine the daily charge. Then the actual number of days in the proration period is determined, and this number is multiplied by the daily charge.

In some cases when a sale is closed on the 15th of the month, the half-month charge is computed simply by dividing the monthly charge by two.

The final proration figure will vary slightly, depending on which computation method is used.

■ SAMPLE CLOSING STATEMENTS

The closing statement lists sales price, earnest money deposit, and all adjustments and prorations between buyer and seller. Figure 9.3 shows a buyer's closing statement, and Figure 9.4 shows a seller's closing statement for the same transaction. The property is being purchased for $89,500, with $49,500 down and the seller taking back a mortgage for $40,000. Closing takes place on August 12.

Prorations

The buyer is taking over a house on which taxes have been paid, in one case until the end of the year. The buyer therefore will reimburse the seller for the time in which the buyer will be living in a tax-paid house. Specifically, the seller has paid city and school taxes of $1,176.35 for the tax year that started July 1 and will receive a large portion of that back as a credit from the buyer. County taxes of $309.06 were paid January 1 for the year ahead, so the buyer will also credit the seller for the four months and 18 days remaining in the year, an adjustment of $118.52.

The buyer owes the seller (total seller's credits) the purchase price plus unearned taxes, for a total of $90,657.68. Toward this sum the buyer receives credit for an earnest money deposit of $500 in a broker's escrow account. (The seller's attorney and the broker will take this sum into consideration later when the commission is paid.) The buyer also receives credit for the $40,000 bond and mortgage given to the seller at closing. The buyer therefore gives the seller cash (or a certified check) for the remaining sum, $50,157.68.

The upper half of the closing statement accounts for the transaction between buyer and seller; the lower part details each one's individual expenses. The buyer pays to record the deed and mortgage, part of the mortgage tax, and the buyer's attorney's fee.

F I G U R E   9.3

Buyer's Closing Statement

SELLER'S CREDITS

Sale Price _____ $ 89,500.00

ADJUSTMENT OF TAXES

School Tax 7/1   to 6/30   Amount $ 1176.35 Adj. 10 mos. 18 days $ 1,039.16

City School Tax 7/1/   to 6/30/   Amount $_____ Adj.____ mos.____ days $_____

County Tax 19____   Amount $ 309.06 Adj. 4 mos. 18 days $ 118.52

Village Tax 6/1/   to 5/31/   Amount $____ Adj.____ mos.____ days $_____

City Tax Embellishments   Amount $_____ Adj.____ mos.____ days $_____

Total Seller's Credits $ 90,657.68

PURCHASER'S CREDITS

Deposit with ___Nothnagle___ $ 500.00

~~(Assumed)~~ (New) Mortgage with Seller $480.07 p/m $ 40,000.00

beg. 9-12 , 12% int. 15 yrs. $_____

$_____

$_____

$_____

$_____

$_____

$_____

Total Purchaser's Credits $ 40,500.00

Cash ~~(Rec'd)~~ (Paid) at Closing $ 50,157.68

EXPENSES OF PURCHASER		EXPENSES OF SELLER	
Mortgage Tax	$ 275.00	Title Search Fee	$_____
Recording Mortgage	$ 11.00	Transfer Tax on Deed	$_____
Recording Deed	$ 12.00	Filing of Gains Tax Affidavit	$_____
		Discharge Recording Fee	$_____
ESCROWS:		Mortgage Tax	$_____
____ mos. insurance $_____		Surveyor's Fees	$_____
____ mos. school tax $_____		Points	$_____
____ mos. county tax $_____		Mortgage Payoff	$_____
____ mos. village tax $_____		Real Estate Commission	$_____
PMI FHA Insurance $_____		Water Escrow	$_____
Total: $_____			$_____
Bank Attorney Fee	$_____		$_____
Points	$_____		$_____
Title Insurance	$_____	Legal Fee	$_____
Interest	$_____	Total	$_____
	$_____		
	$_____	Cash Received:	$
	$_____	Less Seller's Expenses:	$
Legal Fee	$ 500.00	Net Proceeds:	$
Total	$ 798.00		

Cash paid to Seller: $ 50,157.68

Plus Purchaser's Expenses: $ 798.00

Total Disbursed: $ 50,955.68

F I G U R E   9.4

Seller's Closing Statement

SELLER'S CREDITS

Sale Price _____ $ 89,500.00

ADJUSTMENT OF TAXES

School Tax 7/1 to 6/30   Amount $ 1176.35   Adj. 10 mos. 18 days $ 1,039.16

City/School Tax 7/1/ to 6/30/   Amount $_____ Adj.____ mos.____days $_____

County Tax 19____   Amount $ 309.06   Adj. 4 mos. 18 days $ 118.52

Village Tax 6/1/ to 5/31/   Amount $_____ Adj.____ mos.____days $_____

City Tax Embellishments   Amount $_____ Adj.____ mos.____days $_____

Total Seller's Credits $ 90,657.68

PURCHASER'S CREDITS

Deposit with Nothnagle $ 500.00

(Assumed) (New) Mortgage with seller $ 40,000.00

12% interest, 15 years, payments $_____

$ 480.07, beginning 9/12 $_____

$_____

$_____

$_____

Total Purchaser's Credits $ 40,500.00

Cash (Rec'd) (Paid) at Closing $ 50,157.68

EXPENSES OF PURCHASER		EXPENSES OF SELLER	
Mortgage Tax .... $_____		Title Search Fee .... $ 220.00	
Recording Mortgage............... $_____		Transfer Tax on Deed ...... $ 358.00	
Recording Deed................... $_____		Filing of Gains Tax Affidavit .. $ 1.00	
		Discharge Recording Fee ...... $_____	
ESCROWS:		Mortgage Tax .... $ 100.00	
___ mos. insurance $ _____		Surveyor's Fees .... $_____	
___ mos. school tax $ _____		Points .... $_____	
___ mos. county tax $ _____		Mortgage Payoff .... $_____	
___ mos. village tax $ _____		Real Estate Commission ...... $ 4870.00	
PMI/FHA Insurance$ _____		Water Escrow .... $_____	
Total: $_____		...........school tax $ 1,182.14	
Bank Attorney Fee................. $_____		Federal express .... $ 14.00	
Points............... $_____		.... $_____	
Title Insurance.................... $_____		.... $_____	
Interest........................ $_____		Legal Fee.................. $ 550.00	
.... $_____		Total.................... $ 7,295.14	
.... $_____			
.... $_____		Cash Received: $ 50,157.68	
Legal Fee....................... $_____		Less Seller's Expenses: $ 7,295.14	
Total.......................... $_____		Net Proceeds: $ 42,862.54	
Cash paid to Seller: $			
Plus Purchaser's Expenses: $_____			
Total Disbursed: $			

The seller's expenses include last-minute payment of the school tax (plus a small late-payment penalty), for which the seller is largely reimbursed. Also paid by the seller is the required lender's share of the mortgage tax (seller/lender happens to be a corporation). The seller pays the real estate commission, legal costs of proving title, transfer tax, and incidental out-of-pocket expenses incurred by the seller's attorney, who also deducts his or her own fee and turns over the net proceeds to the seller.

■ SUMMARY

The public records give constructive notice to the world of different parties' interests in real estate. Possession of real estate gives notice of possible rights of the person in possession. Actual notice refers to whatever one actually knows; constructive notice is what one could find out by investigating.

Title evidence shows whether a seller is conveying marketable title, one so free from defects that the buyer can be assured title will not be challenged. Four forms of title evidence may be used throughout the United States: (1) abstract of title and lawyer's opinion; (2) owner's title insurance policy; (3) Torrens certificate; and (4) certificate of title. A deed proves that a previous grantor transferred his or her interest but does not prove the grantor actually had any interest in the property.

At closing a buyer may be required to show hazard insurance coverage to a lender. A standard homeowner's insurance policy covers fire, theft, and liability and may be extended to cover less common risks. Insurance covering only personal property is available to those in apartments and condominiums. For some property located in floodplains, flood insurance is needed to obtain a federally related mortgage loan. Many homeowner's policies contain a coinsurance clause requiring that the policyholder insure for at least 80 percent of the replacement cost of the house. Otherwise the policyholder may not be reimbursed for full repair costs in case of loss.

The federal Real Estate Settlement Procedures Act (RESPA) requires disclosure of all settlement costs when a residential real estate purchase is financed by a federally related loan. RESPA requires that lenders use a Uniform Settlement Statement.

The actual amount paid by the buyer at closing is computed by preparing a closing statement. This lists the sales price, earnest money deposit, and all adjustments and prorations between buyer and seller.

QUESTIONS

1. Public records may be inspected by
   a. anyone.
   b. anyone, but only after obtaining permission under the Freedom of Information Act.
   c. New York attorneys and abstractors only.
   d. attorneys, abstractors, and real estate licensees only.

2. An instrument affecting title to a parcel of real estate gives constructive notice to the world when filed with the
   a. county clerk.
   b. city clerk.
   c. Secretary of State.
   d. title company.

3. Barbara Barnes checked the public records. She found that the seller was the grantee in the last recorded deed and that no mortgage was on record against the property. She may assume that
   a. all taxes are paid and no judgments are outstanding.
   b. the seller has good title.
   c. the seller did not mortgage the property.
   d. no one else is occupying the property.

4. An abstractor inspects the county records for documents affecting title and then
   a. writes a brief history of the title.
   b. insures the condition of the title.
   c. personally inspects the property.
   d. issues a certificate of title.

5. If the broker holds the buyer's earnest money in a separate trust account, when does the seller usually receive it?
   a. At the time the offer is accepted
   b. After approval by the buyer's and seller's attorneys
   c. When the buyer receives a firm mortgage commitment
   d. When the property is actually transferred

6. Last year Maureen O'Brien gave a house in Water-town, valued at $110,000, to her son Richard. Richard assumed an existing $30,000 mortgage on the property. Transfer tax due on the gift was
   a. $220.
   b. $320.
   c. $440.
   d. nothing.

7. Ann needs to know how much her parents paid for the Elmira house they bought from a builder in 1954. She finds tax stamps on their old deed totaling $22.55. She can conclude that they paid roughly
   a. $6,000.
   b. $20,500.
   c. $22,550.
   d. $60,000.

8. Last summer Douglas Maloof sold his home in Schenectady to the Auerbachs for $160,000. The Auerbachs assumed his existing mortgage in the amount of $76,578. State transfer tax on the sale came to approximately
   a. $91.85.
   b. $176.
   c. $334.
   d. $640.

9. Susan Johnson, a Manhattan resident, purchases farmland in Clinton County as an investment. The deed she receives should
   a. not be recorded.
   b. be recorded in Manhattan.
   c. be recorded in Clinton County.
   d. be recorded in both the borough of Manhattan and Clinton County.

10. The principle of *caveat emptor* states that if the purchaser buys a faulty title, responsibility for the problem lies with the
   a. buyer.
   b. seller.
   c. broker.
   d. abstractor.

11. Which of the following is *not* acceptable proof of title?
   a. Torrens certificate
   b. Title insurance policy
   c. Abstract with lawyer's opinion
   d. Deed signed by last seller

12. Mortgagee title policies protect which parties against loss?

    a. Buyers only
    b. Sellers only
    c. Buyers and sellers only
    d. Lenders only

13. At closing the seller of a single home must give the buyer an affidavit that the house has

    a. hazard insurance.
    b. title insurance.
    c. a working smoke alarm.
    d. insulation.

14. Robert Dunn is selling a two-family dwelling. The buyer's lending institution is likely to require

    a. proof of hazard insurance.
    b. a certificate of occupancy.
    c. title insurance.
    d. All of the above

15. The terms *basic, broad* and *comprehensive* describe types of

    a. title insurance.
    b. mortgage documents.
    c. homeowner's insurance.
    d. attorney's services.

16. A coinsurance clause can penalize the homeowner who does not carry insurance for at least what part of replacement cost?

    a. 50 percent
    b. 80 percent
    c. 100 percent
    d. 120 percent

17. Flood insurance may be required before mortgaging property if it is

    a. a multiple dwelling.
    b. in a flood-prone area on a special map.
    c. owned by the FHA or the VA.
    d. going to have title insurance.

18. The RESPA Uniform Settlement Statement must be used for

    a. every real estate closing.
    b. transactions financed by FHA and VA only.
    c. residential transactions financed by federally related loans.
    d. all transactions involving commercial property.

19. A mortgage reduction certificate is issued by a(n)

    a. lending institution.
    b. attorney.
    c. abstract company.
    d. grantor.

20. Earnest money left on deposit with the broker or lawyer is a

    a. credit to the seller.
    b. credit to the buyer.
    c. debit to the seller.
    d. debit to the buyer.

21. The buyers are assuming a mortgage loan that had a principal balance of $27,496 as of June 1. Interest is at 12 percent, payable in arrears. The June payment has not been made, and closing is on June 15. Which of the following is true as to the interest adjustment?

    a. Credit buyer $274.96; debit seller $274.95.
    b. Credit buyer $412.44; debit seller $412.44.
    c. Credit seller $137.48; debit buyer $137.48.
    d. No adjustment is necessary.

22. The calendar year's taxes amount to $1,800 and were paid ahead on January 1. If closing is set for June 15, which of the following is true?

    a. Credit seller $825; debit buyer $975.
    b. Credit seller $1,800; debit buyer $825.
    c. Credit buyer $975; debit seller $975.
    d. Credit seller $975; debit buyer $975.

23. Which of the following items is usually not adjusted between buyer and seller?

    a. Recording charges
    b. Property taxes
    c. Rents
    d. Interest on assumed mortgage

24. The seller collected June rent of $800 from the tenant in the upstairs apartment. At the closing on June 15

    a. credit buyer $400; debit seller $400.
    b. credit buyer $400; credit seller $400.
    c. debit buyer $400; credit seller $400.
    d. credit buyer $800; no debit to seller.

25. The O'Briens have been told to bring a cashier's check for the amount they will need to close on the house they're buying. Where can they get an estimate of money needed?

    a. The public records
    b. An abstractor
    c. The broker
    d. Their insurance agent

10

MORTGAGES

Bill and Maria want to buy a home together. They have never purchased a home before, but they read the real estate section of their local newspaper regularly. Even though they have read several articles about home mortgages, they find the many types of loans and rates confusing. The advice they get from relatives and friends is often conflicting and not helpful. What should they do?

Most homebuyers report that they received guidance from a broker or salesperson in obtaining their mortgages. Keeping track of the ever-changing mortgage market is one of the biggest challenges for real estate licensees.

■ KEY TERMS

acceleration clause

adjustable rate mortgatge (ARM)

alienation clause

amortized loan

annual percentage rate (APR)

balloon payment

biweekly mortgage

bond

buydown

default

deficiency judgment

down payment

equity

estoppel certificate

foreclosure

grace period

interest

lien theory

loan servicing

loan-to-value ratio

mortgage

mortgage bankers

mortgage broker

mortgagee

mortgagor

note

PITI

points

prepayment premium (penalty)

primary mortgage market

principal

private mortgage insurance (PMI)

purchase-money mortgage

reduction certificate

satisfaction of mortgage

Sonny Mae (SONYMA)

straight (term) loan

subject to a mortgage

term

title theory

usury

Note

NOTE

April 12 , 20 00   Albany , New York
[City]   [State]

222 Kelly Avenue, Albany, New York 12203
[Property Address]

1. BORROWER'S PROMISE TO PAY

In return for a loan that I have received, I promise to pay U.S. $ 79,000.00 (this amount is called "principal"), plus interest, to the order of the Lender. The Lender is First City Savings and Loan Association of Albany, New York I understand that the Lender may transfer this Note. The Lender or anyone who takes this Note by transfer and who is entitled to receive payments under this Note is called the "Note Holder."

2. INTEREST

Interest will be charged on unpaid principal until the full amount of principal has been paid. I will pay interest at a yearly rate of 9.5 %.

The interest rate required by this Section 2 is the rate I will pay both before and after any default described in Section 6(B) of this Note.

3. PAYMENTS

(A) Time and Place of Payments

I will pay principal and interest by making payments every month.

I will make my monthly payments on the 1st day of each month beginning on May 1 , 20 00. I will make these payments every month until I have paid all of the principal and interest and any other charges described below that I may owe under this Note. My monthly payments will be applied to interest before principal. If, on April 1, 2030 , I still owe amounts under this Note, I will pay those amounts in full on that date, which is called the "maturity date."

I will make my monthly payments at 130 North LaSalle Street, Albany, New York or at a different place if required by the Note Holder.

(B) Amount of Monthly Payments

My monthly payment will be in the amount of U.S. $ 664.29

4. BORROWER'S RIGHT TO PREPAY

I have the right to make payments of principal at any time before they are due. A payment of principal only is known as a "prepayment." When I make a prepayment, I will tell the Note Holder in writing that I am doing so.

I may make a full prepayment or partial prepayments without paying any prepayment charge. The Note Holder will use all of my prepayments to reduce the amount of principal that I owe under this Note. If I make a partial

■ MORTGAGE DEFINED

A **mortgage** is a pledge of property given by a borrower as security for a loan. Some states recognize the lender as the owner of mortgaged land. These states are called **title theory** states. Connecticut, for example, is a title theory state.

New York, however, interprets a mortgage purely as a lien on real property and is called a **lien theory** state. If a mortgagor (borrower) defaults, the lender can foreclose the lien (generally through a court action), offer the property for sale, and apply the funds received from the sale to reduce or pay off the debt.

Loan Instruments

When property is to be mortgaged, the owner must execute, or sign, two separate instruments (sometimes combined into one form):

1. A **note** or **bond,** which is a *personal promise* to repay a loan. It acts as evidence of the promise to repay the debt. The promissory note signed by a borrower (known as the *maker* or *payer*) states the amount of the debt, the time and method of payment, and the rate of interest. Figure 10.1 is an example of a note commonly used in some areas of New York State.

F I G U R E   10.1

Note (continued)

prepayment, there will be no changes in the due date or in the amount of my monthly payment unless the Note Holder agrees in writing to those changes.

5. LOAN CHARGES

If a law, which applies to this loan and which sets maximum loan charges, is finally interpreted so that the interest or other loan charges collected or to be collected in connection with this loan exceed the permitted limits, then: (i) any such loan charge shall be reduced by the amount necessary to reduce the charge to the permitted limit; and (ii) any sums already collected from me which exceeded permitted limits will be refunded to me. The Note Holder may choose to make this refund by reducing the principal I owe under this Note or by making a direct payment to me. If a refund reduces principal, the reduction will be treated as a partial prepayment.

6. BORROWER'S FAILURE TO PAY AS REQUIRED

(A) Late Charge for Overdue Payments

If the Note Holder has not received the full amount of any monthly payment by the end of .....fifteen.... calendar days after the date it is due, I will pay a late charge to the Note Holder. The amount of the charge will be ....5..% of my overdue payment of principal and interest. I will pay this late charge promptly but only once on each late payment.

(B) Default

If I do not pay the full amount of each monthly payment on the date it is due, I will be in default.

(C) Notice of Default

If I am in default, the Note Holder may send me a written notice telling me that if I do not pay the overdue amount by a certain date, the Note Holder may require me to pay immediately the full amount of principal which has not been paid and all the interest that I owe on that amount. That date must be at least 30 days after the date on which the notice is delivered or mailed to me.

(D) No Waiver By Note Holder

Even if, at a time when I am in default, the Note Holder does not require me to pay immediately in full as described above, the Note Holder will still have the right to do so if I am in default at a later time.

(E) Payment of Note Holder's Costs and Expenses

If the Note Holder has required me to pay immediately in full as described above, the Note Holder will have the right to be paid back by me for all of its costs and expenses in enforcing this Note to the extent not prohibited by applicable law. Those expenses include, for example, reasonable attorneys' fees.

7. GIVING OF NOTICES

Unless applicable law requires a different method, any notice that must be given to me under this Note will be given by delivering it or by mailing it by first class mail to me at the Property Address above or at a different address if I give the Note Holder a notice of my different address.

Any notice that must be given to the Note Holder under this Note will be given by mailing it by first class mail to the Note Holder at the address stated in Section 3(A) above or at a different address if I am given a notice of that different address.

MULTISTATE FIXED RATE NOTE—Single Family—**FNMA/FHLMC UNIFORM INSTRUMENT**   Form 3200 12/83

2. A mortgage, which is a pledge of property given by a borrower as security for a loan. The mortgage creates a lien as security for the debt. The **mortgagor** is the one who does the mortgaging, pledging real estate as security for a loan. The **mortgagee** accepts, takes and holds the mortgage, and gives money in exchange. To help in keeping the terms straight, it is useful to note that *bOrrOwer*, like *mOrtgagOr*, contains two *O*s; *lEndEr* and *mortgagEE* each contain two *E*s.

The mortgage document refers to the terms of the note and clearly establishes that the land is security for the debt. It identifies the lender as well as the borrower and includes an accurate legal description of the property. It should be signed by all owners of the property. It also sets forth the obligations of the borrower and the rights of the lender.

In some areas of the country, and in certain situations, lenders prefer to use an instrument known as a *trust deed*, or *deed of trust*, rather than a mortgage. A trust deed conveys the real estate as security for the loan to a third party, called the *trustee*. In case of default the lender with a trust deed can gain possession of the property more promptly and more simply than can a lender who forecloses on a mortgage.

Duties of the Mortgagor

The borrower's obligations usually include the following:

- Paying the debt as promised in the note
- Paying all real estate taxes on the property
- Maintaining adequate hazard insurance to protect the lender if the property is destroyed or damaged
- Obtaining the lender's authorization before making any major alterations
- Maintaining the property in good repair at all times

Failure to meet any of these obligations can result in a borrower's **default.** When this happens, the mortgage usually provides a **grace period** (30 days, for example) during which the borrower can meet the obligation and cure the default. If he or she does not do so, the lender has the right to foreclose the mortgage and collect on the note. The most frequent cause of default is the borrower's failure to pay monthly installments.

Most mortgages contain a *late-payment clause*. For one-family to six-family owner-occupied residences, New York allows a late-payment penalty 15 days after payment is due. An individual may charge a 2 percent penalty; a lending institution may charge 4 percent on government-backed mortgages, 5 percent on conventional loans.

Provisions for Default

A mortgage may include an **acceleration clause** to assist the lender in a foreclosure. If a borrower defaults, the lender has the right to accelerate the debt—to declare the *entire* debt due and owing *immediately*.

Other clauses in a mortgage enable the lender to take care of the property in the event of the borrower's negligence or default. If the borrower does not pay taxes or insurance premiums or make necessary repairs on the property, for example, the lender may step in and do so to protect its security. Any money advanced by the lender to cure such defaults is either added to the unpaid debt or declared immediately due and owing from the borrower.

Foreclosure

When a borrower defaults in making payments or in fulfilling any of the obligations set forth in the mortgage, the lender can enforce its rights through a **foreclosure,** with the property sold at public auction.

There are two general types of foreclosure proceedings—judicial and strict foreclosure. *Strict foreclosure*, in which the lender may regain title to the property, is rarely used. *Judicial foreclosure* is the procedure followed in most cases. On a borrower's default the lender may declare the whole debt immediately due and payable and ask the court to order a public sale, which is advertised. The real estate is sold to the highest bidder. The borrower has the right to redeem the property *until the moment of sale* by producing full payment including back interest and costs incurred in the foreclosure proceedings. In New York the defaulting borrower does not have the right to redeem the property after the foreclosure sale. The buyer at a foreclosure sale receives a deed signed by a court-appointed referee. The buyer receives the property free of the mortgage and all junior liens but subject to any prior liens. (Any unpaid property taxes must be paid out of the proceeds of the sale.)

Deed in lieu of foreclosure.   An alternative to foreclosure is for the lender to accept a *deed in lieu of foreclosure* from the borrower. This is sometimes known as a *friendly foreclosure* because it is by agreement rather than by civil action. The major disadvantage is that the mortgagee takes the real estate subject to all junior liens, whereas foreclosure eliminates all such liens. In addition, the Internal Revenue Service considers the amount of debt that was forgiven as taxable income to the borrower.

Deficiency judgment.   If a foreclosure sale does not produce sufficient cash to pay the loan balance in full after deducting expenses and unpaid interest, the mortgagee may be entitled to seek a *personal judgment* against the signer of the note for the unpaid balance. Such a judgment is called a **deficiency judgment.** It may be obtained against the original borrower and any later owners of the property who assumed the debt by written agreement. If, on the other hand, there are any surplus proceeds from the foreclosure sale after the debt is paid off and expenses and subordinate liens are deducted, they are paid to the borrower.

Sale of Property That Is Mortgaged

Anyone who purchases real estate and takes over the mortgage presently on it may take the property *subject to the mortgage* or may assume the seller's mortgage and *agree to pay* the debt. This technical distinction becomes important if the buyer later defaults and the mortgage is foreclosed.

When property is sold **subject to a mortgage,** the purchaser is not personally obligated to pay the debt in full. The new owner has bought the real estate knowing that he or she should make the loan payments or risk losing the property through a foreclosure sale. If a foreclosure sale did not pay off the entire debt, however, the new owner would not be personally liable for the shortfall.

In contrast, when the new owner not only purchases the property subject to the mortgage but *assumes and agrees to pay the debt* (signs the note or bond), he or she becomes personally responsible. If the mortgage is foreclosed and the court sale does not bring enough to pay the debt in full, a deficiency judgment against both the assumer and the original borrower can be obtained for the unpaid balance.

The divorcing spouse who signs off ownership of a house is still personally responsible for any mortgage, even though no longer a part owner. Only the lender can release a borrower from liability.

When a mortgage is being assumed or paid off early, the borrower requires a statement from the mortgagee detailing the amount currently due. This **reduction certificate** is often referred to as an **estoppel certificate.**

Alienation clause. Real estate lenders frequently wish to prevent future purchasers of property from assuming the existing loans. For this reason most lenders include an **alienation clause** (also known as a *resale clause* or *due-on-sale clause*) in the note. An alienation clause provides that on the sale of the property, the lender has the choice of either declaring the entire debt immediately due or permitting the buyer to assume the loan.

In New York State any mortgage is assumable unless the document contains a specific alienation clause.

Assignment of the mortgage. Sometimes the holder of the bond and mortgage wants to raise immediate cash by selling it (usually at a discount) to an investor. *It may be sold (assigned) to a third party, or assignee.* (It is a negotiable instrument.) An estoppel certificate signed by the borrower will verify the amount owed and interest rate.

Recording of the Mortgage

The mortgage document must be recorded in the recorder's office of the county in which the real estate is located. This gives notice to the world of the borrower's obligations and establishes the lien's priority over future mortgages or other liens.

First and second mortgages. Mortgages and other liens normally have priority in the order in which they have been recorded. A mortgage on land that has no prior mortgage lien on it is a *first mortgage*. When the owner of this land later places another mortgage for additional funds, the new mortgage becomes a *second mortgage*, or *junior lien*, when recorded. In recent years, the term *home equity loan* or *line of credit* is used for what is really a second mortgage.

The first mortgage has first claim to the value of the land pledged as security. The priority of mortgage liens may be changed by the execution of a *subordination agreement* if the first lender agrees to yield first place to the second lender.

Satisfaction of the Mortgage Lien

When all payments have been made and the note is paid in full, the mortgagor wants the public record to show that the debt has been paid and the lien satisfied. The lender is required to execute a *release of mortgage*, or *satisfaction of mortgage*.

This satisfaction should be entered in the public records to show that the mortgage lien has been removed from the property. According to New York law, financial institutions must file a satisfaction of mortgage within 45 days of a request to do so and provide a copy to the mortgagor. Penalties can be imposed for noncompliance, and after a 90-day period the mortgagor may file an affidavit with the recording officer that shows the lien has been satisfied.

■ TYPES OF MORTGAGES

Mortgages may be conventional or sponsored by a government agency, such as the Federal Housing Administration (FHA) or the Department of Veterans Affairs (VA). However, for many different types of mortgages, the source of the financing is the same.

Primary Sources of Real Estate Financing

Funds used to finance the purchase of real estate come from a variety of sources that make up the **primary mortgage market**—lenders who supply funds directly to real estate borrowers. Some lenders then keep the loans in their own portfolios, whereas others later sell them to other investors in the *secondary mortgage market* (discussed more fully in Chapter 11.).

Today most mortgage borrowers begin by browsing mortgage providers on the Internet, on Web sites like *lendingtree.com* and *eloan.com.*

Institutional lenders.   Most of the loans made to finance real estate purchases are obtained from financial institutions designed to hold individuals' savings. Institutional lenders include savings associations ("thrifts"), commercial banks, and savings banks.

Credit unions.   Credit unions are cooperative organizations whose members place money in savings accounts. In the past most made only short-term consumer and home-improvement loans, but in recent years they have been branching out into mortgage loans for their own members.

Insurance companies.   Amassing large sums of money from the premiums paid by policyholders, insurance companies invest much of it in real estate loans, most often large, long-term loans on commercial and industrial properties. They also purchase large blocks of FHA-insured and VA-guaranteed loans on the secondary mortgage market.

Mortgage banking companies.   **Mortgage bankers** are not thrift institutions and offer neither checking nor savings accounts. They are licensed by the New York Banking Department. Mortgage bankers make real estate loans that later may be sold to investors (with the mortgage company receiving a fee if it continues to service the loans). Mortgage bankers originate a large percentage of all home loans. They are not mortgage *brokers*. Mortgage bankers must have a net worth of at least $250,000 and an existing line of credit of at least $1 million from a credit facility approved by the Superintendent of Banks. They must file a $50,000 surety bond with the Superintendent of Banks or establish a trust fund in the same amount that can be used to reimburse customers if it is determined that the mortgage banker has charged improper fees.

Mortgage brokers. Residential **mortgage brokers** act as intermediaries between lenders and borrowers, bringing lenders and borrowers together. They are registered with the state banking department. They charge a fee, often of the borrower, for their services. The Superintendent of Banks may require that a mortgage broker obtain a surety bond or establish a trust fund in the amount of $25,000. They must prove a certain amount of experience in mortgage financing when they register.

The State of New York Mortgage Agency. Sonny Mae (SONYMA) provides lower-interest loans for specific purposes in specific locations. Loans with low down payments are made through local lending institutions to first-time home buyers. Income and home price limits vary from one region to another but are usually in the moderate category. In designated target areas, higher income limits apply, and the purchaser need not be a first-time buyer. The program varies from time to time; information is available by mail from SONYMA, 260 Madison Avenue, New York, NY 10016, or by phone at 1-800-382-HOME (4663). The Web page is *www.nyhomes.org*.

The Rural Economic and Community Development Administration. Formerly the Farmer's Home Administration, this federal agency under the Department of Agriculture channels credit to rural residents. Loan programs fall into two categories: (1) guaranteed loans made and serviced by a private lender and guaranteed by the agency; and (2) insured loans that are made and serviced directly by the agency. For low-income first-time homebuyers in rural areas, mortgage interest may be subsidized and be as low as 1 percent. Only modest residences are eligible. The address of a local office and further information are available from the Rural Economic and Community Development Administration, New York State Office in Syracuse at 1-315-477-6433. Information is also available on the Internet at *www.usda.gov/rhs*.

Among the most basic words needed to discuss mortgages efficiently are *down payment, loan-to-value ratio, equity, interest, servicing,* and *principal.*

The buyer who has only $10,000 to give a seller as a **down payment** on a $100,000 home will have to borrow the rest with a mortgage loan. If $90,000 is being borrowed on property worth $100,000, the loan is said to have a 90 percent **loan-to-value** (LTV) **ratio** (amount borrowed divided by the property's value). **Loan servicing** is provided by the institution that collects and credits payments, issues monthly or annual reports on the status of the loan to the borrower, and handles contact with the borrower.

After the transaction has closed, the buyers will have $10,000 **equity** in the home, *equity* being defined as the amount the owner would receive if the property were sold and all liens against it paid off. In a few years, if the loan has been paid down to $89,000 and the property's value has increased to $110,000, the owner's equity would amount to $21,000 ($110,000 value, minus $89,000 **principal** still owed).

Interest is a charge made by a lender for the use of money. Interest rates charged by lending institutions vary as changes occur in the availability of money to lend.

Low down payments.   For years homebuyers have received help in obtaining low-down-payment mortgage loans through insurance and guarantees from the FHA, the VA, and SONYMA. In addition, **private mortgage insurance (PMI)** companies offer programs to help those who need high LTV ratios on conventional (nongovernment-backed) loans. The various types of loans are discussed in more detail in Chapter 11.

First-time homebuyers of any age are allowed to withdraw up to $10,000 from an IRA to be used within 120 days as down payment on a home, without the usual 10 percent penalty for withdrawal before age 59½. The money is, as always, still subject to income tax, and none of the $10,000 can be used toward the tax.

Types of Amortization

Most mortgage loans are **amortized loans.** Payments over a term of 15 to 30 years are set high enough to include not only interest due but also a portion of the principal owed. At the end of the term the full amount of the principal will have been paid off. *The process is known as amortization of the debt.*

Most amortized mortgage loans are paid in monthly installments. These payments may be computed based on different mortgage plans.

The most common plan requires that the mortgagor pay the same amount in each payment period, usually each month. The lender credits each payment first to the interest due, and then applies the rest to reduce the amount borrowed (the principal). Each month, as the principal is reduced, not quite as much interest is due, so more of the payment can be used to whittle down the debt. At the end of the **term,** that is, the originally scheduled number of years, the entire debt has been paid off. This is known as a **fully amortized loan.**

A mortgagor may choose a *straight payment plan* that calls for payments of *interest only,* with the principal to be paid in full at the end of the loan term. This is known as a **straight** or **term loan.** Such plans are generally used for short-term home improvement loans or construction loans rather than for residential first mortgage loans.

A combination of the two plans already mentioned is a *partially amortized loan.* Monthly payments may include enough to pay down the debt for a specific number of years. At the end of that period the entire remaining principal is due in a final payment, known as a **balloon payment.**

Adjustable-rate mortgages (ARMs) shift the risk or reward of changing interest rates from the lender to the borrower. As rates rise and fall, changes are made in the monthly payment or (occasionally) in the remaining principal.

In recent years some mortgages have offered combinations of fixed and adjustable rates in ways that may fit certain borrowers' own financial situations and future plans. Some mortgage plans remain at a fixed interest rate for the first three, five, or even seven years, with rates adjusted after that.

Biweekly mortgages involve payments every two weeks instead of monthly. Some borrowers wrongly interpret this to mean "twice a month" and feel some magic is involved in the faster repayment of principal. A biweekly schedule, however, can occasionally involve three payments in one month. With 26 half-payments, it produces the equivalent of 13 monthly payments a year. The extra payment is used entirely to reduce the principal debt faster than originally scheduled, so that a 30-year fixed-rate loan can be paid off in about 23 years. Most biweekly loans involve automatic payment from the borrower's checking or savings account. (With adjustable-rate loans, extra principal payments reduce the monthly payment at the time of next adjustment, but they do not affect the term of the loan.)

Borrowers are sometimes offered biweekly payment plans by outside companies. The original traditional mortgage remains in place, but the firm collects 26 bi-weekly payments a year. It makes the borrower's usual monthly payments, then forwards the extra payment annually to reduce principal. A charge is made for the service. Borrowers who have the discipline, however, can make extra prepayments on their own (in separate checks clearly marked "to be applied entirely to principal") and achieve the same results themselves without paying for the service.

Interest

A lender charges a certain percentage of the principal as interest each year the debt is outstanding. The amount of interest due on any payment date is calculated by figuring total yearly interest based on the unpaid balance and dividing that figure by the number of payments made each year.

On an amortized loan of $100,000 for 30 years at an annual interest rate of 8½ percent, the amount due after the first month's payment has been made can be calculated as follows:

a. $100,000 × 8.5% = $8,500 annual interest
b. $8,500 ÷ 12 = $708.33 first month's interest
c. $768.92 monthly payment to amortize the loan in 30 years
d. −$708.33 first month's interest due
e. $60.59 left to reduce principal first month
f. $100,000 original principal at start of month
g. −$60.59 principal reduction
h. $99,939.41 principal due at end of first month

The following month, because less is now owed, not quite so much interest will be due, and the principal can be reduced by a slightly larger amount.

Table 10.1 shows an *amortization schedule* for the first eight months of this 360-payment loan.

T A B L E 10.1

Amortization Table

Loan Amortization Schedule					Simple Interest Loan
			Principal		$100,000.00
			Monthly payment		$ 768.92
			Annual interest rate		8.500
			Term in months		360

Payment	Old Balance	Interest Payment	Principal Payment	Total Payment	New Balance
1	$100,000.00	$708.33	$60.59	$768.92	$99,939.41
2	99,939.41	707.90	61.02	768.92	99,878.39
3	99,878.39	707.47	61.45	768.92	99,816.94
4	99,816.94	707.04	61.88	768.92	99,755.06
5	99,755.06	706.60	62.32	768.92	99,692.74
6	99,692.74	706.16	62.76	768.92	99,629.98
7	99,629.98	705.71	63.21	768.92	99,566.77
8	99,566.77	705.26	63.66	768.92	99,503.11

Interest is usually due at the end of each payment period (payment in arrears, as opposed to payment in advance). The principal and interest on a 30-year mortgage is shown in Figure 10.2. Amortization formulas are complicated. Most real estate practitioners carry special calculators with built-in tables.

Usury. The maximum rate of interest that may be charged on mortgage loans is set by state law. Charging interest in excess of this rate is called **usury.** New York has a *floating usury rate.* The maximum rate that may be charged is adjusted up or down at specific intervals by the New York State Banking Board.

Sellers taking back **purchase-money mortgages** always have been exempt from usury limits. (Purchase-money mortgages secure promissory notes given by buyers to sellers.) Loans in the amount of $2.5 million or more and loans made to corporations are generally exempt from usury laws, except for New York's criminal usury limit of 25 percent on loans up to $2.5 million. Lending institutions are also exempt up to the criminal usury limit. *Other individuals making mortgage loans, however, are still bound by the New York usury limit.*

Such an individual might be an employer making a mortgage loan to an employee or a real estate broker lending the buyer money to help with a sale (which the broker should not do without the consent of the seller). In those cases, the person making the loan should check with the state banking department to make sure the interest charged is within current limits.

Points. When a new mortgage is placed, the lending institution may ask for a lump-sum payment of extra prepaid interest in the form of up-front **points.** *Each point is 1 percent of the new loan.* On an $80,000 loan each point would be $800; a charge of two points would total $1,600. Payment of points is

FIGURE 10.2

Level-Payment Amortized Loan

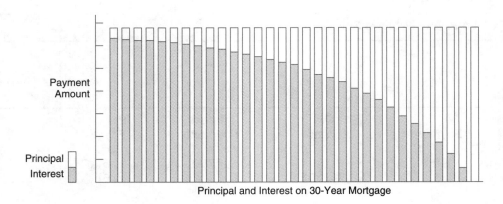

Payment Amount

Principal ☐
Interest ▨

Principal and Interest on 30-Year Mortgage

a one-time affair, usually at the time of closing but occasionally at mortgage application or issuance of a mortgage commitment by the lender. Points may be paid by either the buyer or the seller, depending on the terms of the sales contract.

Annual percentage rate. If a mortgage loan is made at 7 percent but also requires three points in prepaid interest or other service fees, the loan really costs more than 7 percent. The exact rate depends on the length of the proposed mortgage and requires some complicated calculations. The rate, which would total slightly more than 7 percent, is known as the **annual percentage rate (APR).** Federal regulations (Regulation Z of the Truth-in-Lending Act, discussed in Chapter 11) require that the borrower be advised of the APR in advertisements and in writing when a loan is placed. It is intended to help borrowers compare widely differing mortgage plans, but often simply adds to their confusion.

Buydowns. With some mortgage plans, lending institutions are willing to lower the interest rate in return for payment of extra points. The arrangement is known as a **buydown.** Many buydowns lower the rate for a period of time, for example, by 3 percent the first year of the loan, 2 percent the second year, and 1 percent the third year (3-2-1-buydown). Other buydowns last for the whole term of the loan.

Tax-Deductible Interest Payments

Taxpayers may deduct on income tax returns the interest paid on mortgage loans up to a total of $1 million if borrowed to acquire and/or improve both a first and a second (vacation) residence. Interest on additional borrowing (second mortgages, home equity loans) of up to $100,000 also qualifies for income tax deduction, no matter what the money is used for. Homeowners also may deduct all property taxes, prepaid interest points (whether paid by buyer or seller). and any mortgage prepayment penalties. Somewhat different income tax regulations apply to mortgage loans on investment property and to refinance mortgages.

Prepayment

Some mortgage notes charge a **prepayment premium**, or **penalty,** if the loan is paid off before its full term. For a one to six-family dwelling used as a principal residence, the maximum prepayment premium a lender may charge in New York is 90 days' interest on the unpaid balance if the loan is paid in full during the first year. No penalty may be charged after the loan is a year old. No prepayment penalties may be charged on FHA or VA loans.

Tax and Insurance Reserves

Many lenders require that borrowers provide a reserve, or escrow, fund to meet future real estate taxes and insurance premiums. When the mortgage loan is made, the borrower starts the reserve by depositing funds to cover partial payment of the following year's tax bill. The insurance premium reserve is started with the deposit of one-twelfth of the annual tax and insurance premium liability. After that the monthly payments will include principal, interest, and escrow for tax and insurance reserves **(PITI)**.

To be certain that these important bills are being paid, the lender accumulates the borrower's money in the escrow account. Property tax bills and insurance premium bills are sent directly to the lending institution, which pays them and renders an accounting to the borrower. The homeowner is entitled to 2 percent interest on the money thus held. When the mortgage loan is eventually paid off, any money remaining in the escrow account is returned to the borrower.

RESPA, the federal *Real Estate Settlement Procedures Act*, limits the amount of tax and insurance reserves a lender may require.

■ SUMMARY

Mortgage loans involve a borrower, called the *mortgagor*, and a lender, called the *mortgagee*.

The borrower is required to execute a note agreeing to repay the debt and a mortgage placing a lien on the real estate to secure the note. The mortgage document is recorded in the public record to give notice to the world of the lender's interest. Payment in full entitles the borrower to a satisfaction, or release, which is recorded to clear the lien from the public records.

Default by the borrower may result in acceleration of payments and a foreclosure sale. If the proceeds fail to clear the debt, the mortgagee may seek a deficiency judgment against the borrower. A subsequent owner who assumes the loan is also personally responsible and liable for a deficiency judgment; one who takes the property subject to the mortgage is not.

The note for most common forms of mortgage loans provides for amortization, the gradual repayment of principal borrowed along with interest. The note also sets the rate of interest the borrower must pay as a charge for borrowing the money.

Charging more than the maximum interest rate allowed by state statute is called *usury* and is illegal. Sellers taking back purchase-money mortgages are exempt from usury limits.

QUESTIONS

1. The Scotts' new home cost $150,000, and they borrowed $135,000 on a mortgage loan, paying $15,000 in cash as a down payment. That $15,000 now represents their
   a. loan-to-value ratio.
   b. equity.
   c. qualifying ratio.
   d. underwriting.

2. A mortgage broker generally
   a. brings borrower and lender together.
   b. makes mortgage loans using investors' funds.
   c. provides credit and appraisal reports.
   d. places packages of loans in the secondary market.

3. A borrower obtains a 30-year mortgage loan for $176,000 at 7.5 percent interest. If monthly payments of $1,230.62 are credited first to interest and then to princpal, what will be his principal balance after the first payment is made?
   a. $174,990.00
   b. $175,110.00
   c. $175,123.62
   d. $175,869.38

4. When Tiny Tim buys his house, Old Scrooge allows monthly mortgage payments to be figured on a 30-year basis so that Tim can handle them. At the end of the fifth year, however, Scrooge wants the whole remaining debt paid off in a
   a. graduated payment.
   b. shared-equity payment.
   c. balloon payment.
   d. blanket payment.

5. With some exceptions, a homeowner may take as an income tax deduction any cost for
   a. a title insurance premium.
   b. interest on a mortgage.
   c. a homeowner's insurance premium.
   d. mortgage application fees.

6. New York's usury limits do not apply to interest on mortgage loans made by
   a. sellers.
   b. individuals other than sellers.
   c. regular lending institutions.
   d. the Rural Economic and Community Development Administration.

7. John Reilly sells his home for $200,000 and agrees to pay three points to his buyer's lending institution. The buyer is putting 20 percent down on the property. How much will the points cost John?
   a. $900
   b. $1,600
   c. $4,800
   d. $6,000

8. A lending institution may require that the buyer send in an extra monthly payment to cover future bills for
   a. property taxes and insurance premiums.
   b. major repairs.
   c. possible default in monthly payments.
   d. water and municipal utilities.

9. The buyer of a $96,000 property is offered a mortgage with 10 percent down and a loan origination fee of 1.5 percent. Disregarding other possible closing costs, how much cash must the buyer produce to complete the transaction?
   a. $1,290
   b. $1,440
   c. $9,600
   d. $10,896

10. Bill and Maria are looking for a mortgage loan. They will be most likely to apply to a(n)
    a. savings and loan association.
    b. mortgage banking company.
    c. insurance company.
    d. credit union.

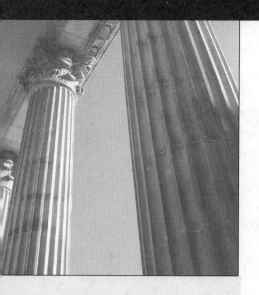

11

REAL ESTATE FINANCE I

Bill and Maria want to buy a home together, but they're not married, Bill is self-employed and they have only $10,000 available for a down payment. They assume those are three reasons to be turned down for a mortgage loan. Are they right?

Keeping track of the changing standards for loan qualifications is vital. A real estate agent who does not know how much money his or her customer will be able to borrow does not know how expensive a home that customer can afford to buy.

■ KEY TERMS

blanket mortgage	Ginnie Mae (GNMA)	package loan
bridge loan	home equity loan	Regulation Z
cap	imputed interest	reverse mortgage
ceiling	index	sale-and-leaseback
construction loan	interim financing	secondary mortgage
conventional loan	jumbo loan	market
convertibility	margin	shared-equity mortgage
Equal Credit Opportunity Act (ECOA)	mortgage insurance premium (MIP)	swing loan
Fannie Mae (FNMA)	negative amortization	underwriting
FHA loan	nonconforming mortgage	VA loan
Freddie Mac (FHLMC)	open-end mortgage	wraparound mortgage

■ TYPES OF LOANS

Most of the loans described in this chapter are long-term mortgages intended for the purchase, improvement, or refinance of real estate. Before discussing those, however, we can examine other common types of borrowing.

Temporary loans.   The homeowner who is selling one residence and buying another may find it necessary to buy the new home before the closing date on the present one. In that situation a temporary loan, variously called a bridge loan, a swing loan, or interim financing, may be arranged.

Shared-equity mortgages.   Under the shared-equity mortgage the purchaser receives help with the down payment, a low interest rate, or assistance with monthly payments from a partner. The "partner" may be a lending institution, the seller, or a relative. Typically the partner receives a share of the profit when the property is sold.

Package loans.   Package loans include not only the real estate but also appliances and furniture on the premises. In recent years this kind of loan has been used to finance furnished condominium units.

Open-end mortgages.   Open-end mortgages (not to be confused with "open mortgages") are used by borrowers to obtain additional funds to improve property. The borrower "opens" the mortgage to increase the debt after the debt has been reduced by payments over a period of time. (An *open mortgage* is one that may be repaid in full at any time without any prepayment penalty by the lender.)

Blanket mortgages.   Blanket mortgages cover more than one parcel or lot and are often used to finance subdivision developments. When one parcel or lot is sold, the borrower makes a partial payment to release it from the overall mortgage.

Wraparound mortgages.   Wraparound mortgages frequently are used to refinance or finance a purchase when an existing mortgage is to be retained. The buyer gives a large mortgage to the seller, who will collect payments on the new loan, usually at a higher interest rate, and continue to make payments on the old loan. *Wraparound mortgages, like all unusual arrangements, require careful study by attorneys. The broker who negotiates one should exercise special care not to give legal advice.*

Reverse mortgage.   A reverse mortgage allows senior citizens on fixed incomes to tap the equity buildup in their homes without having to sell. The homeowner receives a monthly check, a lump sum, a line of credit against which to draw, or a combination. No payments are due while the homeowner remains in the property, and a gradual debt, including interest, builds up against the real estate. The American Association of Retired Persons (AARP) has an excellent booklet titled "Home Made Money" available to those who write to Equity Information, AARP, 601 E. St., NW, Washington, DC 20049. The Web site *www.reversemortgage.org* offers useful information.

WWWeb.Link

Among the better reverse mortgage plans is that backed by HUD (FHA), which requires counseling so that the borrower understands exactly what is involved. HUD's is called a *home equity conversion mortgage.*

Private Mortgages

Purchase-money mortgages. Strictly speaking, a purchase-money mortgage is any loan that enables the purchase of real estate, as opposed to a second mortgage for further borrowing or a refinance mortgage that is used to pay off the original one.

The term is often used, however, for the situation in which a seller lends the buyer money to complete the purchase. The seller "takes back financing" and acts as the lender. A purchase-money mortgage may cover a portion of the purchase price or may be a first mortgage to finance the entire price.

Imputed interest. A purchase-money mortgage held by the seller is exempt from usury limitations on interest rate. If seller financing is at an artificially low interest rate, however, the Internal Revenue Service will invoke imputed interest; that is, it will "impute" a higher rate and tax the recipient accordingly. The seller must charge at least 9 percent or a rate equal to the applicable federal rate (AFR), whichever is lower. The AFR is set monthly by the federal government and is usually somewhat below current national average rates. A seller who charges less will be taxed as if income were received at the required rate. An exception is made for certain transfers of vacant land within a family.

When a third party—employer, perhaps, relative, or individual investor—makes a private mortgage loan, it is important to follow the rules on applicable federal rate.

Construction loans. Also called building loan agreements, construction loans are made to finance the construction of improvements on real estate. A construction loan can be difficult to secure unless the applicant works through a recognized builder or contractor. Payments are made on a scheduled basis to the general contractor or owner for work that has been completed since the previous payment. The lender usually inspects the work before each payment. This kind of mortgage loan generally bears a higher interest rate because of risks assumed by the lender. It is short term. The borrower arranges for a permanent mortgage loan (also known as an *end,* or *takeout, loan*) when the work is completed.

Land contracts. As discussed in Chapter 8, real estate can be purchased under a *land contract.* Real estate is often sold on contract when mortgage financing is not available or is too expensive or when the purchaser does not have a sufficient down payment.

Sale-and-leaseback arrangements. Sale-and-leaseback agreements are sometimes used as a means of financing large commercial or industrial plants. The land and building used by the seller are sold to an investor such as an insurance company. The investor then leases back the real estate to the seller, who continues to conduct business on the property as a tenant. This enables a business firm that has money invested in a plant to free that money for working capital. The buyer benefits from an assured long-term tenant. Real estate brokers should consult legal and tax experts when involved in this type of complex transaction.

Home equity loans.   A form of second mortgage, the **home equity loan** has grown in popularity in recent years. Homeowners whose property has appreciated in value may borrow up to new loan-to-value (LTV) ratios or, in one popular version, establish a line of credit that is based on the equity position in their home, borrowing against it as they choose. Some sellers do not realize that their home equity line of credit is really a second mortgage and must be paid off when they sell, as any other nonassumable mortgage must be.

■ METHODS OF FINANCE

Mortgage loans fall into several classifications:

- Conventional loans are those arranged entirely between borrower and lending institution.
- Government-backed loans include those insured by the FHA or guaranteed by the VA. With both types the actual loan comes from a local lending institution.
- Loans directly from the government include State of New York Mortgage Agency (SONYMA) mortgages and Rural Economic and Community Development Administration (formerly Farmer's Home Administration) (FmHA) loans.
- Private loans are those made by individuals, often the seller of the property or a relative of the buyer.

Conventional Loans

In making conventional loans, lending institutions set their own standards, governed always by banking regulations. As a result, a variety of mortgage plans is often offered, and some flexibility is occasionally available. A conventional loan may be useful where a short processing time is needed or where an unusual house or unusual buyer is involved. Conventional loans are also popular when interest rates for mortgage loans are low. Conventional mortgages may be fixed rate, adjustable rate, or a combination of plans.

Most fixed-rate conventional mortgages are not assumable by a subsequent buyer of the property; some adjustable-rate mortgages are assumable, but only when the buyer can prove financial qualification.

Private mortgage insurance.   In general, conventional loans call for higher down payments (lower LTV ratio) than government-backed mortgages. Banking theory holds that it risks depositors' money to lend more than 80 percent of the value of real estate. With any down payment below 20 percent, therefore, a conventional loan in New York State must be accompanied by *private mortgage insurance (PMI)*. The borrower pays a yearly premium (or, optionally, a lump sum at closing) for insurance that protects the lender in case of loss after a foreclosure. (Private mortgage insurance should not be confused with life insurance.) New York State law requires that the lender discontinue

MORTGAGE LOANS HAVE SEVERAL CLASSIFICATIONS

- Conventional loans
- Government-backed loans
- Loans direct from the government
- Private loans

collecting PMI premiums when the loan has been paid down to 75 percent of the value of the property as appraised at the time of purchase.

For conventional mortgage loans placed after July 29, 1999, the federal government requires that lenders drop PMI coverage at the borrower's request when equity reaches 20 percent, and that coverage be dropped automatically when it reaches 22 percent. Equity calculated from current value or original appraisal, whichever is lower.

Adjustable-rate mortgages.   An adjustable-rate mortgage, particularly popular when interest rates are high, offers the borrower a chance at lower interest rates when national interest levels drop. When rates across the country rise, however, the borrower may find his or her rate being raised.

The vocabulary of ARMs includes the following:

- *Adjustment period:* The anniversary on which interest rate and monthly payment adjustments may be made. Most borrowers elect one-year adjustments, but they might be made more frequently or only after three or five years.
- *Index:* The interest rate on the loan changes following an increase or decrease in a national indicator, or **index,** of current rates. The most commonly chosen index is the rate paid on one-year U.S. Treasury bills.
- *Margin:* The borrower pays a specific percentage above the index. That percentage is known as the **margin.** If Treasury bills were selling at 6 percent interest, for example, the borrower with a 2 percent margin over Treasury bills would be charged 8 percent.
- *Cap:* The loan agreement may set a **cap** of, for example, 2 percent on any upward adjustment. If interest rates (as reflected by the index) went up 3 percent by the time of adjustment, the interest rate could be raised only 2 percent. Depending on the particular mortgage, the extra 1 percent might be treated one of three ways:
    1. It could be saved by the lender to be added at the next adjustment period.
    2. It could be absorbed by the lender with no future consequences to the borrower.
    3. It could be added to the amount borrowed so that the principal would increase instead of decreasing (negative amortization).
- *Ceiling:* A **ceiling** (sometimes called a *lifetime cap*) is a maximum allowable interest rate. Typically a mortgage may offer a five-point ceiling. If the interest rate started at 8 percent, it could never go beyond 13 percent, no matter what happened to national rates.
- *Negative amortization:* **Negative amortization** could result from an artificially low initial interest rate. It also could follow a hike in rates larger than a cap allows the lender to impose. Not all mortgage plans include the possibility of negative amortization. Sometimes the lender agrees to absorb any shortfalls. The possibility must always be explored, however, when an ARM is being evaluated. The debt would be increasing, rather than being paid down.

- *Convertibility:* Some ARMs are **convertible,** that is, the borrower may choose to change to a fixed-rate mortgage at then-current interest levels. With some plans any favorable moment may be chosen. More commonly the option is available on the third, fourth, or fifth anniversary of the loan. The borrower may be charged a slightly higher interest rate in return for this option.
- *Initial interest rate:* With many loan plans the rate during the first year, or the first adjustment period, is set artificially low (discounted) to induce the borrower to enter into the agreement ("teaser" rate). Buyers who plan to be in a home for only a few years may be delighted with such arrangements. Other borrowers, however, may end up with negative amortization and payment shock.
- *Assumability:* Many ARMs are assumable by a financially qualified next owner of the property, with the lender's approval and the payment of service fees.

To help consumers compare different ARMs, lenders must give anyone considering a specific ARM a uniform disclosure statement that lists and explains indexes, history of past interest rate changes, and other information. A method for calculating the highest possible payment is included. The disclosures must be furnished before the loan applicant has paid any nonrefundable application fee.

FHA-Insured Loans

WWWeb.Link

The Federal Housing Administration (FHA), which operates under the Department of Housing and Urban Development (HUD), does not lend money itself. Rather it insures mortgage loans made by approved lending institutions. It does not insure the property, but it does insure the lender against loss. The common term **FHA loan,** then, refers to a loan that is not made by the agency but insured by it. Because the federal government insures the lending institution against loss, borrowers can place FHA mortgages with very low down payments. Information is available at *www.hud.gov/mortprog.html.*

FHA 203(b).   The most widely used FHA mortgage is known as 203(b) and may be placed on one to four-family residences. The following are among the requirements set up by the FHA before it will insure a loan.

Owner/occupants.   The loan is available only to an owner/occupant, someone who intends to live in the property as a primary residence. (Investors may sometimes buy HUD foreclosures with 25 percent down.)

Mortgage insurance premium.   In addition to paying interest, the borrower is charged a lump sum as a **mortgage insurance premium (MIP).** This amount is payable in cash at the closing or may be financed for the term of the loan. If the loan is subsequently paid off within the early years of the loan, some refund of unused premium is due the borrower from HUD.

On FHA loans made since July 1991, borrowers are charged the initial lump-sum premium at closing and also .05 percent MIP (mortgage insurance premium) per month as interest for a number of years, depending on the size of the down payment. First-time homebuyers who complete a course in financial counseling are entitled to a small reduction in the size of their initial MIP.

For an FHA loan placed after 2000, the FHA will drop MIP payments when the principal balance has been reduced to 78 percent of original purchase price, but only after the first five years.

Estimate of value. The real estate must be evaluated by an FHA-approved appraiser. The maximum loan will be a percentage of the appraised value. If the purchase price is higher than the FHA appraisal, the buyer must pay the difference in a higher cash down payment or may decide not to purchase. On Section 203(b) loans, minimum down payment requirements are less than 3 percent. For really inexpensive houses (appraised at less than $50,000), the required down payment is 1.25 percent. This allows a loan-to-value ratio of 98.75 percent. On a house appraised at $40,000, the minimum down payment would be $500.

For houses appraised between $50,000 and $125,000, the LTV ratio is 97.75 percent. For houses valued at more than $125,000, it is 97.15 percent, slightly higher in what are considered high-closing-cost areas.

FHA borrowers are allowed to finance a portion of their closing costs. The amount is added to the base loan amount. Sometimes the total amount borrowed may actually exceed the purchase price of the property.

The FHA sets top limits on its loans, which vary within the state. The highest levels in New York are set for areas in and around New York City, in parts of Long Island, and in Tioga County. The FHA raises its limits from time to time. In 2003, the limits for single dwellings were $154,897 in low-cost areas and more than $280,749 in high-cost counties.

Repairs. The FHA requires its borrowers to be notified, before a purchase contract becomes binding, that its appraisers estimate value rather than condition in detail, and that use of a home inspector is recommended. The FHA may, however, stipulate repair requirements that must be completed before it will issue mortgage insurance on a specific property. Certain energy-saving improvements may be financed along with an FHA mortgage.

Assumability. Older FHA loans may be assumed by the next owner of the property with no change in interest rate, no credit check on the buyer, and only a small charge for paperwork. The assumer could be a nonoccupant/investor. The original borrower is not released from liability, however, unless the new borrower is willing to go through a formal assumption, which involves the lender's approval of credit and income.

For FHA loans made after December 15, 1989, the buyer wishing to assume the mortgage must be a prospective owner/occupant and prove financial qualification; the original borrower is then relieved of liability. Optionally, the new borrower may pass a simple credit check and the property a new appraisal, with the original borrower sharing joint liability for five years after the assumption.

Refinancing.   The FHA offers a "streamline" refinancing for its loans, with minimal closing costs.

Other FHA programs.   Among other FHA programs, which may or may not be handled by a particular local lender at any given time, are ARMs and special plans intended for veterans, for rehabilitation of housing being purchased, and for no-down-payment purchase of modest homes. Other FHA programs are sometimes available to finance mobile homes, manufactured housing, and condominiums. For first-time purchasers, the FHA offers special discounts for teachers, firefighters, and police officers buying HUD-foreclosed houses in "revitalization zones," and for first-time buyers who complete a course in financial management.

The program, known as 203(k), allows money to be borrowed to cover both the purchase and the rehabilitation of a house in need of substantial repair.

VA-Guaranteed Loans

The Department of Veterans Affairs (VA), formerly the Veterans Administration, can guarantee lending institutions against loss on mortgage loans to eligible veterans. Because the VA guarantees part of the loan, no down payment is required (though individual lenders may sometimes ask for a small down payment). The VA has raised its maximum guarantee from time to time. It sets no limit on the amount borrowed, but in 2002, the guarantee was for up to $75,175. It is used to guarantee the top 25 percent of the loan, so that in practice that amount could cover a loan of up to $300,700.

VA loans are intended only for owner-occupied property that is owned by veterans, or veterans and their spouses, and may be placed on one to four-family residences. While the guarantee comes from the federal government, the loan itself is made by a local lending institution. The veteran pays a funding fee directly to the VA at closing. The amount of the funding fee depends on the size of the down payment:

- Nothing down or less than 5 percent: 2 percent
- Down payment between 5 and 10 percent: 1.5 percent
- 10 percent or more down payment: 1.25 percent
- Assumptions of VA loans: .5 percent

Those eligible through national guard/reservist service pay an extra .75 percent in funding fee.

Eligibility.   The right to a VA guarantee does not expire. To qualify, a veteran must have a discharge that is "other than dishonorable" and the required length of service:

- For those in the National Guard or the reserves, six years' service
- For those who enlisted before September 7, 1980, at least 90 days' continuous active service since September 16, 1940 (or 90 days' service during a war)

■ For those who first enlisted after September 7, 1980, two years' active duty
■ Reservists called up for at least 90 days during the Persian Gulf War, whether or not they went overseas

The veteran who applies for a VA loan must furnish a certificate of eligibility, which can be obtained by writing to:

<table>
<tr><td>VA Regional Office
Federal Building
111 West Huron Street
Buffalo, NY 14202
1-800-827-0619</td><td>or</td><td>VA Regional Office
252 Seventh Avenue
New York, NY 10001
1-800-827-8954</td></tr>
</table>

Information is available at *www.valoans.com.*

Veterans who have used some or all of their eligibility to guarantee one loan sometimes can place another VA mortgage. Eligibility may still be available if

■ the first loan used only part of the guarantee;
■ the original VA loan has been paid off and the home sold, o;
■ the original VA loan was formally assumed by another veteran;
■ the applicant is the widow or widower of a veteran who died of a service-connected disability and has not remarried.

Qualified veterans' home loan entitlement will be restored one time only if the veteran has repaid the prior VA loan in full but has not disposed of the property securing that loan. If veterans wish to use their VA entitlement again, they must dispose of all property previously financed with a VA loan, including the property not disposed of under the "one time only" provision.

Assumability.   Any VA mortgage loan made before March 1, 1988, may be assumed by the next owner of the property, who need not be a veteran and need not prove qualification to the lender or the VA. For loans made after March 1, 1988, the assumer (who need not be a veteran) must prove credit-worthiness, and the original borrower is free of future liability.

Refinancing.   VA loans may be refinanced with a streamline process for a fee of .5 percent.

Government Backing via the Secondary Market

Lenders in the primary mortgage market originate loans directly to borrowers. Some keep the loans in their own portfolios. (See Portfolio Loans below.) Other primary lenders may sell packages of loans to large investors in what is known as the secondary mortgage market. A lender may wish to sell a number of loans when it needs more money to meet the mortgage demands in its area. The federal government is active in the secondary mortgage market.

A major source of secondary mortgage market activity is a warehousing agency, which purchases mortgage loans and assembles them into large packages of loans for resale to investors such as insurance companies and pension funds. The major warehousing agencies are Fannie Mae (formerly the Federal National Mortgage Association [FNMA]); Ginnie Mae (formerly the Government National Mortgage Association [GNMA]); and Freddie Mac (formerly the Federal Home Loan Mortgage Corporation [FHLMC]).

Fannie Mae. Fannie Mae (FNMA) is (despite its name) a privately owned corporation. It raises funds to purchase loans by selling government-guaranteed FNMA bonds.

Mortgage bankers are actively involved with FNMA, originating loans and selling them to FNMA while retaining the servicing functions. FNMA is the nation's largest purchaser of mortgages.

When Fannie Mae talks, lenders listen. Because FNMA eventually purchases one mortgage out of every ten, it has great influence on lending policies. When Fannie Mae announces that it will buy a certain type of loan, local lending institutions often change their own regulations to meet the requirements. When lenders are experimenting with new types of loans, a Fannie Mae announcement can standardize the innovative mortgage plans and bring order out of chaos.

Ginnie Mae. Ginnie Mae (GNMA) was formerly called the Government National Mortgage Association. The Ginnie Mae pass-through certificate lets small investors buy a share in a pool of mortgages that provides for a monthly "pass through" of principal and interest payments directly to the certificate holder.

Freddie Mac. Freddie Mac (FHLMC) also provides a secondary market for mortgage loans. Freddie Mac buys mortgages, pools them, and sells bonds with the mortgages as security.

Most lenders use a standardized mortgage application and other forms that are accepted by Freddie Mac and Fannie Mae.

Nonconforming loans. When Fannie Mae and Freddie Mac announce that they will buy loans only up to a certain size (recently at more than $322,000 for one-family homes), many local lenders set that as their own limit. Loans higher than Fannie Mae's or Freddie Mac's maximum loan limit are known as jumbo loans. The borrower who wants to place one would search for a local lending institution that either sells jumbo mortgages to private investors or makes portfolio loans, lending its own money and taking mortgages it intends to keep and collect. A jumbo loan usually carries a slightly higher rate of interest.

Nonconforming mortgages (portfolio loans) do not have to meet uniform underwriting standards, and can be flexible in their guidelines. The borrower with an unusual credit situation or a unique house may need a nonconforming loan. A lending institution may want such loans at one time but not at other times. Following the rapidly changing mortgage market is often the greatest part of a real estate broker's work.

■ FINANCING LEGISLATION

The federal government regulates the lending practices of mortgage lenders through the Truth-in-Lending Act, Equal Credit Opportunity Act (ECOA), and Real Estate Settlement Procedures Act (RESPA).

Regulation Z

The Truth-in-Lending Act, enforced through Regulation Z, requires that credit institutions inform the borrower of the true cost of obtaining credit so that the borrower can compare the costs of various lenders and avoid the uninformed use of credit. All real estate transactions made for personal or agricultural purposes are covered. The regulation does not apply to business or commercial loans.

Regulation Z requires that the customer be fully informed of all finance charges, as well as the true annual interest rate, before a transaction is consummated. In the case of a mortgage loan made to finance the purchase of a dwelling, the lender must compute and disclose the annual percentage rate (APR) in a written Truth-in-Lending statement provided to the mortgagor.

Three-day right of rescission.   In the case of most consumer credit transactions covered by Regulation Z, the borrower has three days in which to rescind (cancel) the transaction merely by notifying the lender. This right of rescission does not apply to residential purchase-money first mortgage loans but does apply to refinances. Lenders sometimes close on the loan but withhold the actual check until they are sure the borrower will not rescind. In situations where the money is needed immediately, borrowers may avoid the three-day wait by waiving their right to rescind.

Advertising.   Regulation Z provides strict regulation of real estate advertisements that include mortgage financing terms. General phrases like "liberal terms available" may be used, but if specifics are given they must comply with this act. The APR, which includes all charges rather than the interest rate alone, must be stated.

Specific credit terms, known as *triggering terms*—such as the down payment, monthly payment, dollar amount of the finance charge, or term of the loan—may not be advertised unless the following information is set forth as well: cash price; required down payment; number, amounts, and due dates of all payments; and APR. The total of all payments to be made over the term of the mortgage must also be specified unless the advertised credit refers to a first mortgage to finance acquisition of a dwelling.

Penalties.   Regulation Z provides substantial penalties for noncompliance, ranging from a fine of $5,000 to $10,000 for each day the misleading advertising continues to a year's imprisonment.

Federal Equal Credit Opportunity Act

The federal Equal Credit Opportunity Act (ECOA) prohibits lenders and others who grant or arrange credit to consumers from discriminating against credit applicants on the basis of race; color; religion; national origin; sex; marital status; age (provided the applicant is of legal age); or dependence on public assistance. Lenders must inform all rejected credit applicants in writing of the principal reasons why credit was denied or terminated.

The *National Affordable Housing Act* requires that borrowers be presented with a statement of their rights if their loan servicing is transferred. The borrower must be notified at least 15 days before the date of transfer and provided with a toll-free or collect-call telephone number of the new servicer. Servicers are also required to acknowledge borrowers' inquiries within 20 days, and act on them within 60 days.

■ LENDER'S CRITERIA FOR GRANTING A LOAN

All mortgage lenders require that prospective borrowers file an application for credit that provides the lender with basic information. A prospective borrower must submit personal information including age, family status, employment, earnings, assets, and financial obligations. Details of the real estate that will be the security for the loan also must be provided, including legal description, improvements, and taxes. For loans on income property or those made to corporations, additional information is required, such as financial and operating statements, schedules of leases and tenants, and balance sheets. Self-employed applicants will be asked to show two years' income tax returns. Anyone employed by a family member will be asked to show a current pay stub and the most recent tax return.

Evaluating the Property

The value of the property is an important element of the lender's underwriting process. The amount of the loan is based on the sales price of the property or appraised value, whichever is less. The lender then applies its LTV ratio to this figure. For example, suppose the property's sales price is $150,000, its appraised value is $152,000, and the buyer is applying for a 90 percent loan (which means he or she is making a 10 percent downpayment). To determine the maximum loan amount, the lender would multiply $150,000 (the lesser of the sales price and appraised value) by 90 percent. The maximum loan amount would be $135,000. (The borrower would have to make a $15,000 down payment.)

To determine the appraised value of the property, the lender will order that an appraisal be performed. When valuing the property, the appraiser will take into consideration such elements as the property's location, its size and square footage, the number of bedrooms and bathrooms, the size of the lot, and the condition of the property. If the property is a condominium or cooperative unit, the appraiser also will look at the project as a whole and examine the condominium declarations and bylaws filed with the attorney general or the cooperative's proprietary lease and bylaws. Appraisal is discussed in detail in Chapter 14.

The lender is concerned about the value of the property because if the borrower defaults on the loan, the lender will have the property sold through a foreclosure process and use the proceeds of the sale to pay off the mortgage debt.

Because a credit report will be part of the application process, homebuyers are well advised to check their own reports early in the homebuying process, to allow time for clearing up any errors. The three main reporting agencies are

WWWeb.Link

- Equifax, 1-800-685-1111, *www.equifax.com;*
- Experian (formerly TRW) 1-800-682-7654, *www.experian.com;* and
- Transunion 1-800-916-8800, *www.transunion.com.*

Evaluating the Potential Borrower

Of course, a lender would much rather have its borrowers pay off their mortgage loans as agreed. If the applicant does not appear financially able to handle the mortgage payments comfortably or if the applicant's continued employment is doubtful, the loan application may be rejected. In recent years, however, some lenders offer special programs, perhaps at higher interest rates, to applicants with less-than-perfect credit scores. The Fannie Mae Foundation (800-605-5200; in Spanish 800-916-8000) offers free pamphlets on understanding, evaluating, and repairing credit history.

Lenders like to see a reasonably stable income history, with at least two years' continuous employment or employment in the same line of work. Bonuses, commissions, and seasonal and part-time income are considered with certain time limits and employer verifications. Dividend and interest income, Social Security income, and pension income are included in qualifying the borrower. Projected rental income is accepted in varying amounts (for example, 50 percent on VA applications, 95 percent toward FHA qualification, 75 percent of actual cash flow with conventional loans). Unrelated coborrowers may pool their incomes to qualify, just as a married couple might.

If the borrower's income is marginal, the lender may look at the borrower's education and training to determine whether his or her skills are in demand in the employment marketplace and whether his or her income is likely to increase in the future.

In judging whether a borrower qualifies to carry the requested loan, lenders analyze the present debts, including any with more than six months (VA and FHA) or ten months (conventional) to run. Lenders sometimes consider potential, as well as actual, balances on credit cards.

Borrowers usually must show that they have liquid assets amounting to the cash that will be required at closing without further borrowing. Some mortgage programs, however, allow a willing seller to pay part of the buyer's closing costs (*seller concessions*). A credit report also will be ordered on the applicant. An applicant who has gone through a bankruptcy may have to wait between one and five years after discharge, depending on the type of loan desired, and show good credit history since.

Through the process known as underwriting, the lender analyzes the application information. Verification forms are sent to the applicant's employers, financial institutions, and lenders. These forms are returned to the lender and examined to make sure the information on the loan application is correct.

LENDER'S CRITERIA FOR GRANTING A LOAN:

- Evaluating the property
- Evaluating the borrower
- Qualifying ratio

The lender also studies the credit reports and the appraisal of the property before deciding whether to grant the loan.

Today when computers analyze borrowers' qualifications, one numeric score summarizing credit history is useful. The widely-used FICO score ranges from 300 to 850, with most people scoring in the 600s and 700s. A score of 750 might bring the offer of a low interest rate; below 620 it could be difficult to mortgage property at all.

FICO analyzes the subject's payment (on-time) record for 35 percent of the score. Current borrowing and credit limits account for 30 percent. Length of credit history (the longer the better) makes up 15 percent, and the rest evaluates types of credit used, number of recent accounts, credit cards, installment loans, and the like.

The lender's acceptance is written in the form of a loan commitment, which creates a contract to make a loan and sets forth the details. This loan commitment must be signed by the borrower and returned to the lender within a specific time period.

Predatory lending.   A few lenders have been known to make mortgage loans to unqualified borrowers regardliess of repayment ability. Such loans often end with the property lost in foreclosure.

Predatory loans are usually at high rates of interest and carry large closing costs. Predatory lenders often urge borrowers to refinance again and again (flipping) to clear past debt, each time increasing the financial burden.

New York State has enacted laws against predatory lending, defined as loans at an interest rate eight or more percentage points over the yield on comparable Treasury notes. Predatory closing costs are defined as anything over 5 percent of the amount being borrowed. The law also addresses the problems of flipping and unreasonable balloon payment arrangments.

Qualifying ratios.   With each mortgage plan offered, the lender has certain qualifying ratios that will be applied to each borrower. A typical ratio for a conventional loan is 28/36; the borrower will be allowed to spend up to 28 percent of gross monthly income for housing expenses (PITI—principal, interest, taxes, and insurance) and up to 36 percent of income for both housing expenses and other payments on long-term debts. The applicant must qualify under both ratios before the loan will be approved.

For example, suppose a prospective buyer earns $3,000 a month. She pays $350 a month on long-term debts, including a car loan and credit card balances. If a lender applies the qualifying ratios to her income, the results will be as follows:

- 28 percent of $3,000 is $840. This is the maximum monthly payment for the loan amount she will qualify for under the housing expense-to-income ratio.

- 36 percent of $3,000 is $1,080; $1,080 minus $350 (monthly long-term payments) equals $730. This is the maximum monthly payment for the loan amount she will qualify for under the total expenses-to-income ratio.

Because a borrower must qualify under both ratios, the highest monthly loan payment this borrower would qualify for is $730.

Other loan programs can have different ratios. For example, to qualify for an FHA loan, applicants can spend no more than 29 percent of their gross monthly income on housing expenses and no more than 41 percent of their gross monthly income on both housing expenses and payments on long-term debts.

To qualify for a VA loan, applicants must spend no more than 41 percent of their gross income on both housing expenses and long-term debt payments, and must also meet the VA's cash flow guidelines (called residual income requirements). Ratio requirements can be changed from time to time.

■ SUMMARY

Mortgage loans include conventional loans, those insured by the FHA or an independent mortgage insurance company, those guaranteed by the VA, and loans from private lenders. Lenders may charge discount points; each point is 1 percent of the new mortgage. FHA and VA mortgages are generally assumable, with some exceptions and regulations.

Other types of real estate financing include purchase-money mortgages, buydowns, graduated-payment loans, shared-equity loans, reverse-annuity mortgages, blanket mortgages, package mortgages, open-end mortgages, wraparound mortgages, construction loans, sale-and-leaseback agreements, land contracts, and investment group financing.

Adjustable-rate mortgages are those under which the interest rate is changed each adjustment period to a stipulated margin above a national index of current mortgage rates. A cap may limit the size of possible adjustments, and a ceiling may limit the adjustment over the life of the loan. In instances where monthly payments do not cover the interest due, negative amortization is possible, with the total debt increasing instead of decreasing as it does with normal amortization.

The federal government affects real estate financing by participating in the secondary mortgage market. The secondary market is composed of investors who purchase and hold the loans as investments. Fannie Mae (Federal National Mortgage Association); Ginnie Mae (Government National Mortgage Association); and Freddie Mac (Federal Home Loan Mortgage Corporation) take an active role in creating a secondary market by regularly purchasing mortgage loans from originators and retaining, or warehousing, them until investment purchasers are available.

Regulation Z, the federal Truth-in-Lending Act, requires that institutional lenders inform borrowers of all finance charges involved. Severe penalties are imposed for noncompliance. The federal Equal Credit Opportunity Act prohibits creditors from discriminating against credit applicants on the basis of race, color, religion, national origin, sex, marital status, age, or dependence on public assistance. The Real Estate Settlement Procedures Act (RESPA) requires that lenders inform both buyers and sellers in advance of all fees for the settlement of a residential mortgage loan.

A lender underwrites a loan by examining the borrower's income, employment history, credit history, net worth and the value of the property. The lender is concerned about the borrower's income and employment history because the lender wants to make sure that the borrower is likely to repay the mortgage debt as agreed. The lender is concerned about the value of the property because if the borrower does default, the property will be sold at a foreclosure sale and the proceeds used to repay the mortgage debt.

When evaluating the borrower's income, lenders typically use two ratios: the borrower may not spend more than a certain amount (for example, 28 percent) of his or her gross monthly income on housing expenses or more than a certain amount (for example, 36 percent) of his or her gross monthly income on both housing expenses and other long-term debt payments.

QUESTIONS

1. Private mortgage insurance (PMI) is required whenever the
   a. loan is to be placed with the FHA.
   b. property covers more than 2.5 acres.
   c. loan exceeds $67,500.
   d. conventional LTV ratio exceeds 80 percent.

2. The Department of Housing and Urban Development insures mortgage loans made through
   a. the FHA.
   b. the VA.
   c. Fannie Mae.
   d. Freddie Mac.

3. Bill and Maria want to buy a home together. A mortgage application is likely to fail, though, if
   a. they are not married.
   b. they are self-employed.
   c. Bill declared bankruptcy eight months ago.
   d. they have less than 10 percent down payment.

4. The terms *index*, *margin*, and *cap* are used in evaluating what type of mortgage?
   a. Package
   b. Blanket
   c. Conventional
   d. Adjustable-rate

5. Negative amortization refers to a situation in which the
   a. debt is gradually reduced through monthly payments.
   b. debt grows larger instead of smaller each month.
   c. regular adjustments reduce the interest rate.
   d. interest rate may rise or fall according to an index.

6. The Williamses are purchasing a lakefront summer home in a new resort development. The house is completely equipped and furnished, and the Williamses have obtained a loan that covers all the personal as well as the real property. This kind of financing is called a(n)
   a. wraparound mortgage.
   b. package mortgage.
   c. blanket mortgage.
   d. unconventional loan.

7. A developer obtains one mortgage for a whole subdivision. As he sells each lot, he obtains a release of one parcel from the
   a. package mortgage.
   b. reverse mortgage.
   c. balloon mortgage.
   d. blanket mortgage.

8. Martin Tones buys a local factory from a company that intends to remain and rent it from him. Martin has put together a
   a. participation transaction.
   b. sale-and-leaseback.
   c. secondary market.
   d. reserve for escrow.

9. A savings and loan institution offers a mortgage plan with an 80 percent LTV ratio. On the purchase of a property appraised at $150,000, how much down payment will be required?
   a. $12,000
   b. $20,000
   c. $30,000
   d. $120,000

10. Fannie Mae's purpose is to
    a. insure loans.
    b. buy loans.
    c. make loans.
    d. service loans.

11. Regulation Z protects the consumer from
   a. misleading advertising.
   b. fraudulent mortgage plans.
   c. discrimination in lending.
   d. substandard housing.

12. Fannie Mae is
   a. the leading purchaser of mortgages on the secondary market.
   b. a lender for homes in rural areas.
   c. a government agency that regulates interest rates.
   d. a government agency that regulates commercial banks.

CHAPTER TWELVE

12

LAND-USE
REGULATIONS

*L. J. Blake owns a house containing eight studio apartments, but it is in an area
zoned for one-family to four-family residences. He thinks it has been used that way
for 100 years. Now he is ready to sell the property and worries about whether another
owner can continue using it for studios.*

To serve buyers and sellers properly, the real estate licensee needs to understand
government—and private—regulations as they affect an owner's use of real property.

■ KEY TERMS

abutting
accessory (apartment) uses
ad valorem tax
assessed value
building codes
building permit
census tract
CERCLA
certificate of occupancy
   (C of O)
cluster zoning
condemnation
deed restriction
demography

development rights
   (transfer of)
direct public ownership
eminent domain
escheat
family (defined)
group home
home occupations
infrastructure
laches (doctrine of)
lead agency
master plan
moratorium
nonconforming use

OPRHP
police power
restrictive covenant
SARA
setbacks
special assessments
special-use permit
spot zoning
subdivision regulations
taking
taxation
variance
zoning boards of appeal
zoning ordinances

■ PLANNING FOR THE FUTURE

While private property owners generally own the complete bundle of rights—that is, the rights to use, sell, lease, and improve their property—governments on all levels also have an interest in private property. It is in the government's interest to make sure that property owners do not use their property in such as way as to harm the public at large. For instance, a property owner may not use his or her property to unduly pollute the air or water; to create a nuisance for neighbors; or to substantially decrease the value of a neighbor's property (such as by operating a factory within a residential neighborhood). The government protects its interest in the use of private property through broad land-use regulations, which range from zoning to environmental protection laws.

■ PRIVATE LAND-USE CONTROLS

The government is not the only entity that can regulate land use. Individual property owners and subdivision developers can restrict the uses to which land can be put. An individual seller or donor can set deed restrictions, such as giving property to a grandchild, for example, with the restriction that no intoxicating liquors ever be served on the premises. The restriction would be binding on future owners as well. The restriction is set by including a **restrictive covenant** in the deed. In the past, deed restrictions might have forbidden any future sale of the property to a member of a particular religious or ethnic group. Today such restrictions are in violation of human rights laws and are not enforceable. Neither are restrictions that forbid owners from selling or mortgaging in the future.

A subdivider may establish restrictions on the right to *use* land through a *covenant* in a deed or by a separate recorded declaration. These restrictions are usually considered valid if they are reasonable and for the benefit of neighboring owners. They are binding on all future buyers in that subdivision. Such restrictions usually relate to type of building, use to which the land may be put, type of construction, height, setbacks, square footage, and cost. "No dwelling of less than 2,000 square feet ever to be constructed in this subdivision" is an example. Some restrictions have a *time limitation*, for example, "effective for a period of 25 years from this date."

Where a deed restriction and a zoning provision cover the same subject, *the more limiting restriction will prevail*. If deed restrictions say lots in a subdivision must measure at least two acres but the town allows half-acre lots, the two-acre restriction can be enforced by neighbors.

Enforcement of Deed Restrictions

Each lot owner has the right to apply to the court for an injunction to prevent a neighboring owner from violating the recorded restrictions. If granted, the court *injunction* will direct the violator to stop the violation or be in contempt of court. If neighbors stand idly by while a violation is being committed, they can lose the right through *laches*, that is, loss of a right through undue delay or failure to assert it in time. In New York, neighboring owners have a two-year statute of limitations from the completion of the alteration or construction for objecting to violations of the general plan (type of building, height, setbacks).

■ GOVERNMENT POWERS

■ Taxation: **Taxation** is a charge on real estate to raise funds to pay for government services.

■ Police power: **Police power** is the government's power to preserve order, protect the public health and safety, and promote the general welfare. It involves more than simply police protection. In the field of real estate, the use and enjoyment of property is subject to restrictions including environmental protection laws, and zoning and building ordinances regulating the use, occupancy, size, location, construction, and rental of real estate.

■ Eminent domain: Through a **condemnation** suit a government may exercise **eminent domain** to acquire privately owned real estate for public use. Three conditions must be met:

1. The proposed use must be declared by the court to be a public use.
2. Just compensation must be paid to the owner.
3. The rights of the owner must be protected by due process of law.

Condemnation proceedings are instituted only when the owner's consent cannot be obtained. Otherwise public agencies acquire real property through negotiation and purchase from the owner. When the courts find that a landowner's right to develop the land is restricted by government controls so that the land becomes essentially useless, courts have sometimes found that an illegal **taking** has occurred and that the landowner is entitled to compensation.

■ Escheat: State laws provide for ownership of real estate to revert, or **escheat,** to the state when an owner dies leaving no natural heirs and no will disposing of real property.

> **GOVERNMENT POWERS OVER LAND INCLUDE**
>
> ■ taxation;
> ■ police power;
> ■ eminent domain; and
> ■ escheat.

Taxation

Ad valorem taxes are charged against each parcel according to the **assessed value** placed on land and improvements by a public official known as an assessor. Tax rates are set to raise whatever sum is needed for the public budget. A rate might be quoted as, for example, $26 per $1,000 of assessed valuation. The same rate, in a different community, might be expressed as $2.60 per $100, or 26 mills (a mill being one-tenth of a cent) per $1 of assessed value. At that rate a house assessed at $100,000 would have a property tax bill of $2,600. Municipalities frequently assess real property at less than 100 percent of its full value.

Special assessments are additional taxes that run for a few years to enable certain neighborhoods to pay for particular improvements. Property on one street might be subject to special assessment property taxes, for example, to install sidewalks or streetlights on that particular street.

Protesting assessments.   Taxpayers who feel their assessment is unfair can research tax records to see how their valuation compares with that of their neighbors. Obtaining solid data on comparative parcels is of prime importance in protesting an assessment. Recent nearby sales are particularly relevant.

Some assessors will visit the property and discuss the matter. If no agreement results, the next step is to present a grievance to the local assessment board of review. The taxpayer who wants to take matters beyond that point may go to court or take advantage of New York State's simple small claims procedure intended for review of grievances on residential property. When other actions have failed, a property owner may bring a *certiorari proceeding* asking for judicial review by a higher court, board, or tribunal.

In New York partial reduction of some property taxes may be available to qualified veterans, religious organizations, homeowners who claim a school tax relief or STaR reduction, and homeowners aged 65 or older who have limited income.

Property taxes have first priority as liens. Foreclosure of a tax lien is often *in rem*, against the property and not against the delinquent taxpayer personally. Property taxes are discussed at greater length in Chapter 26.

■ GOVERNMENT LAND-USE CONTROLS

The government controls and regulates land use through (1) public land-use controls; and (2) public ownership of land, including parks, schools, and expressways, by the federal, state, and local governments.

■ PUBLIC LAND-USE CONTROLS

The increasing demands placed on our limited natural resources have made it necessary for cities, towns, and villages to increase their limitations on the private use of real estate. We now have controls over noise, air, and water pollution, as well as population density. Regulations governing use of privately owned real estate include planning; zoning; subdivision regulations; codes that regulate building construction, safety, and public health; and environmental protection legislation. (See Figure 12.1.) Subdivision regulations and the real estate agents' duties regarding subdivisions are discussed in Chapter 23.

The Master Plan

A local government recognizes development goals through a comprehensive **master plan,** also referred to as a general plan. The federal government's statistical gathering of information for small **census tracts** aids in the process. Cities and counties develop master plans to ensure that social and economic needs are balanced against environmental and aesthetic concerns. Plans take into account the **demography,** or makeup of the population in terms of age, social, and economic status. Physical surveys are also essential in preparing a master plan. Countywide plans must coordinate numerous civic plans to ensure orderly growth, including provision of **infrastructure**—roads, public utilities, schools, and the like. Occasionally a municipality may put a temporary halt to further construction by declaring a **moratorium**. City plans are put into effect by zoning ordinances.

FIGURE 12.1

Environmental Protection Legislation

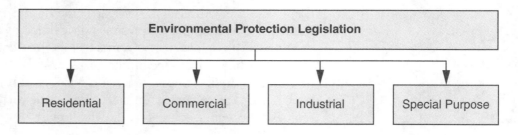

Zoning

Zoning ordinances are laws of local government authorities that control the use of land and structures within designated districts. Zoning regulates such things as use of the land; lot sizes; types of structures permitted; building heights; **setbacks** (the minimum distance from streets or sidewalks that structures may be built); and density (the number of units that can be built in an area). Often the purpose of zoning is to implement a local master plan.

In New York State, zoning powers are given to municipal governments; there are no statewide zoning ordinances. These local authorities enact zoning ordinances, grant any zoning variations, hold planning meetings, and listen to zoning appeals. As with other governmental agencies and departments, their meetings must be open to the public (*Sunshine Law*).

Zoning ordinances generally divide land use into residential, commercial, industrial, vacant, agricultural, open space, institutional, and recreational classifications. Now many communities include **cluster zoning,** which allows **abutting** housing closely grouped, usually in return for community open space, and *multiple-use zoning*, which permits unusual planned unit developments. Zoning classifications found in a typical New York State community might include R-1, one-family residential; R-2, multifamily residential; C-1, commercial-retail; C-2, heavy commercial; and I-1 or M-1, industrial.

Residential areas may be subdivided to provide for detached single-family dwellings, semidetached structures containing not more than four dwelling units, walkup apartments, highrise apartments, and so forth. Variations exist among municipalities, and some may have as many as 15 classifications. In some cases the use of land located *within one to three miles* of an incorporated area must receive approval and consent even though the property is not next to the village, town, or city.

With the growth of unconventional **family** units, including **group homes,** New York has set definitions for what constitutes the allowable occupation of a single-family home as persons related by blood, marriage, or adoption, or a group of up to three people who are not related, living together as a household unit. Court challenges to the definition of a family for residential purposes often arise, particularly in the case of group homes.

Tests commonly applied to determine if zoning violates the rights of individuals require that the

■ power be exercised in a reasonable manner;
■ provisions be clear and specific;
■ ordinance be free from discrimination;
■ ordinance promote public health, safety, and general welfare under the police power concept; and
■ ordinance apply to all property in a similar manner.

Zoning laws are enforced through local requirements that **building permits** be obtained before property owners build on their land. A permit will not be issued unless a proposed structure conforms to the permitted zoning, among other requirements.

Accessory building/use.   An accessory building is one used for a purpose other than that of the principal building on the same lot. For example, a detached garage, pool house, or a storage shed would be considered an *accessory building*.

An accessory use is a use other than that normally allowed. An example of an **accessory use** would be an apartment allowed by special permit and under prescribed conditions in a single-family residence (a mother-in-law apartment).

Home occupations are sometimes allowed in residential zones if they are not the main use of the building, and they are subject to local ordinances.

Nonconforming use.   A frequent problem is a building that does not conform to the zoning use because it was used that way prior to the enactment of the zoning law. Such a **nonconforming use** is allowed to continue. If the building is destroyed or torn down, however, any new structure must comply with the current zoning ordinance. Local laws may say that the right to a nonconforming use is lost if it is discontinued for a certain period, usually one or two years.

Zoning boards of appeal have been established in most communities to hear complaints about the effects of zoning ordinances on specific parcels of property. Petitions may be presented to the appeal board for exceptions to the zoning law. The board's determinations can be challenged in state courts through an Article 78 proceeding.

Zoning variations.   Each time a plan is created or a zoning ordinance enacted, some owners are inconvenienced to the point of hardship. To alleviate some of the problems caused by zoning ordinances, two zoning variations are provided.

A **special-use permit** may be granted to allow a use of property that is in the public interest. For example, a restaurant may be built in an industrially zoned area if it is necessary to provide meal services for area workers, or a church might be allowed in a residential area. Also, a property owner who has suffered hardship as a result of a zoning ordinance may seek a **variance.** For example, if an owner's lot is level next to a road but slopes steeply 50 feet back from the road, the zoning board may be willing to allow a variance so the owner can build closer to the road than normally would be allowed.

Spot zoning.   A special-use permit that is not in harmony with the neighborhood (a chemical plant in a residential area, for example) is considered **spot zoning.** When it benefits only the user and not the neighborhood, spot zoning is illegal in New York State.

A *use variance* requires "unnecessary hardship." The property owner must show that

■ he or she is deprived of all economic use or benefit;
■ the hardship is unique, not universal to the area or neighborhood;
■ the variance will not change the essential character of the neighborhood; and
■ the alleged hardship is not self-created.

An *area variance* requires "practical difficulty," affecting the health, safety, or welfare of the community. The property owner must show that

■ the variance will not cause an undesirable change or detriment to neighboring properties;
■ the benefit sought by the person seeking the variance could not be achieved through other means;
■ the variance would not have an adverse effect on environmental or physical conditions in the neighborhood or district;
■ the difficulty suffered by the property owner was not self-created (does not preclude granting); and
■ the requested variance is not substantial.

Building Codes

Most cities and towns have enacted ordinances to specify *construction standards* that must be met during building construction or repair. These are called building codes, and they set minimum requirements for kinds of materials, sanitary equipment, electrical wiring, fire prevention standards, and the like. New York has a *statewide building code* that applies where no local code exists or where local codes are less restrictive.

Most communities require the issuance of a building permit by a building department or another authority before anyone can build a structure or alter an existing building. Officials can verify compliance with building codes and zoning ordinances by examining the plans and inspecting the work. After the new construction is found satisfactory, the inspector issues a **certificate of occupancy (C of O)** or, for an altered building, a *certificate of compliance.* The certificate of occupancy is also required for some transfers of existing buildings. If the construction violated a private deed restriction (discussed earlier in this chapter), a building permit still might be issued. A *building permit is merely evidence of the applicant's compliance with municipal regulations.* It does not, however, give the landowner the right to ignore private deed restrictions that may apply.

Subdivision Regulations

Article 9-A of the real property law governs subdivided lands. Among the requirements before land can be subdivided or built on are those set by the *Interstate Land Sales Full Disclosure Act,* and the environmental impact statement mandated by the State Environmental Quality Review Act. Where several agencies may be involved, the one that makes final decisions is known as the **lead agency.** Subdivision requirements are discussed in detail in Chapters 16 and 23.

Most communities have adopted **subdivision regulations,** often as a part of a master plan. Subdivision regulations usually provide for

■ location, grading, alignment, surfacing, and widths of streets, highways, and other rights-of-way;
■ installation of sewers and water mains;
■ minimum dimensions of lots;
■ building and setback lines;
■ areas to be reserved for public use, such as parks or schools; and
■ easements for public utilities.

Development Rights

In areas where the right to build commercial buildings is limited in height or square footage, particularly in New York City, the owners of small parcels that do not intend to use their rights (a church, for example, or a small landmark building) may sell their **development rights,** which can be transferred and used to construct a building on another lot, higher or larger than would otherwise be allowed.

In some suburban areas, communities have bought development rights from the owners of agricultural properties. The owners are permitted to continue farming, thus preserving the rural atmosphere and avoiding additional residential subdivisions.

Environmental Protection Legislation

Federal and state legislators have passed a number of environmental protection laws in an attempt to respond to public concern over preservation of America's natural resources. Of particular importance are the *New York Environmental Conservation Law* and the federal *Comprehensive and Environmental Response, Cleanup, and Liability Act of 1980* **(CERCLA),** discussed at greater length in Chapter 16. CERCLA places responsibility for cleanup of environmental disasters on the original offenders and also on current and future owners of the property, including lending institutions that might acquire the property through foreclosure.

In 1986 the *Superfund Amendments and Reauthorization Act* (SARA) further defined responsibility for cleanup caused by past activities. The "innocent" purchaser has a defense against liability for previous owners' actions, provided there is proper diligent investigation of possible contamination before his or her purchase. Proof of an environmental audit before purchase would be a good defense.

Where several agencies are involved in an environmental audit, the work is coordinated by a *lead agency*.

The *New York State Navigation Law*, originally intended to cover liability for oil spills, includes an *Environmental Lien Amendment* under which the state can hold any property owner accountable for environmental cleanup.

Many of these laws were triggered by the 1978 Love Canal disaster, in which a toxic waste dump started leaking and contaminated a residential area and school, which had to be abandoned (although the government later claimed that the dangerous conditions were overstated).

Even when the federal and state officials declared part of the neighborhood cleaned up and safe, banks were unwilling to offer would-be buyers any mortgage loans on the boarded-up houses, fearing liability if future problems arose. Lawsuits to determine who was liable for the cleanup involved Hooker Chemical and Plastics Corp., which originally buried the chemicals; Occidental Chemical Corp., which bought the Hooker company in 1968; and the school board and city of Niagara Falls, which built a grade school and roads on the site.

Wetlands. New York has legislated requirements to protect designated wetlands, those areas listed by the state as having groundwater on or near the surface of the land or meeting other definitions. Improvements may be constructed only with a state permit; most agricultural uses are exempt from the law. The federal government's *Clean Waters Act* also requires a permit from the Army Corps of Engineers and EPA approval for building on designated wetlands. Cities and counties also frequently pass environmental legislation of their own.

Real estate practitioners must be alert to possible environmental problems so that sellers and prospective buyers will be fully informed about potential liabilities. The subject is discussed more fully in Chapter 16.

Landmark Preservation

In New York State, local governments may enact regulations intended to preserve individual buildings and areas of historic or architectural significance. Regulations setting up local historic areas or landmark preservation districts may restrict owners' rights to alter the exteriors of certain old buildings. Interior remodeling is typically free from regulation. Individual buildings located outside an historic area also may be designated as landmarks. Applications for listing on the National Historic Register are made to New York's Office of Parks, Recreation and Historic Preservation **(OPRHP),** which passes them on to the federal government. If a building is listed on the National Register, it is automatically listed also on the state's.

■ DIRECT PUBLIC OWNERSHIP

A certain amount of land is owned by the government for such uses as municipal buildings, state legislature houses, schools, and military stations. **Direct public ownership** is a means of land control.

Publicly owned streets and highways serve a necessary function for the entire population. In addition, public land is often used for such recreational purposes as parks. National and state parks and forest preserves create areas for public use and recreation and at the same time help to conserve our natural resources. At present the federal government owns approximately 775 million acres of land. Much of that is in Alaska.

■ SUMMARY

Private land use controls are exercised by owners, often subdividers, who control use of subdivision lots through deed restrictions that apply to all lot owners. The usual recorded restrictions may be enforced by neighboring lot owners' obtaining a court injunction to stop a violator.

Government powers limiting private rights in land include taxation, eminent domain, police power, and escheat. The control of land use is exercised through public controls, private (or nongovernment) controls, and public ownership.

Public controls are ordinances based on the states' police power to protect the public health, safety, and welfare. Cities and municipalities enact master plans and zoning ordinances.

Zoning ordinances segregate residential areas from business and industrial zones and control not only land use but also height and bulk of buildings and density of population. Zoning boards of appeal can grant special-use permits and variances and recognize nonconforming uses. Subdivision regulations maintain control of development.

Building codes control construction by specifying standards for plumbing, sewers, electrical wiring, and equipment. A building inspector may issue a certificate of occupancy when a completed building meets standards.

In addition to land-use control on the local level, the state and federal governments have intervened to preserve natural resources through environmental legislation. Important are CERCLA and SARA, which placed responsibility on landowners for environmental cleanups, and wetlands legislation that limits building on designated lands.

Public ownership provides land for such public purposes as parks, highways, schools, and municipal buildings.

QUESTIONS

1. In New York State the most effective way to protest a high property tax assessment is to
   a. show that neighboring similar property is assessed at lower figures.
   b. produce proof of the cost basis of the property, purchase price plus improvements.
   c. place the property on the market and see how much is offered for it.
   d. offer to sell to the assessor for the assessed value.

2. A homeowner who is dissatisfied with assessed valuation can take a complaint to
   a. the assessor personally.
   b. a board of review.
   c. a small claims hearing.
   d. Any of the above

3. When the Thruway was constructed, the route ran through the Adams farm. Mr. Adams refused to sell the necessary land. The state then used its right of eminent domain through a court proceeding known as
   a. escheat.   c. condemnation.
   b. variance.   d. downzoning.

4. The right of escheat allows New York State to acquire land
   a. through a developer's dedication of property.
   b. when someone dies without leaving a will or natural heirs.
   c. through a gift from a donor.
   d. when property taxes are not paid as due.

5. L. J. Blake's house contains eight studio apartments, four more than zoning laws allow on his street. To receive a permit for a nonconforming use, Blake must prove that the
   a. present use is in the public interest because the neighborhood is short of rental units.
   b. house has been used that way every year since before the zoning ordinance was adopted.
   c. deed he received specifically lists eight apartments in the building.
   d. zoning ordinance is unreasonably restrictive.

6. Doctor Spock goes before her local zoning board asking for permission to open an office in her residential neighborhood because the area has no medical facilities. She is asking for a
   a. variance.
   b. nonconforming use.
   c. special-use permit.
   d. restriction.

7. Dan Hill asks the zoning board to allow him to build a fence to keep his children safe on a busy corner, though he does not have room for the required ten-foot setback. He is asking for a
   a. variance.
   b. nonconforming use.
   c. special-use permit.
   d. restriction.

8. Private land-use controls include
   a. subdivision regulations.
   b. deed restrictions.
   c. environmental protection laws.
   d. master plan specifications.

9. The building inspector who is satisfied that construction is satisfactory may issue a

   a. certificate of occupancy.
   b. subdivision regulation.
   c. restrictive covenant.
   d. conditional-use permit.

10. The purpose of a building permit is to

    a. override a deed restriction.
    b. maintain municipal control over the volume of building.
    c. provide evidence of compliance with municipal regulations.
    d. regulate area and bulk of buildings.

11. The New York State Navigation Law is concerned with

    a. riparian rights.
    b. environmental cleanups.
    c. the Barge Canal system.
    d. Niagara Falls.

12. CERCLA and SARA are federal laws establishing

    a. restrictions on wetlands development.
    b. national building code standards.
    c. liability for past environmental contamination.
    d. regulations for environmental safety in the workplace.

13. Miss Muffet's Greek Revival home is located in a historic preservation district. She probably can't change

    a. the number of bathrooms in the building.
    b. the exterior of the building.
    c. the interior of the building.
    d. either the exterior or the interior.

14. The term *laches* refers to

    a. loss of a right if it isn't exercised in time.
    b. responsibility for environmental cleanup.
    c. land set aside for recreational use in a master plan.
    d. the process of downzoning.

15. The grantor of real estate may place effective deed restrictions forbidding

    a. any future sale of the property.
    b. rental of the property to a member of a particular ethnic group.
    c. division of the parcel into small building lots.
    d. mortgaging of the property.

16. A deed restriction requires 250 feet of road frontage per lot. The town building code requires only 100 feet, and a builder constructs two houses on his 250-foot lot. The neighbors may

    a. ask the court to order one house torn down.
    b. act only before the builder has obtained certificates of occupancy.
    c. do nothing because the builder complied with all town regulations.
    d. enforce their rights by calling the police.

13

INTRODUCTION TO CONSTRUCTION

The Mortensons' house was brand-new when they bought it seven years ago. Over the years they've had a host of problems. Now they've realized that the shingles the builder used were defective, the heating system was improperly installed, and the foundation is settling. They're wondering if it's too late to sue their builder for any or all of these problems.

Buyers and sellers often consult real estate brokers for advice on renovations and repairs. The agent who has a knowledge of basic construction is often able to judge quality and spot problems. It's also important, though, to know when outside expertise is needed, and to advise hiring a professional building inspector and/or engineer. The salesperson or broker who tries to appear expert on building or engineering systems is inviting lawsuits.

■ KEY TERMS

amperage
basement
beam
bearing walls
blueprint
British thermal unit (BTU)
casement window
circuit breaker box
concrete slab foundation
crawlspace
double-hung window
eave
fascia
floating slab foundation
foundation

framing
frieze board
fuse box
girder
headers
heat pump
insulation
jalousie window
joist and rafter roof
Lally™ columns
110-volt circuit
percolation rate
pier and beam foundation
pitch
plasterboard/wallboard

platform framing
  construction
post-and-beam
  construction
R-value
septic system
sheathing
siding
sill plates
soffit
solar energy
specifications
studs
truss roof
220-volt circuit
voltage

■ SITE PREPARATION

In real estate practice, the term site is used to refer to a parcel of land that has been prepared for construction of some sort of an improvement. Site preparation involves clearing the land and grading it to provide drainage and a building location. Large trees on the property may be marked for retention as the land is cleared.

Siting of the building may take into account which rooms will receive morning and evening sunlight and which side of the house will receive the prevailing winds. Access and utilities also must be provided for. In locations that are not served by public utilities, an on-site well and/or sanitary waste (septic) system may need to be installed. On-site wells and septic systems must meet standards established by the state Department of Health and enforced by county Departments of Health. Other systems, including heating, ventilation, and cooling (HVAC); hot water; and electrical systems must meet standards set by the New York State Energy Code.

■ REGULATION OF RESIDENTIAL CONSTRUCTION

Building construction begins with the construction documents: the plans and specifications. Plans and blueprints are scale drawings of the building and its various components, including floor plans, elevations, sections, and construction details. Separate plans are often drawn to show the locations and features of electrical, plumbing, HVAC, and sewage-disposal systems. **Specifications** are written text; they tell the builder what materials to use and may suggest what construction techniques to follow, which have a great impact on construction costs.

With construction documents in hand, the builder or owner's next step is to obtain a building permit from the local permitting agency. This process involves payment of a permit fee, and the agency then will review the plans to ensure that the building meets all the requirements of the building codes that are in effect in the locality. Separate permits may be required from agencies regulating construction, electrical systems, plumbing systems, and other aspects of the construction. Approval from environmental protection agencies may be required as well.

As construction progresses, the permitting agency or agencies will perform inspections of the building in progress. If construction has progressed in accordance with the approved plans and specifications, the inspector(s) will issue the necessary approvals. The final approval results in a certificate of occupancy, which means the building has been approved as in substantial compliance with requirements and fit for human habitation.

New York State has a minimum standards building code, but local municipalities may *add* to it or *impose tighter restrictions*. Examples of local codes in various New York communities: requiring sprinkler systems, underground wiring, or sump pumps in all new residential construction; banning the use of polyvinyl chloride for plumbing; requiring that plumbers, electricians, or builders be licensed and that they carry liability and workers' compensation insurance. New York's Board of Fire Underwriters must approve all electrical installations, independent of local approval.

■ WOOD-FRAME CONSTRUCTION

Most houses in New York State are built with underlying wood-frame construction covered with an exterior of brick, stone, wood, vinyl, or aluminum siding. Wood-frame houses are preferred because they are less expensive than other kinds of construction, they can be built rapidly, they are easy to insulate, and they allow flexibility of design.

Architectural Styles

Although details of construction are rigidly specified by building codes, architectural styles may vary greatly. Some popular styles include colonial, Georgian, ranch, Cape Cod, contemporary, split-level, Dutch colonial, French provincial, and Spanish. Examples of several typical architectural styles are shown in Figure 13.1.

Throughout this chapter, certain terms are followed by a bold number in brackets that refers to the numbered terms in the house diagram in Figure 13.2.

Foundations

The term foundation includes footings, foundation walls, columns, pilasters, slab and all other parts that provide support for the house. Foundations are constructed of cut stone, stone and brick, concrete block, poured concrete, and even specially treated wood. Poured concrete and concrete block are the most common foundation materials because of their strength and resistance to moisture. In recent years Styrofoam has been used to insulate foundation walls. The two major types of foundations are concrete slab and pier and beam.

Concrete slab. A concrete slab foundation is supported around the perimeter and in the center by concrete footings dug into the earth. It is made of poured concrete reinforced with steel rods. It rests directly on the earth, with usually a minimum of damproofing between the concrete and the ground. Foundations formed by a single pouring of concrete are called *monolithic*, whereas those in which the footings and the slab are poured separately are referred to as **floating slab foundations.**

Pier and beam. In a pier and beam foundation, shown in Figure 13.3, the foundation slab rests on an interconnected concrete footing. The house framing is connected to the foundation by a treated wood **sill plate** bolted down with *anchor bolts.* The *floor joists* that provide the major support for the flooring rest on top of the treated *sills* (floor girders). The slab or concrete floor rests on top of the projecting parts of the footings. The space between the slab and the foundation is called the **crawlspace** or **basement.** The *piers* support the main **girder** or **beam** and are attached by lag bolts through the **Lally™ column** top plate.

Termite protection. In some areas of New York State the earth is infested with termites, active antlike insects that are destructive to wood. After con-

FIGURE   13.1

Architectural Styles

SPLIT LEVEL

MULTILEVEL

GARAGE UNDER SECOND STORY

SPANISH

TILE ROOF

STUCCO WALLS

OVAL DOORS

CENTRAL COURTYARD

RANCH

1 STORY - LOW TO THE GROUND

PICTURE WIND

CAPE COD

1½ STORIES

SHINGLES

CENTRAL ENTRANCE

Architectural Styles (continued)

DUTCH COLONIAL

2 – 2½ STORIES

GAMBREL ROOF

DORMERS

DUTCH DOOR

FRENCH PROVINCIAL

STEEP HIP ROOF

1½-2½ STORIES

CURVED WINDOW TRIM
THAT EXTENDS THROUGH
THE CORNICE

GEORGIAN

2 STORIES

CHIMNEYS AT
EITHER END

HIP ROOF

COLONIAL

2-3 STORIES

COLUMN-SUPPORTED
COLONNADE

SYMMETRICAL

F I G U R E   13.2

House Diagram

1. **FOOTING**	22. **MUNTIN**	43. **FIRESTOP**
2. **FOUNDATION DRAIN TILE**	23. **WINDOW SASH**	44. **DOWNSPOUT**
3. **CRUSHED WASHED STONE**	24. **EAVE (ROOF PROJECTION)**	45. **LATHS**
4. **FOUNDATION WALL**	25. **WINDOW JAMB TRIM**	46. **PLASTER BOARD**
5. **DAMPPROOFING OR WEATHERPROOFING**	26. **WINDOW HEADER**	47. **PLASTER FINISH**
6. **BACKFILL**	27. **CEILING JOIST**	48. **MANTEL**
7. **ANCHOR BOLT**	28. **TOP AND TIE PLATES**	49. **ASH DUMP**
8. **SILL PLATE**	29. **GABLE STUD**	50. **BASE TOP MOULDING**
9. **TERMITE SHIELD**	30. **RAFTERS**	51. **BASEBOARD**
10. **FLOOR JOIST**	31. **COLLAR TIES**	52. **SHOE MOULDING**
11. **BAND OR BOX BEAM**	32. **GABLE END OF ROOF**	53. **FINISH MOULDING**
12. **SOLE PLATE**	33. **RIDGE BEAM**	54. **CROSS BRIDGING**
13. **SUBFLOORING**	34. **CHIMNEY FLUES**	55. **PIER**
14. **BUILDING PAPER**	35. **CHIMNEY CAP**	56. **GIRDER**
15. **WALL STUD**	36. **CHIMNEY**	57. **FOOTING**
16. **CORNER STUDS**	37. **CHIMNEY FLASHING**	58. **RISER**
17. **INSULATION**	38. **ROOFING SHINGLES**	59. **TREAD**
18. **HOUSE WRAP**	39. **ROOFING FELT/ICE AND WATER MEMBRANE**	60. **STRINGER**
19. **WALL SHEATHING**	40. **ROOF SHEATHING**	61. **CLEANOUT DOOR**
20. **SIDING**	41. **EAVE TROUGH OR GUTTER**	62. **CONCRETE BASEMENT FLOOR**
21. **MULLION**	42. **FRIEZE BOARD**	63. **CRUSHED/WASHED STONE**

FIGURE   13.3

**Pier and Beam
Foundation**

structing the slab for the foundation, the ground may be chemically treated to poison termites and prevent them from coming through or around the foundation and into the wooden structure. Chemical or pressure treatment of lumber is used for sills and beams that are close to ground level. The installation of metal *termite shields* [9] also will provide protection.

■ EXTERIOR CONSTRUCTION

Walls and Framing

When the foundation is in place, the first floor deck is built and then the interior and exterior walls are framed. The exterior and some interior walls are known as **bearing walls,** because they support the floors, ceilings, and roof. (Some interior partitions, installed later, may be nonbearing.) The skeleton members of a building are called its **frame.** The walls of a frame are formed by vertical members called **studs [15],** spaced at even intervals and attached to the sill. Many building codes require that for a one-story house the stud spacing not exceed 24 inches on centers. For a two-story house the spacing may not exceed 16 inches. Studs rest on sole plates [12], which are secured to and rest on the *foundation wall* [4] in balloon framing. In constructing walls and floors, if the wall height is more than eight feet, the framer may install *firestops* [43], blocks nailed between studs or joists to stop drafts and retard the spread of fire.

Where there is an opening in a wall frame, such as for a door or window, a horizontal **header** is used to support the weight of the structure over the opening. Wider openings require larger headers for structural support. In masonry walls, the weight over a door or window opening may be supported by an arch or by a lintel. A *lintel* is a piece of stone, steel, or wood that is used to span the opening and support the wall above.

In framing, many builders are moving away from the traditional 2 × 4s placed 16 inches on center, using 2 × 6s instead. This allows a deeper wall for more extensive insulation.

Three basic types of wood-frame construction—platform, balloon, and post and beam—are shown in Figure 13.4.

Platform frame construction.   The most common type of wall framing for both one-story and two-story residential structures is platform framing construction, also known as *western frame construction*. Only one floor is built at a time, and each floor serves as a platform for the next story. Wall studs are attached to the upper and lower plates, and the entire assemblage is then raised into place and anchored to the sill.

Balloon frame construction.   This type of construction differs from the platform method in that the studs extend continuously from the foundation sill plate to the ceiling of the second floor. The second-floor joists rest on *ledger boards* or *ribbon boards* set into the interior edge of the studs. The balloon method gives a smooth, unbroken wall surface on each floor level, thus alleviating the unevenness that sometimes results from settling when the platform method is used. The balloon method is usually employed when the exterior finish will be brick, stone veneer, or stucco.

Post-and-beam frame construction.   With **post-and-beam construction** the ceiling planks are supported on beams that rest on posts placed at intervals throughout the exterior of the house. Because the posts provide some of the ceiling support, rooms can be built with larger spans of space between the supporting side walls. In some houses the beams are left exposed and the posts and beams are stained to serve as part of the decor.

Lumber.   Lumber used in residential construction is graded according to moisture content and structural quality as established by the 1970 National Grade Rule. Grading rules require that dimension lumber (2″ × 4″, 2″, 2″ × 6″) that is classified as *dry* have a moisture content of 19 percent or less. Lumber that has a higher moisture content is classified as *green*. All species and grades are assigned stress ratings to indicate their strength when used in spanning distances between two supports. Actual dimensions of lumber differ from nominal measurements. A 2″ × 4″ actually measures 1½″ × 3½″.

Exterior walls.   After the skeleton is constructed, the exterior wall surface must be built and **sheathing [19]** and **siding [20]** applied. Sheathing is nailed directly to the *wall studs* [15] to form the base for siding and add rigidity to the wall system. Sheathing is generally hardboard, insulated board, or chipboard. If the house is to have a masonry veneer, the sheathing may be moisture-resistant gypsum board. Fabricated sheathings are available in both strip and sheet material. Sheathing is wrapped in tar paper or, more recently, in house wrap.

The final exterior layer, called *siding*, may be vinyl, wood, aluminum, stone, stucco, brick, or other material.

F I G U R E   13.4

F I G U R E   13.4

Frame Construction

Insulation

To ensure adequate protection, **insulation [17]** should be placed in exterior walls and upper-floor ceilings. *Band insulation* of fiberglass is placed above the foundation walls. A sill sealer is placed between the foundation and the treated sill plate to reduce the infiltration of air and insects. The New York code requires varying amounts of insulation in different regions of the state, as well as storm windows and doors. For conversion of existing oil-fired units to gas or electric heat, *cap insulation* (under the attic floor) is required and storm windows or insulated glass where single-glazing had been used.

Insulation is rated according to its R-value, which indicates its resistance to heat transfer. The higher the R-value, the better the insulation. The most commonly used insulation material is fiberglass, which comes in either Kraft (paper) or foil-faced batts that can be placed between the studs. Other materials used are rigid Styrofoam, cellulose fiber (usually blown into existing structures), rock wool, or sprayed-in-place foam. Proper insulation will contribute to the efficiency of both heating and air-conditioning systems.

Each set of building plans must be certified by a licensed architect or engineer, who puts the appropriate energy code on the plan. Different styles and designs and different regions have varying code requirements. For example, the manufacturer of a log house may certify that no insulation is necessary (because the logs do the job and the windows are small), whereas a contemporary-style home with vast areas of glass could require a great deal of insulation.

Window and Door Units

After the exterior walls are framed, the next step is installation of exterior window and door units. Windows may be either side-hinged or vertically hinged **(casement windows)** or may slide up and down (*sash*). Basic window styles include the following:

- Single-hung window: A sash window with only one movable sash, usually the bottom one.
- Double-hung window: A sash window with two vertically sliding sashes; both single-hung and double-hung window sashes are controlled and held in place by springs or weights.
- Slider window: A sash window that opens by moving horizontally.
- Casement/awning window: A window hinged like a door that opens or closes by the action of a gear handle.
- Jalousie window: A jalousie window is formed by horizontal slats of glass that open or close vertically by the action of a gear.

Many modern windows can be removed from the inside for easy cleaning. Window frames are most commonly vinyl, wood, steel, or aluminum. The quality of a window depends on its construction, additional security, and insulating factors. State code requires either double-glazing (two panes of sealed glass with insulating airspace between) or storm windows.

The thickness of an interior door is usually 1⅜ inches; an exterior door is usually 1¾ inches. Most are made of mahogany, birch, walnut, or oak. Glass doors, screen doors with aluminum or steel frames, and insulated metal doors are primarily exterior doors used for patios, porches, or garden areas. Energy considerations dictate *triple-glazing* for many windows in recent years.

Roof Framing and Coverings

The construction of the skeleton framing for the roofing material is the next step in building. Residential roofs are made in several styles, including gabled, shed, salt box, and flat. Roof construction includes the *rafters* or *collar ties* [31], *sheathing* [40], and *exterior trimming* [42]. Skeleton framings are classified as either conventional (site built) or trusses. (See Figures 13.5 and 13.6.)

The slant of the roof is referred to as its **pitch;** shallow roofs sometimes give more trouble than steep ones that shed rain and snow more readily. Pitch is expressed as a ratio. If the total roof rise is 6 feet and the total span is 24 feet, the pitch would be 1/4. *Slope* is the term more commonly used to designate the incline. If the roof rises at a rate of 6" for every 12" of run (half the total span), the roof is said to have a *6 in 12 slope*. The triangular symbol above the roof in a set of architectural plans is where the numbers may be found.

Joist and rafter roof framing.   A **joist and rafter roof** consists of *rafters* [30], *collar beams* [31], *ceiling joists* [27], and *ridge beam* [33]. Rafters are the sloping timbers that support the weight of the roof and establish the roof's pitch, or slant. Collar beams give rigidity to the rafters, and the ridge board aligns and receives the rafters.

Truss roof framing.   A **truss roof** has four parts. It has *lower chords, upper chords,* "W" *diagonals,* and *gusset plates.* The lower chords are similar to ceiling joists, and the upper chords are the equivalent of rafters in a joist and rafter roof. The "W" diagonals are the equivalent of the collar ties. Gusset plates are solid pieces of metal or wood that add rigidity to the roof. All integral parts are assembled and held in place by gusset plates, bolt connections, or nails. A truss roof is generally prefabricated at a mill and set in place in sections by a crane, while a joist and rafter roof is assembled piece by piece on the site.

Exposed rafter and roof framing.   *Exposed,* or *sloping, rafter roofs* are often used with post-and-beam frame construction. The rafters are supported by central support posts at the exterior walls. There may be no ceiling joists or lower chords to provide additional support. The rafters in this type of roof are often left exposed for decorative purposes.

Exterior trim.   The overhang of a pitched roof that extends beyond the exterior walls of the house is called the **eaves** [24], or *cornice.* The cornice is composed of the **soffit,** *frieze board, fascia board, and extended rafters* and recently includes *soffit vents.* The **frieze board** [42] is the exterior wood trim board used to finish the exterior wall between the top of the siding and eaves, or overhang, of the roof framing. The **fascia** board is exterior trim used along the line of the butt end of the rafters where the roof overhangs the structural walls. The overhang of the cornice provides a decorative touch to the exterior of a house as well as some protection from sun and rain. (See Figure 13.7.)

Roof sheathing and roofing.   With the skeleton roof in place, the rafters are covered with sheathing. The type and thickness of sheathing to be used depends on the choice of outside roofing material and rafter spacing. Shingles are commonly of *fiberglass* or *asphalt* and are laid over plywood covered with

FIGURE   13.5

Roof Construction

In a truss roof the upper and lower chords are joined together by either a gusset plate or a split ring and bolt.

Roof Styles

GABLE

HIP

SINGLE DORMER

SHED DORMER

GABLE WITH DORMERS

SALT BOX

SHED

FLAT

GAMBREL

MANSARD

F I G U R E   13.7

Eave or Cornice

tar paper. In recent years the first three to six feet of a roof (depending on location and slope) are covered with an "ice and water" type membrane, which adheres to the sheathing and rip edge. If wood shingles are used, spaced sheathing of 1″ × 4″ boards may be used to provide airspace to allow the shingles to dry after rain.

■ INTERIOR CONSTRUCTION

Walls and Finishing

Interior walls are usually covered with *drywall* (also called **plasterboard** or **wallboard)** [46], although *lath* [45] and *plaster* [47] may be used. Drywall is finished by a process known as *taping and floating*. Taping covers the joints between the sheets of drywall. Floating is the smoothing out of the walls over the joints and the rough edges where nails attach drywall to the studs. Texturing may be applied with a roller prior to painting.

Final features added include (1) *floor covering*, (2) *trim*, (3) *cabinet work*, and (4) *wall finishings* of paint, wallpaper, or paneling. Floor coverings of vinyl, asphalt tile, wood (either in strips or blocks), carpet, brick, stone, or ceramic tile are applied over the wood or concrete subflooring. Trim masks the joints between the walls and ceiling and gives a finished touch to the room. Cabinet work in the home may be either built in on the job or prefabricated in the mill.

Plumbing

If the house is supplied by a well, the state Department of Health sets various requirements for its location, for example, 25 feet from a cast iron sewer pipe and as much as 150 feet from the seepage pit of a **septic system.** It is also generally required that a well produce at least five gallons of water per minute of water supply.

Septic systems also are regulated as to their distance from a house or a well. **Percolation rate** tests must be performed to determine whether the soil will absorb effluent neither too quickly nor too slowly.

Plumbing must be installed subject to strict inspections and in accordance with local building codes that dictate materials and the method of installation. Sewer pipes are of cast iron, concrete, or plastic, whereas water pipes are of copper, plastic, or (in older homes) galvanized iron. Recently, plastic has been used more frequently for waste lines because it eliminates piping joints in the foundation slab and may be less expensive.

All drain pipes must be connected to vents leading out of the building to operate properly. Water supply pipes must be sized adequately to provide sufficient flow of water to faucets or fixtures. The main water lines in a home are usually 1-inch or ¾-inch diameter, while the branch lines running to individual outlets are ½-inch diameter.

Domestic hot water may be supplied directly from a coil in the heating system or by a separate hot-water heater. If a separate unit is used, the water is heated by electricity, gas, or oil. Well-water supplies may require water softeners.

Lead-tin solder, used widely for copper plumbing, has been under scrutiny by the Environmental Protection Agency, which limits lead content to 8 percent and recommends the use of tin-antimony solder instead.

Bathtubs, toilets, and sinks are made of cast iron or pressed steel coated with enamel, plastic, artificial marble, or, increasingly in recent years, fiberglass.

Heating and Air-Conditioning

Warm-air heating systems and hot-water baseboards are the most common heating systems in use today. Steam heat is found in some older homes. In recent years some areas of northern New York have seen increasing dependence on wood as a fuel. A forced-warm-air system consists of a furnace, air handlers, warm-air distributing ducts, and ducts for the return air. Combination heating-cooling systems are common in new homes; the most common is the conventional warm-air heating system with a cooling unit attached.

Heating systems can be powered by electricity, oil, or natural gas. Oil-fired systems use oil from a storage tank located on the property, either above ground (AST) or buried underground (UST). (Note that should USTs leak, costly cleanup procedures will be required.) Natural gas may be supplied through a utility pipeline or from a separate pressurized gas tank on the property.

Each furnace has a capacity rated in British thermal units (BTUs). The number of BTUs given represents the furnace's heat output from gas, oil, or electric firing. A heating and cooling engineer can determine the cubic area of the building as well as its construction, insulation, and window and door sizes and from these data compute the furnace capacity required in the coldest possible weather and the cooling capacity needed for air-conditioning. Air-conditioning units are rated either in BTUs or in tons. Twelve thousand BTUs is equivalent to a one-ton capacity.

Most gas pipes for heating and cooking are made of black iron. A flexible plastic tubing is coming into use, although not all jurisdictions allow it yet. It requires fewer joints and is easier to install. Gas pipes are installed in the walls or run overhead in the attic, where adequate ventilation is possible. They are never placed in the slab.

Solar heating.   One of the most promising sources of heat for residential buildings is solar energy. Most solar heating units suitable for residential use operate by gathering the heat from the sun's rays with one or more solar collectors. Water or air is forced through a series of pipes in the solar collector to be heated by the sun's rays. The hot air or water then is stored in a heavily insulated storage tank until it is needed to heat the house or for use as a hot-water heater.

More immediately practical in the New York State area is *passive solar heating*. Without any additional special equipment, a house may be built or remodeled to take advantage of the sun's rays. Large areas of glass on a southern exposure and few windows on the north side of a building are typical of passive solar arrangements. Substantial savings in fuel may be obtained.

Heat pumps, which utilize heat from outside air in a form of reverse air-conditioning, are often used in conjunction with backup heating units of more conventional design. Where electricity is expensive, use of a heat pump may bring down costs. The heat pump also serves in summer for air-conditioning. Geothermal systems utilize the constant temperature underground to aid in heating and cooling. At depths of four to six feet and greater, the earth maintains about the same temperature year-round, approximately 51°F to 56°F in New York State.

Ventilation.   Ventilation in a home is important for several reasons: to provide fresh air for the occupants to breathe, to prevent the accumulation of moisture that could damage the structure, and to eliminate harmful or offensive gases and odors.

With today's emphasis on insulation and close-fitting windows and doors, proper ventilation can sometimes be overlooked. Enclosed unheated spaces such as attics and crawlspaces must be ventilated by screened openings in the structure. An attic may have vents through the roof, or (more sightly from the street) a ridge beam (number 32 in Figure 13.2) that contains hidden vents. Bathrooms and kitchens are normally ventilated by means of fans that connect to ducts leading out of the building. Exhaust fumes from oil or gas-fired equipment also must be vented to the outside through ducts.

Electrical Services

Electrical power lines can be run underground or strung from power poles. Electrical services are brought into the home through a transformer and meter into a distribution panel (circuit breaker box or fuse box). The utility company owns and maintains the parts of the system up to and including the meter. The rest of the system, including the distribution panel and interior circuits, is the responsibility of the homeowner.

Electricity is measured in terms of volts, amperes (amps), and watts. Voltage indicates the strength of the electrical charge. Amperage indicates the amount of current that is flowing in response to the voltage. *Wattage* is equal to volts times amps; a 100-watt light bulb operating at 100 volts would draw a current of 1 amp. Wattage measures the amount of electric power that is being delivered and used. One thousand watts of power, used for one hour, is called a kilowatt hour.

Most residential circuits operate at approximately 110 volts and are rated to carry 15 or 20 amps of current. Larger appliances require 220-volt circuits and may draw 30 to 60 amps. The amount of amperage a circuit can carry is limited by the size (rating) of the fuse or circuit breaker that controls the circuit and the size (gauge) of the wire; **110-volt circuits** have two wires, one hot and one neutral, and they may also have a separate ground wire; **220-volt circuits** have two hot wires and one neutral wire, and may have a separate ground wire as well.

Electrical wiring is rated by its gauge or thickness. A lower gauge indicates a larger diameter of wire. The gauge determines how much current (amperage) the wire can safely carry. For example, 15-amp circuits require 14-gauge wire, while 20-amp circuits call for 12-gauge wire. Most residential wiring is made of copper, although aluminum wiring is sometimes used. Aluminum wiring requires the use of specially designed receptacles that are approved for use with this type of wire.

Modern construction uses cable known as *Romex*, which has two or three insulated wires and a bare ground wire covered with a plastic sheathing. Exposed cable or wiring must be run through metal conduit to provide protection from physical damage. Conduit can be either rigid metal or plastic tubes or flexible metal tubing. Flexible conduit is sometimes called *Greenfield*.

The circuit breaker box is the distribution panel for the many electrical circuits in the house. (See Figure 13.8.) In case of a power overload the heat generated by the additional flow of electricity will cause the circuit to open, thus reducing the possibility of electrical fires. All electrical installations are inspected by the New York Board of Fire Underwriters. New York State standards require at least 100-ampere service and, for new home construction, a 110-volt smoke detector and a ground fault interrupter on each water hazard circuit (kitchen, baths, exterior outlets). The ground fault interrupter is a supersensitive form of circuit breaker.

Residential wiring circuits are rated by the voltage they are designed to carry. In the past most residences were wired only for 110-volt capacity. Today, because of the many built-in appliances in use, 220-volt service is standard.

A functioning carbon monoxide detector and smoke detector must be installed in every one or two-family house, co-op, or condo constructed in New York State.

■ NEW YORK LAWS

Home Improvement Law

New York State requires that the sale of home improvement goods and services costing more than $500 to homeowners, co-op owners, or tenants conform to certain regulations.

A copy of a written plain-English contract must be given to the customer before any work is done. It must contain the contractor's name, address and telephone number; approximate start and completion dates; specifics of the work and materials (brands, model number, price); and a notice that the customer has an unconditional right to cancel the contract in writing within three days after it is signed.

Contractors are required to put into a trust (escrow) account in a New York State bank any contract payments by a customer, to be withdrawn only under a reasonable payment schedule agreed to by contractor and customer or on substantial completion of the job. If the customer violates the contract, funds may be withdrawn only to the amount of the contractor's reasonable costs. As an alternative to the escrow account, the contractor may deliver to the customer, within ten days of receiving the funds, a bond guaranteeing that the customer's money will be properly used or returned.

Where the contractor fails to adequately secure customers' deposits, to provide a written contract, or otherwise violates the law, penalties include fines of up to 10 percent of the contract price, with a maximum of $1,000 for a first offense, $2,500 for a second one, and $5,000 for a third or succeeding violation.

New Home Warranty

With a few exceptions, New York requires that the buyer of a new home receive the following warranties: one year's protection against faulty workmanship and defective materials; two years' protection against defective installation of plumbing, electrical, heating, cooling, and ventilation systems; and six years' protection against major structural defects (a foundation that settles, a roof that sags, a wall that bows). Some builders carry warranty insurance at a cost of several hundred dollars per house.

Warranty law allows builders a reasonable time to make repairs and does not cover construction done by the buyer that is beyond the builder's control.

Notice of problems must be given to the builder within 30 days after expiration of the warranty. Lawsuits must be filed within four years for the one-year and two-year warranties and within seven years for the six-year warranty. If the home is sold within the warranty period, the new owner is covered as the original owner was.

F I G U R E   13.8

Main Distribution Panel Interior

Main
Disconnect
Switch

Bonding Screw

Cable to
house
circuits

Cables to
house
circuits

3-wire cables to 240-
volt appliances connect
to double breakers

Bonding
Screw

Space for 6
more breakers

Ground bus bar--often
the ground and neutral
bus bars are contiguous.

■ SUMMARY

State and local building codes set standards for health and safety in construction. Working drawings and written specifications establish the quality of materials and workmanship needed.

Foundations include footings, foundation walls, and slabs. The two major types of foundations are concrete slab and pier-and-beam.

Wood-frame construction is the type most frequently used in building single-family houses in New York State. The three basic types of exterior wall framing are platform, balloon, and post-and-beam. Multilevel balloon construction differs from the platform method in that the studs extend continuously to the ceiling of the second floor, whereas with the platform method only one floor is built at a time. Post-and-beam construction utilizes interior posts to support the roof.

Windows may be sash windows, which are single-hung, double-hung, or sliders; casement windows, side-hinged or vertically hinged; or jalousie windows, which are formed of horizontal slats of glass. Door styles include panel, slab, and hollow or solid core.

Skeleton roof framing may be joist and rafter, exposed rafter, or truss. The skeleton roof rafters or upper chords are covered with sheathing, generally plywood, and then covered with fiberglass, wood, slate, composite, ceramic, concrete type, or asphalt shingles.

Interior walls are generally covered with drywall and finished with paint or wallpaper. Final interior features include wall finishings, trim, floor covering and cabinet work. Plumbing, heating, air-conditioning, and electrical wiring require careful installation to adhere to building codes.

New York State requires that the sale of home improvement goods and services costing more than $500 to homeowners, co-op owners, or tenants conform to certain regulations. New York requires that the buyer of a new home receive certain warranties.

QUESTIONS

1. Most building codes emphasize
   a. safety.
   b. sanitation.
   c. structural strength.
   d. All of the above

2. Which is described as a 1½ story house?
   a. Split-level   c. Colonial
   b. Ranch   d. Cape Cod

3. A gambrel roof is found on which type of house?
   a. Dutch colonial
   b. French provincial
   c. Georgian
   d. Spanish

4. Which is a type of foundation?
   a. Balloon   c. Floating slab
   b. Post-and-beam   d. Chord

5. The components of a pier-and-beam foundation include
   a. the footings.   c. the anchor bolts.
   b. the sill or beam.   d. All of the above

6. Which of the following are installed in horizontal position?
   a. Joists   c. Lally™ columns
   b. Studs   d. Posts

7. Blocks nailed between studs and joists are called
   a. trusses.   c. bolts.
   b. firestops.   d. sills.

8. In a frame or wooden skeleton, studs rest on
   a. plates.   c. joists.
   b. balloons.   d. ridges.

9. Which of the following characteristics is considered when grading lumber?
   a. Age   c. Fragrance
   b. Color   d. Moisture content

10. Sheathing is found on the outside
    a. walls.   c. foundation.
    b. windows.   d. doors.

11. Cap insulation, which has the greatest payback in lowered fuel bills, is found
    a. under the attic floor.
    b. on the basement ceiling.
    c. in sidewalls.
    d. just under the roof.

12. Sloping roof supports are called
    a. trusses.   c. joists.
    b. rafters.   d. studs.

13. Drywall is also known as
    a. plasterboard.   c. sheathing.
    b. siding.   d. paneling.

14. Heat from outside air is utilized through a
    a. reverse conditioner.
    b. passive solar system.
    c. heat pump.
    d. cold air return.

15. A contractor must give the customer a written contract in advance of any work when home improvement goods and services will cost more than
    a. $100.   c. $500.
    b. $250.   d. $750.

16. A new-home buyer receives a warranty of six years' protection against
    a. defective materials.
    b. structural defects.
    c. defective installation of heating systems.
    d. All of the above

17. The Mortensens are worried about possible problems with the Victorian home they have fallen in love with. Before their purchase contract becomes firm, they may want to consult a
    a. building inspection engineer.
    b. soil engineer.
    c. framer.
    d. firestop specialist.

14

VALUATION PROCESS

Dr. and Mrs. Goodhue have been trying to sell their home for many months and reject their broker's advice to drop the price, because, they say, "It's already below market value." Their broker claims it's impossible for real estate to remain unsold if it's priced below market value. That sounds like nonsense to the Goodhues.

If the owner prices property too high, no one comes to see it. Price it too low, and the seller loses out. The listing agent who understands valuation techniques can offer solid advice on pricing when property is put on the market.

■ KEY TERMS

appraisal	depreciation	physical deterioration
Appraisal Institute	direct sales comparison	plottage
arm's-length transaction	approach	reconciliation
assemblage	economic obsolescence	replacement cost
capitalization rate	external obsolescence	reproduction cost
CBS	fee appraiser	special-purpose buildings
comparable property	functional obsolescence	staff appraiser
comparative market	gross income multiplier	subject property
analysis (CMA)	highest and best use	substitution
cost approach	income capitalization	supply
CPA	approach	valuation
demand	locational obsolescence	

■ CHARACTERISTICS OF REAL ESTATE

Unlike other commodities, real estate has unique characteristics that affect its value. These fall into two categories: (1) economic characteristics and (2) physical characteristics.

Economic Characteristics

The basic *economic characteristics* of land that influence its value are relative scarcity, improvements, permanence of investment, and area preference.

> **BASIC ECONOMIC CHARACTERISTICS INFLUENCING VALUE:**
> - Relative scarcity
> - Improvements
> - Permanence of investment
> - Area preference

Relative scarcity.   The total supply of land is fixed. "They aren't making any more."

Improvements.   The building of an improvement on one parcel of land has an effect on the value of neighboring parcels or on whole communities. For example, the construction of a shopping mall or the selection of a site for a landfill can influence values in a large area.

Permanence of investment.   Even if older buildings are torn down, improvements such as drainage, electricity, water, and sewerage remain. The *infrastructure* remains.

Area preference.   This economic characteristic, often called *situs*, refers to people's choices and preferences for a given area. It is what makes one house sell for twice as much as an almost identical one on the other side of town. As the old joke goes, the three most important factors in determining the value of real estate are location, location, and location.

Physical Charcteristics

The basic *physical characteristics* of land are immobility, indestructibility, and nonhomogeneity.

> **BASIC PHYSICAL CHARACTERISTICS OF LAND:**
> - Immobility
> - Indestructibility
> - Nonhomogeneity

Immobility.   Land is immobile. Even if soil is removed, that part of the Earth's surface always remains. The geographic location can never be changed. Because land is immobile, *real estate laws and markets tend to be local in character.*

Indestructibility.   Just as land is immobile, it is *durable and indestructible*.

Nonhomogeneity.   No two parcels of land are ever exactly the same. Although there may be substantial similarity, *all parcels differ geographically* because each has its own location.

■ REAL ESTATE—THE BUSINESS OF VALUE

Value is not the same as price, nor is it the same as cost. *Value* can be defined as *the amount of goods or services that will be offered in the marketplace in exchange for any given product*. It also has been described as the *present worth of future benefits*.

In real estate the concept of *cost* generally relates to the past, *price* to the present, and *value* to the future.

FIGURE   14.1

Supply and Demand

SUPPLY AND DEMAND

Supply Exceeds Demand
"Buyer's Market"

Demand

Supply

Demand Exceeds Supply
"Seller's Market"

Demand

Supply

■ SUPPLY AND DEMAND

The forces of *supply and demand* continually interact in the market to establish price levels. Usually when **supply** goes up, prices drop; when **demand** increases, prices rise. (See Figure 14.1.)

Supply and demand in the real estate market. Because real estate is fixed (immobile), the real estate market is relatively slow to adjust to changes in the factors that influence supply and demand. (See Figure 14.2.) The product cannot be removed from the market or transferred elsewhere, so an oversupply usually results in lower price levels. But because development of and construction on real estate take considerable time, increases in demand may not be met immediately. Thus when demand is high, prices rise.

Factors Affecting Supply

Labor supply and construction costs. A shortage of labor in the skilled building trades, an increase in the cost of building materials, or a scarcity of materials will tend to lower the amount of housing built. High interest rates or scarce loans also reduce construction.

Governmental controls and financial policies. The government can influence the amount of money available for real estate investment through its monetary policies. At the local level, policies on taxation of real estate can have either positive or negative effects. Community *amenities* such as churches, schools, parks, and efficient governmental policies all affect the real estate market.

Factors Affecting Demand

Population. The basic human need for shelter grows or declines as the population changes. At any given time some areas are gaining population while others are losing. In recent years, New York State's population has dropped. The makeup of the population, or *demographics*, also must be taken into account. In recent years, for example, an increasing number of homes have been bought by single persons, one-parent families, and retirees.

F I G U R E   14.2

Factors Affecting Supply and Demand

Employment and wage levels.   Employment levels in the community (the opening or closing of a large company, for example) have a major effect on the real estate market.

Vacancy levels.   Vacancy levels in a community provide a good indication of the demand for housing. A growing shortage of housing will result in increasing rents. On the other hand, an increase in vacancies will force rents down.

■ APPRAISAL

An **appraisal** is an estimate or opinion of value. In the real estate business the highest level of appraisal activity is conducted by professional real estate appraisers who are recognized for their knowledge, training, skill, and integrity in this field and who are licensed or certified by New York State. Formal appraisal reports are relied on in important decisions made by mortgage lenders, investors, public utilities, government agencies, businesses, and individuals. *Not all estimates of value are made by professional appraisers.* Often the real estate licensee must help a seller arrive at a market value for his or her property without the aid of a formal appraisal report. Such assistance is known as **valuation.**

A salesperson may sometimes be approached, however, to furnish a simple paid appraisal to help in division of property during divorce proceedings or to settle an estate. Such an appraisal does not require any special license, but it should be performed under the supervision of the managing broker. This provides guidance and education in the process, and of course only the broker may charge the public for services.

Appraisals may be required in a number of situations:

■ *Estate purposes*, to establish taxable value or facilitate fair division among heirs
■ *Divorce proceedings*, where real estate forms part of property to be shared
■ *Financing*, when the amount to be lent depends on the value of the property
■ *Taxation*, to furnish documentation for a taxpayer's protest of assessment figures

FIGURE   14.3

Kinds of Value

- *Relocation,* establishing the amount to be guaranteed to a transferred employee
- *Condemnation,* arriving at fair compensation for property taken by government
- *Insurance,* estimating possible replacement expense in cases of loss
- *Damage loss,* used to support income tax deductions
- *Feasibility,* to study possible consequences of a particular use for property

A **fee appraiser** works as an independent contractor, offering services to a number of different clients. A **staff appraiser** is an in-house employee of an organization such as the FHA, a lending institution, or a large corporation. A fee appraiser's fees are generally based on time and expenses; fees are never based on a percentage of the appraised value.

■ TYPES OF VALUE

An appraiser may be asked to estimate one of several different types of value, including market value, investment value, insurable value, value-in-use, or some other defined type of value. (See Figure 14.3.) The most frequently sought type is market value.

Market Value

Market value is an important concept defined as the *probable price a property will bring in a competitive and open market, offered by an informed seller, and allowing a reasonable time to find a purchaser who buys the property with knowledge of all the uses to which it is adapted, neither buyer nor seller being under duress.*

Market value also presupposes an **arm's-length transaction,** defined as one between relative strangers, each trying to do the best for himself or herself. A sale between mother and son, for example, is not likely to be an arm's-length transaction and may not yield full market value for the property.

Included in the definition of market value are the following key points:

- Market value is the most *probable price* a property will bring.
- Payment must be made in *cash* or its equivalent.
- Both buyer and seller must act without *undue pressure.*
- A *reasonable length of time* must be allowed for the property to be exposed in the open market.

- Both buyer and seller must be *well informed* about the property's assets, defects, and potential.
- Market value presupposes an *arm's-length transaction.*

Market value versus market price. *Market value* is an estimate based on an analysis of comparable sales and other pertinent market data. *Market price,* on the other hand, is what a property *actually* sells for—its *selling price.* Theoretically, the ideal market price would be the same as the market value. There are circumstances under which a property may be sold below market value, however, as when a seller is forced to sell quickly or when a sale is arranged between relatives.

Market value versus cost. One of the most common errors made in valuing property is to assume that cost represents market value.

Cost and market value are most often equal when a newly constructed house is being appraised. Once the last house in the new subdivision has been sold, however, market value may go up because those who want to live in that particular neighborhood have to compete for whatever houses become available. On the other hand, construction of an expressway nearby may make the houses less desirable, and market value might drop. *Cost hasn't changed; value has.*

Approaches to Appraisal

Real estate is usually appraised using one of three different approaches: *cost approach, income capitalization approach,* or *direct sales comparison approach.* Each is appropriate for a different type of real estate. Some appraisals study the *subject property* (the parcel being evaluated) through all three methods, *reconciling* the results for a final estimate of value.

The **cost approach** estimates the amount needed to reproduce or replace the property being studied. This approach is most appropriate for nonincome-producing buildings that cannot easily be compared with others: hospitals, schools, churches, fire stations. It also is used for insurance purposes.

The cost approach considers not only the cost of reconstructing buildings but also the amount of **depreciation** that already has subtracted value from the property. Depreciation falls into three categories: **physical deterioration; functional obsolescence** (undesirable or outmoded features); and **external (economic** or **locational) obsolescence** (undesirable factors located beyond the property lines).

The **income capitalization approach** to appraisal estimates value by analyzing the income generated by the property being considered. It is appropriate for valuation of rental property.

The **direct sales comparison** (market data) **approach** to appraisal evaluates property through careful study of similar parcels recently sold. The process is based on research and study of data. It is most appropriate for single-family residences.

> **REAL ESTATE IS APPRAISED USING ONE OF THREE DIFFERENT APPROACHES:**
>
> 1. Cost approach
> 2. Income capitalization
> 3. Direct sales comparison approach

■ COMPARATIVE MARKET ANALYSIS

"Real estate properly priced is half sold." The *seller* determines the listing price for the property. Because the average seller usually does not have the background to make an informed decision about a fair market price, the real estate agent should be prepared to offer knowledge, information, and expertise in this area.

WWWeb.Link

A broker or salesperson can help the seller by furnishing a **comparative market analysis (CMA).** This study compares the prices of recently sold homes that are similar in location, style, and condition to the home being put on the market (the *subject property*). Among the Internet sites offering data on recent sales in any given neighborhood is *www.Domania.com.*

A CMA differs from a direct sales comparison appraisal in several ways. It is usually offered as a free service by a salesperson or broker, contrasting with the paid appraisal rendered by a fee appraiser. Both studies analyze recent sales of similar properties, but the CMA does so differently. It includes material not usually considered in regular appraisals: information on nearby properties that failed to sell, for example, and a list of competing properties currently on the market. It also includes significant DOM (days on market before the sale) information. Broker ethics dictate that a CMA is never called a "free appraisal."

Once the broker has information on the subject property, he or she must select properties with the same general characteristics from the neighborhood (or a similar neighborhood) that have sold recently, that are listed, and that have recently failed to sell. The broker then uses the information about these **comparable properties** ("comps") to arrive at an informal estimate of value of the **subject property.**

The broker generally uses a comparative market analysis form, similar to the one illustrated in Figure 14.4, to prepare a written CMA to present to the property owner. A well-researched and well-prepared CMA will help the broker explain that the eventual selling price is set by the buying public through the operation of supply and demand in the open market. The CMA gives the seller an effective way to judge the market and choose a reasonable listing price.

■ THE REAL ESTATE AGENT'S ROLE

In valuing property and presenting the owner with a CMA, the real estate agent must be careful to act competently and with due diligence. The agent should keep a copy of the CMA presented to the owner and also copies of any documentation used to complete the CMA. Agents should make sure that owners understand the estimates of value, how those estimates were determined, and what they mean to the owner.

Basic Principles of Value

A number of economic principles affect the value of real estate. The most important are defined in the following paragraphs.

FIGURE 14.4

Comparative Market Analysis

COMPARATIVE MARKET ANALYSIS

PREPARED FOR: _____ AREA: _____ DATE: _____

ADDRESS: _____

PHONE: (H) _____ (O) _____ PREPARED BY: _____

PROPERTY ADDRESS	BEDROOMS	BATHS	GARAGE	DINING	FAMILY	FIREPLACE	BASEMENT	POOL	CONSTRUCTION	AGE	SPECIAL FEATURES/ REMARKS	LISTED PRICE	SELLING PRICE	DAYS ON MARKET	DATE CLOSED	SQ. FT.	PRICE PER SQ. FT.
SUBJECT PROPERTY																	
SOLD PROPERTIES																	
PENDING PROPERTIES																	
FOR SALE PROPERTIES																	
EXPIRED PROPERTIES																	

AVERAGE PRICE PER SQ. FT. SOLD $ _____

COMPETITIVE MARKET RANGE

HIGH $ _____ LOW $ _____

AREA MARKET CONDITIONS: _____

COMMENTS: _____

Highest and best use.   The most profitable use for which the property is adapted and most likely to be in demand in the reasonably near future is its **highest and best use.** For example, a highest-and-best-use study may show that a parking lot in a busy downtown area should, in fact, be replaced by an office building. An appraisal will estimate highest and best use of the subject property, whether or not that is the present use.

Substitution.   The principle of **substitution** states that no one will pay more for a property if an equally desirable one is available for less. Of two similar houses for sale, the one with the lower asking price normally is purchased first.

Supply and demand.   This principle states that the value of a property will increase if the supply decreases and the demand either increases or remains constant and vice versa. For example, the last lot to be sold in a desirable residential area will probably be worth more than the first lot sold in that area.

Conformity.   Maximum value is realized if the use of land conforms to existing neighborhood standards and a reasonable degree of social and economic conformity exists as well. In residential areas of single-family houses, for example, buildings hold value best if they are similar in design, construction, size, and age and house families of similar social and economic status.

Anticipation.   This principle holds that value can increase or decrease in anticipation of some future benefit or problem affecting the property. For example, the value of a house may be affected by rumors that an adjacent parcel may be converted to commercial use in the near future.

Increasing and diminishing returns.   At a certain point adding improvements to land and structures will no longer increase value. As long as money spent on improvements produces an increase in income or value, the *law of increasing returns* is applicable. But when additional improvements no longer increase income or value, the *law of diminishing returns* applies. Adding a second bath to a five-bedroom house increases value. Adding a third, however, will not increase market value as much as the second one did, if at all.

Regression and progression.   This principle holds that property values are limited by the prevailing type of home in the neighborhood. It's difficult to recoup one's investment when selling, if renovations and additions have made a house much better than its neighbors. On the other hand, the least expensive house in a luxurious neighborhood is usually considered a wise investment because its value is increased by its proximity to more expensive dwellings.

Plottage.   The principle of **plottage** holds that the merging of adjacent lots into one larger parcel may produce a higher total value than the sum of the two sites valued separately. For example, if two adjacent lots are valued at $35,000 each, their total value if consolidated into one larger lot might be $90,000. The process of merging the two lots under one owner is known as **assemblage.**

Contribution.   The value of any component of a property is what its addition contributes to the value of the whole. For example, the cost of installing an air-conditioning system and remodeling an older office building must be analyzed to see if it would be worth doing for the anticipated increase it would bring in rental income.

Competition.   This principle states that excess profits tend to attract competition. For example, the outstanding success of one fast-food outlet may attract investors to open others in the area. This could mean less profit for all. That would be taken into consideration in the type of appraisal known as a *feasibility study*.

Change.   No physical or economic condition remains constant. Real estate is subject to natural phenomena such as tornadoes, fires, and routine wear and tear of the elements. Also, like any business, the real estate business is subject to the demands of its market. An appraiser takes into account the past and possible future effects of natural phenomena and the behavior of the marketplace.

■ THE THREE APPROACHES TO VALUE

To arrive at an accurate estimate of value, three basic approaches, or techniques, are traditionally used by appraisers: the direct sales comparison approach, the cost approach, and the income approach. Each method serves as a check against the others and narrows the range within which the final estimate of value will fall. Each method is generally considered most reliable for certain types of property.

The Direct Sales Comparison Approach

In the *direct sales comparison approach*, an estimate of value is obtained by comparing the **subject property** with recently sold **comparable properties.** Because no two parcels of real estate are exactly alike, each comparable property must be compared with the subject property, and the sales prices must be adjusted for any dissimilar features. The principal factors for which adjustments must be made fall into four basic categories:

1. *Date of sale*: An adjustment must be made if economic changes occur between the date of sale of the comparable property and the date of the appraisal.
2. *Location*: An adjustment may be necessary to compensate for locational differences. For example, similar properties might differ in price from neighborhood to neighborhood or even in more desirable locations within the same neighborhood.
3. *Physical features*: Physical features that may require adjustments include age of building, size of lot, landscaping, construction, number of rooms, square feet of living space, interior and exterior condition, presence or absence of a garage, fireplace, or air conditioning, and so forth.
4. *Terms and conditions of sale*: This consideration becomes important if a sale is not financed by a standard mortgage procedure.

After a careful analysis of the differences between comparable properties and the subject property, the appraiser assigns a dollar value to each of these differences. On the basis of their knowledge and experience, appraisers estimate dollar adjustments that reflect actual values assigned in the marketplace.

The value of a feature present in the subject property but not in the comp is *added* to the sales price actually received for the comparable. The theory is that if the comp had had the fireplace, for example, that the subject property has, it would have brought more in the market. Likewise, the value of a feature present in the comparable but not in the subject property is *subtracted*.

The terms CPA and CBS are useful guides—"*Comparable Poorer: Add*" and "*Comparable Better: Subtract*." The adjusted sales price represents the probable value range of the subject property. From this range a single market value estimate can be calculated using a weighted average that emphasizes those properties most closely comparable. An example is shown in Table 14.1.

The sales comparison approach is essential in almost every appraisal of real estate. It is considered the most reliable of the three approaches in appraising most residential property, except brand-new construction.

The Cost Approach

The *cost approach* to value is based on the principle of substitution and assumes that no one will pay more than the price for which the same item could be constructed new. The cost approach is sometimes called *appraisal by summation*. It consists of five steps:

1. Estimate the value of the land as if it were vacant and available to be put to its highest and best use.
2. Estimate the current cost of constructing the building(s) and site improvements.
3. Estimate the amount of depreciation resulting from physical deterioration, functional obsolescence, and/or external (locational) obsolescence (detailed later in this chapter).
4. Deduct accrued depreciation from the estimated construction cost of new building(s) and site improvements.
5. Add the estimated land value to the depreciated cost of the building(s) and site improvements to arrive at the total property value.

There are two ways to look at the construction cost of a building for appraisal purposes (step 2): reproduction cost and replacement cost. **Reproduction cost** is the amount required to construct an exact duplicate of the subject building using original materials and methods. **Replacement cost** estimates the amount needed for a building that is not necessarily an exact duplicate but serves the same function as the original. Replacement cost is more often used in appraising because it eliminates obsolete features and takes advantage of current construction materials and techniques. An example of the cost approach to value is shown in Table 14.2.

Determining reproduction or replacement cost. An appraiser using the cost approach computes the reproduction or replacement cost of a building using one of the following four methods:

T A B L E   14.1

Direct Sales Comparison Approach to Value

	Subject Property	A	B	C	D	E
Sales price		$118,000	$112,000	$121,000	$116,000	$110,000
Location	good	same	poorer +4,500	same	same	same
Age	6 years	same	same	same	same	same
Size of lot	60' × 135'	same	same	larger −5,000	same	larger −5,000
Landscaping	good	same	same	same	same	same
Construction	brick	same	same	same	same	same
Style	ranch	same	same	same	same	same
No. of rooms	6	same	same	same	same	same
No. of bedrooms	3	same	same	same	same	same
No. of baths	1½	same	same	same	same	same
Sq. ft. of living space	1,500	same	same	same	same	same
Other space (basement)	full basement	same	same	same	same	same
Condition—exterior	average	better −1,500	poorer +4,500	better −1,500	same	poorer +2,000
Condition—interior	good	same	same	better −500	same	same
Garage	2-car attached	same	same	same	same	poorer +5,000
Other improvements						
Financing			1 yr. ago			
Date of sale		current	+3,500	current	current	current
Net adjustments		−1,500	+9,000	−7,000	-0-	+2,000
Adjusted value		$116,500	$121,000	$114,000	$116,000	$112,000

Note: Because the value range of the properties in the comparison chart (excluding comparable B) is close, and comparable D required no adjustment, an appraiser would conclude that the indicated market value of the subject is $116,000.

1. *Square-foot method:* The cost per square foot of a recently built comparable structure is multiplied by the number of square feet in the subject building; this is the most common method of cost estimation. The example in Table 14.2 uses the square-foot method.
2. *Unit-in-place method:* Cost is estimated based on the construction cost of individual building components, including material, labor, overhead, and builder's profit.
3. *Quantity-survey method:* An estimate is made of the quantities, prices, and installation costs of raw materials (lumber, plaster, brick, and so on) needed to replace the subject structure. These factors are added to indirect costs (building permit, survey, payroll taxes, builder's profit) to arrive at the total replacement cost of the structure.
4. *Index method:* The original cost is multiplied by an estimate of the increase in construction costs since then.

TABLE   14.2

Cost Approach to Value

Subject Property: 155 Potter Drive

Land Valuation: Size 60' × 135' @ $450 per front foot	=	$ 27,000
Plus site improvements: driveway, walks, landscaping, etc.	=	8,000
Total		$ 35,000

Building Valuation: Replacement Cost
   1,500 sq. ft. @ $85 per sq. ft. = $127,500

Less Depreciation:
Physical depreciation		
Curable		
(items of deferred maintenance)		
exterior painting	$4,000	
Incurable (structural deterioration)	9,750	
Functional obsolescence	2,000	
External depreciation	-0-	
Total Depreciation	$15,750	

Depreciated Value of Building	$111,750
Indicated Value by Cost Approach	$146,750

Depreciation.   In a real estate appraisal, *depreciation* refers to any condition that reduces the value of an improvement to real property. Land usually does not depreciate. For appraisal purposes (as opposed to depreciation for tax purposes, which is discussed in Chapter 21), depreciation is divided into five classes according to its cause:

1. *Physical deterioration—curable:* Needed repairs that it would pay to make. Routine maintenance, such as painting, falls in this category.
2. *Physical deterioration—incurable:* Needed repairs that may be too expensive to be practical. This would include problems with items like the foundation, which is expected to last for the life of the building.
3. *Functional obsolescence—curable:* Physical or design features that are no longer considered desirable but could be replaced or redesigned at low cost. Outmoded fixtures, such as plumbing, are usually easily replaced. Sometimes a poor floor plan can be easily improved.
4. *Functional obsolescence—incurable:* Poor or outmoded physical or design features that could not be easily remedied or would not pay to fix. An office building that cannot be air-conditioned suffers from functional obsolescence.
5. *External ("locational" or "economic") obsolescence—incurable only:* Caused by factors not on the subject property. Proximity to a nuisance, such as a polluting factory, is an unchangeable factor that could not be expected to be cured by the owner of the subject property, and it detracts from value.

THREE CATEGORIES OF DEPRECIATION:
1. Physical deterioration
2. Functional obsolescence
3. External obsolescence

The cost approach is most helpful in the appraisal of **special-purpose buildings** such as schools, churches, and public buildings. Such properties are difficult to appraise using other methods because there are seldom many local sales to use as comparables, and the properties do not ordinarily generate income.

The Income Capitalization Approach

Vital to the appraisal of investment or income property is the concept of the *present value of money*. It considers the question, "Would you rather have $1 today or $1 a year from now?" Obviously today's dollar is more valuable. The next question is, "Would you rather have $.95 today or $1 a year from now?" Depending on current interest rates and investment opportunities, one might even prefer $.90 today. That figure would be the *present value* of next year's dollar. More complex calculations are used to determine the present value of, for example, rental income or a stream of mortgage payments over a period of many years.

The *income capitalization approach* to value assumes that future income derived from a property will control the value of that property. The income approach is used for valuation of apartment buildings, office buildings, shopping centers, and the like. In using the income approach to estimate value, an appraiser goes through the following five steps:

1. Estimate annual potential *gross rental income,* including income from sources like concessions and vending machines.
2. Based on market experience, deduct an appropriate allowance for vacancy and rent collection losses, to arrive at *effective gross income.*
3. Deduct the annual *operating expenses* of the real estate from the effective gross income to arrive at the *annual net operating income.* (See Chapter 21 for details.)
4. Estimate the price a typical investor would pay based on the rate of return produced by the income from this particular type and class of property. This rate of return is called the **capitalization** (or "cap") **rate** and is determined by comparing the relationship of net operating income to the sales price of similar properties that have sold in the current market. For example, a comparable property that is producing an annual net income of $15,000 has sold for $150,000. The capitalization rate is $15,000 divided by $150,000, or 10 percent. If other comparable properties sold at prices that yielded substantially the same rate, it may be assumed that 10 percent is the rate the appraiser should apply to the subject property.
5. Finally, the capitalization rate is applied to the property's annual net income, resulting in the appraiser's estimate of the property value.

With the appropriate capitalization rate and the projected annual net operating income, the appraiser can obtain an indication of value by the income approach in the following manner:

$$\text{Net Operating Income} \div \text{Capitalization Rate} = \text{Value}$$

Example: $18,000 income ÷ 9% cap rate = $200,000 value

This formula (IRV) and its variations are important in dealing with income property.

$$\frac{\text{Income}}{\text{Rate}} = \text{Value} \qquad \frac{\text{Income}}{\text{Value}} = \text{Rate} \qquad \text{Value} \times \text{Rate} = \text{Income}$$

TABLE   14.3

**Income Approach
to Value**

Gross Annual Rental Income Estimate		$60,000
Less vacancy and collection losses (estimated) @ 6%		− 3,600
Income from other sources		$56,400
Effective Gross Income		+ 600
Expenses:		$57,000
Real estate taxes	$ 9,000	
Insurance	1,000	
Heat	2,800	
Maintenance	6,400	
Utilities, electricity, water, gas	800	
Repairs	1,200	
Decorating	1,400	
Replacements of equipment	800	
Legal and accounting	600	
Management	3,000	
Total Expenses		$27,000
Annual Net Operating Income		$30,000

Capitalization Rate = 10%

Capitalization of annual net income: $\dfrac{\$30,000}{.10}$

Indicated Value by Income Approach = $300,000

A simplified version of the income approach is illustrated in Table 14.3.

The most difficult step in the income approach to value is determining the appropriate capitalization rate for the property. An income property that carries with it a great deal of risk as an investment generally requires a higher rate of return than would a property considered a safe investment.

Gross rent or income multipliers.   As a substitute for a more elaborate income analysis, the **gross rent** (or income) **multiplier** (GRM) method is sometimes used in appraising. The GRM relates the sales price of a property to its rental income. (Gross *monthly* income is used for residential property; gross *annual* income for commercial and industrial property.) The question then becomes "How many times monthly rent do houses in this area seem to sell for?" If local rents are about $900, and sale prices average $90,000, the GRM would be 100.

To establish an accurate GRM, an appraiser should have recent sales and rental data from at least four properties similar to the subject property. Table 14.4 shows some examples of GRM comparisons.

Using multipliers is not a very accurate method because they fail to consider many factors. For example, does the landlord furnish heat or not? Many appraisers view the technique simply as a quick, informal way to double-check a value obtained by one of the other methods.

TABLE 14.4

Gross Rent Multiplier

Comparable No.	Sales Price	Monthly Rent	GRM
1	$93,600	$650	144
2	78,500	450	174
3	95,500	675	141
4	82,000	565	145
Subject	?	625	?

Note: Based on an analysis of these comparisons, a GRM of 145 seems reasonable for homes in this area. In the opinion of an appraiser, then, the estimated value of the subject property would be $625 × 145 or $90,625.

Reconciliation

If more than one approach to value is used, different indications of value may result. **Reconciliation** is the art of analyzing and weighing the findings from the approaches used.

Whenever possible all three approaches should be used as a check on the final estimate of value. The process of reconciliation is more complicated than simply averaging the estimates. Each approach is more valid and reliable with certain kinds of properties than with others.

For example, in appraising a single-family residence the income approach is rarely used, and the cost approach is of limited value unless the home is relatively new; therefore, the direct sales comparison approach is usually given greatest weight. In appraising income or investment property, the income approach is normally given the greatest weight. In appraising churches, libraries, museums, schools, and other special-use properties where there is little or no income or sales revenue, the cost approach is usually assigned the greatest weight. From this analysis, or reconciliation, a single estimate of market value is produced.

■ THE APPRAISAL PROCESS

Figure 14.5 outlines the eight steps an appraiser takes in carrying out an assignment.

1. *State the kind of value to be estimated and the approaches that will be used.*
2. *List the data needed.*
3. *Gather, record, and verify the necessary data.* This may include detailed information on the economic conditions of the neighborhood or even the nation as they might affect the subject property. Specific data about the subject site and improvements must be collected and verified. Depending on the approach(es) used, comparative information on comparable properties must be collected.

F I G U R E 14.5

The Appraisal Process

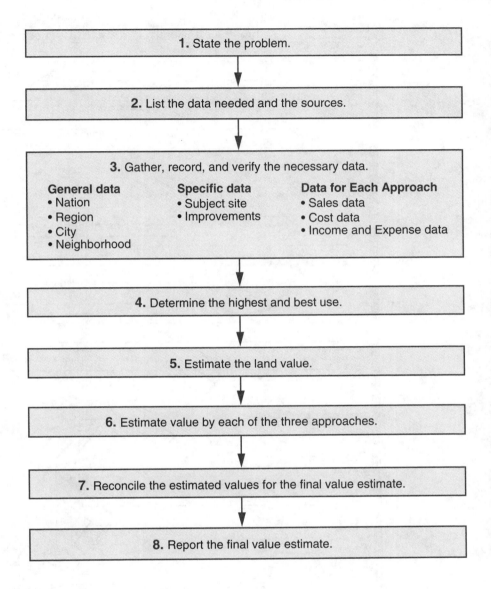

1. State the problem.

2. List the data needed and the sources.

3. Gather, record, and verify the necessary data.

General data	**Specific data**	**Data for Each Approach**
• Nation	• Subject site	• Sales data
• Region	• Improvements	• Cost data
• City		• Income and Expense data
• Neighborhood		

4. Determine the highest and best use.

5. Estimate the land value.

6. Estimate value by each of the three approaches.

7. Reconcile the estimated values for the final value estimate.

8. Report the final value estimate.

4. *Determine highest and best use.*
5. *Estimate land value.*
6. *Estimate value by each of the three approaches.*
7. *Reconcile estimated values for final value estimate.* The appraiser makes a definite statement of conclusions reached, usually in the form of a value estimate of the property.
8. *Report final value estimate.* The formal written report for the client may be a *completed form,* a *letter,* or a lengthy written *narrative.* Figure 14.6 shows a uniform residential form widely used for mortgage financing.

F I G U R E 14.6

Uniform Residential Appraisal Report

Property Description

UNIFORM RESIDENTIAL APPRAISAL REPORT File No. _____

SUBJECT	
Property Address	City State Zip Code
Legal Description	County
Assessor's Parcel No.	Tax Year R.E. Taxes $ Special Assessments $
Borrower	Current Owner Occupant: ☐ Owner ☐ Tenant ☐ Vacant
Property rights appraised ☐ Fee Simple ☐ Leasehold	Project Type ☐ PUD ☐ Condominium (HUD/VA only) HOA$ ____ /Mo.
Neighborhood or Project Name	Map Reference Census Tract
Sale Price $ Date of Sale	Description and $ amount of loan charges/concessions to be paid by seller
Lender/Client Address	
Appraiser Address	

NEIGHBORHOOD

Location	☐ Urban	☐ Suburban	☐ Rural
Built up	☐ Over 75%	☐ 25-75%	☐ Under 25%
Growth rate	☐ Rapid	☐ Stable	☐ Slow
Property values	☐ Increasing	☐ Stable	☐ Declining
Demand/supply	☐ Shortage	☐ In balance	☐ Over supply
Marketing time	☐ Under 3 mos.	☐ 3-6 mos.	☐ Over 6 mos.

Predominant occupancy
☐ Owner
☐ Tenant
☐ Vacant (0-5%)
☐ Vacant (over 5%)

Single family housing
PRICE $(000)   AGE (yrs)
Low
High
Predominant

Present land use %
One family ____
2-4 family ____
Multi-family ____
Commercial ____

Land use change
☐ Not likely ☐ Likely
☐ In process
To: ____

Note: Race and the racial composition of the neighborhood are not appraisal factors.

Neighborhood boundaries and characteristics: _____

Factors that affect the marketability of the properties in the neighborhood (proximity to employment and amenities, employment stability, appeal to market, etc.):

Market conditions in the subject neighborhood (including support for the above conclusions related to the trend of property values, demand/supply, and marketing time - - such as data on competitive properties for sale in the neighborhood, description of the prevalence of sales and financing concessions, etc.):

PUD

Project Information for PUDs (If applicable) - - Is the developer/builder in control of the Home Owners' Association (HOA)? ☐ Yes ☐ No
Approximate total number of units in the subject project ____ Approximate total number of units for sale in the subject project ____
Describe common elements and recreational facilities:

SITE

Dimensions	Topography
Site area	Size
Specific zoning classification and description	Shape
Zoning compliance ☐ Legal ☐ Legal nonconforming (Grandfathered use) ☐ Illegal ☐ No zoning	Drainage
Highest & best use as improved: ☐ Present use ☐ Other use (explain)	View

Corner Lot ☐ Yes ☐ No

Utilities	Public	Other	Off-site Improvements	Type	Public	Private
Electricity			Street			
Gas			Curb/gutter			
Water			Sidewalk			
Sanitary sewer			Street lights			
Storm sewer			Alley			

Landscaping
Driveway Surface
Apparent easements
FEMA Special Flood Hazard Area ☐ Yes ☐ No
FEMA Zone ____ Map Date ____
FEMA Map No. ____

Comments (apparent adverse easements, encroachments, special assessments, slide areas, illegal or legal nonconforming zoning use, etc.): _____

DESCRIPTION OF IMPROVEMENTS

GENERAL DESCRIPTION	EXTERIOR DESCRIPTION	FOUNDATION	BASEMENT	INSULATION
No. of Units	Foundation	Slab	Area Sq. Ft.	Roof
No. of Stories	Exterior Walls	Crawl Space	% Finished	Ceiling
Type (Det./Att.)	Roof Surface	Basement	Ceiling	Walls
Design (Style)	Gutters & Dwnspts.	Sump Pump	Walls	Floor
Existing/Proposed	Window Type	Dampness	Floor	None
Age (Yrs.)	Storm/Screens	Settlement	Outside Entry	Unknown
Effective Age (Yrs.)	Manufactured House	Infestation		

ROOMS	Foyer	Living	Dining	Kitchen	Den	Family Rm.	Rec. Rm.	Bedrooms	# Baths	Laundry	Other	Area Sq. Ft.
Basement												
Level 1												
Level 2												

Finished area **above** grade contains: ____ Rooms; ____ Bedroom(s); ____ Bath(s); ____ Square Feet of Gross Living Area

INTERIOR	Materials/Condition	HEATING		KITCHEN EQUIP.		ATTIC		AMENITIES		CAR STORAGE:	
Floors		Type		Refrigerator	☐	None	☐	Fireplace(s) #	☐	None	☐
Walls		Fuel		Range/Oven	☐	Stairs	☐	Patio		Garage	# of cars
Trim/Finish		Condition		Disposal	☐	Drop Stair	☐	Deck		Attached	
Bath Floor		COOLING		Dishwasher	☐	Scuttle	☐	Porch		Detached	
Bath Wainscot		Central		Fan/Hood	☐	Floor	☐	Fence		Built-In	
Doors		Other		Microwave	☐	Heated	☐	Pool		Carport	
		Condition		Washer/Dryer	☐	Finished	☐			Driveway	

COMMENTS

Additional features (special energy efficient items, etc.): _____

Condition of the improvements, depreciation (physical, functional, and external), repairs needed, quality of construction, remodeling/additions, etc.: _____

Adverse environmental conditions (such as, but not limited to, hazardous wastes, toxic substances, etc.) present in the improvements, on the site, or in the immediate vicinity of the subject property: _____

FIGURE 14.6

Uniform Residential Appraisal Report (continued)

Valuation Section **UNIFORM RESIDENTIAL APPRAISAL REPORT** File No.

COST APPROACH

ESTIMATED SITE VALUE .... = $ _____

ESTIMATED REPRODUCTION COST-NEW-OF IMPROVEMENTS:

Dwelling _____ Sq. Ft @ $ _____ = $ _____

_____ Sq. Ft @ $ _____ = _____

= _____

Garage/Carport _____ Sq. Ft @ $ _____ = _____

Total Estimated Cost New .... = $ _____

Less Physical | Functional | External

Depreciation _____ = $ _____

Depreciated Value of Improvements .... = $ _____

"As-is" Value of Site Improvements .... = $ _____

INDICATED VALUE BY COST APPROACH .... = $ _____

Comments on Cost Approach (such as, source of cost estimate, site value, square foot calculation and for HUD, VA and FmHA, the estimated remaining economic life of the property): _____

SALES COMPARISON ANALYSIS

ITEM	SUBJECT	COMPARABLE NO. 1		COMPARABLE NO. 2		COMPARABLE NO. 3	
Address							
Proximity to Subject							
Sales Price	$		$		$		$
Price/Gross Liv. Area	$ ☑	$	☑	$	☑	$	☑
Data and/or Verification Source							
VALUE ADJUSTMENTS	DESCRIPTION	DESCRIPTION	+ (−) $ Adjustment	DESCRIPTION	+ (−) $ Adjustment	DESCRIPTION	+ (−) $ Adjustment
Sales or Financing Concessions							
Date of Sale/Time							
Location							
Leasehold/Fee Simple							
Site							
View							
Design and Appeal							
Quality of Construction							
Age							
Condition							
Above Grade Room Count	Total ¦ Bdrms ¦ Baths	Total ¦ Bdrms ¦ Baths		Total ¦ Bdrms ¦ Baths		Total ¦ Bdrms ¦ Baths	
Gross Living Area	Sq. Ft.	Sq. Ft.		Sq. Ft.		Sq. Ft.	
Basement & Finished Rooms Below Grade							
Functional Utility							
Heating/Cooling							
Energy Efficient Items							
Garage/Carport							
Porch, Patio, Deck, Fireplace(s), etc.							
Fence, Pool, etc.							
Net Adj. (total)		☐ + ☐ − $		☐ + ☐ − $		☐ + ☐ − $	
Adjusted Sales Price of Comparable			$		$		$

Comments on Sales Comparison (including the subject property's compatibility to the neighborhood, etc.): _____

ITEM	SUBJECT	COMPARABLE NO. 1	COMPARABLE NO. 2	COMPARABLE NO. 3
Date, Price and Data Source, for prior sales within year of appraisal				

Analysis of any current agreement of sale, option, or listing of the subject property and analysis of any prior sales of subject and comparables within one year of the date of appraisal: _____

RECONCILIATION

INDICATED VALUE BY SALES COMPARISON APPROACH .... $ _____

INDICATED VALUE BY INCOME APPROACH (If Applicable) Estimated Market Rent $ _____ /Mo. x Gross Rent Multiplier _____ = $ _____

This appraisal is made ☐ "as is" ☐ subject to the repairs, alterations, inspections or conditions listed below ☐ subject to completion per plans and specifications.

Conditions of Appraisal: _____

Final Reconciliation: _____

The purpose of this appraisal is to estimate the market value of the real property that is the subject of this report, based on the above conditions and the certification, contingent and limiting conditions, and market value definition that are stated in the attached Freddie Mac Form 439/Fannie Mae Form 1004B (Revised _____).

I (WE) ESTIMATE THE MARKET VALUE, AS DEFINED, OF THE REAL PROPERTY THAT IS THE SUBJECT OF THIS REPORT, AS OF _____ (WHICH IS THE DATE OF INSPECTION AND THE EFFECTIVE DATE OF THIS REPORT) TO BE $ _____

APPRAISER:	SUPERVISORY APPRAISER (ONLY IF REQUIRED):
Signature	Signature	☐ Did ☐ Did Not
Name	Name	Inspect Property
Date Report Signed	Date Report Signed	
State Certification # _____ State	State Certification # _____ State	
Or State License # _____ State	Or State License # _____ State	

Freddie Mac Form 70 6-93   10 CH.   PAGE 2 OF 2   Fannie Mae Form 1004 6-93

■ THE PROFESSION OF APPRAISING

Until the early 1990s, when the federal government directed each state to license and certify appraisers, professional designation was made through membership in appraisal societies. Different designations require varying levels of education, specific courses in appraisal, examinations, demonstration appraisals, experience, and continuing education. The **Appraisal Institute,** the largest private society, offers the prestigious designations MAI (Member, Appraisal Institute) and SRA (Senior Residential Appraiser).

Some professional appraisers belong to more than one society. Those along the Niagara frontier, for example, may join an international society, FIABCI. Where expert testimony is provided for court proceedings or before a public body such as a zoning board, specific credentials (MAI, SRA, or state licensing or certification) may be required.

Licensing and Certification

Federal and state governments suggest licensing or certification for all appraisals, but *require* it only for federally related appraisal assignments with a transaction value of at least $250,000. (An appraisal is federally related if there is federal government tie-in, such as when the fact that the appraisal is used for lending purposes and the lender is a federally chartered bank or savings and loan.)

New York's appraisal licensing and certification process provides for four types of appraiser licenses or certifications:

1. *Appraiser Assistant License.* An appraiser assistant must work under the supervision of a state licensed or certified appraiser, who must cosign all the appraisal reports. An appraiser assistant license is good for two years and may be renewed once.
2. *Licensed Real Estate Appraiser.* A licensed real estate appraiser may appraise noncomplex one to four-unit residential real property with a transaction value of less than $1,000,000, and complex ones up to $250,000.
3. *Certified Residential Appraiser.* A certified residential appraiser may appraise any residential property up to four units.
4. *Certified General Appraiser.* A certified general appraiser may appraise any real property.

Education requirements. Various appraisal courses must be completed, depending on the type of license or certification the applicant is seeking. The designated courses include the following:

Course Name	Hours	Hours
Introduction to Real Estate Appraisal	30	R-1
Valuation Principles and Procedures	30	R-2
Applied Residential Property Valuation Case Studies	30	R-3
Elementary Income Capitalization Methods and Techniques	15	R-4
Introduction to Income Property	30	G-1
Principles of Income Property Appraising	30	G-2
Applied Income Property Valuation	30	G-3

To become a licensed appraiser assistant, the applicant must complete courses R-1 and R-2 (60 classroom hours). To become a licensed real estate appraiser, the applicant must complete R-1 and R-2 (60 classroom hours). To become a certified residential appraiser, the applicant must complete R-1, R-2, R-3, and R-4 (105 classroom hours). To become a certified general appraiser, the applicant must complete R-1, R-2, G-1, G-2, and G-3 (150 classroom hours). In addition to these requirements, each applicant also must complete a 15-hour course on Fair Housing, Fair Lending, and Environmental Topics (AQ-1), and a National Course in Ethics and Professional Practice (USPAP).

Examination and Experience.   Licensed assistants are qualified to work at entry-level assignments, assisting under supervision. All other applicants must have at least two years' full-time appraisal experience and pass state examinations of increasing difficulty for various types of license or certification. In addition, they must present evidence of varying numbers of required hours appraising different types of property.

Application.   License and certification applications may be obtained by writing to

> Customer Service Unit
> NYS Department of State
> Division of Licensing Services
> 162 Washington Avenue, 2nd Floor
> Albany, NY 12231

Each application form that is sent out is number-coded. A $250 nonrefundable fee must accompany completed applications. If the application is in order, the applicant will receive an admission card to a scheduled walk-in examination (there is a $50 exam fee). The applicant must score 75 percent or higher on the exam. Renewals require 28 hours of continuing education and a 7-hour USPAP update course.

■ SUMMARY

The economic characteristics of land include scarcity, improvements, permanence of investment, and area preferences (situs). The physical characteristics are immobility, nonhomogeneity, and indestructibility.

A property's value is the present worth of its future benefits. Value is not the same as price; price is determined in the marketplace.

Because of its unique characteristics, real estate is relatively slow to adjust to the forces of supply and demand. Supply is the amount of goods available. Demand is the number of people willing to accept those goods at a given price.

To appraise real estate is to estimate its value. Although there are many types of value, the most common objective of an appraisal is to estimate market value—the most probable sales price of the subject property.

Value is an estimate of future benefits, cost represents a measure of past expenditures, and price is the actual amount of money paid for a property. Basic to appraising are certain underlying economic principles, such as highest and best use, substitution, supply and demand, conformity, anticipation, increasing and diminishing returns, progression, regression, plottage, contribution, competition, and change. A professional appraiser analyzes property through three approaches to value. In the sales comparison approach the subject property is compared with similar nearby properties that have sold recently. Adjustments are made to account for any differences. With the cost approach an appraiser calculates the cost of building a similar structure on a similar site. Then he or she subtracts depreciation (losses in value), which reflects the differences between new property of this type and the present condition of the subject property. The income approach is based on the relationship between the rate of return an investor requires and the net income the property produces.

A special version of the income approach called the *gross rent multiplier* is computed by dividing the sales price of a property by its gross monthly rent.

The application of the three approaches normally results in three different estimates of value. In the process of reconciliation the validity and reliability of each approach are weighed objectively to arrive at the single best and most supportable conclusion of value.

New York State's appraisal licensing and certification process provides for licensure or certification in four categories, requiring various courses and experience. These four categories include licensed appraiser assistant, licensed real estate appraiser, certified residential appraiser, and certified general appraiser.

QUESTIONS

1. The Goodhues will not drop the asking price on their house because "it's already priced below market value." Their agent needs to explain that
   a. if nobody comes forward to offer that sum, by definition it can't be market value.
   b. market value is an ideal figure seldom actually reached in today's real estate climate.
   c. they can expect to get market value only if they find a buyer who is under pressure.
   d. if they wanted to get market value, they should not have put their house into a widespread multiple-listing system.

2. The single most important factor in estimating the value of real property is its
   a. quality of construction.
   b. size.
   c. location.
   d. original cost.

3. Any two parcels of real estate
   a. can never be the same.
   b. can be the same only with identical tract houses.
   c. are considered the same if they have identical sales prices.
   d. are identical because of situs.

4. Real estate markets tend to be
   a. similar across the country.
   b. statewide in their characteristics.
   c. stable despite economic changes.
   d. local in character.

5. Tom Wills is asked to estimate the market value of a church. He will give most emphasis to which appraisal approach?
   a. Cost
   b. Income
   c. Competitive analysis
   d. Direct sales comparison

6. The income approach to appraisal is most appropriate for a(n)
   a. tract ranch house.
   b. library.
   c. apartment house.
   d. vacant lot.

7. The direct sales comparison approach to appraisal utilizes
   a. asking prices for property on the market.
   b. building costs in the area.
   c. analysis of functional obsolescence.
   d. recent sales prices of similar parcels.

8. An example of external obsolescence might be a
   a. faulty heating system.
   b. poor floor plan.
   c. tenant who will not pay rent.
   d. used-car lot next door.

9. The highest price that would be paid by an informed buyer when property is widely exposed on the market is known as
   a. cost.
   b. listing price.
   c. sales price.
   d. market value.

10. In the final analysis, selling price for real estate is set by
    a. the seller.
    b. the broker.
    c. comparative market analysis.
    d. the buying public.

11. Bert Evans is a fully qualified appraiser. As such he
    a. discovers value.
    b. ensures value.
    c. estimates value.
    d. establishes value.

12. The appraiser who works for a number of different clients is known as a(n)
    a. fee appraiser.
    b. freelance appraiser.
    c. staff appraiser.
    d. in-house appraiser.

13. A house should bring $100,000 but is sold for $90,000 by a hard-pressed seller in a hurry, is then mortgaged for $80,000 and insured for $95,000. Its market value is

a. $80,000.
c. $95,000.
b. $90,000.
d. $100,000.

14. Market value is best defined as the

a. gross rental income of the property.
b. cash flow after debt service.
c. most likely price obtainable on the open market.
d. highest and best use of the subject property.

15. An example of an arm's-length transaction is one between

a. father and daughter.
b. employer and employee.
c. broker and salesperson.
d. two strangers.

16. Market value and cost are often equal when property

a. remains in the family a long time.
b. was recently constructed.
c. is sold in an arm's-length transaction.
d. receives a weighted appraisal.

17. Highest and best use of real estate is defined as the use that produces the most

a. benefit to the community.
b. conformity.
c. progression.
d. money.

18. "Why should I pay more when I can buy almost the same house new for less?" is an example of the principle of

a. substitution.
c. anticipation.
b. conformity.
d. change.

19. The principle of value that states that two adjacent parcels of land combined into one larger parcel may have a greater value than the two parcels' value separately is called

a. substitution.
b. plottage.
c. highest and best use.
d. contribution.

20. You are appraising the house at 23 Oak. The house recently sold at 54 Oak is similar but has a fireplace. What use do you make of the value of the fireplace?

a. Subtract it.
c. Ignore it.
b. Add it.
d. Reconcile it.

21. From the reproduction or replacement cost of the building, an appraiser deducts depreciation, which represents

a. the remaining useful economic life of the building.
b. remodeling costs to increase rentals.
c. loss of value due to any cause.
d. costs to modernize the building.

22. The term *external obsolescence* refers to

a. poor landscaping.
b. a faulty floor plan.
c. wear and tear.
d. problems beyond the property line.

23. If a property's annual net income is $37,500 and it is valued at $300,000, what is its capitalization rate?

a. 12.5 percent
c. 15 percent
b. 10.5 percent
d. 18 percent

24. Reconciliation refers to which of the following?

a. Loss of value owing to any cause
b. Separating the value of the land from the total value of the property to compute depreciation
c. Analyzing the results obtained by the three approaches to value to determine a final estimate of value
d. The process by which an appraiser determines the highest and best use for a parcel of land

25. Salesperson Linda O'Brien is asked by a friend's family to appraise a single home for estate tax purposes. She has never done a paid appraisal and has no special training beyond her license-qualifying courses and several years' sales experience. Linda's best course is to

a. refuse the work and explain that she is not certified.
b. offer a free appraisal.
c. accept the assignment and charge a normal fee.
d. do the appraisal under her broker's guidance.

15

HUMAN RIGHTS AND FAIR HOUSING

Mrs. Townsend has the upstairs apartment in her Albany home to rent out. She would prefer renting to a woman, and second-hand cigarette smoke makes her ill. She would like to advertise for a "nonsmoker, woman," but wonders if that would violate human rights laws.

Besides damaging society, unfair housing practices can land property owners and real estate licensees in serious trouble, with ruinous consequences. Understanding the complex laws and regulations concerning human rights is the first step toward fair treatment of all parties.

■ **KEY TERMS**

Americans with Disabilities Act (ADA)
blockbusting
cease and desist order
Civil Rights Act of 1866
Code for Equal Opportunity
Department of Housing and Urban Development (HUD)

Executive Law
familial status
federal Fair Housing Act of 1968
New York Human Rights Law
New York State Division of Human Rights

protected classes
Real Property Law
redlining
reverse discrimination
steering
testers

■ EQUAL OPPORTUNITY IN HOUSING

Federal, state, and local laws about human rights and fair housing affect rentals, sales, and every phase of the real estate sales process from listing to closing.

The goal of these equal opportunity laws and regulations is to create a single, unbiased housing market, one in which every home seeker has the opportunity to buy any home in the area he or she chooses and can afford. The student of real estate must be aware of undesirable and illegal housing practices so as to avoid them. Failure to comply with fair housing practices is not only grounds for loss of license but also an unlawful act.

■ FEDERAL FAIR HOUSING LAWS

The efforts of the federal government to guarantee equal housing opportunities to all U.S. citizens began soon after the Civil War with the **Civil Rights Act of 1866.** This law, an outgrowth of the Civil War, prohibits any type of discrimination based on *race* or *color*. "All citizens of the United States shall have the same right in every state and territory as is enjoyed by white citizens thereof to inherit, purchase, lease, sell, hold, and convey real and personal property." The act provides no exceptions. It is enforceable by a suit in Federal court.

A summary of fair housing laws appears in Table 15.1.

Federal Fair Housing Act of 1968

In 1968 a major event greatly encouraged the progress of fair housing: the passage of the **federal Fair Housing Act of 1968,** which is contained in *Title VIII of the Civil Rights Act of 1968.* This law originally provided that it is unlawful to discriminate on the basis of *race, religion,* or *national origin* when selling or leasing residential property.

TABLE 15.1
Fair Housing Laws Summary

Law	Protected Classes
New York City	Citizenship, lawful occupation, sexual orientation
Civil Rights Act of 1866	Prohibits discrimination in housing based on race or color (without exception)
Title VIII of the Civil Rights Act of 1968 (Federal Fair Housing Act)	Prohibits discrimination in housing based on race, color, religion, or national origin (with certain exceptions)
Housing and Community Development Act of 1974	Extends prohibitions to discrimination in housing based on sex (gender)
Fair Housing Amendments Act of 1988	Extends protection to cover handicaps and families with children (with exceptions)
New York Executive Law	Covers race, creed, color, national origin, sex, disability, age, sexual orientation, and marital status (some exceptions)
New York Real Property Law	Prohibits discrimination based on pres-ence of children in a family or pregnancy
Americans with Disabilities Act	Prohibits discrimination based on disabilities

In 1974 an amendment added *sex* (gender) as a **protected class,** and in 1988 two new classes were added: those with *handicaps* and *familial status* (presence of children in the family). Protection of the handicapped extends to those with hearing, mobility, and visual impairments; recovering alcoholics; AIDS; and mental retardation. Anyone currently using illegal drugs is not protected as handicapped, nor are those who pose a threat to the health or safety of others.

Landlords must make *reasonable accommodations for the disabled,* for example, allowing a guide dog in a no-pets building or setting aside easy-access parking for a handicapped tenant. The tenant who needs to make reasonable modifications to an apartment must be allowed to do so if he or she agrees to restore the property to its original condition when the rental is over. Newly constructed multifamily buildings with four or more units must provide for wheelchair access to all ground floor units and to all upper floor units in buildings with elevators.

Housing developments intended for *older persons* may exclude children if such developments are occupied solely by persons 62 and older, or if 80 percent of the units are occupied by at least one person 55 or older and there are policies and procedures published and adhered to demonstrating an intent to provide housing for persons 55 or older.

Prohibited acts.   The federal Fair Housing Act specifically prohibits the following acts, where they are based on prospective tenants' or buyers' membership in a protected group:

- Refusing to sell, rent, or negotiate with any person, or otherwise making a dwelling unavailable to any person

   Example: Broker Bill is negotiating a listing with Seller Sue. Sue informs Bill that she will not sell her property to anyone who is not a "God-fearing Christian." Because refusing to sell on the basis of religion is a forbidden practice, Bill should refuse to accept the listing.

- Changing terms, conditions, or services for different individuals as a means of discrimination

   Example: The Sky Towers Apartments has a policy of collecting a $500 security deposit from its tenants. However, in the case of families with children, Sky Towers requires a security deposit of $1,000. This variation in the terms of the apartment leases on the basis of familial status is a violation of fair housing laws.

- Practicing discrimination through any statement or advertisement that restricts the sale or rental of residential property

   Example: Jones Realty advertises its listings in the classified section of the local newspaper. The ads include the slogan "Jones Realty—specializing in homes for Asian immigrants." The ad's implication that certain housing is more suitable to persons of a particular race, color, or national origin is a clear violation of fair housing requirements. (This is known as **steering.**)

■ Representing to any person, as a means of discrimination, that a dwelling is not available for sale or rental

Example: When George applies to rent an apartment, the manager takes his application but informs him that there are no units currently available. While it is true that all the units are currently occupied, one of the tenants is due to move out in three days. The manager simply prefers to rent the unit to a woman, since she believes they make better tenants. This is a case of unlawful housing discrimination on the basis of sex.

■ Making a profit by inducing owners of housing to sell or rent because of the prospective entry into the neighborhood of persons of a particular race, color, religion, national origin, handicap, or familial status

Example: Acme Real Estate Company is running a direct mail campaign attempting to solicit listings from the predominantly white Alderbrook neighborhood. Included in the direct mail package are the results of a demographic study that projects that the population of Alderbrook will become increasingly nonwhite in the next few years. Use of such "scare tactics" to generate profit through increased listings puts Acme in violation of fair housing laws. (This is known as **blockbusting.**)

■ Altering the terms or conditions for a home loan to any person who wishes to purchase or repair a dwelling or otherwise denying such a loan as a means of discrimination

Example: Citywide Mortgage Company has a policy of refusing to make loans for properties located in the Valley View neighborhood, claiming that borrowers from Valley View have historically been at higher risk of default. Because this policy does not consider the creditworthiness of individual borrowers from Valley View, it is more than likely intended to discriminate against such borrowers on the basis of some other characteristic, such as race or national origin. (This is known as **redlining.**)

■ Denying people membership or limiting their participation in any multiple-listing service, real estate brokers' organization, or other facility related to the sale or rental of dwellings as a means of discrimination

Example: A multiple-listing service cannot lawfully exclude brokers from participation on the basis of their race, color, sex, religion, age, national origin, familial status, or handicap.

In New York, real estate advertising is often monitored by state and federal government agencies to detect evidence of discriminatory practices. There has been much confusion about what types of property descriptions are and are not appropriate or legal to use in an ad. In an effort to clarify federal regulations regarding real estate advertising, HUD issued the following policy guidelines in January 1995 (see also Figure 15.1):

■ *Race, color, national origin.* Real estate advertisements should state no discriminatory preference or limitation on account of race, color, or national origin. Use of words describing the housing, the current or potential residents, or the neighbors or neighborhood in racial or ethnic terms (e.g., white family home, no Irish) will create liability under this section.

FIGURE 15.1

HUD's Advertising Guidelines

CATEGORY	RULE	PERMITTED	NOT PERMITTED
Race Color National Origin	No discriminatory limitation/preference may be expressed	"master bedroom" "good neighborhood"	"white neighborhood" "no French"
Religion	No religious preference/limitation	"chapel on premises" "kosher meals available" "Merry Christmas"	"no Muslims" "nice Christian family" "near great Catholic school"
Sex	No explicit preference based on sex	"mother-in-law suite" "master bedroom" "female roommate sought"	"great house for a man" "wife's dream kitchen"
Handicap	No exclusions or limitations based on handicap	"wheelchair ramp" "walk to shopping"	"no wheelchairs" "able-bodied tenants only"
Familial Status	No preference or limitation based on family size or nature	"two-bedroom" "family room" "quiet neighborhood"	"married couple only" "no more than two children" "retiree's dream house"
Photographs or Illustrations of People	People should be clearly representative and nonexclusive	Illustrations showing ethnic races, family groups, singles, etc.	Illustrations showing only singles, African-American families, elderly white adults, etc.

However, advertisements that are racially neutral will not create liability. Thus, complaints over use of phrases such as *master bedroom, rare find*, or *desirable neighborhood should not be filed*.

■ *Religion*. Advertisements should not contain an explicit preference, limitation, or discrimination on account of religion (e.g., no Jews, Christian home). Advertisements that use the legal name of an entity that contains a religious reference (for example, Roselawn Catholic Home) or those that contain a religious symbol (such as a cross) standing alone may indicate a religious preference. However, if such an advertisement includes a disclaimer (such as the statement, "This home does not discriminate on the basis of race, color, religion, national origin, sex, handicap, or familial status"), it will not violate the act. Advertisements containing descriptions of properties (apartment complex with chapel) or services (kosher meals available) *do not* on their face state a preference for persons likely to make use of those facilities and are not violations of the act.

The use of secularized terms or symbols relating to holidays, such as Santa Claus or the Easter Bunny, or St. Valentine's Day images, or phrases such as "Merry Christmas," "Happy Easter", or the like, *does not* constitute a violation of the act.

■ *Sex*. Advertisements for single-family dwellings or separate units in a multifamily dwelling should contain no explicit preference, limitation, or discrimination based on sex. Use of the term *master bedroom does not* constitute a violation of either the sex discrimination provisions or the race discrimination provisions. Terms such as *mother-in-law suite* and *bachelor apartment* are commonly used as physical descriptions of housing units and do not violate the act.

■ *Handicap.* Real estate advertisements should not contain explicit exclusions, limitations, or other indications of discrimination based on handicap (e.g., no wheelchairs). Advertisements containing descriptions of properties (great view, fourth-floor walkup, walk-in closets), services or facilities (jogging trails), or neighborhoods (walk to bus stop) do not violate the act. Advertisements describing the conduct required of residents ("nonsmoking," "sober") do not violate the act. Advertisements containing descriptions of accessibility features are lawful (wheelchair ramp).

■ *Familial status.* Advertisements may not state an explicit preference, limitation, or discrimination based on familial status. Advertisements may not contain limitations on the number or ages of children or state a preference for adults, couples, or singles. Advertisements describing the properties (two-bedroom, cozy, family room), services and facilities (no bicycles allowed), or neighborhoods (quiet streets) *are not* facially discriminatory and do not violate the act.

Exceptions.   The following exemptions to the federal Fair Housing Act are provided:

■ The sale or rental of a single-family home is exempted when the home is owned by an individual who does not own more than three such homes at one time and when the following conditions exist: (a) *a broker, salesperson, or agent is not used;* and (b) *advertising is not used.* If the owner is not living in the dwelling at the time of the transaction or was not the most recent occupant, only one such sale by such an individual is exempt from the law within any 24-month period.

■ The rental of units is exempted in an *owner-occupied one to four-family dwelling* (but again, discriminatory advertising may not be used).

■ Dwelling units owned by *religious organizations* may be restricted to people of the same religion, if membership in the organization is not restricted on the basis of race, color, national origin, handicap, or familial status.

■ A *private club* that is not in fact open to the public may restrict the rental or occupancy of lodgings that it owns to its members, as long as the lodgings are not operated commercially.

Jones v. Mayer   The second significant fair housing development of 1968 was the Supreme Court decision in the case of *Jones v. Alfred H. Mayer Company.* In its ruling the Court held that the Civil Rights Act of 1866 "prohibits all racial discrimination, private or public, in the sale and rental of property."

This decision is important because although the 1968 federal law exempts individual homeowners and certain groups, the 1866 law *prohibits all racial discrimination without exception.* So despite any exemptions in the 1968 law, an offended person may seek a remedy for racial discrimination under the 1866 law against any homeowner, regardless of whether the owner employed a real estate broker and/or advertised the property. *Where race or color is involved, no exceptions apply.* (In 1987, U.S. Supreme Court decisions implied that the 1866 law, to which there are no exceptions, extended to ethnic and/or religious groups as well.)

Equal Housing Poster

An equal housing opportunity poster (illustrated in Figure 15.2) can be obtained from HUD. Displayed in a broker's office, it informs the public about fair housing laws and shows the firm's intention to comply. When HUD investigates a broker for discriminatory practices, it considers failure to display the poster evidence of discrimination. The poster should be prominently displayed in any location where the broker conducts business, including model homes.

Blockbusting and Steering

Blockbusting and steering are undesirable housing practices frequently discussed in connection with fair housing. They are prohibited by federal and New York State law.

Blockbusting means *inducing homeowners to sell by using scare tactics about the entry of a certain group into the neighborhood.* The blockbuster frightens homeowners into selling and makes a profit by buying the homes cheaply, then selling them at considerably higher prices to minority persons.

Steering is *the channeling of home seekers to particular areas on the basis of race, religion, country of origin, or other protected class.* Steering is often difficult to detect, because the steering tactics can be so subtle that homeseekers are unaware that their choices have been limited. Steering may be done unintentionally by agents who are not aware of their own unconscious assumptions. Even if unconscious or unintentional, discrimination is still illegal. An increasingly common means of detecting steering is the use of testers, which is described in more detail later in this chapter.

Redlining

Denying applications for mortgage loans or insurance policies in specific areas without regard to the economic qualifications of the applicant is known as *redlining.* This practice, which often contributes to the deterioration of older, transitional neighborhoods, is frequently based on race rather than on any supportable objections to the applicant.

Enforcement.   A person who believes illegal discrimination has occurred has up to one year after the alleged act to file a charge with the **Department of Housing and Urban Development (HUD)** or may bring a federal suit within two years.

For those who think their rights may have been violated, HUD maintains toll-free hot lines: 1-800-669-9777 (voice) and 1-800-927-9275 (TTD). Complaints may also be made by mail to

Fair Housing and Equal Opportunity
HUD Regional Office
26 Federal Plaza
New York, NY 10278-0068

FIGURE   15.2

Equal Housing Opportunity Poster

U.S. Department of Housing and Urban Development

**EQUAL HOUSING
OPPORTUNITY**

We Do Business in Accordance With the Federal Fair Housing Law

(The Fair Housing Amendments Act of 1988)

> ## It is Illegal to Discriminate Against Any Person Because of Race, Color, Religion, Sex, Handicap, Familial Status, or National Origin

- In the sale or rental of housing or residential lots
- In advertising the sale or rental of housing
- In the financing of housing

- In the provision of real estate brokerage services
- In the appraisal of housing
- Blockbusting is also illegal

Anyone who feels he or she has been discriminated against may file a complaint of housing discrimination:
   1-800-669-9777 (Toll Free)
   1-800-927-9275 (TDD)

**U.S. Department of Housing and
Urban Development
Assistant Secretary for Fair Housing and
Equal Opportunity
Washington, D.C. 20410**

Previous editions are obsolete

form HUD-928.1A(8-93)

HUD will investigate, and if the department believes a discriminatory act has occurred or is about to occur, it may issue a charge. Any party involved (or HUD) may choose to have the charge heard in a federal district court. If no one requests the court procedure, the charge will be heard by an administrative law judge within HUD itself.

The administrative judge has the authority to issue an *injunction* (court order). This would order the offender to do something (rent to the complaining party, for example) or to refrain from doing something. In addition, penalties can be imposed, ranging from $10,000 for a first violation to $25,000 for a second violation within five years to $50,000 for further violations within seven years. If the case is heard in federal court, an injunction and actual and punitive damages are possible, with no dollar limit. The Department of Justice may also on its own sue anyone who seems to show a *pattern of illegal discrimination*. Dollar limits on penalties in such cases start at $50,000, with a possible $100,000 penalty for repeat violations.

The guilty party may be required to pay the other side's legal fees and court costs, which can add up to substantial amounts.

Complaints brought under the Civil Rights Act of 1866 must be taken directly to a federal court. The only time limit for action is three years, which is New York's statute of limitations for *torts*, that is, *injuries done by one individual to another*. There is no dollar limit on damages.

Threats or Acts of Violence

The federal Fair Housing Act of 1968 contains provisions protecting the rights of those who seek the benefits of the open housing law as well as the rights of owners, brokers, or salespersons who assist them. Threats and intimidation should be reported immediately to the local police and to the nearest office of the Federal Bureau of Investigation (FBI).

Americans with Disabilities Act of 1992

The **Americans with Disabilities Act (ADA)** of 1992, a federal antidiscrimination law, was enacted primarily to protect disabled persons from discrimination in public accommodations and commercial facilities. It also provides protection from discrimination and mandates easy access in new multifamily housing with four or more units.

In the event a tenant wishes to make alterations at his or her own expense to make an existing dwelling unit more accessible, the tenant may do so. The landlord may require that the tenant restore the premises, as necessary, to their original state when vacating.

■ NEW YORK HUMAN RIGHTS LAW

Protected classes under the *New York Executive Law for Fair Housing* cover race, creed, color, national origin, sex, disability, age, sexual orientation, and marital status (some exceptions).

Blockbusting, forbidden under federal statutes, is specifically mentioned in the **New York Human Rights Law** (Article 15, Executive Law) and also is prohibited by a New York Department of State (DOS) regulation. The DOS has, in the past, responded to complaints by the public by issuing **cease and desist orders** that prohibit canvassing for listings to certain homeowners.

A person charging discrimination may initiate a private lawsuit (with no dollar limit mentioned under state law) and also lodge a complaint with the DOS if the offender is licensed. A complaint also may be filed with the **New York State Division of Human Rights within a one-year period.**

Under sections of the **Executive Law,** New York statutes broaden the non-discrimination rules to cover commercial real estate. They also add several other categories in which discrimination is prohibited, including age and marital status. The age provisions apply only to those 18 and older.

The **Real Property Law** forbids denial of rental housing because of children or an eviction because of a tenant's pregnancy or new child. The rules extend to mobile homes.

Various exceptions are made to the New York State rules, but these exceptions will not apply where the discrimination is racially based, because the federal Civil Rights Act of 1866, which covers race, permits no exceptions. With that in mind, New York State excepts

- public housing that may be aimed at one specific age group;
- restriction of all rooms rented to members of the same sex;
- rental of a room in one's own home; and
- restriction of rentals to persons 55 years of age or older.

Although an owner sometimes may discriminate under these exemptions, *a licensee may not participate in the transaction,* either through ownership or employment. In general the New York statutes cover renting, selling, leasing, and advertising. Public accommodations also are included. The law further forbids any real estate board to discriminate in its membership because of any of the listed categories, which in this case include age. New York regulations are generally more restrictive than federal laws. Table 15.2 summarizes the categories covered by the various federal and New York State laws.

Local Regulations

Local governments may add other groups to the list of protected categories. The New York City Human Rights Commission has adopted the standard of *domestic partner* (an unmarried adult person who can prove emotional and financial commitment and interdependence) for gay or lesbian couples who deal with co-op boards. The definition also has been used in disputes over rights to rent-controlled and rent-stabilized apartments. The city also prohibits discrimination on the basis of *lawful occupation* or *citizenship* and allows no exceptions to fair housing laws for the rental of an owner-occupied two-family house.

TABLE 15.2

Summary of Fair Housing Laws

	Civil Rights Act of 1866	Fair Housing Act of 1968	New York Law	New York City
Citizenship				Yes
Race	Yes	Yes	Yes	Yes
Color	Yes	Yes	Yes	Yes
Religion		Yes	Yes ("creed")	Yes
National origin		Yes	Yes	Yes
Lawful occupation				Yes
Sex		Yes (1974)	Yes	Yes
Age			Yes (older than 18)	Yes
Handicap		Yes (1988)	Yes	Yes
Sexual orientation			Yes	Yes
Marital status			Yes	Yes
Children in family (Familial status)		Yes (1988)	Yes	Yes
Exceptions	No	Yes	Yes	Yes

■ CODE FOR EQUAL OPPORTUNITY

The National Association of REALTORS® has adopted a **Code for Equal Opportunity.** The code sets forth suggested standards of conduct for REALTORS® so that they may comply with fair housing laws. The REALTORS® Code, while it does not have the force of law, asks equal treatment for those classes protected by state and federal law, and also for one more class, *sexual preference*.

Voluntary

The National Association of REALTORS® has a voluntary cooperative agreement with HUD. This agreement, called the *Fair Housing Partnership Agreement*, stipulates that HUD and the National Association of REALTORS® will work together to identify fair housing issues, concerns, and solutions.

■ IMPLICATIONS FOR BROKERS AND SALESPERSONS

To a large extent the laws place the burden of responsibility for effecting and maintaining fair housing on real estate licensees, the brokers and salespeople. *A complainant does not have to prove specific intent, but only the fact that discrimination occurred. In addition, brokers are liable for the discriminatory behavior of their salespeople and employees, even if they have nondiscrimination policies in effect and are not aware of the illegal activities.*

There are a number of steps that a broker can take to ensure compliance with fair housing laws.

■ Include the fair housing logo and/or slogan in all display ads and all classified ads of six column inches or more.

- Prominently display the fair housing logo and/or slogan in all brochures, circulars, billboards, signs, and direct mail advertising, as well as any other forms of marketing.
- When using human models in an advertisement, select the models in such a way as to indicate that the housing is available to all persons without regard to race, color, religion, sex, national origin, familial status, or handicap.
- Prominently display the fair housing poster at all real estate offices, model homes, or other locations where properties are offered for sale or rent.
- Make fair housing information readily available to salespeople and employees, and encourage them to become familiar with it and to attend fair housing education programs.
- Directly inform salespeople and employees of their responsibilities under the fair housing laws through in-house or other training.
- Establish and monitor office procedures to ensure compliance with fair housing regulations and objectives. At a minimum, such procedures should ensure that prospective buyers and renters are made aware of all available properties within their price range and areas of interest and are provided with complete and accurate information.
- Use the "Equal Employment Opportunity" slogan in all employment advertising and take appropriate steps to ensure a broad range of potential recruits.
- Require that salespeople educate sellers regarding their fair housing obligations by providing them with fair housing brochures and other information, and refuse to accept listings from sellers who do not agree to abide by fair housing requirements.

In addition, the National Association of REALTORS® suggests posting a sign stating that it is against company policy as well as state and federal laws to offer any information on the *racial, ethnic, or religious composition of a neighborhood* or to place restrictions on listing, showing, or providing information on the availability of homes for any of these reasons.

If a prospect still expresses a locational preference for housing based on race, the association's guidelines suggest the following response: "I cannot give you that kind of advice. I will show you several homes that meet your specifications. You will have to decide which one you want."

A broker's responsibility for the discriminatory behavior of his or her salespeople presents unique problems. Although brokers may wish to limit their control of salespeople to protect the salesperson's independent contractor status, effective control of behavior in the area of fair housing is essential to protect the broker from liability under civil rights laws. Brokers should have formal office policies regarding discriminatory behavior, and they should require that salespeople acknowledge in writing that they understand those policies and that they have received adequate training to be aware of the requirements of the fair housing laws.

In addition, brokers must have some system for monitoring the activities of salespeople in regard to fair housing compliance. One way to do this is through a record-keeping system that requires that salespeople keep a record of all prospects, including the prospects' qualifying information, the properties that were identified for the prospects, and the prospects' reactions to each individual property. Periodic review of such records by the broker will help identify any instances where a salesperson may be in violation of fair housing standards.

Discrimination involves a sensitive area—human emotions. The broker or salesperson who complies with the law still has to deal with a general public whose attitudes cannot be altered by legislation alone. Therefore, a licensee who wishes to comply with the fair housing laws and also succeed in the real estate business must work to educate the public.

In recent years brokers sometimes have been caught in the middle when local governments enacted well-meaning **reverse discrimination** regulations. Intended to preserve racial balance in given areas, local laws sometimes run counter to federal and state rules, posing a real problem for the conscientious licensee.

From time to time real estate offices are visited by **testers** or *checkers*, undercover investigators who want to see whether all customers and clients are being treated with the same cordiality and are being offered the same free choice within a given price range. For example, two testers—one black and one white—with similar qualifications and interests may separately visit a real estate office to inquire about properties. If the two testers are treated differently by the office or are shown a different range of properties, it may be an indication of unlawful discriminatory behavior by the office. Courts have held that the practice of using testers is permissible as the only way to test compliance with the fair housing laws that are of such importance to American society.

When a broker is charged with discrimination, it is *no defense* that the offense was unintentional or the broker did not know the law. Citing past service to members of the same minority group is of little value. The agent's best course is to study fair housing law, develop sensitivity, and follow routine practices to reduce the danger of unintentionally hurting any member of the public.

These practices include careful record keeping for each customer: financial analysis, properties suggested, houses shown, check-back phone calls. Using a standard form for all qualifying interviews is essential. Special care should be taken to be on time for appointments and to follow through on returning all phone calls. Besides helping to avoid human rights violations, these practices are simply good business and should result in increased sales.

■ SUMMARY

Federal regulations regarding equal opportunity in housing are principally contained in two laws. The Civil Rights Act of 1866 prohibits all racial discrimination, and the federal Fair Housing Act (Title VIII of the Civil Rights Act of 1968) prohibits discrimination on the basis of race, color, religion, sex, national origin, handicap, or familial status (the presence of children in a family) in the sale or rental of residential property. Discriminatory actions include refusing to deal with an individual or a specific group, changing any terms of a real estate or loan transaction, changing the services offered for any individual or group, making statements or advertisements that indicate discriminatory restrictions, or otherwise attempting to make a dwelling unavailable to any person or group because of membership in a protected class. Some exceptions apply to owners but none to brokers and none when the discriminatory act is based on race. Complaints under the federal Fair Housing Act may be reported to and investigated by the Department of Housing and Urban Development and may be taken to a U.S. district court. Complaints under the Civil Rights Act of 1866 must be taken to a federal court.

New York's Executive Law (Human Rights Law) adds age, sexual orientation, and marital status to the grounds on which discrimination is forbidden.

The National Association of REALTORS® Code for Equal Opportunity suggests a set of standards for all licensees to follow, including equal service regardless of a customer's or client's sexual preferences.

QUESTIONS

1. Mrs. Townsend is advertising for a tenant for the other half of her home. Which of these ads would violate human rights law?

   a. No pets
   b. Nonsmoker preferred
   c. No children
   d. No Republicans need apply

2. Salesperson Davis was listing the Johnsons' house. Mr. Johnson informed Davis that he would not sell to a member of a particular religious sect. Davis should

   a. accept the listing, resolving not to discriminate himself.
   b. explain to Johnson why he should change his mind.
   c. discuss the situation with his broker.
   d. refer Johnson to another real estate company.

3. Which of the following acts is permitted under the federal Fair Housing Act?

   a. Advertising property for sale only to a special group
   b. Altering the terms of a loan for a member of a minority group
   c. Refusing to make a mortgage loan to an individual with a poor credit history
   d. Telling nervous owners in a changing neighborhood to sell before their homes lose value

4. The Civil Rights Act of 1866 is unique because it

   a. originally covered only the area of race.
   b. provides no exceptions.
   c. requires a federal court suit by the complainant.
   d. All of the above

5. "I hear they're moving in; there goes the neighborhood. Better sell to me today!" is an example of

   a. steering.   c. redlining.
   b. blockbusting.   d. testing.

6. The broker who suggests only predominantly white areas to a white couple when there are others in their price range is guilty of

   a. blockbusting.
   b. redlining.
   c. steering.
   d. nothing; this is permitted under the Fair Housing Act of 1968.

7. Which would *not* be permitted under the Federal Fair Housing Act?

   a. The Harvard Club in New York will rent rooms only to graduates of Harvard who belong to the club.
   b. A "no-pets" policy, if evenly applied, may refuse rental to the owner of a guide dog.
   c. A convent refuses to furnish housing for a Jewish man.
   d. All of the above

8. Under federal law, families with children may be refused rental or purchase in any building where occupancy is reserved exclusively for those aged at least

   a. 55.   c. 62.
   b. 60.   d. 65.

9. A lending institution may not refuse to make a residential real estate loan simply because of the

   a. questionable financial situation of the applicant.
   b. location of the property.
   c. applicant's not being of legal age.
   d. deteriorated condition of the building.

10. Under federal law, no exceptions apply when the discrimination is based on

    a. race.   c. handicap.
    b. gender.   d. country of origin.

11. A Utica landlord refused to rent to anyone on public assistance and thereby violated

    a. no law.
    b. the New York Executive Law.
    c. the Fair Housing Act of 1968.
    d. the Civil Rights Act of 1866.

12. The Ithaca housewife who refuses to rent rooms to any students is in violation of

a. no law.
b. the New York Executive Law.
c. the Fair Housing Act of 1968.
d. the Civil Rights Act of 1866.

13. Refusing an apartment to a couple because they are unmarried violates

a. no law.
b. the New York Executive Law.
c. the Fair Housing Act of 1968.
d. the Civil Rights Act of 1866.

14. The Fly-by-Night Mortgage Company makes it a practice not to lend money on any inner-city property. This practice is known as

a. redlining.   c. steering.
b. blockbusting.   d. qualifying.

15. A court found Debbie Barnes guilty of illegal discrimination and ordered her to rent her next available apartment to the person who was unfairly hurt. The court order is an example of

a. punitive damages.
b. actual damages.
c. an injunction.
d. a monetary penalty.

16. The seller who requests prohibited discrimination in the showing of a home should be told

a. "As your agent I have a duty to warn you that such discrimination could land you in real trouble."
b. "I am not allowed to obey such instructions."
c. "If you persist, I'll have to refuse to list your property."
d. All of the above

17. A good precaution against even unconscious discrimination is

a. detailed record keeping on each customer.
b. use of a standard financial interview form.
c. routine follow-up phone calls.
d. All of the above

18. The federal Fair Housing Amendments of 1988 added which of the following as new protected classes?

a. Handicap and familial status
b. Occupation and source of income
c. Political affiliation and country of origin
d. Prison record and marital status

19. The fine for a first violation of the federal Fair Housing Act could be as much as

a. $500.   c. $5,000.
b. $1,000.   d. $10,000.

20. The only defense against an accusation of illegal discrimination is proof that it

a. was unintentional.
b. didn't cause financial loss to anyone.
c. arose because the agent was ignorant of the law.
d. didn't occur.

21. Undercover investigations to see whether fair housing practices are being followed are sometimes made by

a. testers.   c. operatives.
b. evaluators.   d. conciliators.

16

ENVIRONMENTAL ISSUES

The Bensons were interested in purchasing a duck and potato farm on eastern Long Island. They were concerned about possible hazardous substances on the farm. How can the Bensons ease their fears about hazardous substances?

■ **KEY TERMS**

asbestos

asbestosis

building-related illness (BRI)

chlorofluorocarbons (CFCs)

Clean Air Act

Comprehensive Environmental Response, Compensation and Liability Act (CERCLA)

due diligence

electromagnetic field

environmental impact statement

Environmental Protection Agency (EPA)

Freon

friable

groundwater

hazardous substances

landfill

lead poisoning

Leaking Underground Storage Tanks (LUST)

mold

percolation test

pollution

polychlorinated biphenyls (PCBs)

potentially responsible parties

radioactive waste

radon gas

Safe Drinking Water Act

septic system

sick building syndrome (SBS)

State Environmental Quality Review Act (SEQRA)

Superfund Amendments and Reauthorization Act

termites

underground storage tanks

urea-formaldehyde foam insulation (UFFI)

■ POLLUTION AND ENVIRONMENTAL RISKS IN REAL ESTATE TRANSACTIONS

Environmental concern has come to the forefront of contemporary issues. Both actual and perceived pollution problems have the ability to stir anger, fear, and other feelings. Indeed, perhaps no other modern issue has a greater ability to elicit strong emotions.

The actual dollar value of real property can be affected significantly by both real and imagined pollution. The desirability and salability of land and buildings may change drastically. Also, the cost of cleaning up and removing pollution may be much greater than the dollar value of the property.

In some areas of the United States, mortgage and title insurance approvals in many cases depend on inspection of the property for **hazardous substances** and proof of their absence.

For all of these reasons real estate professionals should be alert to the possibility of pollution and hazardous substances on property being sold. Knowledgeable real estate professionals should ask property owners about the possibility of hazardous substances. In addition, licensees can expect increasing numbers of questions from concerned customers.

Pollution is an impurity in the environment that was not there originally. The simple act of throwing a piece of paper on the ground creates an unsightly, minor form of pollution. Major pollution problems can result from hazardous substances associated with industrial and other activities, such as farming. Real estate licensees often, however, do not have the technical expertise required to determine if a hazardous material is present on or near the property. Government agencies and private consulting firms may be contacted for information, guidance, and detailed study.

■ LONG-STANDING ISSUES

Water

Water contamination exists in every state in the United States; what varies is the degree of contamination. Contaminants that can endanger health include *bacteria, viruses, protozoa, nitrates, metals such as lead or mercury, fertilizers, pesticides, and radon.* Sources that can also affect the taste and odor of water include industrial discharges; runoff from urban areas (such as landfills); septic systems that are improperly located and maintained; and pesticides and fertilizers from agricultural areas.

Contaminated water can cause a variety of physical symptoms, from mild stomach aches and intestinal cramping to severe nausea and diarrhea, kidney and liver damage, and death. Some adverse effects, even if nonfatal, last for one or two weeks, others last for months or years. There is recent evidence that water contaminants (particularly nitrates and radon) cause cancer.

The quality of drinking water can be tested by a local health authority or water supplier. Federal regulations (the *Safe Drinking Water Act*) require that public water suppliers test the drinking water for contamination periodically. Well water can be tested by health authorities or private laboratories. Some experts advise testing private water supplies at least once a year. If water contamination is suspected, alternate sources of water should be used until it is determined that the water is safe.

Groundwater contamination.   The term *groundwater* includes not only the runoff at ground level but also the underground water systems used for wells, both private and public. Underground streams are formed in the rocks, crevices, and caves under the ground and flow just as dramatically as do rivers above ground. This underground water table can be as shallow as two or three feet below the surface or range all the way down to several hundred feet.

Contamination of this water supply is a serious health threat. Water can be contaminated from a number of sources, including waste disposal sites and underground storage tanks. Heavy regulation in these areas is about the only protection the general public has against water contamination. Once contamination has been identified, its source can be eliminated, but such a process is often time-consuming and extremely expensive. Many times freshwater wells must be relocated.

Waste Disposal Sites

The United States has become increasingly a *throwaway* society. Landfill operations have been the main receptacle for this type of garbage. A **landfill** is a site excavated and lined with either a clay or synthetic liner to prevent leakage of waste material into the local water system. Garbage is then laid at the bottom of the excavation and a layer of topsoil is compacted onto it. The procedure is used again and again until the excavation has been filled. It is then *capped* with from two to four feet of topsoil onto the very top and then planted with some type of vegetation. Completed landfills have been used for such purposes as parks and golf courses.

The construction and maintenance of a landfill operation is heavily regulated by state and federal authorities. Well-run landfill operations do not have to be a source of pollution. However, landfills at improper locations and improperly managed sites have been a source of major problems. Landfills constructed on the wrong type of soil will leak waste into nearby wells, causing major damage. Federal, state, and local authorities and private industry have set up test wells around such landfill operations to monitor the water in the local areas constantly.

Radioactive waste is material that has accumulated as waste from nuclear energy power plants and from various uses of radioactive material in medicine and scientific research. Emissions from such waste can be extremely harmful, sometimes causing cancer or even death.

Radioactive material can have a life expectancy of thousands of years. Much is still to be learned about disposal techniques, and in most cases the only alternative is to put the material in some type of containment facility. The container is then either buried or dropped in the sea. The obvious problem is that sometimes these containers can leak or be damaged in transit.

Although waste disposal is heavily regulated, no one is interested in living next to a hazardous waste dump. Real estate professionals must be aware of such facilities within their areas and take the appropriate action when dealing with potential buyers or sellers.

Septic Systems

Household wastewater is made up of water from toilets, washing machines, dishwashers, sinks, bathtubs, and showers. The average family of four produces about 300 gallons of wastewater every day. A **septic system** is an individual treatment and disposal system that is usually built underground. A septic system consists of a large storage tank (septic tank), in which the wastewater is partially broken down by bacteria, and an absorption (leach) field, which receives and filters the wastewater. Solid material settles out of the wastewater, remains at the bottom of the septic tank, and must be pumped out periodically (at least once every three to five years).

Before a septic tank can be installed, the property owner must have the soil tested to determine how much wastewater the soil can process **(percolation test)**. The septic tank also must be the correct size for the number of occupants, and the proper size is determined by the number of bedrooms in the house. A professional engineer or registered architect must submit "as-built" plans of the system to the Department of Health for approval.

When the septic tank is properly installed and maintained, a septic system is generally adequate for wastewater disposal and treatment. However, if the system is not working properly, there may be serious consequences, including contamination of ground water and wells; contamination of nearby streams, rivers, and lakes; and the pooling of wastewater above the surface.

There are various signs that a septic system is malfunctioning, including wastewater odors inside or outside the home, lush grass and spongy soil over the absorption field, pooled "gray" water over the absorption field, and sluggish or backed-up drains.

If the septic system has failed, pumping the septic tank may solve the problem. More serious malfunctions may require the installation of a new septic system, new fields, new pumps or distribution boxes, or the installation of a sewer system.

Termites

Termites are antlike insects that live in the earth. In some New York regions termites are a common problem for homeowners because these insects are so destructive to wood. In other parts of the state, termites are seldom encountered. In some areas, purchasers may make a contract contingent on a satisfactory termite inspection before closing.

It is vital that when a structure is built, no untreated wood touches the soil. The ground often is treated before laying the foundation, to keep termites from coming up through the foundation. Metal termite shields also may be used.

Termite damage, which typically occurs in homes that are more than five or ten years old, is often hard to detect. Termite inspectors must probe the foundation and base wood structure of a house with a tool similar to an ice pick. If the pick sinks down into the wood, it has probably been eaten away inside (although rot also may be the culprit). Termites may also leave tunnel-like trails as evidence of their presence.

When termite damage or infestation is present, a thorough extermination is required, and the termite damage must be repaired. This must be done only by someone specifically licensed by the New York State Department of Environmental Conservation (DEC). A common method is to drill holes around the property and fill them with a solution that kills the insects.

Asbestos

Asbestos is a mineral, found in rocks, that has been used for many years as insulation on plumbing pipes and heat ducts and as general insulation because it is a poor conductor of heat. It also has been used in floor tile and in roofing material.

Due to its heat-containing property and the fact that it is relatively inexpensive, asbestos has been used in the insulation of almost all types of buildings, especially public buildings such as libraries, schools, and government buildings. Although it remains relatively harmless if not disturbed, it can become life-threatening when removed because of the accompanying dust.

Contemporary environmental concerns affecting real estate include asbestos, lead, radon gas, indoor air quality, and PCBs.

Exposure to the dust can come in several ways. One is when the asbestos material gets old and starts to disintegrate. Remodeling projects that include the removal of asbestos shingles, roof tile, or insulation can cause the dust to form in the air and expose people in the area to the health hazard. Medical problems include **asbestosis,** a chronic lung disease that involves difficult breathing and sometimes death; lung cancer; and mesothelioma, a cancer of the chest and abdominal membranes. They can show up many years after the patient was exposed to asbestos dust.

Testing and, if necessary, removal should be done only by contractors who have been specially trained, and are approved by either the federal **Environmental Protection Agency (EPA)** or the State of New York. Special clothing and respirators are used. Testing is done through bulk sampling of the materials, monitoring of the air, or a technique known as *wipe sampling.*

Once a building has been determined to have an asbestos problem, the owner can take several approaches to eliminating the problem. One is to leave well enough alone. Asbestos roofing, floor tile, and insulation, if undisturbed and not **friable** (fraying or crumbling), do not pose a health problem. An alternative is to remove the material, with the work done, again, only by approved professionals.

The third approach is to encapsulate the material; in other words, if the exposure comes because of the dust in the air, it is possible to contain the dust by enclosing the insulation with a plastic or paint that does not allow the dust to reach the air. Again, such procedures should be carried out by professionals.

Lead Poisoning

Lead has been used for centuries because of its pliability and its ability to block water flow. It has been used as an ingredient in paint and also in the installation of water pipes. Soil around a building may become contaminated as exterior paint deteriorates.

Lead becomes a health hazard when ingested. Once in the body, it can impair physical and mental development in young children and aggravate high blood pressure in adults.

Lead poisoning comes from two main sources. The first is peeling or flaking paint that small children sometimes put into their mouths or that contributes to contaminated dust in the air. The second is the plumbing system. Sometimes lead in connecting water pipes or in insulation for hot-water heaters contaminates the water that flows through them. Concentrated amounts of lead can lead to serious health effects.

Lead was used in many oil-based paints until 1978. Once various health problems were linked to lead poisoning, lead was immediately banned as an ingredient of any paint material. Other limitations have been imposed on all materials that contain lead to keep the lead away from all materials that may be ingested. However, one can still be exposed to lead in many older homes.

Paint is tested for lead by sending a sample to a laboratory. If it is found, it may be left undisturbed if it is not flaking, or it is sometimes covered with drywall, paneling, or wallpaper. Actual removal is a complicated procedure that must not be undertaken by amateurs. Dust released into the air can be highly dangerous and difficult to eliminate.

Lead in the water system also is tested by sending a sample to a qualified laboratory. The water should be drawn directly from the faucet, because lead leaches into water as it stands in the pipes. After a minute or so, a sample may no longer contain enough lead to show up in testing. Remediation includes replacement of old lead plumbing or pipes joined by lead solder.

Both sellers and landlords must disclose information regarding lead-based paint to buyers and renters of pre-1978 residential properties. Sellers and landlords must disclose the location of any lead-based paint that they are aware of, provide a copy of any report concerning lead-based paint in the property to buyers or tenants, give buyers or tenants a copy of a pamphlet on lead-based paint prepared by the government, and offer buyers or tenants a 10-day period in which to have the home tested for lead-based paint.

Although sellers and landlords must make these disclosures, the law does not actually require them to test for lead-based paint or make any repairs. The prospective buyer or tenant could, however, cancel the purchase contract or the lease.

Radon Gas

Radon gas is an odorless, radioactive gas produced by the decay of other radioactive materials in rocks under the surface of the earth. As radon is released from the rocks, it finds its way to the surface and is usually released into the general atmosphere. In some cases it is trapped in buildings and increases in concentration. Radon enters a house through cracks in the foundation or through floor drains. It can become concentrated in crawl spaces or in basements. Long-term exposure to radon gas is said to cause lung cancer.

Radon was identified as being a hazardous problem in homes in 1984. Since that time the EPA has established levels of radon gas that are felt to be unsafe. Testing techniques also have been developed that allow homeowners to determine the exact quantity of radon gas in their homes. The level of radon that necessitates remediation is 4 picocuries (pCi). Its effects are particularly hazardous to a smoker.

Radon testing kits are widely available in hardware stores. The homeowner should follow directions and then send a canister to a laboratory for analysis.

Generally the elimination of radon gas from a home is a relatively simple matter. It can be removed from drinking water by a special filtration system. Gas is removed from the indoor air by ventilation systems or exhaust fans.

For new construction, the federal EPA has guidelines to help builders avoid radon hazards. New York State's radon information line is 1-800-458-1158.

Indoor Air Quality

Indoor air quality has become increasingly significant as two results of poor air quality have become more readily diagnosed. These are *sick building syndrome* and *building-related illness*.

Sick building syndrome (SBS) is the name for a wide range of symptoms suffered by building occupants. These symptoms are present only when the occupants are in the building and subside when the occupants leave the building. They include headaches, dizziness, drowsiness, memory loss, coughing, asthma, hoarseness, stinging skin, runny noses, and watery eyes.

Building-related illness (BRI), caused by toxic substances or pathogens, continues to affect the building occupant even after he or she has left the building. BRI symptoms include hypersensitivity, pneumonitis, asthma, and certain allergic reactions.

The major sources of interior air contamination include *volatile inorganic compounds* (chemical emissions from products such as paints, adhesives, cleaners, pesticides, fixtures, and furnishings), *microorganisms* (fungi, bacteria, viruses, pollen, and mites), and *particulates* (dust and dander). **Urea-formal-**

dehyde foam insulation (UFFI), used in the past as an insulating material, is no longer a concern.

Mold.   In recent years homeowners have become increasingly alert to the presence of **mold** in buildings. Mold grows in moist environments. Some varieties are toxic, others are harmless. Treatment includes remediation of leaks and damp areas. Brokers can alert sellers and buyers to roof leaks, as evidenced by ceiling stains, and to evidence of dampness in basements.

Polychlorinated Biphenyls (PCBs)

Polychlorinated biphenyls (PCBs) are found mostly in electrical equipment. For example, transformers found in electrical vaults within basements of buildings may contain PCBs. Although this type of electrical equipment is slowly being replaced by other equipment, transformers and other electrical equipment should be inspected by the local electric utility experts and replaced if they are found to contain PCBs.

The EPA or New York's DEC can test groundwater and soil around buildings where contamination by leaking PCBs is suspected. The problem is handled by removal and replacement of the soil.

■ FUTURE CONCERNS

Underground Storage Tanks

Underground storage tanks have been used in both residential and commercial settings for many years. One estimate is that there are from 3 million to 5 million underground storage tanks in the United States that contain hazardous substances, including gasoline. The risk comes when such containers become old, rust, and start to leak. The toxic material then can enter the groundwater to contaminate wells and can pollute the soil.

The most obvious source of such pollution is the millions of gas stations scattered around the United States. Older stations sometimes have steel tanks that have developed leaks through oxidation (rusting). Another major source is the underground containers that were used to hold fuel oil for older homes. Many times the homeowner has converted the heating system to natural gas and has abandoned the use of the old oil tank. This, again, raises the risk of leakage and pollution of the general area.

Recent federal legislation has called for the removal of such tanks and all the polluted soil around them. The tank and the soil are then disposed of in a hazardous waste facility. Such a program is extremely expensive, sometimes costing hundreds of thousands of dollars to revamp a gas station, for instance. Legislation regarding underground storage tanks is discussed in more detail later in this chapter.

Electromagnetic Fields

Electromagnetic fields are generated by the presence and movement of electrical charges, that is, electric current. Electromagnetic fields are generally associated with the use of electric power. Common sources of electromagnetic fields (aside from those generated by the earth's magnetic field) include high tension (or high voltage) transmission lines; primary and secondary distribution lines; and electric appliances inside homes, such as televisions, computers, microwave ovens, conventional electric ovens, electric blankets, and electric clocks.

Currently, there is controversy over exactly what, if any, damage is caused by electromagnetic fields. There is some evidence to suggest that exposure to electromagnetic fields may cause cancer, hormonal changes, and changes in behavior. Other studies have found no damage.

Reducing exposure to electromagnetic fields ranges from the simple to the impossible. For example, if a home is built near primary or secondary transmission lines, there is little the occupants can do to reduce their exposure except move. On the other hand, exposure to electromagnetic fields generated by electrical appliances can be reduced by sitting or standing farther away from them—it is generally assumed that standing a distance of two to three feet away from low-voltage electrical appliances is safe.

Figure 16.1 illustrates various potential problems in residential construction.

Chlorofluorocarbons

Chlorofluorocarbons (CFCs) are considered to be a significant cause of the depletion of the ozone layer around the earth, a condition that contributes to the development of cataracts and skin cancer. CFCs are gases produced by the propellants used in older aerosol containers and by a refrigerant called **Freon.** (When used in its liquid form, Freon removes, or absorbs, heat; when released, it becomes a gas.) The **Clean Air Act** mandates that CFCs are no longer legal in aerosol cans, and the use of Freon is no longer allowed. However, old-model refrigerators, automobile air conditioners, residential air conditioners, freezers, and heat pumps may present potential leakage problems. The removal of Freon from older appliances is required by law and must be done in a manner that protects the air from contamination.

■ ENVIRONMENTAL ASSESSMENTS

New York's **State Environmental Quality Review Act (SEQRA)** requires the submission of an **environmental impact statement** for any activity where environmental concerns may be present. In such cases, a *Phase I Environmental Assessment* (or *audit*) should be performed. A Phase I Environmental Assessment is an investigation conducted by an environmental professional to determine whether hazardous substances are present on or being released from the property. It is commonly performed before commercial or industrial property is purchased.

A *Phase I* assessment consists of reviewing the previous ownership and uses of the property by examining all deeds, easements, leases, restrictions, and covenants for a period of 50 years; aerial photographs; any recorded environmental cleanup liens; federal, state, and local government records of sites or facilities where there has been a release of hazardous substances; and a visual site inspection of the property and all its improvements.

FIGURE 16.1

Environmental Hazards

If the Phase I assessment discloses the presence or release of hazardous substances on the property, further action may be necessary to confirm the contamination. If confirmation is necessary, a *Phase II Environmental Assessment* will be performed, which consists of sample testing and evaluation. The Phase II assessment must be conducted by a qualified environmental engineer.

Phase III includes remedying the contamination, if any is confirmed, and *Phase IV* includes management of the environmental hazards.

■ LEGAL CONSIDERATIONS

The majority of legislation dealing with environmental problems has been enacted within the past two decades. Although the **EPA** was created at the federal level to oversee such problems, there are several other federal and state agencies concerned.

> An environmental assessment consists of investigating, testing and confirming, remedying, and managing the contamination.

Federal environmental law is administered by such agencies as the U.S. Department of Transportation under the *Hazardous Material Transportation Act*; the Occupational Safety and Health Administration (OSHA) and the U.S. Department of Labor, which administer the standards for all employees working in the manufacturing sector; and the EPA, which administers such laws as the *Toxic Substance Control Act*, the *federal Clean Water Act*, and the *Resource Conservation and Recovery Act*.

The need for federal legislation was recognized after the Love Canal situation developed in New York. A hazardous waste leak created untold problems from both a physical health and a property standpoint.

The **Comprehensive Environmental Response, Compensation, and Liability Act (CERCLA)** was created in 1980. It established a fund of $9 billion, called the *Superfund*, to clean up uncontrolled hazardous waste dumps and to respond to spills. It created a process for identifying **potentially responsible parties** and ordering them to take responsibility for the cleanup action. A landowner may become liable under this act when there has been a release or there is a threat of release of a hazardous substance. Regardless of whether the contamination is the result of the landowner's actions or those of others, the owner could be held responsible for cleaning up any resulting contamination. The liability includes the cleanup of the landowner's property and any neighboring property that has been contaminated.

WWWeb.Link

On the EPA Web site, *www.epa.gov*, one can search by ZIP code for known or potentially contaminated sites.

Superfund Amendments and Reauthorization Act (SARA)

In 1986 the United States Congress passed the **Superfund Amendments and Reauthorization Act,** reauthorizing the Superfund. The amended statute contains stronger cleanup standards for contaminated sites and provides five times the funding of the original Superfund, which expired in September 1985.

The amendments created a concept called *innocent landowner immunity*. It was recognized that in certain cases a landowner in the chain of ownership had been completely innocent of all wrongdoing and therefore should not be held liable. To establish that an owner is innocent, the damage must have been caused by a previous owner. The innocent landowner must not have had either actual or constructive knowledge of the damage. Most important, the innocent owner must show that *due care* was taken when the land was purchased (the landowner made a reasonable search—preferably an environmental audit—to determine that there was no damage to the property).

Underground Storage Tanks

Underground chemical or petroleum storage tanks have been regulated under a 1984 amendment to the *Resource Conservation and Recovery Act*. A program called **Leaking Underground Storage Tanks (LUST)** was established that governs *installation, maintenance, monitoring, and failure of underground storage tanks*.

The basic provisions of the program require that owners of commercial underground storage tanks and pipes register the present tanks, meet standards for installation, make the tanks leakproof for their entire lives, install leak detection systems, keep the required records, and install no bare steel tanks in soils that will cause rust (otherwise the tanks must be corrosion-proof). Owners also must correct leaks and have funds available to cover potential damage from leaks.

The federal law generally *exempts* farm and residential tanks holding fewer than 1,100 gallons of motor fuel that is used for noncommercial purposes, tanks storing heating oil at the premises where it is consumed, and septic tanks. An important legal point is that LUST places the financial responsibility on the tank owner.

Currently, fuel storage tanks with a capacity of 1,100 gallons or more also are regulated under *New York's Underground Storage Tank Act*. However, owners of small residential tanks are also liable for cleanup costs under the state's Environmental Response Act if there is a leak or spill from their tanks. Because of this liability, it is sometimes difficult to sell property that has an underground tank. Old abandoned gas stations pose a particular problem.

Contamination problems are caused by rusting tanks, leaky piping, and spills or overfills during fuel delivery. A recommended practice is that homeowners replace tanks every 15 years, routinely inspect tank fittings, and monitor fuel levels with a dipstick during summer months to detect any unwarranted fuel losses. Homeowners should use above-ground tanks, if possible, and purchase quality equipment to minimize the risk of any significant contamination problem.

■ IMPLICATIONS OF ENVIRONMENTAL LAW

The real estate professional must be aware of the exposure of all parties involved. Sellers, as mentioned earlier, often carry the majority of the liability. Innocent landowners may be held responsible even though they did not know that the property had been exposed to environmental pollution.

It also is necessary to advise the buyer of the potential for risk posed by neighboring properties. If the broker represents a seller whose property abuts a gas station, the broker must be aware of the possibility of a leak and make the appropriate disclosures. All possible risk should be disclosed to the buyer in any situation in which there might be an environmental problem.

The days of "caveat emptor" (let the buyer beware) are dwindling. Both the statutes and the courts are taking steps to protect the innocent buyer whenever possible. The real estate professional must help protect the buyer in all situations.

Liability of Real Estate Professionals

Additional liability is created for other parties to the transaction. For instance, the real estate appraiser must mention and make the proper adjustments in the estimate of market value. Most of the environmental problems associated with residential units can be cleaned up, and the adjustment to market value typically reflects the cost of that work.

The mortgage lender is protected under certain conditions through the 1986 amendments to the Superfund Act. But in any event the lender must be notified of any potential problems existing with the property.

Also affected may be the insurance carrier. The mortgage insurance companies will protect the lender's investment in the mortgage and may be required to carry part of the ultimate responsibility in case of a loss. More important, the hazard insurance carrier may be deemed directly responsible for damages if environmental concerns were included in the policy.

All parties to the real estate transaction should be certain to ascertain that **due diligence** has been conducted on the property by having an *environmental screening* done before the purchase of the property. The environmental screening may take the form of a report or become a complete environmental audit with complete engineering and scientific tests being conducted.

■ SUMMARY

In today's marketplace, environmental concerns have significant effects on real estate values. The desirability of property is affected by the presence of pollution, and the cost of cleaning up and removing the sources of pollution may be greater than the value of the land itself.

Several long-standing concerns include water pollution (including groundwater pollution), waste disposal sites, contamination caused by septic systems; and damage caused by termites. Some of the more contemporary issues include asbestos, lead poisoning, radon gas, indoor air quality, and PCBs. Some environmental issues that are becoming more important include underground storage tanks, electromagnetic fields, and CFCs.

There are four phases of environmental assessments: Phase I, an investigation to determine where hazardous substances may be present; Phase II, an investigation to confirm the presence of contaminants; Phase III, which includes remedying the contamination; and Phase IV, which includes managing environmental hazards on an ongoing basis.

One of the most important environmental laws that directly affect property owners is the Comprehensive Environmental Response, Compensation, and Liability Act (CERCLA), which established a Superfund to clean up uncontrolled hazardous waste and to respond to spills. It also imposes liability on past, current, and future owners for the costs of cleaning up contaminants. An amendment (SARA) allows some immunity for the subsequent innocent owner who exercised due diligence before buying.

Large underground storage tanks are regulated by both federal and state law: the Resource Conservation and Recovery Act, and the New York Leaking Underground Storage Tank Act.

QUESTIONS

1. Which of the following is a potential polluter of drinking water?
   a. Asbestos
   b. Freon
   c. Termites
   d. Pesticides

2. Owners of older homes must advise prospective buyers or tenants about possible hazards of
   a. iron deposits.
   b. lead paint.
   c. electric transmission wires.
   d. urea-formaldehyde foam insulation.

3. Asbestos has been widely used for
   a. solder.
   b. encapsulation.
   c. insulation.
   d. paint.

4. Which of the following is a hazardous gas?
   a. Radon
   b. Lead
   c. Asbestos
   d. Radioactive waste

5. Eliminating radon from a house is generally
   a. a fairly simple matter.
   b. done by am EPA-trained specialist.
   c. an impossibility.
   d. hazardous.

6. Sick building syndrome (SBS)
   a. requires treatment with insecticides.
   b. subsides when the occupant leaves the building.
   c. is covered by CERCLA.
   d. is associated with contaminated drinking water.

7. A percolation test
   a. is used before a septic tank is installed.
   b. reveals the presence of lead in paint.
   c. can detect the presence of radon.
   d. is proof of due diligence.

8. Asbestos should be removed only by a
   a. seller.
   b. buyer.
   c. handyman.
   d. certified professional.

9. The federal government regulates fuel storage tanks with a capacity of
   a. 550 gallons or larger.
   b. 1,750 gallons or larger.
   c. 1,100 gallons or larger.
   d. 2,000 gallons or larger.

10. A Phase I environmental assessment is common before purchasing a
    a. ranch.
    b. commercial property.
    c. condominium.
    d. residential lot.

11. Documents indicating past uses of the subject property are examined in which phase of an environmental audit?
    a. Phase I
    b. Phase II
    c. Phase III
    d. Phase IV

12. CERCLA established the
    a. EPA.
    b. Landfill Act.
    c. Superfund.
    d. OSHA.

13. Prospective purchasers who are worried about possible contamination of the property they are interested in should ask the seller for a
    a. petition to the Environmental Protection Agency.
    b. Phase I environmental assessment.
    c. percolation test.
    d. lead paint disclosure statement.

REAL ESTATE MATHEMATICS

The Sterns receive two offers for their property at the same time. The Avilas offer $95,000 in cash. The Browns offer $100,000 subject to obtaining a conventional mortgage loan with a 20 percent down payment if the Sterns will pay three points to the bank. Which offer should the Sterns accept?

This review is designed to familiarize students with basic mathematical formulas frequently used in day-to-day real estate transactions and computations required on state licensing examinations. Those who need additional help may want to order the textbook *Mastering Real Estate Mathematics,* Seventh Edition, by Tamper.

■ **KEY TERMS**

acre
front foot

hectare
IRV formula

■ PERCENTAGES

Many real estate computations are based on the calculation of percentages. A percentage expresses a portion of a whole. For example, 50 percent means 50 parts of the possible 100 parts. Percentages greater than 100 percent contain more than one whole unit. Thus 163 percent is one whole and 63 parts of another whole. A whole is always expressed as 100 percent.

Unless a calculator with a percent key is being used, the *percentage must be converted either to a decimal or to a fraction*. To convert a percentage to a decimal, move the decimal two places to the left and drop the percent sign. Thus

$$60\% = .6 \qquad 7\% = .07 \qquad 175\% = 1.75$$

To change a percentage to a fraction, place the percentage over 100. For example:

$$50\% = \frac{50}{100} \qquad 115\% = \frac{115}{100}$$

These fractions then may be *reduced* to make it easier to work the problem. To reduce a fraction, determine the largest number by which both numerator and denominator can be divided evenly. For example

$$\frac{25}{100} = \frac{1}{4} \text{ (both numbers divided by 25)}$$

$$\frac{49}{63} = \frac{7}{9} \text{ (both numbers divided by 7)}$$

Percentage problems contain three elements: *percentage, total,* and *part.* To determine a specific percentage of a whole, multiply the percentage by the whole:

$$\textbf{percent} \times \textbf{whole} = \textbf{part}$$
$$5\% \times 200 = 10$$

For example: A broker is to receive a 7 percent commission on the sale of a $150,000 house. What will the broker's commission be?

$$.07 \times \$150,000 = \$10,500 \text{ broker's commission}$$

This formula is used in calculating mortgage loan interest, brokers' commissions, loan origination fees, discount points, amount of earnest money deposits, and income on capital investments.

A variation, or inversion, of the percentage formula is used to find the total amount when the part and percentage are known:

$$\textbf{whole} = \frac{\textbf{part}}{\textbf{percent}}$$

For example: The Masterson Realty Company received a $9,600 commission for the sale of a house. The broker's commission was 6 percent of the total sales price. What was the total sales price of this house?

$$\frac{\$9,600}{.06} = \$160,000 \text{ total sales price}$$

This formula is used in computing the total mortgage loan principal still due if the monthly payment and interest rate are known. It is also used to calculate the total sales price when the amount and percentage of commission are known and the market value of property when the assessed value and the ratio (percentage) of assessed value to market value are known.

The formula may be used by a real estate salesperson thus: Bertha Buyer has $29,500 available for a down payment, and she must make a 25 percent down payment. How expensive a home can she purchase? The question is $29,500 is 25 percent of what figure?

$$\frac{\$29,500}{.25} = \$118,000$$

Such a problem also may be solved by the use of ratios. Thus, $29,500 is to what number as 25 percent is to 100 percent?

$$\frac{\$29,500}{?} = \frac{25}{100}$$

One type of percentage problem may take several forms. For example, Joe Brown sold property for $90,000. This represents a 20 percent loss from his original cost. What was his cost?

In this problem the student must resist the impulse to multiply everything in sight. Taking 20 percent of $90,000 yields nothing significant. The $90,000 figure represents 80 percent of the original cost, and the question resolves itself into $90,000 is 80 percent of what figure?

$$\frac{\$90,000}{.80} = \$112,500$$

Again: Hester Peters clears $88,200 from the sale of her property after paying a 10 percent commission. How much did the property sell for? Taking 10 percent of $88,200 is an incorrect approach to the problem because the commission was based not on the seller's net but on the full, unknown sales figure; $88,200 represents 90 percent of the sales price.

$$\frac{\$88,200}{.90} = \$98,000$$

To determine the percentage when the amounts of the part and the whole are known:

$$\text{percent} = \frac{\text{part}}{\text{whole}}$$

This formula may be used to find the tax rate when taxes and assessed value are known or the commission rate when sales price and commission amount are known.

The IRV formula, which should be memorized, is basic to investment problems.

Income = Rate × Value

■ **RATES**

Property taxes, transfer taxes, and insurance premiums are usually expressed as rates. A rate is the cost expressed as the amount of cost per unit. For example, tax might be computed at the rate of $5 per $100 assessed value in a certain county. The formula for computing rates is

$$\frac{\textbf{value}}{\textbf{unit}} \times \textbf{rate per unit} = \textbf{total}$$

For example: A house has been assessed at $90,000 and is taxed at an annual rate of $25 per $1,000 assessed valuation. What is the yearly tax?

$$\frac{\$90,000}{1,000} \times \$25 = \text{total annual tax}$$

$$\$90,000 \div \$1,000 = 90 \text{ (increments of } \$100)$$

$$90 \times \$25 = \$2,250 \text{ total annual tax}$$

■ **AREAS AND VOLUMES**

To compute the area of a square or rectangular parcel, use the formula

area = width × depth

The area of a rectangular lot that measures 100 feet wide by 200 feet deep would be

100′ × 200′ = 20,000 square feet

The first figure given always represents **front feet;** a lot described as "80′ × 150′" is 80 feet across and 150 feet deep. Where front footage represents a large part of the value (lakefront, for example), real estate is occasionally priced per front foot, with the amount that extends back from the lake left out of the calculation of value. Area is always expressed in square units.

To compute the amount of surface in a triangular area, use the formula

area = ½ (base × height)

The base of a triangle is the bottom, on which the triangle rests. The height is an imaginary straight line extending from the point of the uppermost angle straight down to the base:

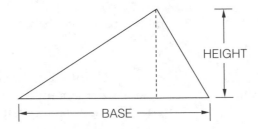

Example: A triangle's base is 50 feet, and its height is 30 feet. What is its area?

½ (50′ × 30′) = area in square feet

½ (1,500) = 750 square feet

To compute the area of an irregular room or parcel of land, divide the shape into regular rectangles, squares, or triangles. Next, compute the area of each regular figure and add the areas together to obtain the total area.

Example: Compute the area of the hallway shown below:

Make a rectangle and a triangle by drawing a single line through the figure:

Compute the area of the rectangle:

area = length × width

16′ × 6′ = 96 square feet

Compute the area of the triangle:

$$\text{area} = \frac{1}{2} (\text{base} \times \text{height})$$

$$\frac{1}{2} (4' \times 6') = \frac{1}{2} (24) = 12 \text{ square feet}$$

Total the two areas:

$$96' + 12' = 108 \text{ square feet in total area}$$

The cubic capacity of an enclosed space is expressed as volume, which is used to describe the amount of space in any three-dimensional area, such as the interior airspace of a room, measured to determine what capacity heating unit is required. The formula for computing cubic or rectangular volume is

$$\textbf{volume} = \textbf{length} \times \textbf{width} \times \textbf{height}$$

Volume is always expressed in cubic units.

For example: The bedroom of a house is 12 feet long, 8 feet wide, 8 feet high to the ceiling. How many cubic feet does the room enclose?

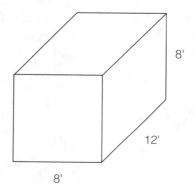

$$8' \times 12' \times 8' = 768 \text{ cubic feet}$$

To compute the volume of a triangular space, such as the airspace in an A-frame house, use the formula

$$\textbf{volume} = \frac{1}{2} (\textbf{length} \times \textbf{height} \times \textbf{width})$$

For example: What is the volume of airspace in the house shown below?

First, divide the house into two shapes, rectangular and triangular, as shown:

Find the volume of *T*:

$$\text{volume} = \tfrac{1}{2}(\text{length} \times \text{height} \times \text{width})$$

$$\tfrac{1}{2}\,(25' \times 10' \times 40') = \tfrac{1}{2}\,(10{,}000) = 5{,}000 \text{ cubic feet}$$

Find the volume of *R*:

$$25' \times 40' \times 12' = 12{,}000 \text{ cubic feet}$$

Total volumes *T* and *R*:

$$5{,}000' + 12{,}000' = 17{,}000 \text{ cubic feet of airspace in the house}$$

Cubic measurements of volume are used to compute the construction costs per cubic foot of a building, the amount of airspace being sold in a condominium unit, or the heating and cooling requirements for a building. When either area or volume is computed, all dimensions used must be given in the same unit of measure. For example, one may not multiply two feet by six inches to get the area; two feet must be multiplied by one-half foot. Thus it is important to remember that

$$1 \text{ yard} = 3 \text{ feet;}$$

$$1 \text{ square yard} = 3' \times 3' = 9 \text{ square feet; and}$$

$$1 \text{ cubic yard} = 3' \times 3' \times 3' = 27 \text{ cubic feet.}$$

■ LAND UNITS AND MEASUREMENTS

Some commonly used land units and measurements follow:

- A *rod* is 16½ feet.
- A *chain* is 66 feet, or 100 links.
- A *mile* is 5,280 feet.
- An *acre* contains 43,560 square feet. Memorize this one.
- A *section* of land is one square mile and contains 640 acres; a *quarter section* contains 160 acres; a *quarter of a quarter section* contains 40 acres.

■ A *circle* contains 360 degrees; a *half segment* of a circle contains 180 degrees; a *quarter segment* of a circle contains 90 degrees. One *degree* (1°) can be subdivided into 60 minutes (60′), each of which contains 60 seconds (60″). One-and-a-half degrees would be written 1°30′.

■ A *mill* is one-tenth of a cent, $.001. When a property tax is quoted as 23 mills, that means $.023 per $1 of assessed value, the same rate as $23 per $1,000.

Where the metric system is used, a hectare is equal to 10,000 square meters, or about 2.471 acres.

QUESTIONS

1. A rectangular lot measures 60 feet wide and has an area of 1,200 square yards. What is the depth of the lot?

   a. 20 feet   c. 20 yards
   b. 180 feet   d. 90 yards

2. A buyer is applying for an FHA mortgage on a house priced at $108,000. The maximum loan-to-value ratio is 97.75. What is the minimum down payment?

   a. $1,054   c. $2,108
   b. $1,080   d. $2,430

3. Ebenezer Scrooge intends to put up a fence between his lot and his neighbor's. The fencing comes in 6-foot sections. For a fence 120 feet long, how many fence posts will be required?

   a. 19   c. 21
   b. 20   d. 22

4. A house is valued at $198,000. It is to be insured for 80 percent of its cost. Insurance will cost $6 per $1,000. What is the annual insurance premium?

   a. $95.40   c. $950.40
   b. $119.80   d. $1,198.00

5. John Walton received a net amount of $74,000 from the sale of his house after paying $1,200 in legal and other fees and 6 percent sales commission. What was the selling price of the house?

   a. $80,000   c. $79,640
   b. $78,440   d. $79,000

6. A lending institution will allow its borrowers to spend 28 percent of their income for housing expense. What will be the maximum monthly payment allowed for a family with annual income of $57,000 and no other debts?

   a. $399   c. $1,596
   b. $1,330   d. None of the above

7. Sally Sellright works on a 50/50 commission split with her broker. If she lists a house at $156,000 for 6 percent commission and sells it for $154,000, how much will Sally receive?

   a. $4,620   c. $9,220
   b. $4,680   d. $9,360

8. Dudley Donnelly's monthly mortgage payment for principal and interest is $628.12. His property taxes are $1,800 a year, and his annual insurance premium is $365. What is his total monthly payment for PITI (principal, interest, taxes, and insurance)?

   a. $808.54   c. $778.12
   b. $1,921.24   d. None of the above

9. A lot measuring 120′ x 200′ is selling for $300 a front foot. What is its price?

   a. $720,000   c. $36,000
   b. $60,000   d. $800,000

10. A five-acre lot has front footage of 300 feet. How deep is it?

    a. 145.2 feet   c. 88 feet
    b. 726 feet   d. 160 feet

11. Broker Sally Smith of Happy Valley Realty recently sold Jack and Jill Hawkins's home for $79,500. Smith charged the Hawkinses 6½ percent commission and will pay 30 percent of that amount to the listing salesperson and 25 percent to the selling salesperson. What amount of commission will the listing salesperson receive from the Hawkins sale?

    a. $5,167.50   c. $3,617.25
    b. $1,550.25   d. $1,291.87

12. Susan Silber signed an agreement to purchase a condominium apartment from Perry and Marie Morris. The contract stipulated that the Morrises replace the damaged bedroom carpet. The carpet Silber has chosen costs $16.95 per square yard plus $2.50 per square yard for installation. If the bedroom dimensions are as illustrated, how much will the Morrises have to pay for the job?

a. $241.54   c. $277.16
b. $189.20   d. $2,494.46

13. Hal, Olive, Ron, and Marvin pooled their savings and purchased a vacation home for $125,000. If Hal invested $30,000 and Olive and Ron each contributed $35,000, what percentage of ownership was left for Marvin?

a. 20 percent   c. 28 percent
b. 24 percent   d. 30 percent

14. Harold Barlow is curious to know how much money his son and daughter-in-law still owe on their predatory mortgage loan. Barlow knows that the interest portion of their last monthly payment was $391.42. If the Barlows are paying interest at the rate of 11½ percent, what was the outstanding balance of their loan before that last payment was made?

a. $43,713.00   c. $36,427.50
b. $40,843.83   d. $34,284.70

15. Nick and Olga Stravinski bought their home on Sabre Lane a year ago for $98,500. Property in their neighborhood is said to be increasing in value at a rate of 5 percent annually. If this is true, what is the current market value of the Stravinskis' real estate?

a. $103,425
b. $93,575
c. $104,410
d. None of the above is within $50

16. The DeHavilands' home on Dove Street is valued at $95,000. Property in their area is assessed at 60 percent of its value, and the local tax rate is $28.50 per thousand. What is the amount of the DeHavilands' monthly taxes?

a. $1,625.50   c. $270.75
b. $570.00   d. $135.38

17. The Fitzpatricks are planning to construct a patio in their backyard. An illustration of the surface area to be paved appears here. If the cement is to be poured as a six-inch slab, how many cubic feet of cement will be poured into this patio?

a. 660 cubic feet   c. 330 cubic feet
b. 450 cubic feet   d. 195 cubic feet

18. Happy Morgan receives a monthly salary of $500 plus 3 percent commission on all of his listings that sell and 2.5 percent on all his sales. None of the listings that Morgan took sold last month, but he received $3,675 in salary and commission. What was the value of the property Morgan sold?

a. $147,000   c. $122,500
b. $127,000   d. $105,833

19. The Salvatinis' residence has proved difficult to sell. Salesperson Martha Kelley suggests it might sell faster if they enclose a portion of the backyard with a privacy fence. If the area to be enclosed is as illustrated, how much would the fence cost at $6.95 per linear foot?

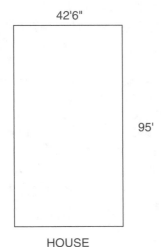

42'6"

95'

HOUSE

   a. $1,911.25   c. $1,615.88
   b. $1,654.10   d. $955.63

20. Andrew McTavish leases the 12 apartments in the Overton Arms for a total monthly rental of $4,500. If this figure represents an 8 percent annual return on McTavish's investment, what was the original cost of the property?
   a. $675,000   c. $54,000
   b. $450,000   d. $56,250

21. A 100-acre farm is divided into house lots. The streets require one-eighth of the whole farm, and there are 140 lots. How many square feet are there in each lot?
   a. 35,004   c. 27,225
   b. 31,114   d. 43,560

22. In a sale of residential property, real estate taxes for the current calendar year amounted to $975 and have already been paid by the seller. The sale is to be closed on October 26; what is the amount of real estate proration to be credited the seller?
   a. $173.33   c. $798.96
   b. $162.50   d. $83.96

23. The buyer is assuming the seller's mortgage. The unpaid balance after the most recent payment (the first of the month) was $61,550. Interest is paid in arrears each month at 13 percent per annum. The sale is to be closed on September 22; what is the amount of mortgage interest proration to be credited to the buyer at the closing?
   a. $666.97   c. $177.82
   b. $488.97   d. $689.01

24. Riley's commission on a sale was $14,100, which was 6 percent of the sales price. What was the sales price?
   a. $235,000.00   c. $846,000.00
   b. $154,255.31   d. $234,500.00

25. A 30-year fixed-rate amortized mortgage for $100,000 at 11 percent interest requires monthly payments of $952.34 for principal and interest. What is the total amount of interest paid on this loan during the life of the mortgage?
   a. $114,280.00   c. $314,272.60
   b. $242,842.40   d. $330,000.00

26. The Duffys are buying a house for $120,000 and seek a fixed-rate loan of $90,000 for 25 years. One lender offers them a 10 percent loan with no points, with monthly payments of $817.85. A second lender requires two points for a 9.5 percent loan, with monthly payments of $786.35. If the Duffys decide to pay the points and take the lower-interest loan, how long will it take before the savings on their lower payments have made up for that extra cost at closing?

   a. Two years, eight months
   b. Three years, two months
   c. Four years, nine months
   d. Seven years, four months

27. The Sterns receive two offers for their property at the same time. The Avilas offer $95,000 in cash. The Browns offer $100,000 subject to obtaining a conventional mortgage loan with 20 percent down payment and ask the Sterns to pay three points to their lending institution. The Sterns decide to accept the all-cash offer. If they had accepted the Browns' offer instead, they would have received

   a. $2,000 more at closing.
   b. $2,400 less at closing.
   c. $2,600 more at closing.
   d. $3,000 less at closing.

28. Diana Fairhaven buys a new ranch house for $178,000 and borrows $150,000 on a mortgage loan. The state's mortgage tax is $.50 per $100 for the first $10,000 borrowed on a one- or two-family residence, and $.75 per $100 on the remainder. How much will Diana owe in mortgage tax at closing?

   a. $1,050   c. $1,400
   b. $1,100   d. $1,500

29. New York State charges a transfer tax of $2 per $500 sale price or fraction thereof when real property is sold. The Currens listed their home for $200,000 and accepted an offer for $198,600 from Mr. and Mrs. Darcy, who obtained a mortgage loan for $160,000. How much did the Currens pay in transfer tax?

   a. $397.20   c. $796.00
   b. $398.00   d. $800.00

30. The Mortensons bought a 1,300-square-foot cooperative apartment on the Upper West Side of Manhattan for $425,000, which was $15,000 less than the listed price. How much did the apartment cost per square foot?

   a. $306   c. $327
   b. $315   d. $338

18

INDEPENDENT CONTRACTOR/ EMPLOYEE

Rhoda Barron is looking for a broker with whose office she can become associated. In interviews with various brokers, she finds that none of them are willing to offer her health insurance coverage. Should she just keep on looking? What's going on?

■ **KEY TERMS**

employee

group boycott

independent contractor

market allocation

price-fixing

restraint of trade

Sherman Antitrust Act

■ SALESPERSON EMPLOYMENT STATUS

All licensed salespeople are required by law to work under the supervision of a sponsoring broker in their real estate activities. In doing so, the salesperson may be employed either as an employee or as an independent contractor. The distinction between an *employee* and an *independent contractor* is an important one, with significant tax consequences as well as important effects on the ability of a broker to control the activities of his or her salespeople.

Employee Status

The employer-employee relationship allows a broker to exercise certain controls over salespeople. The broker can require that an **employee** adhere to regulations affecting working hours, office routine, and dress standards.

As an employer a broker is required by the federal government to withhold Social Security tax and income tax from the compensation paid to employees. An employee is covered by unemployment insurance and workers' compensation. A broker may provide employees with fringe benefits such as health insurance, pension plans, sick leave, and paid vacations. Such benefits are variously estimated to add 25 percent to 50 percent to the cost of an employee's base salary. A broker who chooses to regard salespersons as employees must take such costs into consideration when working out commission schedules.

Independent Contractor Status

Most salespersons, however, act as **independent contractors.** A survey by the National Association of REALTORS® found that nine out of ten real estate firms treated their sales associates as independent contractors. Brokers traditionally have maintained this relationship to avoid the bookkeeping problems of withholding taxes, Social Security payments, unemployment insurance, and other such items that become complex when based not on a regular salary but on unpredictable commissions.

Errors and omissions insurance. A broker may carry errors and omissions insurance on all salespeople, regardless of their status as employees or independent contractors. The cost may be borne by the broker or by the salesperson.

Tests of Employment

The broker who chooses independent contractor status for associates should keep on file agreements signed by the associates, with wording that has been reviewed by the broker's attorney. Recent *safe-harbor guidelines* provide that the IRS will not challenge independent contractor status where the associate (1) is licensed as a real estate broker or salesperson; (2) has income based on sales output and subject to fluctuation; and (3) performs services pursuant to a written contract specifying independent contractor status.

In 1986, New York State adopted similar guidelines on independent contractor status for real estate licensees, whose situation had been unclear with regard to state programs such as unemployment insurance and workers' compensation insurance. The New York Department of Labor, in evaluating associates' status with regard to unemployment insurance, also stresses the importance of a current, written contract between broker and salesperson. A sample contract that meets the Department of Labor requirements, suggested by the New York State Association of REALTORS®, is shown in Figure 18.1.

The requirements for independent contractor status under New York State law are as follows:

1. Substantially all of the licensee's compensation (whether or not paid in cash) for services performed on behalf of the broker must be directly related to sales or other output, rather than to the number of hours worked.
2. There must be a written contract for services between the broker and the licensee, *executed within the past 15 months*, that indicates that the licensee is employed as an independent contractor.
3. The written contract between the broker and licensee must not have been executed under duress (i.e., the broker may not force the licensee to sign the agreement, although the broker may choose not to maintain the licensee's license if he or she refuses to sign).
4. The written contract must contain the following provisions:
   - The licensee will be treated for all purposes by the broker as an independent contractor.
   - The licensee will be paid a commission directly related to gross sales or other output without deduction for taxes.
   - The licensee will not receive any compensation related to the number of hours worked.
   - The licensee will not be treated as an employee for federal or state tax purposes.
   - The licensee may work any hours he or she chooses.
   - The licensee may work out of his or her home as well as out of the broker's office.
   - The licensee is free to engage in outside employment.
   - The broker may provide office facilities and supplies for use by the licensee, but the licensee will otherwise bear his or her own expenses, including automobile, travel, and entertainment expenses.
   - The licensee and broker will act in accordance with the terms of the Real Property Law and Department of State real estate regulations.
   - Either the licensee or the broker may terminate the agreement at any time on notice to the other.

The existence of a written agreement is clearly an important aspect of maintaining an independent contractor relationship between the broker and the salesperson. However, the written agreement will not prevent employee status from being implied as a result of the conduct of the broker and salesperson. For example, if the broker requires that the salesperson attend staff meetings or includes the salesperson in a company pension plan, this may be seen as evidence that the relationship between them is actually that of employer and employee. The consequences of such a determination can be drastic for both the broker and the salesperson.

F I G U R E   18.1

Sample Independent Contractor Agreement

AGREEMENT

THIS AGREEMENT, (hereinafter "Agreement") made and entered into this day of _____ 2___, by and between _____ (hereinafter "Sales Associate") and _____ (hereinafter "Broker").

WHEREAS, the Sales Associate and the Broker are both duly licensed pursuant to Article 12-A of the Real Property Law of the State of New York; and

WHEREAS, the Sales Associate and the Broker wish to enter into this Agreement in order to define their respective rights, duties and obligations.

NOW THEREFORE, in consideration of the terms, covenants, conditions and mutual promises contained herein, and other good and valuable consideration, it is hereby stipulated and agreed as follows:

1. The Sales Associate is engaged as an independent contractor associated with the Broker pursuant to Article 12-A of the Real Property Law and shall be treated as such for all purposes, including but not limited to Federal and State taxation, withholding, unemployment insurance and workers' compensation; and

2. The Sales Associate (a) shall be paid a commission on his or her gross sales, if any, without deduction for taxes, which commission shall be directly related to sales or other output; (b) shall not receive any remuneration related to the number of hours worked; and (c) shall not be treated as an employee with respect to such services for Federal and State tax purposes; and

3. The Sales Associate shall be permitted to work any hours he or she chooses; and

4. The Sales Associate shall be permitted to work out of his or her own home or the office of the Broker; and

5. The Sales Associate shall be free to engage in outside employment; and

6. The Broker may provide office facilities and supplies for the use of the Sales Associate, but the Sales Associate shall otherwise bear his or her own expenses, including but not limited to automobile, travel and entertainment expenses; and

7. The Broker and Sales Associate shall comply with the requirements of Article 12-A of the Real Property Law and the regulations pertaining thereto, but such compliance shall not affect the Sales Associate's status as an independent contractor nor would it be construed as an indication that the Sales Associate is an employee of the Broker for any purposes whatsoever; and

8. This contract and the association created hereby may be terminated by either party hereto at any time upon notice given to the other; and

9. This Agreement is deemed to have been entered into in, and will be construed and interpreted in accordance with the laws of the State of New York; and

10. BY SIGNING BELOW THE UNDERSIGNED STIPULATE AND AGREE THAT THEY HAVE COMPLETELY READ THIS AGREEMENT, THAT THE TERMS HEREOF ARE FULLY UNDERSTOOD AND VOLUNTARILY ACCEPTED BY THEM AND THAT THIS AGREEMENT IS NOT SIGNED UNDER DURESS.

IN WITNESS WHEREOF, the parties hereto have executed this Agreement as of the day and year first above written.

_____
SALES ASSOCIATE

_____
BROKER

PREPARED BY THE NEW YORK STATE
ASSOCIATION OF Realtors®, INC.

Source: Reprinted with permission of the New York State Associations of REALTORS®, Inc.

The employment contract between the broker and the salesperson or associate broker should be renewed each year. The contract should include provisions for the termination of employment.

For the broker, the determination that a salesperson is actually an employee will result in liability for state and federal unemployment insurance premiums; workers' compensation and disability insurance coverages; and federal and state withholding taxes, including the employer's share of Social Security taxes. For the salesperson, the result will be the inability to claim self-employment expense deductions on IRS Form 1040 Schedule C, as well as the fact that the salesperson's commission payments will be subjected to withholding for all applicable state and federal taxes.

The dilemma for brokers who want to maintain independent contractor status for their associates is that this limits the ability of the brokers to control the activity of their salespeople. Too much control often leads to the conclusion that the salesperson is an employee. On the other hand, brokers are legally liable for the actions of their salespeople, and have an obligation under the Real Property Law and Department of State regulations to supervise their salespeople's activities. The New York State law regarding independent contractor status for real estate licensees recognizes part of this dilemma and specifically states that compliance with the Real Property Law and Department of State real estate regulations will not be construed as an indication of employee status. (See Figure 18.2.)

New York City guidelines regarding independent contractor status are detailed in Chapter 19.

■ ANTITRUST LAWS

The real estate industry is subject to federal and state antitrust laws. The most common violations in the real estate industry are *price-fixing* and *allocation of customers or markets*.

Illegal **price-fixing** occurs when competing brokers get together to set commission rates, rather than let competition in the open market establish those rates.

It's not that simple, though. Real estate companies—and agents—have been prosecuted under the **Sherman Antitrust Act** for what appeared to be innocent discussions with agents from other firms. A licensee should walk away immediately from the slightest conversation about rates with someone from another brokerage. (The only exception might be concerning a particular property the two firms have cooperated in selling.)

In the past, discussions about the negative qualities of a third company have been interpreted as a **group boycott,** a conspiracy to boycott that firm and drive it out of business. Licensees must learn which topics must be avoided when engaged in conversation with agents from other companies.

Unemployment Insurance Notice for Real Estate Salesperson

NEW YORK STATE,
DEPARTMENT OF LABOR,
UNEMPLOYMENT INSURANCE DIVISION
NOTICE TO EMPLOYERS

Persons Engaged in Real Estate Sales

Effective October 1, 1986, services performed by a licensed real estate broker or sales associate are excluded from coverage if it can be proven that all of the following conditions are met:

(A) substantially all of the remuneration (whether or not paid in cash) for the services performed by such broker or sales associate is directly related to sales or other output (including the performance of services) rather than to the number of hours worked;

and

(B) the services performed by the broker or sales associate are performed pursuant to a written contract executed between such broker or sales associate and the person for whom the services are performed within the past twelve to fifteen months;

and

(C) such contract was not executed under duress and contains the following provisions:

1. that the broker or sales associate is engaged as an independent contractor associated with the person for whom services are performed pursuant to Article 12-A of the Real Property Law and shall be treated as such for all purposes;

2. that they (a) shall be paid a commission directly related to their gross sales or other output without deduction for taxes; (b) shall not receive any remuneration related to the number of hours worked; and (c) shall not be treated as employees with respect to such services for federal and state tax purposes;

3. that they shall be permitted to work any hours they choose;

4. that they shall be permitted to work out of their own homes or the office of the person for whom services are performed;

5. that they shall be free to engage in outside employment;

6. that the person for whom the services are performed may provide office facilities and supplies for the use of the broker or sales associate, but that they shall otherwise bear their own expenses, including but not limited to automobile, travel, and entertainment expenses;

7. that the person for whom the services are performed and the broker or sales associate shall comply with the requirements of Article 12-A of the Real Property Law and the regulations pertaining thereto, but such compliance shall not affect their status as independent contractors nor should it be construed as an indication that they are employees of such person for any purpose whatsoever;

8. that the contract and the association may be terminated by either party at any time upon notice to the other.

Market allocation might occur when competing firms agree to split up the area and refrain from doing business in each other's territories.

Each real estate company, of course, is free to set its own fee schedule, and to negotiate various rates with individual buyers or sellers if it wishes. The violations occur when competing firms agree to act together, in what the U.S. Justice Department calls **restraint of trade.** More details on the matter can be found in Chapter 19.

■ SUMMARY

Whether a salesperson is employed as an employee or an independent contractor has serious implications for both the salesperson and the broker. Employees are subject to tax withholding and may not file Schedule C to deduct business expenses for federal income tax purposes. Brokers must withhold income and Social Security taxes from employees, but not from independent contractors. Employees are covered by programs such as unemployment insurance and workers' compensation, and the employer is responsible for the premiums and taxes associated with these programs.

The classification of a licensee as an employee or an independent contractor depends on the conduct of the licensee and the broker. A written agreement is important under federal and state law to show independent contractor status, but other factors are of equal or greater significance. The compensation of an independent contractor must be related to performance and not to hours worked, and the broker is limited in the degree of control that may be exerted over an independent contractor's behavior. Participation in benefits such as pension plans or sick pay may indicate that the licensee is an employee.

Antitrust laws prohibit competing brokers from discussing commission rates charged to clients and also the publication of such rates. Brokers also must refrain from negative discussions about other brokers to avoid the appearance of a group boycott.

QUESTIONS

1. When the market was depressed in New Town, New York, the brokers' association decided to lower commission rates to have a better chance to list properties. This would be an antitrust violation called
   a. market allocation.
   b. tie-in arrangement.
   c. price-fixing.
   d. group boycotting.

2. A broker may require a salesperson who is an independent contractor to
   a. work established hours.
   b. comply with Article 12-A of Real Property Law.
   c. accept a regular salary.
   d. have an oral contract.

3. If a salesperson is an independent contractor, he or she is entitled to
   a. unemployment insurance.
   b. workers' compensation.
   c. federal and state withholding.
   d. supervision and guidance.

4. Bob Broker is having breakfast in a coffee shop with his friend Olive Otherbroker. Olive says, "Did you hear about that firm that's charging a flat fee for selling property? Do you think they'll make it?" Bob's proper response is to
   a. explain to Olive that flat fees are allowed by law, just as commissions are.
   b. assure Olive that his commission rates are not going to change.
   c. caution Olive about the dangers of discussing commission rates with competing firms.
   d. immediately say, "Sorry, I've got to go" and walk out.

5. An independent contractor is generally
   a. paid a regular salary, with commissions as a bonus.
   b. reimbursed for all business expenses.
   c. paid commissions on sales.
   d. given two weeks of paid vacation each year.

6. Commission rates are set by
   a. state law.
   b. local custom.
   c. the broker.
   d. agreement between the client and broker.

7. An employee is legally required to receive
   a. an employer-sponsored retirement plan.
   b. unemployment insurance.
   c. health insurance.
   d. commissions on sales.

8. Jose Salesperson is listing a house, and the seller requests a lower commission rate than the firm usually charges. Jose should answer that he'll have to refer the question to
   a. the local Board of REALTORS®.
   b. the Justice Department.
   c. the Department of State.
   d. his broker.

9. The salesperson who joins a real estate company will probably have to pay for his own
   a. office space.
   b. errors and omissions insurance.
   c. contract forms and "For Sale" signs.
   d. hospitalization insurance.

10. The broker whose associates are independent contractors may still insist that they
    a. keep regular office hours.
    b. sign a written contract for services.
    c. attend sales meetings.
    d. be paid by the hour.

19

THE BROKER'S OFFICE

Debby Gould has been general manager for a real estate developer for the past five years, assisting with purchases of land, obtaining financing, construction, and management of apartment complexes and shopping plazas. She'd like to become a broker and has already taken two prelicensing courses, but she has no intention of taking a year off to get experience as a salesperson with a brokerage firm. How can she qualify for a broker's license?

■ **KEY TERMS**

antitrust laws	group boycott	price-fixing
blind ad	independent contractor	restraint of trade
Clayton Antitrust Act	market allocation	Sherman Antitrust Act
consent decree	multiple-listing service	tie-in arrangement
designations	policy and procedures	vicarious liability
employee	guide	
fair employment laws		

■ WHO NEEDS A LICENSE

A license as a real estate broker is required for any of the services listed in Chapter 1, when they are performed *for another and for a fee*. The transactions covered include listing real estate for sale, selling, purchasing, negotiating exchanges, leasing, renting, auctioning, and negotiating the sale of a business with substantial real estate involved.

The license allows the same functions with regard to cooperatives and condominiums.

■ OTHER RELATED LICENSES

As detailed in Chapter 1, licenses are required for apartment information vendors and apartment sharing agents, who must maintain trust accounts and renew their licenses annually. Appraisers who work with federally related loans on property worth more than $250,000 require special licensing or certification (details later in this chapter). Mortgage bankers are licensed by the New York Banking Department, after proving a net worth of at least $250,000 and a line of credit of at least $1 million, at least five years' experience as lenders, and meeting other requirements. Mortgage brokers pass less stringent requirements for registration by the Banking Department.

■ WHO DOES NOT NEED A LICENSE

Licensure is not required for the following:

■ *Attorneys admitted to the New York bar* may act as real estate brokers without any further license, and thus could collect commissions for real estate services. The lawyer who intends to supervise associated salespersons or brokers, however, must apply for a broker's license but need not satisfy the experience, education, or examination requirements.

■ Some individuals may be exempt from license requirements if they *perform services for one employer only*. The exemption might cover, for example, in-house salespersons for the developer of a real estate subdivision or the resident manager in an apartment complex. Often, though, such persons do secure licenses, just to be on the safe side.

■ *Public officers in the performance of their duties* are also exempt. Negotiating the purchase of a tract of land to be used for a park, for example, would not require the town supervisor to be licensed.

■ *Those acting under court order* do not need licenses. Often this is the executor of a will, who negotiates the sale of the home belonging to an estate.

■ A *business broker* does not need a real estate license, unless the business being sold includes a material (significant) amount of its value in real estate.

■ OBTAINING A LICENSE

The Department of State (DOS) issues brokers' licenses to experienced real estate salespersons who have completed what is, in effect, an *apprenticeship* under supervision of a managing broker or to those with extensive other experience in real estate. In addition to the 45-hour qualifying course required of beginning salespersons, the DOS mandates a 45-hour course for prospective brokers. Part of this course consists of a review of license law and agency (Chapters 1, 2, and 3), to be studied in greater detail from the point of view of someone who may soon be supervising others and be responsible for their actions. The remainder of the course covers more advanced specialties within real estate brokerage. The DOS's Web page can be viewed at *www.dos.state.ny.us*.

WWWeb.Link

The education, experience, and examination requirements are the same for all brokers' licenses (except those issued to attorneys and brokers transferring from states with which New York has reciprocity agreements—see Table 1.3 in Chapter 1). The Department issues licenses, however, in several different classes:

- *Class 30* is for the applicant planning to work as an associate broker. Although fully qualified as a broker, the associate nevertheless chooses to work within another broker's firm. As with a salesperson's application, the associate broker's application is signed by a sponsoring broker. Should the associate broker ever wish to operate independently, no further study or examination would be necessary. Application would simply be made to the DOS for a license in the new class.
- *Class 31* is issued to the officer of a corporation who conducts a brokerage business under a corporate name. (Salespersons and associate brokers may not be principals or own voting stock in a licensed brokerage corporation.) For new corporations, the application must include the filing receipt.
- *Class 33* is for the broker who intends to do business under the name of a partnership. A copy of the county clerk's certificate of partnership must accompany the application.
- *Class 35* is for the individual broker who will do business in his or her name only, as "John Smith" or "Jane Brown, licensed real estate broker."
- *Class 37* signifies licensure as a trade-name broker, who will own the business as a sole proprietorship. The local county clerk, after ascertaining that no one else uses the requested trade name, will issue a D/B/A (doing business as) certificate that must accompany the license application; for example, "Juan Sanchez, d/b/a House Calls Realty."
- *Class 49, limited liability company* or *limited liability partnership broker,* is for the member or manager of a brokerage operating under one of these relatively new types of organizations. For a new limited liability company, a copy of the articles of organization or a filing receipt must be filed with the application.

The broker who intends to use anything other than his or her own name for the firm must submit the proposed name for approval to the DOS, which will check, among other things, whether the name is identical with or misleadingly similar to one already in use for a brokerage. *It is prudent to postpone ordering stationery, yellow pages advertising, business cards, or a web page domain until the name has been cleared.*

The Broker's Application

The broker's application (see Figure 19.1) must list the street address of the proposed business. A post office box is not considered sufficient. If the address is outside the state of New York, an agreement giving irrevocable consent (to be sued within the state) must be filed. The required form is available from the DOS's Customer Services Unit (1-518-474-4429).

A check for $150 must accompany each broker's application.

It is possible to hold more than one broker's license at a time. A separate check and application are submitted for each. An associate broker may desire also to operate individually in his or her name or as a partner or member of a corporation dealing in real estate. Some other class of broker may wish to operate as an associate broker also. In either case, a letter from the sponsoring broker involved must be enclosed, indicating that he or she understands about the dual licensure.

Experience Requirement

License law requires that a broker have had at least one year's full-time experience as a licensed salesperson or two years' experience in the general real estate business or a combination of those two requirements. A supplement detailing the claimed experience accompanies the application.

- *Licensed salesperson* (at least one year). At least 1,750 points must be reported on the Supplement A (Figure 19.2) that accompanies the application. It is not necessary that any particular category of experience be included, only that the total number of points has accumulated.
- *General real estate field.* Experience may have been gained over a period of at least two years in buying and selling property, managing property for an employer or a government entity, and the like (no credit, however, for experience illegally gained by doing something for which you should have been licensed). Such experience is reported on Supplement B, which is identical to Figure 19.1, except that twice as many points, 3,500, must be accumulated.
- *Combined experience.* For less than one full year as a licensed salesperson, combined with other general experience, two supplements are filled out. The number of points on each are listed on Supplement C (Figure 19.3), with twice as much weight given to experience gained while licensed. Total points must equal at least 3,500.

It's important that salespersons keep their own files of all transactions, so that in the case of a DOS audit or investigation they can furnish details for all points claimed on their applications.

The broker's examination is given at the test centers listed in Chapter 1, and as with the salesperson's examination, same-day licensure is available for those who pass the exam at the *Albany* and *Rochester* test sites and have completed applications with them. Dates and times for the broker's examination are available by phone from the DOS at 518-474-4429.

F I G U R E   19.1

Broker's Application

FOR OFFICE USE ONLY	CLASS	KEY	UNIQUE ID NUMBER		CASH NUMBER	FEE
	|_|_|	|_|_|	|_|_|_|_|_|_|_|		|_|_|_|_|_|	$150

E W S |_|_|_|_|_| / |_|_| B |_|_|_|_|_| / |_|_| PASSED EXAM |_|_|_|_|_|_|_|

Real Estate Broker/Associate Broker Application   NYS Department of State
DIVISION OF LICENSING SERVICES
84 Holland Avenue
Albany, NY 12208-3490
PLEASE PRINT OR TYPE ALL RESPONSES IN INK

Application as (Check one): ☐ **Individual**   ☐ **Trade Name**   ☐ **Corporation**   ☐ **Associate Broker**
☐ **Partnership**   ☐ **Limited Liability Company**   ☐ **Limited Liability Partnership**

APPLICANT'S NAME   LAST   FIRST   M.I.   SUFFIX

HOME ADDRESS   STREET ADDRESS (REQUIRED)   APT. NUMBER

CITY   STATE   ZIP+4   COUNTY

BUSINESS NAME

BUSINESS ADDRESS   STREET ADDRESS (REQUIRED)

CITY   STATE   ZIP+4   COUNTY

DAYTIME TELEPHONE NUMBER *(IF PROBLEM WITH APPLICATION)*   SOCIAL SECURITY NUMBER *(SEE PRIVACY NOTIFICATION)*   FEDERAL TAXPAYER ID *(SEE PRIVACY NOTIFICATION)*

(   )

E-MAIL ADDRESS (IF ANY)

1 Background Data —

1. What is your date of birth? _____

YES   NO

2. Are you currently a member of the New York State Bar?   _____ _____

3. Have you ever held or do you currently hold a real estate license issued by the State of New York? If Yes, in what year? _____   UNIQUE ID NO. _____   _____ _____

4. Have you ever been convicted in this state or elsewhere of any criminal offense that is a misdemeanor or a felony?   _____ _____
   → IF "YES," you must submit with this application a written explanation giving the place, court jurisdiction, nature of the offense, sentence and/or other disposition. You must submit a copy of the accusatory instrument (e.g., indictment, criminal information or complaint) and a Certificate of Disposition. If you possess or have received a Certificate of Relief from Disabilities, Certificate of Good Conduct or Executive Pardon, you must submit a copy with this application.

5. Are there any criminal charges (misdemeanors or felonies) pending against you in any court in this state or elsewhere?   _____ _____
   → IF "YES," you must submit a copy of the accusatory instrument (e.g., indictment, criminal information or complaint).

6. Has any license or permit issued to you or a company in which you are or were a principal in New York State or elsewhere ever been revoked, suspended or denied?   _____ _____
   → IF "YES," you must provide all relevant documents, including the agency determination, if any.)

For questions 7-9 please answer only the statement which applies to your particular licensing status. (Please enclose a copy of the required certificate)

7. I own this business and the trade name certificate has been filed in the office of the County Clerk where the business is located. (copy enclosed)   _____ _____

8. I am a member of this partnership and the Certificate of Partnership has been filed in the office of the County Clerk where the business is located. (copy enclosed)   _____ _____

F I G U R E   19.1

Broker's Application (continued)

YES   NO

9. a. I am an officer of this corporation and the New York State Certification of Incorporation has been filed with the Department of State, Division of Corporations. (copy enclosed)   _____ _____

   b. I am an officer of this foreign (out of state) corporation and an application for authority to do business has been filed with the Department of State, Division of Corporations. (copy enclosed)   _____ _____

   c. I am currently a licensed real estate salesperson for the above corporation and will be made an officer upon approval of my application.   _____ _____

10. I am a (member) (manager) of this limited liability company, and a copy of the articles of organization have been filed with the Department of State. (copy enclosed)   _____ _____

---

2   Child Support Statement — *You must complete this section. If you do not complete it, your application will be returned.*

"X" A or B, below

I, the undersigned, do hereby certify that (You *must* "X" A or B, below):

A. [ ] **I am not under obligation to pay child support.** (SKIP "B" and go directly to **Applicant Affirmation**).

B. [ ] I am under obligation to pay child support. (You must "X" any of the four statements below that are true and apply to you):

   [ ] I do *not* owe four or more months of child support payments.

   [ ] I am making child support payments by income execution or court approved payment plan or by a plan agreed to by the parties.

   [ ] My child support obligation is the subject of a pending court proceeding.

   [ ] I receive public assistance or supplemental social security income.

Applicant Affirmation — I also affirm, under the penalties of perjury, that the statements made in this application are true and correct. I further affirm that I have read and understand the provisions of Article 12-A of the Real Property Law and the rules and regulations promulgated thereunder.

Applicant's Signature

X _____   Date _____

---

3   For Associate Broker Applicants Only

Association Statement — I am sponsoring this applicant.

*Sponsoring Broker*_____   Date _____

Sponsoring Broker's Unique ID Number _____

F I G U R E   19.2

Broker's Application—Licensed Salespersons Activity

Real Estate Broker/Associate Broker Application
Licensed Salespersons Activity Only

PAGE ___ OF ___

APPLICANT NAME (ENTER NAME EXACTLY AS SHOWN ON APPLICATION PAGE 1)   **Unique ID Number**

Instructions for Completing Supplement A

You must accumulate a minimum of **1750** points* to qualify for a broker's license based on experience as a real estate salesperson.
Applicants must also be licensed as a real estate salesperson for a minimum period of one year*.

1. In the Number of Transactions Performed column, enter the amount of your activity for each category.
2. Multiply the number of transactions performed by the point value indicated to arrive at the points earned for that category.
3. Add the points earned for each category to arrive at your total points.
4. Enter the total figure on the Total Qualifying Points Line. This is your final qualifying points earned.
   *Except those using combined experience.

You must also complete the experience report on the other side of this page to report your qualifying experience. Points earned for that experience must be calculated below.

Category	Point Value X	Number of Transactions Performed	=	Total Points Earned
Residential Sales:				
1. Single Family, condo, co-op unit, multi family (2 to 8 unit), farm (with residence, under 100 acres)	250 X	_____	=	_____
2. Exclusive listings	10 X	_____	=	_____
3. Open listings	1 X	_____	=	_____
4. Binders effected	25 X	_____	=	_____
5. Co-op unit transaction approved by seller and buyer that fails to win Board of Directors approval	100 X	_____	=	_____
Residential Rentals:				
6. Rentals or subleases effected	25 X	_____	=	_____
7. Exclusive Listings	5 X	_____	=	_____
8. Open Listings	1 X	_____	=	_____
9. Property Management - Lease renewal	2 X	_____	=	_____
- Rent collections per tenant/per year	1 X	_____	=	_____
Commercial Sales:				
10. Taxpayer/Storefront	400 X	_____	=	_____
11. Office Building	400 X	_____	=	_____
12. Apartment Building (9 units or more)	400 X	_____	=	_____
13. Shopping Center	400 X	_____	=	_____
14. Factory/Industrial warehouse	400 X	_____	=	_____
15. Hotel/Motel	400 X	_____	=	_____
16. Transient garage/parking lot	400 X	_____	=	_____
17. Multi-unit commercial condominium	400 X	_____	=	_____
18. Urban commercial development site	400 X	_____	=	_____
19. Alternative sale type transaction	400 X	_____	=	_____
20. Single-tenant commercial condo	250 X	_____	=	_____
21. Listings	10 X	_____	=	_____
Commercial Leasing:				
22. New Lease - aggregate rental $1 to $200,000	150 X	_____	=	_____
23. New Lease - aggregate rental $200,000 to $1 million	250 X	_____	=	_____
24. New Lease - aggregate rental over $1 million	400 X	_____	=	_____
25. Renewal - aggregate rental $1 to $200,000	75 X	_____	=	_____
26. Renewal - aggregate rental $200,000 to $1 million	125 X	_____	=	_____
27. Renewal - aggregate rental over $1 million	200 X	_____	=	_____
28. Listings	10 X	_____	=	_____
Commercial Financing (includes residential properties of more than four units):				
29. $1 to $500,000	200 X	_____	=	_____
30. $500,000 to $5,000,000	300 X	_____	=	_____
31. Over $5,000,000	400 X	_____	=	_____
Miscellaneous:				
32. Sale vacant lots, land (under 100 acres)	50 X	_____	=	_____
33. Sale vacant land (more than 100 acres)	150 X	_____	=	_____
34. Other, must be fully explained	___ X	_____	=	_____
Total Qualifying Points	➤			

FIGURE   19.2

Broker's Application—Licensed Salespersons Activity (continued)

Employment History

You must indicate all employment which is commensurate with the experience claimed on the other side of this form. Please make sure that you and the sponsoring broker complete and sign the certification and indicate the total points accumulated. If you were employed with another broker(s) and are claiming experience through that association, you must also have that broker sign the certification and indicate points accumulated while working under his/her sponsorship.

Current Sponsoring Broker/Agency (please print or type)

NAME   LAST   FIRST   M.I.   SUFFIX

WORK ADDRESS   STREET ADDRESS (REQUIRED)

CITY   STATE   ZIP+4   COUNTY

UNIQUE ID NUMBER

Additional Salesperson Experience (if applicable)

Salesperson Experience - I was actively engaged as a licensed real estate salesperson as indicated below:

Broker's Name and Address:	Number of Hours/Week	From: Month/Day/Year	To: Month/Day/Year

Notice to Applicant: The information given on this application is subject to verification. In order to prevent any unnecessary return of your application, we request your cooperation by providing us with information that will help us contact you by telephone if needed.

Business Phone: (   )   *Home Phone:* (   )   *Alternate:* (   )

All claimed transactions are subject to verification. In order to claim experience points, both the broker and salesperson applicant must be able to provide documentation which clearly demonstrates the active participation of the applicant in each transaction.

Failure to provide satisfactory supporting documentation may result in denial of the application and/or disciplinary action initiated against the applicant and broker.

We, the undersigned, jointly certify that the named applicant has accumulated a total of _____ points as indicated in the preceding qualifying experience report. We further certify that the information given above is true to the best of our knowledge and belief. We understand that any material misstatement made may result in the revocation or suspension of the license, if issued, as well as any existing license of the applicant and/or the broker.

Applicant Signature/Date _____   *Broker Signature/Date* _____

Additional Affirmations if Necessary:

We, the undersigned, jointly certify that the named applicant has accumulated a total of _____ points as indicated in the preceding qualifying experience report. We further certify that the information given above is true to the best of our knowledge and belief. We understand that any material misstatement made may result in the revocation or suspension of the license, if issued, as well as any existing license of the applicant and/or the broker.

Applicant Signature/Date _____   *Broker Signature/Date* _____

DOS-036A (Rev. 11/02)

FIGURE 19.3

Broker's Application—Experience

C *Real Estate Broker/Associate Broker Application*
Experience

PAGE ___ OF ___

APPLICANT NAME (ENTER NAME EXACTLY AS SHOWN ON APPLICATION PAGE 1)   **Unique ID Number**

Combined Experience as a Licensed Real Estate Salesperson and Equivalent Experience in General Real Estate Business
Instructions for Completing Supplement C

You must accumulate a minimum of **3500** points to qualify for a broker's license based on combined experience in General Real Estate Business and Licensed Real Estate Salesperson Experience. Applicants must also possess at least two years of experience in the real estate business equivalent to that of an active real estate salesperson.

1. You must complete both sides of Supplement A for all licensed salesperson activity of less than one year. Please disregard the minimum point requirement indicated in Supplement A.
2. You must complete both sides of Supplement B for all equivalent experience in general real estate business. Please disregard the minimum point requirement indicated in Supplement B.
3. After completing Supplements A and B, use the following table for computing your total combined experience.

Enter in the box at right your qualifying points earned from Licensed Salesperson Activity (from the Total Qualifying Points box on Supplement A). *Multiply by two.* Enter this number in the box at the far right.	X 2	
Enter in the box at right your qualifying points earned from Equivalent Experience in General Real Estate Business (from the Total Qualifying Points box on Supplement B).		
Add your qualifying points from Licensed Salesperson Activity and Equivalent Experience in General Real Estate Business and enter in the box at right. This is your total qualifying points earned.		

IMPORTANT — You must earn at least **3500** total points (from Supplement A and Supplement B) to qualify under combined experience. Please be sure that Supplement A and Supplement B are completely filled out.

DOS-036C (Rev. 11/02)

■ RENEWAL OF LICENSE

The DOS sends renewal applications near the end of the two-year license period to all brokers and salespersons, which is one reason change of address notifications are important. If the application is not received, however, it is the licensee's obligation to ask for it and to complete the renewal process. The renewal application includes the signature of the sponsoring broker (for salespersons and associate brokers); the fee of $50 for a salesperson and $150 for a broker; and a statement about continuing education completed during the preceding two years. Successful completion of 22½ hours of approved courses is required for broker renewal, just as it is for salespersons, with two exceptions. Attorneys are exempt from the education requirement, and so is anyone active as an associate or active broker at the time of renewal who has been continuously licensed (as either a salesperson and/or broker) for 15 years.

■ REVIEW OF CHAPTER ONE

The prospective broker should review Chapter 1 carefully, with special attention to the broker's responsibility for notifying the DOS whenever there is a change of address or change in a salesperson's or associate broker's status. *It must always be remembered that brokers are legally responsible for their associates' real estate activities.* When the DOS investigates violations of license law, the broker's defense that "I didn't know what that salesman was doing" probably will be countered by, "You should have known." The broker is expected to furnish close, regular supervision and guidance. This legal responsibility for the actions of others is known as **vicarious liability.**

Advertising Guidelines

When the new broker orders business cards or places advertisements, DOS rules will apply.

Regulation 175.25a states that all advertisements placed by a broker must make it clear that the advertiser is indeed a broker (no **blind ads**). The ad also must include the broker's telephone number. Once it does, salespersons' names also may be included.

Advertisements claiming the property is in a "vicinity" must also name the geographic area where the property is actually located ("near Fancy Heights" may really be "in Swillburg Flats").

The DOS is strict in its regulations concerning business cards. No matter how creative the broker's advertising artist, the card must contain the individual's full name, the type of license held, and name and business address of the firm. Type of license may be abbreviated ("Lic. Assoc. R. E. Broker"). Residence phone numbers may be included if they are identified as "Home," "Residence," or "Res." Additional items may include the individual's field of specialization ("Commercial Properties"); position in the firm ("Vice-President"); or nickname ("Buster"). A salesperson's name may not be published in type larger than the name of the licensed broker.

The same regulations have been extended to Web sites. Any Internet advertising by a salesperson must contain a link to a Web site that makes clear the status of the brokerage firm.

The Truth-in-Advertising Act, known as Regulation Z, provides for the strict regulation of real estate advertisements that include mortgage financing terms. General statements like "liberal terms available" or "low down payment" are acceptable, but certain details, known as "triggering terms," require that additional information be included. Triggering terms are

- amount or percentage of down payment (except for "nothing down" or "no down payment");
- number of payments or period of repayment ("five years left on mortgage");
- amount of any payment ("only $700 a month"); or
- amount of any finance charge.

If any of those items is listed, the advertisement also must contain

- the amount or percentage of down payment;
- the number of payments or term of loan; and
- the words *annual percentage rate*, which takes into consideration all credit costs rather than the interest rate alone.

■ ANTITRUST LAWS

Antitrust laws are designed to prevent the unreasonable restraint of trade (business) as a result of the cooperation or conspiracy of various members of the trade. One of the most important antitrust acts is the **Sherman Antitrust Act** of 1890. The Sherman Act prohibits any kind of contract, combination, or conspiracy in the **restraint of trade.** A *conspiracy* is defined as two or more separate business entities participating in a common scheme or plan, the effect of which is the restraint of trade. Antitrust laws prohibit practices such as

ANTITRUST LAWS PROHIBIT

1. price fixing;
2. group boycotting;
3. market allocation; and
4. tie-in arrangements.

- **price-fixing:** an agreement between members of a trade to artificially maintain prices at a set level;
- **group boycott:** an agreement between members of a trade to exclude other members from fair participation in the activities of the trade;
- **market allocation:** an agreement between members of a trade to refrain from competition in specific market areas; and
- **tie-in arrangements:** arrangements by which provision of certain products or services is made contingent on the purchase of other unrelated products or services.

In 1950, in the case of *United States v. National Association of Real Estate Boards*, the Supreme Court recognized that trade, as used in the Sherman Act, included the real estate brokerage business. Therefore, the real estate business is subject to the restraints of antitrust laws. In this case, the mandatory fee schedules that were set and enforced by real estate boards were held to violate the Sherman Act.

In the 1970s several more real estate boards and associations, including some in New York State, were prosecuted under antitrust laws for unfair restraint of trade, following investigations by Assistant Attorney General Richard McLaren (whose investigations also considered firms of architects and accountants). The result of those cases is that real estate agents and professional real estate associations must exercise extreme care to avoid any appearance of price-fixing in regard to real estate commissions.

In *U.S. v. Prince Georges County Board of REALTORS®, Inc.*, the case was settled by a **consent decree,** under which the Board admitted no wrongdoing but agreed to change its ways. In 1972 the Long Island Board of REALTORS® agreed, in a consent decree, never to fix the rate or amount of any commission, recommend or publish a schedule of commission rates, limit the REALTOR®'s right to negotiate commissions with a client, mandate the amount of commission split between cooperating brokers, refuse to accept a listing in its MLS because of its commission rate, or establish high fees for Board membership beyond what was necessary to operate the organization properly. (In some boards, unduly high membership fees and entrance requirements had the effect of blocking minority brokers from membership.)

Violation of the Sherman Act is a felony, and penalties can be as high as $350,000 for an individual and $10 million for corporations. A jail term of up to three years is also possible.

The **Clayton Antitrust Act** supplements the Sherman Act. Under the Clayton Act private parties are allowed to sue antitrust violators, and if successful, they can recover three times the damages incurred plus court costs and attorneys' fees.

The Federal Trade Commission (FTC) has the power to declare trade practices unfair and to enforce compliance with the Sherman Act and some sections of the Clayton Act, but it cannot impose penal sanctions. The Department of Justice also has the power to fine antitrust law violators.

Most states, including New York, also have laws against monopolies, restraints of trade, and unfair trade practices.

Commissions

Any conversation between two brokers from different brokerages regarding commission rates charged to clients is strictly off limits. The only permissible discussion of commissions between two competing brokers would be a discussion of the commission split between a listing broker and a selling broker in a cooperative sale.

Brokers may discuss client commission rates with their salespeople as a matter of office policy. Potential salespersons being interviewed certainly may inquire about the company's typical rates and how commissions are shared with the salesperson who earned them. Such conversations are perfectly proper. The danger comes when any discussion about rates takes place with brokers or salespersons from other offices.

In *United States v. Foley*, a conspiracy to fix commission rates was found when a member of a board of REALTORS® announced at a board function that he was raising his gross commission rate, and that he did not care what others did. The court viewed the announcement as an invitation to conspire, and the subsequent actions of the other board members were viewed as an acceptance of this invitation. This case is important, because it illustrates the fact that alleged conspirators do not actually have to consult with each other to be judged guilty of conspiring to fix commission rates.

The prohibition against discussion of commission rates among independent brokers extends to publication as well as conversation. Many years ago, certain real estate associations maintained mandatory commission rates for their members, but today an association would be in trouble if it attempted to publish recommended rates or even a survey of going rates. For the same reason, multiple-listing services (MLSs) do not publish the commission rates that are charged to owners, only the amount of commission offered to cooperating brokers.

Group Boycotts

The object of a *group boycott* is to hurt or destroy a competitor; it takes only two brokers to form a group that can be found guilty of a group boycott. For example, if two brokers agree to refuse to cooperate with a third broker or agree to cooperate with that third broker but on less-favorable terms, that action is an *automatic violation* of the antitrust act.

Two independent brokers should never engage in negative conversation regarding the business practices of a third broker, because such a conversation could be construed as an attempt at a group boycott of the third broker. A broker who questions the ethics or practices of another broker may freely choose not to do business with such a broker but may not convey his or her feelings to other brokers in any manner that might lead them to take similar action.

Market Allocation

Agreements between brokers to divide their markets or customers and refrain from competing with each other's business violate antitrust laws. These agreements could be about geographic territories, price ranges, types of properties, sociological divisions of business, or the refusal to deal with a competitor.

Tie-in Agreements

A *tie-in*, or *tying*, *agreement* is defined as an agreement to sell one product only on the condition that the buyer purchase another product as well. An example of a real estate tying agreement would be a so-called list-back clause. For example, a subdivision developer may sell a lot to a builder on the condition that the builder agree to list (or list back) the improved property with the developer for resale to a home buyer. A property management agreement that requires that the owner list the managed property with the manager should the owner decide to sell it is another example of a tying agreement. Tie-in agreements are violations of the antitrust laws.

Enforcement

The Sherman Act is enforced by the U.S. Attorney General through the Antitrust Division of the Department of Justice. Both civil and criminal actions can be brought against those who violate antitrust laws. A corporation found guilty of violating the Sherman Act can be fined up to $10 million; an individual may be fined up to $350,000 and/or be sentenced to three years in prison.

Risk Reduction

Brokers are liable both for their own actions and the actions of their licensees; therefore, it is imperative that brokers educate themselves on antitrust issues. Brokers also should train their licensees to be aware of what may constitute an antitrust law violation. Brokers never should use forms that contain pre-printed commission rates, listing periods, or protection periods. Each of these provisions should include a blank that will be filled in after negotiation between the parties.

Brokers always should take care to establish their fees and other listing terms independently, without consulting any competing firms. Each business judgment and negotiated term should be documented in the form of a confidential memo. Brokers also must avoid discussing business plans with competitors.

■ MULTIPLE-LISTING SERVICES

Multiple-listing services play an important role in the marketing of property, especially residential property. The ability to participate in an MLS greatly enhances the exposure of a property in the market, providing advantages not only to the seller but to the participating listing broker as well. The importance of MLSs in the real estate industry has been recognized in a number of court cases that have imposed obligations on these services to provide open access on a nondiscriminatory basis.

Access to MLS

An MLS must permit access by any licensed real estate broker who can satisfy the requirements of the MLS. These requirements must be reasonable, and they may not be discriminatory in nature or effect. The charge for membership in the MLS must be equivalent to the cost involved in setting up the new member, and fees must be reasonable and nondiscriminatory.

MLS regulations may not unreasonably restrict the operations of its members. Participating brokers may not be prohibited from membership in another MLS or from cooperating with non-MLS brokers. The MLS may not regulate a broker's office hours, and it may not restrict the types of properties that can be advertised through the MLS.

A court decision from the 11th Circuit Federal Court of Appeals (which includes Florida, Georgia, and Alabama) has held that a REALTORS® MLS may not exclude non-REALTORS® from membership. The decision affected only those states, but the implications of this case may well lead to elimination of such restrictions on a nationwide basis.

■ INDEPENDENT CONTRACTOR STATUS

The managing broker who takes on associates to work as independent contractors should carefully avoid the words *employ, employer,* and *employee.* Merely using the words **independent contractor** is not enough, however, to establish the relationship in the eyes of the Internal Revenue Service (which is concerned with income tax withholding and employer-paid Social Security) or the State of New York (which mandates unemployment insurance and workers' compensation coverage for all **employees**).

Careful review of the independent contractor *safe-harbor guidelines* detailed in Chapter 18 is important. (The broker's own attorney can review the sample independent contract shown in Figure 18.1.) While safe-harbor guidelines require a contract at least every 15 months, it is wise to set an annual date, perhaps the first of each year, on which to review and re-sign the contract with each associate.

**New York City
Business Taxation**

The New York City Department of Finance has issued a Statement of Audit Procedure that exempts salespersons and associate brokers from the New York City Unincorporated Business Tax if the following 11 requirements are met:

1. The individual must hold only one license as a salesperson or associate broker.
2. The individual must be affiliated with only one real estate brokerage firm at a time, and that firm must hold the individual's license and be named on such license.
3. All printed material used by the individual must display the name of the real estate brokerage firm with which the individual is affiliated.
4. The brokerage firm must provide the individual with office facilities, that is, a desk, telephone, supplies, etc., at the office of the brokerage firm at no cost to the individual.
5. All listings produced by the individual must be subject to approval by a supervising employee of the brokerage firm. The individual must not have any legal authority to bind the brokerage firm in any agreements.
6. The individual must qualify for nonemployee status under the Internal Revenue Code.
7. The individual may not have any employees. If the individual claims a deduction on Form 1040 Schedule C for commissions or other compensation paid, this requirement is not met.
8. The individual may not take a deduction on Form 1040 Schedule C for a home office. Separate deductions for telephone, automobile, entertainment, travel or postage, or contributions to a Keogh plan are permitted.
9. The individual may not engage in purchases or sales of real estate as a dealer.
10. The individual may not engage in any other regular trade or business activities related to real estate.
11. The individual may not, in his or her own name and as a salesperson or associate broker, receive checks for commissions or other payments from any person other than the brokerage firm with which he or she is

affiliated, be a party to a brokerage or cobrokerage agreement, or advertise a property for sale or lease.

In addition, an individual must meet at least three of the following five requirements:

1. The individual must be subject to minimum office hours or performance goals in terms of commissions earned or listings obtained by the brokerage firm with which the individual is affiliated.
2. The individual must be subject to standards of behavior or to direction or training as to real estate sales techniques or be required to attend periodic meetings of sales staff.
3. The individual may not claim a deduction on Form 1040 Schedule C for advertising expenses.
4. The individual must be subject to periodic written performance evaluation.
5. If the brokerage firm with which the individual is affiliated carries errors and omissions insurance, the individual must be covered at no additional cost to the individual.

■ THE BROKER'S RESPONSIBILITY TO MANAGE AND SUPERVISE

A broker has many special responsibilities. A broker must be an effective real estate sales agent, a business manager, a financial analyst, a marketer, a personnel manager, and a leader. A broker should also be familiar with basic real estate law. Here we will focus on some of the basic tasks that must be accomplished before a real estate brokerage can operate effectively and within the parameters of the license law.

Organization of the Brokerage Company

Naturally, one of the first steps a broker takes when starting a brokerage business is deciding what form of ownership the company will take. The form of ownership is essentially the framework for the brokerage business. The way a business is organized will determine the broker's legal obligations for the company's debts, his or her tax obligations, and his or her decision-making powers.

Because the form of ownership has so many legal and tax implications, brokers should always consult an attorney and an accountant before making a decision.

Various forms of ownership can accommodate sole ownership or joint ownership. These include the sole proprietorship, corporation, S corporation, general partnership, limited partnership, and limited liability company.

Sole proprietorship. The broker is the sole owner of a sole proprietorship. The broker bears all the responsibility for the company and is solely responsible for all debts and other liabilities; the broker also may claim all the earnings and profits of the company.

Many small businesses are sole proprietorships because they are relatively simple to create and the legal paperwork is minimal. However, the existence of a sole proprietorship depends largely on the broker. If the broker dies or becomes incapacitated, the company may not survive.

Corporation.   A corporation is a separate legal entity (often referred to as a *legal fiction* or an *artificial person*) created under state laws. A corporation consists of an association of one or more individuals or other corporations (shareholders) but has an existence that is separate from those shareholders. A corporation has the legal capacity to enter into contracts and own property.

There are several advantages to the corporate form of business ownership. The owners (or shareholders) of a corporation are not liable for the debts of the corporation (other than employee wages) unless they have signed a personal guarantee of the corporation's obligations. In other words, the debts, judgments, or bankruptcies of the corporation will not affect the individual shareholders. All the shareholders risk is their original investment in the corporation.

A corporation has a perpetual existence—it does not die. Therefore, if a managing broker dies or becomes incapacitated, the brokerage can continue to operate (as long as another broker is found to carry on the business). The ownership of the corporation can be easily transferred to another person simply by selling the corporate stock. In addition, a corporation may have an unlimited number of owners and may earn an unlimited amount of income.

S corporation.   An S corporation has nearly all of the advantages of a regular corporation. An added benefit is that the profits and losses of the business are passed on directly to the shareholders. There is no double taxation. The shareholders pay the taxes on the corporate profits or deduct corporate losses on their individual tax returns.

There may be no more than 75 shareholders in an S corporation, and no more than 20 percent of the income may come from passive investments (such as investment property rentals). There are also strict rules on when the corporation may declare S corporation status. If any of these rules are violated, the corporation will be deemed a regular corporation.

General partnership.   A *partnership is a business in which two or more co-owners engage in a business for profit.* All owners have an equal say in management and share equally in the profits or losses of the business. The partnership is not a taxable entity like the corporation, so the individual partners pay the taxes on the earnings. A partnership may dissolve on the death, bankruptcy, or disability of one of the partners, unless the partnership agreement provides otherwise.

Limited partnership.   In a limited partnership, one person organizes, operates, and is responsible for the entire partnership venture. This person is called the *general partner* and is responsible not only for the management of the partnership but also for its debts. The other members of the organization are known as *limited partners*. They are merely investors who have no say in the organization and direction of the operation. They share in the profits and compensate the general partner for his or her efforts. Their possible losses are limited to the amount of their investment. The general partner, on the other hand, has unlimited liability.

Limited partnerships are often used for real estate ventures because they allow investors with relatively small amounts of capital to participate in real estate projects.

Limited liability companies.   New York allows limited liability companies and limited liability partnerships to be formed. These companies enjoy the limited liability of corporate shareholders and the tax advantages of partnerships. These companies are similar in effect to S corporations, but have fewer restrictions on their formation and income sources.

Recruiting Licensees

Once a brokerage company is formed, the broker must find salespeople to recruit. Recruiting is an important part of any broker's job. Not only must the broker choose the best associates available, the broker also must be careful not to violate any antidiscrimination laws.

Before taking on associates, the owner must consider the company's overall goals, public image, and available space. Whether the firm wants part-time salespersons or only full-timers should be decided beforehand. Recruiting must be coordinated with training. The small office that offers informal one-on-one training may recruit on a continuing basis. The large firm may prefer a single recruitment campaign followed by a number of classroom training sessions. Advertising, career nights, and trial training sessions are often used for recruitment. Classified or small display ads in newspapers are common.

The broker who takes on anyone who walks in the door risks a loss in office morale, the financial drain of an unproductive associate, and legal problems arising from unethical associates. Common methods of selection include application forms, aptitude tests, and personal interviews.

Among topics explored during an interview may be the applicant's attitude toward number of hours worked, weekend and evening work, and the amount of income anticipated from commissions. Other jobs presently held should be discussed. The prospective associate's attitudes toward ethics and civil rights should be explored. The manager often cautions the applicant that no income may be forthcoming for three to six months and explains that a regular draw against future commissions is inconsistent with independent contractor status. In explaining the nature of real estate brokerage, the manager can stress the necessity for a salesperson to handle stress, face disappointments, and accept occasional rejection. The decision to take on a particular salesperson should consider not only the profit potential but also whether the individual fits the company image and will contribute to office harmony.

While going through the recruiting process, the broker must keep **fair employment laws** in mind. The broker must be sure that recruiting tools such as classified ads do not run afoul of these laws. These employment laws include *Title VII of the Civil Rights Act of 1964, the Civil Rights Act of 1866, the Age Discrimination in Employment Act, and the Americans with Disabilities Act.* Naturally, state laws also apply. The U.S. Department of Housing and Urban Development (HUD) has stated that *employee,* as used in the act, also refers to *independent contractor.*

Fair employment laws are designed to prevent employers from basing hiring and firing decisions on factors that are unrelated to job performance. When recruiting new licensees (as well as hiring office staff and unlicensed assistants), a broker should avoid asking questions regarding marital status, children or plans to have children, age, origin or nationality, religion, and physical and mental condition. Any applications that are used should comply with all fair employment laws. Advertisements should include such phrases as *equal opportunity employer.* All recruiting and interviewing activities should remain consistent, no matter who is applying for the job.

All managerial decisions, not just hiring decisions, should be based on job performance rather than on protected characteristics. Other types of management decisions include those regarding advancement, salary or compensation increases, fringe benefits, and firing.

Training

A good company training program aids in recruitment and builds reputation. The well-trained associate requires less attention during early transactions and is eager to try out the techniques taught. An educated salesperson is more likely to succeed and to remain with the company. The broker is legally responsible for training (and supervising) his or her affiliated salespeople.

Even a small office can usually offer excellent one-on-one, on-the-job training, with the newcomer led step by step through the first few transactions. The sales meeting technique is often used in medium-sized offices. Periodic training sessions are integrated into sales meetings. Full coverage of the material requires a number of months with this method. Organized classrooms are most often run by multiple-office companies or franchise operations. They offer efficient instruction and are one of the main inducements for franchise affiliation. Occasionally several small independent firms combine to operate an organized classroom.

It is important to include various legal issues in training sessions. Information on licensing laws, agency duties and liabilities, discrimination laws, and antitrust laws should be included.

Policy and Procedures Guide

A written **policy and procedures guide** contributes to the smooth running of the company, heads off misunderstandings, serves as a reference for settling disputes, and can be an excellent tool for recruiting and training associates. A loose-leaf format makes revisions simple. Care must be taken not to violate a salesperson's independent contractor status through inappropriate wording.

Suggested Procedures Guide is a suitable title. Except where legal and ethical considerations are under discussion, the word *must* is inappropriate. "Sales meetings are held each Monday morning at 9:30" is better than "Associates are required to attend each Monday. . . ." The guide should be as concise as possible. It should say nothing, for example, about how to secure a listing; instead, it can detail procedures to follow after the listing is obtained.

Company policy. A typical guide starts with a sketch of the company's history and goals. Background information on the owner and manager is appropriate, with names and responsibilities of personnel. A job description for the associates follows. Independent contractor status is briefly reviewed, with a list of items provided by the company and another list of those to be provided by the associate. A concise treatment of ethical and legal considerations is appropriate: civil rights guidelines to be followed both within the office and in listing and selling (see Chapter 15), a review of the fiduciary duty to clients, policy on buyers' brokers, the theory of hidden defects, non-solicitation orders that may be in effect in the area, and local sign restrictions or regulations. Company policy regarding the termination of a salesperson is also discussed.

The associate needs to know the procedures followed in relationships with attorneys, the franchise or MLS to which the office belongs, and cooperating offices. The guide may suggest (but not dictate) appropriate goals for an associate in terms of number of listings and sales, hours of floor duty, and attendance at sales meetings, and it may discuss the desk cost per associate.

Paperwork should be described in detail: what forms are available; what reports are to be turned in with listings, contracts, or deposits, and to whom. A sample of each form and sales aid used in the office should be included. Supplies, signs, lockboxes, business cards, and use of equipment such as the copier, fax machine, or computer terminal are discussed. Housekeeping information includes rules on desk use, lights, heat, ashtrays, coffee or kitchen equipment, parking, and office hours.

Sales meetings, caravan tours, open houses, and floor duty (opportunity time, office time) should be covered in the guide. The responsibilities and opportunities of the associate on floor duty are spelled out in detail to prevent misunderstandings. Advertising policy includes a discussion of frequency and size of ads, discrimination consideration, paperwork procedures, deadlines, individual budgets, and follow-up reports to be turned in. A section on telephones describes the answering service used, specifies policy on long-distance calls and entries in a long-distance log, briefly discusses standard telephone-answering techniques, and sets standards for customer rotation and the channeling of calls.

The Supervision Requirement

The New York real estate law requires that real estate brokers manage and supervise their affiliated licensees. The broker must ensure that all licensees comply with the license laws and the duties imposed by agency law. According to Regulation 175.21, a broker's supervision must consist of "regular, frequent and consistent personal guidance, instruction, oversight and superintendence by the real estate broker with respect to the general real estate brokerage business conducted by the broker, and all matters relating thereto."

By law, brokers are responsible for the actions of their salespeople. In fact, in many cases, if an affiliated licensee violates the license law, the broker may be subject to disciplinary action along with the affiliated licensee. According to Section 442-c of the *Real Property Law*, a violation of the license law by a real estate salesperson or employee of the broker is cause for a reprimand. It is also a cause for revocation or suspension of the broker's license if the broker (1) had actual knowledge of the violation, or (2) retained the benefits, profits, or proceeds of a transaction wrongfully negotiated by the salesperson or employee after notice of the salesperson's or employee's misconduct.

Furthermore, both the broker and any affiliated salesperson must keep written records of all the real estate listings obtained by the salesperson and of all sales and other transactions effected by the salesperson during the period of his or her affiliation with that broker.

Brokers should review the list of license violations listed in Chapter 1. Violations found by the DOS include

- failure to make timely written disclosure of agency;
- commingling money with that of principals;
- failure to maintain proper escrow accounts;
- improper handling of deposits, good-faith binders, earnest money deposits;
- inducing breach of contract of sale or lease ("get out of that deal and I'll find you a better one");
- negotiating with another exclusive agent's client;
- failure to deliver duplicate originals of documents signed by client or customer;
- writing an automatic extension clause in a listing contract; and
- soliciting listings in prohibited areas.

■ AUDITS FOR COMPLIANCE

In 1999, the Environmental Protection Agency began a series of unannounced audits of real estate offices to check whether its lead-paint disclosure requirements were being observed. The firm's files should contain signed acknowledgments from tenants and homebuyers that they had received the required information before their leases or sales contracts became final. One of the first fines, for $11,000, was levied against a broker in Oklahoma who, according to the EPA, failed to give a tenant information about the danger of lead-based paint. A fine of more than $400,000 was sought against a military housing office that did not give the disclosures to tenants of 11 housing units before finalizing leasing arrangements.

Associates in an office should be instructed to contact the managing broker whenever auditors arrive unannounced. The Department of State conducts random audits to monitor compliance with state regulations on business signs, display of brokers' licenses, and management of the escrow account. Auditors also may want to verify the amount of experience listed in a broker-license application, and will check transaction files for proof of proper agency disclosure, as mandated by Article 443 of the Real Property Law.

The U.S. Department of Housing and Urban Development works with local organizations to fund and train sets of checkers, or testers, who present themselves as would-be tenants or buyers and keep records of their treatment by real estate firms. Discrimination is not limited to differences in the choice of housing offered to members of different groups who are equally qualified financially. A Rochester firm was fined after a pair of white testers who walked into an office were greeted with a handshake, offers to hang up their coats, and cups of coffee. The African-American couple who entered the office soon after received none of these welcoming gestures. In its defense, the managing broker pointed out that the two couples, whose financial situations were similar, were offered the same wide choice of listed homes in their price range. The difference in the initial greeting occurred because they just happened to encounter two different associates, whose methods were different. HUD replied, "It's your job to see that they're not."

To avoid unintentional discrimination, it's helpful to establish routine procedures for phone conversations and interviews. The goal should be to treat all clients and customers in the same fashion. To make sure the same questions are asked in the same order during a financial analysis, for example, it's helpful to use a standard written interview form. *The best protection against violation of fair housing laws is a thorough knowledge of the laws themselves.*

■ PROFESSIONAL ORGANIZATIONS

Years ago real estate brokers realized the need for an organization to help improve their business abilities and to educate the public to the value of qualified ethical brokers. The National Association of REALTORS® (NAR) was organized in 1908 to meet this need. This association is the parent organization of most local real estate boards and associations that operate throughout the United States, and the professional activities of all REALTORS®—active members of local boards that are affiliated with the national association—are governed by the association's Code of Ethics. Listings and much additional information is available at its Web site, *www.realtor.com.*

The term REALTORS® is a registered trademark. A similar organization, The National Association of Real Estate Brokers (Realtists), was founded in 1947. Members subscribe to a code of ethics that sets professional standards for all Realtists.

These are trade associations. Licensed brokers and salespersons are not required to join.

New York State Association of REALTORS®

WWWeb.Link

The New York State Association of REALTORS®, which represents more than 32,000 REALTORS® and REALTOR®-ASSOCIATES in New York State, is a member board of the National Association of REALTORS®. The staff consists of an executive director; an administrator; and directors of education, legislation, communications, and membership services. The New York State Society of Real Estate Appraisers is a division of the state association, as is the New York State Commercial Association of REALTORS®, Inc. NYSAR's Web site can be found at *www.nysar.com.*

Educational services.   The National Association of REALTORS® and The New York REALTORS® Institute administer a structured educational program. The course of study leads to the designation Graduate, REALTORS® Institute (GRI). To earn the GRI designation, the candidate must successfully complete courses that cover business skills, law, and advanced real estate specialties. All are approved by the state for continuing education credit. GRI courses are offered during the year at various locations around the state.

■ DESIGNATIONS

Designations, like college degrees, are awarded by various real estate organizations after study, examinations, and experience. Various real estate bodies award these designations. Some are associated with the National Association of REALTORS®, and some are independent organizations. Among the more well-known designations are

- American Society of Appraisers: ASA;
- American Society of Home Inspectors: M, Member (highest designation);
- American Society of Real Estate Counselors: CRE, Counselor of Real Estate;
- Appraisal Institute: MAI, Member of the Appraisal Institute; SRA, Senior Residential Appraiser;
- Commercial Investment Real Estate Institute: CCIM, Certified Commercial-Investment Member; Counselors of Real Estate: CRE;
- Institute of Real Estate Management: CPM, Certified Property Manager; ARM, Accredited Residential Manager; AMO, Accredited Management Organization;
- International Real Estate Federation (FIABCI): CIPS, Certified International Property Specialist;
- National Association of REALTORS®: GRI, Graduate, REALTORS® Institute;
- National Council of Exchangors: EMS, Equity Marketing Specialist;
- National Association of Exclusive Buyer's Agents: EBA, Exclusive Buyers Agent;
- Real Estate Educators Association: DREI, Distinguished Real Estate Instructor;
- Real Estate Securities and Syndication Institute: SRS, Specialist in Real Estate Securities;
- REALTORS® Land Institute: ALC, Accredited Land Consultant;
- REALTORS® National Marketing Institute: CRB, Certified Real Estate Brokerage Manager; CRS, Certified Residential Specialist;

- REALTORS® Real Estate Buyer's Agent Council: ABR, Accredited Buyer's Representative;
- Real Estate Buyers Agent Council: ACR, Accredited Buyers Represenative;
- Society of Industrial and Office REALTORS®: SIOR; PRE, Professional Real Estate; and
- Women's Council of REALTORS®: LTG, Leadership Training Graduate; RRC, Referral and Relocation Certification.

■ LAW OF AGENCY

The prospective broker should undertake a careful review of Chapters 2 and 3, on law of agency, at this point.

In the situation where a buyer-client seems right for one of the firm's own listings, the managing broker and the firm can find themselves in a position of dual agency. An agent is legally bound to put the client's interests first, and of course there is only one "first." The Department of State has offered a way out of the dilemma with the following suggestion:

> Under the following circumstances, you can designate one of your agents to represent the buyer and another to represent the seller. You must, of course, make full disclosure to both buyer and seller, and you must obtain their informed consent to the arrangement prior to appointing the designated agents.

When a buyer [who is a client] expresses an interest in a property listed with your firm, you must obtain the consent of both the buyer and seller to proceed as a dual agent, and you use the "Agency Disclosure" form for that purpose. At the same time, you can explain the benefits of appointing a designated agent for the buyer and another for the seller. If after full disclosure, the buyer and seller agree, [one of the firm's salespersons may act as single agent for the buyer, and another for the seller].

If designated agents are appointed, the firm continues as a dual agent representing both the buyer and seller in the transaction. The designated agents, however, will, by virtue of the new agreement with the buyer and seller, function as single agents giving undivided loyalty to their respective clients.

If effected properly, an agreement for the appointment of designated agents does not violate any provision of Article 12-A or the rules of the Department of State. That is, of course, premised on (1) making full disclosure to the buyer and seller, and (2) obtaining the informed consent of both. In addition, to avoid future misunderstandings, it is good practice to reduce these agreements to writing, and to provide all of the parties with a signed copy.

A Designated Agency form suggested by the New York State Association of REALTORS® can be found in Figure 19.4.

Suggested Designated Agent Agreement

DESIGNATED AGENT AGREEMENT

We, the undersigned, Buyer and Seller, regarding the purchase and sale of premises known as _____, New York, acknowledge our consent to _____ ("Broker") acting as a dual agent with respect to this transaction. We acknowledge that the Broker will be working for both the Buyer and the Seller in this transaction and we understand that we are giving up our respective rights to the Broker's undivided loyalty. We have carefully considered the possible consequences of a dual agency relationship and understand that instead each of us could have engaged our own agent as a seller's agent or buyer's agent, respectively.

We hereby agree that _____ is appointed to represent only the Buyer (the "Buyer's Designated Agent") and _____ is appointed to represent only the Seller (the "Seller's Designated Agent") in this transaction. We understand that the Broker continues to be a dual agent representing both of us in this transaction with honesty and fairness, but that the Buyer's Designated Agent and the Seller's Designated Agent will each function as a single agent providing each of us, respectively, with undivided loyalty.

SELLER:

_____,   _____
                                                     Date

_____,   _____
                                                     Date

BUYER:

_____,   _____
                                                     Date

_____,   _____
                                                     Date

■ **SUMMARY**

Vicarious liability is created not because of a person's actions but because of the relationship between the liable person and other parties. Subagency can create circumstances or situations that result in vicarious liability.

Antitrust laws prohibit competing brokers from discussing commission rates charged to clients and also the publication of such rates. Brokers also must refrain from negative discussions about other brokers to avoid the appearance of a group boycott.

MLSs must operate in such a manner as not to deny reasonable access to any interested party. Membership requirements must be reasonable, and the charge for membership must be related to the costs involved. Discriminatory policies are forbidden.

An MLS may not impose restrictions on the operations of its members, such as prohibiting membership in other MLS organizations or cooperation with nonmembers. Attempts by an MLS to regulate the business hours of its members or to restrict the types of properties advertised through the MLS also are forbidden.

While recruiting and training licensees, brokers must pay attention to more than selecting effective, successful salespeople. Brokers must also keep fair employment laws in mind. Office policies and procedure guides should emphasize the broker's commitment to the principles of fair employment, fair housing, and full compliance with licensing regulations. In an office where salespersons and associate brokers are considered independent contractors, the state's requirement for close supervision by the broker must be observed without violating the guidelines for independent contractor treatment.

Designations are awarded after study, examinations, and experience by various organizations. The New York State Association of REALTORS® awards the GRI designation to graduates of the REALTORS® Institute.

For the agency dilemma posed by a buyer/client who wishes to see one of the firm's own listings, for which the company is already a seller's agent, the DOS has offered an acceptable solution. After full disclosure and informed consent by both parties, the managing broker, who becomes a dual agent, may designate one associate to represent the buyer and another the seller. Consent forms to the resulting dual agency and designated agencies must be properly executed, and fiduciary duties carefully observed.

QUESTIONS

1. XYZ Realty and MLN Real Estate decide that they will not cooperate with the new broker in town, Homes Bought Realty. This would be an antitrust violation called
   a. market allocation.
   b. tie-in arrangement.
   c. price-fixing.
   d. group boycotting.

2. Town House Realty offered new condominiums for sale. Buyers were told they must make their selections for appliances from Town House Realty's catalog. No other appliances would be permitted. Appliances were furnished through a distributor owned by Town House Realty. This would be an antitrust violation called
   a. market allocation.
   b. tie-in arrangement.
   c. price-fixing.
   d. group boycotting.

3. Broker Margo Marz and broker Nate National decided each could make more money if Margo took the east side of town and Nate took the west side of town. This would be an antitrust violation called
   a. market allocation.
   b. tie-in arrangement.
   c. price-fixing.
   d. group boycotting.

4. An MLS may
   a. regulate a broker's office hours.
   b. prohibit membership in another MLS.
   c. set reasonable and nondiscriminatory membership fees.
   d. restrict the types of property advertised through the MLS.

5. New salesperson Ann Apple wants to be able to claim self-employment expense deductions on IRS Form 1040 Schedule C. She should
   a. have an independent contractor agreement with her broker in writing.
   b. keep a detailed record of her expenses.
   c. pay her own state and federal taxes and Social Security.
   d. All of the above

6. In an independent contractor agreement with Ann Apple, the broker should include
   a. that she will be compensated only by commissions directly based on sales.
   b. the days and hours that she will work.
   c. that she may not work outside the office.
   d. that she will be paid both a salary and commissions.

7. A broker for North End Realty tells a broker from Valley Realty that a house has been listed "at a 7 percent commission, and we will be glad to cooperate with you and give you half, if your company sells it." There may be an antitrust violation in
   a. the offer to cooperate in marketing the property.
   b. the promise of a 50/50 split.
   c. the phrase "7 percent commission."
   d. There is no antitrust problem here.

8. The broker candidate who has not previously been licensed as a salesperson
   a. must show twice as much real estate experience as a licensed salesperson needs.
   b. cannot become a broker at all.
   c. takes a different and more difficult state examination.
   d. must file an irrevocable consent form.

9. A blind ad is one that does not include the
   a. address of the property.
   b. name of the broker.
   c. asking price.
   d. salesperson's home phone number.

10. A licensed salesperson's business card may not
    a. use the licensee's nickname.
    b. list a home telephone under any circumstances.
    c. print the salesperson's name in larger type than the broker's.
    d. carry the Fair Housing logo.

11. Which of the following persons needs a license to sell someone else's real estate and collect a fee for the service?
    a. The executor of an estate
    b. An auctioneer
    c. An attorney
    d. A subdivision's in-house salesperson

12. The term *vicarious liability* refers to
    a. failure to disclose type of agency.
    b. broker's duty to supervise.
    c. independent contractor guidelines.
    d. principal's responsibility for agent's acts.

13. Which of the following phrases might violate Regulation Z advertising guidelines?
    a. "No down payment"
    b. "Assume low-interest mortgage"
    c. "Only 5% down"
    d. "Less than you're paying for rent"

14. The contract setting up an associate's independent contractor status with the broker should be
    a. either oral or written.
    b. re-signed every 15 months.
    c. specific as to number of hours to be worked.
    d. forwarded to the Department of State.

15. The partial protection from legal liability afforded by a corporation can be combined with the tax advantages of a partnership in a
    a. sole proprietorship.
    b. general partnership.
    c. limited liability company.
    d. limited partnership.

16. To preserve independent contractor status, a policy and procedures manual should probably avoid use of the word
    a. "must."
    b. "discrimination."
    c. "ethics."
    d. "termination."

17. The real estate office is sometimes visited by inspectors or auditors from the
    a. EPA.
    b. NYSAR.
    c. FTC.
    d. MLS.

18. The acronym "GRI" stands for
    a. General Real Estate Instructor.
    b. Graduate REALTOR® Institute.
    c. General Realty Insurance.
    d. Guaranteed Realty Information.

19. In-house sales where the buyer wants individual representation after agreeing to dual agency can be handled by the use of
    a. referral sales.
    b. cooperative brokerage.
    c. designated agents.
    d. supplement A.

20. Not all brokers are
    a. REALTORS®.
    b. licensed.
    c. older than 19.
    d. experienced.

20

REAL ESTATE FINANCE II

Farmer Macdonald is approached by a corporation that wants to build a small shopping mall on the far end of his property. He wouldn't mind some extra income, but he hates to see the land go out of the family, which has owned it since 1800. Is there a way to have his cake and eat it, too?

■ KEY TERMS

blanket mortgage	index	sale-leaseback agreement
bridge loan	joint venture	secondary mortgage
bullet loan	negative amortization	market
construction loan	open-end mortgage	shared-equity mortgage
disintermediation	package loan	swing loan
Fannie Mae (FNMA)	participation loan	takeout loan
FHA loan	private mortgage	underwriting
Freddie Mac (FHLMC)	insurance (PMI)	VA loan
Ginnie Mae (GNMA)	purchase-money	wraparound mortgage
home equity loan	mortgage	

■ THE USE OF THE MORTGAGE

Most real estate purchases in New York state are financed through mortgage loans. The word itself comes, like so many legal terms, from Old French—*mort*, meaning *death*, and *gage*, which is still used occasionally in English for *pledge*. (When the mortgage is paid off, the real estate is no longer pledged or promised as security for the loan, and the gage will then be dead.)

A mortgage is a *voluntary lien on real estate*. The person who owns or intends to buy the property gives the lender the right to foreclose and have that property sold at public auction if the borrower fails to repay the loan. The borrower, the *mortgagor*, pledges the land to the lender, or *mortgagee*, as security for the loan. The loan itself is made in return for a *note* or *bond*, the borrower's personal promise to repay the debt.

In *title theory states*, the mortgagor actually gives title to the mortgagee or to a third party, who will hold it in trust until the loan is paid off. The document involved is called a *trust deed*, rather than a mortgage, because title is actually transferred. When the loan is paid off, a *release deed*, or *deed of reconveyance*, returns title to the original owner. If the mortgagor defaults, it is a relatively simple matter for the lender to obtain immediate possession, as opposed to the foreclosure process used in states like New York.

New York is, however, a *lien theory state*. The mortgage does not transfer title, but merely pledges the property to serve as security for the loan. Formal, and more lengthy, legal procedures are necessary to foreclose the loan.

■ HOME MORTGAGES

Brokers who specialize in residential sales will have most experience with single-family loans and those for one to four-unit buildings. As detailed in Chapters 10 and 11, these fall into two categories. Those backed by government agencies include FHA (HUD), VA, RECDA (FmHA), and SONYMA mortgages. In recent years, all of these agencies have relaxed their guidelines to enable buyers who were formerly considered marginally qualified to buy their own homes. Municipalities, particularly larger cities, also may offer special assistance in mortgage lending, particularly for those who buy in "target" neighborhoods. New York State banking regulations allow zero-down mortgage loans.

The second source for home mortgage borrowing is the private sector. In recent years, conventional mortgage loans have often been offered with low down payments, to the point where at the turn of the century, almost half of first-time borrowers agreed to carry **private mortgage insurance (PMI)** so that they could make down payments of less than 20 percent.

Chapters 10 and 11 should be consulted for details on these mortgages, intended for owner-occupied property.

■ TYPES OF MORTGAGES

The **purchase-money mortgage** is the most common, and the proper, term for any loan used in the *original purchase of property*. (In some areas, the term is reserved for seller-take-back financing, when the owner accepts a purchase-money mortgage in return for part or all of the sale price.) Contrasted with purchase-money mortgages are *refinance loans*, which borrow more money against property already owned.

Chapter 11 discussed **shared-equity mortgages** in which the lender receives some share of future profits on the property; **package loans,** which cover both real and personal property, such as furnishings; **open-end mortgages,** which allow for further borrowing; **blanket mortgages,** which cover more than one piece of realty; **wraparounds,** which are a complex method of retaining an old mortgage while accepting a new one; and *gap* **(bridge, swing)** *loans*, which cover a short-term need for funds when a new home is being purchased and the contracted sale of the old one has not yet closed.

Subordinate mortgages are those recorded after initial loans have already been placed against the property. They are considered junior to first mortgages, and in case of foreclosure they would wait in line to see if enough funds remained to satisfy them. Some lenders today offer them under the designation of **home equity loans,** but if the property already has a first mortgage on it, a home equity loan is really just a second mortgage. As a rule, it carries higher interest than a first mortgage, because the property usually has a substantial lien against it already.

■ BROKERS' ISSUES IN REAL ESTATE FINANCE

There are several issues that brokers should become familiar with. These include commercial mortgages, construction loans, sale-leasebacks, and how the economy affects real estate finance.

Commercial Financing

Commercial property includes property that produces income, such as apartment and office buildings, restaurants, shopping centers, hotels and motels, and gas stations. The sources of much of the financing for commercial properties are insurance companies and pension plans, which have large amounts of money to invest in long-term mortgages. Both types of lenders often work through loan correspondents such as mortgage brokers. There are other sources of commercial mortgage funds as well, including commercial banks, savings and loans, sellers, syndicates, and industrial revenue bonds.

Commercial lenders tend to have exacting **underwriting** standards and require low loan-to-value (LTV) ratios. When lenders underwrite a commercial loan, they complete a detailed analysis of the project's ability to generate adequate cash flow. The project's cash flow must be adequate to pay for principal and interest payments, property taxes, insurance, and maintenance costs. (All of these expenses must be paid before the project can reach a breakeven point.) Lenders examine existing leases and lease pledges to determine cash flow and overall financial health. Because of this, every planned and existing large commercial real estate project includes an ongoing marketing program to secure tenants.

Lenders use the property's rental income to estimate the property's value, then apply a low LTV ratio to determine the loan amount. Most commercial loans have maximum LTV ratios of between 70 percent and 75 percent, depending on the financial rating.

There are several types of common commercial real estate loans. Note that many require balloon payments.

Bullet loans (also called *intermediate* or *conduit financing*).   A bullet loan has an intermediate term of three to five years; a *conduit loan*, seven to ten years. It is virtually always a fixed-rate loan. It is partially amortized, so a substantial balloon payment is required at the end of the loan term. In some cases, only the interest is paid in the first years of the loan.

Miniperm loans.   A *miniperm loan* is a variable-rate loan that has an interest accrual feature. This type of loan is used by borrowers who want to increase their cash flow in the early years of a project.

Floating rate loans with accrual.   These commercial loans are adjustable-rate loans, similar to those available on residential property. The interest rate is based on a standard **index** and then fluctuates throughout the life of the loan, depending on the movements of the index. However, unlike residential ARMs, the debt service on this loan is a fixed amount. Any deficiency in interest is added to the principal **(negative amortization).** Loan terms are quite short, usually no longer than five years.

Participation loans.   **Participation loans** give lenders the opportunity to enhance their profits by earning extra revenue from an increase in a project's net income and resale value. During periods of high interest rates and tight money, lenders will offer financing at lower-than-market rates in exchange for a percentage of net income and/or increases in value. Participation loans are often available when other types of permanent financing are not.

Land-leaseback.   In a *land-leaseback*, the investor buys the land, then leases it back to the developer under a long-term lease. The developer then constructs a building on the land. This type of transaction reduces the equity the developer needs to fund a project. Land-leasebacks are related to sale-lease-backs, discussed later.

Joint ventures.   Traditionally, when a lender or investor and borrower decide on a **joint venture,** the lender or investor puts up 100 percent of the funds and the developer does all the work. Ownership may be divided between the two 50/50, or any other split (75/25, 90/10, etc.) that equitably reflects the work and risk involved. The lender or investor generally has the first claim to any income generated from the project up to an amount that equals an agreed-on return on the original investment (a *safety-first position*). The rest of the income is divided between the partners according to a previously agreed-on formula.

Construction Loans

Construction loans (also called *interim loans*) finance the construction of improvements on real estate. A construction loan is temporary; when the construction is completed, the loan is replaced with permanent financing. One of the unique features of this loan is the fact that the building that is used as security for the loan does not exist when the loan is made. Because only the land exists at the time the loan is made, construction lenders use various methods to protect their security interest. These methods include strict underwriting procedures and unique ways of disbursing the loan funds.

Loan application.   Construction loans vary in size from one small enough to finance the construction of a home to one large enough to finance the construction of a shopping center or a multistory office building. However, the application process is essentially the same, regardless of the size of the loan. The first step the borrower takes when applying for a construction loan is to submit plans and specifications for the proposed building. Typically, the borrower already owns the lot on which the building will be constructed. Some lenders insist that the lot be owned lien-free, so that the construction lender will have the security of a first-lien position. Other lenders allow the lot to be encumbered with a mortgage loan, as long as the mortgage contains a subordination clause that gives the construction loan first priority over the previously existing mortgage.

The construction loan amount is based on the total value of the land and the future building. The LTV ratio rarely exceeds 75 percent. For instance, a borrower owns a $40,000 lot and wants to construct a $150,000 house on it. The total value of the property after the house is constructed will be $190,000. Seventy-five percent of the combined value of the lot and home is $142,500. That is the maximum loan amount the lender will agree to. Construction loans are usually large enough to cover all or most of the costs of the construction, with the owner's equity being represented by ownership of the lot.

Disbursement of funds.   Construction loan funds are virtually never disbursed in one lump sum when the application process is completed. Disbursing all the funds at once would be too risky; it would be too easy for the borrower to squander the loan funds on cost overrides, on last-minute changes, or by mismanagement, leaving the lender with an incomplete building as security for the loan. Instead, the loan funds are disbursed according to a prearranged plan. One of the most common plans is that of a series of draws as construction is completed. For instance, the lender may utilize a five-stage plan, whereby 20 percent of the loan funds are distributed each time another one-fifth of the construction is completed. The last 20 percent is typically held by the lender until all labor and materials have been paid for (i.e., lien waivers have been received from contractors and subcontractors, and certificates of completion and approval for occupancy have been issued by a building inspector) and the period for filing a mechanic's lien has passed.

Another method of disbursing construction funds requires that the borrower submit the construction bills to the lender, who pays the bills as they arrive. The benefit of this method is that it gives the lender greater control over the possibility that mechanic's liens will be filed.

Note that interest is charged on the funds only after they have been disbursed. Both lenders and borrower must keep careful records showing when each disbursement was made.

Paying off construction loans.   Construction loans are short-term loans. Terms may range from six months for a house to three years for a commercial project. Construction loans are set up so that the lender will be paid in full—including all accrued interest—at the end of this short loan term. Typically, the construction loan is paid off (replaced) with a permanent **takeout loan.** Often the borrower makes arrangements for permanent financing before the construction loan is even applied for. This kind of arrangement is called a *standby loan commitment.* Naturally, permanent lenders impose conditions on their standby loan commitments. For instance, when completed, the building must meet all building codes and conform to the plans and specifications that were submitted at the time of the loan application. Some lenders refuse to fund the permanent loan until the project has been leased up to its breakeven point.

Release from blanket loan.   When a lender holds a blanket mortgage on a whole subdivision, the developer may not sell an individual lot or completed house until obtaining a release of that one lot from the overall blanket mortgage. As each lot is sold, the lender receives a proportional percentage of the total debt, and releases that parcel so that it can be sold to (and individually financed by) the new homebuyer.

Sale-Leasebacks

Sale-leasebacks are used to finance larger projects, nearly always commercial. The property owner sells it to an investor and then immediately leases it back. The lease is usually a full net long-term lease. The sale of the property frees up the original owner's equity in the property, and the lease is for a long enough period for the investor to recover the sale funds plus make a fair profit on the investment.

As a method of financing, sale-leasebacks offer a number of advantages. For the seller-lessee, the benefits include staying in possession of the property while receiving cash from the sale and getting a tax deduction for the full amount of the rental payments. Many sellers-lessees use the cash from the sale to expand or remodel their facilities.

The primary advantage of this arrangement for the buyer-lessor is the receipt of the rental payments. The rental payments usually include a fair profit on the investment and the return of the investment capital itself.

Sometimes a sale-leaseback includes an option for the tenant to repurchase the property at the end of the lease term. This type of arrangement is called a *sale-leaseback-buyback*. At the time of the original sale, the parties will generally set the repurchase price. If the repurchase price is the same as the original sales price, the parties may run into problems with the Internal Revenue Service. Special tax and legal advice should be sought in sale-leaseback and sale-leaseback-buyback transactions.

In recent years, legal battles have arisen in New York State as 99-year leases expired for whole towns built on land leased from Native American tribes.

■ GROUND LEASES

A lease of land on which the tenant intends to construct a building is usually long-term, which makes it worthwhile for the tenant to construct buildings and other improvements on the property. A farmer who does not want to give up all rights to his land might give a 99-year lease to a developer, who then has enough confidence to construct a shopping mall on the property. In the usual arrangement, the farmer (or his heir) receives rent, and the developer pays property taxes and other expenses. Legal wrangles developed over expired leases on entire towns in the Southern Tier that were built on land leased from Native American tribes 99 years earlier.

■ FHA FINANCING

In the early 1900s, homeowners generally borrowed on short-term mortgages, for perhaps four or five years, and made only interest payments, often once a year. At the end of the term, the friendly local small-town banker would renew the loan for the same amount. But when the Great Depression hit in the early 1930s, the flaws in this system became evident. As factories closed down, homeowners who still owed the full value of their homes were unable to negotiate renewals and were forced into foreclosure. Banks failed, and in a vicious circle, more businesses closed down and more unemployment resulted.

The New Deal, begun by President Franklin Roosevelt in 1932, attacked the problem on many fronts. In the field of housing, a fresh idea was proposed by a secretary at the University of Rochester, whose professor went to Washington as part of the administration's Brain Trust. She conceived the idea of the long-term amortized loan. Instead of paying just interest, the homeowner would pay a bit more, in small monthly installments that would gradually whittle down the debt. The *National Housing Act of 1934* set up the Federal Housing Administration (FHA), which not only adopted the idea of amortization but also set up an insurance program to protect lenders, so that the nation's growing inventory of vacant houses could be bought with low down payments. In 1968, FHA became part of the Department of Housing and Urban Development (HUD). The amortized loan quickly became a standard, both for the Veterans Administration (VA), now the Department of Veterans Affairs, when it was established after World War II and for conventional lenders as well.

On the **secondary mortgage market, Fannie Mae (FNMA)** and **Ginnie Mae (GNMA)** were set up to purchase packages of **VA** and **FHA loans,** thus returning mortgage money to the communities where it could be used to serve more borrowers. Together with **Freddie Mac (FHLMC),** they also tend to standardize and encourage certain types of loans, by announcing the requirements for loan packages they will buy.

Details on FHA and VA loans should be reviewed in Chapter 11. Terms of FHA loans are frequently changed to meet the country's current needs: new allowances for contributions by the seller to the buyer's closing costs, relaxed qualification standards for marginal buyers, raising of maximum loan limits as median prices change. Brokers should stay abreast of current developments, and keep track of which local lenders handle these loans, which can be so useful to cash-poor homebuyers.

■ THE ECONOMY AND REAL ESTATE CYCLES

Brokers should understand the basic ways in which our economy as a whole affects the real estate market. The two are closely tied together: when interest rates and unemployment are high, real estate sales and financing activities are low, and vice versa. The general economy has some obvious impacts on real estate finance. Stock market activity, employment rates, inflation rates, and income levels all affect real estate values and the ability of potential homebuyers to purchase real estate. For example, when unemployment rates are high, interest rates are high, and income levels are low, fewer potential buyers will be able to obtain or afford the financing necessary to purchase a home. On the other hand, when the economy is healthy and interest rates and inflation are low, more people feel confident enough to apply for mortgage loans, and more applicants will qualify for those loans.

Economic Influences

Several economic factors affect real estate cycles, including supply and demand, population characteristics, social attitudes, and property value fluctuations.

The influence of supply and demand encompasses two different commodities: real property and mortgage funds. A demand for property will encourage building and cause prices to increase. For instance, in an area with a healthy economy, employment levels are high and incomes are steady. As a result of these factors, the demand for housing increases. (More people can afford to buy homes—the supply of property cannot keep pace with the demand.) This demand spurs building and causes the prices of already built homes to increase.

At the same time, the demand for mortgage funds also is increasing. As more people are able to purchase homes, more people will want to finance those homes. Thus, there needs to be a healthy supply of money to lend for a strong housing market to continue. If money is tight and interest rates are too high, fewer people will be able to qualify for mortgages and the demand for housing will decrease. Supply will outstrip demand, and housing prices will decrease.

Money may become tight because of the actions of those forces that compete for mortgage funds. The two largest competitors for mortgage funds are the federal government and industry. Both are heavy borrowers: the federal government to cover the enormous federal deficit and industry because it usually takes large sums of money to expand operations.

Economic indicators help the broker stay abreast of economic changes. Rates of *inflation* (an increase in the amount or money or credit in relation to available goods or services) and *stagflation* (persistent inflation combined with stagnant consumer demand and high unemployment rates) are important gauges of the relative health of the economy. And to judge future opportunities in real estate markets, brokers must keep aware of the possibility of *recessions* (period of low general economic activity) or, in extremely rare cases, *depressions* (periods of low general economic activity marked by rising levels of unemployment).

Influence of Individuals

The behavior of the population has a dramatic impact on real estate cycles. Demographic trends include the rate of homeownership and which kinds of homes are desired. The savings habits of individuals also affect real estate cycles. For example, when individuals invest their funds in stocks, bonds, or mutual funds instead of in savings accounts, lenders no longer have as much money to lend, and real estate loans become harder to get. This phenomenon is known as **disintermediation.**

Influence of the Federal Government

The actions of the federal government have a significant impact on real estate cycles. The federal government, through the Federal Reserve, tries to lessen the likelihood of economic downturns (recessions, depressions, and inflation) and decrease the impact of those downturns should they occur. The secondary mortgage market also helps lessen the impact of local real estate cycles by creating a national market for real estate mortgages.

Tax laws.   Tax laws also affect real estate cycles. For example, the *Tax Reform Act of 1986* eliminated many tax benefits once enjoyed by real estate owners and investors. With limited exceptions, losses from property investments can no longer shelter other income. Depreciation time periods were increased significantly (making the yearly tax deduction much smaller).

On the other hand, the *Taxpayer Relief Act of 1998* was a stimulus to the resale market. In previous years, homesellers who wanted to move to smaller and less expensive quarters often faced large capital gains taxes. After 1998, almost no one owed any tax on the sale of their own home, and moving around as often as every two years became a tax-free possibility.

Federal Reserve System.   The role of the Federal Reserve System (also known as the "Fed") is to maintain sound credit conditions, help counteract inflationary and deflationary trends, and create a favorable economic climate. The Federal Reserve System divides the country into 12 federal reserve districts, each served by a federal reserve bank. All nationally chartered banks must join the Federal Reserve and purchase stock in its district reserve banks.

The Federal Reserve regulates the flow of money and interest rates in the marketplace indirectly, through its member banks, by controlling their reserve requirements and discount rates.

The Federal Reserve requires that each member bank keep a certain amount of its assets on hand as reserve funds unavailable for loans or any other use. This requirement was intended primarily to protect customer deposits, but more important, it provides a means of manipulating the flow of cash in the money market.

By increasing its reserve requirements the Federal Reserve in effect limits the amount of money that member banks can use to make loans, thus causing interest rates to rise. In this manner, the government can slow down an overactive economy by limiting the number of loans that would have been directed toward major purchases of goods and services. The opposite is also true: by decreasing the reserve requirements the Federal Reserve can allow more loans to be made, thus increasing the amount of money circulated in the marketplace and causing interest rates to drop.

Federal Reserve member banks are permitted to borrow money from the district reserve banks to expand their lending operations. The interest rate that the district banks charge for the use of this money is called the *discount rate*. This rate is the basis on which the banks determine the percentage rate of interest that they, in turn, charge their loan customers. Theoretically, when the Federal Reserve discount rate is high, bank interest rates are high; therefore, fewer loans will be made, and less money will circulate in the marketplace. Conversely, a lower discount rate results in lower interest rates, more bank loans, and more money in circulation.

Influence of Lending Policies

As mentioned earlier, the availability of mortgage money influences real estate cycles. When interest rates are high or money is tight, real estate sales decrease. Other ways lenders influence the real estate market include how stringent their lending criteria are (who can qualify for a mortgage); documentation requirements; the time frame for loan approval; and LTV ratios.

Publications

To keep up with all the elements that influence real estate cycles, real estate brokers should read various publications, including the *Wall Street Journal*, local or regional newspapers, and professional publications. All of these publications are excellent sources for various economic indicators, such as the discount rate, unemployment rate, inflation rate, interest rates, and housing starts.

Condominiums and Cooperatives

In some parts of the state, condominiums do not hold or increase their value as quickly as detached houses. The Manhattan market, however, is subject to periodic swings, closely tied to the health of the stock market. At one time condos and co-ops may be a drag on the market; six months later they may sell like hotcakes.

Loan Processing   With the growth of the Internet, systems for credit scoring, and sophisticated software programs, mortgage lending continues a trend toward streamlining. Even appraisal time may be shortened, with some loans calling for only "drive-by" appraisals. "One-stop shopping," with all the services for the transaction available from one all-purpose company, may be the real estate transaction of the future.

■ SUMMARY

New York is a lien theory state, considering mortgages as liens on the property, not as transfer of title.

Mortgage loans include conventional loans, loans insured by the FHA or an independent mortgage insurance company, those guaranteed by the VA, and loans from private lenders. In addition to the types of loans described in Chapters 10 and 11, shared-equity arrangements (known as *participation loans* in commercial lending) and subordinate or junior mortgage loans are possible.

Commercial loans include miniperm and floating interest mortgages, sometimes structured to allow lower payments at the start of the repayment term. Other commercial financing techniques include sale-and-leasebacks and ground leases.

Construction loans usually provide for the funds to be disbursed in installments, as the work is finished and inspected.

The federal government affects real estate financing by participating in the secondary mortgage market. The secondary market is composed of investors who purchase and hold the loans as investments. Fannie Mae (Federal National Mortgage Association), Ginnie Mae (Government National Mortgage Association), and Freddie Mac (Federal Home Loan Mortgage Corporation) take an active role in creating a secondary market by regularly purchasing mortgage loans from originators and retaining, or warehousing, them until investment purchasers are available.

Real estate brokers need to stay informed about the factors that influence the real estate market. Locally, employment levels have a major influence. Nationally, the state of the economy in general brings buyers into the market or discourages them, as the economic cycle moves from inflation to stagflation, recession, depression, and back again.

QUESTIONS

1. Farmer Macdonald wouldn't really mind a small shopping mall on the far end of his land, but he hates to see those acres go out of the family. He can solve the problem by negotiating a
   a. sale-leaseback.
   b. miniperm loan.
   c. ground lease.
   d. release deed.

2. Ginny's Minimart does a booming business, and Ginny would like to expand her store. There's plenty of room to build, but she isn't sure she could finance the construction. One remedy might be to find an investor and negotiate a
   a. sale-leaseback.
   b. ground lease.
   c. SONYMA mortgage.
   d. gap loan.

3. With the commercial loans that involve interest accrual, the borrower faces the possibility of
   a. underwriting.
   b. negative amortization.
   c. assignment.
   d. alienation.

4. Construction loans are
   a. insured by the Fed.
   b. considered subordinate.
   c. subject to disintermediation.
   d. disbursed in installments.

5. The strongest governmental influence on the country's interest rates is
   a. the Federal Reserve.
   b. SONYMA.
   c. GNMA.
   d. HUD.

6. In the future, mortgage origination is likely to become a faster process because of
   a. relaxed FNMA regulations.
   b. the Internet.
   c. Federal Reserve policies.
   d. increased use of PMI.

7. The commercial equivalent of a shared-equity home mortgage is
   a. a participation loan.
   b. a miniperm mortgage.
   c. a junior lien.
   d. cooperative financing.

8. Ginnie Mae and Fannie Mae were created to warehouse
   a. land for development by the government.
   b. assigned leases.
   c. home equity loans.
   d. FHA and VA mortgages.

9. Most home equity loans are really
   a. long-term leases.
   b. junior mortgages.
   c. purchase-money mortgages.
   d. trust deeds.

10. When a developer sells one home in a new subdivision, the blanket mortgage on that lot is
    a. secured.
    b. refinanced.
    c. accrued.
    d. released.

21

REAL ESTATE INVESTMENTS

The Agostinos are being transferred out of town and can't decide what to do about their home. If they rent it out, they can clear about $400 a month over their mortgage payment, which would help with payments on their new home. If they sell it, they will have about $60,000 after paying off their present loan. They have asked a real estate broker whether they would be wise to keep the house as an investment.

Often customers want a real estate broker or salesperson to act as an investment counselor. The licensee should understand the fundamentals of income property but should also recommend that a potential real estate investor consult a tax accountant, attorney, or investment specialist who can give expert advice regarding the investor's needs.

■ KEY TERMS

adjusted basis
appreciation
basis
boot
capital gain
cash flow
cost recovery
current rent roll
debt service
depreciation
discounted cash-flow analysis
discounting
discount rate
disposition
general partnership

gross rental income
holding period
installment sales
leverage
limited liability company (LLC)
limited liability partnership (LLP)
limited partnership
marginal tax rate
mortgage debt service
negative cash flow
net operating income
passive income
pro forma statement
pyramid

rate of return
real estate investment syndicate
real estate investment trust (REIT)
real estate mortgage investment conduit (REMIC)
return
Section 1031 property exchange
silent partner
straight-line depreciation
tax basis
tax credit
tax-deferred exchange

■ THE NATURE OF REAL ESTATE INVESTMENT

Investing in real estate usually means buying property and holding it for the production of income. Real estate has been called the best way to build an estate.

Real estate investment, though, takes a constant investment of effort. One can buy shares of stock and then limit further effort to checking the quotations every week in the Sunday paper. Not so with a duplex three blocks from home. The owner must be ready for a 6 A.M. phone call about a burst water heater, have a prompt replacement delivered, and arrange for someone to meet the plumber that very day. For small properties it is very difficult to be an absentee landlord.

In addition, real estate investment is not liquid. Money can be taken out of the stock market with a simple phone call to a stockbroker. Investors in real estate, however, should not count on taking out their capital within perhaps six months. When local unemployment is high, investors may not be able to take out their money until the economic cycle changes.

■ PREPARING TO BE AN INVESTOR

An investor faces two challenges: finding and buying the right property, then managing it. The beginning investor needs

- a lawyer who specializes in real estate;
- an accountant; and
- a real estate broker familiar with investment real estate.

All three should be lined up before the first purchase so they can assist in locating and analyzing the proposed investment. Meanwhile, the new investor should get information about the market by reading the papers and visiting open houses to develop the expertise needed to recognize a bargain.

Start small.   Investors would be wise to start small for the first few transactions so they do not risk too much capital or take on too much liability while learning. A one to six-unit building, located reasonably close to the investor's own home, is often best. Out-of-town property that cannot be monitored or controlled can be disappointing.

Avoid vacant land.   Building lots in resort areas and vacant land held in anticipation of development are not for the beginning investor. Land would have to appreciate markedly before it would pay off, because it produces no income, ties up money, cannot be depreciated, and requires property tax payments. Judging which areas will be in demand in years to come takes skill and expertise, and even experienced investors can be burned.

Leverage

Pyramiding. Traditionally real estate investors have used **leverage** (other people's money) to **pyramid** a small amount of capital. If, for example, an investor had $100,000 and bought one property that went up in value by 5 percent in the next year, the investor would make $5,000 in **appreciation.** To use leverage, one might search for ten such parcels, putting $10,000 down on each and getting sellers to take back $90,000 mortgages. If each went up by 5 percent, the investor would have appreciation totaling $50,000 in one year and would control $1 million worth of real estate.

This technique runs into problems, however, where local conditions change, employment drops, and finding tenants who will pay enough to cover those ten mortgage payments becomes difficult. The investors who delighted in *owning* $1 million worth of real estate now find themselves *owing* on $1 million worth, which is a different matter.

Risk and Reward

The purpose of investing is to generate a **return,** or profit. An investor expects both a return *of* capital (recovery of the invested funds) and a return *on* capital (profit or reward). The **rate of return** that an investor expects is directly related to the degree of risk in the investment. Real estate investments must offer the promise of higher returns to attract capital away from other, safer investments.

One of the most important risks for a real estate investment is the possibility that the property will decline in value during the investment holding period. On the other hand, an increase in property value can be a significant component of an investment's profit. For this reason, real estate investors must give considerable attention to the trends that affect real estate values. Statistical data from government agencies and private research groups are an important source of information in this regard. Such data can help to identify economic and social trends that will affect property values over time.

■ ANALYZING PROPERTY INCOME

A key factor in any investment is the amount of income that can be expected. In the case of income-producing real estate, an investor is concerned with the amount of rent that the property can generate and also with the amount of expenses that are necessary to maintain the property. A property's income and expenses are typically recorded in the form of operating statements.

Operating Statements

An *operating statement* is basically a list of revenues and expenses associated with a property for a given time period, such as one month or one year. The different categories of revenue (rent, parking fees, etc.) are listed at the top, along with their amounts, and the amounts are totaled. Next come the various expenses associated with the property, which are also totaled. At the bottom of the statement, total expenses are subtracted from total revenues and the resulting *net operating income (NOI)* is noted. Net operating income (the "bottom line") is a critical factor in investment analysis. Figure 21.1 is an example of a completed operating statement.

Current Rent Roll

An operating statement for a property will show the total amount of rent generated for the period of the statement, but it does not go into the details. This information is found in a **current rent roll** or rent schedule, which lists the current rent for each tenant of the property. This information is important to investment analysis for several reasons. It indicates the level of vacancies

F I G U R E   21.1

Operating Statement

15-Nov-94	ANNUAL PROPERTY OPERATING DATA	9:27 AM

Owner: XYZ APARTM\ENTS	PREPARED BY:	PRICE: 3,750,000
Location: 621 DALE ROAD	R. BARRY DEICKLER, CRB, EMS	LOANS:
City: NORTH LAUDERDALE, FL 33068	DEICKLER REAL ESTATE	
Type: APARTMENT	40 WEST MAIN STREET	EQUITY: 3,750,000
Size: 100	MT. KISCO, NY	FEE:
Purpose: Owner's Statement	Financing	

Assessed/Appraised: Value %	Existing:	Amount	Int. Rate	Due	Mo. Pymnt. Annual Pymt.
Land	1st Loan				
Improvements	2nd Loan				
Personal Property	3rd Loan				
TOTAL	Potential:				
Adjusted Cost Basis:	1st Loan				
Net Rentable Sq. Ft.:	2nd Loan				

#	ANNUAL INCOME/EXPENSES	$SQ.FT.	GSI %	EXPENSES	INCOME	COMMENTS / FOOTNOTES	#
1	GROSS SCHEDULED INCOME		100.00%		721,560	THE FIGURES AND DATA HEREIN	1
2	Less Vac. & Cr. Losses		2.99%		21,560	ARE NOT GUARANTEED, BUT	2
3	EFFECTIVE RENTAL INCOME		97.01%		700,000	ARE BELIEVED TO BE RELIABLE.	3
4	Plus: Other Income					PLEASE GET ADVICE FROM	4
5	GROSS OPERATING INCOME		97.01%		700,000	YOUR CPA and ATTORNEY.	5
6	OPERATING EXPENSES					COMMENTS / FOOTNOTES	6
7	Accounting & Legal		1.00%	7,000			7
8	Advertising		0.71%	5,000			8
9	Insurance		1.57%	11,000			9
10	Maintenance & Repair		3.57%	25,000			10
11	Management		3.57%	25,000			11
12	Payroll		4.57%	31,980			12
13	Payroll Taxes		0.36%	2,500			13
14	Postage						14
15	Real Estate Taxes		9.687%	67,808			15
16	Telephone						16
17	Other						17
18	Gas						18
19	Electric		2.87%	20,090			19
20	Water/Sewer		2.31%	16,200			20
21	Rubbish		2.48%	17,348			21
22	Reserves		2.14%	15,000			22
23	Leasing Commissions						23
24	Licenses & Permits						24
25	Supplies						25
26	Miscellaneous		0.71%	5,000			26
27	Contract Services						27
28	Lawn/Snow Removal		0.19%	1,345			28
29	Pool		0.71%	5,000			29
30	Janitorial						30
31	TOTAL EXPENSES		36.47%	255,271			31
32	NET OPERATING INCOME				444,729	CAP RATE 11.86%	32
33	Less Annual Debt Service					LTV RATIO	33
34	CASH FLOW BEFORE TAXES				44,729	CASH ON CASH 11.86%	34

in the property, and it also shows the rates at which various units are currently leased. It would be a disadvantage to the investor, for example, if units were subject to long-term leases at below-market rental rates.

**Pro Forma
Statements**

While the owner's operating statements and rent roll are important sources of information for investment analysis, they do not predict what the property will earn in the future. And *future earnings* are precisely what investors are concerned with. Consequently, investment analysis makes use of **pro forma statements,** which are hypothetical future operating statements for a property.

Pro forma statements differ from regular operating statements in several key features. First of all, as just noted, pro forma statements list *potential* future revenues and expenses, while operating statements show actual past revenues and expenses. Second, in a pro forma statement the amount of rent is based on current market rates, as opposed to the currently scheduled rents for the property, unless the scheduled rents are locked in by long-term lease agreements. A pro forma statement shows the total amount of rent that the property is *capable of generating,* and then records a separate deduction for anticipated vacancies and collection losses. A regular operating statement simply shows the amount of rent that actually was collected.

Expense items also may be listed *differently* on a pro forma statement. Two critical items are *depreciation* and *mortgage debt service.* **Depreciation** is an expense item that is listed on operating statements for income tax purposes. The amount of depreciation expense is related to the owner's **tax basis** in the property and also to the relevant tax code provisions. The current owner's depreciation expense is irrelevant to investment analysis, so it is not included in a pro forma. In its place, a line item expense is shown for *replacement reserves,* the anticipated costs for replacing parts of the property (such as a roof or heating equipment) as they wear out.

Mortgage debt service refers to the *payments of principal and interest that must be made on loans that are secured by a property.* Here again, the current owner's debt service is essentially irrelevant to investment analysis, as the new investor will need to obtain new financing. In any case, *debt service is never considered to be a component of net operating income in investment analysis.* Net operating income is calculated independently, and then any debt service (current or pro forma) is deducted to determine the investment's *cash flow* (pretax cash flow). Like net operating income, *pretax cash flow* is a key figure in investment analysis.

A typical pro forma statement would first list the investment's *potential gross operating income.* Market rate rental figures may be used, unless the present rentals are locked in with long-term leases, which would survive a sale.

From potential gross rents, the following items would then be subtracted:

■ An estimated allowance for vacancies and uncollected rents (normally 5 percent or so of gross rental income)

- Utilities paid by the landlord including, if applicable, electric power, fuel for heating and cooling, water, sewer, trash collection, and so forth
- Property taxes
- Hazard and liability insurance premiums
- Estimate for repairs
- Maintenance services such as janitor service, snow removal, lawn care, and the like
- Property management salaries or fees, if applicable
- A reserve for future large improvements such as a new roof or furnace, with the estimated amount based on the building's present condition and perhaps running to 2 percent of the value of the property

Projected expenses subtracted from gross rental yields annual **net operating income.** Next subtracted is **debt service** (mortgage payments). The resulting figure shows **cash flow**—actual dollars one can expect to take out of the property each year. If the figure is a minus, the investment is likely to yield **negative cash flow,** requiring a contribution from the investor's pocket each year.

■ INVESTMENT OWNERSHIP STRUCTURE

Ownership structure refers to the type of entity that will make the investment. For example, an individual may wish to purchase property through a corporation, either to limit personal liability exposure or for tax or accounting purposes. Ownership also may be structured in the form of a real estate syndicate or other specialized investment group.

A **real estate investment syndicate** is a form of business venture in which a group of people pool their resources to own and/or develop a particular piece of property. In this manner people with only modest capital can invest in large-scale, high-profit operations, such as highrise apartment buildings and shopping centers. A certain amount of profit is realized from rents collected on the investment, but the main return usually comes when the syndicate sells the property.

Syndicate participation can take many different legal forms, from tenancy in common and joint tenancy to various kinds of partnerships, corporations, and trusts.

In 1994, the *New York Limited Liability Company Law* was enacted, which allows the formation of **limited liability companies (LLCs)** and **limited liability partnerships (LLPs).** Both LLCs and LLPs allow investors to take advantage of the federal tax benefits and flexibility of a partnership and the limited liability of a corporation. It is anticipated that LLCs will become a popular form of business organization.

Private syndication, which generally involves a small group of closely associated and/or widely experienced investors, is distinguished from *public syndication,* which generally involves a much larger group of investors who may or may not be knowledgeable about real estate as an investment. Any pooling of individuals' funds raises questions of registration of securities under federal securities laws and state securities laws, commonly referred to as *blue-sky laws*.

Securities laws control and regulate the offering and sale of securities to protect members of the public who are not sophisticated investors but may be solicited to participate. Real estate securities must be registered with state officials and/or with the federal Securities and Exchange Commission (SEC) *when they meet the defined conditions of a public offering*. The number of prospects solicited, the total number of investors, or participants, the financial background and sophistication of the investors, and the value or price per unit of investment are pertinent facts. Salespeople of such real estate securities may be required to obtain special licenses and register with the state's attorney general and the SEC.

Forms of Syndicates

A **general partnership** is organized so that *all members of the group share equally in the managerial decisions, profits, and losses*. A certain member (or members) of the syndicate is designated to act as trustee for the group, holding title to the property and maintaining it in the syndicate's name.

Under a **limited partnership** agreement *one party* (or parties), usually a property developer or real estate broker, organizes, operates, and is responsible for the entire syndicate. This person is called the *general partner*. The other members of the partnership are merely investors; they have no voice in the organization and direction of the operation. These passive investors are called *limited partners* (and may also be called *silent or passive partners*).

The *limited partners* share in the profits and compensate the general partner out of such profits. The limited partners stand to lose only as much as they invest, nothing more. The *general partner(s)* is (are) totally responsible for any excess losses incurred by the investment. The sale of a limited partnership interest involves the sale of an *investment security*, as defined by the SEC. Therefore, such sales are subject to state and federal laws concerning the sale of securities. Unless exempt, the securities must be registered with the SEC and the appropriate state authorities.

Real Estate Investment Trusts

By directing their funds into **real estate investment trusts (REITs)**, real estate investors can take advantage of the same tax benefits as mutual fund investors. A real estate investment trust does not have to pay corporate income tax as long as 90 percent of its income is distributed to its shareholders and certain other conditions are met. There are three types of investment trusts: *equity trusts, mortgage trusts*, and *combination trusts*. To qualify as a REIT, at least 75 percent of the trust's income must come from real estate.

Equity trusts. Much like mutual fund operations, *equity REITs* pool an assortment of large-scale income properties and sell shares to investors. This is in contrast to a real estate syndicate, through which several investors pool their funds to purchase one particular property. An equity trust also differs from a syndicate in that the trust realizes and directs its main profits through the income derived from the various properties it owns rather than from the sale of those properties.

Mortgage trusts. *Mortgage trusts* operate similarly to equity trusts, except that the mortgage trusts buy and sell real estate mortgages (usually short-term, junior instruments) rather than real property. A mortgage trust's major sources of income are mortgage interest and origination fees. Mortgage trusts also may make construction loans and finance land acquisitions.

Combination trusts. *Combination trusts* invest shareholders' funds in both real estate assets and mortgage loans. It has been predicted that these types of trusts will be best able to withstand economic slumps because they can balance their investments and liabilities more efficiently than can the other types of trusts.

Real Estate Mortgage Investment Conduits

The **real estate mortgage investment conduit (REMIC),** which issues securities backed by a pool of mortgages, has complex qualification, transfer, and liquidation rules. Qualifications include the "asset test" (substantially all assets after a start-up period must consist of qualified mortgages and permitted investments) and the requirement that investors' interests consist of one or more classes of regular interests and a single class of residual interests. Holders of regular interests receive interest or similar payments based on either a fixed rate or a variable rate. Holders of residual interests receive distributions (if any) on a pro rata basis.

■ HOLDING PERIOD AND DISPOSITION

One of the key considerations in an investment strategy is the question of when to get out of the investment, when to sell. This is especially true of real estate investments, due to the relative illiquidity of real estate. Choosing to sell at the wrong time can more than wipe out any gains that were realized during the ownership of a property. For this reason, real estate investment strategy must focus on both the *holding period* of the investment and the timing of its *disposition*.

The **holding period** is the length of time between the date the investor purchases the property and the date the investor resells the property. During this period, investment strategy is focused on the property's income and cash flow. Will the property generate enough income to cover the investor's financing costs and the expenses of maintaining the property? Does the investor have the resources to handle any periods of negative cash flow that may arise? Is the projected rate of return sufficient to compensate for the degree of investment risk posed by the property?

The strategy of **disposition** is *interrelated* with the strategy of the holding period. An anticipated gain or loss from the sale of the property will obviously affect the overall rate of return on the investment, which must be commensurate with the risk. The investor must balance the anticipated income during the holding period against the likelihood of a change in property value. A lower rate of income during the holding period may be acceptable if there is a strong probability of appreciation in value, whereas market uncertainty may demand a high rate of holding period income.

Financing considerations also come into play in the *investor's timing strategy*. Loan rates are dependent on the term of the loan, with lower rates often available for shorter term financing. An investor might be able to obtain a more favorable rate on a five-year balloon loan, for example, but then assumes the risk of needing to refinance on less desirable terms if market conditions preclude a profitable resale of the property after five years.

TYPES OF INVESTMENT PROPERTIES

There are several types of properties investors are interested in, including the following:

- *Retail.* Retail properties include freestanding buildings and traditional shopping centers (which range from strip centers to superregional malls).
- *Office.* Office properties can be small properties with one or two tenants, highrise complexes, or office parks. They may be situated in downtown urban areas or in suburban developments.
- *Apartment.* Multifamily housing is a popular type of investment property. Apartment buildings can range from five or six units to highrise complexes.
- *Mixed Developments.* Mixed developments are increasing in popularity. These developments combine several types of property uses, such as residential (apartments), office space, and retail space.
- *Hotels/Motels.* Hotels and motels are a very specialized type of property and require expert management. While the failure rate for hotels and motels is quite high, they can be a good investment if the properties are in a good location and are well managed.

INVESTMENT ANALYSIS TECHNIQUES

To a certain extent, investment analysis is a subjective operation, because it depends on the *goals* and the *situation* of the particular investor. One investor may have $50,000 to invest, and another may wish to invest $500,000. Some investors are naturally conservative, while others thrive on risky ventures. Often an investor has definite ideas about the type(s) of properties he or she is interested in. Although these subjective factors will affect any given investment analysis, certain techniques are widely used by a broad spectrum of real estate investors. The broker counseling a potential investor must have knowledge and expertise in the analysis of many types of investments.

Discounted Cash-Flow Analysis

Discounting is a mathematical technique for calculating the present value of a future amount. In discounting, the value of $1 that will be received at some future date depends on two factors: the length of *time* until the money is paid and the *rate* at which the payment is discounted. In general, a shorter repayment term or a lower discount rate means a higher present value.

Selecting the *discount rate* is a critical part of **discounted cash-flow analysis.** This rate corresponds to the investor's expected rate of return on the investment. The **discount rate** must take into account *the time value of money, anticipated inflation or deflation, and the particular risks associated with the future cash flows.* For example, a discount rate of 12 percent may be based on a "safe" rate of 5 percent, anticipated inflation of 3 percent, and an additional 4 percent to account for investment risk.

Although discounted cash-flow analysis often is used to analyze a series of regular annual cash flows, it also can be applied to *individual cash flows that vary from year to year*. Different discount rates may be used for different payments, to reflect differences in risk. Assume, for example, that a property is subject to a long-term lease with a highly reputable tenant. Because the income from lease payments is at relatively low risk in this case, it may be discounted at a lower rate than the income that will come from resale of the property at the conclusion of the investment.

■ INCOME TAX CONSIDERATIONS

Depreciation

Depreciation allows an investor to recover the cost of an income-producing asset by way of tax deductions over the period of the asset's useful life. *Land cannot be depreciated*—technically, it never wears out or becomes obsolete. If depreciation is taken in equal amounts over an asset's useful life, the method used is called *straight-line depreciation*.

In past years, tax rules allowed depreciation over as little as 15 years, allowing deduction of one-fifteenth of the cost of real property each year. For property placed in service after January 1, 1987, the *Tax Reform Act of 1986* increased the **cost recovery** period for residential rental property to 27.5 years and for nonresidential property to 39 years.

Subtracting depreciation from net operating income yields the profit or loss the investor can declare on an income tax return. An accountant can determine whether any loss can be taken as a loss against other sources of income. The rules are complex. If total income is less than $100,000, the investor who actively manages the property may be able to claim up to $25,000 in losses against other types of income, such as salary or dividends. (An owner actively manages property when he or she is involved in management decisions such as setting rental rates.) With total income up to $150,000, part of a loss may be deducted. Otherwise a paper loss can be taken only against other **passive income** (the category into which all rental income now falls for tax purposes). In the 1990s real estate brokers and investors campaigned strenuously for Congress to change these passive loss tax rules. As a result, rental income is no longer considered passive for persons involved full time in real estate.

Income tax considerations are calculated at the investor's **marginal tax rate** (highest applicable tax bracket).

Capital Gains

Capital gain is defined as the difference between the adjusted basis of property and its net selling price. At various times tax law has excluded a portion of capital gains from income tax or set lower rates on long-term gains. As of 2003, the long-term holding period (minimum length of time an asset must be owned to qualify for special capital gains treatment) was 12 months. For long-term assets sold before May 6, 2003, the maximum capital gains rate was

20 percent (10 percent for any gain that fell within the lowest income tax bracket). Long-term assets sold after that date are taxed at 15 percent (5 percent for low-income taxpayers). Any part of the gain attributable to depreciation that was claimed or could have been claimed as an expense while the property was rented, however, is taxed at 25 percent.

Basis.   The **basis** of property is the investor's initial cost for the real estate, plus the cost of any subsequent capital improvements. Any depreciation claimed as a tax deduction is then subtracted to arrive at the property's **adjusted basis.** Sales price also is adjusted, with commissions and legal costs of selling deducted. When the property is sold, adjusted sales price minus adjusted cost basis equals the capital gain taxable as income.

For example, an investor purchased a small one-family dwelling for use as a rental property. Purchase price was $45,000. The investor is now selling the property for $100,000. The investor made $3,000 worth of capital improvements to the house. Depreciation of $10,000 has been taken during the investor's ownership. The investor will pay a broker's commission of 7 percent of the sales price and also will pay closing costs of $600. The investor's capital gain is computed as follows:

Selling price:		$100,000
Less:		
7% commission	$ 7,000	
closing costs	+600	
	$ 7,600	–$7,600
Net sales price:		$92,400
Basis:		
original cost	$45,000	
improvements	+3,000	
	$48,000	
Less:		
depreciation	–10,000	
Adjusted basis:	$38,000	
Total capital gain:		–$38,000
		$54,400

$44,400 of the total gain will qualify for capital gains tax rates; the remaining $10,000, which represents past depreciation, will be taxed at 25 percent.

Exchanges

Real estate investors can postpone taxation of capital gains by arranging what is known as a **Section 1031 property exchange.** To qualify as a **tax-deferred exchange,** the properties involved must be of *like kind* and be investment property or a property used in trade or business (as defined by the IRS). For example, vacant land held as an investment may be exchanged for a shopping center, or an apartment building may be exchanged for water rights to a stream in Colorado. State law determines what qualifies as real estate. For example, a cooperative in New York and in 17 other states is considered real estate for the purpose of exchanging. Any additional capital or personal property included to even out the exchange is called **boot,** and the party receiving boot is taxed on it at the time of the exchange.

Suppose investor Brown owns an apartment building with an adjusted basis of $225,000 and a market value of $375,000. Brown exchanges the building plus $75,000 cash for another apartment building having a market value of $450,000. That building, owned by investor Grey, has an adjusted basis of $175,000. Brown's basis in the new building will be $300,000 (the $225,000 basis of the building exchanged plus the $75,000 cash boot paid), and Brown has no tax liability on the exchange. Grey must pay tax on the $75,000 boot received and has a basis of $175,000 (the same as the previous building) in the building now owned. In a 1031 exchange, the investor's basis is transferred to the new
property.

Brown	Exchanges with	Grey
$375,000	Price	$450,000
$225,000	Basis	$175,000
$ 75,000	Boot	

Amount necessary to exchange: $375,000 + $75,000 cash = $450,000
The $75,000 cash/boot is taxable to Grey
Brown's new basis = $300,000 ($225,000 + $75,000)
Grey's basis = $175,000

Some Section 1031 exchanges involve strict time limitations and require accurate paperwork. Property to be purchased must be identified within 45 days and the transactions completed within 180 days. In some cases proceeds must be held in escrow by a qualified intermediary third party. For these "Starker" (delayed) exchanges, the use of an attorney and/or accountant familiar with the procedure is essential.

Tax Credits

A **tax credit** is a direct reduction in tax due, rather than a deduction from income before tax is computed. A tax credit is therefore of far greater value.

Investors in older building renovations and low-income housing projects may use designated tax credits to offset tax on up to $25,000 of other income. This is a major exception to the rule requiring active participation in the project. Even passive investors can take advantage of the tax credits. The maximum income level at which the credits can be taken is also higher. Investors with adjusted gross income of up to $200,000 are entitled to the full $25,000 offset, which is reduced by $.50 for every additional dollar of income and eliminated entirely for incomes above $250,000.

Tax credits of up to 20 percent of money spent are available for taxpayers who renovate historic property. Historic property is property so designated by the Department of the Interior and listed in the *National Register of Historic Landmarks* or property of historic significance located in a state or locally certified *historic district*. The property may be depreciated, but the full amount of the tax credit must be subtracted from the basis derived by adding purchase cost and renovation expenses.

The work must be accomplished in accordance with federal historic property guidelines and must be certified by the Department of the Interior or other state, county, or local entity. After renovation, the property must be used as a place of business or rented; it cannot be used as the personal residence of the person taking the tax credit.

There is also a credit of 10 percent of rehabilitation costs for nonhistoric buildings placed in service before 1936. Nonhistoric buildings must be non-residential property.

Also available are tax credits ranging from 4 percent to 9 percent each year over a ten-year period for expenditures on new construction or renovation of certain low-income housing.

Installment Sales

A taxpayer who sells real property and receives payment on an *installment basis* may report and pay taxes on any profit on the transaction year by year as it is collected. Many complex provisions apply to **installment sales.**

■ SUMMARY

Traditionally, real estate investment has offered a high rate of return while at the same time acting as an effective inflation hedge and allowing an investor to make use of other people's money to make investments through leverage. There may also be tax advantages to owning real estate. On the other hand, real estate is not a highly liquid investment and often carries with it a high degree of risk. Also, it is difficult to invest in real estate without expert advice, and a certain amount of involvement is usually required to establish and maintain the investment.

Net operating income on an investment is calculated by subtracting expenses (including vacancies and reserve for expected improvements) from gross rental income. Subtracting debt service (mortgage payments) then yields the figure representing actual cash flow. Total return is composed of cash flow plus mortgage amortization plus appreciation and tax benefits. A property's operating statements indicate its historical performance, while future performance must be estimated through the use of pro forma statements.

An investor hoping to use maximum leverage in financing an investment will make a small down payment, pay low interest rates, and spread mortgage payments over as long a period as possible. By holding and refinancing properties, known as *pyramiding,* an investor may substantially increase investment holdings without contributing additional capital. The process can run into trouble if vacancy rates rise and rental income falls.

Individuals may invest in real estate through an investment syndicate; these include general and limited partnerships. Other forms of real estate investment are the real estate investment trust (REIT) and the real estate mortgage investment conduit (REMIC).

The holding period of an investment and its eventual resale are important factors in investment analysis. Discounted cash-flow analysis is commonly used to evaluate investments.

Depreciation allows an investor to recover in tax deductions the basis of an asset over the period of its useful life. Only costs of improvements to land may be recovered, not costs for the land itself.

Capital gain represents the taxable profit when property is sold, calculated by subtracting adjusted cost basis from adjusted sales price. Adjusted cost basis represents original cost plus improvements, minus depreciation claimed.

By exchanging one property for another with an equal or greater selling value, an investor can defer paying tax on the gain realized until a sale is made. Any extra cash or property received in the exchange is called *boot* and is taxed.

An investor may defer federal income taxes on gain realized from the sale of an investment property through an installment sale of property.

The real estate licensee should be familiar with the rudimentary tax implications of real property ownership, but should refer clients to competent tax advisers for answers to questions to specific matters.

QUESTIONS

1. Many experts advise that a first real estate investment be
   a. within a short drive of the investor's own home.
   b. in a popular resort area.
   c. located only where professional management is available.
   d. a handyman-special property in need of upgrading.

2. The beginning investor should first consult an accountant when
   a. preparing the present year's income tax return.
   b. establishing cost basis for depreciation.
   c. analyzing a prospective purchase.
   d. researching fair market rentals.

3. Among the disadvantages of real estate investment is
   a. leverage.
   b. the need for physical and mental effort.
   c. tax shelter.
   d. equity buildup.

4. Jim's property has a gross rental income of $12,000 a year and total expenses, including debt service, of $13,000. Jim is experiencing
   a. leverage.
   b. negative cash flow.
   c. recapture.
   d. deflation.

5. A small multifamily property generates $50,000 in rental income with expenses of $45,000 annually, including $35,000 in debt service. The property appreciates about $15,000 a year. The owner realizes another $5,000 through income tax savings. On this property, the cash flow is
   a. $5,000.   c. $20,000.
   b. $15,000.   d. $35,000.

6. In question 5, the owner's return is
   a. $5,000.   c. $25,000.
   b. $15,000.   d. $35,000.

7. Leverage involves the extensive use of
   a. cost recovery.
   b. borrowed money.
   c. government subsidies.
   d. alternative taxes.

8. Property that has a net operating income of $28,000 with annual depreciation of $10,000 and debt service of $18,000, which includes $17,000 interest, has taxable income of
   a. $38,000.   c. $10,000.
   b. $28,000.   d. $1,000.

9. The primary source of tax shelter in real estate investments comes from the accounting concept known as
   a. recapture.
   b. boot.
   c. depreciation.
   d. net operating income.

10. For tax purposes the initial cost of an investment property plus the cost of any subsequent improvements to the property, less depreciation, represents the investment's
    a. adjusted basis.   c. basis.
    b. capital gain.   d. salvage value.

11. The money left in an investor's pocket after expenses, including debt service, have been paid is known as
    a. net operating income.
    b. gross income.
    c. cash flow.
    d. internal rate of return.

12. The concept of depreciation of income property is of most value to the taxpayer in
    a. the top income bracket.
    b. a marginal income tax bracket.
    c. the lowest income tax bracket.
    d. any tax bracket.

13. Julia Kinder is exchanging her apartment building for an apartment building of greater market value and must include a $10,000 boot to even out the exchange. Which of the following may she use as boot?
    a. $10,000 cash
    b. Emeralds with a current market value of $10,000
    c. A used automobile with a current market value of $10,000
    d. Any of the above if acceptable to the exchangers

14. In question 13, which of the following is true?
    a. Julia may owe income tax on $10,000.
    b. Each may owe tax on $10,000.
    c. The other investor *may* owe tax on $10,000.
    d. No one owes any tax at this time.

15. An investment syndicate in which all members share equally in the managerial decisions, profits, and losses involved in the venture would be an example of which of the following?
    a. Real estate investment trust
    b. Limited partnership
    c. Real estate mortgage trust
    d. General partnership

16. The term *debt service* refers to
    a. total operating expenses.
    b. real estate and income taxes only.
    c. principal and interest on mortgage loans.
    d. interest payments only.

17. In an installment sale of real estate, taxable gain is usually received and reported as income by the seller
    a. in the year the sale is initiated.
    b. in the year the final installment payment is made.
    c. in each year that installment payments are received.
    d. at any one time during the period installment payments are received.

18. Depreciation allows the investor to charge as an expense on each year's tax return part of the
    a. purchase price minus land value.
    b. down payment.
    c. mortgage indebtedness.
    d. equity.

19. A separate license and/or registration is required for the sale of
    a. all investment property.
    b. real estate securities.
    c. installment property.
    d. boots.

20. An investor bears unlimited liability for a share of possible losses in a
    a. general partnership.
    b. limited partnership.
    c. real estate investment trust.
    d. corporation.

21. Harvey, a limited partner in a partnership that is renovating a historic waterfront property, is entitled to offset up to $25,000 in tax credits against
    a. no more than the amount he has at risk.
    b. income up to $100,000.
    c. income up to $200,000.
    d. income up to $250,000.

22. Helen has purchased a dilapidated town house that is 40 years old and of no particular historic value. Helen intends to renovate the town house and live in it. For her renovation expenditures Helen will be entitled to tax credits of

   a. $25,000.
   b. $0.
   c. $12,500.
   d. 25 percent.

23. Jim exchanged his office building, purchased for $475,000 and valued at $650,000, for an office building valued at $750,000. Jim also paid $100,000 cash to the owner of the other building. Jim

   a. received $100,000 "boot."
   b. must report $100,000 as income.
   c. must reduce his adjusted basis by $100,000.
   d. now has a property basis of $575,000.

24. A new tax entity that issues securities backed by a pool of mortgages is a

   a. REIT.
   b. REMIC.
   c. TRA.
   d. general partnership.

25. The Agostinos are being transferred out of town. They decide to keep their current home as an investment property. They ask a real estate broker to manage the property for them. In the first year, they end up losing $1,500 on the investment property, due to a combination of depreciation and a three-month vacancy. For income tax purposes, they can deduct this loss

   a. against any passive income.
   b. against salary, as long as they make less than $200,000.
   c. against a 1031 exchange.
   d. under no circumstances.

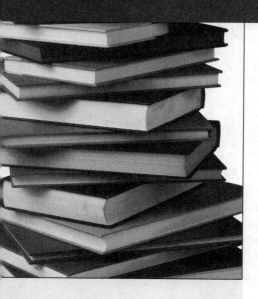

22

GENERAL BUSINESS LAW

Clint and Clifford Buntsen owned their real estate brokerage business as partners. Last month Clint died, leaving everything he owned to his wife, who is a licensed salesperson. Clifford knows that the Department of State will not allow a nonbroker to be part owner of a real estate firm and worries because now he and his sister-in-law will be partners.

Real estate brokers are familiar with many aspects of law: agency, contract, and real property law. Other areas of general business law may, however, unexpectedly impinge on the practice of real estate.

■ KEY TERMS

administrative law	corporation law	personal property law
administrator	criminal law	real property law
arbitration	due process	security agreement
bankruptcy	endorsement	small claims court
case law	executor	statute of limitations
certificate of incorporation	financing statement	statutory law
civil law	injunction	torts
commercial law	law of agency	trustee
commercial paper	litigation	trusts and wills
common law	mediation	Uniform Commercial Code
constitutional law	negotiable instrument	(UCC)
contract law	partnership law	

■ SOURCES OF LAW

The principal *sources of law* in the United States, all of which affect the ownership and transfer of real estate, are *the Constitution of the United States; laws passed by Congress; state constitutions; laws passed by state legislatures; ordinances passed by cities, towns, and other local governments; regulations adopted by agencies created by Congress, state legislatures, and local governments;* and *court decisions.*

The *U.S. Constitution and the individual state constitutions* establish the rights of citizens and set forth the limits of governmental authority. The term **due process** refers to our constitutional protection against the unfair taking of life, liberty, or property, and guarantees of the right to a fair hearing, notice, and the opportunity to be heard before a judge.

Laws passed by Congress and by state and local legislative bodies (**statutory law**) may establish specific provisions on any issue, from procedures for recording deeds and mortgages to taxation, or they may simply set broad standards of conduct and establish agencies to administer and enforce the laws.

Government agencies that enact rules and regulations range from the EPA through state real estate commissions to local zoning boards. These regulations implement and enforce legislative acts; they provide detailed information on legal and illegal actions and designate penalties for violations. These regulations have the effect of law.

Court decisions of federal, state, and municipal courts clarify and interpret laws, regulations, and constitutional provisions. By applying the laws to a specific event, a court decision expands the meaning of the law. For example, an attorney draws up what is considered a valid contract under the provisions of state law. If the court finds the contract is not valid, it will render an opinion as to why the contract does not fulfill the legal requirements for such a document. Future contracts in the state then will be based on the precedent of the court decision **(case law)** as well as on the statutes governing contracts.

The courts are not always bound by established precedent. Courts in one jurisdiction (area of authority) may not be bound by the decisions of courts in other jurisdictions. In addition, a court with superior authority in its jurisdiction may at its discretion reverse the ruling of a lower court.

Common law. In addition to these sources of law, real estate ownership and transfer are affected indirectly by what is known as the **common law,** that body of rules and principles founded on custom and usage, as well as the precedents of court decisions.

■ UNIFORM COMMERCIAL CODE

The **Uniform Commercial Code (UCC)** represents commercial law that has been adopted, wholly or in part, in all states. While this code generally does not apply directly to real estate, it has replaced state laws relating to chattel mortgages; conditional sales agreements; and liens on chattels, crops, or items that are to become fixtures. Shares in an apartment cooperative are personal property, and lenders to whom they are pledged as security for a loan generally use UCC filings.

To pledge a chattel as security, including chattels that will become fixtures, the code requires the use of a **security agreement,** which must contain a complete description of the items against which the lien applies. A short notice of this agreement, called a **financing statement** or UCC-1, which includes the identification of any real estate involved, must be filed *for fixtures* with the clerk of the county where the debtor resides and *for other personal property* with the Secretary of State in Albany. The recording of the financing statement constitutes notice to subsequent purchasers and mortgagees of the security interest in chattels and fixtures on the real estate.

Many mortgagees require the signing and recording of a financing statement when the mortgaged premises include chattels or readily removable fixtures (washers, dryers, and the like) as part of the security for the mortgage debt. If the financing statement has been properly recorded, on the borrower's default the creditor could repossess the chattels and cause them to be sold, applying the proceeds to the debt payment.

■ NEGOTIABLE INSTRUMENTS

A written promise to pay money is known as **commercial paper.** *Promissory notes, checks, drafts,* and *certificates of deposit*, all forms of commercial paper, are also known as **negotiable instruments.** *Negotiability* means that they can be freely transferred from one person to another. Commercial paper serves as a convenient substitute for actual money. The Uniform Commercial Code (UCC) divides commercial paper into four types: notes, drafts, checks, and certificates of deposit.

The simplest form of commercial paper, the *note*, is a promise by one person (the *maker*) to pay money to another (the *payee*) *with interest*. A promissory note may be made payable to a specific payee or simply to anyone who presents it for payment (the *bearer*). If it can be collected at any time, it is a *demand* note. Often, however, notes are not due until a specified time in the future. The bond or note accompanying a mortgage, for example, is a form of promissory note.

A *draft* is a form of commercial paper involving three parties. Sometimes known as a *bill of exchange*, a draft is issued by the *drawer*, who orders another party (the *drawee*) to pay money to the payee. Like a note, a draft may be payable either to a specific payee or to a bearer and may be payable on demand or on a certain date. Drafts are often used in connection with goods being shipped from seller to buyer. A *trade acceptance* is a form of time draft.

A *check* is a special type of draft that orders a bank to pay money to the payee on demand. A check may name a specific payee or be payable to the bearer (often, in that case, made out to "cash"). A *cashier's check,* issued by the bank, is a type of draft in which the bank orders itself to make the payment.

A *certificate of deposit* is a bank's receipt for a sum of money with a promise to repay it with interest. Certificates of deposit (CDs) are devices for investing large amounts of cash. They run for a specific length of time.

The Uniform Commercial Code sets standards for a negotiable instrument that is freely transferable. It must be in writing, be signed by the maker or drawer, contain an unconditional promise or order to pay a specific sum of money either on demand or at a definite time, and be payable either *to order* or *to a bearer.* If a third-party instrument, it must identify the drawee.

Writing.   The instrument must be written on material relatively permanent and portable. It may be written in ink or pencil, typed or printed. Standard printed forms are used most often.

Signed.   A simple X made by a person unable to write can constitute a legal signature. Initials or a thumbprint are also acceptable. A trade name or a rubber stamp, when used by someone authorized to do so, is also permitted.

Promise.   The promise or order to pay must be *unconditional.* Because it may pass from one person to another and be used in place of money, the instrument cannot be dependent on other happenings. The promise or order to pay must be clear. A simple IOU acknowledging that "I owe you $1,000" is not a promise to pay and not a negotiable instrument. A promise to pay "to Mary Doe" implies no promise to pay to anyone else. To enable Mary to sell the instrument or otherwise turn it over to someone else, it should contain a promise to pay "*to the order* of Mary Doe." Mary could then order the sum paid to another party.

Specific sum.   Negotiable paper must be payable *only in money.* It cannot promise payment in goods or services. If interest is involved, it must be stated so clearly that a computation of the sum promised is possible.

Demand or time.   A negotiable instrument must be payable "on *demand*" or at a *definite time.* Most checks are payable immediately (*on* sight, or *on* pre-sentation). A note also may be payable *after* sight—for example, one month after it is presented for payment. It may state that it will be paid "on or before" a specific date. If it is payable in installments, it may contain an acceleration clause, allowing the full amount to fall due immediately if some event occurs, like default on payment.

Endorsement.   Instruments payable to the bearer may be transferred by *delivery.* Instruments payable to order must be transferred by **endorsement.** A note may be transferred from one party to another by one of four types of endorsements:

1. *Blank endorsement,* in which the payee signs the back of the note without further explanation. It is the riskiest form of endorsement because the

note remains negotiable for any purpose, even if the holder acquired it illegally. It is almost equivalent to cash.

2. *Restrictive endorsement,* in which the negotiability of the instrument is restricted to a specific purpose, stated in the endorsement: "For deposit only."

3. *Special endorsement,* in which the payee specifically names the next holder in due course: "Pay to the order of John Smith."

4. *Qualified endorsement,* in which the phrase *without recourse* is written as part of the endorsement to relieve the person making the endorsement from any liability if the check or note is not honored. A qualified endorsement specifies that the person who originated the check remains liable for the note.

If an instrument is payable to John *or* Mary Doe, one endorsement is sufficient to transfer it. If it is payable to John *and* Mary Doe, both must endorse it.

Defenses. Legal defense against paying on an instrument might include claims that the maker was under duress, that the instrument was intended for some illegal purpose (payment of a gambling debt or for the purchase of illegal drugs), that the instrument was obtained by fraud, or that the instrument was altered after it was signed.

The most common method of discharging commercial paper is by *payment.* It also may be *canceled* by the holder, either by marking it *paid* or by destroying it. The destruction must be deliberate, not accidental, for the instrument to be discharged. The instrument also may be *renounced* by the holder, or, in the case of a check, the maker may issue a *stop-payment* order.

■ BUSINESS ORGANIZATIONS

Partnerships

The nature of a *partnership,* defined by partnership law as an *association of two or more persons to carry on a business for profit as co-owners,* has been discussed in earlier chapters. Many brokerage firms are set up as general partnerships; limited partnerships are generally formed for commercial investment.

A *partnership agreement* sets up the powers and duties of the partners. Unless the agreement specifies otherwise, new members usually must be approved by all existing partners. When the question arises as to whether two persons are in fact partners, the chief test is whether each receives a share of profits. If one partner assigns his or her share of profits to a third person, that person may be entitled to profits but does not become a partner and has no right to share in management or examine the firm's books. Partners have a fiduciary duty to each other; notice given to one is considered given to all.

Partnership property. Property contributed to the partnership when it is formed is considered to be *partnership property.* Creditors of the individual partners may not attach the assets of the partnership for a partner's personal debts but may attach the partner's interest in the partnership.

Dissolution.   The partnership is dissolved at a specific time originally agreed on, when requested by any partner or on the death or bankruptcy of a partner. A court order can dissolve the partnership if it is shown that one partner is insane or incapacitated, that the business cannot be operated at a profit, or that one partner is involved in impropriety affecting the partnership.

On dissolution the partnership may no longer transact new business, but the partnership continues through the process of *winding up*. Assets are distributed first to creditors who are not partners, next to partners who have lent money to the partnership, then in a refund of capital contributed by each partner. Anything remaining is distributed among the partners according to their respective interests.

Partners often buy special life insurance designed to ensure that the surviving partner can buy out the deceased partner's estate and continue the business.

Corporations

A *corporation* is an organization that is recognized by the law as a legal person. It may buy, sell, lease, mortgage, make contracts, and perform most other acts allowed to persons. It is entitled to most of the same protection guaranteed other persons by the Bill of Rights.

In most cases the persons who own shares in it bear no individual liability for the corporation's actions or debts. The corporation, in turn, cannot be held liable for the shareholders' debts.

Creation of a corporation.   A corporation is created by the filing of a **certificate of incorporation** with the Secretary of State. The incorporator(s) must sign the certificate, giving their names and addresses; the name of the intended corporation and its purposes; intended duration (usually perpetual); address; and number of shares of stock authorized to be issued. On payment of a fee and approval of the Secretary of State, the corporation becomes a legal entity. Bylaws, the rules and regulations under which the corporation will operate, are usually adopted at the first organizational meeting after the certificate of incorporation has been secured.

Management.   A corporation is managed by a *board of directors* elected by shareholders. Shareholders who cannot attend meetings, which are usually held annually, may vote by proxy. Once elected, the board of directors selects officers who administer the business of the corporation. Directors and officers have a fiduciary duty to the corporation and may not profit personally at its expense. Each shareholder has the right to examine the company's books.

A *closely held corporation* is one owned by a single individual or a small number of shareholders, perhaps members of the same family. The shareholders usually manage the business themselves.

Corporations are subject to the New York State franchise tax (also called *corporate income tax*) and if they do business in New York City, the city's general corporation tax.

One of the major advantages of corporate organizations, however, is the ability to shelter some income through pension and profit-sharing plans and to consider as business expense fringe benefits such as health or life insurance. Nevertheless, in recent years, liberalized tax-deferment possibilities for individuals through various retirement plans have lessened the appeal of this aspect of incorporation.

S corporations. With an *S corporation*, profits are passed directly to shareholders so that profits are taxed only once. Losses also may be passed to shareholders (although only to the limit of their investments) and used to offset ordinary income.

Limited liability companies and partnerships. *Limited liability companies* (LLCs) allow investors to take advantage of the limited liability of a corporation and also the tax advantages of a partnership, with earnings and profits taxed only to the individual members. A *limited liability partnership* is available to professionals, who have all the advantages of a limited liability company, except that their professional work is still subject to liability, as, for example, in cases of malpractice.

Termination. *Dissolution* is the legal death of the corporation. *Liquidation* is the winding-up process. A corporation may be dissolved by an act of the legislature, expiration of the time originally planned for the business, approval of the shareholders and board of directors, unanimous action of all the shareholders, failure to pay franchise taxes, or court order. A *certificate of dissolution* is filed with the Secretary of State, and assets are distributed first to creditors, next to holders of preferred stock, and last to holders of common stock.

Security Offerings

Like other securities, shares in real estate investment trusts (described in Chapter 21) may be issued as either private or public offerings.

Public offerings. After the stock market crash of 1929, the federal government began requiring certain disclosures by companies and others who wish to issue securities (stock, bonds, debentures, or warrants) in an effort to prevent fraud and insider trading. The Securities and Exchange Commission (SEC) administers the law.

The process includes the filing of a written registration statement and a prospectus with the SEC. They describe, among other factors, the securities being offered; the registrant's business; management, including compensation; competition in the industry; and any special risk factors. No advertisements or offers to sell the securities may be made during the prefiling period. Certain advertising is allowed during the waiting period between filing and SEC approval. The SEC does not pass on the merits of the securities offered but merely states that the issuer has met the disclosure requirements.

A simpler process, *Regulation A,* is available for issues of up to $5 million to be raised during a 12-month period. Any offering for more than $100,000 requires that an offering statement be filed with the SEC. It requires less information than a registration statement and is less costly to prepare.

Private offerings.   It is also possible to offer securities without SEC registration, if the investors are *accredited*. In general, they must be insiders of the issuer (partners, officers of the company, etc.) or "sophisticated" investors who are considered financially capable of judging for themselves: anyone with net worth of at least $1 million; anyone with annual income of at least $200,000 for the past two years; or corporations, partnerships, or business trusts with total assets in excess of $5 million.

Up to 35 *nonaccredited investors* also may buy part of a private offering, but only if they have a certain amount of financial sophistication. For private offerings, no general selling efforts or advertising to the public are allowed. Private placement securities may not be resold for a year after they are issued and in only limited amounts for the second year. After that period, there are usually no restrictions on resale.

■ THE FEDERAL COURT SYSTEM

The federal court system includes specialized courts, district courts, courts of review (appellate courts), and the Supreme Court. Federal judges receive lifetime appointments, subject to confirmation by the Senate.

District courts cover specific geographic areas, with at least one in each state. New York has four districts, referred to as the *northern, eastern, southern,* and *western districts*. District courts are the point of origin for civil cases arising from federal law and for federal crimes. They also serve as appellate courts for the U.S. bankruptcy court.

Specialized courts are established by Congress. Among them are tax court, court of claims, and bankruptcy court. The U.S. court of appeals provides review for district courts, tax courts, the court of claims, and decisions made by federal agencies such as HUD. The United States is divided into 13 judicial circuits. Appeals from district courts located in New York are heard by the second circuit court of appeals, which also covers Vermont and part of Connecticut. Decisions of this court are generally final, with further appeal to the Supreme Court the only possibility.

The Supreme Court of the United States consists of nine justices. It serves mainly as a court of appeals for cases involving federal law or constitutionality, but it also has original, or trial, jurisdiction in a few situations.

■ NEW YORK COURT SYSTEM

In New York State the supreme court is paradoxically one of the lowest courts in the system; it is so named because of its wide civil jurisdiction and because it originates most lawsuits. It is the lowest court of unlimited dollar amount of claims. It has branches in every county. Supreme court justices are also assigned to criminal cases when the caseload requires it.

County courts (outside New York City and the criminal court in New York City) have criminal jurisdiction. County courts also handle some civil cases and appeals from lower courts. The *surrogate court* handles decedents' estates, will contests, probates, adoptions (with family court), and incompetency proceedings. *Family court* handles family complaints, delinquencies, child abuse, and adoptions. Divorces, however, are heard in the supreme court. The *court of claims* has jurisdiction over claims against the state.

Small claims courts are set up for prompt and informal treatment of disputes and complaints involving less than $3,000. Fees and paperwork are nominal, and the parties generally appear for themselves, with no lawyers involved except in the case of corporations. Small claims courts may issue monetary awards and judgments but may not compel specific performance. They are part *of city, town,* or *village justice courts.* Corporations, partnerships, and associations may initiate up to five claims a month in commercial claims court. An inexpensive small claims procedure is also available for homeowners protesting their tax assessments.

The *appellate divisions* of the supreme court handle appeals by parties dissatisfied with lower court findings. The state is divided into four departments; the first and second departments cover New York City, Long Island, and the surrounding counties. The third is based in Albany and the fourth in Rochester. Five judges serve, taking no testimony but basing their decisions on the record and arguments by the parties' attorneys. Appeals are usually based on questions of law and procedure and not on disputes about the facts in the case. Occasionally the appellate division will rule, however, that the original verdict was against the weight of evidence. Those dissatisfied may, in some instances, take the case further, to the court of appeals.

The *court of appeals* is the highest court in the state. Seven judges sit. There is generally no further appeal from this court, although U.S. constitutional questions may be taken to the Supreme Court of the United States.

■ SUBSTANTIVE AND PROCEDURAL LAW

Law can be defined as either *substantive,* that portion of the law that defines our rights and responsibilities, and *procedural,* which deals with the methods for enforcing our rights.

Real estate licensees already will be familiar with at least three branches of substantive law: the **law of agency, contract law,** and **real property law.** Other branches include **administrative law,** through which government agencies regulate business practices; **commercial law; constitutional law, corporation law, personal property law, partnership law; trusts and wills;** and **criminal law.**

■ CIVIL LAW

The state prosecutes criminals who commit acts that injure the state or society as a whole under the provisions of criminal law. **Civil law,** on the other hand, deals with the injuries one person does another. These injuries can result from wrongful actions against persons or property (the legal term of which is **torts**) or from failure to perform contractual obligations. In a lawsuit for breach of contract, a court may award money damages to the plaintiff (the person bringing the complaint) or issue an *injunction,* ordering the defendant to perform his or her obligations.

While criminal law concentrates on punishing the culprit, the law of torts is intended to compensate the injured party. A single act may result in both civil and criminal court action as well as administrative procedure. The commission of a fraud, for example, may result in criminal prosecution, a civil suit by the defrauded person, and administrative action such as the revocation of a real estate license.

For a tort to be committed, three factors must exist: the plaintiff must have suffered a loss or injury; the damage must have been caused by the defendant; and depending on the type of tort, the defendant must usually have failed to exercise reasonable care or intended to do the act that caused the harm. Torts are generally classified into three groups: *intentional torts, negligence,* and *strict liability.*

Wrongs against the person include *assault* (threatening behavior); *battery* (physical contact; even without actual injury); *false imprisonment* (sometimes charged, for example, in the detention of a suspected shoplifter); and the *infliction of mental distress. Defamation* covers *slander* (oral) and *libel* (written), actions that tend to hold a person up falsely to contempt, ridicule, or hatred. Slander or libel arises when third parties can read or overhear the oral or written material. Among the grounds for libel that may concern real estate brokers are statements that a person has committed improprieties while engaging in a profession or trade. In a lawsuit the truth of the statement is almost always a complete defense. False statements about products, businesses, or title to property also can result in tort liability if actual damages occur. Torts against the person also include *misrepresentation, fraud,* and *invasion of the right to privacy.*

Wrongs against property include *trespass,* unauthorized intrusion on another's land. No actual damage need be shown; the landowner's right to exclusive possession is violated by the trespass. *Trespass to personalty* occurs when personal property is injured or the owner's right to enjoyment of it is interfered with. When property is stolen, the tort of *conversion* (to someone else's use) has occurred. *Nuisances* are acts that interfere with another's enjoyment or health. Barking dogs, searchlights that shine onto another's property, and business activities that cause unpleasant odors are typical nuisances. In addition to seeking money damages, the plaintiff may ask the court for an **injunction,** an order forbidding the offending activity.

Negligence covers actions that tend to wrong another through carelessness without any intent to cause damage. Such torts are often committed in accidents, and the court may apportion negligence between the parties. *Business torts* include infringement of copyrights, patents, and trademarks, as well as unfair competition. A business venture that is entered into for the single purpose of harming another established business becomes the tort known as *malicious injury to business. Strict liability* (usually in product liability cases) covers damages caused by unusual and abnormally dangerous activities in the course of business, such as improper manufacturing procedures that create dangerous products. Failure to warn the user of the dangers in using such an item is also covered by strict liability.

Civil Procedure

The term **litigation** refers to the process of a civil lawsuit. To start the process, the plaintiff serves or files a complaint with the proper court. A summons also is issued, directing the defendant to appear in court and answer the complaint. The defendant serves a written answer to the complaint or faces the possibility of a default judgment in the plaintiff's favor. A defendant who believes he or she has been injured by the plaintiff may file a counter-complaint or cross-complaint, which the original plaintiff must answer with a written reply.

The process of litigation continues with a procedure known as *discovery*, during which either party and witnesses give oral testimony known as *depositions*. Either party may submit *interrogatories*, written questions that must be answered in writing within a specified time. Either party may request that the other produce documents relevant to the case.

Still prior to the trial, parties may make pretrial motions in an attempt to dispose of all or part of the lawsuit immediately. One of the most common is a *motion for summary judgment*, which asks the judge to rule on the matter there and then when there is no dispute about the facts of the case. A pretrial hearing, also known as a *settlement conference*, brings the attorneys or parties together in an attempt to reach agreement before the trial begins.

The average layperson is more familiar with the trial itself, so often dramatized in movies and on TV. It begins with jury selection and opening statements by each side. The plaintiff then presents his or her case, calling witnesses and introducing evidence to support the complaint. The defendant's case follows, and then each side has a further chance to present a rebuttal and rejoinder. Closing arguments are made by each party's attorney, following which the judge instructs the jury on the law to be applied to the case. The jury then retires to deliberate and returns a verdict, after which the judge enters a judgment to the successful party.

Dispute Resolution

Disputes also can be resolved by **arbitration** or **mediation,** without using the courts. These procedures are less formal than lawsuits, much quicker, and less expensive for the parties. In most cases of arbitration, the disputing parties agree in advance that they will abide by the ruling of a disinterested third party. The arbitrator need not be a lawyer; often he or she is an expert in the matter being contested. The American Arbitration Association has a set of rules for the proceedings. (REALTORS® agree to submit disputes with fellow REALTORS® to binding arbitration rather than litigate.) The decision imposed by the arbitrator is seldom subject to appeal.

The process of mediation, often used today in cases of divorce, is growing in popularity as a less expensive, less time-consuming alternative to arbitration. It differs in that the mediator has no authority to issue a decision on the matter being disputed. Instead, a skilled attempt is made to facilitate an agreement between the parties.

Bankruptcy

Bankruptcy is a federal proceeding that allows someone whose debts have become unmanageable to be protected from creditors, gives the debtor a chance to start over, and distributes the debtor's available assets fairly to the creditors.

Bankruptcy is handled through a special federal court. Three general types of bankruptcy are known by chapter numbers. *Chapter 7* provides for the total liquidation of the debtor's assets (less certain exempt items available to individuals). *Chapter 11* and *Chapter 13* provide for the debtor's retention of assets and a corresponding adjustment in the payment of the outstanding debts.

Chapter 7, often known as *straight bankruptcy*, requires that the debtor (either an individual, partnership, limited liability company, or corporation) disclose all debts and surrender all assets to a trustee. The process starts with the filing of a petition in bankruptcy court, either by the debtor (*voluntary bankruptcy*) or by creditors (*involuntary bankruptcy*). Filing of the petition automatically freezes actions against the debtor, *including any pending foreclosure suit (automatic stay)*. Lawsuits in progress against the debtor are halted, and no new actions may be commenced. However, if a creditor is *secured* (the debt is backed by a lien on the debtor's real property or personal property), the secured creditor may request the court to permit the creditor to pursue foreclosure or repossession remedies. The bankruptcy judge may or may not grant this request or may require that the debtor make some payments to the secured creditor to forestall foreclosure.

An interim **trustee** is appointed. A meeting of the creditors provides an opportunity for questioning of the debtor and confirmation of the amounts owed. The creditors also may vote for the election of a permanent trustee. The trustee takes over the debtor's assets and distributes the net proceeds proportionately to creditors. With certain exceptions, the remaining debts are canceled or *discharged*. The law provides guidelines for the priority or payment of the claims.

In New York an individual debtor is allowed by law to retain up to $5,000 worth of household furnishings, equity in an automobile up to $2,400, and up to $10,000 equity in a homestead. A husband and wife filing for bankruptcy together may protect up to $20,000 in homestead equity.

Property acquired after the bankruptcy petition is filed is not administered by the trustee and belongs to the debtor (with the exception of an inheritance within six months after the petition was filed).

A *corporation, partnership, limited liability company,* or *individual* may file for *Chapter 11* relief and receive the same automatic stay or freeze on creditors' actions as provided by Chapter 7. The goal of Chapter 11, however, is not immediate liquidation of the debtor's business or total distribution of assets. Instead, the debtor and a creditors' committee formulate a plan for paying a portion of the debts while the debtor continues in business under the scrutiny of the bankruptcy court and the creditors' committee. Chapter 11 plans may provide for a gradual, orderly winding up of the business or may aim at total recovery.

Persons holding mortgages on real property may be delayed in foreclosing those mortgages by order of the bankruptcy judge until a plan is proposed by the bankrupt party and either accepted or rejected by the creditors and the court. A mortgagee may have to wait a considerable time, sometimes years, before the mortgage can be foreclosed. *Bankruptcy does not, however, free the debtor or the property of a mortgage.*

After the Chapter 11 petition is filed, the debtor continues to operate the business, free of claims and judgments. *Debtor-in-possession* (DIP) is the term for this situation. The court may allow the debtor to continue in the operation of the business or may appoint a trustee. In either event, if a creditors' committee is appointed by the United States Trustee (part of the Department of Justice), that committee will oversee the management. After a plan is proposed (by the debtor or by the creditors' committee), a vote of the creditors is taken. If they favor the plan and the court approves, it is put into effect. If no plan is presented or one is turned down, the proceeding is generally converted into a straight Chapter 7 bankruptcy.

Chapter 13 is available only to *individuals* with regular income (including those with welfare, Social Security, and retirement income) or those who operate a small business. It offers a chance to work out financial problems over a period of up to five years. Creditors may be paid in part or in full as in Chapter 11, but under Chapter 13 the proposed plan is not voted on by creditors. The court makes the decisions. Chapter 13 can be initiated only by a voluntary petition and tends to avoid the stigma of bankruptcy. The automatic stay halting all pending actions and prohibiting new actions exists, just as under Chapter 7 and Chapter 11.

Certain claims may not be discharged in bankruptcy:

- Income taxes accruing within three years of the bankruptcy filing
- Sales taxes and withholding taxes collected from customers and employees but not paid over to the taxing authorities
- Claims not listed on the bankruptcy schedule
- Claims based on fraud (misrepresentation or false pretenses)
- Alimony and child support

- Claims based on willful injury (except under Chapter 13)
- Some fines or penalties due the government
- Some student loans (except where the court determines there is undue hardship or under Chapter 13)

Occasionally, debtors do not receive their discharge. Discharges may be withheld where proof is offered that the debtor has concealed assets, obtained credit under false financial statements, or failed to cooperate with the trustee.

Estates

A decedent's estate is administered and *settled by a personal representative* appointed by the surrogate court. A will may name an **executor** to serve as personal representative. If no will can be found or no executor is named, the court will appoint an **administrator,** who serves as a personal representative and performs the same duties as an executor. The executor first inventories the estate to determine its extent and value. The will, insurance policies, deeds, car registrations, and birth and marriage certificates are located. Safe deposit boxes are inventoried, and the executor takes possession of bank accounts, real estate, and personal property. Names, addresses, and Social Security numbers of all heirs are obtained. The executor files claims for Social Security, pension, and veteran's benefits.

The personal representative administers the estate as the decedent would have done, collecting debts, managing real estate, collecting insurance proceeds, continuing a family business, and arranging for the support of survivors pending final distribution of the estate. The executor also pays rightful claims against the estate, negotiates the most favorable treatment for taxes, and sells selected assets to pay taxes in time to avoid any penalties.

Final winding up of the estate involves proper division of assets, selling some to pay cash bequests and transferring title to real and personal property. Final estate costs are paid, and an accounting is prepared.

Estate and gift taxes.   Any amount may be transferred between spouses during a lifetime or at death with no federal or New York State gift or estate tax due. Transfer to a spouse is known as the *marital deduction.*

The remainder of an estate may pass to anyone tax-free up to $1.4 million in 2003, $1.5 milion in 2004, $2 million in 2006, and $3.5 million in 2009. An estate of any amount can pass untaxed in 2010.

In 2011 the law establishing those amounts is scheduled to expire, and estate taxes would be due on any amount greater than $1 million (not counting anything left to a spouse). It is expected that Congress will make changes in the estate tax law before that date.

The figures cited above are known as *unified credits*, and may be used to cover gifts made during the donor's lifetime as well as the estate at death. In addition, any number of gifts may be made to individuals, free of federal tax, to a limit of $11,000 each (scheduled to rise yearly with inflation).

New York has no gift tax, and currently has a limit of $1 million before estate tax is due, not counting anything left to a spouse.

If estate or gift tax is due and not paid, the government may impose a lien on property. With certain exceptions, after a tax lien attaches to property, it continues even though the property is transferred to another. Thus until taxes are paid, a cloud on the title may render property subject to the lien unmarketable.

Divorce in New York

Divorce in New York State is not granted on the grounds of incompatibility or irreconcilable differences. No-fault divorce is possible after one year of living apart under a separation agreement or a court-ordered separation decree. Four grounds for divorce in New York hold one party at fault: cruel and inhuman treatment, abandonment for one or more years, imprisonment for three years or more, and adultery.

Equitable distribution. In New York, the courts may order division of marital property (all property acquired during the marriage except inheritance, gifts from third parties, and compensation for personal injuries). Court-ordered division can take place, no matter who holds title to the property, and need not be made on a 50/50 basis. Maintenance may be ordered for one spouse on a limited or permanent basis.

When real property is to be divided, thought must be given to the income tax liability of the person who will eventually sell the property. Cost basis for income property should be considered as carefully as the present value of the real estate.

No gift tax consequences apply when property is transferred between spouses incident to a divorce.

The ex-spouse who has moved out of a home may still be able to use the homesellers' capital gains exclusion on his or her share of a sale, if the one remaining in the home qualifies to use it.

■ STATUTE OF LIMITATIONS

Lawsuits must be commenced within a given period after damages have occurred, or the plaintiff's right to sue may be lost through *laches*. In some cases it is necessary only to file notice within the period that a suit may be instituted (a *lis pendens*). The **statute of limitations** (time within which a suit must be commenced) varies for different matters in New York State:

- To sue a governmental agency: notice of claim within 90 days
- To recover real property: 10 years
- Contracts, foreclosures, fraud: 6 years
- Personal or property injury, malpractice (other than dental and medical): 3 years
- Medical or dental malpractice: 2½ years (1 year after discovery of a foreign object in the body)

■ Assault, battery, false imprisonment, right of privacy, libel and slander:
1 year

As detailed in Chapter 5, a mechanic's lien must be filed within four months
of completion of work on a single dwelling, eight months on other buildings.

■ SUMMARY

The seven sources of law in the United States are the U.S. Constitution, laws
passed by Congress, federal regulations, state constitutions, laws passed by
state legislatures, local ordinances, and court decisions.

Common law in the United States evolved predominantly from custom and
usage in England. Gradually the basis of common law expanded to include
prior court decisions as well as custom. Much of real property law is founded
in common law.

Under the Uniform Commercial Code, security interests in chattels must be
recorded using a security agreement and financing statement.

Commercial paper, or negotiable instruments, refers to written promises or
orders to pay money that may be transferred from one person to another. The
Uniform Commercial Code divides commercial paper into notes, drafts,
checks, and certificates of deposit. Commercial paper must be in writing,
signed by the maker or drawer, payable either to bearer or a specific payee,
for a specific sum of money, at a definite time or on demand. It may be
transferred by four types of endorsement: blank, restrictive, special, or qualified.

A partnership is an association of two or more persons to carry on a business
for profit as co-owners. Profit and loss are passed directly through to individual
partners for taxation. Partners have unlimited individual liability for the
partnership's debts.

A corporation is a legal person owned by any number of shareholders who
have limited individual liability for the corporation's debts. It is formed
through the approval of a certificate of incorporation by the secretary of state.
A board of directors, elected by the shareholders, selects officers to manage
the business.

Organization as an S corporation, limited liability company, or limited liability
partnership offers the liability protection of a corporation without the burden
of double taxation.

The federal court system includes district courts, specialized courts, courts of
review, and the Supreme Court. New York State has four federal judicial
district courts, which originate federal cases. Appeals from this state are heard
by the second circuit court of appeals.

New York's lowest court of general jurisdiction is the supreme court. Small claims courts are courts of local jurisdiction for the prompt and informal treatment of disputes. Appeals from lower courts are handled by the appellate divisions of the supreme court. The highest court in the state is the court of appeals.

Criminal law covers acts that injure society or the state; civil law is concerned with torts, the injuries one person does another. Torts may be against a person or against property. Civil lawsuits are intended to recompense the injured party.

The process of civil litigation begins with the filing of a complaint by the plaintiff and a summons to the defendant, who files an answer. Pretrial procedures involve discovery through depositions, interrogatories, and the production of documents. Last-minute requests may include a motion for judgment on the pleadings or summary judgment. A pretrial hearing or settlement conference may bring the parties to agreement before trial.

The trial itself involves jury selection, opening statements, the plaintiff's case followed by the defendant's case, rebuttal and rejoinder, closing arguments, and the judge's instructions to the jury. Jury deliberation is followed by the verdict and judgment.

Less costly, time-consuming, and expensive than litigation are arbitration, in which the arbitrator's decision is usually binding on both parties, and mediation, which involves a skilled attempt to bring the parties into agreement.

Bankruptcy is a federal proceeding through which a debtor seeks relief from overwhelming financial problems. Chapter 7 provides for immediate liquidation of debts, Chapter 11 for reorganization or the orderly winding up of businesses, and Chapter 13 for gradual payment over a period of time, either in part or in full, by individual debtors.

A decedent's estate is settled by a personal representative, either an executor named in a will or an administrator appointed by the court. The executor inventories the estate, administers it, collects debts and pays claims, divides the assets, and distributes them to heirs. Federal and state governments levy estate taxes.

No-fault divorce is available in New York State after a year's living apart under a separation agreement or court decree. The court uses its judgment in ordering equitable distribution of marital property.

Under the statute of limitations, various time limits apply for bringing suit for different types of damage.

QUESTIONS

1. The parties are not legally bound when a dispute is settled by
   a. litigation.
   b. arbitration.
   c. laches.
   d. mediation.

2. Clifford Buntsen had a real estate brokerage in partnership with his brother Clint, who died leaving everything to Clint's wife, Brenda. Clifford is concerned because his sister-in-law is licensed only as a salesperson. In this situation
   a. Brenda must take over Clint's broker's license.
   b. Clint's death immediately dissolves the partnership.
   c. Brenda has lost her license.
   d. Clifford becomes full owner automatically on his brother's death.

3. To be negotiable, an instrument must
   a. mention a consideration.
   b. conform with Chapter 11 rules.
   c. mention a specific sum of money.
   d. qualify for dissolution.

4. The debtor who has filed for bankruptcy is still required to pay
   a. credit card debt.
   b. child support.
   c. car loans.
   d. past utility bills.

5. The Uniform Commercial Code covers
   a. bequests.
   b. realty.
   c. chattels.
   d. services.

6. A REIT is a form of
   a. litigation.
   b. debt consolidation.
   c. equitable distribution.
   d. investment.

7. Co-owners have no individual liability for the debt of a
   a. corporation.
   b. partnership.
   c. private offering.
   d. marital deduction.

8. The general partner has unlimited liability in a
   a. corporation.
   b. real estate investment trust.
   c. limited partnership.
   d. closely held corporation.

9. Most federal lawsuits and prosecution for federal crimes originate in the
   a. supreme court.
   b. court of claims.
   c. district court.
   d. court of appeals.

10. New York State's highest court is the
    a. supreme court.
    b. court of claims.
    c. district court.
    d. court of appeals.

11. Disputes of limited dollar value may be settled at nominal cost and without the use of lawyers in the
    a. small claims court.
    b. court of claims.
    c. civil court.
    d. justice court.

12. When a property owner facing foreclosure files for bankruptcy, the foreclosure
    a. is automatically stopped.
    b. proceeds against the trustee.
    c. requires permission from the creditors' committee to continue.
    d. may never be pursued.

13. Slander, libel, assault, and battery are types of torts known as
    a. negligence.
    b. wrongs against property.
    c. wrongs against the person.
    d. strict liability.

14. A court order forbidding a certain activity is known as
    a. specific performance.
    b. an injunction.
    c. conversion.
    d. a rejoinder.

15. Legal relief through the immediate canceling of most debts can be sought through which form of bankruptcy?

    a. Chapter 26
    b. Chapter 7
    c. Chapter 11
    d. Chapter 13

16. The debtor who files bankruptcy is allowed to keep

    a. household furnishings.
    b. income-producing real estate.
    c. a vacation home worth up to $20,000.
    d. income tax refunds.

17. Bankruptcy proceedings are heard in

    a. federal court.
    b. small claims court.
    c. surrogate court.
    d. family court.

18. The personal representative who handles a decedent's estate may be a(n)

    a. referee.
    b. administrator.
    c. plaintiff.
    d. proxy.

19. Federal tax law provides that one spouse may give another

    a. any amount without gift taxes due.
    b. up to $250,000 without gift taxes due.
    c. no more than $250,000 tax-free during a lifetime.
    d. up to $20,000 tax-free in any year.

20. New York's estate tax has always allowed a spouse to inherit without any estate tax due

    a. any amount.
    b. one-half the estate.
    c. $675,000.
    d. up to $250,000.

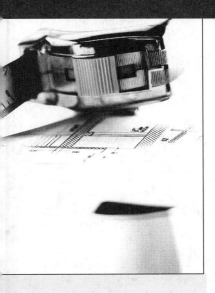

23

CONSTRUCTION AND DEVELOPMENT

Farmer Jensen's widow has been offered a substantial amount for their land, which includes half a mile of road frontage. She has calculated how many lots a subdivider could get from the acreage and how much those lots would sell for. Why not just sell off lots herself, she wonders, and end up with much more money? How hard can it be?

Subdivision and development is a complex branch of real estate involving specialized knowledge, some financial risk, and compliance with ever-increasing state, federal, and local regulation.

■ KEY TERMS

board of directors
board of managers
bylaws
common elements
completion bond
conversions
covenants, conditions, and restrictions (CC&Rs)
curvilinear system
declaration
density zoning
Department of Environmental Conservation (DEC)

developer
disclosure statement
environmental impact studies
eviction plan
gridiron pattern
HVAC
impact fees
Interstate Land Sales Full Disclosure Act
noneviction plan
planned unit development (PUD)
planning board

plat of subdivision
preliminary prospectus
proprietary lease
public offering
red herring
reserves
sponsor
subdivider
subdivision
time-sharing
town house
wetland survey

■ CONSTRUCTION STANDARDS

All real estate agents should be aware of the various sources of construction standards. These standards are established at many levels of government and by a variety of agencies.

Federal Agencies

Federal regulatory agencies include the Department of Housing and Urban Development (HUD), the Army Corps of Engineers, and the Environmental Protection Agency.

The *Department of Housing and Urban Development (HUD)* establishes construction standards for homes that in some way are funded through HUD programs; for instance, homes that are financed with FHA funds.

The *Army Corps of Engineers* regulates certain waterways and drainage into them. These regulations affect building sites and the manner in which homes may be constructed.

The *Environmental Protection Agency* has established standards for the protection of the environment. One of the major effects of these standards has been a general increase in the time and money required to plan and secure the necessary approvals for new developments.

State Agencies

New York State regulates minimum building standards and requires that various codes and regulations be followed, including building codes, fire codes, sanitary regulations, and environmental requirements. The state also has different code requirements for special types of construction, such as schools (for example, a state inspector must inspect schools for compliance each year).

The various state codes and other regulations are *minimum standards*. Local counties and municipalities may require stricter standards. For instance, a particular county code may require sprinkler systems in all new residential construction, even though the state code does not. The enforcement of the state codes is largely carried out on a local basis (by county or municipal inspectors), but the state agency also may become involved in enforcement.

The New York State *Board of Fire Underwriters* sets standards for electrical service systems in all buildings. District inspectors enforce the Board's electrical code.

The New York State *Department of Transportation* regulates traffic and must authorize any curb cuts onto a state highway. Naturally, transportation, ingress onto, and egress from state highways are important considerations for any type of development, especially commercial and large residential developments.

The New York State Department of State (DOS) is responsible for the *Coastal Zone Management Program*. Any project on the coast, navigable rivers, lakes, or islands, such as projects in Long Island Sound, must have DOS approval.

DOS is also responsible for the *Local Waterfront Revitalization Program (LWRP)*. The DOS Office for Local Government Services oversees this program and is a resource for local officials.

Regional Agencies

The counties of Nassau, Putnam, Suffolk, Rockland, and Westchester, plus the city of New York, are under some regulation from the *Metropolitan Transportation Authority (MTA)*. The MTA has taxing powers and controls air rights as well as land rights to all properties within these counties.

■ **EXAMPLE:** The owner of an office building wanted to build a pedestrian bridge over the adjacent railroad tracks to provide more convenient access to his building from the parking lot for his tenants. To do so, he had to acquire air rights over the tracks and install a prefabricated pedestrian bridge to MTA specifications and with the supervision of MTA personnel. He also had to get approvals from Penn Central (the landowner), from the local Planning Board, and from the Zoning Board of Appeals.

New York City. The *New York City Department of Environmental Protection (DEP)* has regulatory powers over New York City's water supply system, from upstate down through the aqueducts and reservoirs and the extensive drainage basins. Land in several counties is included in New York City's watershed. The New York City DEP actually stopped the construction of a modest subdivision that had already received all final approvals from the county board of health and the local planning board, based on its effect on the water supply system (Somers, N.Y.).

Counties. *County boards of health* have jurisdiction over sanitary systems and facilities; local water supplies (water potability); food purveyors or suppliers, and so forth.

County planning boards are largely advisory but can establish certain reporting requirements and intermunicipal standards. In more rural counties, they exercise more authority.

Local municipalities. Most municipalities have a building department that is responsible for ensuring that minimum standards of construction are met. The building department issues a *certificate of occupancy (C of O)* when the construction is completed to its satisfaction. Lenders sometimes require a C of O on resale properties as well as on new construction. In some jurisdictions a *certificate of compliance (C of C)* is issued to indicate that the structure meets certain standards, particularly those regarding safety.

Before a building inspector may issue a C of O on a newly constructed building, the inspector must have proof that all other required permits have been issued, such as permits from the Board of Health; from the Board of Fire Underwriters; and for highway curb cuts, blasting, excavation, tree cutting, and so on. Wetlands review boards, conservation review boards, environmental review boards, architectural review boards, or historical district commissions or fire marshals also may need to inspect and approve a project.

Minimum construction standards offer a consumer some assurance of safety and quality. However, building inspectors are not expert on all matters, and their inspections only assure the consumer that *minimum* standards have been met, not that *higher* standards of quality or the parties' contractual standards have been met.

All the various permit processes, including any required inspections, could directly increase the cost of construction. In some areas the preconstruction permit process for even a small subdivision can take up to ten years and may include exorbitant costs for all kinds of specialists, such as engineers and architects, who must review and alter the plans to meet the demands of local and state agencies. The permit process poses a financial drain on the developer, who must continue to pay the property taxes as well as the other expenses of the permit process while receiving no return on his or her investment. In turn, these expenses drive up the final purchase cost to the homebuyer.

■ THE ROLE OF THE REAL ESTATE AGENT

Real estate agents must be knowledgeable about their products; that is, the property and its surrounding area, including any geographic and topographic peculiarities. When listing a property, agents must exercise *due diligence* when inspecting the premises. In addition to calculating the square footage and describing the style, acreage, and location of the property, the agent should take note of its general condition, including the condition of the roof; interior and exterior siding; cracks in any masonry (chimney, foundation, porches); broken windows; the type and condition of heating and cooling systems; septic or sewer systems; and the water supply (whether well, municipal, or private). Some of this information is readily obtained by a visible inspection; some must be obtained from the owner.

An agent should avoid making any judgment or statement that could cause trouble later or even result in a lawsuit.

An astute agent will use a checklist or the a seller's disclosure form in addition to the listing form. The more information available to the agent, the smoother the sales transaction. Recommending that the buyer use a qualified inspector is a prudent precaution.

■ BUILDING INSPECTIONS

Various building inspections are required for new construction, including inspections of the

- footing forms;
- foundation;
- framing;
- roof;
- insulation;
- sheetrock;
- electrical system;

T A B L E   23.1

New Home Construction Schedule

Preliminary work: Site engineering, evaluation, preliminary plan, environmental review, etc., county and local agency reviews, signatures, and filing of plan. Obtain financing. Site development.

Construction schedule:

Building and other permits	Insulation
Surveyor stakes out lot and house	Drywall, hanging and finishing
Excavator digs basement	Mason pours concrete floors
Plumber installs sanitary sewer/water service	Interior trim
Building inspector inspects sewer or County Board of Health inspects septic system	Interior painting
	Kitchen cabinets and vanities
Excavator backfills sewer/water trench and digs trench for footings	Ceramic tile walls and floors
	Finish flooring—hardwood, vinyl
Mason forms the footings and pours concrete footings; lays up concrete block walls or pours concrete foundation	Finish plumbing, set fixtures
	Finish heating
Framer sets steel beams and columns	Finish electrical, fixtures, switches
Framer frames house	Electrical inspection—final
Roofing	Mirror/shower doors
Rough HVAC	Storms and screens
Rough plumbing and heating	Blacktop
Rough electric, security, cable TV, phone	Landscaping
Backfill basement walls after framing	Appliances
Building inspector reviews framing, plumbing, and heating	Cleanup
Electric inspection, rough wiring	Certificate of Occupancy inspection
Simultaneous with other work:	Surveyor prepares instrument survey "as built"
Concrete block wall dampproofing	Building department issues Certificate of Occupancy
Box out driveway and spread gravel	Buyer reviews and does a final inspection prior to closing and prepares a punch list if necessary
Mason builds fireplace	
Mason lays up exterior brick or stone	Close on title
Set windows, do exterior siding	
Exterior painting/staining	
Gutters, leaders, garage doors	

- plumbing system and HVAC systems; and
- all hook-ups including water and sewer.

Table 23.1 is a sample schedule of procedures to be followed when construction of a new house is undertaken.

Professional home inspections performed for potential buyers or for sellers generally include

- systems: heating, air-conditioning, septic or sewer, electric, and plumbing;
- water: potability and occasionally other (radon, lead);
- storm windows and screens;
- general condition;
- radon, lead, asbestos;
- insulation;
- termites, dry rot; and
- roof, grading, and decks/porches.

A seller would be wise to have a professional inspection performed before marketing the property. Any defects that might kill the sale or cause a last-minute problem for closing can be corrected in advance. The sale price and marketability of the property are directly affected by its condition.

A buyer always should have a professional inspection done before committing to a purchase, even for new construction. Serious defects affect the marketability and value of the property.

Unlike some other states, New York does not license home inspectors. Many, however, are licensed engineers. Some belong to the American Society of Home Inspectors (ASHI), which requires training, experience, and examinations from its members.

■ SUBDIVISION

Subdivision refers to the process of dividing a single tract of land into smaller parcels. Land in large tracts must receive special attention before it can be converted into sites for homes, stores, or other uses. A **subdivider** buys undeveloped acreage and divides it into smaller lots for sale to individuals or developers or for the subdivider's own use. A **developer** (who also may be a subdivider) builds homes or other buildings on the lots and sells them. Developing is generally a much more extensive activity than subdividing. A developer may have a sales staff or may use the services of local real estate brokerage firms.

Restrictions on Land Use

No uniform city planning and land development legislation affects the entire country. Most laws governing subdividing and land planning are controlled by state and local government bodies. New York State sets standards for villages, cities, and towns. Local governments may adopt more restrictive policies. *Article 9-A* of New York's *Real Property Law* governs subdivision.

A subdivision development plan must comply with any overall local master plan adopted by the county, city, village, or town. The developer must consider zoning laws and land-use restrictions adopted for health and safety purposes. Basic city plan and zoning requirements are not inflexible, but long, expensive, and frequently complicated hearings are usually required before alterations can be authorized. Chapter 12 includes details on zoning board of appeals, and the process for securing area and use variances.

Most villages, cities, and other areas incorporated under state laws have **planning boards** and/or *planning commissioners*. Communities establish strict criteria before approving new subdivisions. Frequently required are *dedication* of land for streets, schools, and parks; assurance by *bonding* that sewer and street costs will be paid; and *compliance* with zoning ordinances governing use and lot size and with fire and safety ordinances.

Zoning ordinances that systematically exclude certain groups or classes of people from certain areas are *exclusionary* and can be considered discriminatory as well as a violation of a person's right to travel interstate, as provided by the U.S. Constitution.

Local authorities usually require that land planners submit information on how they intend to satisfy sewage disposal and water supply requirements. Developments with septic tank installation may first require a *percolation test* of the soil's absorption and drainage capacities. A planner usually will have to submit an *environmental impact report*.

Regulatory taking occurs when rules, regulations, or ordinances essentially deprive a property owner of the use or the fair return on the value of the owner's property. In these circumstances, the rules, regulations, or ordinances can be considered confiscatory and therefore unlawful or unreasonable.

Environmental Regulations

The Environmental Protection Agency (EPA) has identified 403 chemicals as highly toxic, and innocent future purchasers of land can be held liable. Previous use of land being considered for development should be carefully investigated at the outset. Chemical companies, dry cleaners, old farms with trash dumps or underground gas tanks, airports, warehouses, gas stations, and factories of all sorts may have produced potentially dangerous chemical wastes.

Problems faced by unaware future owners could include liability for cleanup, liability for health problems, unfavorable publicity, and restrictions on future use of the land. More and more, developers are turning to specialists trained in environmental compliance and documentation.

In the early 1990s New York directed each county clerk or recording officer to compile an index of past and present owners and operators of sites listed on the *Inactive Hazardous Waste Registry*.

The New York State Environmental Quality Act is commonly referred to as SEQRA. Every application to a planning board or a zoning board of appeals must be viewed in light of its environmental impact. Classifications of proposed actions are

- *Type I*—An *environmental impact statement (EIS)* is required unless the applicant demonstrates conclusively that one is not needed. The next step is to fill out a Preliminary Environmental Review Form (PERF).
- *Type II* or *Exempt Action*—No environmental impact statement is needed.
- *Unlisted Action*—Pending analysis of further information, an environmental impact statement may be required. An environmental assessment form must be prepared.

Most applications to a zoning board of appeals are considered Type II or exempt. Most applicants for subdivision or development before a planning board are required to prepare at least a short form. Larger projects require an EIS and could include hydrologic studies, traffic impact, population density, and even light pollution.

In some instances construction requires a permit from the New York **Department of Environmental Conservation (DEC).** Permits are necessary for work in a protected wetland or the 100-foot buffer zone around a wetland. Depending on the circumstances, permits may be needed for work that disturbs the banks of streams, for using some water supplies, for sewage discharges, and for sewer extensions. The sale of more than 1,000 tons of fill dirt or gravel per year requires a DEC mining permit. **Environmental impact studies** of varying complexity may be required when the parcel is ruled environmentally sensitive—large projects or those located on floodplains, wetlands, steep slopes, or other environmentally fragile areas.

A **wetland survey** is based on the EPA and DEC statutes and is coordinated by the U.S. Army Corps of Engineers. A wetland survey examines everything from types of plant and animal life to soil composition. Based on the findings, a parcel of land may or may not be classified as wetlands, with severe restrictions on development.

Value of Land for Subdivision

> Value for subdivision depends on land-use restrictions, nature and location of the land, availability of services, and access.

The value of a given tract of land for subdivision purposes depends on many factors. Government land-use restrictions such as minimum lot size requirements, use restrictions, and building standards limit the type of development that is possible for a given tract of land. The nature of the land itself is also a factor, particularly if significant portions of the tract are unbuildable owing to soil conditions, wetlands, slopes, or other considerations.

Location is always a prime consideration in determining real estate value as well. Land will be more valuable for subdivision purposes if it is in a desirable location in an area with strong economic growth and an increasing population.

The availability of utility services and access roads is another factor that has a major impact on the cost and practicality of development.

■ THE PROCESS OF SUBDIVISION

The process of subdivision involves three distinct stages of development: *initial planning, final planning,* and *disposition* or *start-up*.

During the *initial planning stage* the subdivider seeks raw land in a suitable area. The property is analyzed for *highest and best use,* and preliminary subdivision plans are drawn up. Close contact starts with local planning officials. If the project requires zoning variances, negotiation begins along these lines. The subdivider also locates financial backers and initiates marketing strategies.

In the *final planning stage,* plans are prepared, approval of the **plat of subdivision** is sought from local (and, if necessary, state and federal) officials, financing is actually obtained, the land is purchased, final budgets are prepared, and marketing programs are designed.

Once final approvals are granted by all the various government agencies, the subdivider may then become the developer (or contractor), sell to a developer, or enter into a joint venture with a contractor.

The *disposition,* or *start-up,* carries the subdividing process to a conclusion. Subdivision plans are recorded with local officials, and streets, sewers, and utilities are installed. Buildings, open parks, and recreational areas are constructed and landscaped if they are part of the subdivision plan. Marketing programs then are initiated, and title to the individual parcels of subdivided land is transferred as the lots or buildings are sold or leased.

■ COSTS AND FINANCING

Subdivision development involves a range of different costs. In addition to the direct costs of acquiring the land and making improvements such as clearing, grading, roads, and utilities, there are indirect costs for subdivision and development permit fees and professional fees for engineers, attorneys, and marketing specialists. A large development also may be charged **impact fees,** intended to help a community cope with increased demand for schools, roads, and other services. If approval of the subdivision is contingent on the subdivider's making public improvements such as roads or sewers, there is usually a requirement to obtain a **completion bond** guaranteeing completion of these improvements.

With all of the costs involved, it is common for subdivision developers to rely on borrowed funds to help finance a project. Development financing is secured by a mortgage lien against the entire project. When a new lot or unit is first sold, the buyer needs to be sure that it is no longer covered by any blanket mortgage lien that applied to the overall project. Blanket mortgage liens commonly have lot release provisions that allow clear title to be passed to a buyer in these situations.

■ RESTRICTIVE COVENANTS

Often a subdivider creates and records deed restrictions as a means of *controlling and maintaining the desirable quality and character of the subdivision*. Deed restrictions can be set forth in a separate document, which is recorded later, or they can be included in the subdivision plat. When a separate document is used, that document is generally called a *declaration of restrictions*.

Sometimes a deed restriction and a zoning provision cover the same subject. When this happens, the more limiting restriction prevails. For example, if deed restrictions require that subdivision lots be used only for single-family residences but local zoning ordinances allow duplexes, the single-family restriction found in the declaration of restrictions will govern the situation and can be enforced by subdivision residents.

To be valid, a deed restriction must be both reasonable and for the benefit of neighboring owners. Deed restrictions are binding on all future property owners in that subdivision. Common types of deed restrictions include the use to which the land may be put, the type of construction, height, setbacks, square footage and cost, and parking limitations. "No off-road or recreational vehicle may be parked on the subdivision streets" is an example. Some restrictions have a time limitation; for example, "effective for a period of 25 years from this date."

FIGURE   23.1

Street Patterns

Enforcement of Deed Restrictions

Neighboring lot owners may apply to a court to prevent a neighbor from violating subdivision deed restrictions. In New York State, lot owners have up to two years from the completion of the alteration or construction in which to object. After that time they lose their right through *laches*, the failure to assert a right in time.

Types of Subdivisions and Subdivision Density

Zoning ordinances often include population density requirements as well as minimum lot sizes. A zoning restriction, for example, may set the minimum lot area on which a subdivider can build a single-family housing unit at 10,000 square feet. The developer would be able to build four houses per acre. Many zoning authorities now establish special **density zoning** standards for certain subdivisions. **Density zoning** ordinances restrict the average maximum number of houses per acre that may be built within a particular subdivision. If the area is density-zoned at an average maximum of four houses per acre, for example, by clustering building lots the developer is free to achieve an open effect.

Street patterns.   By varying street patterns and clustering housing units, a subdivider can dramatically increase the amount of open and recreational space in a development. Some of these patterns are illustrated in Figure 23.1.

The **gridiron pattern** evolved out of the government rectangular survey system. Featuring large lots, wide streets, and limited-use service alleys, the system works reasonably well. It can result in busy streets and monotonous neighborhoods, however, and sometimes provides little or no open, park, or recreational space. The **curvilinear system** integrates major arteries of travel with smaller secondary and cul-de-sac streets carrying minor traffic. In addition, small open parks are often provided at intersections. The *loop* features serpentine streets that wind through the development, and the *radius pattern* is built on a series of cul-de-sacs that radiate from the main street.

Clustering for open space.   By slightly reducing lot sizes and clustering them around varying street patterns, a developer can house as many people in the same area as could be done using traditional subdividing plans, but with substantially increased tracts of open space.

FIGURE   23.2

**Clustered
Subdivision Plan**

🌱 Conventional Gardens 🌱	C̲E̲ Cluster Estates
12,500-square-foot lots	7,500-square-foot lots
368 housing units	366 housing units
1.6 acres of parkland	23.5 acres of parkland
23,200 linear feet of street	17,700 linear feet of street

For example, the first illustration in Figure 23.2 is a plan for a conventionally designed subdivision containing 368 housing units. It leaves only 1.6 acres open for park areas. Contrast this with the second subdivision pictured. Both subdivisions are equal in size and terrain. But when lots are minimally reduced in size and clustered around limited-access, cul-de-sac streets, the number of housing units remains nearly the same (366), with less street area and drastically increased open space (23.5 acres). In addition, with modern building designs this clustered plan could be modified to accommodate 550 patio homes or 1,100 town houses. Cluster housing may take the form of a **planned unit development (PUD),** with some or all of an entire community's land use established by the developer's original plan.

■ LAND-USE REGULATIONS

Local governments pass zoning ordinances to control the use of land and building within designated districts. Zoning regulates such things as use of the land; lot sizes; types of structures permitted; building heights; setbacks (the minimum distance from streets or sidewalks that structures may be built); and density (the number of units that can be built in an area). An important purpose of zoning is to implement a local master plan.

Zoning ordinances generally divide land use into residential, commercial, industrial, vacant, agricultural, open space, institutional, and recreational classifications. Now many communities include cluster zoning and multiple-use zoning, which permit unusual planned unit developments. Zoning and other land-use regulations are discussed in more depth in Chapter 12.

Nonconforming use. When zoning laws are changed, there are usually already-existing buildings that do not conform to the new zoning laws. These buildings are referred to as *nonconforming uses*, and are allowed to continue. However, if the building is destroyed or torn down, any new structure must comply with the current zoning ordinance.

Building Codes

Most cities and towns have enacted ordinances to specify construction standards that must be met during building construction or repair. These are called *building codes*, and they set requirements for kinds of materials, sanitary equipment, electrical wiring, fire prevention standards, and the like. New York has a statewide building code that applies where no local code exists or where local codes are less restrictive.

Interstate Land Sales Full Disclosure Act

The **Interstate Land Sales Full Disclosure Act** requires those engaged in the interstate sale or leasing of 25 or more lots to file a statement of record and register the details of the land with HUD.

The seller also is required to furnish prospective buyers with a property report containing all essential information about the property, such as distance over paved roads to nearby communities, number of homes currently occupied, soil conditions affecting foundations and septic systems, type of title a buyer will receive, and existence of liens. The property report must be given to a prospective purchaser at least three business days before any sales contract is signed.

If a buyer does not receive a property report, the purchaser may cancel such a contract without further liability within two years. Any buyer of land covered by this act has the right to rescind a contract within seven days after signing. If the seller misrepresents the property in any sales promotion, a buyer induced by such a promotion is entitled to sue the seller for civil damages. Failure to comply with the law also may subject a seller to imprisonment and fines.

New York State Subdivided Land Sales Law

New York considers land to be covered by subdivision regulations as soon as a fifth lot is carved from the original parcel. Land sold within New York State on the installment plan by a subdivider and out-of-state land offered for sale in New York in any manner may not be offered for sale until at least two documents have been filed with the Department of State. The first covers the identity and address of the offerer, the names of owners of the land, a statement on the subdivider's previous experience with vacant land, any criminal activity, a description of the land complete with maps, a title statement including any encumbrances or liens, and the terms on which the land will be sold, with a copy of the contract to be used.

The second document is a copy of the offering statement to be furnished to each buyer with a full financial statement of the assets and liabilities of the subdivider; a description of the subdivision and each lot; information on

Condominium Ownership

The owner of unit 4 owns his or her unit, plus an undivided one-fifth share of the elevator, lobby, grounds, and structure.

Elevator

Grounds

Lobby

Condominium

existing liens and encumbrances, existing or proposed utilities and area, community, and recreational facilities; and even the weather conditions of the area, as well as the terms of sale.

A copy of any advertising to be used must be filed with the Department of State. The state allows any purchaser who is not represented by an attorney to cancel a contract within ten days.

In addition, New York's Public Health Laws require that any subdivider offering for sale or rent five or more residential building lots file a map of the proposed subdivision with the Department of Health, showing adequate water supply and sewerage facilities. The department must approve the plan before it can be filed. A development of 50 lots or more must have a central municipal water supply rather than individual wells. (These rules are found in the summary of Article 9-A; see page 408.)

■ CONDOMINIUMS

The buyer of a condominium receives a *deed* conveying *fee simple ownership* of the unit and an undivided interest in the **common elements.** (See Figure 23.3.) The unit itself usually consists of little more than airspace bounded by the innermost layers of construction, often interior drywall.

Chief among the common elements are the land and the exteriors of the buildings. Also common property are foyers; hallways; main walls; basements; elevators; stairwells; heating, plumbing, and electrical systems; and in suburban locations, driveways, private roads, sidewalks, lawns, landscaping, and recreational facilities. In addition, the condominium typically has an underlying loan on the land and common elements.

In most respects the law regards a residential condominium owner as it would the owner of a single detached house. The unit receives an individual tax account number and tax bill and may be mortgaged as a house would be. The owner places a separate insurance policy on the living space. Income tax advantages are identical to those for single homes. Owners are free to sell the property, lease it, give it away, or leave it to heirs. Each unit is financially independent, and if an adjoining unit is foreclosed, no obligation is incurred by the other owners.

Owners are, however, bound by the **bylaws** of an *owners' association* to which all belong. Monthly fees are levied for the maintenance, insurance, and management of common elements. If unpaid, these *common charges* become a lien against the individual unit and even may be enforced by foreclosure. The bylaws also set up **covenants, conditions, and restrictions (CC&Rs),** for example, may prohibit the display of For Sale signs or painting the front door bright red. Owners even may adopt bylaws that restrict leasing of the units.

A condominium is usually managed by an elected **board of managers.** When there are more than 25 units, a board often hires professional management.

Selling Condominiums

The selling of condominiums or town houses is now among the activities covered by a broker's or a salesperson's license. The broker who deals in such properties must be concerned with some items that do not apply to the marketing of single homes. The buyer of a condominium must receive detailed statements about the property, should read the CC&Rs, and must be alerted to any unpaid common charges against the unit. Prospective buyers should also examine the **reserves,** funds set aside to accumulate for large expenses like new roofs or heating units. The sale of a condominium is arranged on a special form of contract.

Although it is most widely used for residential property, condominium ownership is growing for professional buildings, office buildings, and shopping malls.

■ COOPERATIVE OWNERSHIP

Cooperative ownership is common in the New York City metropolitan area and in some resort areas. Under the usual *cooperative arrangement*, title to land and building is held by a *corporation*. Each purchaser of an apartment in the building receives stock in the corporation and a **proprietary lease** for his or her apartment.

Real estate taxes are paid on the whole building by the corporation. A single mortgage, known as the *underlying* or *overlying mortgage*, covers the entire building. Taxes, mortgage interest and principal, and operating and maintenance expenses on the property are shared by the tenants/shareholders as monthly *maintenance charges*. Proprietary leaseholders may individually finance their apartments with a cooperative loan. Most proprietary leases provide that they may not be assigned, transferred, or sublet without the consent of the **board of directors.**

Although cooperative tenants/owners do not actually own an interest in real estate (they own stock, which is *personal property*), they do control the property through their *board of directors*.

One disadvantage of cooperative ownership became particularly evident during the Great Depression and still must be considered. If enough owner/occupants become unable to make prompt payment of their monthly assessments, the corporation may be forced to allow mortgage and tax payments to go unpaid. The entire property could be sold by court order in a foreclosure suit. Such a sale would destroy the interests of all occupant/shareholders, even those who paid their assessments. Accumulation of a substantial reserve fund offers some protection to the cooperative as a whole.

The tenant/owner, not owning actual real estate, may not place a regular mortgage against the unit. Instead shares are pledged against a personal loan. Boards of directors, sensitive to the financial dependence of one tenant on the others, sometimes set down payment requirements that are more stringent than those asked by lending institutions. In some cases they may even refuse prospective tenants unless the purchase is to be made for all cash.

The Internal Revenue Service, however, offers the owner of a cooperative apartment the same income tax treatment as the owner of a condominium or a single home. That portion of maintenance charges that covers property taxes and mortgage interest may be taken as a deduction as long as no more than 20 percent of the cooperative's income comes from nonshareholder sources like rental of commercial space and washing machine concessions. Interest paid on the individual's own loan is treated as mortgage interest would be.

■ CONDOMINIUM/COOPERATIVE CONSTRUCTION AND CONVERSION

Many condominium and cooperative projects, particularly in the New York City area, are **conversions** from rental properties. The sale of any form of shared housing is considered a **public offering** and falls under the jurisdiction of the New York attorney general's office. If the proposal is for a condominium, a **declaration,** together with floor plans for each unit, must be filed with the county clerk. The declaration contains a complete description of the land, building, and individual units. Common elements are described, and the percentage of ownership for each unit is stated. Bylaws also are included.

Whether for new construction or a conversion, the developer or **sponsor** must file a **disclosure statement** (or *offering plan*) with the attorney general's office. The statement includes an architect's or engineer's report of the physical condition of the building; a statement of past and projected expenses; prices for each unit and expected amount of tax deductions; management arrangements; a description of the corporation (if a cooperative); and a sample unit deed (for a condominium). The declaration is forwarded along with the disclosure statement. If the offering is for a cooperative, the disclosure statement includes the form of the proprietary lease.

After it has been reviewed by the attorney general's office, the **preliminary prospectus** for a conversion, or **"red herring,"** is available for inspection by present tenants. At this point it is subject to modification. When a plan is accepted for filing by the attorney general's office (usually within four to six months in the case of a conversion and 30 days in the case of new construction), it is issued as a black book to potential buyers.

Conversion Restrictions

If the property is occupied, special regulations safeguarding the rights of tenants are in effect in New York City and in parts of Westchester, Nassau, and Rockland counties. Under a **noneviction plan** in Westchester, Nassau, and Rockland counties, unless at least 15 percent of present tenants agree to purchase their units, the property may not be converted to condominium or cooperative ownership. In New York City the property may be converted under a noneviction plan if purchase agreements are signed for 15 percent of the apartments (whether by tenants or outsiders). If the sponsor intends to evict present tenants **(eviction plan)** at the expiration of their leases, the requirement is that at least 51 percent of the tenants must evince their intention to purchase. Other communities across the state are eligible to adopt the regulations if they choose. Disabled persons and those older than 62 are exempt from eviction. To encourage tenant participation, the sponsor may offer discounts that frequently average one-third off the list price.

Nonpurchasers may have three-year protection from eviction under an **eviction plan** and tenants in occupancy have a 90-day exclusive right to purchase and other benefits. If the sponsor elects the noneviction (15 percent) route, all those tenants who do not wish to purchase may remain as tenants under whatever rent regulations may be in effect. The sponsor's inside sales staff, working as employees, do not require any real estate license.

■ TOWN HOUSES, PUDS, AND TIME-SHARING

The term **town house,** as it refers to shared housing, describes a type of ownership rather than an architectural style. Although the organization, similar to a *planned unit development,* often takes the form of town houses (attached row houses), it also may refer to attached ranch homes or even to small single dwellings in close proximity to each other.

A town house owner has title to the land beneath the individual unit and owns a share in the common elements, most often in the form of shares in a corporation.

A form of ownership known as **time-sharing** or *vacation ownership* has become popular in resort and vacation areas. The buyer of a time-share receives a fraction of a year's ownership of property, which might be a condominium, town house, single-family detached home, campground, or even a motel. Although the concept is most popular in resort areas such as the Caribbean,

Colorado, Vermont, and Florida, it has been used in Long Island, the Catskills, and a few other areas of New York State.

In New York, time-sharing is regulated under the blue-sky securities statute administered by the Department of Law and the Department of State. Sellers must file a public offering statement, and buyers have a ten-day rescission period in which to withdraw from a contract. Real estate licenses are required of those handling such sales.

■ SUMMARY

A subdivider buys undeveloped acreage, divides it into smaller parcels, and sells it. A land developer builds homes or other improvements on the lots and sells them, either through an in-house sales organization or through local real estate brokerage firms. City planners and land developers, working together, plan whole communities that are later incorporated into cities, towns, or villages.

Land development must generally comply with master land plans adopted by counties, cities, villages, or towns. This may entail approval of land-use plans by local planning boards or commissioners.

Environmental impact studies are generally required and for sensitive areas may involve increasingly detailed environmental audits.

The process of subdivision includes dividing the tract of land into lots and blocks and providing for utility easements, as well as laying out street patterns and widths. A subdivider generally must record a completed plat of subdivision with all necessary approvals of public officials in the county where the land is located. Subdividers usually place restrictions on the use of all lots in a subdivision as a general plan for the benefit of all lot owners.

By varying street patterns and housing density and clustering housing units, a subdivider can dramatically increase the amount of open and recreational space within a development.

Subdivided land sales are regulated on the federal level by the Interstate Land Sales Full Disclosure Act. This law requires that developers engaged in interstate land sales or the leasing of 25 or more units register the details of the land with HUD. Developers must provide prospective purchasers with a property report containing all essential information about the property at least three business days before any sales contract is signed.

Subdivided land sales also are regulated by New York laws. For the sale of subdivided land on an installment basis, and for sale of any out-of-state land offered in New York, documents must be filed in advance with the Department of State and an offering statement furnished to buyers. The sale of any subdivision of five or more lots requires approval of a water and sewerage plan

SUMMARY OF ARTICLE 9-A
OF THE REAL PROPERTY LAW

Subdivided lands. No real estate broker or real estate salesperson should be involved in any way, in the State of New York, with the sale or lease of subdivided lands located within or outside the state, unless the subdivider offering the property for sale or lease has complied with the provisions of Article 9-A of the Real Property Law.

Article 9-A of the Real Property law is designed to protect the residents of New York State in the purchase or lease of subdivided lands located within the State of New York where sold on an installment plan and located outside the State of New York, whether offered on the installment or any other plan, terms and conditions of sale or lease.

Safeguards are inserted into the law to prevent fraud or fraudulent practices that might be employed to include the purchase or lease of vacant subdivided lands. Among such safeguards is the requirement that the subdividers file with the Department of State a statement with substantiating documentation including a certified copy of a map of the subdivided lands and a search of the title to the land reciting in detail all the liens, encumbrances and clouds on the title that may or may not render the title unmarketable.

A subdivider, in addition to the statement required under the law, must file an Offering Statement with the Department of State. The Offering Statement must contain, among other facts, detailed information about the subdivision, including a description of the land, existence of utilities, area, community and recreational facilities, restriction, weather conditions, and financial statement of the subdivider. The Offering Statement must be revised yearly. It must clearly indicate that the Department of State has not passed on the merits of the offering.

No sale or lease of subdivided lands shall be made without prior delivery of an Offering Statement to the prospective customer. Any offer to sell or lease subdivided lands prior to filing both the Offering Statement and the statement constitutes a felony.

Where the land is affected by mortgages or other encumbrances, it is unlawful for the subdivider to sell such vacant lands in the subdivision unless appropriate provisions in the mortgage or lien enable the subdivider to convey valid title to each parcel free of such mortgage or encumbrance. A mortgage on an entire subdivision will usually provide for a release of individual lots from that mortgage on payment of a specified amount of money. If the land is being sold on an installment plan, the law provides that where the amount paid to the subdivider by the purchaser reaches the point where the balance owing is the amount required to release that lot from the mortgage, all monies thereafter received by the seller from the purchaser must be deemed trust funds, be kept in a separate account, and applied only toward clearance of title from the lien of the mortgage.

If, after investigation, the Secretary of State believes that the subdivider is guilty of fraud or that certain sales methods may constitute a fraud on the public, court proceedings to stop these practices may be instituted. The Secretary of State may also withdraw the acceptance previously granted and may order that all sales and advertising in New York State stop.

The law, as amended, also makes it mandatory that all advertising prior to publication be submitted to the Department for acceptance for filing. Misrepresentations in the sale or lease of subdivided lands constitute a misdemeanor.

The law now also provides that in every contract of sale or lease of subdivided lands, if the purchaser or lessee is not represented by an attorney, he or she has a ten-day cancellation privilege.

Sales may not be made based on the representation that the purchase of the property is a good investment, that the purchaser will or may make money on the transaction, or that the property can be readily sold. Nothing may be promised that is not contained in the written contract and offering Statement.

by the Department of Health, and 50 or more lots requires a central municipal water system.

Condominium and cooperative arrangements for homeowning are becoming more frequent due to scarcity of land, the need for economy of construction and operation, and changing lifestyles. Both terms refer to forms of ownership and not to the type of buildings involved.

Condominiums provide fee simple ownership of real property: the living unit and an undivided interest in common elements. Owners may mortgage their units, and they receive individual tax bills and arrange homeowner's insurance. Owners bear no direct financial liability for adjoining units. Management of common elements is administered by a homeowners' association, which levies monthly fees. Bylaws provide regulations binding all owners in the form of covenants, conditions, and restrictions.

The owner of a cooperative apartment receives personal property: shares in a corporation that owns the entire building and a proprietary lease to an apartment. Financing is arranged through a single mortgage on the entire property; individual financing comes through personal loans. Each owner shares responsibility for the debts of the corporation. The corporation usually has the right to reject prospective buyers.

Plans for construction or conversion of a condominium or cooperative must be filed with the county recorder and reviewed by the attorney general's office. In the New York City area at least 15 percent of present tenants must agree to buy their apartments before conversion may take place. Regulations in some communities may differ. Certain disabled persons and senior citizens are exempt from eviction in any case.

A town house development involves fee simple ownership of the living unit and the land beneath it. All other land and common elements are owned by a homeowners' association, in which owners are members. Time-sharing involves the purchase of a resort or vacation property for a portion of the year.

Subdivision regulations are complex and require a good deal of expertise. Any property owner who wishes to subdivide and/or develop his or her land must be aware of these regulations and comply with all of them. In many cases, it is a safer course of action to sell the property to an experienced developer.

QUESTIONS

1. In New York State, building plans must be signed by a
   a. fire underwriter.
   b. licensed architect or engineer.
   c. site planner.
   d. primary contractor.

2. Joe Builder is constructing a new single-family residence. The local building inspector must inspect and certify
   a. all electrical systems.
   b. all general construction.
   c. the septic system.
   d. the financing.

3. Which of the following would *not* benefit from a professional house inspection?
   a. The buyer
   b. The seller
   c. The broker
   d. The Department of State

4. New York State law requires
   a. minimum building and electrical standards.
   b. written and signed property condition disclosures.
   c. professional property inspections.
   d. that new houses have underground wiring.

5. Overall subdivision guidelines are set by
   a. the federal government.
   b. New York State.
   c. the Department of Health.
   d. the Department of Environmental Conservation.

6. Local governments often regulate subdivision through their
   a. planning boards.
   b. conservationists.
   c. site planners.
   d. building inspectors.

7. A map illustrating the sizes and locations of streets and lots in a subdivision is called a
   a. gridiron pattern.
   b. survey.
   c. plat of subdivision.
   d. property report.

8. A subdivider turns over streets to public ownership through
   a. development
   b. eminent domain.
   c. dedication.
   d. condemnation.

9. Deed restrictions are usually placed on an entire subdivision by the
   a. building inspector.
   b. state government.
   c. planning board.
   d. subdivider.

10. The Marshes received a property report and consulted a lawyer before they signed a contract to buy a lot in a retirement community in Florida covered by the Interstate Land Sales Full Disclosure Act. They may change their minds and cancel the contract within
    a. seven days.
    b. ten days.
    c. two years.
    d. zero days; they may not cancel.

11. Separate tax account numbers, insurance policies, and mortgages are available to the owners of
    a. cooperative apartments.
    b. condominiums.
    c. neither co-ops nor apartments.
    d. both co-ops and apartments.

12. Condominium common elements may include

   a. closets.
   b. kitchen equipment.
   c. personal property.
   d. elevators.

13. The owner of a cooperative apartment receives

   a. a deed.
   b. a property tax bill.
   c. a life estate.
   d. shares in a corporation.

14. The land immediately under the unit is owned individually in a

   a. condominium.   c. town house.
   b. cooperative.   d. time-share.

15. The changing of a rental building into shared ownership is called

   a. conversion.   c. disclosure.
   b. declaration.   d. offering.

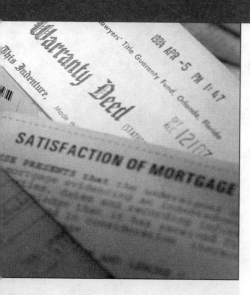

24

CONVEYANCE OF REAL PROPERTY

Every year since Henry can remember, his father planted a vegetable garden in the extra lot attached to their house. After his father died last year, Henry planted a garden himself. Last week he looked over the lot size on his property tax bill and discovered he is not being taxed for the extra land. He investigated and found out the lot really belonged to someone who moved to Alaska and later died. How can Henry gain title to that extra lot? Or does he already own it?

A parcel of real estate may be transferred from one owner to another (alienated) in a number of different ways. It may be given voluntarily by sale, devise, or gift or it may be taken involuntarily by operation of law. In a way, the process of alienation is the central point of all of a real estate broker's activity.

■ **KEY TERMS**

adverse possession	escheat	last will and testament
condemnation	executor	probate
dedication	heir	testate
descent	intestate	testator/testatrix
devise	involuntary alienation	voluntary alienation

■ TITLE

Title to real estate means the right to or ownership of the land; in addition it represents the *evidence* of ownership. The term *title* has two functions. It represents the "bundle of rights" the owner possesses in the real estate and denotes the facts that, if proved, would enable a person to recover or retain ownership or possession of a parcel of real estate.

Title to real estate in New York may be transferred during an owner's lifetime by *voluntary alienation* or *involuntary alienation*, and after an owner's death by *will* or *descent*.

■ VOLUNTARY ALIENATION

There are four forms of **voluntary alienation:** *sales, gift, dedication,* and *grant.* In a sale, property is transferred from a seller to a buyer in exchange for something of value, known as *consideration.* A transfer without something of value in return (without consideration) is a gift. To sell property or give it to someone, the owner uses a deed of conveyance.

FOUR FORMS OF VOLUNTARY ALIENATION:

1. Sale
2. Gift
3. Dedication
4. Grant

The word *dedication* is used for a gift from a landowner to the government. A developer passes ownership of subdivision lands earmarked for streets and roads to a city, town, or village by dedicating the streets. **Dedications** are often required as a condition of subdivision approval. They benefit the subdivider by allowing development of public access and utilities for the subdivision and relieving the subdivider of responsibility for maintenance, and they benefit the local government by providing lands for these purposes at no cost to taxpayers.

In contrast to dedication, land owned by the government may be transferred to individuals through *public grant,* as when public land (still available in Alaska, for example) is transferred to persons who have created homesteads on it.

■ INVOLUNTARY ALIENATION

Title to property can be transferred during the owner's lifetime by **involuntary alienation,** without the owner's consent. Land may be taken for public use (condemnation) or it may be sold at foreclosure of an unpaid lien (mortgage, judgment, property taxes). Natural processes such as *erosion* and *accretion* can result in the gain or loss of title to land, and title may also transfer involuntarily by *partition* or *adverse possession.*

Condemnation

Federal, state, and local governments; school boards; some government agencies; and certain public and quasi-public corporations and utilities (railroads and gas and electric companies) have the power of *eminent domain.* Private property may be taken for public use through a *suit for* **condemnation.** Eminent domain may be exercised only when a court determines that the use is for the benefit of the public and that equitable (just) compensation, as set by the court, will be paid to the owner. Whenever private property is taken in New

York, the owner is given the opportunity to challenge in court the amount of money offered. Former property owners are entitled to a 90-day grace period when they continue to occupy the property for residential purposes after state acquisition.

Foreclosure

Land also may be transferred without an owner's consent to satisfy debts contracted by the owner. In such cases the debt is foreclosed, the property is sold, and the proceeds of the sale are applied to pay off the debt. Debts that could be foreclosed include mortgage loans, real estate taxes, mechanics' liens, or general judgments against the property owner.

Natural Processes

> Involuntary alienation can occur by condemnation, foreclosure, natural processes, partition, or adverse possession.

In addition to the involuntary transfer of land by legal processes, land may be transferred by natural forces. Owners of land bordering on rivers, lakes, and other bodies of water may acquire additional land through the process of *accretion*, the slow accumulation of soil, rock, or other matter deposited by the movement of water on an owner's property. The opposite of accretion is *erosion*, the gradual wearing away of land by the action of water and wind. In addition, property may be lost through *avulsion*, the sudden tearing away of land by natural means such as earthquakes or tidal waves.

Partition

A partition is a legal proceeding used to divide a property that is jointly owned by two or more persons, such as in a joint tenancy or tenancy in common. If co-tenants cannot agree on the use or disposition of the property, one of them may start a *partition proceeding* in court. If possible, the court will attempt to physically divide the property among the co-owners, but if this is not possible, the court may order the property to be sold and the proceeds of sale to be distributed among the co-owners in proportion to their shares of ownership.

Adverse Possession

Adverse possession is another means of involuntary transfer. An owner who does not use his or her land or does not inspect it for a number of years may lose title to another person who has some claim to the land, takes possession, and, most important, uses the land. In New York a person may acquire title by adverse possession to land owned by another by the continuous, open, notorious, hostile, and exclusive occupation of the property for *ten years*. After that time the user may perfect the claim of title to land by adverse possession by bringing a court suit to quiet title.

Through a process known as *tacking*, continuous periods of adverse possession may be combined by successive users, thus enabling a person who had not been in possession for the entire ten years to establish a claim of adverse possession. The process is not automatic; legal action is necessary to *perfect* the claim. This is known as an *action to quiet title*, which is used in cases where the ownership of land is in dispute. The original owner may defend title by proving that he or she objected to the unauthorized use of the land or on the other hand specifically gave permission for the use. Adverse possession of publicly owned property is not possible.

■ TRANSFER OF A DECEASED PERSON'S PROPERTY

Even the person who dies (the decedent) transfers property in one of two ways: either voluntarily (through a will) or involuntarily (through **descent** or **escheat**). Every state has a law known as the *statute of descent and distribution.* When a person dies **intestate** (without a valid will), the decedent's real estate and personal property pass to the spouse or *natural* **heirs** according to this statute. In effect the state makes a will for such decedents. In contrast a person who dies **testate** has prepared a will indicating the way his or her property will be disposed of after death.

Legally, when a person dies, title to his or her real estate immediately passes either to the heirs by descent or to the persons named in the will. Before the heirs can take possession of the property, however, the estate must be probated and all claims against it satisfied.

Probate Proceedings

Probate or administration is a legal process by which a court determines who will inherit the property of a deceased person and what the assets of the estate are. Surrogate court proceedings must take place in the county where the deceased person lived. In the case of a person who has died testate, the court also rules on the validity of the will. If the will is upheld, the property is distributed according to its provisions.

If a person has died without a will, the court determines who inherits by reviewing a *proof of heirship.* This statement, usually prepared by an attorney, gives personal information regarding the decedent's spouse, children, and relatives. From this document the court decides which parties will receive what portion of the estate.

To initiate probate or administration proceedings, the custodian of the will, an heir, or another interested party must petition the court. The court then holds a hearing to determine the validity of the will and/or the order of descent, should no valid will exist. If for any reason a will is declared invalid by the court, any property owned by the decedent will pass by the laws of descent. The court will appoint an **executor,** usually named in the will, or an administrator to oversee the administration and distribution of the estate.

Transfer of Title by Will

A **last will and testament** is an instrument made by an owner to convey title to the owner's property after death. A will takes effect only after the death of the owner of the property; until that time, devisees named in the will have no claim to the property.

A party who makes a will is known as a **testator** or **testatrix** (female); the gift of real property by will is known as a **devise,** and a person who receives real property by will is known as a *devisee.* A gift of personal property is a *legacy* or *bequest;* the person receiving the personal property is a *legatee.*

In New York, children of legal age can be disinherited, but a surviving spouse is entitled to at least one-third of the estate, or $50,000 plus one-half of the remainder of the estate, whichever is greater. In a case where a will does not provide the minimum statutory inheritance, the surviving spouse may inform the court that he or she will claim the minimum rather than the lesser share provided in the will. This practice, called a *right of election*, is a right reserved only for a surviving spouse.

A will differs from a deed in that a deed conveys a present interest in real estate during the lifetime of the grantor, while a will conveys no interest in the property until after the death of the testator. To be valid, a deed must be delivered during the lifetime of the grantor. The parties named in a will have no rights or interests as long as the party who has made the will is still alive; they acquire interest or title only after the owner's death.

Legal requirements for making a will.   A person must be of *legal age* and of *sound mind* when he or she executes the will. Usually the courts hold that to make a valid will the testator must have sufficient mental capacity to understand the nature and effect of his or her acts and to dispose of the property according to some plan. The courts also hold that the execution of a will must be a voluntary act, free of any undue influence by other people.

New York provides that any person of sound mind who is 18 years of age or older can make a will devising his or her real property. All wills must be in writing and signed by the testator in the presence of at least two witnesses. A holographic will is one that is written entirely in the testator's own hand-writing and is not properly attested in the manner just described. Such a document will be enforced by New York courts only under limited circumstances.

A later addition or revision may be added to a will; such an addendum is known as a *codicil*.

Transfer of Title by Descent

Title to real estate and personal property of a person who dies intestate passes to what the law regards as natural heirs. Under the descent statutes the primary heirs of the deceased are his or her spouse and close blood relatives. When children have been legally adopted, New York treats them as natural children. In most states illegitimate children inherit from the mother but not from the father unless he has admitted parentage in writing or parentage has been established legally. Such a child who is legally adopted, however, will inherit.

Intestate property will be distributed according to the laws of the state in which the property is located. The New York law of descent and distribution provides that real property belonging to an individual who has died intestate is distributed in the following order. This law and the estate discussed apply only to what remains of the estate after payment of all debts. If a decedent is survived by

■ a spouse and children or grandchildren, the spouse receives money or personal property not to exceed $50,000 in value and one-half of what remains of the estate, and the balance of the estate passes to the children or grandchildren;

■ a spouse and parents only, the spouse receives the entire estate;

- a spouse only, the spouse receives the entire estate;
- children only, the children receive the entire estate;
- parent or parents only, the parents receive the entire estate; or
- siblings only or their children, they receive the entire estate.

If there are no heirs, the decedent's property **escheats** to the state of New York.

TITLE CLOSING AND COSTS

The student is advised to review the material in Chapter 9, on title closings, which will mean more at this point than it did originally to the beginner who had no real estate experience.

SUMMARY

Title to real estate is the right to and evidence of ownership of the land. It is transferred by (1) voluntary alienation; (2) involuntary alienation; (3) will; and (4) descent.

Title may be conveyed voluntarily by gift or sale during the owner's lifetime. It may be transferred without the owner's permission by a court action such as a foreclosure or judgment sale, a tax sale, condemnation under the power of eminent domain, adverse possession, or escheat. Land also may be transferred by the natural forces of water and wind, which either increase property by accretion or decrease it through erosion or avulsion.

Adverse possession allows someone to claim title to someone else's land that has been used openly for at least ten years without protest by the owner.

The real estate of an owner who makes a valid will (who dies testate) passes to the devisees. Generally, an heir or a devisee does not receive a deed, because title passes by the law or the will.

The title of an owner who dies without a will (intestate) passes according to the provisions of the laws of descent of the state in which the real estate is located.

QUESTIONS

1. Title to real estate may be transferred during a person's lifetime by
   a. devise.
   b. descent.
   c. involuntary alienation.
   d. escheat.

2. Title to an owner's real estate can be transferred at the death of the owner by which of the following documents?
   a. Warranty deed
   b. Quitclaim deed
   c. Referee's deed
   d. Last will and testament

3. Matilda Fairbanks bought acreage in a distant county, never went to see the acreage, and did not use the ground. Harold Sampson moved his mobile home onto the land, had a water well drilled, and lived there for 12 years. Sampson may become the owner of the land if he has complied with the state law regarding
   a. requirements for a valid conveyance.
   b. adverse possession.
   c. avulsion.
   d. voluntary alienation.

4. Which of the following is *not* one of the ways in which title to real estate may be transferred by involuntary alienation?
   a. Eminent domain   c. Erosion
   b. Escheat   d. Seisin

5. A person who has died leaving a valid will is called a(n)
   a. devisee.   c. legatee.
   b. testator.   d. intestate.

6. Claude Johnson, a bachelor, died owning real estate that he devised by his will to his niece, Annette. In essence, at what point does title pass to his niece?
   a. Immediately on Johnson's death
   b. After his will has been probated
   c. After Annette has paid all inheritance taxes
   d. When Annette executes a new deed to the property

7. An owner of real estate who was adjudged legally incompetent made a will during his stay at a nursing home. He later died and was survived by a wife and three children. His real estate will pass
   a. to his wife.
   b. to the heirs mentioned in his will.
   c. according to the state laws of descent.
   d. to the state.

8. Henry inherited his father's house last year and continued the garden his father had planted on a side lot for decades. Henry recently discovered his father never owned the lot. Which of the following is true?

   a. Henry has no claim because he himself used the land for only one year.
   b. Henry automatically owns the land under the doctrine of adverse possession.
   c. Henry might succeed with a suit to quiet title and declare the land his.
   d. No suit will succeed unless Henry makes bona fide efforts to locate the owner and offer to pay rent.

9. The acquisition of land through deposit of soil or sand washed up by water is called

   a. accretion.
   b. avulsion.
   c. erosion.
   d. condemnation.

10. The person whose land is taken for public use in New York State may

   a. or may not receive compensation.
   b. refuse to give up the property.
   c. still devise it by will.
   d. challenge a money award in court.

PROPERTY MANAGEMENT

Broker Larry has managed a small ten-unit apartment house for years and never faced a quandary like this one. A prospective tenant, who is handicapped, has good credit and Larry would like to rent to her. He does not want to discriminate against the handicapped, but the property owner has told Larry that he should not accept as a tenant someone who intends to widen doorways and add grab bars in the bathroom. What should Larry do?

Tenant protection regulations are among the important matters to be mastered by property managers, who administer rentals either on their own properties or as the hired agents of investors.

■ **KEY TERMS**

anchor stores
boiler and machinery
   coverage
business interruption
   insurance
capital expense
capital reserve fund
casualty insurance
Certified Property Manager
   (CPM)
contents and personal
   property insurance
corrective maintenance
Division of Housing and
   Community Renewal
   (DHCR)

fire and hazard insurance
industrial property
liability insurance
management agreement
management proposal
market analysis
maximum base rent (MBR)
multiperil policies
neighborhood analysis
office property
operating budget
preventive maintenance
property analysis
property maintenance

property management
   report
property manager
regional analysis
rent control
rent stabilization
replacement cost
residential property
retail property
Section 8
security deposit
surety bond
workers' compensation
   acts

■ PROPERTY MANAGEMENT

In recent years the increased size of buildings; the technical complexities of construction, maintenance, and repair; and the trend toward absentee ownership by individual investors and investment groups have led to the expanded use of professional property managers for both residential and commercial properties. HUD maintains a useful Web site at *www.hud/gov/groups/landlords.cfm.*

Property management has become so important that some brokerage firms maintain separate management departments. Many corporations that own real estate have also established property management departments. Many real estate investors manage their own property, however, and must acquire the knowledge and skills of a property manager. Although the license law allows an exception for those who work for one employer alone, in other instances property managers must hold real estate licenses.

Property managers may look to corporate owners, apartment and condominium associations, homeowners' associations, investment syndicates, trusts, and absentee owners as possible sources of management business.

■ THE PROPERTY MANAGER

A **property manager** does more than just find tenants and collect rents. A property manager's job is to maximize income while maintaining the value of the property. Thus the property manager is closely involved in a variety of activities related to generating income, including budgeting, market analysis, advertising, and negotiating leases. Because it is important that the value of the property be maintained or enhanced as well, the manager is also involved in property maintenance, security supervision, and insurance evaluation.

A property manager may be an individual, a part of a property management firm, or a member of a real estate firm. He or she also may be in charge of managing corporate-owned property or work for a trust.

■ TYPES OF PROPERTY THAT ARE MANAGED

Property can be divided into four major categories for management purposes:

1. Residential property (including condominiums, cooperatives, and subsidized housing)
2. Office space
3. Retail property
4. Industrial property

Residential Property

Residential property includes any type of property that is used for dwelling space. Both single-family homes and multifamily residences can be managed by a professional property manager, although the management of multifamily properties is more common. Multifamily residences include garden apartments, walkup buildings, highrise complexes, cooperatives, and condominiums. Multifamily residences may have a live-in *resident manager.*

Office Space

Office properties include lowrise buildings, highrise complexes, and office or business parks. The ownership and occupancy of office property varies widely, from one owner-occupant to a multitude of individual tenants with a single, nonoccupant owner. Some office properties attract certain types of tenants, such as medical professionals, financial consultants, and so forth. Office properties can be found in both downtown urban areas and suburban areas.

Retail Property

Retail properties come in a wide range, from free-standing buildings to traditional shopping centers. Shopping centers come in many different sizes, including strip centers, neighborhood centers, community centers, regional shopping centers, and superregional malls. Discount and factory outlet shopping centers also are becoming increasingly common.

Industrial Property

Industrial property is defined as all land and facilities used for manufacturing and the storage and shipment of goods. Industrial property may be a large, individually owned and occupied property or a large industrial park with several tenants.

■ THE MANAGEMENT AGREEMENT

The first step in taking over the management of any property is to enter into a **management agreement** with the owner. This agreement creates an agency relationship between the owner and the property manager. A property manager usually is considered a *general agent,* whereas a real estate broker usually is considered a *special agent.* As agent the property manager is charged with the usual fiduciary duties.

The management agreement should be in writing and should cover the following points:

- *Identification of the parties.* The name of the owner of the property should appear in the agreement just as it does on the deed to the property. If the owner is a partnership, each partner should sign the contract. If the owner is a corporation, a duly authorized officer of the corporation must sign the contract.
- *Description of the property.* Typically, the street address of the property is sufficient, but it is always wise to use a legal description in real estate documents. It is important that the contract be clear on the extent of the property to be managed. For instance, if an office building is the subject of the management agreement but the building contains a coffee shop that is to be managed separately, that exclusion should be carefully noted.
- *Time period the agreement will be in force.* The length of the term is purely a matter of negotiation between the parties. Property owners generally want a shorter time period, to allow them to seek other management if they are not satisfied with the current arrangements. On the other hand, property managers usually insist on a contract term that is long enough to make all the extra work required during the initial start-up period

worthwhile. One year is usually the minimum time period. It is also a good idea to include provisions for canceling or renewing the agreement on proper notice.

■ *Definition of management's responsibilities.* All duties should be stated, and exceptions should be noted. The manager's responsibilities include preparing monthly earnings statements (itemizing income and expenses) and making the necessary disbursements to keep the property operating smoothly. It is important to detail what will happen if the property's account does not contain enough funds to cover the required disbursements.

■ *Extent of manager's authority as an agent.* This provision should state what authority the manager is to have in such matters as hiring, firing, and supervising employees; fixing rental rates for space; making expenditures; and authorizing repairs within certain limits.

■ *Owner's responsibilities.* The owner's responsibilities need to be as clearly defined as the manager's. For instance, is the owner responsible for maintaining proper insurance? The owner also should be responsible for providing the manager with a list of monthly payments, including debt service, taxes, and special assessments.

■ *Reporting.* Frequent detailed **property management reports** allow the owner to monitor the manager's work and serve as a basis for planning policy.

■ *Management fee.* The fee can be based on a percentage of gross or net income, a commission on new rentals, a fixed fee, or a combination of these. A fixed fee is often to the manager's disadvantage, because he or she has to negotiate a new fee with the owner before the fee is increased, no matter how much work the manager is completing. A percentage fee will increase if the manager is effective in generating income from the property and decrease if the property's income decreases. A minimum guaranteed fee plus a percentage guarantees the manager at least a certain amount per unit to reimburse the manager for spending time on jobs that do not necessarily increase revenues immediately.

■ *Allocation of costs.* The agreement should state which of the property management expenses, such as custodial and other help, advertising, supplies, and repairs, are to be paid by the owner.

■ FUNCTIONS OF THE PROPERTY MANAGER

A property manager preserves the value of an investment property while generating income as an agent for the owners. A property manager is expected to merchandise the property and control operating expenses to maximize income. A manager should maintain and modernize the property to preserve and enhance the owner's capital investment. The manager carries out these objectives by securing suitable tenants, collecting rents, caring for the premises, budgeting and controlling expenses, hiring and supervising employees, keeping proper accounts, and making periodic reports to the owner.

■ PLANNING AND BUDGETING

One of the first things a property manager does when a property management agreement is signed (and sometimes even before a property management agreement is signed) is to develop a **management proposal.** A management proposal includes, at the minimum, a market analysis, an operating budget, financing proposals, and recommendations as to how the property should be managed.

Market Analysis

The **market analysis** includes a regional analysis, a neighborhood analysis, and a property analysis. The purpose of the market analysis is to give the manager information about the local economic conditions, the supply of and demand for similar properties in the neighborhood, and the competitiveness of other properties that are similar to the property to be managed.

Regional analysis. A **regional analysis** includes economic and demographic information about the regional or metropolitan area in which the property is located. For example, the regional analysis may include figures on local wage levels, employment levels, major employers, population trends, and the availability of transportation and government services. All of these separate pieces of information are used to derive a clear picture of the local economy. Essentially, the property manager is seeking the answer to the question, "Is there a healthy demand for this type of property in this regional or metropolitan area?"

Neighborhood analysis. A **neighborhood analysis** is similar to the regional analysis in its focus on economic factors, government services, demographics, and transportation. However, a neighborhood analysis focuses on the local rather than the regional level.

Generally speaking, property management activities take place on a local, or neighborhood, level, so it is important to be familiar with neighborhood trends. A neighborhood usually is defined as an area whose limits are defined by some natural or artificial boundaries, such as major arterial thoroughfares, a body of water, or a type of land use. Sometimes a neighborhood is only a few square blocks; sometimes it may be a few square miles.

The health of a neighborhood's economy can be measured by several factors: the number and type of businesses in the area, growth trends, wage levels, and current rental and occupancy rates. Obviously, areas that contain well-diversified businesses, have low occupancy rates and high rents, and are experiencing growth are more economically healthy than neighborhoods that are experiencing the opposite trends. A property manager generally will have an easier time finding and keeping tenants in economically prosperous neighborhoods.

The presence of government and utility services is important. Adequate fire and police protection; well-maintained roads; and the easy availability of electricity, gas, water, and a sewage disposal system are all necessary to attract both residential and office tenants. Transportation also is important. A neigh-

---

A MANAGEMENT PLAN INCLUDES

■ a market analysis;
■ an operating budget;
■ financing proposals; and
■ recommendations for managing a property.

borhood that is served by good arterial roads, highways, or freeways; bus or train travel; or other means of transportation tends to be valued more highly by tenants. Good transportation makes commuting to and from work and places of entertainment easier for residential tenants, makes the transportation of goods and services easier for industrial and office tenants, and makes shopping access easier for retail tenants.

Especially for residential tenants, extra amenities that can be found in the neighborhood also are important. For example, convenient access to parks, schools, restaurants, playgrounds, theaters, and places of worship are all important to potential tenants.

Special attention should be paid to vacancy rates for similar properties in the neighborhood. Not only do vacancy (or occupancy) rates indicate the economic climate in the neighborhood, they also reflect the supply of and demand for similar properties in the neighborhood. Supply and demand has a tremendous impact on the rental levels that can be charged for the subject property. For example, an oversupply of rental space means a high vacancy rate and probably a demand for lower rates. On the other hand, an undersupply of rental space usually translates into low vacancy rates and rent increases.

Property analysis.   Examining the region and the neighborhood gives the property manager a good idea of the economic climate and the supply of and demand for similar types of properties. From the information gathered, the property manager also should be able to tell what the optimum rental rates are for competitive space in the neighborhood.

At this point, the property manager needs to turn his or her attention to the subject property itself. The property manager must determine how the subject property compares with competitive properties. Is the subject property in a stronger or a weaker position than competing properties to attract tenants?

In the **property analysis,** the property manager examines the terms of each tenant's existing lease, the quantity and quality of the rentable space, and the physical condition of the property itself.

As the property manager studies the existing leases, he or she is gauging the amount and durability of the rental income. The manager also examines the lease renewal rate for the building (tenant turnover); vacancy rate; and bad debt rate. These elements help determine whether tenant relations are managed wisely and whether the rental rate is right for the current market.

Curb appeal—the building's overall appearance—is one of the more important elements the manager studies. Curb appeal includes the building's age, design, and condition. The manager also checks the interior space, including measuring the total amount of usable space or number of units, the layout, and the hardware and fixtures (such as carpeting and plumbing). The physical condition of all aspects of the property is inspected in light of housekeeping and maintenance requirements.

Part of the property analysis includes studying the features of comparable properties in the neighborhood to determine how the subject property measures up. If the subject property has less curb appeal and higher tenant turnover than competing properties, this may mean that maintenance has been ignored in the past, that current rental rates are too high, or that tenant services are lacking.

Owner objectives.   After the property manager has analyzed the region, neighborhood, and subject property, he or she then must analyze the *goals of the owner*. Those goals may vary from maximizing income or cash flow to increasing the value of the property. It is the manager's job to put the owner's goals into concrete terms so that the management plan can reflect those goals (and the manager can more easily achieve them).

Budgeting

An important part of the planning stage includes preparing a *detailed operating budget*. A property manager should develop an **operating budget** based on anticipated revenues and expenses and reflecting the long-term goals of the owner. The manager begins by allocating money for continuous fixed expenses such as employees' salaries, real estate taxes, property taxes, and insurance premiums. Next the manager establishes a *capital reserve fund* for such *variable expenses* as repairs, decorating, and supplies. The amount allocated for the reserve fund can be computed from the previous yearly costs of variable expenses.

If an owner and a property manager decide that modernization or renovation of the property will enhance its value, the manager should budget money to cover the costs of remodeling, which are called **capital expenses.** The manager should be thoroughly familiar with the principle of contribution (an improvement is only worth the additional value it adds to the property, not its cost) or seek expert advice when estimating any increase in value expected from an improvement. In the case of large-scale construction, the expenses charged against the property's income should be spread over several years. Although budgets should be as accurate an estimate of cost as possible, adjustments may sometimes be necessary, especially in the case of new properties.

■ MARKETING

One of the first steps a property manager must take when beginning to manage a new property is to develop a marketing plan. Unless a property is effectively marketed, well-qualified tenants will be difficult to find and existing tenants will fail to renew their leases.

Marketing plans will vary widely, depending on the type of property that is being managed. Obviously, a property manager will develop an entirely different marketing plan for residential property than for industrial property. However, there are some marketing principles that apply to any type of property. First, a property manager must be thoroughly acquainted with the property he or she is trying to market. The property's features, as well as the property's layout, should be known and noted. The manager must be familiar with the property's strengths as well as its weaknesses. And the manager should make sure the property is "prepared" for the marketing effort—that is, that the space is clean and in good condition.

Another marketing principle property managers should be aware of is that satisfied tenants are the best, most cost-effective way to market the property. Happy tenants give good referrals and can often supply names of other prospective tenants.

Marketing Activities

A successful marketing plan includes both advertising/promotional efforts and person-to-person selling. A property manager must be able to engage effectively in all three types of activities.

Advertising.   The way in which a property manager advertises property depends a great deal on the type of property. Residential, commercial, and industrial properties draw tenants from different sectors of the public. Furthermore, new properties are often advertised in a different manner from established concerns. For example, a newly completed large apartment complex needs to find hundreds of new tenants at the same time, whereas an existing apartment complex needs to find only "replacement" tenants on an ongoing basis.

Several media can be effectively used to market rental space, including

- the Internet;
- signs;
- newspaper advertising;
- periodicals;
- radio and television; and
- direct mail.

Most advertising plans combine one or more of these media.

Signs that identify the management firm for the building and the contact person should be placed outside residential, office, and retail properties. When space is currently available, "For Rent" signs describing the type of space can be posted outside the building or in vacant store windows. Billboards are sometimes used for large industrial or commercial properties.

Newspaper advertising is perhaps the most commonly used medium. Classified advertisements are used for residential properties, and the larger display ads are used for large residential complexes and sometimes retail or office space. Regional periodicals and other publications are used to advertise large residential and retail properties. Many newspapers also post their classified ads on the Internet.

Radio advertising sometimes is used for large residential, commercial, and industrial properties. Its major disadvantage is that radio audiences cannot be targeted very effectively; there are likely to be few potential tenants among the listeners. The same is true for television, with the added disadvantage that television advertising is costly.

Direct mail can be used effectively for some industrial and commercial properties. Well-tailored mailing lists often can be obtained for likely prospects, so direct marketing can be targeted to an appreciative audience. Of course, the direct mail pieces must look professional. Brochures often are developed for large residential, commercial, and industrial properties and are given to prospects who actually inquire about available space.

Promotions. *Promotional efforts* include any activities that serve to improve the reputation of the building and increase its desirability to tenants. For example, the property manager may speak in front of various interest groups, offer to share professional expertise, prepare press releases and send them to various local publications, and send news releases to real estate sections of newspapers or real estate journals. Promotional activities generally translate into free advertising, which is why they can be so valuable to a property manager.

Personal selling activities. This aspect of marketing involves the responses of the property manager or management staff to a prospective tenant. The manager or employee needs expert selling skills to deal effectively with qualifying the prospect, creating interest, dealing with objections, and negotiating and closing the agreement.

Qualifying the prospect includes determining the prospective tenant's space needs, price range, parking needs, and required improvements. In selecting commercial or industrial tenants, a manager should be sure that each tenant will "fit the space." The manager should be certain that (1) the size of the space meets the tenant's requirements; (2) the tenant will have the ability to pay for the space for which it contracts; (3) the tenant's business will be compatible with the building and the other tenants; and (4) if the tenant is likely to expand in the future, expansion space will be available. After a prospect becomes a tenant, the manager must be sure that the tenant remains satisfied.

If the tenant's needs coincide with the available space, the manager can move to the next step, creating interest and desire on the tenant's part. Note that it is a waste of time and money to try to interest a tenant in available space when it will not suit that tenant's needs. The tenant either will reject the space or will sign a lease but vacate the premises before the end of the lease term.

In selecting tenants, the property manager must comply with all federal and local fair housing laws. Tenants with handicaps must be allowed to make appropriate modifications at their own expense if they agree to return the property to its original state when they leave.

Creating interest and desire is largely a matter of describing the property's special features and benefits while showing the prospect the building. Taking a tour of both the exterior and interior of the building and of both the rentable space and the common areas is virtually always advisable. Any questions the prospect may have about the space should be answered promptly, and objections should be dealt with persuasively. Once all answers have been given and objections resolved, the manager then moves to the negotiation and closing stage of marketing. Getting the tenant to sign on the dotted line is, naturally, the prime objective of marketing.

■ MANAGING LEASES AND TENANT RELATIONS

The manager who has moved through the marketing stages and found rental prospects then must attend to managing leases and tenant relations.

Renting the Property

The role of the manager in managing a property should not be confused with that of a broker acting as a leasing agent and solely concerned with renting space. The property manager may use the services of a leasing agent, but that agent does not undertake the full responsibility of maintaining and managing the property.

For low-income or moderate-income residential rentals, managers and owners may want to consider participating in the FHA's **Section 8** program. Qualified tenants pay no more than 30 percent of their income in rent, with HUD carrying the rest.

Setting rental rates.   A basic concern in establishing rental rates is that income from the rentable space must cover the fixed charges and operating expenses and also provide a fair return on the investment. Consideration also must be given to prevailing rates in comparable buildings and the current level of vacancy in the property to be rented—supply and demand. Following a detailed survey of the competitive space available in the neighborhood, prices should be adjusted for differences between neighboring properties and the property being managed. Annual rent adjustments are often warranted.

Office and commercial space rentals are usually quoted according to either annual or monthly rate per square foot of space.

If a high level of vacancy exists, an immediate effort should be made to determine why. *A high level of vacancy does not necessarily indicate that rents are too high.* The trouble may be inept management or defects in the property. Conversely, *a high percentage of occupancy may appear to indicate an effective rental program, but it could also mean that rental rates are too low.* With an apartment house or office building, whenever the occupancy level exceeds 95 percent, serious consideration should be given to raising rents.

Negotiating Leases

A lease is a contract and like any other contract, it must satisfy certain requirements to be valid. These requirements include competent parties, consideration, offer and acceptance, and a lawful purpose. Many leases also must be in writing, according to the provisions of the statute of frauds.

Leases also must contain a description of the property, the amount of rent and when it is due, the term of the lease, the use of the premises, and the rights and obligations of each party.

Typically, the tenant's main obligation is the prompt payment of rent. The lease usually provides for a late penalty if the rental payment is paid after a certain date and termination of the lease if the rent remains unpaid after proper notice by the landlord.

Security deposits usually are required. Security deposits protect the landlord from tenant default. They are available to the landlord should the tenant fail to pay accrued rent or should the tenant damage the property (beyond normal wear and tear). Security deposits should be in a separate account, and the tenant is entitled to all but 1 percent of the interest earned on the deposit. The 1 percent may be retained by the owner as compensation for managing the account.

Tenants usually also are required to comply with local laws and regulations (such as land-use laws and health and safety codes); seek permission before altering or improving the property; and remove personal property on vacating the premises.

Landlords generally are required to maintain the common areas and guarantee the tenant's "quiet enjoyment" of the premises. That is, the tenant has exclusive possession of the premises, and the landlord may gain entrance only for certain purposes with the proper notice or in emergency situations.

Other lease provisions may address such items as

- possession of the premises;
- rental rate adjustments;
- tax and insurance requirements;
- condemnation;
- assignment and subletting; and
- fire and casualty damage.

One of the most important elements involved with managing leases is negotiating tenant alterations and tenant concessions. The property manager must maintain a proper balance between flexibility and practicality. While the manager wants to offer the tenant the proper incentives to enter into the lease, he or she also must keep the "bottom line" in mind and not enter into a transaction that is not in the ultimate best interests of the property owner. Some concessions commonly made to tenants are rental rebates; expansion options (guaranteeing the tenant the option to lease additional space); and reimbursement of moving expenses.

Collecting Rents

Once the tenant has signed the lease and moved onto the premises, a major responsibility of the manager becomes rent collection. The best way to minimize problems with rent collection is to make a *careful selection* of tenants in the first place. A desire for a high level of occupancy should not override good judgment. A property manager should investigate financial references, local credit bureaus, and, when possible, the prospective tenant's former landlord.

The terms of rental payment should be spelled out in detail in the lease agreement. A *firm and consistent collection plan* with a sufficient system of notices and records should be established. In cases of delinquency every attempt must be made to make collections without resorting to legal action. When it is required, a property manager must be prepared to initiate and follow through with legal counsel.

Tenants' Rights

New York's *Multiple Dwelling Law*, in effect in New York City and Buffalo, sets the following requirements for buildings with three or more living units: automatic self-closing and self-locking doors; two-way voice buzzers (for buildings with eight or more units); mirrors in each self-service elevator; and peepholes and chain door-guards on the entrance door of each apartment. Tenants may install their own additional locks but must provide the landlord with a duplicate key on request. Heat must be provided from October 1 to May 31. Additional regulations apply in various communities.

Postal regulations require that landlords of buildings with three or more units provide secure mailboxes. *Smoke detectors* always are required. In New York City, tenants with children younger than 11 must receive *window guards* on request. Protective guards also must be installed on all public hall windows.

Throughout the state the landlord of a building with three or more apartments is specifically required to keep apartments and public areas in good repair and electrical, plumbing, sanitary, heating, and ventilation systems in good working order. Landlords also must maintain appliances that are furnished to tenants. Landlords have a legal duty to keep buildings free of vermin, dirt, and garbage. Landlords also have the duty to inform their tenants of hazards posed by lead-based paint.

A landlord may enter the tenant's apartment only with reasonable prior notice, to provide repairs or service in accordance with the lease or to show the apartment to prospective tenants or purchasers. The landlord may enter without prior permission only in an *emergency*.

A tenant who is disabled has the right to make alterations to improve accessibility at his or her own expense. The landlord may not charge this tenant more rent or a larger security deposit, but may require that the tenant post a bond to ensure that the property is restored as much as is necessary on vacating.

Mobile home park tenants must be offered at least a one-year written lease. If they do not have leases, they are entitled to 90 days' written notice before rent increases. Rules must not be changed without 30 days' written notice. Rules must be posted conspicuously or a copy given to each tenant who moves in. Late rent payment charges are limited to 5 percent after a 10-day grace period. Mobile home park tenants, whether they own or rent the home itself, are governed by the same rules as any other tenants with regard to security deposits, subleasing, sharing space, eviction, and related matters. (In New York, a mobile home is not considered real property unless it is permanently affixed to the land on a foundation.)

Owners may not discriminate against mobile home tenants with children and may not charge extra for children. Owners have the right to sell their homes within the park with the consent of the park owner, which consent may not be unreasonably withheld. Park owners may not require any fee or commission in connection with the sale of a mobile home unless they act as sales agents pursuant to a written contract. Owners may not foster park monopolies.

Owners of mobile home parks with more than two units must register with the New York **Division of Housing and Community Renewal (DHCR)**, which enforces the rights of mobile home tenants in the state.

■ MAINTAINING THE PROPERTY

One of the most important functions of a property manager is the supervision of **property maintenance.** A manager must learn to balance services and costs to satisfy the tenants' needs while minimizing operating expenses. *Maintenance* covers several types of activities. First, the manager must *protect the physical integrity* of the property to ensure that the building and grounds stay in good condition over the long term. Repainting the exterior or replacing the heating system will help keep the building functional and decrease routine maintenance costs. **Preventive maintenance** is performed to head off future trouble, as contrasted with **corrective maintenance**, which repairs damage already incurred.

A property manager also must *supervise routine cleaning and repairs* of the building, including cleaning of common areas; minor carpentry and plumbing; and regularly scheduled upkeep of heating, air-conditioning, and landscaping.

In addition, especially when dealing with commercial or industrial space, a property manager will be called on to make tenant improvement alterations to the interior of the building to meet the functional demands of the tenant. These alterations can range from repainting to completely gutting the interior and redesigning the space. Tenant improvements are especially important when renting new buildings, because the interior is usually left incomplete so that it can be adapted to the needs of individual tenants ("make-ready").

Supervising the modernization or renovation of buildings that have become functionally obsolete and thus unsuited to today's building needs is also important. The renovation of a building often increases the building's marketability and thus its possible income.

Hiring Employees versus Contracting for Services

One of the major decisions a property manager faces is whether to contract for maintenance services from an outside firm or hire on-site employees to perform such tasks. This decision should be based on a number of factors, including size of the building, complexity of tenants' requirements, and availability of suitable labor.

■ OWNER RELATIONS, REPORTS, AND INSURANCE

A property manager is an agent of the property owner, and thus must act in a fiduciary capacity. The manager must act in the best interests of the owner and owes the owner the duties of loyalty and good faith.

Owner Relations

When a property manager first takes over managing a property, he or she should begin building a good foundation for effective owner/manager relations immediately. In the planning process, the manager should have learned the owner's goals and developed the management plan accordingly. The manager should have obtained all the necessary vital information about the owner, including the owner's name; address; telephone number; Social Security number; state employment number; and information on the owner's accountant, attorney, and insurance broker. Information about the owner's property financing is also vital. If the property is already operational, current tenant security deposits must be accounted for and long-term accounting procedures established. It also may be necessary for the manager to have the owner set up a working capital fund for operating expenses.

Once the relationship has been established, the manager should go about setting up a procedure for *regular owner contact*. Typically, the major form of communication between the manager and owner is a *monthly earnings report*. This report includes information on receipts, expenses, and cash flow. The report should be accompanied by a personal letter from the manager, enumerating any special concerns or other information that the manager feels the owner should know.

The property manager should quickly get to know how involved each owner wishes to be in the management of his or her property. Some owners want to be very involved, and expect frequent communication from the manager.

Insurance Coverage

One of the most important responsibilities of a property manager is to protect the property owner against all major insurable risks. In some cases a property manager or a member of the management firm may be a licensed insurance broker. To avoid charges of *self-dealing*, the owner should be made aware of the situation and consent to it.

In any case a competent, reliable insurance agent who is well versed in all areas of insurance pertaining to property should be selected to survey the property and make recommendations. Final decisions, however, must be made by the property owner. *An insurance broker must have passed a state examination to secure a special license to sell insurance.*

Many kinds of insurance coverage are available to income property owners and managers. Some of the more common types include the following:

■ **Fire and hazard:** Fire insurance policies provide coverage against direct loss or damage to property from a fire on the premises. Standard fire coverage can be extended to cover hazards such as windstorm, hail, smoke damage, or civil insurrection. Most popular today is the all-risks or special form.

■ **Business interruption:** Most hazard policies insure against the actual loss of property but do not cover loss of revenues from income property. Interruption insurance covers the loss of income that occurs if the property cannot be used to produce income.

■ **Contents and personal property:** Inland marine insurance covers building contents and personal property during periods when they are not actually located on the business premises.

■ **Liability:** Public liability insurance covers the risks an owner assumes when the public enters the building. Medical expenses are paid for a person injured in the building as a result of landlord negligence. Another liability risk is that of medical or hospital payments for injuries sustained by building employees in the course of their employment. These claims are covered by state laws known as **workers' compensation acts.** These laws require that a building owner who is an employer obtain a workers' compensation policy from a private insurance company.

■ **Casualty:** Casualty insurance policies include coverage against theft, burglary, vandalism, and machinery damage as well as health and accident insurance. Casualty policies usually are written on specific risks such as theft, rather than being all-inclusive.

■ **Surety bonds:** Surety bonds cover an owner against financial losses that result from an employee's criminal acts or negligence while carrying out his or her duties. A blanket crime policy is most often chosen.

■ **Boiler and machinery coverage:** This covers repair and replacement of heating plants, central air-conditioning units, and other major equipment.

Lower premiums may be offered on property that qualifies as a *highly protected risk (HPR)*, based on the quality of water supply, sprinklers, alarms, security personnel, and loss control programs. Many insurance companies offer **multiperil policies** for apartment and business buildings. These include standard types of commercial coverage: fire, hazard, public liability, and casualty.

Claims. When a claim is made under a policy insuring a building or other physical object, either of two methods can determine the amount of the claim. One is the depreciated, or actual, cash value of the damaged property; the other is replacement cost. If a 30-year-old building is damaged, the timbers and materials are 30 years old and therefore do not have the same value as new material. Thus in determining the amount of the loss under what is called *actual cash value*, the cost of new material would be reduced by the estimated depreciation, based on the time the item had been in the building.

The alternate method is to cover **replacement cost.** This represents the actual amount a builder would charge to replace the damaged property at the time of the loss, including materials. When purchasing insurance, a manager must assess whether the property should be insured at full replacement cost or at a depreciated cost. As with homeowners' policies, commercial policies usually carry *coinsurance* clauses that require coverage up to 80 percent of the building's replacement value.

Many property managers, faced with filing an insurance claim, call on professional *private adjusters*, who are skilled in representing owners in negotiations with insurers.

■ SKILLS REQUIRED OF A PROPERTY MANAGER

As is evident from the detailed description of a property manager's functions, a wide variety of skills are required of a property manager. During his or her career, a property manager will "wear many hats" and be called on to display expertise in a number of areas.

The property manager needs to be a *human relations expert*, because he or she handles owner–tenant relations. *Research and planning skills* are required to prepare a marketing plan and perform market analyses. The manager needs excellent *accounting skills* to prepare budgets and monthly reports and to help ensure that the owner's income goals are reached. *Marketing skills*, such as advertising, promotional activities, and person-to-person selling skills, are a must to maintain a high occupancy rate. *Negotiating skills* are required for entering into lease agreements. And of course the property must be *well maintained*, so the manager must know enough about physical operations to see to it that both the exterior and interior of a building are kept in good condition.

■ THE MANAGEMENT FIELD

Office building management requires attention to local economic conditions and planning for the specific type of tenants who are likely to suit the space best. For example, dentists and doctors are likely to remain as tenants, because they hesitate to change addresses.

Managing retail space like shopping malls involves the careful selection for the right blend of tenants. Large **anchor stores**, especially with nationally known names (Sears, Macy's), will set the tone for a mall and make it easier to attract other tenants. One goal is to find the right balance: for example, too many shoe stores may make for ruinous competition, but it takes a certain number of shoe stores to attract shoebuyers to that location.

Managers of residential property handle every sort of dwelling from single houses to mobile homes. Their main concern, besides maintenance of the property, is the selection and servicing of tenants.

Professional management is usually hired by the homeowners association of a condominium or the corporation that owns a cooperative. While management is not involved with selection of tenants, maintaining harmonious relationships while enforcing the organization's rules and regulations can be a major challenge. Security, repairs, and maintenance form a large part of the manager's duties.

For those interested in pursuing a career in property management, most large cities have local associations of building and property owners and managers that are affiliates of regional and national associations. The Institute of Real Estate Management is associated with the National Association of REALTORS®. Members may earn the designation **Certified Property Manager (CPM).** The Building Owners and Managers Association International (BOMA International) is a federation of local associations of owners and managers, primarily of office buildings. Participation in groups like these allows property managers to gain valuable professional knowledge and to discuss their problems with other managers facing similar issues. Management designation also is offered by the National Association of Home Builders, the New York Association of Building Owners, and the International Council of Shopping Centers.

A growing field is management of cooperatives and condominiums. The manager hired by a homeowners' organization must develop different techniques because owners and tenants are one and the same. The Community Associations Institute (CAI) is a nonprofit organization founded in 1974 to research and distribute information on association living and offers training and designation for specialized management.

■ RENT REGULATIONS

Rent regulation in New York State is administered by the Office of Rent Administration of the New York State DHCR. It includes two programs: *rent control* and *rent stabilization*.

Rent Control

Rent control dates back to the housing shortage that followed World War II and generally covers property containing three or more units constructed before February 1947 and located in one of the 64 municipalities where the system is in effect. These include New York City, Albany, Buffalo, and parts of Albany, Erie, Nassau, Rensselaer, Schenectady, and Westchester counties. Also covered are tenants who have been in continuous residence since May 1, 1953, in one or two-family dwellings in the participating communities.

For buildings with three or more units, the regulations apply to an apartment continuously occupied by the present tenant since July 1, 1971 (with some exceptions in Nassau County). When such an apartment is vacated, it moves to rent stabilization status or is removed from regulation, depending on the municipality.

Rents in controlled apartments initially were based on rentals in effect when rent control was first imposed in 1943. Outside New York City the DHCR determines maximum allowable rates of rent increases, which are available to landlords every two years. Within New York City a **maximum base rent (MBR)** is established for each apartment and is adjusted every two years. Tenants may challenge proposed increases if the building has been cited for violations or the owner's expenses do not warrant an increase.

Under rent control, rent may be increased (1) if the landlord increases services; (2) if the landlord installs a major capital improvement; (3) in cases of hardship; and (4) to cover high labor and fuel costs. Rents will be reduced if the landlord fails to correct violations or reduces essential services. The law prohibits harassment of rent-controlled tenants or retaliatory eviction of tenants who exercise their right to complain to a government agency about violations of health or safety laws.

Rent Stabilization

In New York City **rent stabilization** applies to apartments in buildings of six or more units constructed between February 1, 1947, and January 1, 1974. Tenants in older buildings are covered if they moved in before January 1, 1971. Buildings with three or more units that were constructed or extensively renovated since 1974 with special tax benefits are also subject to rent stabilization while the tax benefits continue.

Outside New York City rent stabilization applies in those communities that have adopted the *Emergency Tenant Protection Act (ETPA)*. Each community sets a limit on the size of buildings to be covered; in no case is the program applied to property with fewer than six living units.

Where rent stabilization applies, maximum allowable rent increases are set annually by local rent stabilization boards. Tenants may choose one-year or two-year renewal leases.

The DHCR has set up a special unit to assist the owners of buildings with fewer than 50 rental units in filling out registration forms and with record keeping and bookkeeping. The department's main office is located at 25 Beaver St., New York, NY 10004. Telephone: (212) 480-6700.

■ SUMMARY

Property management is a specialized service to owners of income-producing properties in which a manager, as agent of the owner, becomes administrator of the property.

A management agreement must be prepared carefully to define and authorize the manager's duties and responsibilities.

The manager draws up a budget of estimated variable and fixed expenses. The budget also should allow for any proposed expenditures for major renovations or modernizations. These projected expenses, combined with the manager's analysis of the condition of the building and the rent patterns in the neighborhood, will form the basis on which rental rates for property are determined.

The property manager is responsible for soliciting tenants whose needs are suited to the space and who are capable of meeting the proposed rents. The manager usually collects rents, maintains the building, hires employees, pays taxes for the building, and deals with tenant problems.

One of the manager's primary responsibilities is supervising maintenance, which includes safeguarding the physical integrity of the property and performing routine cleaning and repairs as well as adapting interior space and design to suit tenants' needs.

In addition the manager is expected to secure adequate insurance coverage for the premises. The basic types of coverage applicable to commercial structures include fire and hazard insurance on the property and fixtures; business interruption insurance to protect the owner against income losses; and casualty insurance to provide coverage against such losses as theft, vandalism, and destruction of machinery. The manager also should secure public liability insurance to insure the owner against claims made by people injured on the premises and workers' compensation policies to cover the claims of employees injured on the job. The Multiple Dwelling Law in New York City and Buffalo sets health and safety standards for apartment buildings. Local communities have additional regulations. The state also regulates mobile home parks.

The Institute of Real Estate Management, a branch of the National Association of REALTORS®, awards the most widely recognized designation in the field, the CPM, Certified Property Manager.

QUESTIONS

1. Must a manager allow modifications of the premises to accommodate a handicapped tenant who offers to pay for the work?
   a. Yes, and the landlord must pay for the adaptations.
   b. No, if more suitable accommodations are for rent within a reasonable distance.
   c. No, unless the apartment is located in a rent-controlled building.
   d. Yes, but the tenant must return the premises to its original condition on leaving.

2. An operating budget for income property usually is prepared on what basis?
   a. Daily
   b. Weekly
   c. Monthly
   d. Annually

3. In the absence of rent regulations the amount of rent charged is determined by the
   a. management agreement.
   b. principle of supply and demand.
   c. operating budget.
   d. local apartment owners' association.

4. Office rentals usually are figured by the
   a. front foot.
   b. amount of desk space.
   c. number of rooms.
   d. square foot.

5. From a management point of view, apartment building occupancy that reaches as high as 98 percent would tend to indicate that
   a. the building is poorly managed.
   b. the building is run-down.
   c. the building is a desirable place to live.
   d. rents should be raised.

6. Which of the following should not be a consideration in selecting a tenant?
   a. The size of the space versus the tenant's requirements
   b. The tenant's ability to pay
   c. The racial and ethnic backgrounds of the tenant
   d. The compatibility of the tenant's business with other tenants' businesses

7. A property manager may be reimbursed with
   a. a percentage of rentals.
   b. rebates from suppliers.
   c. key money.
   d. a rebate from fees paid outside workers.

8. The term *make-ready* refers to
   a. cleaning a vacant apartment for the next family.
   b. obtaining clearance for Section 8 tenants.
   c. the inspection of an insurance underwriter.
   d. adaptation of space for a commercial tenant.

9. While her tenants are at work, Laura Landlady may enter their apartment
   a. to leave them a note.
   b. to check on their housekeeping.
   c. in case of fire.
   d. for any purpose.

10. Which insurance insures the property owner against the claims of employees injured on the job?
    a. Business interruption
    b. Workers' compensation
    c. Casualty
    d. Surety bond

11. A delivery man slips on a defective stair in an apartment building and is hospitalized. A claim against the building owner for medical expenses will be made under which of the following policies held by the owner?

    a. Workers' compensation
    b. Casualty
    c. Liability
    d. Fire and hazard

12. Property manager Frieda Jacobs hires Albert Weston as the full-time janitor for one of the buildings she manages. While repairing a faucet in one of the apartments, Weston steals a television set. Jacobs could protect the owner against liability for this type of loss by purchasing

    a. liability insurance.
    b. workers' compensation insurance.
    c. a surety bond.
    d. casualty insurance.

13. The initials CPM stand for

    a. chargeback percentage mortgage.
    b. contract priority maintenance.
    c. Certified Property Manager.
    d. cardiopulmonary manipulation.

14. Rent regulations in New York are administered by

    a. the New York City Housing Bureau.
    b. the Department of State.
    c. HUD.
    d. the New York Department of Housing and Community Renewal.

15. Rent control regulations are found mainly around the

    a. Adirondacks.
    b. southern tier.
    c. Finger Lakes.
    d. New York City area.

16. When the original tenant dies or moves out, a rent-controlled apartment may become eligible for

    a. rent control.
    b. rent stabilization.
    c. comparative hardship.
    d. freeze.

17. The rent stabilization program is known outside New York City as

    a. ETPA.   c. CPR.
    b. DHCR.   d. HPR.

18. The DHCR's special unit for helping owners with registration, bookkeeping, and record keeping is aimed at apartment buildings with fewer than

    a. 3 units.   c. 50 units.
    b. 8 units.   d. 100 units.

26

TAXES AND ASSESSMENTS

Broker Edwina Abbott is listing a house owned by an elderly minister who does not have much money. Even though the house is modest and in need of repair, the property tax figure mentioned by the owner seems low to Edwina, who asks to see a bill. Sure enough, though, the owner had the right amount. How could this be?

The listing broker who gives the buying public information about the property taxes on a parcel of real estate must exercise great care that the figures are accurate. It helps to understand how taxes are levied and what special provisions apply.

■ **KEY TERMS**

ad valorem tax	homestead	taxable status date
aged exemption	in rem	tax certiorari
appropriation	levy	tax foreclosure
assessment roll	mill	tax lien
assessments	nonhomestead	tax sale
equalization factor	statutory redemption	true tax
full-value assessment	period	
grievance		

■ TAX LIENS

State and local governments impose *taxes* on real estate to support their services. Because the location of real estate is permanently fixed and ownership cannot be hidden, the government can levy taxes with a high degree of certainty that they will be collected. Liens for property taxes, which usually have priority over other previously recorded liens, may be enforced by the court-ordered sale of the real estate.

Real estate taxes can be divided into two types: *general real estate tax*, or *ad valorem tax*, and *special assessment tax*, or *improvement tax*. Both are levied against specific parcels of property and automatically become liens on those properties.

General Tax (Ad Valorem Tax)

The general real estate tax is made up of taxes levied by the state, cities, towns, villages, and counties. Other taxing bodies are school districts, park districts, lighting districts, drainage districts, water districts, and sanitary districts. Municipal authorities operating recreational preserves such as forest preserves and parks also may be authorized by the legislature to levy real estate taxes.

General real estate taxes are known as **ad valorem** (to the value) **taxes** because the amount of the tax is determined by the value of the property being taxed.

Special Assessments (Improvement Taxes)

Special assessments are levied only on the parcels of real estate that will benefit from improvements in a limited area. They may be levied, for example, to pay for sidewalks, curbs, or streetlights in a particular neighborhood.

Property owners may request the improvements, or the local government may propose them. Hearings are held and notices given to owners of the property affected. An *ordinance* may be adopted that sets out the nature of the improvement, its cost, and a description of the area to be assessed. The assessment is then spread over the various parcels of real estate that will benefit. The assessment often varies from parcel to parcel, because not all will benefit equally from the improvement.

Exemptions

Most property owned by cities, various municipal organizations (schools, parks and playgrounds), the state and federal governments, religious corporations, hospitals, or educational institutions is tax-exempt. The property must be used for tax-exempt purposes; if not, it is subject to tax.

New York also allows special exemptions to reduce real estate tax bills for certain property owners or land uses. Veterans may be eligible for reductions in some property taxes. Real estate tax reductions are sometimes granted to attract industries or to encourage construction of multifamily housing. In specific agricultural districts New York may offer reductions for agricultural land to encourage the continuation of agricultural uses. Farmers may claim exemption from school taxes for some or all of their acreage. New York State allows local taxing authorities to grant partial exemptions to homeowners who construct in-law apartments, to the disabled, and to "Gold Star" parents who have lost a child in combat.

Every homeowner is entitled to school tax relief (STaR), as described below.

Elderly exemption.   The state allows local governments (towns, counties, and school districts) to offer partial exemption from property taxes on a primary residence to certain homeowners aged 65 or older with modest incomes, at levels that change from year to year. Exemptions can range from 10 percent to 50 percent, depending on income levels, including Social Security payments. Application is made through the local village, town, or city hall assessor's office and must be renewed each year.

Applicants who do not understand how early in the year tax rolls are closed **(taxable status date)** are often disappointed to find that they must wait up to two years before receiving any benefit. This special tax treatment is known officially by the inelegant title **aged exemption,** and is only an option that the towns, counties, and school districts may adopt. Those who receive it also will receive the STaR abatement described below. New York's tax status date, before which applications should be made, is March 1.

Veterans exemption.   Qualified veterans who served during a conflict may receive partial property tax exemption of 15 percent of the value of a primary residence (co-op apartments are not eligible). Those who served in combat are eligible for an additional 10 percent. The exemption, which may not total more than $5,000, is calculated differently for older veterans discharged before newer regulations took effect. The tax abatement is partial, applying to general municipal taxes but not to school tax. It renews automatically each year.

The real estate broker taking the listing of a parcel of real estate should be alert to the possibility of exemptions and exercise diligence in ascertaining the **true tax** figure, before any special exemptions held by the present owner are subtracted.

STaR program.   In the late 1990s, the state instituted a *School Tax Relief program (STaR)*, giving every homeowner who applied a permanent reduction in school taxes on a main residence.

Elderly homeowners with income of less than $60,000 may apply for higher "enhanced" STaR reductions, but must reapply yearly. Any senior receiving the aged exemption described above automatically receives an enhanced STaR reduction as well.

■ THE TAXATION PROCESS

Assessment

Assessments in New York are made by municipal officials known as *assessors.* Assessments are made by towns, villages, cities, and, in a few cases, counties. The **assessment roll,** open to public inspection, contains assessments for all lands and buildings within the area.

In 1788 New York law mandated **full-value assessment.** The requirement was largely ignored, with most municipalities assessing at less than full value. In

1975 the court of appeals ordered the state either to enforce the law or to change it. More than 400 communities then went to full-value assessment voluntarily or under court order. In 1982 the legislature repealed the 200-year-old requirement. Under the regulations that went into force at that time, Upstate communities were simply required to assess all property at a *"uniform percentage of value,"* while New York City and Long Island were allowed to divide real property into four different classes for tax purposes. The question of full-value assessment remains controversial and hotly debated, with court challenges occurring frequently.

Protesting assessments. Property owners who claim that errors were made in determining the assessed value of their property may present their objections and request adjustments. Those who investigate records in the assessor's office may be able to show that the description on file for their property lists more lot size, floor space, or amenities than they actually have. Also persuasive are comparisons with neighboring parcels that indicate the protester's assessment is unreasonably high. Documentation to back up the claims can be compiled from the public records.

Problems should be discussed first with the local assessor; it is not necessary to wait for an official *grievance day*. The next step is to apply for a hearing, filing a document known as a **grievance** with the local tax appeals board. At the next level a simple and inexpensive small claims procedure is available in New York State for owner-occupied one to four-family dwellings if the property has an equalized value of less than $150,000 or if the reduction being sought is less than 25 percent. Protests also can be taken to the regular court system in a **tax certiorari** proceeding.

Equalization. Uniformity among districts that may assess at different rates is achieved through use of an **equalization factor.** The New York State Board of Equalization and Assessment receives reports on sales prices and calculates an equalization rate for each municipality. This factor is intended to equalize the assessments in every taxing jurisdiction across the state. No equalization factor applies where full-value assessment is used.

The assessed value of each property is multiplied by the equalization factor, and the tax rate then is applied to the equalized assessment. For example, the assessments in one district are determined to be 20 percent lower than average assessments throughout the rest of the state. This underassessment can be corrected by applying an equalization factor of 125 percent to each assessment in that district. Thus a parcel of land assessed for tax purposes at $98,000 would be taxed on an equalized value of $122,500 ($98,000 + 1.25 = $122,500).

Tax rates. The process of arriving at a real estate tax rate begins with the *adoption of a budget* by each county, city, school board, or other taxing district. The budget covers financial requirements for the coming fiscal year, which may be the January through December calendar year or some other 12-month period. The budget must include an estimate of all expenditures for the year and indicate the amount of income expected from all fees, revenue sharing, and other sources. The net amount remaining to be raised from real estate taxes is then determined from these figures.

Separate tax rates may be established for **homestead** and **nonhomestead** real estate. Homestead property in New York includes dwellings with no more than four units, mobile homes if owner-occupied and separately assessed, residential condominiums, farms, and some vacant land suitable for homestead-qualified buildings. Nonhomestead property includes industrial and commercial property and most vacant land.

Tax shares are sometimes negotiated between different taxing authorities, as when two towns support one school district or villages share the expense for a county sheriff's department.

Appropriation

The next step is *appropriation*, the action that authorizes the expenditure of funds and provides for the sources of the money. Appropriation involves the adoption of an ordinance or the passage of a law setting forth the specifics of the proposed taxation.

The amount to be raised from the general real estate tax then is imposed on property owners through a tax **levy,** the formal action taken to impose the tax.

The tax rate for each individual taxing body is computed separately. To arrive at a tax rate, the total monies needed for the coming fiscal year are divided by the total assessments of all real estate located within the jurisdiction of the taxing body. For example, a taxing district's budget indicates that $300,000 must be raised from real estate tax revenues, and the assessment roll (assessor's record) of all taxable real estate within this district equals $10 million. The tax rate is computed thus:

$$\$300,000 \div \$10,000,000 = .03 \text{ or } 3\%$$

The tax rate may be stated in a number of different ways. In many areas it is expressed in mills. A **mill** is *¹⁄₁₀ of a cent or $.001*. The tax rate may be expressed as a mill ratio, in dollars per hundred or in dollars per thousand. The tax rate computed in the foregoing example could be expressed as

30 mills (per $1 of assessed value) or $3 per $100 of assessed value
or $30 per $1,000 of assessed value

Tax bills.   A property owner's tax bill is computed by applying the tax rate to the assessed valuation of the property. For example, on property assessed for tax purposes at $90,000, at a tax rate of 3 percent, or 30 mills, the tax will be $2,700 ($90,000 × .030 = $2,700). If an *equalization factor* is used, the computation on a property with an assessed value of $120,000 and a tax rate of 4 percent with an equalization factor of 120 percent would be as follows:

$$\$120,000 \times 1.20 = \$144,000$$
$$\$144,000 \times .04 = \$\ \ 5,760 \text{ tax}$$

Penalties in the form of monthly interest charges are added to all taxes that are not paid when due. The due date also is called the *penalty date*. (Where a lending institution maintains an escrow account to meet a mortgagor's taxes, tax bills may be sent directly to the lender. After the taxes are paid, the receipted bills are forwarded to the property owner.)

New York cities, towns, villages, and school districts generally send out their own tax bills, which may include the county tax levy. Improvement district charges are usually included in the town tax bill; benefit charges are often billed separately. State, town, and county taxes run from January to December and are payable in advance. Villages may begin their tax year either in March or, more commonly, in June. School taxes are levied from July 1 through June 30, but the tax may not be payable until September or October in some areas and may be payable in installments. School taxes, therefore, are paid in arrears for several months. City taxes frequently are payable in two or four installments during the year.

Enforcement of Tax Liens

To be enforceable, real estate taxes must be *valid*, which means they must be levied properly, used for a legal purpose, and applied equitably to all affected property. Real estate taxes that have remained delinquent for the period of time specified by state law can be collected through either **tax foreclosure** (similar to mortgage foreclosure) or **tax sale.** Many cities and villages enforce their own **tax liens** through tax sales; in most cases towns do not. Some foreclosures are **in rem,** against the property on which taxes are delinquent, without proceeding against the individual owner. When a lienholder, often a municipality, decides to go to court for an in rem foreclosure and subsequently takes title to the property, the lienholder becomes the owner, and the owner and the former owner lose any right or claim to the property. The lienholder (new owner) may then keep the property or dispose of it by sale.

Tax sales are held after a published notice and often are conducted by the tax collector as an annual public sale. The purchaser of the lien must pay at least the amount of delinquent tax and penalty owing. The delinquent taxpayer may redeem the property at any time before the tax sale by paying the delinquent taxes plus interest and charges (any court costs or attorney's fees); this is known as an *equitable right of redemption*. State laws also grant a period of redemption *after the tax sale* during which the defaulted owner or lienholders (creditors of the defaulted owner) may redeem the property by paying the amount paid at the tax sale plus interest and charges. This is known as the *statutory right of redemption*. During the **statutory redemption period** the property owner and other parties who have an interest in the property, including a mortgagee, may redeem the property by paying the back taxes together with penalties and interest.

Once property has been sold at a tax sale, the property owner is usually free of any personal liability for the unpaid taxes.

Counties, cities, and villages have different statutory redemption periods. New York City, for example, allows at least four months after taxes are foreclosed, and the period sometimes is extended.

County tax sales.   The owner of the property encumbered by the delinquent tax lien is entitled to redeem the property from the tax lien (as sold) within one year following the date of the tax sale. If the property is actually occupied (not vacant land) or if the property is mortgaged, the period for redemption is extended for an additional two years (three years total, following the date of the tax sale). This period may be shortened by a procedure involving service on the owner of a notice to redeem.

Village tax sales.   The owner of the property encumbered by the delinquent tax lien is entitled to redeem the property from the tax lien (as sold) within two years following the date of the tax sale.

In most cases the purchasers of tax titles in New York secure title insurance or bring actions to quiet any outstanding claims against the property and do not rely only on the tax deed issued by the municipality. The buyer at a tax foreclosure takes the property free of any junior liens, which is why lending institutions require escrow accounts to give them some control over tax payments.

■ SUMMARY

Real estate taxes are levied by local authorities. Tax liens generally are given priority over other liens. Payments are required before stated dates, after which penalties accrue. Special assessments are levied to spread the cost of improvements such as new sidewalks, curbs, or paving over the particular parcels of real estate that benefit from them.

Partial exemption from property taxes is granted to certain senior citizens on modest incomes (aged exemption), to some veterans, and to others for various reasons.

The appraisal process begins with assessment of the taxable value of each parcel. New York mandates either equitable or full-value assessment with variations from one jurisdiction to another adjusted through the use of equalization rates. The money to be raised through taxation is then divided by the total assessment roll to arrive at the tax rate. The tax bill for each parcel is determined by multiplying the tax rate by assessed valuation.

Various taxing authorities send tax bills at different times of the year. Unpaid taxes become a lien against property, usually taking precedence over other liens, and may be enforced through tax foreclosure or sale.

An owner may lose title to property for nonpayment of taxes if the real estate is sold at a tax sale. New York allows a time period during which a defaulted owner can redeem his or her real estate from a tax sale.

QUESTIONS

1. The broker seeking a property's true tax figure should watch for exemptions granted to certain
   a. veterans.
   b. senior citizens.
   c. religious organizations.
   d. Any of the above

2. Which of the following taxes is used to distribute the cost of civic services among all real estate owners?
   a. Personal property tax
   b. Inheritance tax
   c. Ad valorem tax
   d. Sales tax

3. Sidewalk repairs in one area of the town of Brighton will be paid for through a(n)
   a. mechanic's lien.
   b. special assessment.
   c. ad valorem tax.
   d. utility lien.

4. Which of the following steps is usually required before a special assessment becomes a lien against a specific parcel of real estate?
   a. The State of New York verifies the need.
   b. An ordinance is passed.
   c. The improvement is completed.
   d. A majority of affected property owners approve.

5. New York statutes require that property be assessed for taxes at which percentage of its value?
   a. 33⅓
   b. 50
   c. Any uniform percentage
   d. 100

6. When real estate is assessed for tax purposes
   a. the homeowner may appeal to a local board of review.
   b. a protest must take the form of a personal suit against the assessor.
   c. the appeal process must start in state court.
   d. no appeal is possible.

7. A specific parcel of real estate has a market value of $180,000 and is assessed for tax purposes at 25 percent of market value. The tax rate for the county in which the property is located is 30 mills. The tax will be
   a. $180.   c. $1,350.
   b. $450.   d. $5,400.

8. What is the annual real estate tax on a property that is valued at $135,000 and assessed for tax purposes at $47,250 with an equalization factor of 125 percent, when the tax rate is 25 mills?
   a. $1,417.50   c. $4,050.00
   b. $1,476.56   d. None of the above

9. An in rem foreclosure proceeds against
   a. the property.
   b. the owner of the property.
   c. the mortgagee of the property, if any.
   d. All of the above

10. During the statutory period of redemption, New York property sold for delinquent taxes may
    a. be redeemed by paying back taxes, penalties, and interest.
    b. be redeemed by paying four times the delinquent taxes.
    c. be redeemed only through a court proceeding.
    d. not be redeemed.

11. The elderly homeowner who wants a large STaR property tax reduction must
    a. be qualified to receive welfare.
    b. reapply every year.
    c. have no school children living in the home.
    d. consent to a lien being placed on the property.

1. A broker legitimately may pay all or part of a real estate commission to a
   a. seller.
   b. salesperson.
   c. buyer.
   d. friend who provides a listing lead.

2. The minimum age for a New York real estate broker's license is
   a. 19. c. 20.
   b. 18. d. 21.

3. Which of the following acts would require a real estate license in New York?
   a. Sale of one's own property
   b. Sale by the owner's lawyer
   c. Sale of land by an auctioneer
   d. Foreclosure sale by court order

4. An associate broker may
   a. sponsor a person for a salesperson's license.
   b. collect his or her own real estate fees.
   c. act as a principal broker for another broker.
   d. work as a salesperson for a principal broker.

5. Violation of the license law is a misdemeanor, punishable by up to a year in jail and a fine of up to
   a. $500. c. $1,000.
   b. $2,000. d. $1,500.

6. When salesperson Tom Jones left ABC Realty and went to work with XYZ REALTORS®, Tom's listings
   a. became null and void.
   b. remained with ABC Realty.
   c. went with him to XYZ REALTORS®.
   d. required the sellers' signatures to remain in the local MLS.

7. A salesperson's license must be
   a. displayed on the firm's wall.
   b. kept in the salesperson's wallet.
   c. retained by the principal broker.
   d. sent to the local REALTORS® association.

8. When does offering a client's business for sale require a real estate license?
   a. Never
   b. Always
   c. When the business includes any real estate
   d. When more than half the value is in real estate

9. Broker Bobbs had received a commission of $4,225 for a transaction for which she later was found to be in violation of license law. In addition to having her license suspended, she could be held liable for up to
   a. three times $4,225.
   b. two times $4,225.
   c. five times $4,225.
   d. four times $4,225.

10. When a license is revoked, how long must a licensee wait before applying to have the license reinstated?
    a. 18 months c. 6 months
    b. 1 year d. 2 years

11. The form of listing whereby an owner lists property for sale with a number of brokers is known as a(n)
    a. exclusive agency.
    b. open listing.
    c. exclusive right to sell.
    d. net listing.

12. To avoid possible liability for the actions of cooperating members of a multiple-listing system, the owner who lists property for sale may decline to offer
    a. commission to the selling agent.
    b. subagency.
    c. cooperation with buyer brokers.
    d. vicarious responsibility.

13. In New York one can under some circumstances legally enforce an oral
    a. listing agreement.
    b. deed.
    c. mortgage.
    d. option to purchase.

14. Jan Lipson gave Sun City Realty an exclusive agency listing on her property. If she sells the property herself without involving Sun City, she will owe Sun City
    a. half of the commission.
    b. all of the commission.
    c. no commission.
    d. only reimbursement for Sun City's expenses.

15. When selling a property in New York, the licensee is required to disclose to a potential buyer that
    a. there is a group home 1½ miles away.
    b. the property lies in an agricultural district.
    c. there is a fundamentalist church three blocks away.
    d. the former owners were divorced.

16. The commission to be paid in a written listing agreement is the
    a. rate set by law.
    b. amount of money over the net listing amount.
    c. customary rate in the area.
    d. percentage of the sales price as negotiated and agreed or a flat fee.

17. The relationship between an agent and his or her principal is
    a. fiduciary.   c. allodial.
    b. alluvial.   d. executory.

18. If you are selling a house in New York, it is necessary to disclose that
    a. there is a utility surcharge.
    b. the former owner committed suicide.
    c. the train station is eight miles away.
    d. a shopping center in the nearby town is closing.

19. Seller is legally required to reveal to a buyer anything seller knows about
    a. crimes committed on the property in the past three years.
    b. how much seller paid for the house.
    c. repairs that have been made to a roof leak.
    d. lead paint hazards on the property.

20. To create an agency relationship, it is necessary that
    a. a listing contract be registered with the DOS.
    b. the principal and agent sign a written agreement.
    c. the principal pay the agent's fees.
    d. the parties act as principal and agent.

21. A listing would still be in effect after
    a. the death of the seller.
    b. the broker's bankrupcy.
    c. a kitchen fire on the property.
    d. sale of the property by another broker.

22. The type of listing illegal in New York State is a(n)
    a. net listing.
    b. exclusive agency.
    c. exclusive right to sell.
    d. open listing.

23. What must the sale price be if the owner wishes to clear (net) $247,000 and the broker's commission will be 6 percent?
    a. $232,180   c. $261,820
    b. $262,766   d. $264,208

24. A salesperson sells another firm's listing of a commercial building for $462,500. The 7 percent commission is split 50/50 between the two companies. The salesperson received 60 percent of her office's share. How much does she receive?
    a. $1,619.75   c. $9,712.50
    b. $3,237.50   d. $10,850.00

25. A broker may be entitled to a commission in the event that the sale does not close if the problem was caused by the
    a. seller.   c. bank.
    b. buyer.   d. title company.

26. Big Apple Realty is concerned that its commission on a sale will not be paid. Big Apple Realty may
    a. file a lis pendens.
    b. request a de minimis gift.
    c. file an affidavit of entitlement.
    d. file a mechanic's lien.

27. A real estate salesperson's compensation is set by
    a. the local realty association.
    b. the Department of State, Division of Licensing Services.
    c. agreement between broker and salesperson.
    d. the cooperating broker in a transaction.

28. The *Duncan and Hill* decision cautioned real estate licensees against
    a. misrepresentation.
    b. consumer fraud.
    c. the unauthorized practice of law.
    d. undisclosed dual agency.

29. When a buyer-client wants to see property listed by his or her agent's company, the possible conflict of interest can be solved by the use of
    a. undisclosed dual agency.
    b. designated agents.
    c. exclusive-right-to-sell.
    d. fiduciary duties.

30. Buyers should be careful not to reveal the top price they're willing to pay to a(n)
a. buyer's agent.
b. principal broker.
c. seller's agent.
d. associate broker.

31. If a selling broker is not acting as the seller's agent, he or she owes the seller which of the following duties?
a. Fair and honest business dealing
b. Loyalty
c. Confidentiality
d. Disclosure

32. The acknowledgment of the parties to the contract in the NYS disclosure form need not be signed if
a. the real estate agent had the rest of the form correctly filled out.
b. the title company forgets to ask to have it signed.
c. the seller has already moved to Virginia.
d. both seller and buyer are represented by attorneys throughout.

33. Agency relationships in an in-house sale require
a. no notice to the principal broker.
b. full discussion and disclosure in writing to all parties.
c. notice to the title company.
d. notice to the MLS.

34. In a buyer-agency relationship the broker owes the seller
a. care.
b. accounting.
c. obedience.
d. fair and honest dealing.

35. What is the amount of New York State transfer tax to be paid on the sale of a property for $405,575?
a. $405.00
b. $811.15
c. $1,240.00
d. $1,624.00

36. In a real estate transaction, a broker had a written representation agreement with the buyer but was paid 6 percent of the selling price at the closing by the seller. Under these facts, whose agent was this broker?
a. The seller's
b. The buyer's
c. The broker is a dual agent.
d. The broker has violated New York's real estate license laws, and may have his or her license suspended or revoked.

37. A broker signed a listing agreement with the Ghents to market their luxury downtown condominium. A few days later, the broker signed a buyer representation agreement with the Smiths, who were looking for a modest suburban single-family home. If the buyers decide they're in the market for a luxury downtown condominium instead, and want to see the Ghents' property, what should the broker do?
a. Say nothing, and collect a commission from the sellers and a fee from the buyers.
b. Disclose the unintended dual agency, and obtain both parties' written consent.
c. Withdraw from representing one of the parties, to avoid any appearance of self-dealing.
d. Nothing: as long as the broker accepts compensation from only one of the parties, there is no undisclosed dual agency issue.

38. DOS regulation 175.7: "A real estate broker shall make it clear for which party he is acting . . . ." applies to
a. the sale or lease of one to four-unit residential properties.
b. only condominiums and cooperatives.
c. the sale or lease of commercial space only.
d. all types of transactions, not just residential.

39. Broker Norman listed the home of a woman who then died the next week. Norman is sure her children want to sell the house. In this situation, Norman should
a. write to the heirs, informing them he will continue his efforts.
b. request that the executor of the estate put his probable commission in an escrow account.
c. ask the executor to sign a new listing contract.
d. do nothing special, because the old listing is still in effect.

40. In which clause in a deed would you find metes and bounds and monuments?
a. Demising
b. Defeasance
c. Description
d. Habendum

41. If Mr. Jones owns his home free and clear of encumbrances and has the right to devise it to his daughter, he owns a(n)
a. life estate.
b. fee simple.
c. estate at will.
d. leasehold.

42. The Goodmans purchased a cottage bounding on a stream. They have rights to the stream known as
    a. reversionary.   c. laches.
    b. littoral.   d. riparian.

43. Which of the following would *not* be considered chattel?
    a. A tractor   c. The draperies
    b. The barn   d. A trade fixture

44. The most complete type of ownership in real estate is
    a. fee on condition.   c. qualified fee.
    b. life estate.   d. fee simple.

45. Deed restrictions may be established only by the
    a. grantor.
    b. local government.
    c. zoning board of appeals.
    d. grantee.

46. One future action that may *not* be limited by a deed restriction is
    a. the free transfer of the property.
    b. the use of alcoholic beverages on the premises.
    c. further subdivision.
    d. the total number of lots in a subdivision.

47. Any right to or interest in the land interfering with its use or transfer is called an
    a. encumbrance.   c. easement.
    b. encroachment.   d. appurtenance.

48. A deed is valid when it is
    a. delivered and accepted.
    b. recorded.
    c. signed.
    d. notarized.

49. Which type of deed is used to convey title to a parcel of land through a foreclosure proceeding?
    a. Trust   c. Referee's
    b. Quitclaim   d. Warranty

50. Title to real property is conveyed by a
    a. contract.   c. lease.
    b. lien.   d. deed.

51. Daniel paid Robert $2,000 for the right, if he chooses, to lease a store within 60 days at a specified annual rental. The agreement was a(n)
    a. lease-option.   c. implied contract.
    b. open lease.   d. option.

52. The tenant who pays property taxes and heating bills for the store he or she rents probably has what type of lease?
    a. Net   c. Percentage
    b. Participation   d. Gross

53. A contract transferring the rights to possession of real property for a specified term is known as a
    a. lis pendens.   c. lease.
    b. lien.   d. deed on condition.

54. Under the New York General Obligations Law, security deposits by a tenant
    a. become the property of the landlord.
    b. are held in trust by the landlord.
    c. may be commingled with the landlord's funds.
    d. can be retained by the landlord after he or she sells the property.

55. A tenant learns her building has been sold to a new landlord. The sale of the property
    a. automatically terminates all preexisting leases.
    b. under New York's tenant protection law, automatically renews the lease for an additional term, although the tenant has the option of declining the renewal.
    c. has no effect on existing leases, and the tenant must make timely rent payments to the new owner.
    d. terminates the lease, but the tenant is entitled to a legal holdover tenancy for the remainder of the lease term.

56. A legally enforceable agreement between competent parties in which each party acquires a right is called a
    a. certiorari.   c. contract.
    b. consideration. d. clause.

57. The usual listing agreement between a seller and a real estate agent is a(n)
    a. implied contract.
    b. breach of contract.
    c. express contract.
    d. discharge of contract.

58. When the agreement of the parties is demonstrated by their acts and conduct, this is known as what type of contract?
    a. Express   c. Implied
    b. Voidable   d. Unilateral.

59. When a new contract is substituted for an existing agreement, the process is known as
    a. novation.   c. assignment.
    b. innovation.   d. default.

60. Except for the amount of mortgage that may be assumed, a sale in New York State is subject to a transfer tax of
  a. $.55 per $500 or fraction thereof of the consideration paid.
  b. 1 percent on a sale of less than $500,000.
  c. 10 percent where the consideration is more than $1 million.
  d. $2 per $500 or fraction thereof of the consideration paid.

61. Which of the following items would be credited to the buyer at closing?
  a. Sales price
  b. Prepaid insurance
  c. Unpaid water bills
  d. Fuel oil on hand

62. The Flintstones sold their house to the Simpsons and are to close on July 1. The Flintstones paid their annual town taxes in April. At the closing the Simpsons will reimburse the Flintstones for
  a. the tax for the balance of the year.
  b. the tax due in November.
  c. nothing.
  d. the tax due in January.

63. RESPA explicitly prohibits the payment of kickbacks or unearned fees. This does not prohibit a
  a. referral fee from an insurance agent.
  b. fee to a furniture supplier.
  c. brokerage referral fee.
  d. fee to a moving company.

64. An instrument in writing that is the security for a debt with specific property as a pledge is a
  a. bond.   c. deed.
  b. mortgage.   d. lease.

65. A Department of Veterans Affairs mortgage is
  a. insured.   c. conventional.
  b. guaranteed.   d. prepaid.

66. When a house purchase is financed by a federally related mortgage loan, RESPA requires that loan closing information be prepared on the
  a. Uniform Settlement Statement.
  b. Fannie Mae form.
  c. Mortgage Reduction Certificate.
  d. Affidavit of Title.

67. A mortgage with a final payment larger than the preceding ones is known as a(n)
  a. blanket mortgage.
  b. balloon mortgage.
  c. open mortgage.
  d. variable-rate mortgage.

68. Discount charges imposed by a lender to raise the yield on a loan are called
  a. negative amortization.
  b. points.
  c. laches.
  d. lis pendens.

69. Margo and Clarence Stilton have applied for an FHA-insured loan. The mortgage will be
  a. backed by the full faith and credit of the U.S. Government.
  b. insured by a fund set up by HUD.
  c. guaranteed by the federal government at no cost to the borrower.
  d. paid for by PMI premiums.

70. U Kan Tu Realty negotiated a sale at $172,000. The buyers need a mortgage of $142,000. The lender will approve only an 80 percent LTV mortgage. U Kan Tu prepares a fake second sales contract with a purchase price of $177,500, has the sellers and the buyers sign it and presents that to the lender.
  a. U Kan Tu is properly putting the buyer's interests first.
  b. The buyers and sellers have no liability because they followed their broker's guidance.
  c. Both the realty firm and the buyers and sellers are committing fraud.
  d. U Kan Tu is entitled to commission based on $177,500.

71. What type of mortgage loan has an interest rate that may become higher or lower at specified intervals, keyed to an economic indicator?
  a. Pledged account
  b. Shared equity
  c. Growing equity
  d. ARM

72. Charging more than the legal interest rate is known as
  a. points.   c. discounting.
  b. usury.   d. novation.

73. A lot zoned for business use was 95′ by 125′. It sold for $155,000. What was the price per front foot?
    a. $1,631.58
    c. $1,187.50
    b. $1,240.00
    d. $950.74

74. One common zoning category is
    a. municipal.
    c. historic.
    b. suburban.
    d. commercial.

75. Rezoning is the responsibility of the
    a. state government.
    b. municipal government.
    c. environmental conservation board.
    d. zoning board of appeals.

76. The owner whose five-unit apartment building would not be allowed by a new zoning law may be entitled to a(n)
    a. nonconforming use.
    b. variance.
    c. accessory use.
    d. special-use permit.

77. Among other methods, land use is controlled or regulated by
    a. the local assessor.
    b. subdivision regulations.
    c. demographics.
    d. the economic cycle.

78. When a building is located in a historic district, owners usually lose the right to
    a. make any renovations in the building.
    b. sell without the approval of the landmark preservation board.
    c. change the exterior of the building.
    d. mortgage the property.

79. Even though a building permit is issued, new construction will still need
    a. a certificate of occupancy.
    b. a variance from the zoning board of appeals.
    c. approval by an architectural review board.
    d. an environmental survey.

80. In recent years, bathtubs are increasingly made of
    a. cast iron.
    c. marble.
    b. enameled steel.
    d. fiberglass.

81. Electrical systems are routed through a
    a. pier and beam.
    c. stringer.
    b. circuit box.
    d. muntin.

82. A lakefront home sold for $385,000. The broker received $27,912.50. What rate of commission did this broker charge?
    a. 7¼%
    c. 10%
    b. 8.5%
    d. 14%

83. The most commonly used insulation material is
    a. rock wool.
    b. cellulose fiber.
    c. urea formaldehyde foam.
    d. fiberglass.

84. Value of real property is best defined as
    a. cost.
    b. price.
    c. present worth of future benefits.
    d. attractiveness and location.

85. A comparative market analysis resembles which approach to real estate evaluation?
    a. Income approach
    b. Direct sales comparison
    c. Cost approach
    d. Guesstimate

86. The definition of *market value* includes
    a. most recent sale price.
    b. amount of owner's equity in the building.
    c. potential income tax consequences of a sale.
    d. neither buyer nor seller under undue pressure.

87. It can be dangerous for a real estate broker to
    a. discount the firm's usual commission rates for a particular client.
    b. discuss commission rates with another broker.
    c. pay one salesperson 50 percent of earned commissions and another salesperson 60 percent.
    d. charge more for selling vacant land than for selling single-family houses.

88. Federal civil rights legislation forbids housing discrimination based on
    a. political affiliation.
    b. source of income.
    c. country of origin.
    d. prison record.

89. The Civil Rights Act of 1866
    a. prohibits any type of discrimination based on race.
    b. prohibits discrimination only in federally funded housing.
    c. allows an exception for an owner-occupied two-family house.
    d. does not apply to nonlicensed persons.

90. Redlining is defined as
    a. steering home seekers to a particular neighborhood.
    b. drawing red lines on a local map indicating what areas to look in for listings.
    c. denying or restricting loans in a certain area by a lending institution.
    d. a zoning procedure.

91. New York State law goes beyond federal human rights law when it forbids discrimination based on
    a. race.
    b. marital status.
    c. religion.
    d. children in a family.

92. PDQ Realty advertises that it specializes in areas suitable for European immigrants. This is a fair housing violation called
    a. redlining.
    b. steering.
    c. blockbusting.
    d. sexual bias.

93. Using "scare tactics" regarding the possible change in the demographics of a neighborhood when soliciting listings is a violation called
    a. redlining.
    b. steering.
    c. blockbusting.
    d. harassment.

94. Although a property owner may be exempted sometimes from discrimination laws, a real estate licensee
    a. is exempt as an owner.
    b. may list the property for sale noting the exemption.
    c. may advertise the noted exemption.
    d. may not participate in the transaction in any way.

95. The Sherman Antitrust Law is intended to promote
    a. a uniform commission rate schedule in any given area.
    b. cooperation among brokers for the benefit of consumers.
    c. free competition in the open market.
    d. protection for small independent firms.

96. The Underground Storage Tank Act in New York regulates underground fuel storage tanks that are
    a. 2,000 gallons or larger.
    b. 550 gallons or larger.
    c. 1,100 gallons or larger.
    d. 750 gallons or larger.

97. A certified professional need not be hired for the removal of
    a. radon.
    b. asbestos.
    c. lead.
    d. UFFI.

98. Janice has just received her salesperson's license and has joined a firm. She will probably be taken on as a(n)
    a. associate broker.
    b. salaried employee.
    c. independent contractor.
    d. REALTOR®.

99. An asbestos problem is sometimes best treated by
    a. installing new distribution boxes.
    b. proper ventilation of the building.
    c. removal of chipping paint.
    d. leaving it alone.

100. An environmental screening that examines a suspected site and reviews documents affecting the subject property for the past 50 years is known as a(n)
    a. Phase I audit.
    b. abstract.
    c. certificate of occupancy.
    d. building permit.

BROKER'S PRACTICE EXAMINATION

1. Samantha Shore's first listing was of a house whose owner asked Sally not to mention to potential buyers that the house had drainage problems. If Sally does not mention this to buyers or other brokers, she will be guilty of
   a. fraudulent misrepresentation.
   b. no violation, because of the fiduciary duty of obedience.
   c. innocent misrepresentation.
   d. human rights violations.

2. Broker Bob Brown and Broker Sally Shore together purchased a property at a very low price from a distressed owner. Bob and Sally did not tell the owner that they were brokers. They then proceeded to sell the property, making a profit of 125 percent. This was a(n)
   a. legitimate business transaction.
   b. violation of Article 12-A.
   c. antitrust violation.
   d. example of cooperative brokerage.

3. In a real estate business organized as a corporation
   a. the death of the broker automatically terminates the company.
   b. profits are taxed twice.
   c. the broker would enjoy the best tax advantages for a small office.
   d. the broker has unlimited financial liability.

4. Members of a limited liability company
   a. are taxed twice on earnings.
   b. are personally responsible for the company's debts.
   c. must all be licensed as real estate brokers.
   d. enjoy advantages similar to those of an S corporation.

5. Errors and omissions insurance covers
   a. intentional acts of a broker to deceive.
   b. punitive damages.
   c. the defense of "nuisance cases."
   d. negligence when buying or selling for one's own account.

6. The mixing of clients' or customers' funds with an agent's personal funds is known as
   a. commingling.   c. collateral.
   b. consideration.   d. codicil.

7. The Internal Revenue Service will challenge "independent contractor" status if the sales associate
   a. is licensed as a real estate broker or salesperson.
   b. receives health and life insurance as an employment benefit.
   c. has income based on sales output, subject to fluctuation.
   d. performs services pursuant to a written contract specifying independent contractor status.

8. Operating a real estate office in restraint of trade violates the
   a. General Obligations Law.
   b. Sherman Antitrust Act.
   c. Civil Rights Act.
   d. statute of frauds.

9. A salesperson who is an independent contractor
   a. has income tax and Social Security withheld from wages.
   b. has health and life insurance supplied as a benefit.
   c. can be told what to do but not how to do it.
   d. must keep hours as assigned by the broker.

10. The process of placing something with a neutral third party to be held and later delivered to another person after a certain condition is met is known as
    a. equity.   c. escrow.
    b. contingency.   d. consideration.

11. A real estate broker is most generally a(n)
    a. universal agent.   c. special agent.
    b. general agent.   d. ostensible agent.

12. Which of the following is a negotiable instrument?
    a. A mortgage
    b. A stock certificate
    c. A check
    d. A UCC filing

13. In real estate advertising which of the following is correct?
    a. The listing salesperson's name must appear in the ad.
    b. The advertisement must indicate that the advertiser is a broker.
    c. A property may be listed as being "in the vicinity of" without stating the exact location.
    d. The ad may indicate only the rate of interest on available financing.

14. A principal broker is responsible for
    a. getting listing leads for sales associates.
    b. training sales associates.
    c. sales associates' clothing allowance.
    d. salespersons' business calls placed from their home phones.

15. Several brokerage firms may legitimately get together to
    a. collaborate to establish reasonable fees for services rendered.
    b. cooperate to divide up various market areas so as to limit the competition between them.
    c. work together to prevent a "discount broker" from getting business or cobrokerage.
    d. cooperate to enhance the ethical practices in their area.

16. An associate broker may
    a. sponsor an applicant for a salesperson's license.
    b. work as a salesperson under the name and supervision of another principal broker.
    c. collect his or her own real estate fees.
    d. act as a principal broker.

17. When handling funds for others, a broker must
    a. place all monies in his or her own business account.
    b. use the interest to take care of the expenses he or she incurs.
    c. maintain a separate escrow account to hold other people's money.
    d. not give a full account of the funds to a principal.

18. When a broker is recruiting new salespersons, which of the following laws does *not* apply to the recruiting process?
    a. Title VII of the Civil Rights Act of 1964
    b. Article 9-A of the Real Property Law
    c. The Age Discrimination in Employment Act
    d. The Americans with Disabilities Act

19. The requirements for Truth-in-Lending (Regulation Z) would be triggered if an advertisement said
    a. "no down payment."
    b. "annual percentage rate 7%."
    c. "owner may finance."
    d. "just $850 a month will buy."

20. A legal proceeding through which a debtor may seek relief from overwhelming financial problems and have a chance at a fresh start is called
    a. certiorari.
    b. bankruptcy.
    c. capital recapture.
    d. dispossess proceedings.

21. A clause in a mortgage instrument that states that in the event of the default of the mortgagor the entire debt is due and payable is called the
    a. habendum clause.
    b. acceleration clause.
    c. demising clause.
    d. granting clause.

22. The document in which a borrower (mortgagor) certifies the amount owed on a mortgage loan and the rate of interest is called a(n)
    a. affidavit.
    b. estoppel certificate.
    c. mortgage statement.
    d. covenant.

23. An FHA (Federal Housing Administration) loan is always
    a. conventional.   c. insured.
    b. guaranteed.   d. prepaid.

24. The amount that may be borrowed on a house appraised at a certain figure is called the
    a. percentage.
    b. LTV ratio.
    c. negative amortization.
    d. equity loan.

25. Discount charges imposed by lenders to raise the yields on their loans are called
    a. negative amortizations.
    b. points.
    c. garbage fees.
    d. novations.

26. RESPA requirements do not apply when the
    a. sale of property is paid in cash and in full.
    b. loan is made by a federally insured lender.
    c. loan is insured by FHA or guaranteed by VA.
    d. loan is administered by the U.S. Department of Housing and Urban Development.

27. Stockholders of a corporation are liable
    a. only to the extent of their investment in the firm.
    b. personally for losses.
    c. for the debts of any another shareholder.
    d. for the entire debt of the corporation.

28. A Real Estate Investment Trust (REIT)
    a. has its profit taxed twice.
    b. has a general partner running a project as a fiduciary.
    c. may stay in the business indefinitely by investing in further projects.
    d. must be managed by a licensed broker.

29. A real estate limited partnership
    a. is often traded on stock exchanges.
    b. is managed by a board of directors.
    c. has a reinvestment plan.
    d. usually liquidates one project in five to seven years.

30. A broker may provide a salesperson working as an independent contractor with
    a. paid vacations not to exceed two weeks a year.
    b. medical and hospitalization insurance.
    c. unemployment insurance.
    d. the services of a secretary.

31. A transaction in which an owner sells his or her improved property and, as part of the same transaction, arranges to continue occupying the property as a tenant is called a(n)
    a. lease-option.
    b. land contract.
    c. sale and leaseback.
    d. installment sale.

32. A statutory accounting concept in real estate investments known as *depreciation* is also called
    a. cost recovery.   c. amortization.
    b. appreciation.   d. rehabilitation.

33. The store owner who rents his building from the owner and agrees to pay property taxes, repairs, and all other charges himself has a
    a. ground lease.   c. net lease.
    b. holdover.   d. participation lease.

34. "Regular, frequent, and consistent personal guidance, instruction, oversight, and superintendence" is owed to the
    a. associated salesperson by the managing broker.
    b. buyer by the buyer's broker specifically hired with a written contract.
    c. homeowner by the listing agent.
    d. managing broker by the DOS.

35. The broker must take care that a firm's policy and procedures manual does not violate
    a. independent contractor status.
    b. associates' privacy.
    c. DOS advertising guidelines.
    d. MLS regulations.

36. A portfolio loan is one that
    a. is purchased by Fannie Mae.
    b. is guaranteed by the federal government.
    c. covers a large development.
    d. will not be sold on the secondary market.

37. The term *quiet enjoyment* refers to
    a. no loud radios or TV permitted after 11 P.M. in an apartment building.
    b. a warrant that premises are suitable for human habitation.
    c. the tenant's right against unauthorized intrusion by anyone, including the landlord.
    d. permitted wording in a classified "For Sale" ad.

38. A property manager would be expected to secure
    a. liability insurance.
    b. health and hospitalization insurance.
    c. life insurance.
    d. valuable items insurance.

39. Peter manages a large apartment house for the owner, Bruce. He rents an apartment to Julie, and collects a security deposit of one month's rent. Interest earned on the deposit can be kept by
   a. Peter.
   b. Bruce.
   c. Julie.
   d. Julie, except 1 percent to Bruce.

40. If a tenant is actually removed from possession of a premises either by force or by process of law, it is known as
   a. partial eviction.
   b. actual eviction.
   c. constructive eviction.
   d. tentative eviction.

41. Mr. Landlord allows Ms. Tenant to occupy an apartment without any agreement as to the amount of rent or term of occupancy. This is known as a tenancy
   a. at sufferance.   c. at will.
   b. by the entirety.   d. for life.

42. New York rent stabilization rules apply to
   a. commercial space only.
   b. all residential housing in the state.
   c. buildings officially deemed of historic value.
   d. some housing in New York City.

43. Which of the following is illegal for a New York landlord?
   a. Ejectment
   b. Retaliatory eviction
   c. Constructive eviction
   d. Actual eviction

44. At a closing, the buyer reimburses the seller for
   a. unpaid water bills.
   b. the earnest money deposit.
   c. prepaid taxes.
   d. the broker's commission.

45. If one agent in a firm lists a house and another is working as buyer's agent for someone who wants to see that house, the fiduciary problem is sometimes avoided by making them
   a. dual agents.   c. nonagents.
   b. express agents.   d. designated agents.

46. A written agreement between two or more parties providing that a certain property will be placed with a third party and will be delivered to a designated person on the performance of some act or condition is called an
   a. estate.   c. equity.
   b. escrow.   d. egress.

47. Under the Uniform Vendor and Purchaser Risk Act in New York, the party who bears any loss to property that occurs before the title passes or the buyer takes possession is the
   a. seller.   c. bank.
   b. buyer.   d. title company.

48. Fred Freeman and Apple Annie together own 20 acres. Each has an undivided interest in severalty, without right of survivorship. This form of ownership is known as
   a. tenancy by sufferance.
   b. tenancy by the entirety.
   c. tenancy in common.
   d. joint tenancy.

49. A history of conveyances and encumbrances affecting a title as far back as records are available is known as a(n)
   a. color of title.   c. chain of title.
   b. marketable title.   d. abstract of title.

50. In every contract for sale or lease of subdivided lands, if the purchaser or lessee is not represented by an attorney, he or she has
   a. a 30-day cancellation privilege.
   b. a 90-day cancellation privilege.
   c. a 10-day cancellation privilege.
   d. no cancellation privilege.

51. Farmer Brown could sell off how many building lots before subdivision regulations would apply?
   a. Two   c. Six
   b. Four   d. As many as he wants

52. The sale or lease of subdivided lands in New York is primarily governed by
   a. Article 9-A of the Real Property Law.
   b. the statute of limitations.
   c. the Uniform Commercial Code.
   d. the Civil Rights Act of 1866.

53. Misrepresentation in the sale or lease of subdivided lands constitutes
   a. a misdemeanor.   c. escheat.
   b. a felony.   d. insubordination.

54. The absolute ownership of an apartment or a housing unit plus an undivided interest in the ownership of the common elements that are jointly owned is called a
a. leasehold.
b. cooperative.
c. condominium.
d. dominant tenement.

55. A residential multiunit building with title held by a trust or corporation that is owned and operated for the benefit of persons living within the building, each of whom has a proprietary lease, is called a
a. leasehold.
b. cooperative.
c. condominium.
d. dominant tenement.

56. The owners of a cooperative apartment are treated by the IRS as homeowners even though strictly speaking they do not own
a. equity.
b. securities.
c. real property.
d. an equitable interest.

57. New York State allows partial property tax reductions for some
a. social workers.
b. public officials.
c. corporations.
d. senior citizens.

58. A mill represents how much money?
a. $1.00
b. $0.10
c. $0.01
d. $0.001

59. Taxes levied on only one neighborhood to pay for streetlights or sewers are
a. ad valorem taxes.
b. in rem proceedings.
c. special assessments.
d. corporation taxes.

60. A legal proceeding against the realty directly, as distinguished from a proceeding against a person, is considered
a. a tax lien.
b. in rem.
c. a mill.
d. an ad valorem tax.

61. If a reassessment finds the total value of real estate in the community to be higher than previously listed, tax rates are likely to
a. drop.
b. remain the same.
c. rise.
d. be challenged by Albany.

62. At the closing the seller is usually required to pay the
a. mortgage tax.
b. transfer tax.
c. buyer's attorney.
d. FHA MIP.

63. The transfer tax in New York State is
a. 1 percent on a sale of less than $500,000.
b. 10 percent on any sale of over $1 million.
c. $2 per $500 or any fraction thereof.
d. $.55 per thousand or any fraction thereof.

64. Private mortgage insurance is required on conventional loans in New York State when
a. the down payment is less than 20 percent.
b. there is a 5 percent down payment on an FHA loan.
c. the buyer is only marginally qualified.
d. there is a VA mortgage.

65. A buyer puts $20,000 down on a $200,000 house and will finance the rest. In this example 90 percent represents
a. the buyer's equity
b. the loan-to-value ratio.
c. a deficiency judgment.
d. the amortization of the mortgage.

66. In terms of real estate appraisal, *the present worth of future benefits arising from the ownership of real property* is the definition of
a. cost.
b. value.
c. price.
d. amenities.

67. UCC filings are used to
a. protect assets in bankruptcy.
b. settle an estate.
c. pledge personal property as security for a loan.
d. institute litigation in New York's supreme court.

68. To find the value of a property when you know the income and the capitalization rate, you
a. divide the cap rate by the income.
b. divide the income by the cap rate.
c. multiply the cap rate by the income.
d. add the income to the cap rate.

69. The art of analyzing and effectively weighing the findings of value on a property when all the basic approaches to appraisal are used is called
a. regression.
b. averaging.
c. calculation.
d. reconciliation.

70. An appraiser must have licensure or certification from New York State for any federally related appraisal assignment
    a. with a dollar value of at least $250,000.
    b. done under the supervision of a licensed appraiser.
    c. unless the appraiser has an MAI or SRA designation.
    d. used for securing a mortgage loan.

71. Which of the following should be included in the calculation of square feet of living area in a house?
    a. Front porch
    b. Bathrooms
    c. Garage
    d. Below-grade family room

72. The level of government that is responsible for the standards and policing of water supply and sewage disposal is
    a. local.   c. state.
    b. county.   d. federal.

73. In New York, building plans must be signed by a(n)
    a. builder.   c. architect.
    b. developer.   d. land planner.

74. A house that is completely factory built, delivered to the site by truck, already joined, and with systems hooked up ready to be installed on a foundation is called a
    a. bilevel.   c. mobile home.
    b. rambler.   d. modular home.

75. The merging of two or more adjacent lots under one owner is
    a. contribution.   c. assemblage.
    b. competition.   d. anticipation.

76. To find the cubic yards of space in a warehouse, you
    a. multiply the height and length.
    b. multiply the length and width.
    c. divide the height by the length and width.
    d. multiply the height, length, and width.

77. John and his brother own a summer cottage together. When the brother dies, John automatically becomes sole owner. They must have owned it as
    a. tenants by the entirety.
    b. joint tenants.
    c. tenants in common.
    d. life tenants.

78. The Wallaces are worried about possible problems with the Victorian house they plan to buy. Before the contract is firm, they should consult a
    a. building inspection engineer.
    b. soil engineer.
    c. framer.
    d. firestop specialist.

79. The Environmental Protection Agency considers solder materials dangerous when they contain more than 8 percent
    a. copper.   c. tin.
    b. lead.   d. antimony.

80. Federal law requires that a landlord modify an older building at the request of a handicapped tenant who
    a. qualifies for a handicap parking certificate.
    b. produces a doctor's letter.
    c. agrees to a rent increase.
    d. is willing to pay for the modifications.

81. Federal law prohibits discrimination based on
    a. handicap.
    b. political affiliation.
    c. legal source of income.
    d. sexual preference.

82. Primary responsibility for dealing with and/or correcting problems with a new structure lies with the
    a. County Board of Health.
    b. building inspector.
    c. Board of Fire Underwriters.
    d. builder/contractor.

83. If a property is located in an agricultural district or if there is a lack of available utilities, a purchaser should
    a. ask the seller about it.
    b. be given written notice.
    c. ask the building inspector.
    d. sue the agent.

84. The federal law that prohibits any type of discrimination based on race, with no exception, is
    a. the Civil Rights Act of 1964.
    b. the Civil Rights Act of 1866.
    c. the Fair Housing Act of 1968.
    d. Executive Order No. 11063.

85. Failure to display the equal housing opportunity poster is considered by HUD to be
    a. evidence of discrimination.
    b. illegal.
    c. redlining.
    d. blockbusting.

86. Susan Subdivide has one mortgage on her large tract of land. When she sells off a single lot, she requests the lender to release that lot from the
    a. package mortgage.
    b. balloon mortgage.
    c. subordinate mortgage.
    d. blanket mortgage.

87. An undercover individual who visits real estate offices to check on compliance with fair housing laws is
    a. always a HUD employee.
    b. sometimes a disgruntled customer.
    c. known as a *tester*.
    d. usually a welfare recipient.

88. The Larsens have owned the house they live in for the past four years. When they sell, they will be entitled to how much capital gain free of federal tax?
    a. None   c. $250,000
    b. $125,000   d. $500,000

89. To be granted a use variance by a zoning board of appeals, the applicant must prove
    a. convenience.
    b. hardship.
    c. permanence.
    d. benefit to the community.

90. A lien on real estate
    a. binds only the current owner.
    b. runs with the land.
    c. prevents the sale of the property.
    d. expires after 20 years.

91. Which type of lien generally holds priority over all others?
    a. First mortgage   c. Unpaid property taxes
    b. Mechanic's lien   d. Vendor's lien

92. The easement granted to New York State Electric and Gas to put electric service across another's property is a(n)
    a. easement appurtenant.
    b. easement in gross.
    c. dominant easement.
    d. servient easement.

93. Anything given to induce entering into a contract, such as money or personal services, is called
    a. consideration.   c. conversion.
    b. condemnation.   d. caveat emptor.

94. Nancy and Chris sign a contract under which Nancy will convey Blackacre to Chris. Nancy changes her mind, and Chris sues for specific performance. What is Chris seeking in this lawsuit?
    a. A forced sale of the property
    b. Money damages
    c. A new contract
    d. A deficiency judgment

95. An example of a unilateral contract is
    a. a land contract.
    b. a contract on a house sale.
    c. the offer of a reward.
    d. a contract to sell a car.

96. A person who delays taking steps to enforce a contractual right within the statute of limitations may lose that right through
    a. lis pendens.   c. litigation.
    b. laches.   d. lien.

97. Agreements written into deeds that promise performance or nonperformance of certain acts or stipulate certain uses or nonuses of the property are known as
    a. covenants.   c. curtesy.
    b. considerations.   d. certioraris.

98. The legal description of a property always should include
    a. an exact description.
    b. metes and bounds.
    c. monuments.
    d. government survey data.

99. To be valid, a warranty deed must include
    a. the full price paid.
    b. the buyer's signature.
    c. an adequate description.
    d. an acknowledgment.

100. The deed that provides the grantee with the least protection of any deed is the
    a. bargain and sale deed.
    b. referee's deed.
    c. warranty deed.
    d. quitclaim deed.

GLOSSARY

abstract of title The condensed history of the title to a particular parcel of real estate.

abstract of title with lawyer's opinion An abstract of title that a lawyer has examined and has certified to be, in his or her opinion, an accurate statement of fact.

abutting Lying immediately next to, as with two parcels of real estate with a common lot line.

acceleration clause The clause in a note or mortgage that can be enforced to make the entire debt due immediately if the mortgagor defaults.

accessory apartment/uses An additional apartment, usually small, sometimes allowed in an area zoned for one-family homes, which might be used for elderly grandparents; an accessory use would be something in addition to occupation of a home, possibly a small home business.

accountability The agent's fiduciary duty to account to the principal, particularly for any money involved in the transaction.

accretion The increase or addition of land by the deposit of sand or soil washed up naturally from a river, lake or sea.

accrued items On a closing statement, items of ex-pense that have been incurred but are not yet payable, such as interest on a mortgage loan.

acknowledgment A formal declaration made be-fore a duly authorized officer, usually a notary public, by a person who has signed a document.

acre A measure of land equal to 43,560 square feet, 4,840 square yards, 4,047 square meters, 160 square rods, or 0.4047 hectare.

act of waste *See* waste.

actual eviction Action whereby a defaulted tenant is physically ousted from rented property pursuant to a court order. *See also* eviction.

actual notice That which is known; actual knowledge.

adjacent Lying near to but not necessarily in actual contact with.

adjoining Contiguous; attaching, in actual contact with.

adjustable-rate mortgage (ARM) A mortgage loan in which the interest rate may increase or decrease at specific intervals, following an economic indicator.

adjusted basis Basis minus depreciation.

adjustments Divisions of financial responsibility between a buyer and seller (also called *prorations*).

administrative discipline The Department of State's enforcement of license laws, rules, and regulations through the use of reprimands and denial, suspension, or revocation of licenses.

administrative law Laws concerned with the conduct of government agencies.

administrator A person appointed by court to administer the estate of a deceased person who left no will, i.e., who died intestate.

ad valorem tax A tax levied according to value; generally used to refer to real estate tax. Also called the *general tax*.

adverse possession The actual, visible, hostile, notorious, exclusive, and continuous possession of another's land under a claim of title. Possession for ten years may be a means of acquiring title.

affidavit A written statement sworn to before an officer who is authorized to administer an oath or affirmation.

affirmative marketing Program to inform all buyers in a minority community about housing opportunities available, without discrimination.

aged exemption New York state's partial exemption of school tax for low-income elderly homeowners.

agency That relationship wherein an agent is employed by a principal to do certain acts on the principal's behalf.

agency coupled with an interest An agency relationship in which the agent has an interest in the property.

agent One who undertakes to transact some business or to manage some affair for another by authority of the latter.

agricultural real estate Farms, timberland, pasture land, and orchards.

air rights The right to use the open space above a property, generally allowing the surface to be used for another purpose.

alienation The act of transferring property to another.

alienation clause The clause in a mortgage stating that the balance of the secured debt becomes immediately due and payable at the mortgagee's option if the property is sold.

alluvion Extra soil deposited on shore by the action of water.

Americans with Disabilities Act (ADA) Federal law requiring reasonable accommodations and accessibility to goods and services for persons with disabilities.

amenities Elements of a property or its surroundings that contribute to its attractiveness to potential buyers and to owner satisfaction.

amortized loan A loan in which the principal as well as the interest is payable in monthly or other periodic installments over the term of the loan.

amperage Amount of electrical current, measured in amperes ("amps").

anchor stores Large stores, often nationally-known department stores, whose presence attracts other tenants to a shopping mall.

annual percentage rate (APR) Rate of interest charged on a loan, calculated to take into account up-front loan fees and points. Usually higher than the *contract interest rate*.

antitrust laws Laws designed to preserve the free enterprise of the open marketplace by making illegal certain private conspiracies and combinations formed to minimize competition.

apartment information vendor A person who, for a fee, brings landlords and tenants together.

apartment-sharing agent One who brings together roommates and house-mates.

appeals Complaints made to a higher court requesting the correction of errors in law made by lower courts.

appellate division Courts of appeal.

apportionments Adjustment of the income, expenses, or carrying charges of real estate usually computed to the date of closing of title so that the seller pays all expenses to that date.

appraisal An estimate of a property's valuation by an appraiser who is usually presumed to be expert in this work.

Appraisal Institute Largest private organization for professional appraisers.

appreciation An increase in the worth or value of a property due to economic or related causes.

appropriation The process of levying property taxes; *also,* the setting aside of part of a subdivision for public use. *See* dedication.

appurtenances Those rights, privileges, and improvements that belong to and pass with the transfer of real property but are not necessarily a part of the property, such as rights-of-way, easements, and property improvements.

APR *See* annual percentage rate.

arbitration A hearing before a person chosen by the parties or appointed to hear a dispute and render a determination.

ARM *See* adjustable-rate mortgage.

arm's-length transaction A transaction between relative strangers, each trying to do the best for himself or herself.

Army Corps of Engineers Federal body responsible for regulating waterways and drainage.

Article 9A The section of New York State's Real Property Law relating to subdivision.

Article 12A The section of New York State's Real Property Law relating to real estate licenses.

Article 78 procedure Legal process for contesting the action of a governmental body.

asbestos Commonly used insulating mineral that becomes toxic when it is exposed and fibers and dust are released into the air.

asbestosis Lung disease caused by exposure to asbestos.

"as is" Contract words indicating that the seller makes no guarantees or warranties about the property; not always effective if challenged in court.

assemblage The merging of two separate parcels under one owner.

assessed value A valuation placed on property by a public officer or a board as a basis for taxation.

assessment The imposition of a tax, charge, or levy, usually according to established rates.

assessment review board A local body empowered to hear protests by property-tax payers, and to lower or raise assessments.

assessment roll Public record listing assessed value for all real property in a village, town, city, or county.

assignment The transfer in writing of interest in a bond, mortgage, lease, or other instrument.

associate broker A broker who chooses to work as a salesperson under the name and supervision of another broker.

assumption of mortgage Acquiring title to property on which there is an existing mortgage and agreeing to be personally liable for the terms and conditions of the mortgage, including payments.

attorney-in-fact A person who has been given a power of attorney on behalf of a grantor. The power must be recorded, and ends on the death of the grantor.

attorney's opinion of title Report in which a lawyer examines and evaluates an abstract of title.

avulsion The removal of land when a stream suddenly changes its channel.

balloon payment The final payment of a mortgage loan that is considerably larger than the required periodic payments because the loan amount was not fully amortized.

bankruptcy A federal court procedure to relieve an over-burdened debtor of certain liabilities.

bargain and sale deed A deed that carries with it no warranties against liens or other encumbrances but that does imply that the grantor has the right to convey title.

bargain and sale deed with covenant A deed in which the grantor warrants or guarantees the title against defects arising during the period of his or her tenure and ownership of the property but not against defects existing before that time.

basement Space wholly or partly below grade, usually not used for living accommodations.

basis The cost that the Internal Revenue Service attributes to an owner of an investment property for the purpose of determining annual depreciation and gain or loss on the sale of the asset.

beam Structural member, usually horizontal, used for support.

bearing walls Walls that serve as more than simple partitions, that support ceiling, upper stories, or roof.

benchmark A permanent reference mark or point established for use by surveyors in measuring differences in elevation. *See* datum.

beneficiary The person who receives or is to receive benefits resulting from certain acts.

bequeath To give or hand down by will; to leave by will.

bequest That which is given by the terms of a will.

bilateral contract A contract in which both parties promise to do something; an exchange of promises.

bill of sale A written instrument given to pass title of personal property from vendor to vendee.

binder An agreement that may accompany an earnest money deposit for the purchase of real property as evidence of the purchaser's good faith and intent to complete the transaction.

biweekly mortgage   A loan that is paid in 26 half (biweekly) payments each year, resulting in an earlier payoff and lower interest costs over the life of the loan.

black book   Offering plan for a cooperative or condominium as accepted for filing by the attorney general and used for marketing.

blanket mortgage   A mortgage covering more than one parcel of real estate.

blanket unilateral offer of cooperation   A seller's option to agree to a commission split with the selling broker without subagency.

blanket unilateral offer of subagency   Traditionally, a seller's automatic consent to subagency by submitting a listing to a MLS.

blind ad   An advertisement that does not name the person placing the ad, or indicate that it was placed by a licensed real estate broker.

blockbusting   The illegal practice of inducing homeowners to sell their property by making representations regarding the entry or prospective entry of minority persons into the neighborhood.

blueprint   An architect's or engineer's plan for a building, including floor plan, dimensions, and specifications, to be followed by the builder.

blue-sky laws   Common name for those state and federal laws that regulate the registration and sale of investment securities.

board of directors   Elected managing body of a corporation, specifically of a cooperative apartment building.

Board of Fire Underwriters   New York state agency responsible for oversight of electrical systems and for enforcing its electrical code.

board of managers   Elected managing body of a condominium.

boiler and machinery coverage   Insurance policy covering repair and replacement of major equipment and systems such as central air-conditioners and heating plants.

bond   The evidence of a personal debt that is secured by a mortgage or other lien on real estate.

boot   Money or property given to make up any difference in value or equity between two properties in an *exchange*.

branch office   A secondary place of business apart from the principal or main office from which real estate business is conducted.

breach of contract   Violation of any terms or conditions in a contract without legal excuse; for example, failure to make a payment when it is due.

bridge loan   A short-term loan designed to cover a gap between the sale of one property and the purchase of another (also called a *swing loan*, *temporary loan*, or *interim financing*).

British thermal unit (BTU)   A unit of measure of heat that is used to rate air-conditioning and heating equipment capacity. One BTU raises one pound of water one degree Fahrenheit.

broker   One who buys and sells for another for a fee. *See also* real estate broker.

brokerage   The business of buying and selling for another for a fee.

broker's agent   A broker who assists the listing broker in marketing a property under a formal agency agreement.

building codes   Regulations established by state and local governments fully stating the structural requirements for building.

building line   A line fixed at a certain distance from the front and/or sides of a lot, beyond which no building can project.

building loan agreement   An agreement whereby the lender advances money to an owner with partial payments at certain stages of construction.

building permit   Written permission from the local government to build or alter a structure.

building-related illness (BRI)   Symptoms such as hypersensitivity, asthma, and allergic reactions caused by toxic substances and pathogens in a building that remain with the affected individual even when he or she is away from the building. *See* sick building syndrome.

bullet loan   A short- or intermediate-term (3 to 5 years) interest-only loan with a balloon payment at the end of the term (also called an *intermediate loan* or *conduit financing*).

bundle of legal rights   The concept of land ownership that includes ownership of all legal rights to the land—for example, possession, control within the law, and enjoyment.

business interruption insurance   Insurance policy coverage against a financial loss resulting from a property's inability to generate income.

buydown   A financing technique used to reduce the monthly payments for the first few years of a loan. Funds in the form of points are given to the lender by the builder or seller to buy down or lower the effective interest rate paid by the buyer, thus reducing the monthly payments for a set time.

buyer agency   An agency relationship in which the broker/agent represents the interests of the buyer.

buyer's broker   A broker who has entered into an agreement to represent a buyer (the broker's principal and client) in finding a suitable property.

bylaws   Rules and regulations adopted by an association.

cap   With an adjustable-rate mortgage, a limit, usually in percentage points, on how much the interest rate or payment might be raised in each adjustment period. For *lifetime cap, see* ceiling.

capital expense   Money spent on permanent improvements that add value to property.

capital gains   Profits realized from the sale of assets such as real estate.

capitalization   A mathematical process for estimating the value of a property using a proper rate of return on the investment and the annual net income expected to be produced by the property.

capitalization rate The rate of return a property will produce on the owner's investment.

capital reserve budget Money set aside to meet anticipated large expenditures for major improvements.

case law Law resulting from past court decisions.

casement window A window that opens on hinges.

cash flow The net spendable income from an investment.

casualty insurance Insurance policy coverage against theft, burglary, vandalism, physical damage to systems, and health and accident coverage on a specific-risk basis.

caveat emptor A Latin phrase meaning "Let the buyer beware."

CBS Memory aid for an appraiser's adjustments: Comparable Better, Subtract.

CC&Rs Covenants, conditions, and restrictions of a condominium or cooperative development.

cease and desist order A prohibition against brokers' canvassing for listings, either from certain individual homeowners or in certain areas.

ceiling With an adjustable-rate mortgage, a limit, usually in percentage points, beyond which the interest rates or monthly payment on a loan may never rise. Sometimes known as a *lifetime cap*.

census tract A small geographic area designated by the Bureau of the Census.

CERCLA The federal Comprehensive Environmental, Responsibility, Compensation, and Liability Act, which established procedures for remediation of contaminated areas.

certificate of compliance (C of C) Verification that a construction project meets certain standards, primarily safety-related.

certificate of occupancy (C of O) Document issued by a municipal authority stating that a building complies with building, health, and safety codes and may be occupied.

certificate of title A statement of opinion of title status on a parcel of real property based on an examination of specified public records.

Certified Property Manager (CPM) A real property manager who has completed specific educational requirements, demonstration reports, and qualified for the CPM designation, which is granted by the Institute of Real Estate Management of the National Association of REALTORS®.

certiorari proceeding A judicial proceeding seeking higher court review of a lower court's decision in a case or proceeding.

chain of title The conveyance of real property to one owner from another, reaching back to the original grantor.

Chapter 7, Chapter 11, Chapter 13 Different forms of bankruptcy.

chattel Personal property such as household goods or fixtures.

chattel mortgage A mortgage on personal property.

checkers *See* testers.

chlordane An insecticide banned in the 1980s.

chlorofluorocarbons (CFCs) Gases produced by propellants once used in aerosol sprays and the common coolant Freon. CFCs are linked to depletion of the earth's ozone layer.

civil law The laws dealing with wrongs one person does another.

Civil Rights Act of 1866 Federal law that prohibits racial discrimination in the sale and rental of property.

Clean Air Act The law prohibiting the use of Freon in refrigerators and spray cans.

client The principal.

closing date The date on which the buyer takes title to the property.

closing statement A detailed cash accounting of a real estate transaction showing all cash received, all charges and credits made, and all cash paid out in the transaction.

cloud on the title An outstanding claim or encumbrance that, if valid, would affect or impair the owner's title.

clustering The grouping of home sites within a subdivision on smaller lots than normal with the remaining land used as common areas.

cluster zoning Zoning that allowed the grouping of buildings on small lots to allow for extra parcels of open space.

CMA *See* comparative market analysis.

Code for Equal Opportunity Professional standard of conduct for fair housing compliance, promulgated by the National Association of REALTORS® (NAR).

C of C *See* certificate of compliance.

C of O *See* certificate of occupancy.

coinsurance clause A clause in insurance policies covering real property that requires that the policyholder maintain fire insurance coverage generally equal to at least 80 percent of the property's actual replacement cost.

commercial law The division of law dealing with business and industry.

commercial paper Notes, checks, certificates of deposit, and other promises to pay money.

commercial real estate Business property, including offices, shopping malls, theaters, hotels, and parking facilities.

commingling The illegal act of a real estate broker who mixes other people's money with his or her own.

commission Payment to a broker for services rendered, such as in the sale or purchase of real property; usually a percentage of the selling price.

common elements Parts of a property normally in common use by all of the condominium residents.

common law The body of law based on custom, usage, and court decisions.

community property A system of property ownership not in effect in New York.

company dollar   A broker's net commission income after cooperating brokers and the firm's own salespersons have been paid.

comparable property   In appraisal, a similar nearby property, recently sold, whose price can be analyzed in relation to the property being appraised.

comparables   Properties listed in an appraisal report that are substantially equivalent to the subject property. Also called *comps.*

comparative market analysis (CMA)   A study, intended to assist an owner in establishing listing price, of recent comparable sales, properties that failed to sell, and parcels presently on the market.

competent parties   Those recognized by law as being able to contract with others; usually those of legal age and sound mind.

completion bond   Bond furnished by a subdivider, guaranteeing completion of the undertaking.

Comprehensive Environmental Response, Compensation, and Liability Act (CERCLA)   Enacted in 1980 and reauthorized by the Superfund Amendments and Reauthorization Act of 1986 (SARA), this federal law imposes liability on lenders, occupants, operators and owners, for correcting environmental problems discovered on a property.

concrete slab foundation   Foundation made of poured concrete and steel rod reinforcement, resting on a waterproof sheet directly on the ground; supported by sunken concrete beams (footings).

condemnation   A judicial or administrative proceeding to exercise the power of eminent domain through which a government agency takes private property for public use and compensates the owner.

condominium   The absolute ownership of an apartment or a unit (generally in a multiunit building) plus an undivided interest in the ownership of the common elements, which are owned jointly with the other condominium unit owners.

confidentiality   An agent's duty to keep the principal's information confidential.

consent decree   Agreement by which an accused party promises not to do something illegal in the future, without admitting it was done in the past.

consideration   (1) That received by the grantor in exchange for a deed. (2) Something of value that induces a person to enter into a contract. Consideration may be *valuable* (money) or *good* (love and affection).

constitutional law   That law arising from the federal and state constitutions.

construction loan   *See* interim financing.

constructive eviction   Landlord actions that so materially disturb or impair the tenant's enjoyment of the leased premises that the tenant is effectively forced to move out and terminate the lease without liability for any further rent.

constructive notice   Notice given to the world by recorded documents. Possession of property is also considered constructive notice.

contents and personal property insurance   Coverage of personal property and other building contents when they are not on the insured premises.

contingency   A provision in a contract that requires that a certain act be done or a certain event occur before the contract becomes binding.

continuing education   The Department of State's requirement that licensees complete additional study before licenses can be renewed.

contract   An agreement entered into by two or more legally competent parties by the terms of which one or more of the parties, for a consideration, undertakes to do or refrain from doing some legal act or acts.

contract for deed   A contract for the sale of real estate wherein the purchase price is paid in periodic installments by the purchaser, who is in possession of the property even though title is retained by the seller until final payment. Also called an *installment contract* or *land contract.*

contract law   That law dealing with contracts between parties.

conventional loan   A loan not insured or guaranteed by a government.

conversions   Process by which an existing residential property is changed into a cooperative or condominium.

convertibility   An adjustable rate mortgage in which the borrower may elect to change to a fixed-rate mortgage, either whenever current rates are favorable or at specific set conversion dates.

convey   In real estate, to transfer interest or rights to another party.

conveyance   The transfer of title of land from one to another. The means or medium by which title to real estate is transferred.

cooperating broker   A broker other than the listing broker who is involved in a real estate transaction. In an MLS transaction, a subagent of the seller, unless a declared agent of the buyer.

cooperative   A residential multiunit building whose title is held by a corporation owned by and operated for the benefit of persons living within the building, who are the stockholders of the corporation, each possessing a proprietary lease.

co-ownership   Ownership by two or more persons.

corporation   An entity or organization created by operation of law whose rights of doing business are essentially the same as those of an individual.

corporation franchise tax   Tax levied on corporations as a condition of allowing them to do business in New York State.

corporation law   Those laws dealing with the creation, conduct, and dissolution of corporations.

corrective maintenance   Repairs made on damage already occurred (contrasted with *preventive maintenance*).

cost approach   The process of estimating the value of property by adding to the estimated land value the appraiser's estimate of the reproduction or replacement cost of the building, less depreciation.

cost basis *See* basis.

cost recovery Internal Revenue Service term for the accounting use of depreciation.

counteroffer A new offer made as a reply to an offer received.

county boards of health County-level boards with authority over public health issues, such as sanitary systems, water supplies, and food standards.

county planning boards Primarily advisory county agencies that promulgate reporting requirements and standards; county planning boards have greater authority in rural counties.

covenants Agreements written into deeds and other instruments promising performance or nonperformance of certain acts.

covenants, conditions, and restrictions (CC&Rs) Provision in condominium bylaws restricting the owners' usage of the property.

CPA Appraiser's memory aid in making adjustments: Comparable Poorer, Add.

CPM Certified Property Manager, a designation awarded by the Institute of Real Estate Management.

crawlspace Space too low for standing upright, usually in basement but occasionally in attic.

credit On a closing statement, an amount entered in a person's favor.

criminal law That branch of law defining crimes and providing punishment.

cubic-foot method A technique for estimating building costs per cubic foot.

current rent roll List of present tenants' rent.

curtesy/dower Legal rights each spouse has in the other's real property, no longer observed in New York state.

curvilinear system Street pattern system that integrates major arteries with smaller winding streets and cul-de-sacs.

customer A potential buyer of real estate; should not be confused with a property seller (i.e., listing broker's client).

damages The indemnity recoverable by a person who has sustained an injury, either to person, property, or rights, through the act or default of another.

datum Point from which elevations are measured. Mean sea level in New York harbor, or local datums.

DBA "Doing business as"; an assumed business name.

dealer An IRS classification for a person whose business is buying and selling real estate on his or her own account.

debit On a closing statement, a charge or amount a party owes and must pay at the closing.

debt service Mortgage payments, including principal and interest on an amortized loan.

DEC The New York Department of Environmental Conservation.

decedent A person who has died.

declaration A formal statement of intention to establish a condominium.

dedication The voluntary transfer of private property by its owner to the public for some public use such as for streets or schools.

deed A written instrument that, when executed and delivered, conveys title to or an interest in real estate.

deed restriction An imposed restriction in a deed for the purpose of limiting the use of the land by future owners.

default The nonperformance of a duty, whether arising under a contract or otherwise; failure to meet an obligation when due.

deficiency judgment A personal judgment levied against the mortgagor when a foreclosure sale does not produce sufficient funds to pay the mortgage debt in full.

delinquent taxes Unpaid past-due taxes.

delivery and acceptance The transfer of the possession of a thing from one person to another.

demising clause A clause in a lease whereby the landlord (lessor) leases and the tenant (lessee) takes the property.

demography The statistical study of populations: births, deaths, ages, etc.

denial, suspension, or revocation of license Actions by which the Department of State enforces real estate laws, rules, and regulations.

density zoning Local ordinances that limit the number of housing units that may be built per acre within a subdivision.

Department of Environmental Conservation (DEC) Agency that issues permits for developments in or around a protected wetland or other environmentally sensitive area.

Department of Housing and Community Renewal The New York State department charged with administering rent regulations.

Department of Housing and Urban Development (HUD) Federal agency that administers the Fair Housing Act of 1968.

Department of State (DOS) The New York state agency that supervises real estate licensees, through its Division of Licensing Services.

Department of Transportation State agency with oversight of New York's highway system.

deposition Sworn testimony that may be used as evidence in a suit or trial.

depreciation In appraisal, a loss of value in property due to any cause, including physical deterioration, functional obsolescence, and external (locational) obsolescence.

descent Acquisition of an estate by inheritance in which an heir succeeds to the property by operation of law.

description In real estate, the portion of a document that defines the subject property in specific legal terms.

designation An indication of special training and expertise, awarded by various real estate organizations.

determinable fee estate A fee simple estate in which the property automatically reverts to the grantor on the occurrence of a specified event or condition.

developer One who improves land with buildings, usually on a large scale, and sells to homeowners and/or investors.

devise A gift of real property by will; the act of leaving real property by will.

devisee One who receives a bequest of real estate made by will.

devisor One who bequeaths real estate by will.

direct public ownership Land-use control method through which land is owned by the government for such public uses as municipal buildings, parks, schools, and roads.

direct sales comparison approach An appraisal method in which a subject property is evaluated in comparison with similar recently sold properties; most useful for single residential properties.

disclosure A broker is responsible for keeping a principal fully informed of all facts that could affect a transaction. If a broker fails to disclose such information, he or she may be liable for any damages that result.

disclosure statement Document that must be filed by the developer of a new or converted condominium or co-operative project, including an architect's or engineer's evaluation of the structure, an expense statement, prices per unit, and other financial and administrative information.

discounted cash-flow analysis Mathematical model of variables inherent in an investment.

discounting Method for mathematically calculating present value of money, based on time and the discount rate.

discount points An added loan fee charged by a lender to make the yield on a lower-than-market-value loan competitive with higher-interest loans.

discount rate Rate of return needed to compensate an investor for risk; the Federal Reserve's loan rate for eligible banks.

disintermediation A tight-money real estate lending market (in which real estate loans are more difficult to obtain) that results when investors choose to invest in stocks, bonds, and mutual funds rather than savings accounts, limiting the funds available to lenders.

disposition Investment strategy for reconciling anticipated gain or loss with the risk involved.

Division of Housing and Community Renewal (DHCR) New York agency that administers rent control and stabilization programs.

documentary evidence Evidence in the form of written or printed papers.

dominant estate A property that includes in its ownership the right to use an easement over another person's property for a specific purpose.

DOS New York Department of State; administers license law.

down payment The amount of cash that a purchaser will pay at closing.

dual agency Representing both parties to a transaction.

due diligence A fair and responsible degree of care.

due-on-sale *See* alienation clause.

due process Legal procedures that protect the rights of the individual.

duress Unlawful constraint or action exercised on a person who is forced to perform an act against his or her will.

earnest money deposit Money deposited by a buyer under the terms of a contract, to be applied to the purchase price if the sale is closed.

easement A right to use the land of another for a specific purpose, as for a right-of-way or utilities; an incorporeal interest in land. An easement appurtenant passes with the land when conveyed.

easement appurtenant An easement involving adjacent parcels that runs with the land (is permanently attached), so that subsequent owners are bound by it, and it passes with the land when conveyed.

easement by grant An easement given (usually by deed) by one landowner to another.

easement by necessity An easement allowed by law as necessary for the full enjoyment of a parcel of real estate; for example, a right of ingress and egress over a grantor's land.

easement by prescription An easement acquired by continuous, open, uninterrupted, exclusive, and adverse use of the property for the period of time prescribed by state law.

easement in gross An easement that is not created for the benefit of any *land* owned by the owner of the easement but that attaches *personally to the easement owner.*

eave Overhang or roof projection beyond the outside walls of a house.

economic obsolescence *See* external obsolescence.

electromagnetic field (EMF) Invisible energy fields created by the movement of electrical currents in high tension wires and electrical appliances. EMFs may be responsible for occurrences of cancer, hormonal changes, and behavioral disorders.

emblements Growing crops, such as grapes and corn, that are produced annually through labor and industry; also called *fructus industriales.*

eminent domain The right of a government or quasi-public body to acquire property for public use through a court action called *condemnation.*

encroachment A building or some portion of it—a wall or fence, for instance—that extends beyond the land of the owner and illegally intrudes on some land of an adjoining owner or a street or alley.

encumbrance Any claim by another—such as a mortgage, a tax or judgment lien, an easement, an encroachment, or a deed restriction on the use of the land—that may diminish the value of a property.

endorsement An act of signing one's name on the back of a check or note with or without further qualifications.

environmental impact study Report detailing the effect of a proposed development on the existing environment, including possible alternative measures to remedy or repair environmental damage.

Environmental Protection Agency (EPA)   A federal agency involved with the problems of air and water pollution, noise, pesticides, radiation, and solid-waste management. EPA sets standards, enforces environmental laws, conducts research, allocates funds for sewage-treatment facilities, and provides technical, financial and managerial assistance for municipal, regional, and state pollution control agencies.

Equal Credit Opportunity Act (ECOA)   The federal law that prohibits discrimination in the extension of credit because of race, color, religion, national origin, sex, age or marital status.

equalization   The raising or lowering of assessed values for tax purposes in a particular county or taxing district to make them equal to assessments in other counties or districts.

equalization factor   A multiplier that adjusts for different communities' tax assessment policies.

equitable title   The interest held by a vendee under a land contract or an installment contract; the equitable right to obtain absolute ownership to property when legal title is held in another's name.

equity   The interest or value that an owner has in property over and above any mortgage indebtedness and other liens.

equity of redemption   A right of the owner to reclaim property before it is sold through foreclosure by the payment of the debt, interest, and costs.

erosion   The gradual wearing away of land by water, wind, and general weather conditions; the diminishing of property caused by the elements.

errors and omissions insurance   A form of malpractice insurance for real estate brokers.

escape clause   A provision in a contract that allows one party to unilaterally void the contract without penalty; for instance, a seller may be allowed to look for a more favorable offer, while the purchaser retains the right to drop all contingencies or void the contract if another offer is received.

escheat   The reversion of property to the state or county, as provided by state law, in cases where a person dies intestate without heirs capable of inheriting or when the property is abandoned.

escrow   The closing of a transaction through a third party called an *escrow agent*. Also can refer to earnest money deposits or to a mortgagee's trust account for insurance and tax payments.

estate   The degree, quantity, nature, and extent of interest that a person has in real property.

estate at will   The occupation of lands and tenements by a tenant for an indefinite period, terminable by one or both parties at will.

estate for years   An interest for a certain, exact period of time in property leased for a specified consideration.

estate in land   The degree, quantity, nature, and extent of interest a person has in real property.

estate tax   Federal tax levied on property transferred on death.

estoppel certificate   A document in which a borrower certifies the amount he or she owes on a mortgage loan and the rate of interest. Often used for *reduction certificate*.

eviction   A legal process to oust a person from possession of real estate.

eviction plan   Method of converting a rental property into a condominium or cooperative, in which existing tenants will be evicted when their leases expire.

evidence of title   Proof of ownership of property; commonly a certificate of title, a title insurance policy, an abstract of title with lawyer's opinion, or a Torrens registration certificate.

exchange   A transaction in which all or part of the consideration for the purchase of real property is the transfer of *like-kind* property (that is, real estate for real estate).

exclusive-agency listing   A listing contract under which the owner appoints a real estate broker as his or her exclusive agent. The owner reserves the right to sell without paying anyone a commission.

exclusive right to represent   The most common form of buyer agency agreement.

exclusive-right-to-sell listing   A listing contract under which the owner appoints a real estate broker as his or her exclusive agent and agrees to pay the broker a commission when the property is sold, whether by the roker, the owner, or another broker.

executed contract   A contract in which all parties have fulfilled their promises and thus performed the contract.

execution   The signing and delivery of an instrument. Also, a legal order directing an official to enforce a judgment against the property of a debtor.

Executive Law   New York State Human Rights Law.

executor   A male person, corporate entity, or any other type of organization designated in a will to carry out its provisions.

executory contract   A contract under which something remains to be done by one or more of the parties.

executrix   A woman appointed to perform the duties of an executor.

express agency   An agency that is specifically stated, orally or in writing.

express contract   An oral or written contract in which the parties state the contract's terms and express their intentions in words.

external obsolescence   Reduction in a property's value caused by factors outside the subject property, such as social or environmental forces or objectionable neighboring property.

fair employment laws   Laws designed to prevent employers from making their hiring and firing decisions on factors unrelated to job performance.

Fair Housing Amendment Act of 1988   Effective March 12, 1989, this amendment to the federal Fair Housing Act added two more classes protected from discrimination: those physically and mentally handicapped, and those with children under age 18.

Fair Housing Partnership Agreement Voluntary agreement between NAR and HUD to cooperate in identifying fair housing problems, issues, and solutions.

familial status A protected class under fair housing laws, which refers to the presence of children in a family.

family For the purposes of defining single-family residence, New York state considers a family one or more persons related by blood, marriage, or adoption; or up to three persons not so related who live together.

Fannie Mae A quasi-government agency established to purchase any kind of mortgage loans in the secondary mortgage market from the primary lenders.

fascia Flat board on the outside of a soffit.

federal Fair Housing Act of 1968 The federal law that prohibits discrimination in housing based on race, color, religion, sex, handicap, familial status, or national origin. Amended in 1988 to include persons with physical and mental disabilities, and those with children under 18.

Federal Home Loan Mortgage Corporation (FHLMC) *See* Freddie Mac.

Federal National Mortgage Association (FNMA) *See* Fannie Mae.

fee appraiser An appraiser who works as an independent contractor, performing appraisal services for various clients.

fee simple estate The maximum possible estate or right of ownership of real property, continuing forever. Sometimes called a *fee* or *fee simple absolute*.

FHA loan A loan insured by the Federal Housing Administration and made by an approved lender in accordance with the FHA's regulations.

fiduciary One in whom trust and confidence is placed; a reference to a broker employed under the terms of a listing contract or buyer agency agreement.

fiduciary duties The specific legal duties an agent owes to the principal.

fiduciary relationship A relationship of trust and confidence as between trustee and beneficiary, attorney and client, or principal and agent.

financing statement *See* Uniform Commercial Code.

fire and hazard insurance Policy providing coverage for direct loss of or damage to property resulting from fire, storms, hail, smoke, or riot.

first substantive contact The point at which agents must disclose and obtain signed acknowledgments of their agency relationships.

fixture An item of personal property that has been converted to real property by being permanently affixed to the realty.

flashing Waterproofing material used to seal seams of roof, chimney, and walls.

floating slab foundation Type of concrete slab foundation in which the footings and slab are poured separately.

forbearance A legally binding promise to refrain from doing some act.

foreclosure A procedure whereby property pledged as security for a debt is sold to pay the debt in the event of default in payments or terms.

franchise An organization that leases a standardized trade name, operating procedures, supplies, and referral service to member real estate brokerages.

fraud Deception that causes a person to give up property or a lawful right.

Freddie Mac A corporation established to purchase primarily conventional mortgage loans in the secondary mortgage market.

freehold estate An estate in land in which ownership is for an indeterminate length of time, in contrast to a leasehold estate.

Freon Chemical substance, formerly used in refrigerators and spray cans, now prohibited because it contributes to air pollution.

friable Crumbly, breaking off (as in some asbestos insulation).

front foot A standard measurement, one foot wide, of the width of land, applied at the frontage on its street line.

full covenant and warranty deed A deed that provides the greatest protection, in which the grantor makes five legal promises (covenants of seisin, quiet enjoyment, further assurances, warranty forever, against encumbrances) that the grantee's ownership will be unchallenged.

full-value assessment Practice of assessing property at its full value, rather than by a percentage of full value.

functional obsolescence A loss of value to an improvement to real estate due to functional problems, often caused by age or poor design.

fuse box Area where electric service enters a building and is distributed to various circuits.

future interest A person's present right to an interest in real property that will not result in possession or enjoyment until some time in the future.

gap A defect in the chain of title of a particular parcel of real estate; a missing document or conveyance that raises doubt as to present ownership.

general agent One authorized to act for the principal in a specific range of matters.

general contractor A construction specialist who enters into a formal contract with a landowner or lessee to construct a building or project.

general lien The right of a creditor to have all of a debtor's property—both real and personal—sold to satisfy a debt.

general partnership *See* partnership.

general tax *See* ad valorem tax.

Ginnie Mae A government agency that plays an important role in the secondary mortgage market. It sells mortgage-backed securities that are backed by pools of FHA and VA loans.

girder The heavy beam, wood or steel, that furnishes the main support for the first floor.

Government National Mortgage Association (GNMA) *See* Ginnie Mae.

grace period Additional time allowed to perform an act or make a payment before a default occurs.

graduated lease A lease that provides for a graduated change at stated intervals in the amount of the rent to be paid; used largely in long-term leases.

grant A sale or gift of real property.

grantee A person who receives a conveyance of real property from the grantor.

granting clause Words in a deed of conveyance that state the grantor's intention to convey the property. This clause is generally worded as "convey and warrant," "grant," "grant, bargain and sell," or the like.

grantor The person transferring title to or an interest in real property to a grantee.

GRI (Graduate, REALTORS® Institute) A professional designation earned by any member of a state-affiliated Board of REALTORS® who completes specific courses approved by the board.

gridiron pattern Street pattern systems that evolved out of the government rectangular survey, featuring a regular grid of straight-line streets and alleys.

grievance A complaint, particularly that made by a taxpayer protesting property tax assessment figures.

gross income Total income from property before any expenses are deducted.

gross income multiplier The figure used as a multiplier of the gross annual income of a property to produce an estimate of the property's value.

gross lease A lease of property under which a landlord pays all property charges regularly incurred through ownership, such as repairs, taxes, and insurance.

gross operating income Rent actually collected on an income property.

gross rental income Total amount collected in rents, from which expenses must be paid.

gross rent multiplier (GRM) A figure used as a multiplier of the gross rental income of a property to produce an estimate of the property's value.

ground lease A lease of land only, on which the tenant usually owns a building or is required to build as specified in the lease. Such leases are usually long-term net leases; the tenant's rights and obligations continue until the lease expires or is terminated through default.

groundwater Surface runoff and underground water systems.

group boycott An agreement among members of a trade to exclude other members from fair participation in the activities of the trade.

group home A living unit housing more than three unrelated individuals.

habendum clause That part of a deed beginning with the words "to have and to hold" following the granting clause and defining the extent of ownership the grantor is conveying.

hazardous substances Materials such as chemicals, industrial and residential by-products, biological waste, and other pollutants that pose an actual or suspected threat to human health, quality of life, and the environment.

headers Horizontal supports above doors and windows.

heat pump Mechanism that uses heat from outside air to reduce heating and air-conditioning costs.

hectare Land measurement equivalent to 10,000 square meters, or approximately 2.471 acres.

heir One who might inherit or succeed to an interest in land under the state law of descent when the owner dies without leaving a valid will.

highest and best use That possible use of land that would produce the greatest net income and thereby develop the highest land value.

holding period The time an investment or asset is possessed.

holdover tenancy A tenancy whereby a lessee retains possession of leased property after his or her lease has expired and the landlord, by continuing to accept rent, agrees to the tenant's continued occupancy.

holographic will A will that is written, dated, and signed in the testator's handwriting but is not witnessed.

home equity loan A loan (sometimes called a *line of credit*) under which a property owner uses his or her residence as collateral and can then draw funds up to a prearranged amount against the property.

home occupations Small business or creative activities, allowed to residents in an area otherwise zoned entirely residential.

homeowners' association A nonprofit group of homeowners in a condominium, cooperative, or PUD that administers common elements and enforces covenants, conditions, and restrictions.

homeowner's insurance policy A standardized package insurance policy that covers a residential real estate owner against financial loss from fire, theft, public liability, and other commercial risks.

homestead Land that is owned and occupied as the family home. The right to protect a portion of the value of this land from unsecured judgments for debts.

impact fees Charges levied by a local government to help the community absorb the public costs involved in the development of a new subdivision.

implied agency An agency established not by words, but by the actions of the parties.

implied contract A contract under which the agreement of the parties is demonstrated by their acts and con-duct.

implied creation of a subagency The unintended creation of a fiduciary relationship through an informal cooperation arrangement between brokers.

implied warranty of habitability A theory in landlord/tenant law in which the landlord renting residential property implies that the property is habitable and fit for its intended use.

improvement Any structure erected on a site to enhance the value of the property—buildings, fences, driveways, curbs, sidewalks, or sewers.

imputed interest An IRS concept that treats some concessionary low-interest loans as if they had been paid and collected at a statutory rate.

income capitalization approach The process of estimating the value of an income-producing property by capitalization of the annual net income expected to be produced by the property during its remaining useful life.

incompetent A person who is unable to manage his or her own affairs by reason of insanity, imbecility, or feeblemindedness.

independent contractor Someone retained to perform a certain act but subject to the control and direction of another only as to the end result and not as to the way in which he or she performs the act; contrasted with employee.

index With an adjustable-rate mortgage, a measure of current interest rates, used as a basis for calculating the new rate at the time of adjustment.

index lease A lease in which the rental figure is adjusted periodically according to the government's cost-of-living index.

industrial real estate Warehouses, factories, land in industrial districts, and research facilites (sometimes referred to as *manufacturing property*).

informed consent Agreement to an act based on the full and fair disclosure of all the facts a reasonable person would need in order to make a rational decision.

infrastructure Basic public works such as utilities, roads, bridges, sewer and water systems, etc.

inheritance tax New York State tax levied on those who inherit property located in the state.

injunction An order issued by a court to restrain one party from doing an act deemed to be unjust to the rights of some other party.

in rem A proceeding against the realty directly as distinguished from a proceeding against a person.

installment contract *See* land contract.

installment sale A method of reporting income received from the sale of real estate when the sales price is paid in two or more installments over two or more years.

instrument A written legal document created to effect the rights of the parties.

insulation Material that protects a surface from cold or heat.

interest A charge made by a lender for the use of money.

interest rate The percentage of a sum of money charged for its use.

interim financing A short-term loan usually made during the construction phase of a building project (in this case often referred to as a *construction loan*).

internal rate of return (IRR) Discount rate that, when applied to both positive and negative cash flows, results in zero net present value.

Interstate Land Sales Full Disclosure Act A federal law that regulates the sale of certain real estate in interstate commerce.

intestate The condition of a property owner who dies without leaving a valid will.

involuntary alienation Transfer of real estate without the owner's initiative, as in foreclosure or condemnation.

involuntary bankruptcy A bankruptcy proceeding initiated by one or more of the debtor's creditors.

involuntary lien A lien imposed against property without consent of the owners, i.e., taxes, special assessments.

irrevocable consent An agreement filed by an out-of-state broker stating that suits and actions may be brought against the broker in the state where a license is sought.

joint tenancy Ownership of real estate between two or more parties who have been named in one conveyance as joint tenants. On the death of a joint tenant, his or her interest passes to the surviving joint tenant or tenants.

joint venture The joining of two or more people to conduct a specific business enterprise.

joist and rafter roof Roofing system that relies on sloping timbers supported by a ridge board and made rigid by interconnecting joists.

judgment The formal decision of a court regarding the respective claims of the parties to an action.

jumbo loan A loan that exceeds FNMA and FHLMC maximum loan limits.

junior lien An obligation such as a second mortgage that is subordinate in priority to an existing lien on the same realty.

kickbacks The return of part of the commission as gifts or money to buyers or sellers.

laches Loss of a legal right through undue delay in asserting it.

Lally™ columns Upright columns that support the main beams of a building.

land The earth's surface, extending downward to the center of the earth and upward infinitely into space.

land contract *See* contract for deed.

landfill A site for the burial, layering, and permanent storage of waste material, consisting of alternating layers of waste and topsoil.

landlord One who rents property to another.

last will and testament An instrument executed by an owner to convey the owner's property to specific persons after the owner's death.

latent defects A hidden defect that is not discoverable by ordinary inspection.

law of agency The law that governs the relationships and duties of agents, clients, and customers. *See* agent.

lead agency In an environmental survey, the one agency that coordinates the process.

lead poisoning Illness, including the impairment of physical and mental development in children and aggravated blood pressure in adults, resulting from the ingestion of lead toxins, primarily in paint or plumbing.

Leaking Underground Storage Tanks (LUST) Federal environmental protection program to protect the nation's groundwater by identifying underground tanks and preventing or correcting leakage of hazardous materials.

lease A written or oral contract between a landlord (the lessor) and a tenant (the lessee) that transfers the right to exclusive possession and use of the landlord's real property to the lessee for a specified period of time and for a stated consideration (rent).

leasehold estate   A tenant's right to occupy real estate during the term of a lease; generally considered personal property.

legacy   A disposition of money or personal property by will.

legal description   A description of a specific parcel of real estate complete enough for an independent surveyor to locate and identify it.

legality of object   The requirement that a valid and enforceable contract may not involve an illegal purpose or one that is against public policy.

lessee   Tenant.

lessor   Landlord.

leverage   The use of borrowed money to finance the bulk of an investment.

levy   The placing of tax liens against real property.

liability insurance   Standard package homeowner's insurance policy coverage for personal injuries to others resulting from the insured's acts or negligence; voluntary medical payments and funeral expenses for accidents sustained by guests or resident employees on the property and physical damage to other's property.

license   (1) A privilege or right granted to a person by a state to operate as a real estate broker or salesperson. (2) The revocable permission for a temporary use of land.

lien   A right given by law to certain creditors to have their debt paid out of the property of a defaulting debtor, usually by means of a court sale.

lien theory   Some states interpret a mortgage as being purely a lien on real property. The mortgagee thus has no right of possession but must foreclose the lien and sell the property if the mortgagor defaults.

life estate   An interest in real or personal property that is limited in duration to the lifetime of its owner or some other designated person.

life tenant   A person in possession of a life estate.

like-kind property   *See* exchange.

limited liability company (LLC)   A hybrid business entity that combines the managerial freedom of partnerships with the limited liability for owner and avoidance of income taxes offered by corporations.

limited partnership   *See* partnership.

liquidated damages   An amount of money, agreed to in advance, that will serve as the total compensation due to the injured party if the other does not comply with the contract's terms.

liquidity   The ability to sell an asset and convert it into cash at a price close to its true value in a short period of time.

lis pendens   A recorded legal document giving constructive notice that an action affecting a particular property has been filed in court.

listing agent   The broker with whom a seller enters into a valid listing agreement for the sale of his or her real estate.

listing agreement   A contract between a landowner (as principal) and a licensed real estate broker (as agent) by which the broker is employed as agent to sell real estate on the owner's terms within a given time, for which service the landowner agrees to pay a commission or fee.

listing broker   The agent hired by a property owner to assist in the marketing of real estate.

litigation   Lawsuits.

littoral rights   (1) A landowner's claim to use water in large navigable lakes and oceans adjacent to his or her property. (2) The ownership rights to land bordering these bodies of water up to the high-water mark.

LLP   A limited liability corporation.

loan servicing   The lender's duties in administering a loan, such as collecting payments, accounting and bookkeeping, maintaining records, and issuing loan status reports to the borrower.

loan-to-value (LTV) ratio   The relationship between the amount of the mortgage loan and the market value of the real estate being pledged as collateral.

locational obsolescence   *See* external obsolescence.

loyalty   The fiduciary duty that requires an agent to put the principal's interest above all others, including the agent's.

management agreement   Employment contract between property owner and manager, under which the manager assumes the responsibility for administering and maintaining the property as the owner's general agent.

management proposal   A property manager's report to the owner of his or her plan for supervising the property.

margin   With an adjustable-rate mortgage, the number of points over an *index* at which the interest rate is set.

marginal tax rate   Percentage at which the last dollar of income is taxed; top tax bracket.

marital status   A protected class under New York state law that does not allow sellers or landlords to base decisions on whether prospective occupants are married or not.

marketable title   Good or clear title reasonably free from the risk of litigation over possible defects.

market allocation   An agreement among members of a trade to refrain from competition in specific areas.

market analysis   Study undertaken by a property manager of the local and regional market, as well as the underlying property itself, to provide information about the economic conditions, supply, demand, and similar competing properties.

market data approach   *See* direct sales comparison approach.

market price   The actual selling price of a property.

market value   The probable price a ready, willing, able and informed buyer would pay and a ready, willing, able and informed seller would accept, neither being under any pressure to act.

master plan   A comprehensive plan to guide the long-term physical development of a particular area.

maximum base rent (MBR)   Under rent control, the maximum rent allowable for an individual unit.

mechanic's lien A statutory lien created in favor of contractors, laborers, and material suppliers who have performed work or furnished materials in the erection or repair of a building.

mediation Method for dealing with disputes; the person running the session does not make a determination, but rather brings the parties into agreement.

meeting of the minds *See* offer and acceptance.

memorandum of sale A nonbinding information sheet prepared by brokers in some New York localities that states the essential terms of the agreement; the final contract is later drawn up by an attorney.

metes-and-bounds description A legal description of a parcel of land that begins at a well-marked point and follows the boundaries, using direction and distances around the tract, back to the place of beginning.

Metropolitan Transport Authority (MTA) Regional agency with taxing power and jurisdiction over certain air and land rights.

mill One-tenth of one cent. A tax rate of 52 mills would be $.052 tax for each dollar of assessed valuation of a property.

minimum building standards Degree of quality and care mandated by the state; local codes and regulations may require adherence to a higher standard.

minor A person under 18 years of age.

MIP Mortgage insurance premium.

misdemeanor A crime less than a felony but greater than a violation.

misrepresentation A false statement or concealment of a material fact made with the intent of causing another party to act.

month-to-month tenancy A periodic tenancy; that is, the tenant rents for one period at a time. In the absence of a rental agreement (oral or written), a tenancy is generally considered to be month to month.

monument A fixed natural or artificial object used to establish real estate boundaries for a metes-and-bounds description.

moratorium A period of delay; in real estate usually refers to a community's temporary halt to development.

mortgage A conditional transfer or pledge of real estate as security for the payment of a debt. Also, the document creating a mortgage lien.

mortgage bankers Companies that are licensed to make real estate loans that are sold to investors.

mortgage broker An individual who acts as an intermediary between lenders and borrowers for a fee.

mortgage debt service Property owner's expense for payments (usually monthly) on mortgages.

mortgagee A lender in a mortgage loan transaction.

mortgage insurance premium (MIP) Lump sum premium for mortgage insurance coverage, payable either in cash at closing or financed over the mortgage term.

mortgage lien A lien or charge on the property of a mortgagor that secures the underlying debt obligations.

mortgage reduction certificate An instrument executed by the mortgagee setting forth the present status and the balance due on the mortgage as of the date of the execution of the instrument.

mortgagor A borrower who conveys his or her property as security for a loan.

multiperil policies Insurance policies offering protection from a range of potential perils, such as fire, hazard, public liability, and casualty, in a single policy.

multiple-listing service A marketing organization composed of member brokers who agree to share their listings with one another in the hope of procuring ready, willing, and able buyers more quickly and efficiently.

negative amortization Gradual building up of a large mortgage debt when payments are not sufficient to cover interest due and reduce the principal.

negative cash flow Negative figure resulting when expenditures on an investment exceed the income it produces.

negligence An unintentional tort caused by failure to exercise reasonable care.

negotiable instrument A signed promise to pay a sum of money.

neighborhood analysis A property manager's study of nearby rental availability and market rental figures.

net lease A lease requiring that the tenant pay not only rent but also some or all costs of maintaining the property, including taxes, insurance, utilities, and repairs.

net listing A listing based on the net price the seller will receive if the property is sold. Under a net listing the broker is free to offer the property for sale at any price to increase the commission. Outlawed in New York.

net operating income (NOI) The income projected for an income-producing property after deducting losses for vacancy and collection and operating expenses.

net present value (NPV) Difference between the present value of all positive and negative cash flows.

New York City Department of Environmental Protection (DEP) Local agency with authority over the city's water supply (from its source to local reservoirs), and which ensures that construction projects do not interfere with the watershed.

New York General Obligations Law The state's version of the Statute of Frauds, which requires, among other provisions, that any agreements relating to the sale of real estate must be in writing.

New York Human Rights Law State law prohibiting discrimination in housing.

New York State Division of Human Rights Agency with which a complaint of housing discrimination may file a complaint within one year of the alleged act.

nonconforming mortgage Flexible loan that does not meet standard uniform underwriting requirements, usually structured for borrowers who have unique credit situations or who wish to purchase an unusual property.

nonconforming use Use of land that is not allowed by the local zoning ordinance.

noneviction plan Method of converting a rental property into a condominium or cooperative.

nonhomestead Not used as the owner's primary residence: buildings with more than four dwelling units, industrial and commercial property, most vacant land.

nonhomogeneity A lack of uniformity; dissimilarity. Because no two parcels of land are exactly alike, real estate is said to be nonhomogeneous.

notary public A public officer who is authorized to take acknowledgments to certain classes of documents such as deeds, contracts, and mortgages and before whom affidavits may be sworn.

note An instrument of credit given to attest a debt.

novation Substituting a new obligation for an old one or substituting new parties to an existing obligation.

nuisance An act that disturbs another's peaceful enjoyment of property.

NYSAR New York State Association of REALTORS®.

obedience The agent's fiduciary duty to obey all lawful instructions of the principal.

obsolescence *See* external obsolescence; functional obsolescence.

offer and acceptance Two essential components of a valid contract; a "meeting of the minds," when all parties agree to the exact terms.

office property Any type of structure (lowrise, highrise, complex, or campus) used by nonmanufacturing, nonretail tenants such as medical, legal, and financial professionals.

open-end mortgage A mortgage loan that is expandable to a maximum dollar amount, the loan being secured by the same original mortgage.

open listing A listing contract under which the broker's commission is contingent on the broker's producing a ready, willing, and able buyer before the property is sold by the owner or another broker.

operating budget A property manager's detailed plan for expenses.

option An agreement to keep open for a set period an offer to sell or purchase property.

package loan A real estate loan used to finance the purchase of both real property and personal property, such as the purchase of a new home that includes carpeting, window coverings, and major appliances.

package mortgage A method of financing in which the loan that finances the purchase of a home also finances the purchase of items of personal property such as appliances.

parcel A specific piece of real estate.

parol evidence rule A rule of evidence providing that a written agreement is the final expression of the agreement of the parties, not to be varied or contradicted by prior or contemporaneous oral or written negotiations.

participation financing A mortgage in which the lender participates in the income of the mortgaged venture.

participation loan A mortgage arrangement in which the lender receives a share of the venture's profits or the real estate's appreciation.

partition The division of real property made between those who own it in undivided shares.

partnership An association of two or more individuals who carry on a continuing business for profit as co-owners. A *general partnership* is a typical form of joint venture in which each general partner shares in the administration, profits and losses of the operations. A *limited partnership* is administered by one or more general partners and funded by limited or silent partners who are by law responsible for losses only to the extent of their investments.

party wall A wall that is located on or at a boundary line between two adjoining parcels of land and is used by the owners of both properties.

passive income Income derived from an investment activity in which the investor does not take an active management or participatory role.

percentage lease A lease commonly used for commercial property whose rental is based on the tenant's gross sales at the premises.

percolation The soil's ability to process water.

percolation rate A figure establishing how quickly liquid can drain through the ground.

percolation test A test to see if a septic tank will work successfully in a specific location.

periodic estate An interest in leased property that continues from period to period—week to week, month to month, or year to year.

personal property Items, called *chattels*, that do not fit into the definition of real property; movable objects.

personal property law That section of the law dealing with chattels.

personal representative The administrator or executor appointed to handle the estate of a decedent.

physical deterioration Loss of value due to wear and tear or action of the elements.

pier and beam foundation Foundation style in which partly-submerged columns (piers) support the foundation slab, with an air pocket (crawlspace) between the slab and the ground.

pitch Slope of a roof expressed as a ratio of height to span.

PITI Principal, interest, taxes, and insurance: components of a regular mortgage payment.

planned unit development (PUD) A planned combination of diverse land uses such as housing, recreation, and shopping in one contained development or subdivision.

planning board Municipal body overseeing orderly development of real estate.

plasterboard/wallboard Prepared 4' by 8' boards often used as wall finish in place of plaster.

plat A map of a town, section, or subdivision indicating the location and boundaries of individual properties.

platform framing construction Common form of construction for one- and two-story residential buildings; one floor is built at a time, with the lower floor providing a platform on which the upper floor is built.

plat of subdivision A map of a planned subdivision, entered in the public records.

plottage The increase in value or utility resulting from the consolidation (assemblage) of two or more adjacent lots into one larger lot.

PMI Private mortgage insurance.

pocket card Copy of a real estate license, issued by the Department of State, to be carried in the licensee's wallet.

point A unit of measurement used for various loan charges; one point equals 1 percent of the amount of the loan. *See also* discount points.

point of beginning In a metes-and-bounds legal description, the starting point of the survey, situated in one corner of the parcel. Also called *place of beginning*.

police power The government's right to impose laws, statutes, and ordinances, including zoning ordinances and building codes, to protect the public health, safety, and welfare.

policy and procedures guide A broker's compilation of guidelines for the conduct of the firm's business.

pollution Artificially created environmental impurity.

polychlorinated biphenyls (PCBs) Potentially hazardous chemical used in electrical equipment, principally transformers.

post-and-beam construction An old framing method in which ceiling planks are placed on beams (often left exposed).

potentially responsible parties (PRPs) Under Superfund, the landowners suspected of contaminating a property.

power of attorney A written instrument authorizing a person, the *attorney-in-fact*, to act as agent on behalf of another person.

precedent A court decision that serves as authority for later cases.

preliminary prospectus Description of new or converted condominium or cooperative property, subject to change, available for inspection by present tenants after review by the attorney general (also referred to as a *red herring*).

premises Lands and tenements; an estate; the subject matter of a conveyance.

prepaid item A bill paid by the seller for something the buyer will benefit from: the coming year's property taxes, for example. Buyer will reimburse seller at closing for the unused portion.

prepayment clause A clause in a mortgage that gives the mortgagor the privilege of paying the mortgage indebtedness before it becomes due.

prepayment premium (penalty) A charge imposed on a borrower who pays off the loan principal early.

present value of money Money's value changes over time: For example, the present value of $1 receivable in one year is $1 minus the lost potential interest on the dollar. If the interest rate is 7 percent, then the present value of $1 to be received in one year is 93¢ today.

preventive maintenance Maintenance done to avoid possible future damage.

price-fixing An agreement between members of a trade to artificially maintain prices at a set level.

primary mortgage market Lenders who make loans directly to real estate borrowers.

principal (1) A sum lent or employed as a fund or an investment as distinguished from its income or profits. (2) The original amount (as in a loan) of the total due and payable at a certain date. (3) A main party of a transaction; the person for whom the agent works.

principal broker *See* supervising broker.

priority The order of position or time.

private mortgage insurance (PMI) Insurance that limits a lender's potential loss in a mortgage default, issued by a private company rather than by the FHA.

probate To establish the will of a deceased person.

procuring cause of sale The effort that brings about the desired result. Under an open listing the broker who is the procuring cause of the sale receives the commission.

professional home inspections Examination of a property's structure and systems performed by a trained professional for either prospective buyers, lenders, or home owners.

pro forma statement Financial statement showing what is expected to occur, particularly with income property.

progression Economic principle that a lower-quality property's worth will be enhanced by its proximity to higher-quality properties.

property manager Someone who manages real estate for another person for compensation.

property management report A property manager's regular report to the owner.

property analysis A property manager's examination of leases and rental rates.

proprietary lease A written lease in a cooperative apartment building, held by the tenant/shareholder, giving the right to occupy a particular unit.

prorations Expenses, either prepaid or paid in arrears, that are divided or distributed between buyer and seller at the closing.

prospectus A printed statement disclosing all material aspects of a real estate project.

protected classes Groups of individuals who have been found to be in need of protection by federal, state, or local laws and regulations against discriminatory actions or conditions.

public offering A transaction falling under the jurisdiction of the New York attorney general's office, requiring certain specific transactional and financial disclosures. The sale of any form of shared housing in New York is a public offering.

PUD *See* planned unit development.

puffing Exaggerated or superlative comments or opinions not made as representations of fact and thus not grounds for misrepresentation.

pur autre vie   For the life of another. A life estate pur autre vie is a life estate that is measured by the life of a person other than the grantee.

purchase-money mortgage (PMM)   A note secured by a mortgage or deed of trust given by a buyer, as borrower, to a seller, as lender, as part of the purchase price of the real estate.

pyramid   Investment strategy of refinancing existing properties and using the borrowed money.

quiet enjoyment   The right of an owner or a person legally in possession to the use of property without interference of possession.

quiet title suit   *See* suit to quiet title.

quitclaim deed   A conveyance by which the grantor transfers whatever interest he or she has in the real estate, if any, without warranties or obligations.

radioactive waste   Hazardous by-product of uses of radioactive materials in energy production, medicine, and scientific research.

radon gas   Odorless, naturally occurring radioactive gas that becomes hazardous when trapped and accumulated in unventilated areas of buildings. Long-term exposure to radon is suspected of causing lung cancer.

rate of return   The ratio between earnings and the cost of the investment.

ratification   Method of creating an agency relationship in which the principal accepts the conduct of someone who acted without prior authorization as the principal's agent.

ready, willing, and able buyer   One who is prepared to buy property on the seller's terms and is ready to take positive steps to consummate the transaction.

real estate   A portion of the earth's surface extending downward to the center of the earth and upward infinitely into space, including all things permanently attached thereto, whether by nature or by a person.

real estate broker   Any person, partnership, association, or corporation that sells (or offers to sell), buys (or offers to buy), or negotiates the purchase, sale, or exchange of real estate, or that leases (or offers to lease) or rents (or offers to rent) any real estate or the improvements thereon for others and for a compensation or valuable consideration.

real estate investment syndicate   Business organization in which individuals combine their resources to invest in, manage or develop a particular property.

real estate investment trust (REIT)   Trust ownership of real estate by a group of individuals who purchase certificates of ownership in the trust.

real estate mortgage investment conduit (REMIC)   A tax vehicle created by the Tax Reform Act of 1986 that permits certain entities that deal in pools of mortgages to pass income through to investors.

real estate sales contract   A contract for the sale of real estate, in which the purchaser promises to pay the agreed purchase price and the seller agrees to deliver title to the property.

real estate salesperson   A person licensed by the state to assist a licensed broker in the field of real estate.

Real Estate Settlement Procedures Act (RESPA)   The federal law that requires certain disclosures to consumers about mortgage loan settlements. The law also prohibits the payment or receipt of kickbacks and certain kinds of referral fees.

real property   Real estate plus all the interests, benefits, and rights inherent in ownership. Often referred to as *real estate*.

Real Property Law   New York law governing the real estate profession, including prohibitions against discrimination in housing.

REALTORS®   A registered trademark term reserved for the sole use of active members of local REALTOR® boards affiliated with the National Association of REALTORS®.

reasonable care   A broker's duty to perform duties properly.

reciprocity   An arrangement by which states agree to honor each other's licenses, as with real estate salespersons or brokers.

reconciliation   The final step in the appraisal process, in which the appraiser weighs the estimates of value received from the direct sales comparison, cost, and income approaches to arrive at a final estimate of value for the subject property.

recording   The act of entering or recording documents affecting or conveying interests in real estate in the recorder's office established in each county.

rectangular survey system   A system established in 1785 by the federal government providing for surveying and describing land outside the 13 original colonies by reference to principal meridians and base lines.

redemption period   A period of time established by state law during which a property owner has the right to redeem his or her real estate from a tax sale by paying the sales price, interest and costs.

red herring   Preliminary offering plan for a cooperative or condominium project submitted to the attorney general and to tenants and subject to modification.

redlining   The illegal practice of a lending institution denying loans or restricting their number for certain areas of a community.

reduction certificate   A statement from the lender detailing the amount remaining and currently due on a mortgage, usually sought when a mortgage is being assumed or prepaid (also referred to as an *estoppel certificate*).

referee's deed   A deed delivered when property is conveyed pursuant to court order.

reference to a plat   A form of legal description, which cites the book and page on which the subject property can be identified on a map.

regional analysis   Study of the economic and demographic character of the larger regional or metropolitan area in which a property is located.

regression Economic principle that the worth of a higher-quality property will be diminished by its proximity to lower-quality properties.

Regulation Z Law requiring credit institutions and advertisers to inform borrowers of the true cost of obtaining credit; commonly called the *Truth-in-Lending Act.*

release The act or writing by which some claim or interest is surrendered to another.

release clause A mortgage clause that permits part of the mortgaged property to be released from the lien; often used with blanket mortgages.

remainder The remnant of an estate that has been conveyed to take effect and be enjoyed after the termination of a prior estate, as when an owner conveys a life estate to one party and the remainder to another.

remainder interest The remnant of an estate that has been conveyed to take effect and be enjoyed after the termination of a prior estate, such as when an owner conveys a life estate to one party and the remainder to another.

remainderman The person who is to receive the property after the death of a life tenant.

rent A fixed, periodic payment made by a tenant of a property to the owner for possession and use, usually by prior agreement of the parties.

rent control State or local regulations restricting the amount of rent that may be charged for particular properties.

rent stabilization Local regulations that stem from the adoption of the Emergency Tenant Protection Act, and which limit maximum allowable rent increases.

replacement cost The construction cost at current prices of a property that is not necessarily an exact duplicate of the subject property but serves the same purpose or function as the original.

reproduction cost The construction cost at current prices of an exact duplicate of the subject property.

rescission The canceling of a contract.

reserves Money set aside to accumulate for future expenses.

residential property Real estate used as a dwelling.

residential real estate All property used for housing, from acreage to small city lots, both single-family and multifamily, in urban, suburban, and rural areas.

resident manager A property manager who resides on the site.

restraint of trade The unreasonable restriction of business activities as the result of the cooperation or conspiracy of members of the trade.

restrictive covenant Provisions placed in a deed by the grantor, restricting future uses for the property.

restriction A limitation on the use of real property, generally originated by the owner or subdivider in a deed.

retail property Any type of property used for commercial retail purposes, including storefronts, shopping centers, and enclosed malls.

return The income from a real estate investment, calculated as a percentage of cash invested.

reverse-annuity mortgage (RAM) A loan under which the homeowner receives monthly payments based on his or her accumulated equity rather than a lump sum. The loan must be repaid at a prearranged date or upon the death of the owner or the sale of the property.

reverse discrimination (*benign discrimination*) Housing discrimination, usually based on quotas, designed by a municipality to achieve a racial balance perceived as desirable.

reversion The remnant of an estate that the grantor holds after he or she has granted a life estate to another person, if the estate will return, or revert, to the grantor; also called a *reverter.*

reversionary right The return of the rights of possession and quiet enjoyment to the lessor at the expiration of a lease.

reversionary interest The remnant of an estate that the grantor holds after he or she has granted a life estate to another person, if the estate will return, or revert, to the grantor; also called a *reverter.*

revocation An act of recalling a power of authority conferred, such as the revocation of a power of attorney, a license, or an agency.

rider An amendment or attachment to a contract.

right of first refusal A provision that a condominium or cooperative association has the first right to purchase if a member wishes to sell his or her unit.

right of survivorship *See* joint tenancy.

right-of-way The right to pass over another's land more or less frequently according to the nature of the easement.

riparian rights An owner's rights in land that borders on or includes a stream, river, or lake. These rights include access to and use of the water.

R-value Numerical measurement of insulating material's resistance to heat transfer; a higher R-value indicates superior insulation.

Safe Drinking Water Act Federal law requiring local public water suppliers to periodically test the quality of drinking water.

sale-and-leaseback A transaction in which an owner sells his or her improved property and, as part of the same transaction, signs a long-term lease to remain in possession of the premises.

sales comparison approach The process of estimating the value of a property by examining and comparing actual sales of comparable properties.

sales contract A contract containing the complete terms of the agreement between buyer and seller for the sale of a particular parcel of real estate.

salesperson A person who performs real estate activities while employed by or associated with a licensed real estate broker.

SARA The federal Superfund Amendments and Reauthorization Act, concerned with environmental clean-ups.

satisfaction of mortgage *See* satisfaction piece.

satisfaction piece   A document provided by the mortgagee, stating that the debt has been paid off. A document acknowledging the payment of a debt. Also called *satisfaction of mortgage*.

S corporation   A form of corporation taxed as a partnership.

secondary mortgage market   A market for the purchase and sale of existing mortgages, designed to provide greater liquidity of mortgages.

section   A portion of a township under the rectangular survey (government survey) system. A section is a square with mile-long sides and an area of one square mile, or 640 acres.

Section 8   Federal housing assistance program administered by the FHA, in which low- and moderate-income tenants pay a fixed portion of their income in rent, with HUD paying the remainder.

Section 1031 property exchange   A tax-deferred exchange of like-kind investment or commercial property.

security agreement   A document pledging personal property as security for a debt.

security deposit   A payment by a tenant, held by the landlord during the lease term and kept (wholly or partially) on default or destruction of the premises by the tenant.

seisin   The possession of land by one who claims to own at least an estate for life therein.

self-dealing   The act of a broker who lists property and then buys it and collects the agreed-on commission.

seller agency   The practice of representing the seller in a real estate transaction.

selling broker   The broker who successfully finds a ready, willing, and able buyer for a property (may or may not be the listing broker).

sensitivity analysis   Analysis of a projected investment, to discover which variable is most significant in anticipated cash flow.

septic system   Wastewater treatment and disposal system used by individual households.

SEQRA   New York's State Environmental Quality Review Act, requiring environmental impact statements before certain development projects.

servient tenement   Land on which an easement exists in favor of an adjacent property (called a *dominant estate*); also called *servient estate*.

setback   The amount of space local zoning regulations require between a lot line and a building line.

severalty   Ownership of real property by one person only; also called *sole ownership*.

shared-appreciation mortgage   A mortgage loan in which the lender, in exchange for a loan with a favorable interest rate, participates in the profits (if any) when the property is eventually sold.

shared-equity mortgage   A loan in which the lender will receive part of any appreciation on the property.

sheathing   Material applied to framing members to form walls, often plywood, insulating material, or sheetrock.

Sherman (and Clayton) Anti-Trust Acts   Federal legislation prohibiting business practices that limit competition.

sick building syndrome (SBS)   Range of symptoms, such as asthma, coughing, and hoarseness, that are related to the individual's presence in the affected building, but that disappear when he or she is not exposed to the building's environment. *See* building-related illness.

siding   Exterior wall finish of a building: commonly brick, shingles or clapboard, wood or vinyl.

silent partner   One who takes no part in managing the enterprise, and whose possible losses are usually limited to his or her investment.

sill plates   Horizontal supports on top of the foundation.

single agency   An agency relationship in which the agent represents a single party.

situs   The location of a property.

slab-on-grade construction   Concrete slab poured on prepared earth as a foundation.

small claims court   A special local court for settling disputes without the need for attorneys or expensive court costs.

soffit   Horizontal finish for the underside of a roof overhang.

solar energy   Use of solar collectors to convert heat from the sun into usable heat and energy for a building.

sole proprietorship   A business owned by one individual.

Sonny Mae (SONYMA)   The state of New York Mortgage Agency.

special agent   One authorized by a principal to perform a single act or transaction.

special assessment   A tax or levy customarily imposed against only those specific parcels of real estate that will benefit from a proposed public improvement like a street or sewer.

special-purpose buildings   Real estate neither residential, commercial, industrial or agricultural. Includes schools, hospitals, churches, and government-held property.

special purpose real estate   Religious institutions, schools, cemeteries, hospitals, and government-held land.

special-use permit   Permission granted by a local government to allow a use of property that, although in conflict with zoning regulations, is nonetheless in the public interest (a house of worship in a residential neighborhood, for instance, or a restaurant in an industrial zone).

special warranty deed   A deed in which the grantor warrants, or guarantees, the title only against defects arising during the period of his or her tenure and ownership of the property and not against defects existing before that time, generally using the language "by, through, or under the grantor but not otherwise."

specifications   The architect's or engineer's detailed instructions for material used in construction.

specific lien   A lien affecting or attaching only to a certain specific parcel of land or piece of property.

specific performance suit A legal action brought in a court of equity in special cases to compel a party to carry out the terms of a contract.

sponsor The developer or owner organizing and offering for sale a condominium or cooperative development.

sponsoring broker The principal broker in a real estate firm, who undertakes to train and supervise associated licensees.

spot zoning Special zoning actions that affect only a small area. Uses that are not in harmony with the surrounding uses are illegal in New York.

staff appraiser A professional appraiser employed in-house to perform appraisals solely for the employer.

statute of frauds The part of state law requiring that certain instruments, such as deeds, real estate sales contracts, and certain leases, be in writing to be legally enforceable.

statute of limitations That law pertaining to the period of time within which certain actions must be brought to court; in New York, six years for contracts.

statutory lien A lien imposed on property by statute—a tax lien, for example—in contrast to a voluntary lien such as a mortgage lien that an owner places on his or her own real estate.

statutory redemption The right of a defaulted property owner to recover the property after its sale by paying the appropriate fees and charges.

statutory redemption period Period of time after a tax sale in which the delinquent taxpayer may regain the property by paying the back taxes, penalties, interest, and costs.

statutory law Law that is established by legislative bodies.

steering The illegal practice of channeling home seekers to particular areas for discriminatory ends.

straight-line depreciation An accounting "expense" against rental income, arrived at by dividing the cost of the building by the number of years allowed by the Internal Revenue Service.

straight-line method A method of calculating cost recovery for tax purposes, computed by dividing the adjusted basis of a property by the number of years chosen.

straight (term) loan A loan in which only interest is paid during the term of the loan, with the entire principal amount due with the final interest payment.

studs Upright supports that form a wall.

subagency An agency relationship in which the broker's sales associate, or a cooperating broker, assumes a fiduciary duty to the principal who has designated the broker as an agent.

subagent A broker's sales associate in relation to the principal who has designated the broker as an agent.

subchapter S corporation *See* S corporation.

subcontractor *See* general contractor.

subdivide Partitioning a tract of land to sell it as individual lots.

subdivision A tract of land divided by the owner, known as the *subdivider*, into blocks, building lots, and streets according to a recorded subdivision plat.

subdivision regulations New York state requirements for subdivisions, which apply as soon as the fifth lot is sold off a larger parcel.

subject property The property being appraised.

subject to a mortgage When a property is taken "subject to" a mortgage, the purchaser is not personally liable to the mortgagee for satisfaction of the pre-existing debt (unless he or she agrees to be held liable).

sublease *See* subletting.

subletting The leasing of premises by a tenant to a third party for part of the tenant's remaining term. *See also* assignment.

subordination agreement Relegation to a lesser position, usually in respect to a right or security.

subrogation The substitution of one creditor for another with the substituted person succeeding to the legal rights and claims of the original claimant.

subscribing witness One who writes his or her name as witness to the execution of an instrument.

substitution An appraisal principle stating that the maximum value of a property tends to be set by the cost of purchasing an equally desirable and valuable substitute property.

subsurface rights Ownership rights in a parcel of real estate of any water, minerals, gas, oil, and so forth that lie beneath the surface of the property.

suit for possession A court suit initiated by a landlord to evict a tenant from leased premises after the tenant has breached one of the terms of the lease or has held possession of the property after the lease's expiration.

suit to quiet title A court action intended to establish or settle the title to a particular property, especially when there is a cloud on the title.

Superfund Amendments and Reauthorization Act (SARA) Federal law defining landowner responsibility for cleanup of environmental contamination resulting from past activities. Establishes innocent landowner defense against liability for contamination caused by prior owners.

supervising broker The one broker registered with the Department of State as in charge of a real estate office, responsible for the actions of salespersons and associate brokers.

surety bond Bond covering an owner against financial losses resulting from the criminal acts or negligence of an employee in the course of performing his or her job.

surface rights Ownership rights in a parcel of real estate that are limited to the surface of the property and do not include the air above it (air rights) or the minerals below the surface (subsurface rights).

surrender The cancellation of a lease by mutual consent of the lessor and the lessee.

surrogate's court (probate court) A court having jurisdiction over the proof of wills, the settling of estates, and adoptions.

survey The process by which a parcel of land is measured and its area ascertained; also, the map showing the measurements, boundaries, and area.

suspension or revocation The action of punishing violations of the license law by recalling a license temporarily (*suspension*) or permanently (*revocation*).

swing loan A short term loan similar to a bridge loan that uses the strength of the borrower's equity in the property he or she is selling to purchase a new property.

syndicate A combination of people or firms formed to accomplish a joint venture of mutual interest.

tacking Adding or combining successive periods of continuous occupation of real property by several different adverse possessors.

takeout loan A loan commitment obtained prior to a lender extending a construction loan, under the terms of which the takeout lender will pay off the construction loan once the work is finished. Provides assurance for the construction lender that the initial short-term loan will be satisfied.

taking Government restriction on use of property, to the extent that the owner must be compensated for loss of value.

taxable status date The date, often in March, on which a community's tax assessment rolls are fixed for the coming year.

taxation The process by which a government or municipal quasi-public body raises monies to fund its operation.

tax basis The original cost basis for property, reduced by depreciation and increased by the amount spent on capital improvements.

tax certiorari Appeal in state court of a ruling by the local assessment board of review.

tax credit A direct reduction in tax payable, as opposed to a deduciton from income.

tax deed An instrument, similar to a certificate of sale, given to a purchaser at a tax sale.

tax-deferred exchange A means by which one investment property can be exchanged for a similar one of equal value, with no immediate or capital gain tax consequences.

tax depreciation *See* straight-line depreciation

tax foreclosure Legal proceeding (comparable to a private mortgage foreclosure) brought by a taxing body against the property itself (*in rem*); former owner loses all rights and claims.

tax lien A charge against property created by operation of law. Tax liens and assessments take priority over all other liens.

tax rate The rate at which real property is taxed in a tax district or county. For example, real property may be taxed at a rate of .056 cents per dollar of assessed valuation (56 mills).

tax sale A court-ordered sale of real property to raise money to cover delinquent taxes.

tax shelter Property throwing off an income-tax loss that can offset other income.

tenancy at will An estate that gives the lessee the right to possession until the estate is terminated by either party; the term of this estate is indefinite.

tenancy by the entirety The joint ownership acquired by husband and wife during marriage. On the death of one spouse, the survivor becomes the owner of the property.

tenancy in common A form of co-ownership by which each owner holds an undivided interest in real property as if he or she were sole owner. Each individual owner has the right to partition. Tenants in common have no right of survivorship.

tenant One who holds or possesses lands or tenements by any kind of right or title.

tenant at sufferance One who comes into possession of land by lawful title and keeps it afterward without any title at all.

term The originally scheduled period of time over which a loan is to be paid.

termination of association notice Notice sent to the Department of State by a principal broker, stating that a particular licensee is no longer under the broker's supervision.

termites Wood-boring insects whose presence causes structural damage.

testate Having made and left a valid will.

testator The (male) maker of a valid will.

testatrix The (female) maker of a valid will.

testers Members of civil rights and neighborhood organizations, often volunteers, who observe real estate offices to assess compliance with fair housing laws.

tie-in arrangement An arrangement by which provision of certain products or services is made contingent on the purchase of other, unrelated products or services.

time is of the essence A phrase in a contract that requires the performance of a certain act within a stated period of time.

time-sharing Undivided ownership of real estate for only a portion of the year.

title Evidence that the owner of land is in lawful possession thereof; evidence of ownership.

title insurance A policy insuring the owner or mortgagee against loss by reason of defects in the title to a parcel of real estate, other than the encumbrances, defects, and matters specifically excluded by the policy.

title search An examination of the public records to determine the ownership and encumbrances affecting real property.

title theory Some states interpret a mortgage to mean that the lender is the owner of mortgaged land. Upon full payment of the mortgage debt, the borrower becomes the landowner.

Torrens system A method of evidencing title by registration with the proper public authority, generally called the *registrar*.

tort A civil wrong done by one person against another.

town house A hybrid form of real estate ownership in which the owner has fee simple title to the living unit and land below it, plus a fractional interest in common elements.

township The principal unit of the rectangular survey (government survey) system, a square with six-mile sides and an area of 36 square miles.

trade fixtures Articles installed by a tenant under the terms of a lease and removable by the tenant before the lease expires.

transfer of development rights Method by which one developer can buy unused rights belonging to a landowner.

transfer tax Tax stamps required to be affixed to a deed by state and/or local law.

trespass An unlawful intrusion on another's property.

true tax Actual taxes payable for a property after all exemptions and reductions for which the property or its owner is qualified.

truss roof Particularly strong roofing system composed of chords, diagonals, and gusset plates, preassembled at a mill.

trust A fiduciary arrangement whereby property is conveyed to a person or an institution, called a *trustee*, to be held and administered on behalf of another person, called a *beneficiary*.

trust account Escrow account for money belonging to another.

trust deed An instrument used to create a mortgage lien by which the mortgagor conveys his or her title to a trustee, who holds it as security for the benefit of the note holder (the lender); also called a *deed of trust*.

trustee *See* trust.

trustor The individual who establishes a trust.

UFFI Urea-formaldehyde foam insulation, considered carcinogenic, no longer used.

umbrella policy An insurance policy that covers additional risk beyond several underlying policies.

underground storage tanks Buried containers used for storage or disposal of chemicals, fuel, and gas that pose an actual or potential environmental hazard in the event of a leak.

underwriting The process by which a lender evaluates a prospective borrower's application through verification of employment and financial information and analysis of credit and appraisal reports.

undisclosed dual agency Representation of both principal parties in the same transaction without full written disclosure to and approval of all parties.

undivided interest *See* tenancy in common.

undivided loyalty Fiduciary duty owed by the agent to the principal or client.

unenforceable contract A contract that seems on the surface to be valid, yet neither party can sue the other to force performance of it.

Uniform Commercial Code A codification of commercial law, adopted in most states, that attempts to make uniform all laws relating to commercial transactions, including chattel mortgages and bulk transfers.

Uniform Settlement Statement (HUD Form 1) A special form designed to detail all financial particulars of a transaction.

unilateral contract A one-sided contract wherein one party makes a promise so as to induce a second party to do something. The second party is not legally bound to perform; however, if the second party does comply, the first party is obligated to keep the promise.

unity of ownership The four unities traditionally needed to create a joint tenancy: unity of title, time, interest, and possession.

universal agent One empowered by a principal to represent him or her in all matters that can be delegated.

usury Charging interest at a rate higher than the maximum established by law.

valid contract A contract that complies with all the essentials of a contract and is binding and enforceable on all parties to it.

VA loan A mortgage loan on approved property made to a qualified veteran by an authorized lender and guaranteed by the Department of Veterans Affairs to limit the lender's possible loss.

valuation Estimated worth or price. The act of valuing by appraisal.

value The power of a good or service to command other goods in exchange for the present worth of future rights to its income or amenities.

value-in-use Present worth of future benefits of ownership of a parcel of real estate.

variance Permission obtained from zoning authorities to build a structure or conduct a use that is expressly prohibited by the current zoning laws; an exception from the zoning ordinances.

vendee A buyer under a land contract or contract of sale.

vendor A seller under a land contract or contract of sale.

vicarious liability Liability that is created not because of a person's actions but because of the relationship between the liable person and other parties.

voidable contract A contract that seems to be valid on the surface but that may be rejected or disaffirmed by one of the parties.

void contract A contract that has no legal force or effect because it does not meet the essential elements of a contract.

violation An infraction of the law less serious than a misdemeanor.

voltage Force of an electric current, measured in volts.

voluntary alienation Transfer of title by gift or sale according to the owner's wishes.

voluntary lien A lien created by the owner's voluntary action, such as a mortgage.

waiver The renunciation, abandonment, or surrender of some claim, right, or privilege.

warranty deed A deed in which the grantor fully warrants good clear title to the premises.

waste   An improper use or an abuse of a property by a possessor who holds less than fee ownership, such as a tenant, life tenant, mortgagor, or vendee.

wetland survey   An intensive examination of property, coordinated by the U.S. Army Corps of Engineers, to determine whether or not it should be classified and protected as a wetland.

will   A written document, properly witnessed, providing for the transfer of title to property owned by the deceased, called the *testator*.

without recourse   Words used in endorsing a note or bill to denote that the future holder is not to look to the endorser in case of nonpayment.

workers' compensation acts   State insurance program, paid for by employers, to compensate those hurt on the job.

wraparound loan   A method of refinancing in which the lender refinances a borrower by lending an amount over the existing first mortgage amount without disturbing the priority of the first mortgage.

wraparound mortgage   An additional mortgage in which another lender refinances a borrower by lending an amount including the existing first mortgage amount without disturbing the existence of the first mortgage.

year-to-year tenancy   A periodic tenancy in which rent is collected from year to year.

zone   An area set off by the proper authorities for specific use subject to certain restrictions or restraints.

zoning boards of appeal   Official local government bodies established to hear complaints about the impact of zoning ordinances on individual properties, and to consider variances and special-use permits.

zoning ordinances   An exercise of police power by a municipality to regulate and control the character and use of property.

ANSWER KEY

CHAPTER 1
License Law

1. c
2. d
3. c
4. c
5. d
6. d
7. c
8. b
9. d
10. c
11. b
12. d
13. a
14. b
15. c
16. a
17. b
18. c
19. b
20. d
21. b
22. a

CHAPTER 2
The Law of Agency

1. a
2. b
3. b
4. b
5. c
6. c
7. c
8. c
9. d
10. d
11. b
12. c
13. c
14. c
15. a
16. d

CHAPTER 3
Agency and Real Estate
Brokerage

1. d
2. b
3. c
4. a

5. b
6. d
7. d
8. c
9. c
10. d
11. d
12. a
13. a
14. c

CHAPTER 4
Estates and Interests

1. b
2. d
3. b
4. b
5. c
6. c
7. a
8. c
9. c
10. c
11. a
12. b
13. d
14. b
15. a
16. b
17. b
18. a
19. b
20. b
21. b
22. b
23. b
24. b
25. a

CHAPTER 5
Liens and Easements

1. b
2. b
3. b
4. a
5. c
6. a
7. d
8. d
9. a
10. b

11. d
12. d
13. b
14. d
15. b
16. a
17. d
18. a
19. c
20. a
21. a

CHAPTER 6
Real Estate Instruments:
Deeds

1. a
2. c
3. c
4. d
5. c
6. a
7. c
8. b
9. b
10. b
11. b
12. b
13. a
14. d
15. d

CHAPTER 7
Real Estate Instruments:
Leases

1. b
2. a
3. c
4. d
5. d
6. c
7. d
8. d
9. c
10. b
11. d
12. c
13. d
14. a
15. b
16. a
17. a

18. b

CHAPTER 8
Real Estate Instruments:
Contracts

1. b
2. b
3. d
4. c
5. b
6. a
7. b
8. d
9. c
10. c
11. d
12. c
13. a
14. d
15. d
16. b
17. b
18. b
19. a
20. d
21. c
22. b
23. b
24. d
25. c

CHAPTER 9
Title Closings and Costs

1. a
2. a
3. c
4. a
5. d
6. d
7. b
8. c
9. c
10. a
11. d
12. d
13. c
14. d
15. c
16. b
17. b
18. c

21. b
22. d
23. a
24. a
25. c

CHAPTER 10
Mortgages

1. b
2. a
3. d
4. c
5. b
6. a
7. c
8. a
9. d
10. a

CHAPTER 11
Real Estate Finance I

1. d
2. a
3. c
4. d
5. b
6. b
7. d
8. b
9. c
10. b
11. a
12. a

CHAPTER 12
Land-Use Regulations

1. a
2. d
3. c
4. b
5. b
6. c
7. a
8. b
9. a
10. c
11. b
12. c
13. b
14. a
15. c
16. a

CHAPTER 13
Introduction to Construction

1. d
2. d
3. a
4. c
5. d
6. a
7. b
8. a
9. d
10. a
11. a
12. b
13. a
14. c
15. c

16. b
17. a

CHAPTER 14
Valuation Process

1. a
2. c
3. a
4. d
5. a
6. c
7. d
8. d
9. d
10. d
11. c
12. a
13. d
14. c
15. d
16. b
17. d
18. a
19. b
20. a
21. c
22. d
23. a
24. c
25. d

CHAPTER 15
Human Rights and Fair Housing

1. c
2. c

3. c
4. d
5. b
6. c
7. b
8. c
9. b
10. a
11. a
12. a
13. b
14. a
15. c
16. d
17. d
18. a
19. d
20. d
21. a

CHAPTER 16
Environmental Issues

1. d
2. b
3. c
4. a
5. a
6. b
7. a
8. d
9. c
10. b
11. a
12. c
13. b

CHAPTER 17
Real Estate Mathematics

1. **b. 180 feet**
1,200 square yards × 9 = 10,800 square feet

area = length × width
10,800 = length × 60
10,800 ÷ 60 = 180 feet

2. **d. $2,430**
$108,000 × 97.75% maximum loan amount

$108,000 × 97.75% = $105,570

$108,000 − $105,570 = $2,430 minimum down payment

3. **c. 21**
120 feet ÷ 6 feet per section = 20 sections
One fence post must be added to anchor the other end.

20 + 1 = 21 fence posts

4. **c. $950.40**
$198,000 × 80% = $198,000 × .80 = $158,400 insured value

$158,400 ÷ 1,000 = 158.4 thousands

158.4 × $6 per thousand = $950.40

5. **a. $80,000**
$74,000 + $1,200 = $75,200 sales price less commission

$75,200 = 94% of sales price

$75,200 ÷ .94 = $80,000 sales price

6. **b. $1,330**
$57,000 ÷ 12 = $4,750 monthly income

$4,750 × .28 = $1,330 permissible mortgage payment

7. **a. $4,620**
$154,000 × .06 = $9,240 total commission

$9,240 × .50 = $4,620 Sally's share

8. **a. $808.54**
$1,800 ÷ 12 = $150 monthly property taxes

$365 ÷ 12 = $30.42 monthly insurance premium

$150 + $30.42 + $628.12 = $808.54 total monthly payment

9. **c. $36,000**
120 front feet × $300 = $36,000 sales price

10. **b. 726 feet**
43,560 feet per acre × 5 = 217,800 square feet

217,800 ÷ 300 = 726 feet depth

11. **b. $1,550.25**
$79,500 sales price × 6½% commission =

$79,500 × .065 = $5,167.50 Happy Valley's commission

$5,167.50 × 30% or $5,167.50 × .30 = $1,550.25 listing salesperson's commission

12. **c. $277.16**
12′ × 9.5′ = 114 square feet, area of rectangle

½ (3′ × 9.5′) = ½ (28.5) = 14.25 square feet, area of triangle

114 + 14.25 = 128.25 square feet

To convert square feet to square yards, divide by 9:

128.25 ÷ 9 = 14.25 square yards

$16.95 carpet + $2.50 installation = $19.45 cost per square yard

$19.45 × 14.25 square yards = $277.1625

rounded to $277.16

13. **a. 20%**
$30,000 Hal + $35,000 Olive + $35,000 Ron = $100,000

$125,000 − $100,000 = $25,000 Marvin's contribution

part ÷ whole = percent

$25,000 ÷ $125,000 = .20, or 20%

14. **b. $40,843.83**
391.42 × 12 = $4,697.04, annual interest

part ÷ whole = percent

$4,697.04 ÷ 11½% or $4,697.04 ÷ .115 = $40,843.826

15. **a. $103,425**
$98,500 × 5% = $98,500 × .05 = $4,925, annual increase in value

$98,500 + $4,925 = $103,425, current market value

16. **d. $135.38**
$95,000 × 60% or $95,000 × .60 = $57,000, assessed value

divided by 1,000 because tax rate is stated per thousand dollars

$57,000 ÷ 1,000 = 57

57 × $28.50 = $1,624.50, annual taxes

divide by 12 to get monthly taxes

$1,624.50 ÷ 12 = $135.375

17. **d. 195 cubic feet**
22′ × 15′ = 330 square feet, area of rectangle

½ (4′ × 15′) = ½ (60) = 30 square feet, area of each triangle

30 × 2 = 60 square feet, area of two triangles

330 + 60 = 390 square feet, surface area to be paved

6′ deep = ½ foot

390 × ½ = 195 cubic feet, cement needed for patio

18. **b. $127,000**
$3,675 − $500 salary = $3,175 commission on sales

$3,175 ÷ 2.5% = $3,175 ÷ .025 = $127,000, value of property sold

19. **c. $1,615.88**
Two sides of 95′ plus one side of 42′6″

95′ × 2 = 190 feet

42′6″ = 42.5 feet

190 + 42.5 = 232.5 linear feet

232.5 × $6.95 = $1,615.875

20. **a. $675,000**
$4,500 × 12 = $54,000 annual rental

$54,000 ÷ 8% or $54,000 ÷ .08 = $675,000, original cost of property

21. **c. 27,225 square feet**
100 acres × 43,560 square feet per acre = 4,356,000 total square feet

4,356,000 × ⅞ available for lots = 3,811,500 square feet

3,811,500 ÷ 140 lots = 27,225 square feet per lot

22. a. **$173.33**
$975 ÷ 12 months = $81.25 property tax per month
$81.25 ÷ 30 days = $2.708 property tax per day
$81.25 × 2 months = $162.50
$2.708 × 4 days = $10.832
$162.50 + $10.832 = $173.332 rounded to $173.33, prepaid unused tax

23. b. **$488.97**
$61,550 × 13% = $61,550 × .13 = $8,001.50 annual interest
$8,001.50 ÷ 12 months = $666.792 interest per month
$666.792 ÷ 30 days = $22.226 interest per day
$22.226 × 22 days = $488.972 rounded to $488.97 unpaid back interest

24. a. **$235,000**
$14,100 commission ÷ 6% commission rate =

$14,100 ÷ .06 = $235,000 sales

25. b. **$242,842.40**
30 years × 12 months = 360 payments
360 payments × $952.34 = $342,842.40 total payments for principal and interest
$342,842.40 total payments − $100,000 principal repayment = $242,842.40 total interest paid

26. c. **Four years, nine months**
Two points on a $90,000 loan = $90,000 × .02 or 2 percent = $1,800 paid in points
$817.85 − $786.35 = $31.50 saved each month with lower payment
$1,800 ÷ $31.50 = 57.14 months to recoup the payment of points
57.14 months = 4 years, 9 months

27. c. **$2,600 more at closing**
$80,000 × 3 percent or .03 = $2,400 payment for points
$100,000 − $95,000 = $5,000 received with the higher offer
$5,000 − $2,400 payment for points = $2,600 realized with the higher offer after payment of points

28. b. **$1,100**
$10,000 ÷ $100 = 100
100 × .50 = $50 tax on first $10,000
$150,000 − $10,000 = $140,000
$140,000 ÷ $100 = $1,400
1,400 × .75 = $1,050
$50 + $1,050 = $1,100 total mortgage tax

29. c. **$796**
$198,600 sale price ÷ $500 = 397.2
398 × $2 = $796 transfer tax

30. c. **$327**
$425,000 purchase price ÷ 1,300 square feet =326.92 or $327 per square foot

CHAPTER 18
Independent Contractor
1. c
2. b
3. d
4. d
5. c
6. d
7. b
8. d
9. d
10. b

CHAPTER 19
The Broker's Office
1. d
2. b
3. a
4. c
5. d

6. a
7. d
8. a
9. b
10. c
11. b
12. d
13. c
14. b
15. c
16. a
17. a
18. b
19. c
20. a

CHAPTER 20
Real Estate Finance II
1. c
2. a
3. b

4. d
5. a
6. b
7. a
8. d
9. b
10. d

CHAPTER 21
Real Estate Investment
1. a
2. c
3. b
4. b
5. a
6. c
7. b
8. d
9. c
10. a
11. c

12. a
13. d
14. c
15. d
16. c
17. c
18. a
19. b
20. a
21. c
22. b
23. d
24. b
25. a

CHAPTER 22
General Business Law
1. d
2. b
3. c
4. b

5. c
6. d
7. a
8. c
9. c
10. d
11. a
12. a
13. c
14. b
15. b
16. a
17. a
18. b
19. a
20. a

CHAPTER 23
Construction and Development

1. b
2. b
3. d
4. a
5. b
6. a
7. c
8. c
9. d
10. a
11. b
12. d
13. d
14. c
15. a

CHAPTER 24
Conveyance of Real Property

1. c
2. d
3. b
4. d
5. b
6. a
7. c
8. c
9. a
10. d

CHAPTER 25
Property Management

1. d
2. d

3. b
4. d
5. d
6. c
7. a
8. d
9. c
10. b
11. c
12. c
13. c
14. d
15. d
16. b
17. a
18. c

CHAPTER 26
Taxes and Assessment

1. d
2. c
3. b
4. b
5. c
6. a
7. c
8. b
9. a
10. a
11. b

SALESPER-SON'S REVIEW EXAMINATION

1. b
2. a
3. c
4. d
5. c
6. b
7. c
8. d
9. d
10. b
11. b
12. b
13. a
14. c
15. b
16. d
17. a
18. a
19. d
20. d
21. c

22. a
23. b
24. c
25. a
26. c
27. c
28. c
29. b
30. c
31. a
32. d
33. b
34. d
35. d
36. b
37. b
38. d
39. c
40. c
41. b
42. d
43. b
44. d
45. a
46. a
47. a
48. a
49. c
50. d
51. d
52. a
53. c
54. b
55. c
56. c
57. c
58. c
59. a
60. d
61. c
62. a
63. c
64. b
65. b
66. a
67. b
68. b
69. b
70. c
71. d
72. b
73. a
74. d
75. b

76. a
77. b
78. c
79. a
80. d
81. b
82. a
83. d
84. c
85. b
86. c
87. b
88. c
89. a
90. c
91. b
92. b
93. c
94. d
95. c
96. c
97. a
98. c
99. d
100. a

BROKER'S PRACTICE EXAMINATION

1. a
2. b
3. b
4. d
5. c
6. a
7. b
8. b
9. c
10. c
11. c
12. c
13. b
14. b
15. d
16. b
17. c
18. b
19. d
20. b
21. b
22. b
23. c
24. b
25. b

26. a	45. d	64. a	83. b
27. a	46. b	65. b	84. b
28. c	47. a	66. b	85. a
29. d	48. c	67. c	86. d
30. d	49. d	68. b	87. c
31. c	50. c	69. d	88. d
32. a	51. b	70. a	89. b
33. c	52. a	71. b	90. b
34. a	53. a	72. b	91. c
35. a	54. c	73. c	92. b
36. d	55. b	74. d	93. a
37. c	56. c	75. c	94. a
38. a	57. d	76. d	95. c
39. d	58. d	77. b	96. b
40. b	59. c	78. a	97. a
41. c	60. b	79. b	98. a
42. d	61. a	80. d	99. c
43. b	62. b	81. a	100. d
44. c	63. c	82. d	

INDEX